Teaching Exceptional Children

Mojdeh Bayat

DePaul University

Mc Graw Hill

Connect Learn Succeed™

Connect
Learn
Succeed™

TEACHING EXCEPTIONAL CHILDREN
Published by McGraw-Hill, a business unit of The McGraw-Hill Companies, Inc., 1221 Avenue of the Americas,
New York, NY 10020.

ISBN 978-0-07-337869-5
MHID 0-07-337869-0

Vice President & Editor-in-Chief: *Michael Ryan*
Vice President EDP/Central Publishing Services: *Kimberly Meriwether David*
Publisher: *Mike Sugarman*
Sponsoring Editor: *Allison McNamara*
Editorial Coordinator: *Sarah Kiefer*
Marketing Manager: *Yasuko Okada*
Senior Project Manager: *Lisa A. Bruflodt*
Design Coordinator: *Brenda A. Rolwes*
Cover Designer: *Studio Montage, St. Louis, Missouri*
Cover Image: *Two Friends Interacting in a Classic Little Girl Game: © SuperStock, Inc.; Child Playing.*
Teacher Watches: © IT Stock Free/Alamy Images
Buyer: *Laura Fuller*
Media Project Manager: *Sridevi Palani*
Compositor: *Laserwords Private Limited*
Typeface: *10/12 Times LT Roman*
Printer: *R. R. Donnelley*

Library of Congress Cataloging-in-Publication Data

Bayat, Mojdeh.
    Teaching exceptional children/Mojdeh Bayat.—1st ed.
        p. cm.
    ISBN 978-0-07-337869-5 (alk. paper)
    1. Special education teachers—Handbooks, manuals, etc.   2. Learning disabled children—
Education.   3. Developmentally disabled children—Education. 4. Individualized   instruction.   I. Title.
    LC4704.5.B39 2011
        371.9'043—dc22

                                                                                  2010034735

www.mhhe.com

Dedication

This book is dedicated to the memory of my teacher, Dr. Javad Nurbakhsh, and to Mrs. Parvaneh Daneshvar Nurbakhsh, for all they have taught me.

Preface

During the past two decades, two major developments have influenced the field of disability research and practice: (1) better diagnostic systems and advances in genetics and neuroscience have made it possible to identify a variety of neurodevelopmental problems during the first 5 years of a child's life, and (2) a gradual change in the public perception of disabilities has prompted a paradigm shift and policy change from isolation to inclusion of all children and individuals with disabilities in schools and communities in which they live. Accordingly, early childhood education (ECE) classrooms have gradually become diverse environments, witnessing an increase in the number of young children with a variety of special needs.

Teacher preparation programs have increasingly acknowledged a growing need for programs that address the training needs of preservice early childhood teachers in the area of early childhood special education (ECSE). On the other hand, the provisions of the Individuals with Disabilities Improvement Act of 2004 puts an emphasis on employing science-based methods in working with children with special needs. As a result, currently there is a great need for training tools, such as appropriate textbooks to address scientific theory, as well as evidence-based practices in early childhood epecial education. This book is written in response to this need. It presents theory and practice in the education of children with special needs from birth through third grade.

The Philosophical Framework of this Book

My mentors, Gilkerson and Stott, child development researchers at Erikson Institute, once cited Rousso: "Like other aspects of the child, the disability contributes to a sense of identity, and is in need of acceptance, appreciation, and affirmation" (Gilkerson & Stott, 2000). They emphasized that the acceptance and appreciation of any disability is elemental in having an appreciation and love for the child, as well as in forming a positive relationship with him or her—a relationship that is crucial for the child's healthy development. Although in that specific argument they were referring to the parent–child relationship, their belief about appreciation and affirmation of the child is as valid for professionals and educators who work with children with disabilities as it is for their parents.

In fact, as far as common perceptions about a child with a disability are concerned, distinguishing the disability separate from the child is hardly possible. The two together represent a set of meaning for the parents and for others who might work or interact with the child. Historically, a disability in a child has been viewed as a negative phenomenon, even a tragic end for both the child and the family. However, research and practice, as well as public opinion, have been progressively moving away from such pathological and negative views.

The inclusion movement in education is in part a response to a gradual global change in beliefs about disability and its meaning. We are now moving toward a positive inclusive approach that acknowledges the rights of individuals with disabilities to be active and self-determined members of their increasingly diverse communities.

The philosophy of this book is therefore based on the premise that understanding each disability, the history of its development, and its characteristics are the first steps toward understanding and appreciating the child with that disability. It is because of such an understanding and appreciation that professionals can make judgments about which educational and therapeutic methods to use in educating and enhancing the development of the child, and when and how to use them.

This book does advocate for inclusion of all children and individuals with disabilities within their learning and living communities. However, it also acknowledges that although we have come a long way, our educational settings and our communities are far from being truly inclusive. True inclusion comes with understanding, appreciation, and acceptance. And so, this book aims to not only present methods of working with children with disabilities in both specialized and inclusive settings, but also to promote an understanding of disabilities that might encourage professionals to appreciate, affirm, accept, and love working with children with special needs in early childhood settings.

The Theoretical Background and Scope of this Book

This textbook does not advocate one developmental or educational theory over another, because every child and family deserves to be regarded and treated individually There certainly is not a one-theory-fits-all approach to intervention. However, an overarching theme or philosophy does dominate this textbook. This philosophy is grounded in the attachment theory, as well as in the brain development research of the past 15 years regarding development of the child's self-regulatory and cognitive capabilities through positive relationships with adults. In fact, the importance of a positive adult–child relationship in the treatment of disabilities and in the developmental and academic outcomes of children has been emphasized throughout this book whenever appropriate.

A number of groundbreaking findings in the field of child development has occurred over the past decades; specifically, in the area of genetics and brain development (neuroscience and sensory processing). A growing body of research now provides theoretical explanations regarding the possible explanations for different disorders, such as attention deficit hyperactivity disorder, Autism Spectrum Disorders, various emotional and behavioral disorders, and intellectual disability. Most disorders have specific developmental characteristics that appear during early childhood years. Understanding the different characteristics of each disorder and their etiologies influences the way research-based educational and therapeutic treatments are designed and practiced. This book presents theoretical information grounded in neuroscience and child development underpinning each disability, along with specific behavioral characteristics of that disability. When appropriate, explanations have been presented to address sensory processing deficiencies manifested in regulatory disorders (such as ASD and ADHD) in young children. Research-based methods of working with children related to each disability have been presented in each chapter as well.

The Audience for this Book

This textbook is intended for use in introductory and method courses in early childhood special education (with children from birth through age 8). The text is appropriate for use with undergraduate and graduate students who might be working toward degree and licensure for various therapeutic specialties, case management, social work, and special and general early childhood teaching specialties and administration.

Organization

This book is divided into three sections. Section 1 includes Chapters 1 through 6 and introduces the readers to the field of early childhood education, presenting the scientific, theoretical, and legal issues related to the field. The configurations of chapters are as follows:

- ➢ Chapter 1 introduces the reader to the field. It provides historical, legal, and research foundations of early childhood special education.
- ➢ Chapter 2 presents developmental risk factors before, during, and after birth.
- ➢ Chapter 3 presents disability issues influencing the family system. It presents research in the areas of family resilience and family quality of life. Building on the evolution of models of working with families in the field, the chapter establishes the 21st-century framework of collective empowerment or family–professional partnership as the model of choice in working with families of children with disabilities.
- ➢ Chapter 4 explains the process of the identification and evaluation of children with disabilities and their entry into the special education field.
- ➢ Chapter 5 explains the legal requirements of Individual Family Service Plan and Individualized Education Plan development, along with guidelines to write IFSP outcomes and IEP measurable goals and objectives.
- ➢ Chapter 6 presents modern theories that form the foundations of practice in early childhood special education, and provides examples of these theoretical applications in the field.

Section 2 includes Chapters 7 through 14, and introduces the reader to various disabilities. Each disability chapter is divided into four major parts: (1) history of the disability, (2) causal theories or etiology of the disability, (3) behavioral or developmental characteristics of the disability, and (4) methods of working with children with that disability in inclusive and special education classrooms.

- ➢ Chapter 7 presents Autism Spectrum Disorders. The chapter examines a variety of methods used in the treatment and education of children with autism, and presents evidence-based practices in this disability category.

> Chapter 8 explores attention deficit hyperactivity disorder. The method section of this chapter focuses on strategies for the classroom and in working with families of children with ADHD.

> Chapter 9 discusses children with behavioral and social emotional needs. The method section of the chapter focuses on positive behavioral support and its use as a school-wide, classroom-wide, and individual strategy for children with behavioral needs.

> Chapter 10 explains issues related to communication difficulties, including various types of speech and language impairments. The method section of this chapter focuses on specific strategies to enhance receptive and expressive language development, and the use of alternative and augmentative communication methods.

> Chapter 11 introduces readers to children with intellectual disabilities, issues related to classification, as well as methods of working with these children.

> Chapter 12 describes children with deafness, hearing loss, blindness, and visual impairments. The chapter includes strategies and various methods of working with children with visual impairments and hearing loss.

> Chapter 13 describes issues related to motor development, children with motor problems, as well as children with chronic illnesses. Appropriate strategies and methods of working with these children are presented.

> Chapter 14 focuses on two remaining groups of children whose education merits special attention: children at risk and gifted children. The chapter explains risk factors as well as factors contributing to resilience in children. Issues pertinent to the education of gifted children are also explored in this chapter.

Section 3 of the book is composed of Chapter 15, which focuses on issues related to the education of children with special needs in primary levels of kindergarten through third grade. Since learning disabilities are usually diagnosed during elementary or middle school, they are discussed in this chapter.

> Chapter 15 addresses various types of learning disabilities and the methods of working with children with learning disabilities. In addition, curricular and school-wide issues regarding the education of exceptional children in inclusive settings, such as community-based instruction, physical education, and sexual and hygiene education are also addressed in this chapter.

Features of this Book

The following key features appear in the text:

> **Objectives:** Each chapter begins with learning objectives to help students focus on the key aspects of the chapter.

> **Key Terms:** A key terms list is presented at the beginning of each chapter. Key terminology appears in boldface on the first introduction in the text, and definitions are provided in the comprehensive glossary at the end of the book.

> **Reflection Questions:** Students are given the opportunity to reflect upon their personal opinions and beliefs that are pertinent to early childhood special

education by answering the reflection questions presented at the beginning of each chapter.

> **Opening Stories:** Thought-provoking stories that open each chapter provide students with real-life scenarios to ponder.
> **Critical Thinking Questions:** Critical thinking questions that relate to the chapter-opening story are interspersed within the body of the chapter. Students must rely on critical thinking skills and the knowledge presented in the chapter to answer the questions.
> **Text Boxes:** Text boxes highlight and elaborate upon areas of particular interest to students, including laws, regulations, and pertinent research, to name a few.
> **Research Corner:** Additional research on chapter-related content can be found in Research Corner boxes at the end of certain chapters.
> **Color Photographs:** Color photos appear throughout the book to support the textual material presented.
> **Figures and Tables:** Figures and tables supplement the text to clarify and elucidate key concepts.
> **Summary:** Each chapter summary is an excellent review of the main topics presented in the chapter.
> **Review Questions:** End-of-chapter review questions help reinforce learning and measure students' understanding of the material presented in the chapter.
> **Out-of-Class Activities:** These activities provide students with the opportunity to apply their knowledge to real-life situations and to interact with individuals in their schools and communities. Students complete field-based activities; conduct interviews with children, parents, and school personnel; and perform additional research on key topics presented throughout the text.
> **Recommended Resources:** Each chapter includes a list of recommended online resources for further study.
> **References:** A complete list of references appears at the end of each chapter.

It is hoped that this textbook is beneficial to anyone who seeks to understand and meet the needs of all young children with disabilities in early childhood educational contexts.

Acknowledgments

Writing this book would not have been possible had it not been for the support and encouragement of family members, friends, and colleagues. First and foremost, I am indebted to my family: my husband, Dr. Ali Jamnia, for his continued friendship and advice, for encouraging and supporting me, and for drawing some of the artwork for this book. My daughter, Naseem, for her patience with me, especially during the sensitive time of looking into and applying to colleges, for not complaining when I wasn't available to listen to her, and for copyediting the entire first draft of my book. To my son, Seena, for whom I became interested in the field of disability in the first place, who has inspired me to help all other children with special needs and their families, and from whom I continue to learn numerous lessons daily. I am also grateful to my parents, Mr. Ardashir Bayat and Ms. Badri Merat, for their continued love and support.

My colleagues and good friends—Dr. Gayle Mindes, Dr. Marie Donovan, Dr. John Gabriel, and Alice Moss—were all caring and encouraging through this process, and I am grateful for their collegiality and ongoing support.

My graduate students in T&L 427: Exceptional Child Growth and Development gave me feedback for content clarity and improvement, and generously let me use some of their wonderful artwork for this book. Specifically, my talented students Kathleen Lange and Alison Pouthier wrote and illustrated social stories and task analyses in the book.

A number of special education teachers contributed to this book by welcoming me into their classrooms, generously making instructional materials, and letting me photograph their classrooms. These teachers are truly remarkable and exemplary. They taught my son during his early childhood and elementary school years, and have been responsible for his progress. Over the years, they have become my best friends. Their passion for teaching, creativity, and compassion for children with special needs have been a source of inspiration for me. They are Monica Daly, Chad Kirkpatrick, and Erika Ash. Erika also kindly let me use photographs of her and her son, Dominic, for illustration of some of the book's content.

My editor, Alexis Breen Ferraro, has been very patient with me. She was always kindly available to answer my numerous questions and help me through the writing process. Without her constructive suggestions and input, the completion of this work would not have been possible. I am also grateful to David Patterson and Allison McNamara from McGraw-Hill for giving me the opportunity to write this book, and for replying to my many e-mails when I needed their help. And, my good friend, Mr. Irving Karchmar, who edited several chapters of the book, has always helped me with language clarity and the improvement of my work through the years.

Finally, I am, as always, grateful to all children with disabilities and their families, from whom I have learned and continue to learn. They inspire me and keep my passion for children with disabilities alive.

Reviewers

The author and publisher wish to thank the following reviewers for their valuable feedback, which helped shape the final text:

Karen Applequist, Ph.D., *Northern Arizona University*

Holly Bagby, M.S.Ed., *Three Rivers Community College*

Frances M. Carlson, M.Ed., *Chattahoochee Technical College*

Sharon Carter, M.A., *Davidson County Community College*

Mary Cordell, M.S., *Navarro College and Texas A&M University at Commerce*

Dede Dunst, M.Ed., *Mitchell Community College*

Kelly Hantak, M.Ed., *St. Charles Community College*

Jennifer Johnson, M.Ed., *Vance-Granville Community College*

Cindy Kirk, M.A.Ed., *National Park Community College*

Aida Michlowski, Ph.D., J.D., *Marian University School of Education*

Gayle Mindes, Ed.D., *DePaul University*
Sandra Owen, M.A., *Cincinnati State University*
Michael A. Rettig, Ph.D., *Washburn University*
Joan Robison, M.A., *St. Cloud Community College*
Amy Strimling, M.A., *Sacramento City College*
Kim Sutton, M.Ed., *Ozarks Technical Community College*
Judith Terpstra, M.Ed., Ph.D., *Southern Connecticut State University*
Shawne Thomas, M.A., *Edison State College*
Elaine Wilkinson, B.S., M.Ed., A.B.D., *Collin County Community College*
Julie Williams, M.S.Ed., *Pulaski Technical College*
Kathleen Winterman, Ed.D., M.Ed., *Xavier University*

Reference

Gilkerson L., & Stott F. (2000). Parent–child relationships in early intervention with infants and toddlers with disabilities and their families. In C. H. Zeanah (Ed.), *Handbook of infant mental health* (2nd ed., pp. 457–471). New York: Guilford Press.

Contents

Chapter **3**

Families Are the Most Important of All 73

Chapter **4**

Identification and Intervention 107

Chapter   **5**

Developing IFSP and IEP   143

Chapter   **6**

Theoretical Foundations in Special Education   175

──── *Section* **2** ────

Disabilities and Methods   209

Chapter   **7**

Autism Spectrum Disorders   210

Chapter   **8**

Children with Attention Deficit Hyperactivity Disorder   253

Chapter   **9**

**Young Children with Behavioral and Social
Emotional Needs   286**

Chapter   **10**

**Children with Communication Difficulties:
Speech and Language Impairments   326**

Theoretical and Legal Foundations

Early Childhood Special Education: An Introduction to the Field

Objectives

Upon completion of this chapter, you should be able to:

> Describe who children with exceptional needs are.
> Understand the various programs under early childhood education, early childhood intervention, and early childhood special education in which children with disabilities and their families are served.

➢ Describe the role of various professionals in the field of early childhood special education (ECSE).

➢ Understand and analyze the historical developments that shaped the field of ECSE.

➢ Understand and analyze the legal foundation of special education, and the laws which shaped ECSE.

➢ Evaluate the provisions of IDEA as it relates to early intervention and special education for young children.

➢ Define inclusion and understand arguments for and against inclusion in early childhood education.

➢ Understand and analyze the important research that has shaped ECSE.

➢ List recommendations for early childhood special education and inclusive programs.

Key Terms

Americans with
   Disabilities Act
   (ADA) (20)
children at risk (7)
children with special
   needs (4)
compensatory or prevention
   programs (7)
developmental delay (9)
due process hearing (17)
early childhood
   education (ECE) (4)
early childhood
   intervention (ECI) (7)
early childhood special
   education (ECSE) (8)
early intervention (EI) (8)
elementary special
   education (6)
evidence-based (22)

exceptional children (4)
experimental (27)
free and appropriate
   public education
   (FAPE) (9)
giftedness (4)
Head Start (7)
inclusion (17)
inclusive classrooms (4)
Individualized Education
   Plan (IEP) (15)
Individualized Family
   Service Plan
   (IFSP) (20)
Individuals with
   Disabilities Education
   Act (IDEA) (8)
least restrictive
   environment
   (LRE) (24)

mainstreaming (24)
mixed methodologies (28)
natural environments (21)
No Child Left Behind Act
   (NCLB) (21)
qualitative research (28)
quantitative research (28)
quasi-experimental (27)
regular or general
   classrooms (4)
scientific research-
   based (22)
special education (9)
special education
   classrooms (4)
special education
   regulations (17)
transition (21)

Reflection Questions

Before reading this chapter, answer the following questions to reflect upon your personal opinions and beliefs that are pertinent to early childhood special education.

1. In your opinion, what should an early childhood educator know before working with a child with a disability?

2. In your opinion, what kind of services and support should be provided for children with disabilities?

3. In your opinion, what kind of support and services should be available to teachers who work with children with disabilities?

4. What is your position about inclusion of children with disabilities? Why?

INTRODUCTION

Education, care, and treatment of young **children with special needs** in the United States are accomplished through interaction and collaboration between public health and education fields, both of which are related to a broader system of care and education for all young children. Children with special needs, also referred to as **exceptional children,** are children who, due to a variety of factors such as a diagnosed condition/disability, environmental risks, or **giftedness,** might require a special education, which would differ from the education provided for other children who otherwise do not have exceptional needs.

This chapter introduces the field in which exceptional children are educated. We will examine the forces that have shaped the field of early childhood special education today, and establish a framework for working with young children with special needs. In this book and throughout this chapter, we use the terms **regular** and **general classrooms** interchangeably to refer to the educational settings in which typically developing children are educated, where no specific adaptations are made to the curriculum. We use the term **inclusive classrooms** to describe classrooms in which diverse populations of children, such as children with and without special needs, are educated. Finally, we use **special education classrooms** to refer to specialized and highly structured classrooms where children with disabilities are usually educated.

EARLY CHILDHOOD EDUCATION

Early childhood education (ECE) is a complex system of care and education of children from birth through 8 years (third grade). Its development is a result of the evolution of a series of educational philosophies from the 16th to 20th centuries, such as those of John Locke (1632–1704), Jean-Jacques Rousseau (1712–1778), Friedrich Froebel (1782–1852), and Maria Montessori (1870–1952) (Meisels & Shonkoff, 2000). These individuals formed the initial ideas about kindergarten, which was the first educational setting for young children outside the home.

Early childhood education is a dynamic field, which has continued to be influenced by research in developmental psychology, applied child development, and neuroscience. Gradual changes in the public policy and economic conditions also have influenced the system of care and education of young children in the United States.

The National Association for the Education of Young Children (NAEYC), a professional organization established in 1926 to promote excellence in the education of young children in the United States, has identified over 30 social, economical, and demographic critical issues influencing the education of young children. These issues include demographic changes in the U.S. population, availability of educational programs for young children, and employment resources available for educators of young children. See Table 1.1 for an example of a number of issues that have influenced early childhood education today.

Programs for Children with Exceptional Needs

One of the issues affecting the education of young children is the increasing number of children with disabilities in early childhood programs over the past two decades. In the past, the education and care of young children with special needs was carried out in hospitals or institutions and by professionals. Children with mild disabilities were enrolled in regular classrooms, from which they usually dropped out (Meisels & Shonkoff, 2000).

Over the past 30 years, along with the increasingly diverse needs of young children and their families, various public- and privately funded early childhood

TABLE 1.1   Critical Issues Related to the Education of Young Children as Identified by the National Association for the Education of Young Children (NAEYC)

Issues Related to Children and Families
➢ Growing number of children under age 8 in the United States
➢ Growing amount of racial diversity in families
➢ Growing number of non-native English speaking children in public schools
➢ Extreme poverty rate in young children (17.7% in 2006)
➢ Growing number of mothers in the workforce
➢ Growing number of children being cared for in center-based and home care programs
➢ Growing number of young children with disabilities

Issues Related to Programs for Young Children (Birth–8)
➢ Availability of state and federally funded early childhood programs in relation to the number of young children in the United States in need of publicly funded early education (birth–6 programs)
➢ Availability of high-quality programs
➢ Age and number of children in relation to program availability
➢ Types of care and education available after and before school hours
➢ State policies in regard to reimbursement for early care, and accreditation of early childhood education programs
➢ Ratio of child group size to staff
➢ Licensing requirements for home care programs

Issues Related to Early Childhood Workforce
➢ Qualification requirements for early childhood education professionals
➢ Training requirements for family child care providers
➢ Degree requirements for early childhood teachers
➢ Professional wages and salaries for early childhood professionals
➢ Professional and career development opportunities for early childhood professionals

Source: National Association for Education of Young Children; available at http://www.naeyc.org/ece/critical/facts.asp.

programs have been created to serve children and their families. The scope of intervention and the goals of each early childhood program vary from one to the next. These goals and functions depend on each program's funding source, the developmental and demographic characteristics of children whom the program serves, and the type of services required to address the needs of children in that program. Today, children from birth through age 8 who have special needs are educated in various settings: at home, in clinics, in centers, and in schools, and by a variety of professionals and paraprofessionals. Some of these programs are listed next:

> **Early childhood intervention (ECI) programs:** Serve children at risk or with developmental delays or disabilities from birth to 5 years old.
> **Early intervention (EI) programs:** Serve infants and toddlers at risk for disabilities or diagnosed with developmental delays or disabilities from birth to 3 years old.
> **Early childhood education (ECE) programs:** Serve children with and without disabilities from birth to 8 years old (third grade).
> **Early childhood special education (ECSE) programs:** Serve children with disabilities from birth to 8 years old (third grade).
> **Elementary special education programs:** Serve children with disabilities from age 5 to 13 years old (eighth grade).
> **Elementary education programs:** Serve children with or without disabilities from age 5 to 13 years old (eighth grade).

Although programs are separated by their function, the type of services they offer, and the age of the children whom they serve, they are all interrelated and work together within a larger system that is responsible for providing educational, therapeutic, and compensatory programs for all children in the United States (Figure 1.1).

FIGURE 1.1
System of Care and Education of Children with and without Education Needs

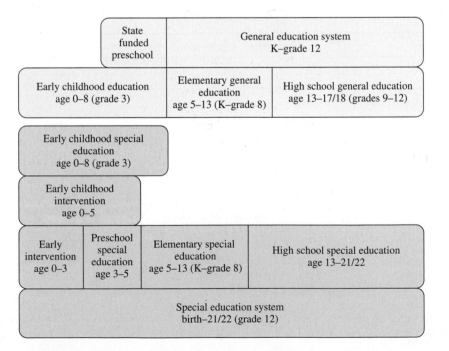

EARLY CHILDHOOD INTERVENTION

The terms early childhood intervention (ECI) and early intervention (EI) have been used interchangeably. However, these terms have specific meanings derived from the purpose of their programs, and the population of children and families they serve. **Early childhood intervention (ECI)** refers to the system of education and care for young children at risk and their families, as well as infants and toddlers with disabilities. Meisels and Shonkoff (2000) define early childhood intervention (ECI) as a field consisting of

> . . . multidisciplinary services provided to children from birth to 5 years of age to promote child health and well-being, enhance emerging competencies, minimize developmental delays, remediate existing or emerging disabilities, prevent functional deterioration, and promote adaptive parenting and overall family functioning. These goals are accomplished by providing individualized, developmental, educational, and therapeutic services to children in conjunction with mutually planned support for their families. (p. 17–8).

By this definition, the field of ECI encompasses **compensatory or prevention programs** as well as early intervention (EI) programs for infants and toddlers with disabilities.

Compensatory Programs

Compensatory or prevention programs target at-risk children in order to improve their school readiness. **Children at risk** are children who by virtue of growing up in sub-optimal environments and conditions, or because of their biological makeup, are at risk for negative developmental outcomes. Compensatory or prevention programs are publicly funded services that offer opportunities for intervention to change the life-course of children at risk.

The **Head Start** program is a compensatory program that was initially founded as an 8-week summer demonstration project by the office of Economic Opportunity in 1965 as part of the War on Poverty movement. In the 1990s, Head Start services expanded to include children from birth to 3 years of age and their families under Early Head Start programs. Head Start and Early Head Start programs offer multiple services, such as nutrition, medical, and parent education. The most important goal of these programs is to diminish the differences between socioeconomic disparities in the preschool years, so that young children will enter school on an equal footing with their more economically advantaged peers. In addition, they provide opportunities to prevent child maltreatment through parental education and support (Rose, 2009; Asawa, Hansen, & Flood, 2008). Both Early Head Start and Head Start programs are considered inclusive programs, within which young children with special needs might be served.

Because at-risk children are likely to be educated in inadequately staffed early childhood centers and schools (Stormont, 2007), there has been a concerted effort in Head Start to increase the criteria for teacher qualification as a critical component to increase the overall quality of its programs. In 2007, Congress approved a bill that boosted teacher qualifications in federally funded Head Start preschools.

The legislation set a goal that by 2013 all Head Start teachers will have at least an associate's degree and 50 percent of Head Start teachers and administrative staff will have a baccalaureate or advanced degree.

EARLY INTERVENTION PROGRAMS

Early intervention programs (EI) consist of educational, therapeutic, and medical programs and services for infants and toddlers (birth to 3 years of age) with disabilities, as well as their families. In some states, early intervention programs are funded and provided by the Department of Health and Human Services, while other states might provide EI to infants and toddlers through their State Board of Education.

The EI programs are commonly considered to be part of the larger system of Early childhood special education (ECSE) since both EI services and services for older children with disabilities are mandated within the same law **(Individuals with Disability Education Act–IDEA),** which governs the education of all children with disabilities in the United States. In later sections of this chapter, we will examine this law and provisions under which EI is to be provided to infants and toddlers and their families.

EARLY CHILDHOOD SPECIAL EDUCATION

Part of the larger special education system, **early childhood special education (ECSE)** provides services to all children with developmental delays or with disabilities (birth–age 8 or third grade) and their families (Bowe, 2007). Children 3 to 5 years old, who have a diagnosed condition, might receive services through special education preschool, or in any inclusive early childhood preschool programs.

Children age 6, 7, and 8 who have a diagnosed disability receive services through elementary education or elementary special education. They might be educated in special education, inclusive, or in general education classrooms (Bowe, 2007).

Children 3 to 5 years old who have a diagnosed condition might receive services through a special education preschool.

Special education means special instruction for children who have special needs and require modified and adapted education (Ysseldyke & Algozzine, 2006). IDEA describes special education as "specially designed instruction, at no cost to the parents, to meet the unique needs of a child with a disability (IDEA as cited by Wright & Wright, 2007, p. 21)."

Who Is Eligible to Receive Early Intervention and Special Education?

Under U.S. laws, all children from birth to age 21 (or 22, in some states) who have disabilities are entitled to receive free and appropriate education at the public expense. The Individuals with Disabilities Education Act (IDEA) is the major law regarding the education of children with disabilities, which has been reauthorized and amended several times since 1975 when it was first introduced to the Congress of the United States under the title: Education for All Handicapped Children Act. The most recent amendment of IDEA took place in 2004 under a new title, Individuals with Disabilities Education Improvement Act, also known as IDEIA.

Under its Part C, governing the regulation for early intervention, Individuals with Disabilities Education Act (IDEA) requires that the eligibility of infants and toddlers be determined by each state's definition of **developmental delay** and whether it includes children at risk for disabilities in the eligibility formula. The use of the term developmental delay has been necessary to allow young children to receive needed services without having to be assigned a specific disability label (Bernheimer, Koegh, & Coots, 1993). Additionally, all aspects of development are still in progress, and a condition in a child might not persist over time to constitute a disability (Brown & Sorensen, 2007). The criteria for assigning the developmental delay label vary by state, and typically involve measures of delay based on standard deviation from the mean, usually between 1.5 and 2 standard deviations below the mean, or a 25 percent delay in one or more of the following areas: adaptive, cognitive, communication, social or emotional, or physical development (Delgado, Vagi, & Scott, 2007). Developmental delay is therefore established as an eligibility category under Part C. A diagnosis of developmental delay is determined by developmental testing conducted by professionals. States rely on an informed clinical decision and the opinion of professionals who are experienced in working with infants and toddlers to determine eligibility. Under IDEA, depending on the states' discretions, at-risk infants and toddlers are also eligible to receive early intervention services.

The eligibility of children 3 years of age and older is determined based on the diagnosis of a specific disability. In general, IDEA requires that both developmental delays and disabilities be measured by appropriate diagnostic instruments and procedures. Table 1.2 displays categories of disabilities and delays defined under IDEA.

What Services Do Children Receive?

Based on provisions of IDEA, school districts are responsible for providing **free and appropriate public education (FAPE)** to children with disabilities. Congress defines free appropriate public education as special education and related services, such as speech pathology, audiology, psychological services, physical and occupational

TABLE 1.2   Categories of Disabilities under IDEIA 2004

Categories of Disabilities under Part B–Special Education	Areas of Developmental Delays under Part C–Early Intervention

➢ Mental retardation
➢ Hearing impairment (including deafness)
➢ Speech or language impairment
➢ Visual impairment (including blindness)
➢ Serious emotional disturbance
➢ Orthopedic impairment
➢ Autism
➢ Traumatic brain injury
➢ Other health impairment
  ➢ Limited strength, vitality, or alertness due to chronic illnesses such as:
    ➢ Asthma
    ➢ ADHD
    ➢ Diabetes
    ➢ Epilepsy
    ➢ Heart condition
    ➢ Hemophilia
    ➢ Lead poisoning
    ➢ Leukemia
    ➢ Nephritis
    ➢ Rheumatic fever
    ➢ Sickle cell anemia
    ➢ Tourette's syndrome
➢ Specific learning disability
➢ Deaf-blindness
➢ Multiple disabilities
➢ Those who, due to disability, need special education and related services
	➢ Infants and toddlers identified as having developmental delays in one or more of the following areas:
	  ➢ Physical development
	  ➢ Cognitive development
	  ➢ Communication development
	  ➢ Social or emotional development
	  ➢ Adaptive development

therapy, recreation, and other supportive services (Ysseldyke & Algozzine, 2006). Special education and supportive services are to be "appropriate" based on the child's special educational needs.

In 1982, the U.S. Supreme Court in *Board of Education v. Rowley* ruled that "appropriate" education is not synonymous with "best" education. Rather, the standard is that adequate education, like the education other children have access to, should be provided (Wright & Wright, 2007; Sands, Kozleski, & French, 2000). Various services available for infants, toddlers, and young children with disabilities are displayed in Table 1.3.

TABLE 1.3   Categories of Developmental Delays and Provision of Services under IDEIA (2004)

Who Receives Services? (Areas of Development Addressed)	What Types of Services Are Provided?	Who Provides Services?
Infants and toddlers identified as having delays in one or more of the following areas:		
Early identification and diagnostic services	Screening and assessment; medical services only for diagnostic purposes	Health and education professionals (e.g., physicians, psychologists, therapists, special education teachers, etc.)
Physical development	Physical therapy	Physical therapists
Cognitive development	Special instruction	Special educators and developmental therapists
Communication development	Speech/language pathology services: ➢ Speech therapy ➢ Audiology services ➢ Sign language and cued language services	Speech language pathologists and audiologists
Fine motor development, feeding, and sensory processing and integration	Occupational therapy	Occupational therapists, developmental therapists, and special education teachers
Social or emotional development	Developmental therapy, special education	Developmental therapists and special education teachers
Adaptive development, family empowerment, and other areas	Developmental therapy, family training, counseling, and home visits	Family therapists
	Psychological services	Psychologists
	Service coordination services	Nurses

TYPES OF EARLY CHILDHOOD SETTINGS FOR SERVICE PROVISION

A variety of home, center, and school-based private and public programs serve children with disabilities. These programs can be inclusive or specialized; they might provide care and education for children for a part of the day or for a full day. In addition, these programs might target specific age groups, such as infants and toddlers, preschoolers, or school-age children. Table 1.4 displays a range of settings available for children with disabilities.

TABLE 1.4   Programs for Young Children with Disabilities

Type of Programs	Funding
Child Care Programs	
≻ Home/family child care	≻ Private
≻ Child care centers	≻ Private or supplemental funding by states
≻ Corporate sponsored child care	≻ Corporate organizations or workplace
Programs for Infants and Toddlers	
≻ Early Head Start	≻ Federal
≻ Birth-to-Three programs	≻ Federal, state, or private/nonprofit
≻ Parent/child programs	≻ Federal, state, or private/nonprofit
≻ Early intervention center-based or home-based	≻ State EI program
≻ Clinics or office therapy visits	≻ State EI and/or private
Preschool Programs	
≻ State Pre-K	≻ States
≻ Head Start	≻ Federal
≻ Private preschools	≻ Private/nonprofit or religious organizations
≻ Preschool for All	≻ Selective states
Schools	
≻ Private schools	≻ Private/nonprofit or religious organizations
≻ Public schools	≻ Federal, state, and local government

A range of settings are available for children with disabilities. These target specific age groups such as infants and toddlers.

WHO ARE THE PROFESSIONALS IN THE FIELD?

A variety of professionals in early childhood education and in early childhood special education provide educational and therapeutic services to children with special needs (age 0–8). These professionals range from early childhood teachers and therapists to support personnel who provide transportation. Table 1.5 lists the professionals in the field.

EARLY CHILDHOOD SPECIAL EDUCATION TODAY

The current early childhood special education system in the United States is a result of (1) a number of historical developments in the education of children with disabilities, (2) a number of landmark legal decisions and laws regarding the civil and educational rights of individuals and children with disabilities and their families, and (3) advances in early education and child intervention research.

A HISTORICAL PERSPECTIVE ON THE EDUCATION OF YOUNG CHILDREN WITH SPECIAL NEEDS

The history of special education began with ideas brought forth by Renaissance philosophers, activists, religious leaders, philanthropists, and intellectuals who had some revolutionary ideas—for their times—about the education of children and individuals with disabilities. The interest of a variety of such individuals, which had been sparked by the development of the scientific method and philosophical enlightenment beginning in the early modern period—the 14th through 16th centuries—set the stage for the development of what we know today as special education.

The formal education of exceptional children has often been cited to have begun sometime in the mid-18th to early 19th century (Braddock & Parish, 2002; Noll & Trent, 2004; Longmore & Umansky, 2001; Winzer, 2007). Prior to that time, children and adults with disabilities were rarely tolerated no matter what the disability, and were lumped together under the broad category of "idiots," who were considered to be inferior and not worthy of having the same rights and privileges in society (Winzer, 2007).

There is no specific date as to when children with special needs began to receive special education and training. The first schools for deaf and blind children opened in Spain and France in the early 1800s. Pedro Ponce de Leon, a Benedictine monk, is credited with being the first teacher of deaf children, who apparently utilized a kind of manual alphabet to teach the deaf children of wealthy Spanish families (Braddock & Parish, 2002). Abbe de l'Epee, a French priest, established the first public residential school for deaf persons in Paris in 1755 (Braddock & Parish, 2002). Special schools for deaf and blind children grew throughout the 19th century, and gradually children with physical and intellectual disabilities were also included in special schools.

Advances in medical science changed public opinion regarding the nature and treatment of disabilities in the late 19th century. A medical model of treatment for

TABLE 1.5   **Meet the Professionals in the Field**

Developmental therapists	Provide therapy to enhance all areas of development in the child (i.e., physical, cognitive, social emotional, language)
Early childhood teachers	Provide early education including developmental and age appropriate experiences
Early childhood special education teachers	Provide special education and services
Early childhood paraprofessional and support personnel:	
Parent liaisons	Provide support for the parents of young children with special needs in matters related to the early intervention system and services
Student's one-on-one aides	Support and help with the child's individual needs in the classroom
Teacher's assistants	Assist the teacher in daily classroom activities
School bus attendants	Ensure children's safety on the bus
Bus drivers	Operate school buses
Volunteers	Support staff and teachers to carry out classroom and school activities
Food service workers	Carry out lunchroom activities
Clerical/office staff	Perform administrative tasks
Speech and language pathologists/therapists	Provide speech and language therapy, and help enhance communication development in the child
Occupational therapists	Provide therapy related to development of fine muscles and sensory integration
Physical therapists	Provide therapy related to development of gross muscles
Service coordinators	Direct and coordinate IFSP development; coordinate provision and delivery of special education and support services for children from birth to 3 years of age
Case managers	Direct and coordinate IEP development; coordinate provision and delivery of special education and support services in schools for children 3 years of age and older
School nurses	Provide medical support for children who need daily medical supervision (e.g., for medication, diet, and other health issues)
School social workers/counselors	Work with parents and children in providing support for issues related to home and school that might have an effect on the child's learning, performance, and development
Learning specialists	Provide tutoring and support, and teach strategies that help children overcome learning difficulties related to specific subjects, such as math and reading
School psychologists	Provide support with issues related to development and learning, as well as conduct psychological, aptitude, and developmental testing
Principals	Oversee all matters related to IEP development, delivery of general and special education and supplemental services to children, and issues related to special education personnel and funding in schools (in kindergarten through twelfth grade)

children with disabilities became popular during this time, which advocated separation of children with special needs from the public, and their education in specialized classes (Winzer, 2007). From the late 19th century through the early 20th century, special and segregated classes for children with disabilities grew in number, and by 1927, 218 U.S. cities had special classes for about 52,000 children with disabilities (Osgood, 1997).

With the expansion of special classes came advances in psychology and cognitive testing, which resulted in welcoming a new group of specialized professionals and clinicians, such as psychologists, social workers, and speech and occupational therapists to the field of special education (Winzer 2007).

Early Pioneers in Special Education

The field of special education has been influenced by the works of a number of pioneers who devised methods of working with children and individuals with special needs for the first time. A brief description of some such pioneers and their work follows.

Itard

Jean-Marc-Gaspard Itard (1775–1850) has been called the father of special education. Itard was a young French physician who joined the medical staff of the National Institution for Deaf Mutes in Paris when he was 25 years old (Humphrey, 1962). In 1799, a boy was found in the outskirts of the forest of Aveyron in southern France, who appeared to be about 12 years old, was naked and apparently had lived in the forest without any human contact all his life. The boy had no language, was dirty, and "trotted and grunted like animals" (Humphrey, 1962, p. 6). He was brought to Paris, and people from all over France came to see the "man in the state of nature," or the "man-animal" (Braddock & Parish, 2002; Humphrey, 1962).

Itard set out to educate the boy, who was named Victor, despite the beliefs of his colleagues and scientists of the time that because of severe sensory deprivation, the boy was not educable. Itard recorded the account of his experience with Victor's education in a diary that was later published in a book, *The Wild Boy of Aveyron*, in 1828. The case description of Victor, along with the educational methods used by Itard in his diary, provide one of the first well-documented case studies of a child who might have been diagnosed with autism had he lived in the 21st century (Frith, 1989; Carrey, 1995).

Devoting 5 years of his life to the education of Victor, Itard provided an individualized instruction for Victor based on what might be considered the first **Individualized Education Plan (IEP)** in history. Victor's IEP consisted of five basic goals (Itard, 1962, pp. 10–11):

> To interest him in social life by rendering it more pleasant to him than the one he was then leading
> To awaken his nervous sensibility by the most energetic stimulation
> To extend the range of his ideas by giving him new needs and by increasing his social contacts
> To lead him to the use of speech by inducing the exercise of imitation through the imperious law of necessity
> To make him exercise the simplest mental operations upon the objects of instruction

Itard used a combination of what we know today as visual strategies, sensory stimulation, and behavioral methods to help Victor learn language, as well as cognitive, social, emotional, and self-help skills. His educational methods have formed the foundations of many educational techniques used to educate young children with special education needs today.

Although Victor made significant progress, he learned only minimal speech and was never able to become fully independent. However, Itard's work triggered further successful interventions for children with intellectual disabilities by his predecessors, such as Seguin and Howe (Braddock & Parish, 2002).

Seguin

Edward Seguin (1812–1881) was Itard's pupil. He expanded Itard's sensory techniques into what he called the "physiological method," which included sensory-motor, intellectual, academic, and speech training (Braddock & Parish, 2002). Seguin's work with children who had mental disabilities eventually became the standard worldwide, and many schools for such children opened around the globe as a result (Simpson, 1999). Seguin's methods focused on self-help skills and vocational training for children and individuals with cognitive and intellectual disabilities. He moved to the United States in 1850 and introduced his methods to U.S. specialized institutions (Simpson, 1999).

Howe

Samuel Howe (1801–1876) supported Seguin's methods and envisioned a set of training efforts that would result in the integration of children with disabilities into their communities as independent and productive members of society (Trent, 1994). He founded a number of training schools in Massachusetts, including the Perkins School for the Blind. His efforts resulted in the establishment of a number of residential asylums and institutions for children and individuals with intellectual disabilities.

Among many other notable persons who pioneered the individualized approach to education are Anne Sullivan Macy (1866–1936), Helen Keller's teacher (refer to Chapter 12); Elizabeth Farrell (1870–1932), the founder of the Council of Exceptional Children (CEC), who taught the first special education classes in New York; and Maria Montessori (1870–1952), whose sensory methods in education continue to be used in many of today's early childhood educational settings.

Helen Keller was taught by Anne Sullivan Macy, one of the pioneers of the individualized approach to education.

LEGAL FOUNDATIONS OF SPECIAL EDUCATION TODAY

The first laws regarding disability in the United States date back to 1817 and established the American Asylum for the education and instruction of the deaf (Ysseldyke & Algozzine, 2006). During the 19th century, a variety of laws were enacted to fund the creation of hospitals, institutions, and rehabilitation centers to educate children and adults with various disabilities. As a result, the number of special schools for children with disabilities such as deafness, blindness, and intellectual disability increased throughout the 19th and 20th centuries (Wright & Wright, 2007). Historically, these schools and institutions segregated children with special needs from their families and communities, and educated them in isolation from their typically developing peers and adults.

Over time, U.S. laws regarding the education of children with special needs have undergone numerous changes, which have resulted in the mandate of the **inclusion** of children with disabilities in the school and community when appropriate. The laws that have shaped the current practices in early childhood and higher grade special education have been legislated partly because parents of children with disabilities have taken legal actions against the existing system and laws governing the education of their children (Ysseldyke & Algozzine, 2006), and partly because of the research that has demonstrated the importance of early childhood intervention. When individuals take legal actions, it usually means the views of the public have changed, and the public is now demanding changes in the law. As a result, Congress may respond by passing new laws. The original federal special education law was titled The Education of All Handicapped Children Act of 1975, which was later amended and renamed the Individuals with Disabilities Education Act, also known as IDEA. Congress publishes a *law* as an act first, and then organizes these subjects in the United States Code (U.S.C.) (Wright & Wright, 2007). The U.S. Department of Education, thereafter, clarifies and explains the federal laws related to the education of children with disabilities, and publishes them as the U.S. **special education regulations.**

The legislation process is a dynamic process. U.S. laws constantly evolve and are redefined based on the changing needs and views of society. Therefore, the special education laws and practices change on an ongoing basis. These changes might be based on litigations brought to the U.S. Supreme Court by family members, and usually start with a special education **due process hearing** (Wright & Wright, 2007).

Changes to special education laws and practices occur on an ongoing basis and may be based on litigations brought to the U.S. Supreme Court by family members.

FIGURE 1.2

Timeline of Landmark
Case Laws and
Public Laws in
Special Education in
the United States

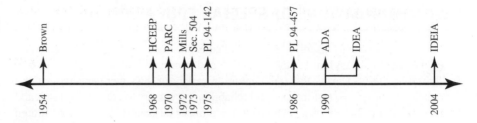

A due process hearing is a process that gives parents the right to legal counsel and to present evidence to contest decisions made about the education of their children with disabilities (Ysseldyke & Algozzine, 2006).

In the following section, we will describe several important pieces of legislation, as well as some U.S. Supreme Court cases (also known as *case laws*), involving children and individuals with disabilities. Although these legal developments have occurred independently of one another, each court ruling, as well as each piece of legislation by Congress, has formed the building blocks of early childhood special education in the United States today. Figure 1.2 displays the timeline for landmark litigations and public laws in early childhood special education.

Brown v. Board of Education (1954)

Many of you may be familiar with *Brown v. Board of Education,* the landmark civil right's case in which the U.S. Supreme Court ruled against segregated schools and found that African American children had the right to equal educational opportunities. In the Brown ruling, the Supreme Court elaborated the negative emotional impacts of segregation on the development and education of African American children. It was this decision that paved the way for parents of children with disabilities to bring lawsuits against their school districts for discriminating against their children with disabilities (Wright & Wright, 2007).

Handicapped Children's Early Education Assistance Act of 1968 (Public Law 90-538)

Public Law 90-538 established the Handicapped Children's Early Education Program, also known as HCEEP, which provided for the establishment of from 75 to 100 model programs designed to develop successful approaches in assisting preschool age children with disabilities (U.S. Department of Health, Education, and Welfare, 1968). This law approved federal funds to be designated to support experimental and model programs providing early intervention services for young children with disabilities (or those at risk for disabilities) and their families. This program no longer exists, and funds for research and demonstration projects are currently dispersed through the general funds that finance all programs for children with disabilities (Allen & Cowdery, 2005).

Pennsylvania Association for Retarded Children (PARC) v. Commonwealth of Pennsylvania

In the early 1970s, the Pennsylvania Association for Retarded Children (PARC) brought a lawsuit against the state of Pennsylvania on behalf of children with mental retardation in that state, contending that the state had failed to provide free public education to children with mental retardation. The Supreme Court found that all children with mental retardation could benefit from education, and because the state had promised to provide free public education to *all* its children, it could not deny any child access to an education (Sands et al., 2000).

Mills v. Board of Education

In 1972, the families of seven children with disabilities sued the District of Columbia public schools, which had refused to pay for the education of their children. The Washington DC public schools had reasoned that it could not afford the high costs of the extended services these children needed. The Supreme Court found that no school district could deny students access to free public education and that the district was responsible for providing services that are appropriate to the students' needs regardless of the degree and severity of disability and the costs (Sands et al., 2000).

Section 504 of the Rehabilitation Act of 1973

In 1973, in Section 504 of the Rehabilitation Act, Congress had prohibited all programs funded by the federal and state government to discriminate against individuals with disabilities solely on the basis of their disabilities. The act mandated that persons with disabilities should have equal access to state and federally funded programs and services and should be able to participate in the activities of these programs. In 1977, Congress determined that this law is applicable to schools as well as social and health service agencies. With this, Congress asked schools to provide auxiliary aid should any student with disabilities need them in order to be able to participate in school programs.

Congressional Committee Findings

Both PARC and Mills prompted Congress to appoint a committee to investigate the status of education of children with disabilities. Congress found that the majority of children with disabilities were either receiving no appropriate education or an inappropriate education. Congress recognized the long-term negative effects of a lack of appropriate education on children with disabilities and their families. Therefore, in 1975 Congress enacted the first public law describing the educational rights of children with disabilities.

Public Law (Public Law 94-142): The Education of All Handicapped Children Act of 1975

Through the Education of All Handicapped Children Act of 1975, Congress held that all children with disabilities have a right to a free appropriate public education.

    This act also provided the following:

> Students with disabilities (age 3–21) should have an Individualized Education Plan (IEP), a written plan developed by professionals and parents outlining the education plan for the child on an annual basis, which should be filed by the school.

> Parents of students with disabilities have a right to examine their children's record, be informed of any changes in regard to their children's education, and have a right to challenge the school's decisions in regard to their children's education via a due process hearing.
> Students with disabilities have the right to be educated in the *least restrictive environment.*
> Students with disabilities must be assessed in a *nondiscriminatory* and fair way.

All Handicapped Children Act Amendments of 1986 (Public Law 99-457): The Birth of Early Intervention and Early Childhood Special Education

Public Law 94-142 was amended in 1986 as PL 99-457 to include infants, toddlers, and preschoolers (age 0–5) with disabilities, to receive free appropriate public education. Under Part B of this law, services were to be provided for children from age 3 to 5.

Part H was also enacted to provide incentives to the states to provide early intervention services (EI) for children from birth through age 2, who either had disabilities or were at risk for disabilities. Part H of this law acknowledged the importance of the family's role in the child's development and education. It emphasized the necessity of the family's participation in the development of an individualized educational program for young children from birth through age 2. The **Individualized Family Service Plan (IFSP)** is an annual plan written by professionals and parents outlining outcomes for the infants and toddlers and their families.

The Americans with Disabilities Act of 1990

In 1990, Congress recognized that segregation and unequal treatment of individuals with disabilities was the major problem with the common perceptions and treatment of individuals with disabilities that needed to be addressed, and not the impairment of the individual (Braddock & Parrish, 2002). The **Americans with Disabilities Act (ADA)** prohibited discrimination against individuals with disabilities in employment settings, public places, transportation, and telecommunication services. ADA required that public places, including public schools, make accommodations to the facilities and programs. In addition, public schools were to provide assistive technology for students with disabilities.

Individuals with Disabilities Education Act of 1990 and Its Subsequent Amendments

Since 1975, Congress has renamed and amended the Education of All Handicapped Children Act several times (1986, 1990, 1992, 1997, and 2004). In the second amendment of this law in 1990, Congress renamed the Act to *Individuals with Disabilities Education Act Amendment of 1990* (P.L. 101-476), commonly known as IDEA. With this act, Congress abandoned the phrase "handicapped child," replacing it with "child with a disability," and acknowledged that children and individuals with disabilities are *people* and *children first.*

In general, IDEA provides a set of guidelines regarding the rights of children with disabilities and their families to services and support. In addition, it provides a mechanism for the appropriation of funds to federal agencies to assist early intervention programs and schools in providing support and services to children with disabilities and their families (Sands et al., 2000).

In 1992, IDEA was amended as (P.L. 102-119) to place an emphasis on **transition** services for infants and young children (under Part H of IDEA) to be placed by the time they reach age 3. Accordingly, services should be provided for toddlers to ensure a smooth transition from Part H service to educational and supplementary services provided for these children under Part B.

IDEA was amended again in 1997 (P.L. 105-17) to revise the early intervention program, which had been previously enacted under Part H, under a new section: Part C. The Part C of IDEA acknowledges that because infants and toddlers spend most of their time at home, their homes should be considered schools, and parents and caregivers should be considered teachers (Shaw & Good, 2008; Brown & Sorenson, 2007). Therefore, the law requires that to the extent possible, infants and toddlers should receive EI services in their **natural environments.** Natural environments have been defined as the environment in which the infants and toddlers without disability grow and develop; namely their homes and community settings (Brown & Sorensen, 2007).

The No Child Left Behind Act of 2001 (Public Law 107-110)

The **No Child Left Behind Act (NCLB)** reauthorized the Elementary and Secondary Education Act (ESEA), which is the main federal law specifying the education that needs to be provided to all children in the United States from kindergarten through high school. The NCLB was signed into law in January 2002 by President George W. Bush, and a proposal for reauthorization of the act was submitted to Congress in 2007. The NCLB Act is based on four principles: (1) accountability of results; (2) choices for parents; (3) more local control; and (4) focus on scientific-based teaching methods (U.S. Department of Education, 2007).

Although the NCLB is a general education act, because its provisions are for *all* children, the act affects the education of children with disabilities. The NCLB's emphasis on accountability mandates that school personnel need to include students with disabilities in their accountability system (Ysseldyke & Algozzine, 2006). In addition, the act's focus on scientific-based (also known as evidence-based) methods of education influenced the new provisions of IDEIA 2004, under which scientific-based intervention is required to be a part of the evaluation and intervention process for all children with disabilities.

Individuals with Disabilities Education Improvement Act 2004

The most recent reauthorization of IDEA took place in 2004 and is known as *Individuals with Disabilities Education Improvement Act–IDEIA 2004* (P.L. 108-446). In general, IDEA, including its latest provisions, is divided into five major parts (Parts A–E) (Table 1.6). As previously specified, the provisions of services to children from age 3 to 21 are addressed under Part B, and the early intervention

TABLE 1.6   **Five Major Parts of IDEIA 2004**

Part A	General provisions (Sections 1400–1409)
Part B	Assistance for Education of All Children with Disabilities (Sections 1411–1419)
Part C	Infants and Toddlers with Disabilities (Sections 1431–1444)
Part D	National Activities to Improve Education of Children with Disabilities (Sections 1450–1482)
Part E	National Center for Special Education Research (Section 9567)

services to infants and toddlers with disabilities are addressed under Part C of IDEA. Text Box 1.1 explains the provisions of IDEA under Part C.

Significant Changes under IDEIA 2004

The new IDEIA includes several changes. Some of the significant changes of IDEIA 2004 influencing the education of young children as cited by the Council for Exceptional Children (2004) and Mandlawitz (2007) are as follows:

- All special education teachers should be highly qualified—that is, teachers should have state special education certification or have passed state licensing exams in regard to the contents of specialization in their teaching certificates.
- To prevent over-identification of children, states provide funding for training teachers in effective teaching techniques and positive behavioral interventions and support.
- The changes in the new IDEIA put an emphasis on **evidence-based** or **scientific research-based** approaches to intervention, which are carried out by qualified teachers and therapists. Evidence-based approaches to intervention are those educational and therapeutic methods that have been supported by empirical research.
- Schools and early intervention programs are required to use a process that determines if the child responds to scientific research-based intervention as a part of a required evaluation process.
- For a young child who has been served under early intervention, the service coordinator may participate in the first IEP after transition to the next educational setting, at the request of the parent.
- An optional state program may be established in which parents of children eligible for preschool special education services, who had been previously receiving EI services under Part C, are allowed to choose to continue early intervention services under Part C until their children enter, or can send their children to kindergarten.
- States are required to include policies and procedures that require infants and toddlers under age 3 to be referred for early intervention services if:
  - They are involved in a substantiated case of child abuse or neglect
  - They are identified as affected by illegal substance abuse or withdrawal symptoms resulting from prenatal drug exposure

IDEA–Part C–Infants and Toddlers with Disabilities (Sections 1431–1444)

Text Box 1.1

By enacting Part C, Congress asked states to establish early intervention programs:

- ≥ To enhance the development of infants and toddlers to minimize the potential for developmental delays during the first 3 years of life
- ≥ To reduce the educational costs to minimize the need for special education and related services after infants and toddlers reach school age
- ≥ To maximize the potential for individuals with a disability to live independently in society
- ≥ To enhance the capacity of families to meet the special needs of their infants and toddlers with disabilities
- ≥ To enhance the capacity of states and local agencies to identify, evaluate, and meet the needs of all children, particularly those at risk

Congress set policy:

- ≥ To develop and implement a statewide comprehensive, coordinated, multidisciplinary, interagency system that provides early intervention services for infants and toddlers with disabilities, as well as their families
- ≥ To facilitate the coordination of payment for EI services
- ≥ To enhance a state's capacity to provide quality early intervention services and expand and improve current services
- ≥ To encourage states to expand opportunities for children under 3 years of age who would be at risk of having substantial developmental delay if they did not receive early intervention services

Source: Wright, P. W. & Wright, P. D. (2006). *Special education law* (2nd ed.). Hartfield, VA: Harbor House Law Press, Inc.

INCLUSION

Scholars and educators have defined inclusion in a variety of ways. The definition of inclusion far exceeds describing a geographic location for education of children with disabilities or a set of pedagogical actions to be used for these children. Rather, inclusion is a philosophy, or an ideology about the educational rights of all children. As a philosophy, inclusion refers to the right of all children to the same education, as well as their right to be active participating members of the same classroom community (Schwartz, 1996). Inclusion "begins with the right of every child to be in the mainstream of education. Students do not have to 'earn' their way into the classroom with their behavior or skills" (Sapon-Shiven, 2007, p. 6).

The term inclusion has not been used in the language of the law. However, IDEA requires that to the maximum extent possible, it is necessary that the schools educate children with disabilities along with typically developing children. Special classes or other removal from regular educational environments should occur only if the nature or severity of the disability is such that education in regular classes with supplementary aides and services cannot be satisfactorily achieved. This is known as the principle of the **least restrictive environment (LRE).** The equivalent of this principle for infants and toddlers is the principle of natural environment. Together these two principles have formed the concept of inclusion in education today. Inclusion ensures that children with disabilities to the maximum extent possible should be educated in general education classrooms and settings along with their typically developing peers. For preschool children, age 3 to 5, inclusive education is emphasized to be provided in community and local preschools, such as Head Start, private and publicly funded early childhood centers where children without disabilities are typically educated.

What Is Mainstreaming?

Traditionally, children with disabilities had to "earn" their way into general education classrooms by showing that they had made enough improvement and progress in their behavioral and academic development that they deserved the right to be educated with their typically developing peers. This model is usually referred to as **mainstreaming.**

Before inclusion found its way into our consciousness, mainstreaming had been the primary method by which children with disabilities were educated in the least restrictive environments (Idol, 2006). Mainstreaming differs from inclusion. In mainstreaming, children with disabilities are educated in a general education setting with or without receiving special education services. Children who are mainstreamed in a general education setting are expected to demonstrate that they are capable of performing the tasks that other students perform in the same classroom. In partial mainstreaming, a child might spend a portion of the day in a general education classroom and a portion of the day in a special education classroom (Idol, 2006).

Inclusion in Early Childhood Education

Although inclusion has been discussed since the 1970s (Allen, Benning, & Drummond, 1972), in the United States, inclusion of children with disabilities has found momentum only since the 1990s. The number of children with disabilities in inclusive classrooms has been on the rise. Between 1985 and 2001, this number doubled in most disability categories, including learning disabilities and autism (Cook, Cameron, & Tankersley, 2007). The Division for Early Childhood (DEC) of the Council for Exceptional Children and the National Association for the Education of Young Children (NAEYC) have articulated a joint position on early childhood inclusion (DEC/NAEYC, 2009). In their position statement, they define early childhood inclusion to embody "the values, policies, and practices that support the right of every infant and young child and his or her family, regardless of ability to participate in a broad range of activities and contexts as full members of families, communities, and society. The desired results of inclusive experiences for children with and without disabilities and their families include a sense of belonging and membership, positive social relationships and friendships, and development and learning to reach their full potential. The defining features of inclusion that can be used to identify high-quality early childhood programs and services are access, participation, and supports" (DEC/NAEYC, 2009, p. 2). You can find the full position statement at http://www.naeyc.org/files/naeyc/file/positions/DEC_NAEYC_EC_updatedKS.pdf.

As articulated by Baily, McWilliam, Buysse, and Wesley (1998), inclusion in early childhood education has been defined to espouse three sets of values:

1. Children should be educated in high-quality educational settings.
2. Services should address the special learning needs of children with disabilities.
3. Services should be family-centered.

These values indicate that any early childhood setting should strive to not only improve the quality of child care for all children, but to facilitate inclusion through training programs for teachers, by means of various support services for children and their families, and by providing individualization of curriculum and instruction so all children will benefit. The concept of inclusion does not involve only students with disabilities. It encompasses the practice of including all children regardless of their talent, disability, socioeconomic background, language, or cultural origin (Karagiannis, Stainback, & Stainback, 1996).

An inclusive educational setting is a classroom within which a variety of supports, such as teaching innovations and adaptations are made for every child in the classroom, and includes all children with diverse developmental and learning needs (Schwarz, 2006). An inclusive classroom is a community in which children with disabilities and other diverse needs are welcomed "into the curriculum, environment, social interaction, and self-concept of the school" (Smith, 1998, p. 18).

Research on Inclusion in Early Childhood Education

Research has been consistent in finding positive outcomes for all young children who are educated in early childhood inclusive settings (Hundert, Mahoney, Mundy, & Vernon, 1998; Hanlin, 1993; Levine & Antia, 1997; Stahmer & Carter, 2005). Most studies on inclusive preschool classrooms report gains in language, cognitive, motor, and social emotional development, which is above the progress that children with disabilities would typically make in special education classrooms (Odom, 2000; Fewell & Oelwein, 1990; Burack & Volkmar, 1992; Stahmer & Carter 2005). Toddlers and preschoolers with special needs seem to make considerable social gains in inclusive settings, especially when their teachers facilitate interactions and play among peers and model appropriate behaviors for all children (Terpstra & Tamura, 2008; Hestenes & Carroll, 2000). In addition, children with disabilities who are educated in inclusive classrooms seem to have a greater number of social interactions and a larger friendship network consisting of peers without disabilities (Kennedy, Shukla, & Fryxell, 1997).

Inclusive classrooms have been found beneficial for children with typical development as well. Young typically developing children appear to develop advanced social skills such as how to get along with others when compared with children in non-inclusive settings (Hestenes & Carroll, 2000). Contrary to common belief, research has shown that children without disabilities are empathetic toward their peers with disabilities. As these children enter primary grade inclusive classrooms, they provide physical and academic assistance for their peers with disabilities and show physical affection to them (Evans, Salisbury, Palombaro, Berryman, & Hollowood, 1992). Typically developing children who are educated in inclusive settings frequently demonstrate increased acceptance, understanding, and tolerance of individual differences, and tend to develop meaningful friendships with their classmates with disabilities

Text Box 1.2   Ten Lessons That Children Learn from Inclusive Classrooms

1. **Understanding differences:** Children understand and value differences when they are surrounded by them.
2. **Perspective taking:** Children learn that not everyone experiences the world the same way they do.
3. **Real safety:** Being different does not automatically mean separation and exclusion. Being in real safety means that children know that they are accepted and supported for who they are regardless of their differences.
4. **Exclusion hurts everyone:** Being in the same classroom with children who are different allows children to reach out and ask "Do you want to play?" as opposed to "We don't want you to play with us."
5. **Compassion:** Being educated with children who have various abilities and disabilities allows children to "feel with" one another and treat each other with an open heart, understanding, and compassion.
6. **Giving and getting help graciously:** Being in inclusive classrooms helps children feel useful and valued for their contributions, and teaches them that every person is involved with various levels of helping and being helped.
7. **Responsibility to one another:** Inclusive classrooms teach children to think about "we" rather than "I." Children who are educated in inclusive classrooms learn that they are a community—that a blow to one is a blow to all.
8. **Honesty about hard topics:** Children who are educated in inclusive classrooms and grow up surrounded with individual differences learn a vast repertoire of skills and attitudes about uncomfortable and painful topics.
9. **Courage:** Inclusive classrooms provide children with examples and opportunities for many kinds of bravery.
10. **Faith and hope:** Inclusive classrooms teach children that acceptance, love, and support are possible and that persons can make a difference even if they may not see the results of their efforts immediately.

Source: Sapon-Shevin, M. (2007). *Widening the circle: The power of inclusive classrooms.* Boston: Beacon Press.

(Salend & Garrick Duhaney, 1999). Text Box 1.2 displays benefits of inclusive classrooms for all children.

In the past, parents of young children have raised concerns that interacting with children with disabilities might negatively impact the behavior and development of their typically developing children (Green & Stoneman, 1989), especially during toddler years when children are at a critical age. However, this perception has not been supported by research. Similar to preschoolers, toddlers with typical development have shown progress in all areas of development in inclusive settings (Stahmer & Carter, 2005).

Teachers' attitudes toward inclusion have been positive for the most part, although teachers generally express a need for support and training in instructional methods and behavioral support for exceptional children (Conderman & Johnston-Rodriguez, 2009; Hanson, Horn, Sandall, Beckman, Morgan, Marquart, et al., 2001). It is important to keep in mind that what determines whether or not inclusion might be effective for children with disabilities is the quality of the classroom setting, the quality of teaching, the types of adaptations and modifications teachers make, and the kind of support available for both teachers and students with disabilities (Fenty, Miller, & Lampi, 2008; Waldron & McLesky, 1998). Availability of support, whether through consultation, co-teaching, teaching assistance, and assistive technology, as well as teacher's skills in adaptations of curriculum and materials, are elemental in providing an effective inclusive environment for all children.

Although we have discussed the merits of inclusion in early childhood settings, you should be aware that arguments continue to be made both for and against inclusion by scholars, teachers, and parents. And the body of research on both sides of these arguments continues to grow. We have presented one side of the argument in this chapter. However, it is important to note the other side of the argument as well. Scholars who argue against inclusion have contended that trying to force students into inclusion is discriminatory, and that children who need specialized services and instruction might lose access to necessary, specially designed instruction and services, which have been otherwise absent in nonspecialized classrooms (Hallahan, 2005).

The topic of inclusion is complex and includes an understanding of both societal and cultural values regarding disability. In addition, the question of appropriateness of inclusion based on the child's severity of disability and needs remains an important question to consider. IDEA recognizes that not all children can be educated in a regular classroom. Decisions regarding inclusion of children with disabilities should therefore be made by the parents and in consultation with the intervention team based on the child's needs. You should examine the research on both sides of these arguments and decide for yourself what position you might choose to take on inclusion.

RESEARCH ON EARLY CHILDHOOD INTERVENTION AND EDUCATION

The majority of studies in early childhood intervention and education use **experimental** or **quasi-experimental** research methodologies. In an experimental study, the researcher tests a hypothesis about the relationship between two factors, called *dependent* and *independent* variables. For example, a study might be designed to examine the efficacy of an intervention program (independent variable) on children's language development (dependent variable). An experimental study requires that the researcher maintain control over all factors, so that the researcher can predict what might occur. For example, the researcher might want a control for the age of the child, or the severity of disability. To control a variety of factors, an experiment might involve using pretest and posttest measuring, employing both experimental and control groups, and randomly selecting research participants.

Maintaining control is not always possible or practical. It might even be unethical in some situations (especially in educational and therapeutic settings). For example, it might not always be possible to have both an experimental and a control group in an early childhood classroom or to randomly assign children to experience intervention methods. For this reason, researchers often use a quasi-experimental design in educational research. In a quasi-experimental study, a random assignment to groups is not used, and the experimenter might choose to manipulate or not manipulate the independent variable. For example, in an early intervention study, the researcher might choose to manipulate the educational or therapy methods or conditions. In both experimental and quasi-experimental research designs, the scientists rely on the statistical significance of their findings, and the results of these types of research is usually reported in numbers. For this reason, experimental methods are also called **quantitative research.**

In the past decade, the use of scientific inquiry in early childhood education and special education has been questioned. The traditional types of research described earlier have been deemed inadequate in capturing the reality of the programs, especially as it relates to underserved children (Hauser-Cram, Erickson-Warfield, Upshur, & Weisner, 2000). In addition, the field of special education research has faced questions regarding the cultural fairness of intelligence testing and bias in placement procedures—which has overwhelmingly placed minority children in special education (Paul, Fowler, & Cranston-Gingras, 2007).

Over the past 10 years, **mixed methodologies,** in which quantitative methods are combined with qualitative/narrative methods to capture the context and essence of teaching and learning experiences, have become increasingly valued in early childhood education and special education. In **qualitative research,** observational or interview methods are used to understand the nature of the experience of the subjects in the study. For example, a study of an early intervention program employing a mixed methodology might indicate that children in a 2-year program had some moderate outcome after completing the program. The qualitative results of parent and teacher interviews and child observations could shed some light on specific conditions under which the intervention program might or might not have been effective.

Studies That Have Shaped the Field

With the emphasis that the No Child Left Behind Act and IDEIA place on scientific-based intervention and educational methods to be used for all children, it has become crucially important that research methodologies that are most appropriate for the field be used to study the educational experience and developmental outcome of children in ECSE programs.

Research has continued to be elemental in shaping both early childhood education and special education fields. In fact, several longitudinal research projects were initiated in the late 1960s and early 1970s that shaped current practices in the field. In addition, the legislation that established the Part C program was developed in response to the findings of such studies, which provided evidence for the importance of early education and intervention services for young children at risk in order to reduce negative developmental outcome. By the late 1970s, several research projects had demonstrated the benefits of early education and intervention for children's development in regard to future academic success. In fact, the phrase "earlier is better," which has long been the assumption of early childhood special education, is derived from these studies (Hemmeter, Santos, Synder, Hyson, Harris-Soloman, Bailey, et al., 2005). In the following sections, we briefly review some of the important research that has shaped the field.

High/Scope Longitudinal Research

One of the oldest longitudinal studies, the Perry Preschool (High/Scope) project was established in 1970 by Weikart and his colleagues. This study has followed a group of research participants from age 3 through 41. The project has collected data at ages 10, 15, 19, 27, and 39 through 41. The Perry Preschool study has been examining the effects of a high-quality child-centered preschool program on 123 African American children who lived in Ypsilanti, Michigan. These children were compared to a control group who did not attend the program. The results of this study, which have been published since 1982, indicate:

> ➢ Fewer children who had been enrolled in the early childhood program were held back a grade or placed in special education classrooms. These children had higher achievement scores through elementary and high school (Schweinhart & Weikart, 1980; Lazar & Darlington, 1982).
> ➢ At adulthood, of the number of children who had attended the Perry Preschool program only 7 percent had been arrested for drug-related or other offenses, compared to 35 percent of the group who had not attended the preschool program (Schweinhart, Barnes, & Weikart, 1993).
> ➢ At adulthood, children who had attended the Perry Preschool program were more likely to have completed high school, be married, hold a job, earn higher salaries, or own their own homes (Schweinhart et al., 1993; Schweinhart, 2003).
> ➢ In the long run, every public dollar spent on the program saved $7.16 in tax dollars (Schweinhart, 2003).

The Carolina Abecedarian Project

The Carolina Abecedarian Project was an early childhood intervention, longitudinal, scientific study that involved four cohorts of at-risk children who were born between 1972 and 1977. About 97 percent of the children who participated in the study were from poor African American families. The study examined the benefits of early education on poor children from infancy throughout their early childhood years in a center-based early childhood setting. The program was individualized for children and had a language-based curriculum.

Participating children in this study have been followed through age 21, and so far the data has been collected of children at ages 12, 15, and 21 years (Campell & Ramey, 1995; Burchinal, Campbell, Bryant, Wasik, & Ramey, 1997; Campbell, Pungello, Miller-Johnson, Burchinal, & Ramey, 2001; Campell, Ramey, Pungello, Sparling, & Miller-Johnson, 2002). The major findings of this study support cognitive gains and academic achievement, especially in math and reading, for participating children during years of their school experience. Children who participated in the study were more likely to complete elementary and secondary school and attend college.

Chicago Child-Parent Centers

The Chicago Child-Parent Center Program was established in 1967 as a center-based early childhood intervention, which provided comprehensive educational and family support services to at-risk children and their parents from preschool through primary school (K–third grade) (Chicago Longitudinal Study, 1999). The program offers a language-based curriculum for children age 3 to 9, provides health and social services for children and their families, and involves parents as the active participants in their children's education (Niles, Reynolds, & Roe-Sepowitz, 2008; Reynolds & Clements, 2005).

In a longitudinal study, Reynolds and his team at the University of Wisconsin followed 1,539 children (93 percent of whom were African American), who took part in the Chicago Child-Parent Center program beginning in the 1983–1984 school year and matched a control group enrolled in an alternative kindergarten program. Children in this study were followed from kindergarten through age 22.

Confirming the Abecedarian and High/Scope research findings, Reynolds' study has resulted in several important findings:

> Early intervention, especially that which involves the family in the child's education, would promote early cognitive and academic advantages, which would in turn culminate in better social competence in adolescence (Miedel & Reynolds, 1999). The benefits are especially higher for children from high family risk status and low parental education levels (Niles et al., 2008).
> Children participating in the Parent-Child Center Program not only had a higher academic achievement in reading and math by seventh grade, but were less likely to be delinquent at age 15, or drop out of high school (Reynolds, Chang, & Temple, 1998; Reynolds & Temple, 1998; Temple, Reynolds, & Miedel, 2000).
> Early childhood programs are the most cost-effective interventions. In the long run, the participants and the general public receive $7.14 in educational, social welfare, and socioeconomic benefits for every single dollar that it spends on early childhood (Reynolds, Temple, Robertson, Mann, & Ou, 2003).

What Have We Learned from Research?

The results of these studies have had several important implications for early childhood special education:

> The younger the age of the child at entry, the more likely that child may benefit from early intervention.
> The higher the quality of the program, the more likely that child may benefit from the program. Of course, the question remains with what standards "quality" might be measured. In addition to the quality, other studies have provided evidence that the more intense the early intervention, the more effective it will be (Lovaas, 1987; Lord & Venter, 1992).
> When parents are involved in the education and treatment of children, children and families both are likely to benefit from the intervention.
> Early intervention is cost-effective in the long run.

Current Research in Early Childhood Special Education and Disabilities

Research in the area of early childhood special education and the disability field has continued to grow during the last 30 years. Areas of current research interest include the efficacy of specific therapy methods with children with disabilities, the effectiveness of inclusion, the benefits of team teaching, self-determination, and the quality of life of families of children with disabilities.

Aside from these areas, research in ECSE continues to provide new information about intervention and the experiences of children with disabilities and their families in early childhood specialized and inclusive settings. The National Early Intervention Longitudinal Study (NEILS) and Pre-Elementary Education Longitudinal Study (PEELS) are two notable longitudinal research projects that employ both qualitative and quantitative methodologies. These studies investigate issues related to intervention and services provision for young children with disabilities in the United States. Both projects are funded by the U.S. Department of Education.

National Early Intervention Longitudinal Study (NEILS)

NEILS is a longitudinal study that began in 1999 by Hebbeler and her colleagues at the Stanford Research Institute (SRI) International. NEILS involves 3,338 children and their families who have entered early intervention programs in the United States since 1997–1998. Children and their families are followed through their experiences in early intervention and through early elementary school years.

NEILS does not involve a comparison group. The investigators are interested in examining characteristics of children and families who receive EI services, the types of services received, outcomes of intervention on families and children, and the relationship between outcome variations and characteristics of children and families and services. Early findings of this study suggest that families receiving early intervention services under Part C are generally satisfied with the services and believe the services to be appropriate, adequate, and individualized based on their child's needs (Spiker, Malik, Hebbeler, & Scarborough, 2009; Bailey, Scarborough, Hebbeler, Spiker, & Mallik, 2004).

The most recent findings of NEILS was reported in 2007 (Hebbeler, Spiker, Bailey, Scarborough, Mallik, Simeonsson, et al., 2007). This report indicates several important findings.

> ➢ As compared with children with diagnosed conditions, children with risk conditions and general developmental delays (about one-third of all children in EI) benefit from EI to the degree that they are more likely not to continue to receive special education services in preschool or kindergarten.
> ➢ A total of 82 percent of the EI participants who go to kindergarten without a disability have literacy and math skills comparable with the general population of kindergarteners around the country.
> ➢ Communication impairments are the most widespread and persistent developmental problems among children who receive EI.
> ➢ Given current EI providers, the field lacks personnel with the necessary training or background to identify and address young children with issues related to infant mental health, such as social emotional and behavioral problems.
> ➢ Children living in poverty who participate in EI are more likely to be in poor health, receive services for multiple areas of delay, have hearing difficulties, and are more likely to be African American or Hispanic.

Pre-Elementary Education Longitudinal Study (PEELS)

PEELS is a longitudinal study conducted by the National Center for Special Education Research Institute of Education Sciences. PEELS began data collection in the spring of 2003, and repeated the effort in winter 2005, 2006, 2007, and 2009. The study involves about 3,000 3-, 4-, and 5-year-old children with disabilities. The investigators have followed these children through their early elementary school years through year 2009. Employing a variety of factors such as disability characteristics and types of early childhood special education services and programs, the study has examined how these children have transitioned from kindergarten to early primary grades (Daley & Carlson, 2009). PEELS' first report detailed developmental characteristics of children receiving services and the types of services provided to children. This report was published in 2006 (Markowitz, Carlson, Frey, Riley, Shimshak, Heinzen, et al., 2006). It indicates the following:

> Many children with disabilities do not begin receiving special education services until they are nearly 3 years old.
> Children who begin receiving services later are more likely to be identified as having speech or language impairment, and least likely to be those identified as having an orthopedic impairment, mental retardation, or other health impairments.
> Speech and language therapy is by far the most common service provided—to about 93 percent of children.
> Teachers of preschoolers with disabilities report they use a variety of practices and techniques to support social interaction between children with and without disabilities. Providing structured play, prompting, and reinforcing children without disabilities are among the most common practices to encourage children without disabilities to interact with children who have disabilities.
> More than half of children with disabilities have teachers with graduate degrees.
> For about one-third of children with disabilities, transition from Part C to Part B brings about a program interruption. For these children, the gap in transition between programs is an average of 5 months.

The transition result reported by PEELS might be different during the study's next cycle of data collection and analysis since the IDEIA 2004 now provides an option for the families if they decide to have the child receive services under Part C until kindergarten, which was not in effect during the first tide of data collection.

RECOMMENDATIONS FOR EARLY CHILDHOOD SPECIAL EDUCATION AND INCLUSIVE PROGRAMS

Results from all of the studies reviewed here have clear implications for intervention. Accordingly, the following recommendations are made for the field of early childhood special education.

> Poor minority children continue to be the largest group of children who are likely to be at risk and/or identified with developmental problems. Therefore, programs that identify these children early and address their special needs should continue to be a priority in early childhood.

> Training in the area of infant mental health, including behavior management, is an area of need in professional development in early intervention, which needs to be addressed as a priority.

> Improving the transition process from Part C to Part B is crucial to the continuum of intervention and success of young children with disabilities.

> For inclusion to be successful, a concerted school-wide effort needs to be underway to model appropriate interaction and socialization between children with and without disabilities so they might learn to interact and play together in their school and home community.

> Emphasis should be put on speech and language services, as well as training in language-based curricula, which would benefit all children in general as well as children with communication disorders (the largest group of children with special needs in ECSE).

SUMMARY

This chapter introduced readers to the field of early childhood special education (ECSE) by examining the variety of programs in which children with special needs are educated. Children with special education needs receive services in various early childhood settings, such as early intervention programs, compensatory programs, preschool special education or inclusive classrooms, and primary special education or inclusive classrooms.

Three important forces have shaped early childhood special education today: (1) historical developments; (2) legal foundations of special education; and (3) research in early childhood education. The history of early childhood special education is shaped by the efforts of pioneers in special education and in early childhood who established philosophies and methods of working with children with disabilities. U.S. laws are shaped by case law, research, and changes in public opinion, which demand the creation of legislation to articulate specific groups' rights, such as those of families with children with disabilities. The most important law articulating the educational rights of children with disabilities was originally mandated in 1975 under the title "Education of All Handicapped Children Act." This law was amended several times and was renamed the Individuals with Disabilities Education Act (IDEA). The most recent amendment of this act took place in 2004.

The educational rights of infants and toddlers with disabilities are articulated under Part C of IDEA, while the educational rights of children 3 years and older are explained under Part B. IDEA requires that children with disabilities receive a free and appropriate education at the public's expense, and, to the maximum extent possible, be educated in inclusive classrooms along with their typically developing peers.

Longitudinal studies beginning in the 1970s in early childhood education and intervention have provided evidence for the importance and efficacy of early intervention for young children at risk and for children with disabilities. Research which employs a mixed methodology—qualitative and quantitative—has been considered the most appropriate for studying children with disabilities. Current research in early childhood special education has identified several areas of strength and needs, which should be addressed as a priority in ECSE.

Review Questions

1. Who are children with special needs?
2. What are the major fields in which children with disabilities (birth–age 8) are educated?
3. What are compensatory and prevention programs?
4. What is special education, who receives special education, and what types of services are provided?
5. Who are two of the most elemental historical figures who shaped special education?
6. Which major case laws influenced special education laws?
7. What is the most important special education law that articulates the educational rights of children with special needs?
8. What are provisions of IDEA under which children (birth–age 8) are served?
9. What are some of the most important changes to IDEA in its 2004 amendments?
10. Define *inclusion* and explain its implications for early childhood classrooms.
11. What are some of the important findings of the major longitudinal studies in early childhood intervention?
12. Describe major findings of NEILS and PEELS. What are some of their implications?

Out-of-Class Activities

1. Conduct inclusion interviews:
   a. Interview an early childhood teacher to find out his or her perceptions, opinions, and feelings about inclusion.
   b. Interview a parent of a child with a disability to find out his or her perceptions, opinions, and feelings about inclusion of his or her child in a general education classroom.
   c. Interview an administrator to find out his or her perceptions, opinions, and feelings about inclusion, as well as his or her experience including children with disabilities in their schools.
   d. Analyze the results of your interviews to see similarities, differences, and issues these people consider important. Write a report of your findings.

Recommended Resources

Books and articles on Inclusion
http://www.inclusion.com/

DEC and NAYC joint position statement on Early Childhood Inclusion
http://www.dec-sped.org/uploads/docs/about_dec/position_concept_papers/PositionStatement_Inclusion_Joint_updated_May2009.pdf

IDEA and its provisions
http://www.ed.gov/policy/speced/guid/idea/idea2004.html

National Early Childhood Technical Assistance Center (NECTAC)
http://www.nectac.org

National Early Intervention Longitudinal Study (NEILS)
http://www.sri.com/neils/

National Network for Child Care
http://www.nncc.org/

No Child Left Behind Act
http://www.ed.gov/nclb/landing.jhtml?src=pb

Pre-elementary Education Longitudinal Study (PEELS)
https://www.peels.org/default.asp

The Carolina Abecedarian Project
http://www.fpg.unc.edu/~abc/#intervention

Wrights law: A law firm providing information in special education laws and advocacy
http://www.wrightslaw.com/

View the Online Resources available to accompany this text by visiting http://www.mhhe.com/bayat1e.

References

Allen, E. K., & Cowdery, E. G. (2005). *The exceptional child: Inclusion in Early Childhood Education* (5th ed.). Clifton Park, NY: Thomson Delmar Learning.

Allen, K. E., Benning, P. M., & Drummond, W. T. (1972). Integration of normal and handicapped children in a behaviour modification preschool: A case study. In G. Semb (Ed.), *Behavior analysis and education* (pp. 127–141). Lawrence, KS: University of Kansas.

Asawa, L., Hansen, D., & Flood, M. (2008). Early childhood intervention programs: Opportunities and challenges for preventing child maltreatment. *Education and Treatment of Children, 31*(1), 73–110.

Bailey, D., Scarborough, A., Hebbeler, K., Spiker, D., & Mallik, S. (2004). *Family outcomes at the end of early intervention.* Menlo Park, CA: SRI International. Retrieved March 13, 2008, from http://www.sri.com/neils/pdfs/FamilyOutcomesReport_011405.pdf

Baily, D. B., McWilliam, R. A., Buysse, B., & Wesley, P. W. (1998). Inclusion in the context of competing values in early childhood education. *Early Childhood Research Quarterly, 13*(1), 27–47.

Bernheimer, L. P., Koegh, B. K., & Coots, J. J. (1993). From research to practice: Support for developmental delay as a preschool category of exceptionality. *Journal of Early Intervention, 17*(2), 97–106.

Bowe, F. G. (2007). *Early childhood special education: Birth to eight.* Clifton Park, NY: Thomson, Delmar Learning.

Braddock, D., & Parish, S. L. (2002). An institutional history of disability. In D. Braddock (Ed.), *Disability at the dawn of the 21st century and the state of the states* (pp. 3–61). Washington, DC: American Association on Mental Retardation.

Brown, E. J. & Sorensen, J. (2007). *An overview of Early Intervention.* Austin: Pro-ed.

Burack, J. A., & Volkmar, F. R. (1992). Development of low and high functioning autistic children. *Journal of Child Psychology and Psychiatry, 33,* 607–616.

Burchinal, M. R., Campbell, F. A., Bryant, D. M., Wasik, B. H., & Ramey, C. T. (1997). Early intervention and medicating processes in cognitive performance of children of low-income African American families. *Child Development, 68,* 935–954.

Campbell, F. A., Pungello, E. P., Miller-Johnson, S., Burchinal, M., & Ramey, C. T. (2001). The development of cognitive and academic abilities: Growth curves from an early childhood educational experiment. *Developmental Psychology, 37,* 231–242.

Campbell, F. A., Ramey, C. T., Pungello, E. P., Sparling, J., & Miller-Johnson, S. (2002). Early childhood education: Young adult outcomes from the Abecedarian Project. *Applied Developmental Science, 6,* 42–57.

Campell, F. A., & Ramey, C. T. (1995). Cognitive and school outcomes for high-risk African-American students at middle adolescence: Positive effects of early intervention. *American Educational Research Journal, 32,* 743–772.

Carrey, N. J. (1995). Itard's 1828 memoire on "Mutism caused by a lesion of the intellectual functions": A historical analysis. *Journal of American Academy of Child and Adolescent Psychiatry, 34*(12), 1655–1661.

Chicago Longitudinal Study. (1999). *Chicago longitudinal study: A study of children in the Chicago public schools.* [User's guide, version 6]. Madison: University of Wisconsin, Waisman Center.

Conderman, G., & Johnston-Rodriguez, S. (2009). Beginning teachers' views of their collaborative roles. *Preventing School Failure, 53*(4), 235–244.

Cook, B. G., Cameron, D. L., & Tankersley, M. (2007). Inclusive teachers' ratings of their students with disabilities. *Journal of Special Education, 40*(4), 230–239.

Council for Exceptional Children. (2004, November). *The new IDEA: CEC summary of significant issues.* Arlington: Author.

Daley, T., & Carlson, E. (2009). Predictors of change in eligibility status among preschoolers in special education. *Exceptional Children, 75*(4), 412–426.

Delgado, C. E., Vagi, S. J., & Scott, K. G. (2007). Identification of early risk factors for developmental delay. *Exceptionality, 15*(2), 119–136.

DEC/NAEYC. (2009). *Early childhood inclusion: A joint position statement of the Division for Early Childhood (DEC) and the national Association for the Education of Young Children (NAEYC).* Chapel Hill: The University of North Carolina, FPG Child Development Institute.

Evans, I. M., Salisbury, C. L., Palombaro, M. M., Berryman, J., & Hollowood, T. M. (1992). Acceptance of elementary-aged children with severe disabilities in an inclusive school. *Journal of the Association for Persons with Severe Handicaps, 17,* 205–212.

Fenty, N., Miller, M., & Lampi, A. (2008). Embed social skills instruction in inclusive settings. *Intervention in School and Clinic, 43*(3), 186–192.

Fewell, R. R., & Oelwein, P. L. (1990). The relationship between time in integrated environments and developmental gains in young children with special needs. *Topics in Early Childhood Education, 10,* 104–116.

Frith, U. (1989). *Autism: Explaining the enigma.* Oxford: Blackwell.

Green, A. L., & Stoneman, Z. (1989). Attitudes of mothers and fathers of nonhandicapped children. *Journal of Early Intervention, 13,* 292–304.

Hallahan, D. P. (2005). We need more intensive instruction. In M. A. Byrnes (Ed.), *Taking sides: Clashing views on controversial issues in special education* (2nd ed., pp. 190–192). New York: McGraw-Hill Co.

Hanlin, M. F. (1993). Inclusion of preschoolers with profound disabilities: An analysis of children's interactions. *Journal of the Association for Persons with Severe Handicaps, 18,* 28–35.

Hanson, M. J., Horn, E., Sandall, S., Beckman, P., Morgan, M., Marquart, J., et al. (2001). After preschool inclusion: Children's educational pathways over the early school years. *Exceptional Children, 68*(1), 65–83.

Hauser-Cram, P., Erickson-Warfield, M., Upshur, C. C., & Weisner, T. S. (2000). An expanded view of program evaluation in early childhood intervention. In J. P. Shonkoff & S. J. Meisels (Eds.), *Handbook of early childhood intervention* (2nd ed., pp. 487–509). Cambridge: Cambridge University Press.

Hebbeler, K., Spiker, D., Bailey, D., Scarborough, A., Mallik, S., Simeonsson, R., et al. (2007). *Early intervention for infants and toddlers with disabilities and their families: Participants, services, and outcomes.* Menlo Park, CA: SRI International. Retrieved March 13, 2008, from http://www.sri.com/neils/pdfs/NEILS_Report_02_07_Final2.pdf

Hemmeter, M. L., Santos, R., Snyder, P., Hyson, M., Harris-Soloman, A., Bailey, D., et al. (2005). Young children with, or at risk for developmental disabilities. In K. C. Lakin & A. Turnbull (Eds.), *National goals and research for people with intellectual and developmental disabilities.*

Washington, DC: American Association on Mental Retardation.

Hestenes, L. L., & Carroll, D. E. (2000). The play interactions of young children with and without disabilities: Individual and environmental influences. *Early Childhood Research Quarterly, 15*(2), 229–246.

Humphrey, G. (1962). Introduction. In J. G. Itard. *The wild boy of Aveyron* (pp. 5–19). New York: Appleton-Century-Crofts.

Hundert, J., Mahoney, B., Mundy, F., & Vernon, M. L. (1998). A descriptive analysis of developmental and social gains of children with severe disabilities in segregated and inclusive preschools in southern Ontario. *Early Childhood Research Quarterly, 13,* 49–65.

Idol, L. (2006). Toward inclusion of special education students in general education: A program evaluation of eight schools. *Remedial and Special Education, 27,* 77–94.

Itard, J. G. (1962). *The wild boy of Aveyron (English Translation).* New York: Appleton-Century-Crofts.

Karagiannis, A., Stainback, W., & Stainback, S. (1996). Rationale for inclusive schooling. In S. Stainback & W. Stainback (Eds.), *Inclusion: A guide for educators* (pp. 3–15). Baltimore: Brooks.

Kennedy, C. H., Shukla, S., & Fryxell, D. (1997). Comparing the effects of educational placement on the social relationships of intermediate school students with severe disabilities. *Exceptional Children, 64,* 31–47.

Lazar, I., & Darlington, R. (1982). *Lasting effects of early education: Report from the consortium for longitudinal studies.* Chicago: University of Chicago Press for the Society for Research in Child Development.

Levine, L. M., & Antia, S. D. (1997). The effects of partner hearing status on social and cognitive play. *Journal of Early Intervention, 21,* 21–35.

Longmore, P. K., & Umansky, L. (Eds.). (2001). *The new disability history: American perspective.* New York: New York University Press.

Lord, C., & Venter, A. (1992). Outcome and follow-up studies of high-functioning autistic individuals. In E. Shopler & G. Mesibove (Eds.), *High-functioning individuals with autism* (pp. 187–199). New York: Plenum.

Lovaas, O. I. (1987). Behavioral treatment and normal education and intellectual functioning in young autistic children. *Journal of Consulting and Clinical Psychology, 55*(1), 3–9.

Mandlawitz, M. (2007). *What every teacher should know about IDEA 2004 laws and regulations.* Boston: Allyn and Bacon.

Markowitz, J., Carlson, E., Frey, W., Riley, J., Shimshak, A., Heinzen, H. et al. (2006). *Preschoolers with disabilities: Characteristics, services, and results.* U.S. Department of Education, Institute of Education Sciences. Retrieved March 13, 2008, from https://www.peels.org/Docs/PEELS%20Final%20Wave%201%20Overview%20Report.pdf

Meisels, S. J., & Shonkoff, J. P. (2000). Early childhood intervention: A continuing evolution. In J. P. Shonkoff & S. J. Meisels (Eds.), *Handbook of early childhood intervention* (2nd ed., pp. 3–31). Cambridge: Cambridge University Press.

Miedel, W. T., & Reynolds, A. J. (1999). Parent involvement in early intervention for disadvantaged children: Does it matter? *Journal of School Psychology, 37*(4), 379–402.

Niles, M. D., Reynolds, A. J., & Roe-Sepowitz, D. (2008). Early childhood intervention and early adolescent social and emotional competence: Second-generation evaluation evidence from the Chicago Longitudinal Study. *Educational Research, 50*(1), 55–73.

Noll, S., & Trent, J. (Eds.). (2004). *Mental retardation in America: A historical reader.* New York: New York University Press.

Odom, S. L. (2000). Preschool inclusion: What we know and where we go from here. *Topics in Early Childhood Special Education, 20,* 20–27.

Osgood, R. (1997). Undermining the common school ideal: Intermediate schools and ungraded classes in Boston, 1838–1900. *History of Education Quarterly, 37,* 375–398.

Paul, J. L., Fowler, K., & Cranston-Gingras, A. (2007). Perspectives shaping and challenging research approaches in special education. In L. Florian (Ed.), *The SAGE handbook of special education* (pp. 175–186). London: Sage Publications.

Reynolds, A. J., Chang, H., & Temple, J. (1998). Early childhood intervention and juvenile delinquency: An exploratory analysis of the Chicago Child–Parent Centers. *Evaluation Review, 22,* 341–372.

Reynolds, A., & Clements, M. (2005). Parental involvement and children's school success. In E. N. Patrikakou, R. P. Weissberg, S. Redding, & H. J. Walberg (Eds.), *School–family partnerships: Promoting the social, emotional, and academic growth of children* (pp. 109–127). New York: Teachers College Press.

Reynolds, A. J., & Temple, J. A. (1998). Extended early childhood intervention and school achievement: Age 13 findings from the Chicago longitudinal study. *Child Development, 69,* 231–246.

Reynolds, A. J., Temple, J. A., Robertson, D. L., Mann, E. A., & Ou, S. R. (2003, April 26). *Prevention and cost-effectiveness in the Chicago child-parent centers.* Paper presented at the Meeting of the Society for Research in Child Development, Tampa, Florida.

Rose, E. (2009). Poverty and parenting: Transforming early education's legacy in the 1960s. *History of Education Quarterly, 49*(2), 222–234.

Salend, S. J., & Garrick Duhaney, L. M. (1999). The impact of inclusion on students with and without disabilities and their educators. *Remedial and Special Education, 20*(2), 114–126.

Sands, D. J., Kozleski, E. B., & French, N. D. (2000). *Inclusive education for the 21st century.* Belmont, CA: Wadsworth/Thompson Learning.

Sapon-Shiven, M. (2007). *Widening the circle: The power of inclusive classrooms.* Boston: Beacon Press.

Schwartz, I. S. (1996). Expanding the zone: Thoughts about social validity and training. *Journal of Early Intervention, 20,* 204–205.

Schwarz, P. (2006). *From disability to possibility: The power of inclusive classrooms.* Portsmouth: Heinemann.

Schweinhart, L. (2003, April 26). *Benefits, costs, and explanations of the High/Scope Perry preschool program.* Paper presented at the Meeting of the Society for Research in Child Development, Tampa, Florida.

Schweinhart, L., Barnes, H. V., & Weikart, D. P. (1993). *Significant benefits: The High/Scope Perry preschool study through age 27.* Ypsilanti, MI: High/Scope Press.

Schweinhart, L. J., & Weikart, D. P. (1980). *Young children grow up: Effects of the Perry preschool program on youth through age 15.* Ypsilanti, MI: High/Scope Press.

Shaw, E., & Good, S. (2008). *Fact sheet: Vulnerable young children.* Chapel Hill: the University of North Carolina, FPG Child Development Institute, National Early Childhood Technical Assistance Center.

Simpson, M. K. (1999). The moral government of idiots: Moral treatment in the work of Seguin. *History of Psychiatry, 10,* 227–243.

Smith, J. D. (1998). *Inclusion: Schools for all students.* Belmont, CA: Wadsworth.

Spiker, D., Malik, S., Hebbeler, K., & Scarborough, A. (2009, April). Overview: Analysis of kindergarten outcomes in the National Early Intervention Longitudinal Study. Paper presented in *Society for Research in Child Development.* Biennial Meeting: Denver, Colorado.

Stahmer, A. C., & Carter, C. (2005). An empirical examination of toddler development in inclusive childcare. *Early Child Development and Care, 17,* 321–333.

Stormont, M. (2007). *Fostering resilience in young children at risk for failure: Strategies for grades K–3.* Upper Saddle River: Pearson/Prentice Hall.

Temple, J. A., Reynolds, A. J., & Miedel, W. T. (2000). Can early intervention prevent high school dropout? Evidence from the Chicago Child–Parent Centers. *Urban Education, 35*(1), 31–56.

Terpstra, J., & Tamura, R. (2008). Effective social interaction strategies for inclusive settings. *Early Childhood Education Journal, 35,* 405–411.

Trent, J. W. (1994). *Inventing the feeble mind: A history of mental retardation in the United States.* Berkeley: University of California Press.

U.S. Department of Education (2007). *Four Pillars of NCLB.* Retrieved February 21, 2008, from http://www.ed.gov/nclb/overview/intro/4pillars.html

U.S. Department of Health, Education, and Welfare (1968). *Programs for the handicapped.* Washington, DC: Author.

Waldron, N. L., & McLesky, J. (1998). The effects of an inclusive school program on students with mild and severe learning disabilities. *Exceptional Children, 64,* 395–405.

Winzer, M. A. (2007). Confronting differences: An excursion through the history of special education. In L. Florian (Ed.), *The SAGE handbook of special education* (pp. 21–45). London: Sage Publications.

Wright, P. W., & Wright, P. D. (2007). *Special education law* (2nd ed.). Hartfield: Harbor House Law Press.

Ysseldyke, J., & Algozzine, B. (2006). *The legal foundations of special education: A practical guide for every teacher.* Thousand Oaks: Corwin Press.

Chapter 2

Typical and Atypical Development

Objectives

Upon completion of this chapter, you should be able to:

> Understand the concepts of typical and atypical development.

> Differentiate between factors that might affect development before, during, and after birth.

> Describe environmental factors that could cause damage to the developing organism during the prenatal period.

> Describe how maternal substance use can lead to maternal and fetal complications.

> Discuss the importance of maternal health, and understand various disorders and infections that might cause developmental problems in the child.

> Discuss the impact of maternal and child nutrition on the healthy development of the fetus and the health of the child after birth.
> Describe possible complications that could occur during the birthing process.
> Differentiate between areas of development in the child and define each area.
> Understand the relationship between brain and behavior in a child's development.
> Discuss the importance of the child/adult relationship in relation to the overall development of the child.

Key Terms

Apgar score (56)
attachment (63)
atypical development (41)
body mass index (BMI) (54)
cells (43)
chromosomes (43)
cognitive development (57)
congenital (49)
deoxyribonucleic acid (DNA) (44)
development (41)
developmental care (57)
developmental domains (57)
developmental milestones (58)

diagnostic test (56)
extremely low birth weight (ELBW) (56)
false negative (56)
false positive (56)
genes (44)
gestational diabetes (53)
growth (41)
large for gestational age (55)
lead (45)
low birth weight (LBW) (55)
mercury (45)
micropreemie (56)
multifactorial genetic disorders (45)
neonate (55)

perinatal period (42)
physical development (57)
polygenic disorders (45)
postnatal period (42)
prenatal period (41)
screening test (56)
single-gene disorder (45)
social emotional development (57)
terotogen (45)
TORCH (49)
umbilical cord prolapse (55)
very low birth weight (VLBW) (56)

Reflection Questions

Before reading this chapter, answer the following questions to reflect upon your personal opinions and beliefs that are pertinent to early childhood special education.

1. In your view, what are some factors that could affect the healthy development of the child before the child is born?
2. Why do you think pregnant women are advised to avoid using drugs, alcohol, and smoking cigarettes during pregnancy?
3. How important is a child's nutrition in his or her development?
4. In your opinion, is it important to stimulate infants through daily interactions? Why or why not?

INTRODUCTION

Development can be defined as anything that changes over time. In terms of human development, it refers to change in human thought, behavior, and function (Pellegrino, 2007a). Development and **growth,** although two related concepts, have different meanings. While growth usually indicates an increase, addition, or maturation of an original organism, development is more concerned with the qualitative changes that the organism undergoes. In other words, development is the process of children's biological and psychological growth, change, and learning.

Growth and development both occur from conception through adulthood. Most children have similar growth patterns, such as gaining in height or weight at certain times; however, not all children follow exactly the same pattern of development (Pellegrino, 2007a). For example, each child might have a unique developmental history because a child's development is influenced by his or her experiences in the environment, as well as his or her biological makeup. Although the developmental process is unique for every child, the course of development itself is predictable. We might say that in development a child's behaviors change in a predictable way provided certain biological and experiential conditions are met.

A human's development depends on the brain and the maturation of the central nervous system (CNS) (Pellegrino, 2007a), as all kinds of behaviors occur based only on the input and commands from the brain. Measuring a child's development depends on that child's level of physical, cognitive, and social emotional development as compared to his or her peers. In general, a child's CNS is expected to mature at a certain rate, and a child's physical, cognitive, and social emotional levels are expected to reach certain milestones around certain periods of time. By looking at these areas, we are usually able to tell whether or not a child's development is healthy.

Although we hope that all children grow to be healthy both biologically and psychologically, not all children have typical developments. When children do not reach their developmental milestones within a reasonable time frame, we might assume that a developmental delay or deviation has occurred. **Atypical development** might occur because of a slower rate of growth, or deviations in patterns and pathways of development. The causes of delays or atypical development are not always easily identified. Numerous problems occurring before, during, or after birth can cause damage to the CNS and create developmental problems. Biological and environmental factors alone or in combination with one another can cause deviation in development.

In this chapter, we will describe some of the important environmental and biological risk factors that might occur before, during, or after birth, which could cause or contribute to developmental problems in children.

DEVELOPMENT AND BIRTH

Different factors can influence development either before, during, or after birth. The period before birth is referred to as the **prenatal period;** the period in which the sperm and ovum unite to form a new living organism, which would become the fetus

(Burk, 2006). The prenatal period begins from conception and ends in birth. It further consists of three periods:

> The *zygote* period in which the organism is formed. It takes about 2 weeks.
> The *embryonic* period, during which the primitive brain and spinal cord develop. It takes about 6 weeks.
> The *fetal* period, during which the fetus rapidly grows. It begins from the 9th week of pregnancy and continues to birth.

The **perinatal period** is the period around childbirth, usually beginning from the 20th week of pregnancy and continuing to about 4 to 6 weeks after birth (American Academy of Pediatrics, 2004). The **postnatal period** begins immediately after birth and ends when the baby is 4 to 6 weeks old. The postnatal period includes the postpartum recovery as well as the neonatal period of the infant's development (American Academy of Pediatrics, 2004).

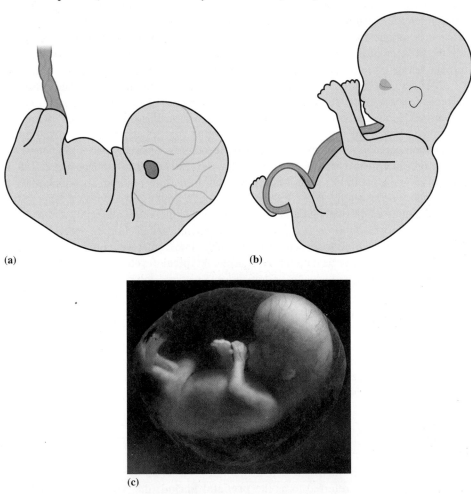

(a)   (b)

(c)

(a) 8-week-old embryo; (b) 3-month-old fetus; (c) developing fetus

FACTORS INFLUENCING DEVELOPMENT

Genetics, environmental, and maternal factors are the most common factors that can influence the development of the infant before and after birth. These factors can determine the health and developmental path of a child. Figure 2.1 illustrates the general factors influencing development during the pre- and postnatal period.

Genetic Disorders

Genetics plays an important role in development. Not only our feature characteristics such as the color of our hair and what we look like, but certain health conditions or illnesses can be inherited from our parents through genes. It is also interesting to know that every individual carries genes for four to eight genetic diseases (Milunsky, 1977).

About 70 percent of developmental disorders are related to genetics (Percy, Lewkis, & Brown, 2007). It is either by active genes alone, or by the genes' interactions with the environment, that developmental problems related to genetics might occur (Batshaw, 2007). Fortunately, the progress made about genetic knowledge has helped scientists advance methods of diagnosis and prevention of developmental disorders that have genetic causes. See Text Box 2.1 for a description of The Human Genome Project.

Human **chromosomes** are small threadlike structures located in the nucleus of over 100 trillion human **cells.** The human body has several different kinds of cells, such as skin cells, muscle cells, and blood cells. Each cell contains 23 pairs of

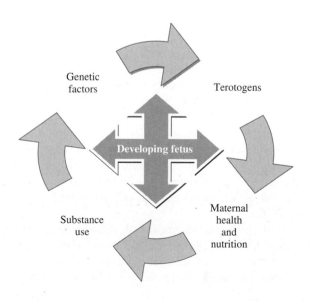

FIGURE 2.1
Factors Influencing the Pre- and Postnatal Development of the Infant

| Text Box 2.1 | The Human Genome Project |

The Human Genome Project (HGP) was the largest international project of its kind. Sponsored by the U.S. Department of Energy and the National Institute of Health, the project involved many scientists in the United States and around the world. It began in 1990 and finished in 2003, although the analysis of its data will continue for many years. The goal of the Human Genome Project was to identify all 20,000 to 25,000 genes existing in human DNA (called the genome) and make them accessible for further biological studies. The findings of this project have enabled scientists to continue to discover various genetic health problems and disorders, and learn possible ways to test individuals for these disorders. This project will enable the design of new technologies for the identification, prevention, and treatment of many gene-based diseases. The project has also devoted about 3 to 5 percent of its funding to examine the ethical, legal, and social implications of human genetics. The U.S. Human Genome Project has encouraged over 18 countries around the world to develop other human genome research projects.

Source: Human Genome Program of the U.S. Department of Energy, available at http://www.ornl.gov/sci/techresources/Human_Genome/home.shtml.

chromosomes, for a total of 46. Chromosomes contain hundreds of **genes.** Humans have about 20,000 to 25,000 genes. Genes are the units of heredity, which determine human traits (Batshaw, 2007). They are made up of a chemical substance called **deoxyribonucleic acid (DNA).** The DNA contains the heredity information as a code. Nearly every cell in the human body has the same DNA. Genetic problems are divided into different types: single-gene disorders, chromosomal abnormalities, multifactorial, and polygenic disorders (Percy et al., 2007).

Chromosomal Abnormalities

Human cells have the capability of dividing into other cells, which have identical genetic information. Cell division occurs through two kinds of processes, called *mitosis* and *meiosis.* In mitosis, two cells are created from one parent cell—each containing 46 chromosomes. In meiosis, four cells are created from one parent cell—each containing only 23 chromosomes. Cell division enables the body to function properly—for example, in recovering from injuries or illnesses. Problems that might occur during cell division could contribute to developmental problems in children—for example, if the chromosomes divide unequally, intellectual impairments, unusual facial appearances, and various congenital malformations might result (Batshaw, 2007).

One of the most common chromosomal abnormalities is Down syndrome or trisomy 21, in which the embryo contains three copies of chromosome 21. Other chromosomal disorders include cri-du-chat syndrome, Turner syndrome, Klinefelter syndrome, Prader-Willi syndrome, Angelman syndrome, and Williams syndrome (see Chapter 11).

Single-Gene Disorders

When chromosomal abnormality affects only one gene, it is called a **single-gene disorder** (Percy et al., 2007). Single-gene disorders are rare. They are also called inborn errors of metabolism. In these cases, the cells cannot produce enzymes or proteins needed to function appropriately. Phenylketonuria (PKU) is a single-gene disorder in which the amino acid phenylalanine is not properly metabolized because of a deficiency in an enzyme needed for its breakdown (Percy et al., 2007). If an infant is diagnosed with PKU, a specific diet should be followed closely. Otherwise, brain damage might occur.

Multifactorial and Polygenic Disorders

Multifactorial genetic disorders are inherited and complex disorders that result from one or more gene abnormalities in combination with environmental factors. Spina bifida is one example of a multifactorial disorder, which usually occurs as a result of chromosomal abnormalities in combination with environmental toxins (Percy et al., 2007). **Polygenic disorders** are caused by defects in more than one gene without the influence of environment, such as certain seizures (Sheffer & Berkovic, 1997). Attention Hyperactivity Disorder (ADHD) has been suspected to be a polygenic disorder as well (Bobb, Castellanos, Addington, & Rapoport, 2005).

TERATOGENS

Any environmental factor that can cause damage to the developing organism during the prenatal period is called a **teratogen.** Teratogens can interfere with physical and/or brain development and therefore cause serious damage to the fetus when exposed to it during pregnancy. Teratogens not only include toxins available in the environment, such as the pollution in the air and chemicals in food, but any hazardous materials that the pregnant woman might consume.

Environmental Toxins

Toxic threats might include exposure to **lead, mercury,** pesticides, radiation, and environmental pollutants, as well as maternal use of drugs, tobacco, and alcohol. Lead and mercury are two common environmental teratogens. Children might be exposed to lead through the air, drinking water, food, contaminated soil, deteriorating lead-based paint, dust, certain types of pottery, and certain cosmetics (Percy, 2007). Exposure to lead can impair cognitive development in the child. Old buildings often contain lead-based materials that were used in their construction. Certain imported toys might contain lead as well. It is important to check all toys and materials that children play with and/or are exposed to, to make sure they are free of lead and toxic materials.

Mercury is a neurotoxin that exists in three forms: metallic, inorganic, and organic (Ricciotti, 2008). An organic kind of mercury, methylmercury, can be found in certain fish. High levels of prenatal exposure to mercury might cause intellectual disability, cerebral palsy, or a visual and auditory deficit in the child (Davidson, Myers, & Weiss, 2004). Because all fish contain a certain amount of mercury, pregnant women and young children should limit consuming seafood, and avoid seafood that is high in mercury content (Ricciotti, 2008).

There has been a great deal of publicity and controversy around mercury as a potential cause of Autism Spectrum Disorders. Many parents of children with autism are concerned that their children's exposure to mercury after birth through immunization—most vaccines contain thimerosal, a mercury-based preservative—might have resulted in their child's autism. Although thimerosal is now removed from most vaccines used for children, parents continue to be concerned about immunizing their children (Davidson & Myers, 2007). This issue will be furthered discussed in Chapter 7.

Burk (2006) describes four factors that can determine the harm done by teratogens to the developing fetus:

> **Dose:** The larger the amount of the terotogen over a longer period of time, the more damage will occur.
> **Heredity:** The mother's genetic makeup along with that of the developing fetus determine whether the fetus will be better able to withstand the harmful environment.
> **Other negative influences:** Several negative factors present at the same time, such as maternal poor nutrition and drug exposure, as well as health status and life style (Zhu, Kartiko, & Finnell, 2009) can exacerbate the effects of the terotogen.
> **Age:** The effect of the terotogen might be different depending on the age of the fetus during exposure.

Generally, teratogens are most dangerous during the embryonic period. This is the time in which the central nervous system begins to develop, and therefore is considered a sensitive period when the living organism is most vulnerable to the harmful effect of environmental toxins.

MATERNAL SUBSTANCE USE

The adverse effects of drugs, alcohol, and tobacco have been examined and documented within a large body of growing research in the past three decades. Today, it is broadly understood that maternal drug use, such as prescribed and nonprescribed medication, alcohol, illegal substances, and tobacco during pregnancy are associated with a variety of maternal and fetal complications. The negative influences of some drugs on the developing central nervous system of the fetus are long lasting and irreversible in some children.

Prescribed and Nonprescribed Medications

Most prescribed and nonprescribed drugs do not have harmful effects on the developing fetus. Some, however, might cause significant problems in the fetus's development. The amount of harm done depends on the type of the medication and the time in which the drug is taken by the mother (Swanson, Entringer, Buss, & Wadhwa, 2009; Riley et al., 2005).

A well-known example is the use of thalidomide by pregnant women in the 1950s. Thalidomide is a sleeping drug which was administered to pregnant women to help with their morning sickness in the 1950s. Children of the mothers who had used thalidomide were born with deformed limbs at the time. In 1961, drug researchers discovered that taking even a small one-time dose of thalidomide early during pregnancy could severely impede the growth of fetal limbs (U.S. Food and Drug Administration, 2005). As a result, the prescription of thalidomide to pregnant women was banned.

In 1979, the Food and Drug Administration (FDA) mandated that drug companies provide a description on all medical drug labels of the possible fetal or maternal harm their products may cause. Despite the increased awareness regarding the adverse effects of medication on fetal development, many women continue to take prescribed and over-the-counter medications during pregnancy (Riley et al., 2005). To reduce the risks of fetal harm, pregnant women are advised to consult with their physicians about the possible risks of prescribed and nonprescribed medication to their health and that of their developing infant.

Illicit Drugs

A large body of information on the effects of illicit drugs on the growing fetus and the neonate has been gathered during the last 20 years due to rigorous research in this area. The National Institute on Drug Abuse (NIDA) reported that in 1992 more than 5 percent of the 4 million women who gave birth in the United States annually used multiple drugs such as marijuana, cocaine, alcohol, and cigarettes while they were pregnant. This study reported that, in general, 11.3 percent of African American women, 4.4 percent of white women, and 4.5 percent of Hispanic women used illicit drugs while pregnant (National Institute on Drug Abuse, 1995).

This alarming rate has put in motion widespread public education efforts regarding the negative influences of drug and alcohol use on infant development. A more recent survey in 2005 indicated that the rate of drug use in pregnant women age 15 to 44 had decreased to only 4.3 percent by 2003, and over 130,000 infants continue to be exposed to drugs in utero each year (National Survey on Drug Use and Health, 2005).

Current studies on use of drugs in pregnant women (Arria et al., 2006; Winslow, Voorhees, & Pehl, 2007; Garcia-Bournissen, Rokach, Karaskov, & Koren, 2007) have focused on the maternal use of methamphetamine, commonly known as meth or crystal meth, a drug that has become popular since the late 1980s. Arria and colleagues (2006) have found that about 5.2 percent of women reported that they have used methamphetamine during pregnancy. This population is more likely to smoke tobacco, drink alcohol, and use other drugs as well. This latter fact makes it difficult to isolate and understand the effects of a specific drug on fetal development in the presence of other drugs used.

These studies show that despite all efforts, drug use during pregnancy remains a major public health concern in the United States Prenatal drug and alcohol use have long been associated with neurodevelopmental problems in the fetus and the neonate. When coupled with other environmental factors, such as poverty, maternal low educational levels, and malnutrition, the negative developmental outcomes of drug exposure is multiplied for the child.

Alcohol

Alcoholic beverages contain ethanol, a toxin that adversely affects neurological development in the fetus. When taken in large quantities, consumption of alcoholic beverages can result in fetal alcohol syndrome (FAS). FAS is discussed in more detail in Chapter 11 (Davidson & Myers, 2007). Ethanol passes easily through the placenta and can result in neurodevelopmental impairments even when alcohol is consumed in low doses (Batshaw, 2007).

Cocaine, Heroin, and Methamphetamine

The effects of prenatal exposure to various drugs are complex and are modulated by the timing, dose, and amount of drug exposure (Thompson, Levitt, & Stanwood, 2009; Bhide, 2009). Although the long-term effects of prenatal exposure to these drugs is not clear, some studies have suggested that children who are born to women who abused drugs during pregnancy are at risk for academic failure and mild physical delays (Winslow et al., 2007). Others (Schneider et al., 2008) have found that prenatal exposure to drugs might increase the risk of sensory processing disorders in children. Finally, a mother's ongoing drug use after birth is associated with the child's poor cognitive and language development, and attention skills in later years (Hurt et al., 2009; Schuler, Nair, & Kettinger, 2003).

Cocaine use has been associated with preterm labor, the infant's reduced head circumference, prematurity, increased perinatal mortality, neonatal seizures, as well as lasting adverse effects on brain structure and function (Hurt et al., 2009; Bhide, 2009; Chasnoff, Burns, Schnoll, & Burns, 1985; Brown, Bakeman, Coles, Sexon, & Demi, 1998). Heroin use causes fetal growth retardation and decreased birth weight and body length, and an increase in neonatal morbidity (Bhide, 2009; Zhu & Stadlin, 2000). Methamphetamine has similar effects to cocaine on developing infants, such as low birth weight and prematurity (Hohman, Oliver, & Wright, 2004). Methamphetamine crosses the placenta and might cause placental abruption and maternal death (Winslow et al., 2007; Garcia-Bournissen et al., 2007). It could also cause increased heart rate and blood pressure in both the mother and the infant (Hohman et al., 2007). Many neonates who are born to mothers who used opiates or methamphetamine have to undergo a period of withdrawal treatment. These infants usually have symptoms such as abnormal sleep patterns, poor feeding, tremors, and hypertonia, which is the reduced ability of the muscles to stretch (Winslow et al., 2007).

Tobacco

Exposure to smoking could happen in two ways: either through exposure in utero, or by being passively exposed to cigarette smoke after birth through inhalation. Weitzman, Kananaugh, and Florin (2006) have argued that inhalation of cigarette smoke is more dangerous to children than being exposed to tobacco in utero, because environmental tobacco smoke contains twice the number of chemicals as the inhaled smoke. In that sense, fathers, mothers, and others who smoke around children put those children at risk for smoke inhalation and the resulting health hazards.

Exposure to cigarette smoke in utero has been associated with slow rate of growth in infants and low birth weight in direct proportion to the number of cigarettes smoked (Swanson et al., 2009; Persson, Grennert, Gennser, & Kullander, 1978; Harrison, Branson, & Vaucher, 1983). Smoking increases the risk of sudden infant death syndrome (Eskenazi, Prehn, & Christianson, 1995). Prenatal smoking has also been known to affect neurological development. Infants who have been exposed to tobacco in utero are more likely to be low in birth weight, develop attention deficit disorders, and have higher rates of hyperactivity, impulsiveness, and anxiety (Andersen, Simonsen, Uldbjerg, Aalkjaer, & Stender, 2009; Huang et al., 2008; Richardson, 1994; Fried, Watkinson, & Gray, 1992; Naeye & Peters, 1984). The effects of maternal smoking are subtle but might persist throughout the child's life (Huang, Liu, Griffith, & Winzer-Serhan, 2007).

MATERNAL HEALTH

A mother's health condition affects the development of the unborn child. There are a variety of maternal diseases and conditions that could threaten the healthy brain and physical development of the fetus. Maternal health conditions might lead to the birth of an infant with a problem or disorder, called a **congenital** condition. As part of the standard care in the United States and other developed countries, pregnant women receive screening and genetic diagnostic testing during their first and second trimester of pregnancy for identification of possible problems. Table 2.1 displays some prenatal screening and diagnostic tests currently available (Schonberg & Tifft, 2007).

Maternal infections during pregnancy are common conditions that can directly damage the neural structure of the fetus, and therefore alter brain development (Bell, 2007). The placenta usually acts as a barrier to many small infections, but certain types of infections can pass through the placenta to the fetus.

A group of prenatal infections called **TORCH** infections, named for **t**oxoplasmosis, **o**ther (HIV, syphilis, and others), **r**ubella, **c**ytomegalovirus, and **h**erpes

The ultrasound uses high-frequency sound waves to observe the fetus.

TABLE 2.1   **Prenatal Screening and Diagnostic Tests**

First Trimester	Second Trimester
Ultrasound: Using high-frequency sound waves to observe the fetus Uses: Determine the number of fetuses; locates placenta position and general stability of pregnancy	Ultrasound: Using high-frequency sound waves to view the fetus and related organs. The three-dimensional ultrasound might be used Uses: Observe the structure of varying organs and limbs forming
Maternal serum screening: Blood sample taken around 10 to 14 weeks of gestation Uses: Identification of birth defects such as Down syndrome, spina bifida, low birth weight, or possible fetal loss	Maternal serum screening: Blood sample taken at around 16 weeks of gestation Uses: A more accurate diagnosis of possible birth defects which might not show up in earlier tests
Chronic villus sampling (CVS): A biopsy of the outer membrane surrounding the embryo via a small needle inserted through the abdominal wall, done at 1 to 12 weeks gestation Uses: Identification of genetic disorders through chromosome analysis, enzyme assay, and DNA analysis	Amniocentesis: Drawing an amniotic fluid sample by inserting a needle through the abdominal wall Uses: To detect possible chromosomal abnormalities, such as Down syndrome
	Magnetic resonance imaging (MRI): A high-resolution ultrasound to observe certain structures in the brain and other organs Uses: To examine the structure of the brain, lungs, and other organs
	Fetal echocardiography: Using ultrasound to carefully examine the fetus's heart Uses: To determine fetal heart abnormalities
	Diagnostic testing of fetal cells: Obtaining fetal cells through amniocentesis or CVS. (Fluorescent in situ hybridization [FISH] might be used, which is a technique to identify chromosomes or detect small deletions in the regions of the chromosome.) Uses: To identify a variety of genetic disorders
	Percutaneous umbilical blood sampling: Obtaining a small sample of fetal blood under ultrasound guidance Uses: To detect chromosomal abnormalities and blood disorders

Source: Schonberg, R., & Tifft, C. (2007). Birth defects and prenatal diagnosis. In M. Batshaw, L. Pellegrino, & N. J. Roizen (Eds.), *Children with disabilities* (6th ed., pp. 83–96). Baltimore: Paul H. Brookes.

TABLE 2.2   TORCH Infections and Other Disorders Affecting the Healthy Development of the Fetus

---

Group B streptococcus

Toxoplasmosis

Cytomegalovirus (CMV)

Herpes simplex viruses

Human immunodeficiency virus (HIV)

Rubella

Diabetes

(Bell, 2007; Deiner, 2009), are dangerous to the developing fetus and are known to cause certain disabilities in the infant. Maternal metabolic disorders, such as diabetes, are another group of health conditions that constitute risks to healthy fetal development. Table 2.2 displays a number of TORCH infections and health conditions which have adverse effects on the development of the infant. A discussion of all conditions that might lead to disabilities in children is outside the scope of this chapter; however, we will briefly examine some of the more common infections and conditions that might impede an infant's healthy development.

Group B Streptococcus

Group B streptococcus (GBS) is the most common cause of perinatal bacterial infection. GBS can cause sepsis (infections in the lungs) and meningitis (infection of the fluid and lining of the brain) during the first month of the infant's life (Bell, 2007). Bacterial colonization occurs in the vaginal wall. During the birth, the infant could contract the bacteria as it passes through the birth canal.

The neonate could show symptoms during the first week of life or several weeks or months after birth (Centers for Disease Control and Prevention, 2008). About 20 percent of infants with GBS die, and others might develop serious brain damage (Deering & Satin, 2002). A routine GBS test for the strep bacteria during weeks 35 to 37 of pregnancy can prompt appropriate care, such as taking antibiotics during labor, that would prevent the transmission of the bacteria to the infant (Bell, 2007).

Toxoplasmosis

Toxoplasmosis is a food-borne disease, which is caused by a parasite known as toxoplasma gondii or *T. gondii.* Toxoplasmosis can be transmitted to humans through meat, eggs, or the feces of infected pet cats. The infection in the mother usually passes through the placenta to the infant (Bell, 2007). If the infection occurs during the first trimester, the child is less likely (17 percent chance) to be born with congenital toxoplasmosis, but the damage to the fetus is usually severe; whereas, if the mother acquires an infection during the later trimesters, the infant will have a 65 percent chance of being infected, but will have a milder toxoplasmosis at birth (Hokelek & Safdar, 2006).

Toxoplasmosis causes inflamed lymph glands in the infant that can lead to brain damage, or might obstruct the flow of cerebrospinal fluid to the brain and cause *hydrocephalous* in the infant (Bell, 2007). Hydrocephalous is marked by an accumulation of cerebrospinal fluid in the brain, which leads to enlargement of the skull or a prominent forehead, and might cause mental deterioration and convulsions.

Cytomegalovirus

Cytomegalovirus (CMV) is a member of the herpes family. It is one of the most common conditions that might be present at birth. According to the Centers for Disease Control and Prevention, about 40,000 infants annually are born with congenital cytomegalovirus; out of this number about 8,000 will suffer from permanent disabilities (Centers for Disease Control and Prevention, 2008).

An infection caused by CMV can be hidden and unnoticed, and except for in utero infections and those patients who have a compromised immune system, it rarely causes a disease (Bell, 2007; Kerzel Andersen et al., 2008). The fetus can acquire the CMV through the placenta. If the infection occurs during the second half of pregnancy, the infant is at greater risk of developing CMV at the time of birth (Bell, 2007).

When CMV is contracted at a critical time during fetal development, the damage to the central nervous system can be considerable. About 15 percent of infants with a CMV infection who have no symptoms at birth will develop intellectual disability or progressive hearing loss within the first 5 years of life or later (Bell, 2007). Other diseases that might develop as a result of CMV infection include jaundice, motor disability, seizures, and hepatitis (Kerzel Andersen et al., 2008). Some reports have supported the existence of a link between CMV and autism in vulnerable children (Sweeten, Posey, & McDougle, 2004).

Herpes Simplex Virus

Herpes simplex virus (HSV) is a sexually transmitted disease. Herpes viruses are categorized into two types: HSV-1, which is acquired by contact with salivary secretions, and HSV-2, or genital herpes, which is acquired genitally, and is replicated in the genital areas (Gonzalez-Villasenor, 1999).

Only 5 percent of all neonatal infections with HSV are acquired in utero through the placenta; 85 percent occur as a result of contact with maternal lesions during the birth process (Bell, 2007). A mother with HSV can deliver a healthy baby, especially using a Cesarean section, which reduces the risk of HSV infection in infants (Bren, 2002). An infant who is infected with HSV could develop intellectual disability, kidney and liver problems, deafness, or blindness; blindness usually occurs if the infection has taken place in utero (Bell, 2007). Some infants infected with herpes, whose CNS is damaged as a result of the infection, might die if untreated (Gonzalez-Villasenor, 1999). Early treatment for the infant who is infected with herpes is critical and can help reverse the outcome for that child.

HIV and AIDS

Human immunodeficiency virus (HIV) has been known for the past 27 years. HIV is the cause of acquired immunodeficiency syndrome (AIDS). The 2006 report published by the United Nations Program on HIV/AIDS estimated that 39.5 million people were living with HIV worldwide in 2006, almost half of whom were women.

This report also indicated that 6 percent of people living with HIV are children (United Nations Program on HIV/AIDS, 2006).

HIV can be passed to the fetus in three ways: in utero, during the birth process, or through breastfeeding (Alvarez & Rathore, 2007; Kamau-Mbuthia, Elmadfa, & Mwonya, 2008). Half of children infected with HIV show symptoms within the first year of their lives, either gradually or acutely. Infants and children infected with HIV are susceptible to a variety of other infections and illnesses. These children might have recurring conditions, such as ear infections, upper respiratory tract infections, pneumonia, or gastroenteritis (Bell, 2007). Infants suspected of having HIV should be tested within 48 hours after birth, at 1 to 2 months of age, and at 4 to 6 months of age, and when confirmed of infection should be treated with a multi-drug regimen (Bell, 2007).

Early intervention and prevention of HIV infection in infants is possible through several screenings during pregnancy. Alvarez and Rathore (2007) recommend that HIV screenings be conducted in women who are at risk for acquiring the virus early in pregnancy and during the third trimester. It is recommended that infected women do not breastfeed their infants at all, or stop breastfeeding their infants during the first months after birth (Kamau-Mbuthia et al., 2008).

Rubella Virus

Rubella virus causes rubella, also known as German measles, in children and adults. Rubella has been under control since 1969 with effective vaccinations. However, a small number of infants continue to be born with congenital rubella in the United States, Canada, and other parts of the world. Congenital rubella syndrome (CRS) occurs in infants as a result of maternal infection during pregnancy (Bell, 2007).

The risks of the fetus contracting rubella in utero are restricted to the first 16 weeks of gestation. Infection of the fetus occurs through the placenta and might lead to stillbirth, spontaneous abortion, or congenital rubella (Bell, 2007). Congenital rubella is a dangerous condition, which can lead to severe disabilities in children. Possible conditions that might occur as a result of congenital rubella include cardiac defects, intellectual disability, deafness, and blindness.

Maternal Diabetes

Diabetes is a condition in which one's blood sugar is too high. In type 1 diabetes, the body makes very little insulin and cannot use sugar effectively. In type 2 diabetes, the body might make enough insulin, but is unable to use it effectively. People with type 1 diabetes require daily insulin shots, whereas those with type 2 diabetes are able to manage their body's metabolic needs with appropriate diet. Another type of diabetes, **gestational diabetes,** refers to the type of diabetes that occurs in women who are pregnant and did not have diabetes prior to pregnancy.

In April 2008, a report indicated that the rate of diabetes in pregnant women had doubled in the United States from 1999 to 2005, regardless of age or ethnic and racial background (Lawrence, Contreras, Chen, & Sacks, 2008). This dramatic increase in the rate of diabetes in young women of childbearing age is a great public health concern. Maternal diabetes during pregnancy poses a significant risk to the infant's developing brain and metabolic function. Too much sugar in the mother's blood during pregnancy leads to a fetal hyperglycemia, which in turn causes a reaction of *hyperinsulinemia,* production of too much insulin in the fetus's blood (Stonestreet, Golstein, Oh, & Widness, 1989; Milley, Papacostas, & Tabata, 1986). This would result in an increased rate of oxygen consumption beyond the capacity of the placenta to supply oxygen to the fetus (Milley et al., 1986). The result is *infant hypoxemia,* lack of oxygen.

Hypoxemia poses a significant risk to the developing brain and can result in damage to specific regions of the brain, such as the hippocampus (Nelson, 2007; Burdo & Conner, 2002). In addition, maternal diabetes results in chronic iron deficiency in the infant, which affects multiple developing brain functions (Nelson, 2007). Aside from the possible neurological and metabolic problems during fetal development, if diabetes is not managed during pregnancy with appropriate diet and close monitoring, the born infant is at risk for obesity and developing diabetes later in life (Centers for Disease Control and Prevention, 2008).

MATERNAL AND CHILD NUTRITION

Good nutrition not only contributes to healthy development of the growing fetus, but to the health and well-being of the child after birth and later in life. A good diet should provide all the nutrients required for the healthy development of the child before and after birth. During prenatal development, nutritional substances pass through the placenta to the child. Similarly, the child who is breastfed receives nutrition from the mother through the breast milk. Therefore, the mother's diet affects the infant both prenatally and postnatally.

Prenatal and Postnatal Nutrition

Recent theories state that maternal malnutrition might contribute to cognitive and other health problems in children that would persist through their adulthood (Ricciotti, 2008; Percy, 2007). Many health risks and diseases, such as low birth weight, obesity and diabetes, have been linked to fetal under-nutrition and over-nutrition. For example, infants who are small for gestational age at birth, and are born to undernourished mothers, are at risk for coronary heart disease (Ricciotti, 2008). As mentioned, the number of women of childbearing age who have diabetes and obesity has grown tremendously during the past decade. With this recent increase, there is a growing concern that maternal overweight might lead to birth complications, increased likelihood of a Cesarean birth, and childhood obesity (Galtier-Dereure, Boegner, & Bringer, 2000).

Determining the correct weight gain in a pregnant woman depends on the woman's **body mass index (BMI).** The appropriate weight gain during pregnancy is usually individualized by the obstetrician based on recommendations by the American Dietetic Association and Institute of Medicine (1990). Nutritionists and physicians take into consideration the mother's age, activity level, and weight before recommending the appropriate diet.

Maternal eating habits influence the child's growth and physical heath. Children who are born to mothers who eat unhealthy food (junk food) during pregnancy, or during the infant's breastfeeding period, are more likely to have unhealthy eating habits and obesity problems later in development (Bayol, Farrington, & Stickland, 2007).

Child Nutrition

A child's nutrition later in development is as important as having a good diet during the prenatal and infancy periods. Malnutrition in children consists of a lack of appropriate minerals, vitamins, and other nutrients necessary for growth. In developing countries around the world, about 143 million children suffer from malnutrition (UNICEF, 2000). Many children around the world, including the United States and Canada, are either underweight and suffer from a lack of certain vitamins, minerals, and protein, or deal with obesity and other health problems that have arisen from having an inappropriate diet (Percy, 2007). Malnutrition not only affects physical and motor development, but cognitive development as well. Children who do not have a healthy diet are at risk for a variety of developmental problems (Bayol et al., 2007; Percy, 2007).

BIRTH AND COMPLICATIONS

A full-term pregnancy refers to a period of between 38 and 42 weeks. Factors affecting birth and the birth process are generally the mother's emotional and physical health, appropriate prenatal care, healthy diet, and good support from the partner and obstetrician or midwife during delivery.

Most deliveries occur through spontaneous vaginal delivery (SVD). In case of fetal distress—when the baby fails to get enough oxygen—operative deliveries might be used to speed the birth process (Deiner, 2009). Operative deliveries might include the use of forceps and other vacuum devices (Brown & Satin, 2007). Cesarean section, which takes place through an incision in the abdomen and uterus, might also take place if the fetus is in jeopardy.

The Newborn

During the first 28 days after birth, a newborn infant is called a **neonate.** A neonate whose weight is less than 2,500 grams (5.5 pounds) is considered an infant with a **low birth weight (LBW),** whereas a neonate whose weight is over 4,000 grams (8.5 pounds) is considered **large for gestational age** (Deiner, 2009).

We have described several maternal health conditions that might put an infant in jeopardy. Other factors, as described by Brown and Satin (2007), that might contribute to complications during labor and the condition of the newborn are:

> ≻ Maternal hypertension—the mother's elevated blood pressure (greater than 140/90)
> ≻ Maternal trauma and abuse, such as abdominal trauma caused by an accident or physical abuse
> ≻ Obstetric conditions, such as preterm labor, membrane rupture, placental abruption, or **umbilical cord prolapse**
> ≻ Special conditions, such as breach presentation and birth injuries or defects
> ≻ Maternal stress, which has recently been found to contribute to vulnerability to disorders such as mood and anxiety disorders (Gillespie, Phifer, Bradley, & Ressler, 2009)

Neonatal Screening

In general, a **screening test** is designed to screen for certain risk factors or possible problems. It is not designed to diagnose or assess a condition (Pellegrino, 2007b). Because screening tests are broad-based instruments, they might produce either **false positive** or **false negative** results. A false positive result indicates a problem, where in fact there is no condition present in the individual, while a false negative indicates the absence of a possible risk factor, when in fact the individual is at risk. Conducting a screening test helps health professionals decide whether or not administering a **diagnostic test** is warranted. A diagnostic test is designed to confirm or exclude the existence of a certain condition.

A number of neonatal screening tests help physicians identify the possibility of significant genetic and medical conditions, such as infectious diseases like HIV, or metabolic disorders like PKU (Pellegrino, 2007b). Neonatal screening helps in timely diagnosis and intervention measures, and the prevention of further conditions that might occur if the original problem is not treated. Most newborn screening tests rely on blood samples (taken during the first few days after birth) and can identify the possibility of conditions such as endocrine disorders, infectious diseases, and metabolic disorders (Pellegrino, 2007b).

The overall well-being of the newborn is assessed by using a scoring system designed by Virginia Apgar (1909–1974). When used to assess an infant, this scoring system will produce what is known as the **Apgar score.** The Apgar score consists of a total of 10 points that are given to the infant's level of **a**ctivity (muscle tone), **p**ulse, **g**rimace, **a**ppearance, and **r**espiration (APGAR) (Gaitatzes, Chang, & Baumgart, 2007). The score is usually given within the first to fifth minute of the infant's birth. The Apgar test is not a diagnostic test. Its score represents the newborn's condition in the immediate postnatal period (Gaitatzes et al., 2007).

Premature Infants

Babies who are born before the 37th week of pregnancy are considered to be premature or preterm infants. A preterm infant usually has a low birth weight (LBW)—or a **very low birth weight (VLBW)**—of under 1,500 grams (3.33 pounds) (Rais-Bahrami & Short, 2007). Some infants might weigh less than 1,000 grams (2.25 pounds), something called **extremely low birth weight (ELBW),** or weigh even less than 800 grams (1.75 pounds), wherein they are called **micropreemies** (Rais-Bahrami & Short, 2007). Premature infants with an extremely low gestational age are at increased risk for structural and functional brain problems (O'Shea et al., 2009).

Since most organs of a preterm infant are not fully formed and ready to perform their tasks, the infant is at risk for developing complications in different organ systems of the body. These complications include respiratory problems; neurodevelopmental problems; hearing loss; apnea and bradycardia—respiratory pauses and a decrease in the heart rate; sudden infant death syndrome (SIDS); cardiovascular problems; gastrointestinal problems; and immunological problems (Rais-Bahrami & Short, 2007; Szatmari, Saigal, Rosenbaum, & Campbell; 1993). Fortunately, advances in the care of premature infants have been effective in reducing the number of mortalities and increasing their health and developmental outcomes.

Premature infants are cared for in the NICU (neonatal intensive care unit) of the hospital. The infant is treated and cared for until the appropriate weight gain is reached and the body organs function appropriately. A preterm infant who is discharged from the hospital may have many special health needs. Owing to an underdeveloped CNS, some premature infants have behaviors that are associated with a difficult temperament, such as crying often, making little eye contact, and difficulties in being soothed (Goldberg-Hamblin, Singer, Singer, & Denney, 2007). Parents might find caring for their preterm infants stressful and challenging. In addition, separation of the infant from his or her parents right after birth might delay the process of bonding between parents and child.

Early intervention, beginning right before discharge from the hospital, can help provide parents with appropriate and needed support in caring for their infant and successfully coping with the stressors of such care. One early intervention strategy being used for premature infants is **developmental care** (Als & Gilkerson, 1997). This strategy focuses on the interaction between the caregiver and the infant.

In this strategy, the caregiver learns to read the infant's cues through his or her autonomic (heart rate), motoric (mobility, muscle tone, position), state (movement between states), and interaction/attention behaviors to understand the infant's capabilities and needs. The caregiver is then coached to devise ways to support the infant to increase his or her self-regulation. For example, if the infant's behaviors indicate over-stimulation of the sensory system, the caregiver would use body positioning, reduction of stimulation, and other adjustments (such as a blanket roll, padding) to help the infant increase self-regulation (Goldberg-Hamblin et al., 2007).

Developmental care strategies have been described as "relationship caregiving" (Als & Gilkerson, 1997), which promote healthy attachment and relationship development between the caregiver and the baby. Later, we will describe the importance of attachment and adult–child relationships in a healthy child's development.

DEVELOPMENT AND THE CHILD

Child developmental scholars have studied the development of the child within different dimensions and through different periods of development. Dimensions of development are commonly known as **developmental domains.** Developmental domains are distinct areas that encompass the development of certain abilities. Domains of development are divided into three major areas, as stated by Santrock (2006): **physical development, cognitive development** (which includes communication and language development), and **social emotional development.**

Early childhood special education is concerned with five areas within these major three domains of development, from birth through the end of early childhood years. Therapists and educators strive to achieve developmental goals related to skill learning in the following areas:

> **Physical development:** Includes biological health, sensory, and motor development
> **Cognitive development:** Includes intelligence, general knowledge, and awareness of the surroundings

FIGURE 2.2
Five Areas of
Development

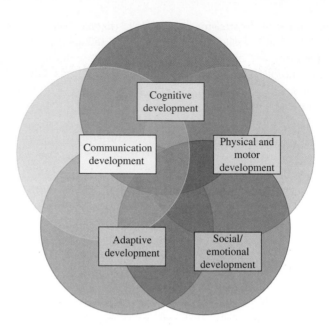

> **Communication development:** Includes speech and language development, vision and hearing
>> **Language development:** Includes expressive language (ability to express oneself and use oral language for communication; and receptive language (ability to listen and understand what is heard)
> **Social/emotional development:** Includes emotions, personality, temperament, and relationship development
> **Adaptive development:** Includes integration of learning and application in day-to-day functioning, such as self-help skills, self-hygiene, and independent functioning

Areas of development are interrelated with each other in that change and growth in one area influences other areas. Figure 2.2 illustrates the interrelation of areas of development.

Arnold Gesell (1880–1961) was a developmental psychologist at Yale University who developed guidelines for the systematic observation of development in children. Gesell described children's development in the first 5 years of life. He suggested that typically developing children go through the same sequences, but might vary in their rates of growth (Crain, 2004). For example, by 1 month of age, infants could observe a ring that is dangled before them and follow its movement, or by 1 year of age a child is able to walk. Based on Gesell's work, there emerged a field of knowledge regarding the range of abilities in various domains of development at different points in time. See Table 2.3 for examples of developmental milestones in five areas of development.

Gesell's work became the foundation for what we know today as **developmental milestones.** Milestones are specific developmental and behavioral markers that can be generally agreed upon to be present around a specific time. Referencing a particular milestone allows us to understand a child's skill level in each area of

TABLE 2.3   Areas of Development with Examples of Developmental Behaviors/Skills

Areas of Development	Descriptions and Examples of Skills during Early Childhood Years
Social emotional development	The ability to interact with others and form various relationships with adults and peers *Skills* Infancy and toddler years: By 3 months of age, able to interact with caregivers through facial expressions, vocal exchange, eye contact, and smiles; by 9 months, enjoys lap games and interactive games with adults; by 2 years, shares many exchanges, such as sharing objects of interest with others; responds and interacts in playful activities with others Preschool: Able to interact and form relationships with peers and adults, take turns in group activities, share objects and toys, get along with peers and adults Early primary school: Able to cooperate with others, function well in small and large groups; understand member roles in a team situation
Cognitive development	Refers to thought processes, including thinking, reasoning, remembering, problem solving, and making decisions *Skills* Infancy and toddler years: Is aware of surroundings and others, curious and able to explore environments and things; by 14 months is able to imitate, has memory of events and episodes Preschool: Able to understand basic concrete and abstract concepts, such as similarities, differences, and time; able to solve simple problems and engage in simple reasoning Early primary school: Able to think logically and apply knowledge to situations; able to use reasoning abilities to solve more complex problems
Communication development	Ability to exchange ideas; includes hearing and vision, as well as receptive and expressive language development *Skills* Infant's vision: By 3 months, able to watch faces intently, follow moving objects with eyes, recognize familiar objects and people Infant's early communication: able to reciprocate early facial and vocal exchanges with caregiver, use gestures and sounds for communicative purposes; by 3 months, smiles at the sound of a caregiver's voice, imitates sounds and begins vocalizing; by 6 months, babbles consonants, responds to own name, imitates sounds; by one year, uses one word sounds for communication Toddler years: Able to point to pictures and objects when named, follows simple directions; uses two- or three-word phrases for communication Preschool: Able to follow two- or three- step directions, recognize and label most common objects, speak in three- or four-word sentences; by 4 years of age, able to use basic rules of grammar, ask and answer questions; by 5 years, able to hold conversations, recall most parts of a story, and tell a story with beginning, middle, and end Early primary school: Able to read and write words; by the end of first grade, able to write and read simple sentences, and hold longer conversations
Physical, sensory, and motor development	Physical/sensory: Includes general health, ability to organize and modulate incoming sensory stimuli, and regulate oneself in a calm manner Gross motor: Ability to use large muscles to sit, stand, walk, run, keep balance, and change position

(Continued)

TABLE 2.3   (Continued)

	Fine motor: Ability to use small muscles to hold objects, eat, draw, dress, write, and perform tasks that require use of fingers and small muscles
	Infant: By 3 months, able to raise head and chest while on stomach, kick and push feet when the feet are on a hard surface; bring hand to mouth, open and shut hands, grasp and shake toys; by 6 months, able to roll, sit with or without support, move objects from one hand to the other; by 1 year, able to crawl, pull self up to stand, use furniture to walk, begin to walk unaided
	Toddlers: Able to walk and begin to run; pull and push toys along, stand on tiptoes, climb furniture; build towers, fill in and empty containers
	Preschool: Able to run, kick, climb, peddle a tricycle; draw vertical, horizontal, and round lines, begin drawing simple geometric shapes, use scissors, begin writing simple letters.
	Early primary school: Begin participating in sports and physical games; able to write words and sentences on a straight line, and draw different geometric shapes
Adaptive development	Consists of a constellation of skills and behaviors related to different areas of development that enable the child to function independently. Includes ability to take care of needs, function sufficiently in the community, take personal and social responsibilities, and adjust to environmental and social demands
	Skills
	Infancy and toddler years: Able to respond reciprocally to caregivers' behaviors; by 2 years, begins to learn the toileting process, put some items of clothing on, eat independently using fingers, and drink out of a cup independently
	Preschool: Able to take care of self-hygiene needs, eat using a fork and spoon, help adults in cleaning a room
	Early elementary school: Able to take care of self-hygiene and grooming needs, and dress independently; play and perform academic tasks independently; participate and help in various home and community activities, such as shopping

development according to his age (Pellegrino, 2007a). They also help us understand whether or not a delay or deviation exists in the development of a child. Developmental milestones have been used in the design of formal developmental screening and assessment instruments (Pellegrino, 2007a).

The importance of each milestone is relevant to the functionality and magnitude of each specific skill. Uttering words for the purpose of communication around age 1 has a different weight as compared with putting together a puzzle at age 2, which relies on development of other fundamental skills in cognition and motor functioning. Therefore, as Pellegrino (2007a) puts it, "therapeutic intervention should not be directed toward achieving milestones per se, but rather toward achieving meaningful functional goals that are represented by milestones" (p. 222).

THE BRAIN BEHAVIOR RELATIONSHIP

The development of skills and milestones are related to the brain developmental process. In the last 20 years, there have been remarkable advances in infant and child brain research that have helped us understand the relationship between brain development and behavior in children with both typical and atypical development. The process of brain development in a human begins from conception continues in an orderly fashion throughout life. Early brain development depends on a series of genetic events that cause establishment of the basic brain structure (Pellegrino, 2007a). Much of this basic structure begins to be built in the fetus in the first trimester of pregnancy.

By the end of the second trimester, the maximum number of neurons is formed in a fetus's brain. And from this time forward neurons begin forming connections and transmitting electrical impulses from one part of the nervous system to the other through synapses. Synaptic development and connections, and myelination—the process of the formation of a sheath around nerve cells—occur rapidly in the first 2 years after birth. By 2 years of age, the brain has gained 80 percent of its adult weight; with 96 percent of the brain weight being gained by age 6 (Lenroot & Giedd, 2007).

The first 3 years of life are critical to the development of the brain. The synaptic activities and the infant's brain development are heavily dependent on the infant's experiences in the environment during these years. Experiences of the infant with outside stimuli cause the firing of neurons and strengthen the synaptic connections.

Synaptic activities in the infant's brain allow for the creation of different components of the brain—each of which carry a different function, such as attention, perception, memory, and emotional regulation (Davies, 2002). Over time, certain brain areas of specialization will result and the brain quickly develops a whole network specialized for a specific area—for example, a network for social behavior function, one for memory function, or another for the language function (Johnson, 2007). Accordingly, a brain specialized network is responsible for developing the specific tasks and abilities related to that specialization. For example, the brain social network is responsible for developing social skills; a constellation of skills such as detecting eye gaze, forming joint attention, or understanding and reacting to others' actions, all of which would gradually form social perceptions and competence in the child (Johnson, 2007).

A constant feedback loop between environmental stimuli and the child's brain network functioning occurs as the infant grows. These interactions cause brain characteristics and activity level changes systematically during childhood, bringing changes in the child's actions, speech, problem solving, concepts, social interactions, and physical development (Immordino-Yang & Fischer, 2007). Brain development goes through periods of sharp spurts as well as discontinuity in different periods of life, which correspond to the development of various complex behaviors and skills in the child. For example, at 8 months of age infants begin to search for hidden objects. This infant behavior corresponds to the electroencephalogram (EEG) power and coherence test, indicating a brain activity spurt around 8 months of age in the cognitive network of the brain (Immordino-Yang & Fischer, 2007).

Because the infant's brain development is dependent upon experience (Rosenzweig, 2002), this phenomenon is often called an "experience dependent" development of the brain (Davies, 2002). Based on this process, the infant not only needs specific stimuli, but another person to interact with in order to stimulate the development of its brain (Davies, 2002). Therefore, early development of the brain is not only dependent on genetic makeup, but on early and later experiences that occur between the infant and the caregiver or between the child and adults. In this section, we will focus on early experiences that are crucial in the promotion of healthy brain development in infants. These experiences will ultimately influence development in all areas.

Early Stimulation and Neurodevelopment

Brain studies have shown that the experiences of infants and young children in enriched environments enhance the cortical development of the brain (Rosenzweig, 2002; Johnston, 2009). Exposure to sensory stimulation and interaction with appropriate materials during early infancy are crucial for both physical and cognitive development. For example, in one study an infant whose eyes had been covered during the first months after birth due to an injury showed specific impairments in the establishment of the neural pathways to the brain related to sight as a result of this early sensory deprivation (Davies, 2002).

Similarly, an infant's ability to become aware of his surroundings and relate to his environment, and eventually develop further cognitive functions, is related to his early experiences in an enriched environment. An enriched environment is defined as an environment that provides appropriate learning stimulations for an infant or a child. For some decades, we have known that early deprivation of infants and young children who grow up in poverty and live with families of a low educational level has been associated with cognitive impairment and further problems in learning (Eckert, Lambardino, & Leonard, 2001; Drews, Yeargin-Allsopp, Decoufle, & Murphy, 1995; Murphy, Yeargin-Allsopp, Decoufle, & Drews, 1995).

For an infant, an enriched environment not only consists of gradual and careful exposure to various sensory stimuli, such as sights, sounds, lights, and textures, but the caregiver's responsiveness to the infant's cues in relationship to the absence or presence of the specific types of the stimuli; for example, when the infant needs stimulation, and when she needs to rest. For toddlers and older children, exploration and manipulation of, and interactions with, appropriate educational materials and toys provide some elements of an enriched environment.

In and of themselves, appropriate educational materials and toys are not sufficient for promoting early brain development in a young child. Rather, it is the specific early relationship experiences, such as daily facial and vocal dialogues, between the infant and caregiver that teaches the infant to feel safe, regulate different sensory stimuli, make sense of his surroundings, and finally be able to explore and interact with his environment and the materials within. With this latter statement, we turn our attention to the process of attachment between the caregiver and the child, and the importance of the adult–child relationship in the development of the child.

Attachment and Neurodevelopment

Infants come into the world with biologically prepared capabilities for self-regulation, as well as the capacity to form relationships with others (Emde, 1989). The most important part of an infant's development is not her adaptations to the environment; rather it is her relationship with the caregiver (or the parent). The first 3 years of life are the years in which the infant begins to develop ways of being with others through her many daily encounters with the adults who care for her (Reyna & Pickler, 2009; Stern, 2000). The infant's brain is wired with a capacity to initiate, maintain, and terminate social interaction, some of which are present at birth, such as eye-to-eye contact, and being soothed by human holding, touching, and rocking (Reyna & Pickler, 2009; Emde, 1989).

The parents are also predisposed to caregiving by a variety of behaviors that seem to spring automatically and naturally. Therefore, both infant and caregiver are biologically prepared to mesh their behaviors in a mutual interchange of behavioral synchrony, such as exchanges of smiles, coos, and facial expressions (Emde, 1989). The tie that bonds the infant to the caregiver (mother, father, or any other primary caregiver) has been referred to as **attachment,** while the aspects of caregiving that bonds the caregiver (parent) to the child is called bonding (Emde, 1989).

Attachment

The responsiveness of the caregiver (parent) to the infant's bids for attention (such as the infant's smiles and vocalizations) and his cues for physical and safety needs (such as the infant's cries, facial expressions, or motoric behavior and body language) not only helps the infant better regulate the sensory stimuli, but causes the infant to learn to engage with and relate to others. Through these early back and forth interactions, the infant learns to trust the caregiver to be there every time the infant needs him. When foundations of trust are established, the infant uses the caregiver as a secure base to and from which he could depart to explore the environment and return whenever he needs the caregiver. Therefore, attachment refers to this early process of relationship building between the caregiver and the infant.

We owe much of our understanding about attachment to John Bowlby (1907–1990), a British psychiatrist who proposed the attachment theory, and to Mary Ainsworth (1913–1999), a student of Bowlby's who conducted numerous studies on attachment between babies and their mothers. Bowlby defined attachment as "the bond that ties" the infant to her caregiver (parent) over time (Bowlby, 1969/1982). According to Bowlby, attachment is a complex biological process that takes time and is different from what is considered simply as bonding between parent and child, which is instantaneous. Bowlby believed that attachment is an innate developmental process for which the infant's brain is wired.

Mary Ainsworth (1984) developed a laboratory procedure called "strange situation" to assess the infant–caregiver attachment relationship. Her studies on attachment have helped us understand that children form different types of attachment with their caregivers (parents), depending on the type of relationship they have with them. Consistency and the kind of responses that infants receive from their caregivers determine the type of relationship and attachment they form with that adult. For example, an infant who receives consistent warm responses from her caregiver will form a *secure attachment* with that adult. This same child is more likely to have a healthy social emotional development later in life and be able to form positive relationships with others.

Earlier, Bowlby had explained this phenomenon under a concept called internal working models. Accordingly, children form internal working models or images of themselves and their attachment figures and internalize their attachment relationships. These early experiences are transferred to serve later behavioral and emotional adaptations in new contexts and with new people. So, for example, if infants do not form a secure attachment with their caregivers, they will be less likely to have positive images of themselves and of others, and therefore are less likely to develop the necessary skills to form positive relationships with others later in life.

Although the early caregiver–child relationship is the key to further social emotional development in the child, it does not follow that a negative relationship will necessarily lead to an atypical development. Rather, as children develop, if they have consistent positive interactions with other adults and under new circumstances, they would be able to establish healthy neurological patterns of adaptations necessary to help them form social emotional skills and competencies (Weinfield, Sroufe, Egeland, & Carlson, 1999).

Bowlby's attachment theory has withstood the test of numerous scientific controlled experimentations from the 1950s to the present, and is among the few developmental theories that have a solid empirical basis. Today, there is no doubt about the importance of positive infant–caregiver relationships in the child's brain social network development. This is indeed the reason why a positive adult–child relationship is considered to have the strongest buffering and therapeutic effect in the development of children who are at risk. Similarly, relationship-based models of intervention for children with developmental delays and disabilities have presented much promise in the field of early intervention and early childhood special education (described further in Chapters 6, 11, and 14).

Breastfeeding and Neurodevelopment

The benefits of breastfeeding have been elaborated upon since the 1920s. The American Academy of Pediatrics recommends that mothers breastfeed infants for at least the first 4 to 8 months of life (American Academy of Pediatrics, 1997). Breastfeeding has been known to be related to the infant's enhanced physical health, specifically the immune system, and higher growth rate (Ljujic-Glisic, Bozinovic-Prekajski, & Glibetic, 2009; Xanthou, 1998; Rogers, Emmett, & Golding, 1997). Breastfeeding is also believed to protect infants from sudden infant death syndrome and early infections (Ford et al., 1993; Cunningham, 1979).

Aside from these benefits, a relationship between breastfeeding and neurodevelopment in children has been described in research as well (Brown, Thoyre, Pridham, & Schubert, 2009; Golding, Rogers, & Emmett, 1997; Lanting, Patandin, Weisgals-Kuperus, Touwen, & Bersma, 1998). For example, children breastfed during their first months have been shown to have better motoric movements, higher school achievement, and better social emotional development and adjustments later in life (Golding et al., 1997; Lanting et al., 1998). In addition, children who are breastfed up to 9 months of age are found to perform better on intelligence tests in adulthood (Mortensen, Michaelsen, Sanders, & Reinish, 2002). In fact, it seems that the longer children are breastfed the greater their gains in intelligence and language abilities (Mortensen et al., 2002; Jacobson, Chiodo, & Jacobson, 1999; Jacobson & Jacobson, 2002).

Research Corner

Genomic Research

The 21st century has seen great advancements in genomic research. The technology is now available for cloning and stem cell production. To date, clones of sheep, mice, cows, goats, and other primates have already been made (Faber, Ferre, Metzger, Robl, & Kasinathan, 2004; Percy et al., 2007). Cloning has not only been used for reproduction purposes, but for generating stem cells. Embryonic stem cells are unspecialized cells that act as the "parents" of additional stem sells, such as nerve or bone cells. They are derived from the inner cell mass of very early embryos, and given the right conditions can be maintained and differentiated into distinct cell types (Roslin Institute Edinburgh, 2006).

Scientists have already been able to conduct animal stem cell studies to transplant stem cells for possible treatment of some neurological disorders, such as Parkinson's disease (Kim, 2004). This may make it possible to apply the technology in the treatment of other neurological, developmental, and intellectual disabilities. However, many complex ethical, social, and legal concerns surround cloning and stem cell research, so any discussion of stem cell research should raise these issues. Such a discussion is outside the scope of this book, however. The Recommended Resources section at the end of this chapter lists some useful web sites that provide further information on this topic. Should you have an interest, it is recommended you examine these sites to learn more about the subject.

Some studies have examined the social emotional benefits of breastfeeding in children. The skin-to-skin contact between mother and child during breastfeeding is thought to decrease stress in the infant and promote mother–child bonding (Uauy & Andraca, 1995). An infant's sucking is known to produce *prolactin* and *oxytocin* in the mother, which contribute to "mothering behaviors" (Drane & Logemann, 2000).

In an 18-year longitudinal study of 1,000 children, Fergusson and Woodward (1999) found that breastfeeding leads to increased levels of parental attachment. In adolescence, children in their study perceived their mothers to be more caring and less overprotective as compared with children who had been bottle fed. Additionally, children in their study reported that they had more positive relationships with their mothers as compared with bottle-fed children. Woodward and Fergusson's study also suggests that breastfeeding may lead to closer parent–child relationships.

It is not exactly clear how breastfeeding might help enhance a child's physical and neurological development. Petryk, Harris, and Jongbloed (2007) claim that the following reasons might explain the relationship between breastfeeding and global, enhanced brain function in children:

> Infants who succeed at breastfeeding may have a better genetically determined neurological system from the moment of conception.

> Several breast milk compounds and hormones that contribute to the physical growth and development of the child also greatly influence the development of the nervous system.

> It is not only the breast milk, but what happens during breastfeeding that is elemental in the social emotional development of the infant. In other words, the attitude and behavior of mothers during breastfeeding are just as important as the substances transferred in breast milk in determining the neurodevelopment of the child.

SUMMARY

Child development is the process of change in a child's biological, psychological, and behavioral functions from conception to death. Development is influenced by many factors, such as biological and genetic makeup, environmental factors, and learning. When development does not follow a reasonable course, a deviation may have occurred. A deviation in development may occur before birth (prenatally), during birth (perinatally), or after birth (postnatally).

Many factors might contribute to a deviation in development. Genetic disorders are one factor that can lead to specific conditions and disabilities, such as fragile-X syndrome or Down syndrome. Terotogens are another group of factors that may contribute to developmental disabilities. Terotogens are any factors that might pose a hazard to fetal development, such as smoking, drinking, drug consumption,

environmental toxins, maternal infections, or other diseases. A series of prenatal screening tests are available that enable professionals to detect certain developmental problems in the fetus.

Development of children after birth is monitored by looking at various areas of development, such as cognitive, language, social, emotional, and physical development. The first 3 years of the child's life are the most critical period for the infant's brain development. It is hypothesized that the brain develops specialized networks, such as social, cognitive, and language networks during this period. The development of the brain's specialized network depends on the early experiences of the infant, such as appropriate sensory stimulations and the quality of interactions that take place between the infant and the caregiver.

Review Questions

1. What are development and deviation in development?
2. How might genetics contribute to developmental disorders?
3. What are terotogens?
4. Describe how environmental terotogens might influence healthy fetal development.
5. How would maternal substance use affect fetal development?
6. What are some maternal health conditions that might threaten the fetal development?
7. What are some effects of maternal diabetes in the fetal development?

8. What is a neonatal screening? What are some of its benefits?
9. How might a premature infant be at risk for developmental problems?
10. What are five areas of developmental domains that are of concern in ECSE?
11. What is the relationship between brain development and a child's behaviors?
12. What is attachment, and why is it important?

Out-of-Class Activities

1. Conduct Internet research of the human genome project. What are this project's implications for treatment of developmental disabilities?
2. Conduct three interviews of pregnant women, and design an interview questionnaire to answer the following research question: How aware are pregnant women of the importance to avoid use of drugs, alcohol, over-the-counter medication, and smoking during pregnancy?
3. Ask three parents of infants how important they think it is for them to interact with their infants on

a daily basis, and why. Compare their answers and write a report.

4. Log on to the Internet and explore the web site of the Beech Center on Disability at www .beachcenter.org. Read the Beach Center newsletter (Fall 2005), Volume 5. This volume expresses the concerns of the disability community regarding the human genome project. Read the information carefully, and write an essay explaining your opinion regarding the arguments made in this newsletter.

Recommended Resources

American Diabetes Association (Diabetes and Pregnancy) http://www.diabetes.org/gestational-diabetes/pregancy.jsp

Attachment research at Stony Brook http://www.psychology.sunysb.edu/attachment/

Human Genome Collection: *Nature: International Weekly Journal of Science* http://www.nature.com/nature/supplements/collections/humangenome

Roslin Institute Edinburgh (cloning and stem cell research) http://www.roslin.ac.uk/

The Human Genome Project: U.S. Department of Energy http://www.ornl.gov/sci/techresources/Human_Genome/home.shtml

View the Online Resources available to accompany this text by visiting http://www.mhhe.com/bayat1e.

References

Ainsworth, M. D. S. (1984). Attachment. In N. S. Endler & J. McV. Hunt (Eds.), *Personality and behavioral disorders* (vol. 1, pp. 559–602). New York: Wiley.

Als, H., & Gilkerson, L. (1997). The role of relationship-based developmentally supportive newborn intensive care in strengthening the outcome of preterm infants. *Seminars in Perinatalogy, 21*(3), 178–189.

Alvarez, A. M., & Rathore, M. H. (2007). Hot topics in pediatric HIV/AIDS. *Pediatrics Annals, 36*(7), 423–432.

Andersen, M., Simonsen, U., Uldbjerg, N., Aalkjaer, C., & Stender, S. (2009). Smoking cessation early in pregnancy and birth weight, length, head circumference, and endothelial nitric oxide synthase activity in umbilical and chorionic vessels: An observational study of healthy singleton pregnancies. *Circulation, 119*(6), 857–864.

American Academy of Pediatrics: Policy Statement. (2004). Age terminology during the perinatal period. *Pediatrics, 114*(5), 1362–1364.

American Academy of Pediatrics: Work Group on Breastfeeding. (1997). Breastfeeding and the use of human milk. *Pediatrics, 100,* 1035–1039.

Arria, A. M., Derauf, C., LaGasse, L. L., Grant, P., Shah, R., Smith, L., et al. (2006). Methamphetamine and other substance use during pregnancy: Preliminary estimates from the infant development, environment, and lifestyle (IDEAL) study. *Maternal and Child Health Journal, 10*(3), 293–302.

Batshaw, M. L. (2007). Genetics and developmental disabilities. In M. L. Batshaw, L. Pellegrino, & N. J. Roizen (Eds.), *Children with disabilities* (6th ed., pp. 3–21). Baltimore: Paul H. Brookes.

Bayol, S. A., Farrington, S. J., & Stickland, N. C. (2007). A maternal "junk food" diet in pregnancy and lactation promotes an exacerbated taste for "junk food" and a propensity for obesity in rat offspring. *British Journal of Nutrition, 98,* 843–851.

Bell, M. J. (2007). Infections and the fetus. In M. L. Batshaw, L. Pellegrino, & N. J. Roizen (Eds.), *Children with disabilities* (6th ed., pp. 71–82). Baltimore: Paul H. Brookes.

Bhide, P. G. (2009). Dopamine, cocaine, and the development of cerebral cortical cytoarchitecture: A review of current concepts. *Seminars in Cell and Developmental Biology, 20*(4), 395–402.

Bobb, A. J., Castellanos, F. X., Addington, S. M., & Rapoport, J. L. (2005). Molecular genetic studies of ADHD: 1991 to 2004. *American Journal of Medical Genetics. B, Neuropsychiatric Genetics, 132,* 109–125.

Bowlby, J. (1969/1982). *Attachment and loss: Vol. 1. Attachment.* New York: Basic Books.

Bren, L. (2002, March/April). Genital herpes: A hidden epidemic. *FDA Consumer, 36*(2), 10–16.

Brown, J. E., & Satin, A. J. (2007). Having a baby: The birth process. In M. L. Batshaw, L. Pellegrino, & N. J. Roizen (Eds.), *Children with disabilities* (6th ed., pp. 35–45). Baltimore: Paul H. Brookes.

Brown, J. V., Bakeman, R., Coles, C. D., Sexon, W. R., & Demi, A. S. (1998). Maternal drug use during pregnancy: Are preterm and full-term infants affected differently? *Developmental Psychology, 34*(3), 540–554.

Brown, L. Thoyre, S., Pridham, K., & Schubert, C. (2009). The mother-infant feeding tool. *Journal of Obstetric, Gynecologic, and Neonatal Nursing, 38*(4), 491–503.

Burdo, J. R., & Connor, J. R. (2002). Iron transport in the central nervous system. In D. Templeton (Ed.), *Molecular and cellular iron transport* (pp. 487–505). New York: Dekker.

Burk, L. E. (2006). *Child development* (7th ed.). Boston: Pearson/Allyn & Bacon.

Center for Disease Control and Prevention: Department of Health and Human Services. (2008). *Birth defects: Diabetes and pregnancy, frequently asked questions.* Retrieved May 1, 2008, from http://www.cdc.gov/ncbddd/bd/diabetespregnancyfaqs.htm

Centers for Disease Control and Prevention: Department of Health and Human Services. (2008). *Cytomegalovirus (CMV).* Retrieved April 30, 2008, from http://www.cdc.gov/cmv/facts.htm

Centers for Disease Control and Prevention: Department of Health and Human Services. (2008). *Newborns and group B strep.* Retrieved April 29, 2008, from http://www.cdc.gov/groupBstrep/general/gen_public_faq.htm#section1

Chasnoff, I. J., Burns, W. J., Schnoll, S. H., & Burns, K. A. (1985). Cocaine use in pregnancy. *New England Journal of Medicine, 313,* 666–669.

Crain, W. (2004). *Theories of development: Concepts and applications* (5th ed.). Upper Saddle River: Pearson, Prentice Hall.

Cunningham, A. S. (1979). Morbidity in breastfed and artificially fed infants. II. *Journal of Pediatrics, 95,* 685–689.

Davidson, P. W., & Myers, G. J. (2007). Environmental toxins. In M. L. Batshaw, L. Pellegrino, & N. J. Roizen (Eds.), *Children with disabilities* (6th ed., pp. 61–70). Baltimore: Paul H. Brookes.

Davidson, P. W., Myers, G. J., & Weiss, B. (2004). Mercury exposure and child development outcomes. *Pediatrics, 113,* 1023–1029.

Davies, M. (2002). A few thoughts about the mind, the brain, and a child with early deprivation. *Journal of Analytical Psychology, 47,* 421–435.

Deering, S. H., & Satin, A. J. (2002). Having a baby: The birth process. In M. L. Batshaw (Ed.), *Children with disabilities* (5th ed., pp. 55–68). Baltimore: Paul H. Brookes.

Deiner, P. L. (2009). *Infants and toddlers: Development and curriculum planning* (2nd ed.). Clifton Park, NY: Delmar Engage Learning.

Drane, D. L., & Logemann, A. J. (2000). A critical evaluation of the evidence on the association between type of infant feeding and cognitive development. *Pediatric and Perinatal Epidemiology, 14,* 349–356.

Drews, C. D., Yeargin-Allsopp, M., Decoufle, P., & Murphy, C. C. (1995). Variation in the influence of selected sociodemographic risk factors for mental retardation. *American Journal of Public Health, 85,* 329–334.

Eckert, M. A., Lambardino, L. J., & Leonard, C. M. (2001). Planar asymmetry tips the phonological playground and environment raises the bar. *Child Development, 72,* 988–1002.

Emde, R. N. (1989). The infant's relationship experiences: Developmental and affective aspects. In A. J. Sameroli & R. N. Emde (Eds.), *Relationship disturbances in early childhood* (pp. 33–51). New York: Basic Books.

Eskenazi, B., Prehn, A. W., & Christianson, R. E. (1995). Passive and active maternal smoking as measured by serum cotinine: The effect on birth weight. *American Journal of Public Health, 85,* 395–398.

Faber, D. C., Ferre, L. B., & Metzger, J., Robl, P., & Kasinathan, P. (2004). Review: Agro-economic impact of cattle cloning. *Cloning Stem Cells, 6,* 198–207.

Fergusson, D. M., & Woodward, L. J. (1999). Breastfeeding and later psychosocial adjustment. *Paediatric and Perinatal Epidemiology, 13,* 144–157.

Ford, R. P. K., Taylor, B. J., Mitchell, E. A., Enright A. A., Stewart A. W., Becroft, D. M. O., et al. (1993). Breastfeeding and the risk of sudden infant death syndrome. *International Journal of Epidemiology, 22,* 885–890.

Fried, P., Watkinson, B., & Gray, R. (1992). A follow-up study of attentional behavior in 6-year-old children exposed prenatally to marijuana, cigarettes, and alcohol. *Neurotoxicology and Teratology, 14,* 299–311.

Gaitatzes, C., Chang, T., & Baumgart, S. (2007). The first weeks of life. In M. L. Batshaw, L. Pellegrino, & N. J. Roizen (Eds.), *Children with disabilities* (6th ed., pp. 47–59). Baltimore: Paul H. Brookes.

Galtier-Dereure, F., Boegner, C., & Bringer, J. (2000). Obesity and pregnancy: Complications and cost. *American Journal of Clinical Nutrition, 71,* 1242S–1248S.

Garcia-Bournissen, F., Rokach, B., Karaskov, T., & Koren, G. (2007). Methamphetamine detection in maternal and neonatal hair: Implications for fetal safety. *Archives of Disease in Childhood–Fetal and Neonatal Edition, 92,* 351–355.

Gillespie, C, Phifer, J., Bradley, B., & Ressler, K. J. (2009). Risk and resilience: Genetic and environmental influences on development of the stress response. *Depression and Anxiety, 26*(11), 984–992.

Goldberg-Hamblin, S., Singer, J., Singer, G. H., & Denney, M. K. (2007). Early intervention in neonatal nurseries: The promising practice of developmental care. *Infants & Young Children, 20*(2), 163–171.

Golding, J., Rogers, I. S., & Emmett, P. M. (1997). Association between breast feeding, child development, and behaviour. *Early Human Development, 49*(Suppl.), S174–S184.

Gonzalez-Villasenor, L. I. (1999). A duplex PCR assay for detection and genotyping of herpes simplex virus in cerebrospinal fluid. *Molecular and Cellular Probes, 13,* 309–314.

Harrison, G., Branson, R., & Vaucher, Y. (1983). Association of maternal smoking with body composition of the newborn. *American Journal of Clinical Nutrition, 38,* 757–762.

Hohman, M., Oliver, R., & Wright, W. (2004). Methamphetamine abuse and manufacture: The child welfare response. *Social Work, 49*(3), 373–381.

Hokelek, M., & Safdar, A. (2006). Toxoplasmosis. *E Medicine Specialties.* Retrieved April 28, 2008, from http://www.emedicine.com/med/topic2294.htm

Huang, L. Z., Liu, X, Griffith, W. H., & Winzer-Serhan, U. H. (2008). Chronic neonatal nicotine increases anxiety but does not impair cognition in adult rats. *Behavioral Neuroscience, 121*(6), 1342–1352.

Huang, Y., Gao, X., Zhang, X. W., Xiang, Y., Fu, Y., Meng, H. Q., et al. (2007). Examining the comorbidity of attention deficit and hyperactivity disorder and conduct disorder in a population-based twin sample. *Zhonghua Yi Xue Yi Chuan Xue Za Zhi, 25*(1), 23–26. Retrieved May 20, 2010, from http://www.ncbi.nlm.nih.gov/pubmed/18247298

Hurt, H., Betancourt, L. M., Malmud, E. K., Shera, D. M., Giannetta, J. M., Brodsky, N. L., ct al. (2009). Children with and without gestational cocaine exposure: A neurocognitive systems analysis. *Neurotoxicology and Teratology, 31*(6), 334–341.

Immordino-Yang, M. H., & Fischer, K. W. (2007). Dynamic development of hemispheric biases in three cases: Cognitive/hemispheric cycles, music, and hemispherectomy. In D. Coch, K. W. Fischer, & G. Dawson (Eds.), *Human behavior, learning, and the developing brain: Typical development* (pp. 74–111). New York: The Guilford Press.

Institute of Medicine. (1990). *Nutrition during pregnancy: Weight gain and nutrient supplements.* Report of the Subcommittee on Nutritional Status and Weight Gain During Pregnancy, Subcommittee on Nutritional Status During Pregnancy and Lactation, Food and Nutrition Board. Washington, DC: National Academy Press.

Jacobson, S. W., & Jacobson, J. L. (2002). Breastfeeding and IQ: Evaluation of the socio-environmental confounders. *Acta Paediatrica, 91,* 258–266.

Jacobson, S. W., Chiodo, L. M., & Jacobson, J. L. (1999). Breastfeeding effects on intelligence quotient in 4- and 11-year-old children. *Pediatrics, 103*(5), e71.

Johnson, M. H. (2007). The social brain in infancy: A developmental cognitive neuroscience approach. In D. Coch, K. W. Fischer, & G. Dawson (Eds.), *Human behavior, learning, and the developing brain: Typical development* (pp. 115–137). New York: The Guilford Press.

Johnston, M. (2009). Plasticity in the developing brain: Implications for rehabilitation. *Developmental Disabilities Research Reviews, 15*(2), 94–101.

Kamau-Mbuthia, E., Elmadfa, I., & Mwonya, R. (2008). The impact of maternal HIV status on infant feeding patterns in Nakuru, Kenya. *Journal of Human Lactation, 24*(1), 34–41.

Kerzel Andersen, H., Brostrom, K., Brogard Hansen, K., Leerhoy, J., Pedersen, J., Osterballe, O., et al. (2008). A prospective study on the incidence and significance of congenital cytomegalovirus infection. *Acta Pediatrica, 68*(4), 329–336.

Kim, S. U. (2004). Human neural stem cells genetically modified for brain repair in neurological disorders. *Neuropathology, 24,* 159–171.

Lanting, C. I., Patandin, S., Weisglas-Kuperus, N., Touwen, B. C., & Bersma, E. R. (1998). Breastfeeding and neurological outcome at 42 months. *Acta Paediatrica, 87,* 1224–1229.

Lawrence, J. M., Contreras, R., Chen, W., & Sacks, D. A. (2008). Trends in the prevalence of preexisting diabetes and gestational diabetes mellitus among a racially/ethnically diverse population of pregnant women. *Diabetes Care, 31,* 899–904.

Lenroot, R. K., & Giedd, J. N. (2007). The structural development of the human brain as measured longitudinally with Magnetic Resonance Imaging. In D. Coch, K. W. Fischer, & G. Dawson (Eds.), *Human behavior, learning and the developing brain: Typical Development* (pp. 50–73). New York: The Guilford Press.

Ljujic-Glisic, M., Bozinovic-Prekajski, N., & Glibetic, M. (2009). Biochemical and antropometric monitoring of growth in preterm infants. *Acta Chirurgica Lugoslavica, 56*(2), 93–96.

Milley, J. R., Papacostas, J. S., & Tabata, B. K. (1986). Effects of insulin on uptake of metabolic substrates by the fetus. *American Journal of Physiology Endocrinology and Metabolism, 251,* E349–E359.

Milunsky, A. (1977). *Know your genes.* Boston: Houghton Mifflin Company.

Mortensen, E. L., Michaelsen, K. F., Sanders, S. A., & Reinisch, J. M. (2002). The association between duration of breastfeeding and adult intelligence. *Journal of the American Medical Association, 287,* 2365–2371.

Murphy, C. C., Yeargin-Allsopp, M., Decoufle, P., & Drews, C. D. (1995). The administrative prevalence of mental retardation in 10-year-old children in metropolitan Atlanta, 1985–1987. *American Journal of Public Health, 85,* 319–323.

Naeye, R., & Peters, E. (1984). Mental development of children whose mothers smoked during pregnancy. *Obstetrics and Gynecology, 64,* 601–607.

National Institute on Drug Abuse: The Science of Drug Abuse and Addiction. (1995). *NIDA notes: Survey provides first national data on drug use during pregnancy.* Retrieved April 26, 2008, from http://www.drugabuse.gov/NIDA_Notes/NNVol10N1/NIDASurvey.html

National Survey on Drug Use and Health. (2005). *The NSDUH report: Substance use during pregnancy: 2002–2003 update.* Retrieved April 25, 2008, from http://www.oas.samhsa.gov/2k5/pregnancy/pregnancy.html

Nelson, C. A. (2007). A developmental cognitive neuroscience approach to the study of atypical development: A model system involving infants of diabetic mothers. In D. Coch, G. Dawson, & K. W. Fischer (Eds.), *Human behavior, learning, and the developing brain: Atypical development* (pp. 1–25). New York: The Guilford Press.

O'Shea, T., Allred, E., Dammann, O., Hirtz, D., Kuban, K. C. K., Paneth, N., et al. (2009). The ELGAN study of the brain and related disorders in extremely low gestational age newborns. *Early Human Development, 85*(11), 719–725.

Pellegrino, J. E. (2007b). Newborn screening: Opportunities for prevention of developmental disabilities. In M. L. Batshaw, L. Pellegrino, & N. J. Roizen (Eds.), *Children with disabilities* (6th ed., pp. 97–106). Baltimore: Paul H. Brookes.

Pellegrino, L. (2007a). Patterns in development and disability. In M. L. Batshaw, L. Pellegrino, & N. J. Roizen (Eds.), *Children with disabilities* (6th ed., pp. 217–228). Baltimore: Paul H. Brookes.

Percy, M. (2007). Factors that cause or contribute to intellectual and developmental disabilities. In I. Brown & M. Percy (Eds.), *A comprehensive guide to intellectual and developmental disabilities* (pp. 125–148). Baltimore: Paul H. Brookes.

Percy, M., Lewkis, S. Z., & Brown, I. (2007). Introduction to genetics and development. In I. Brown & M. Percy (Eds.), *A comprehensive guide to intellectual and developmental disabilities* (pp. 87–108). Baltimore: Paul H. Brookes.

Persson, P., Grennert, L., Gennser, G., & Kullander, S. (1978). A study of smoking and pregnancy with special reference to fetal growth. *Acta Obstetrica et Gynecologica Scandinavica, 78,* 33–39.

Petryk, A., Harris, S. R., & Jongbloed, L. (2007). Breastfeeding and neurodevelopment: A literature review. *Infants and Young Children, 20*(2), 120–134.

Rais-Bahrami, K., & Short, B. L. (2007). Premature and small-for-dates infants. In M. L. Batshaw, L. Pellegrino, & N. J. Roizen (Eds.), *Children with disabilities* (6th ed., pp. 107–122). Baltimore: Paul H. Brookes.

Reyna, B., & Pickler, R. (2009). Mother-infant synchrony. *Journal of Obstetric, Gynecologic, and Neonatal Nursing, 38*(4), 470–477.

Ricciotti, H. A. (2008). State of the art reviews: Nutrition and lifestyle for a healthy pregnancy. *American Journal of Lifestyle Medicine, 2*(2), 151–158.

Richardson, G. A. (1994). Comparative teratogenicity of alcohol and other drugs. *Alcohol Health & Research World, 18*(1), 42–48.

Riley, E. H., Fuentes-Afflick, E., Jackson, R. A., Escobar, G. J., Brawarsky, P., Schreiber, M., et al. (2005). Correlates of prescription drug use during pregnancy. *Journal of Women's Health, 14*(5), 401–409.

Rogers, I. S., Emmett, P. M., & Golding, J. (1997). The growth and nutritional status of the breastfed infant. *Early Human Development, 49*(Suppl.), S157–S174.

Rosenzweig, M. R. (2002). Animal research on effects of experience on brain and behavior: Implications for rehabilitation. *Infants and Young Children, 15*(2), 1–10.

Roslin Institute Edinburgh: Annual report. (2006). Edinburgh: Author. Retrieved May 2, 2008, from http://www.ri.bbsrc.ac.uk/publications/ AnnRep06.pdf

Santrock, J. W. (2006). *Lifespan development* (10th ed.). Boston: McGraw Hill.

Schneider, M. L., Moore, C. F., Gajewski, L. L., Larson, J. A., Roberts, A. D., Converse, A. K., et al. (2008). Sensory processing disorder in a primate model: Evidence from a longitudinal study of prenatal alcohol and prenatal stress effect. *Child Development, 79*(1), 100–113.

Schonberg, R. L., & Tifft, C. J. (2007). Birth defects and prenatal diagnosis. In M. L. Batshaw, L. Pellegrino, & N. J. Roizen (Eds.), *Children with disabilities* (6th ed., pp. 83–96). Baltimore: Paul H. Brookes.

Schuler, M. E., Nair, P., & Kettinger, L. (2003). Drug-exposed infants and developmental outcome. *Archives of Pediatrics and Adolescent Medicine, 157,* 133–138.

Sheffer, I. E., & Bercovic, S. F. (1997). Generalized epilepsy with febrile seizures plus: A genetic disorder with heterogeneous clinical phenotype. *Brain, 120,* 479–490.

Stern, D. N. (2000). *The interpersonal world of the infant: A view from psychoanalysis and developmental psychoanalysis.* New York: Basic Books.

Stonestreet, B. S., Goldstein, M., Oh, W., & Widnes, J. A. (1989). Effect of prolonged hyperinsulinemia on erythropoiesis in fetal sheep. *American Journal of Physiology, 257,* R1199–R1204.

Swanson, J., Entringer, S., Buss, C., & Wadhwa, P. (2009). Developmental origins of health and disease: Environmental exposures. *Seminars in Reproductive Medicine, 27*(5), 391–402.

Sweeten, T. L., Posey, D. J. & McDougle, C. J. (2004). Brief report: Autistic disorder in three children with cytomegalovirus infection. *Journal of Autism and Developmental Disorders, 34*(5), 583–586.

Szatmari, P., Saigal, S., Rosenbaum, P., & Campbell, D. (1993). Psychopathology and adaptive functioning among extremely low birth weight children. *Journal of Child Psychology and Psychiatry, 38,* 315–326.

Thompson, B., Levitt, P., & Stanwood, G. (2009). Prenatal exposure to drugs: Effects on brain development and implications for policy and education. *Nature Reviews. Neuroscience, 10*(4), 303–312.

Uauy, R., & Andraca, I. (1995). Human milk and breastfeeding for optimal mental development. *Journal of Nutrition, 125,* S2278–S2280.

UNICEF. (2000). *UNICEF statistics: Malnutrition.* Retrieved April 28, 2008, from http://childinfo.org/ areas/malnutrition/

United Nations Program on HIV/AIDS. (2006). *Reports on the global AIDS epidemic: A UNAIDS 10th anniversary special edition.* Joint United Nations Programme on HIV/AIDS: Author. Retrieved

April 30, 2008, from http://www.unaids.org/en/ KnowledgeCentre/HIVData/GlobalReport/ Default.asp

U.S. Food and Drug Administration: Center for Drug Evaluation and Research. (2005). *Thalidomide: Important patient information.* Retrieved April, 24, 2008, from http://www.fda.gov/cder/news/ thalidomide.htm

Weinfield, N., Sroufe, L. A., Egeland, B., & Carlson, E. A. (1999). The nature of individual differences in infant-caregiver attachment. In J. Cassidy, & P. R. Shaver (Eds.), *Handbook of attachment: Theory, research, and clinical applications* (pp. 68–88). New York: The Guilford Press.

Weitzman, M., Kananaugh, M., & Florin, T. A. (2006). Parental smoking and children's behavioral and cognitive functioning. In P. W. Davidson,

G. J. Myers, & B. Weiss (Eds.), *International review of mental retardation research: (Vol. 30). Neurotoxicology and developmental disabilities* (pp. 237–261). New York, NY: Elsevier.

Winslow, B. T., Voorhees, K. I., & Pehl, K. A. (2007). Methamphetamine abuse. *American Family Physician, 76*(8), 1169–1174.

Xanthou, M. (1998). Immune protection of human milk. *Biology of the neonate, 74,* 121–133.

Zhu, H., Kartiko, S., & Finnell, R. (2009). Importance of gene-environment interactions in the etiology of selected birth defects. *Clinical Genetics, 75*(7), 409–423.

Zhu, J. H., & Stadlin, A. (2000). Prenatal heroin exposure: Effects on development, acoustic startle response, and locomotion in weanling rats. *Neurotoxicology and Teratology, 22,* 193–203.

Chapter 3

Families Are the Most Important of All

Objectives

Upon completion of this chapter, you should be able to:

> Define *family*.
> Discuss Bronfenbrenner's system theory.
> Understand family system factors and their relationships with the disability in the family.

> List and describe the different dimensions of family functioning.
> Understand the influence of culture on parenting and perceptions of disability.
> Discuss how poverty impacts the family of a child with a disability.
> Understand negative and positive influences of having a child with a disability in the family.
> Understand family adjustment and coping models.
> Understand the evolution of various models of working with families.
> Understand the current model of collective empowerment and partnership with families and its principles.
> Understand the concept of family quality of life and its dimensions.

Key Terms

cohesion (83)	family (76)	socioeconomic
collective	family functioning (83)	status (SES) (87)
empowerment (96)	family resilience (91)	subsystem (80)
cultural codes (84)	family structure (80)	systems theory (77)
cultural competence (87)	flexibility (83)	values (84)
cultural reciprocity (87)	partnership with	
culture (84)	families (97)	

Reflection Questions

Before reading this chapter, answer the following questions to reflect upon your personal opinions and beliefs that are pertinent to early childhood special education.

1. How do you think families of children with disabilities should be involved in their children's education?
2. How do you think your cultural beliefs about parenting, education, and disability have influenced your answers to the preceding question?
3. How do you think teachers can establish a positive relationship with families?

Portrait of a Family

Maria, Cindy, and Christopher are a family. Christopher is Maria's 8-year-old son who has special needs. Soon after Maria gave birth to Christopher, the doctors informed Maria that Christopher had Down syndrome. The months following Christopher's birth constituted a difficult period for Maria and her family. Christopher began receiving different early intervention services such as speech and developmental therapy after he and Maria came home. The family had to make many changes to meet the medical and therapeutic needs of Christopher. These changes put a lot of strain on relationships in the family. Maria's husband blamed Maria for Christopher's condition, and Maria contested that her husband did not provide the needed emotional support for the family at this time of crisis. Despite efforts made on each side of the family, Maria and her husband divorced before Christopher had reached age 1.

Being a single mother and raising a child with a disability has not been easy for Maria. She has had to work two jobs for the past 7 years in order to provide for her family. Finding child care has been one of the most challenging aspects of parenting a child with a disability for Maria. When Christopher was 1 year old, Maria, who had been struggling with meeting the costs of living and caring for Christopher, had to go back to work. Although Maria had some college education, it was difficult for her to find a job that would pay enough to cover the high costs of child care as well as living expenses. Fortunately, she found a job in an early childhood education and care center as a teacher's assistant. For a reduced tuition, Maria was allowed to take Christopher to the classroom in which she worked. This provided the best child care option for Maria, where she could supervise and care for Christopher herself.

Christopher received early intervention in the center several times a week. In the evenings, Maria worked in a restaurant, while her aunt cared for Christopher. When Christopher turned 3, he was enrolled in a neighborhood public school that had an early childhood special education program. Maria could no longer complete her full-time work shifts in the child care center because she had to be home when the school bus dropped off Christopher. Therefore, she found a part-time job as an office administrative assistant for a community service agency during school hours, and she continued to work in the restaurant every night.

A couple of years ago, her friend and previous coworker, Cindy, suggested they share the rent of a bigger apartment in a better neighborhood together. Cindy had been an early childhood teacher in the classroom where Maria worked several years before. She was fond of Christopher and had learned to work with him from observing and consulting with the developmental and speech therapists who had regularly come to the center to work with him. For the past 2 years, Maria, Cindy, and Christopher have been living together in a nice apartment in the city. Christopher is enrolled in an after-school therapeutic recreation program for children with special needs funded by the city's park district. The school bus takes Christopher to the park program after school, and Cindy picks up Christopher every day on her way home and cares for him while Maria is at work. Cindy is paid by a local respite provider agency for caring for Christopher during the time that Maria works. Because of this new living arrangement, Maria has been able to take courses at a local community college, and complete a certificate program in accounting. She was recently hired by her community college as an accounting clerk, and while she still needs to work some evenings at the restaurant, she is now able to be at home with Christopher more nights and for longer hours.

INTRODUCTION

Today, an increasing number of people like Maria, Cindy, and Christopher consider and define themselves as a **family** unit. Forms and types of family have been rapidly changing during the past several decades. Today, we no longer define a family as a unit comprised of parents and children. In fact, with the diverse forms and configurations of families, it is becoming more difficult to explain just what we mean when we use the term family.

Working with young children usually includes working with families as well. However, working with children with special needs almost always requires working with the family members, especially with parents and the primary caregivers. In fact, forming collaboration and partnership with families of children with special needs is a cornerstone of any successful early childhood and early intervention program.

In this chapter, we will examine what family is and how it may influence child development. We will examine the issues a family might face when a child with a disability is born into a family. We will introduce the new concept of positive contributions of disability to the family and will focus on establishing a partnership between families and professionals that would not only promote the child's developmental and educational outcomes, but enhance the quality of life of families of children with disabilities.

WHAT IS A FAMILY?

It is common to refer to our own understanding of what a family is and what a "normal family" should look like as a point of reference. Our understanding of family is often based on our own family background and experiences. Frequently, we may consider anything that deviates from our definition of family as dysfunctional or abnormal. It is important therefore to ask ourselves "What is a family?"

The term family has over one hundred definitions. We use two definitions in this book: (1) "a family is considered to be any unit that defines itself as a family including individuals who are related by blood or marriage as well as those who have made a commitment to share their lives" (Hanson, Lynch, & Wayman, 1992, p. 285). The other

Today we no longer define a family unit as a unit comprised of parents and children. This family consists of mother, child, and grandmother.

When working with families, it is crucial to look at every family within its own form, characteristics, and culture.

definition we use describes family as: (2) "those people who; (a) consider themselves as a family (whether or not they are related by blood or marriage), and (b) support and care for each other on a regular basis" (Park, Turnbull, & Turnbull, 2002, p. 153).

These definitions are inclusive of different types of families such as nuclear and extended families, single parent, biracial families, minority families, dual working parents, divorced or two-family households, as well as gay and lesbian, and non-married or kinship families. As we work and interact with families, it is crucial we look at every family within its own form, characteristics, and culture. It is also important to look at the family within its own system, as well as consider the family's interactions with other systems.

Critical Thinking Question 3.1   Refer back to the story presented at the beginning of the chapter. As early childhood educators working with families, should we or should we not accept Maria, Cindy, and Christopher as a family unit? Why or why not?

THE SYSTEMS THEORY: A FRAMEWORK FOR UNDERSTANDING FAMILIES OF CHILDREN WITH DISABILITIES

Our educational ideas about working with children with special needs have often been influenced by the medical model, in which disability is viewed as a negative condition or illness that needs treatment (Seligman & Darling, 2007). This model calls for the treatment of the child in isolation from other factors. It was not until the 1970s when Urie Bronfenbrenner brought forth the idea of human ecology that we began to look at working with children in the ecology of the family and environment. Why have we found it important to work with a child and the family together? Bronfenbrenner's **systems theory** is based on the premise that a child develops within the context of family, society, culture, and time. And if we are to examine the development of the child, we need to consider all different systems in which the child grows and develops. He claimed that programs which put an emphasis on working with parents and child together are more likely to be successful and have a positive impact on the child's development (Bronfenbrenner, 1979).

A child's development is influenced by many elements. The most important element in shaping a child's health and development is the family. Children constantly interact with and learn from their environment, as well as from adults and other children they grow up with. In turn, a family is also influenced by the development and growth of a child. For example, a child who is developing typically influences a family differently from a child who has special needs. According to the systems theory, a family itself is a system in which its members interact with one another and with other systems, and influence each other (Bronfenbrenner, 1979). These other systems include community, school, workplace, ethnic culture, societal values, and rules that govern the society. We might say that children and families are part of an ecosystem (Patterson, 1999). See Table 3.1 for Bronfenbrenner's ecological or systems theory of development.

The systems theory provides a useful framework in understanding families of children with disabilities. When a child with a disability is born or diagnosed in a

TABLE 3.1   Bronfenbrenner's Systems Theory of Development

Microsystem	Children, parents, siblings, and other immediate family members interact with each other and develop in the center of the family's ecosystem within what is called a microsystem.
Exosystem	The surrounding community, consisting of neighbors, school, church, friends, workplace, and peers are part of the proximally close system called the exosystem. The family system has a close relationship with the exosystem. What happens in the exosystem directly affects the family. For example, how many hours children are in school, or what kind of community and workplace support is available to parents for child care may influence a parent's decisions about career and work, which in turn may affect their socioeconomic status as well as the amount of time they might spend with their children.
Mesosystem	Interactions between the family system and the exosystem are called the mesosystem. The family system is not only affected by what happens in the proximally close systems, but by what happens in the removed systems.
Macrosystem	Laws, socioeconomic status of a family, cultural beliefs and values, attitudes of society, crime and violence, and social stigma are examples of the proximally removed system which Bronfenbrenner called the macrosystem. This proximally removed system also impacts the family system. For example, when the society stigmatizes having a child with a disability, parents of that child may become isolated and decide not to participate in typical activities that other families take part in. Another example would be the influence of the culture on a family's attitude—the way we behave, dress, eat, raise our children, and interact with one another is influenced by the culture in which we have grown up. This is an example of the influence of the macrosystem on the microsystem.
Chronosystem	A final system, chronosystem, refers to the patterns of events over time that are influenced by sociohistoric conditions. For example, the influence of Hurricane Katrina on children who were affected by it would be determined over a certain period of time as these children grow up.

Source: Bronfenbrenner, U. (1979). *The ecology of human development: Experiments by nature and design.* Cambridge, MA: Harvard University Press.

family, the family system is inevitably affected. The family begins to interact with different people in settings within the mesosystem and exosystem, which it otherwise would not have had much contact with had it not been for the needs of its member (child) with special needs (Seligman & Darling, 1997, 2007). For example, the family of a child with special needs may need to form relationships and interact with medical and health care workers, early intervention or special education personnel, private therapists, and other parents of children with disabilities. These would form elements of the family's new exosystem.

What happens within each of these settings and in connection with the family and the child will influence not only the welfare of the child with special needs but the dynamics of the family. In addition, how friends, neighbors, and extended family members react to the disability—for instance, provide support or distance themselves from the family—also has a direct influence on the way a family copes with the disability and manages its daily functions. In the same way, the available services in the community, the quality of the early intervention services, the special education system, and so on, impact the way a family deals and copes with the disability of its member. Finally, ethnic and cultural views of disability, including the way media portrays disability, as well as existing policies on disability, are important factors that influence the family and the child with a disability (Figure 3.1).

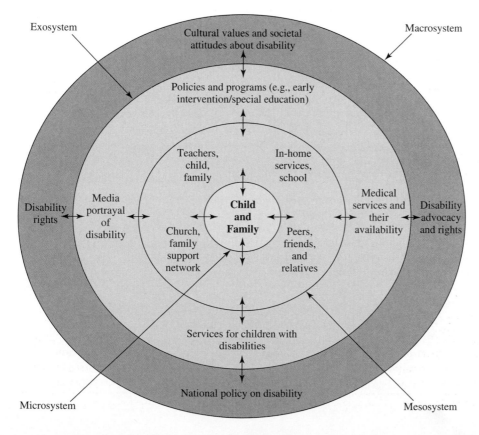

FIGURE 3.1
Application of Bronfenbrenner's Systems Theory to Families of Children with Disabilities

As we can see in Figure 3.1, when a child with special needs is considered as an element of an ecosystem, in order to influence the child's development, it becomes almost necessary to not only work with the child but work with other elements of the most influential systems within this ecosystem. As far as development of the child is concerned, family is the most influential system.

A mobile analogy has frequently been used in the early intervention field (Satir, 1972). In this analogy, if we liken every member of the family to a piece of a toy mobile, the pieces are grouped together, and the mobile is balanced when all pieces carry a similar weight. Accordingly, if the focus of intervention is only on the child with special needs and not on the family as a unit, it is as if a weight is put on one piece of the mobile, whereby the balance is tilted toward one side. Thus, we cannot work with one piece of the mobile without thinking about other pieces, and, in order for us to help keep the balance, we need to put an equal weight on all pieces of the mobile. Working with a child involves working with the family as well. In fact, the child and family intervention models, in which the intervention takes place at the family's level, are more likely to be effective as compared with the traditional medical intervention models, in which the intervention takes place only at the child's level.

FAMILY SYSTEM FACTORS AND DISABILITY

As we work with families, we should be aware of certain factors within each family system. The interaction of these factors in the system determines how a family may adjust to and cope with the demands of having a child with a disability. In addition, intervention is only effective when all factors within a family system are considered. For example, a family's structure and subsystems are two important elements that should be considered when working with families.

Family Structure

Consider the definitions of the family that were provided earlier. In both definitions, a family itself defines who is in the family and who is not. Therefore, the size of a family depends on the number of members whom the family itself considers as belonging to that unit. Who is in a family is also defined as **family structure** (Patterson, 1999). In the opening story, Maria's family structure consisted of three members: two unmarried same-sex members and one child. Other family structures may be smaller or larger consisting of heterosexual, homosexual, married, unmarried with or without children, or unrelated members (Walsh, 2003).

The family system carries out its function through **subsystems,** which are part of the structure of each family. Each individual in the family belongs to a different subsystem, and each individual in each subsystem has a certain power and a specific role (Minuchin, 1974; Turnbull, Turnbull, Erwin, & Soodak, 2006; Seligman & Darling, 1997, 2007). Turnbull and her colleagues (2006) describe four subsystems in the family: marital subsystem, parental subsystem, sibling subsystem, and extended family subsystem.

Marital Subsystem

Couples develop complementary roles in which they can carry out a family's functions and support other members. Often, the birth of a child with special needs adds stress to the marriage, in that the couple might have two different views about the meaning of the disability, and what it means for them to have a child with a disability (Patterson, 1993). They might need to examine and redefine their role as it relates to the care of the child with a disability and the child's relationship to other members in the family. New attitudes and roles that have to be taken on by each spouse or parent may affect their relationship.

In some cases, each parent may not view the disability of their child in the same light. They might blame one another, or have conflicting views regarding how to provide care for the child. For example, one parent might think that a child who has a disability must be cared for by expert outsiders, while another parent may believe that parents are responsible for the care of the child no matter what the circumstances. In this case, discord may occur (McCubbin, Thompson, Thompson, & McCubbin, 1993; Patterson, 1999), as was the case with Maria and her husband in the opening story. On the other hand, the disability of the child might bring spouses closer to each other in an effort to mobilize their efforts to help the child (Bayat, 2007; Patterson, 1999).

Parental Subsystem

A child's birth demands new roles for the spouses, as well as guidance, nurturance, support, and authority from parents, so that the child may develop in a healthy environment. The parenting process varies at different times depending on the child's age

Often, the birth of a child with special needs brings new stressors to the family. Spouses might have two different views about the meaning of the disability and what it means for them to have a child with a disability.

and needs (Cowan & Cowan, 2003). For example, when children are very young, nurturing is required. Firmer control and authority are also needed when young. As children grow older, however, giving them autonomy and independence becomes an important issue.

Raising a child with a disability may demand constant care or a more hands-on involvement. Parents may have many roles and functions to perform, including being in charge of the education and therapy of the child. It is important that these new roles are balanced for parents, and one role is not overemphasized (Seligman & Darling, 1997). For example, raising a child with autism has frequently resulted in parents playing a therapist's role, or providing educational support at home (Gray, 2002). It is important for parents to be careful that emphasis on one role does not negatively affect the parent and other family members (Marcus, Kunce, & Schopler, 1997).

Sibling Subsystem

The sibling subsystem is the first place where children can experiment with a peer relationship (Seligman & Darling, 1997). In this subsystem, children learn to share, cooperate, and negotiate. Children apply what they have learned in their sibling relationships to the outside world when they begin interacting with peers. When a brother or sister of a child has special needs, siblings and their relationship with one another and with other family members are affected (Seligman & Darling, 1997).

In some families brothers and sisters of children with disabilities have household responsibilities, and they frequently take care of their sibling with a disability (Strohm, 2005; Wilson, Blacher, & Baker, 1989). Siblings of children with disabilities might feel left out, burdened, alone, angry, or envious of their brother or sister with special needs. They might feel guilty for having negative feelings toward their sibling with a disability, or might develop anxiety as a result of unresolved conflicting feelings (Strohm, 2005).

On the other hand, there is some strong empirical evidence indicating that siblings of children with disability have warm and supporting relationships with their brother and sister with special needs (Kaminsky & Dewey, 2001; Fisman, et al., 1996). Many such siblings have articulated positive lessons they have learned from having a brother and sister with a disability (Bayat, 2007; Summers, Behr, & Turnbull, 1988). It is important to be aware of the needs of siblings of children with a disability, and provide support for them so they may articulate their feelings. Participating in sibling support groups is one way of addressing the needs of brothers and sisters of children with special needs. Sibling support groups are often available through early intervention programs. They provide emotional support for siblings and give them an outlet to discuss their issues. Brothers and sisters of children with disabilities can be valuable collaborators in the inclusion of children with disabilities in typical activities (Turnbull et al., 2006).

Extended Family Subsystem

Depending on the family's ethnic background, many families live in an extended family structure. In these families, the extended family members—such as grandparents or aunts and uncles—form a subsystem. The roles of the members of the extended family members might be defined differently in every family. For example, in some families, grandparents might have caregiving roles for the young children. In families of children with disabilities, the extended family members could provide support for the family and the child with special needs on a daily basis (Turnbull et al., 2006). However, it should be kept in mind that the extended family members also need to be supported themselves. Providing information—and when needed, special skills training—regarding disability would enable these members to participate and help other family members (Seligman & Darling, 2007; Turnbull, 2006).

FAMILY FUNCTIONING

No matter who is in a family and what roles the members have, every family performs four functions: (1) forms membership, (2) provides for the basic physical and emotional needs of its members, (3) nurtures, educates, and socializes its adults and children, and (4) protects its vulnerable member (Patterson, 1999). The way in which the members of a family interact with each other to fulfill these functions is called **family functioning.**

Family functioning has different dimensions: cohesion and flexibility (Patterson, 1999). **Cohesion** refers to the closeness between family members. There may be different degrees of cohesion between family members at different times (Walsh, 2003). For example, when children in a family are young, adults have tighter supervision of the children, and are closer to them. Cohesion has also been characterized by using the concepts of *enmeshment* and *disengagement* (Beavers & Hampson, 2003). Families who are enmeshed are families who have weak boundaries between subsystems and are considered as overprotective. In this situation, the behavior of one member immediately affects other members in the family. On the opposite end, the families who are considered disengaged are those who have inappropriately rigid boundaries between subsystems. In this case, individuals hardly get involved with one another (Beavers & Hampson, 2003; Minuchin, 1974).

Overly protective families might have difficulties in letting go of their children. In the case of having a child with a disability, such families might have a hard time promoting independence of the child with a disability. Conversely, in a disengaged family, a child with a disability might have independence, but might not feel fully supported by his or her family (Seligman & Darling 2007, 1997). In some families, having a child with a disability brings family members closer together. In such a situation, family members may close ranks in order to provide emotional support for one another (Bayat, 2007; Patterson & Garwick, 1994).

Flexibility refers to the degree by which family members are willing to accept change in a family when it becomes necessary (Patterson, 2002, 1999). During the life cycle of every family, transitional changes are inevitable, such as changes necessary when a child is born, or when a child grows older and moves out of the family's home. When a child is born in a family, the family undergoes an important transition. This transition includes new parenting roles for the adult members of the family.

Here the adult members need to decide how parenting and breadwinning responsibilities might be divided. This necessitates some role changes as well as changes in work and home arrangements, and in behaviors of the family members (Cowan & Cowan, 2003). The degree to which a family is willing to change its members' roles defines how flexible each family is.

When a child with a disability is born into a family, or when a child is diagnosed with a disability, family flexibility plays an important role in the overall family functioning. When families are flexible, members are able to take on new or additional responsibilities so they can respond to the new demands of the disability in the family (Patterson, 2002, 1999). On the other hand, too much flexibility might create chaos in the family. This means that a family that changes too quickly and too often is not stable enough to sustain a lasting influence on any situation (Patterson, 2002). Caring for a child with a disability requires a healthy amount of flexibility in the family so that members can change their habits and behaviors in order to meet the special needs of the child (Patterson, 1999).

CULTURE, PARENTING, AND DISABILITY

The term **culture** refers to values and beliefs that set the standards for how people behave within their family, community, and larger society (Turnbull et al., 2006). Culture has frequently been referred to as national origin as well as race (Gollnick & Chinn, 2002). Different elements influence the way an individual identifies with a specific culture. For example, one's religion, language, gender, race, age, income, or one's geographic location interact together to shape the cultural beliefs of a person (Turnbull et al., 2006). Family is the first teacher of cultural behavior and values. **Values** are the standards of what we consider as proper and improper (Stonik & Jezewski, 2005). Some values held by middle-class Caucasians in the United States form what we might call the dominant "American culture." While the dominant U.S. culture values specific concepts, other groups and individuals within the United States may not value the same things (Stonik & Jezewski, 2005).

Every culture consists of different components, such as behavioral codes, which dictate how an individual should behave. **Cultural codes** are the way in which a group conducts its food practices, child-rearing practices, and spiritual practices (Stone, 2005). Cultural codes articulate one's parenting style and the way the parent interacts, educates, or disciplines his or her children.

Although there is usually a dominant culture within a society, people living in a common geographic area do not necessarily share the same set of cultural beliefs in child rearing. In the United States, diverse sets of cultural beliefs abound in child development. Different groups of people might have different parenting styles. For example, African American parents emphasize shared parenting (Giles-Sims & Lockhart, 2005; Hurd, Moore, & Rogers, 1995), whereas white middle-class families in the United States have an individualistic or *laissez-faire* (Baumrind, 1971) parenting style, in that discipline is used infrequently and parents are generally permissive (Giles-Sims & Lockhart, 2005). Culture not only has a strong influence on how parents raise their children, but on how they might view the phenomenon of disability within their family.

Views on Disabilities in Other Cultures

A diverse country, the United States has attracted people from different cultures around the world. Since the 1980s, one million people annually have migrated to the United States (Stone, 2005). For immigrant families, having a child with a disability might add to the many challenges they already face, such as learning a new language, finding employment, and learning to live in a new society. These families have to learn how to secure services, navigate the system, and communicate with the service providers. Misunderstandings and miscommunications between the service providers and families of children with a disability who have a different cultural background is common. Many of these misunderstandings stem from differences in cultural perspectives regarding disability. How a family's culture defines disability and the causes of disability influences the way that family views the intervention program as well as the service providers.

Historically, American society has looked at the disability of a child in the family as a tragic end to the family. Not long before reauthorization of the Americans with Disabilities Act mandated that "person first language" should be used in addressing children and individuals with disabilities, we used to refer to children with disabilities as "handicapped children." This phrase indicated that children who are *handicapped* are unable to accomplish something which their typically developing peers are able to accomplish.

Today we believe that, although in some circumstances a child with a disability might not be able to accomplish certain tasks, with appropriate education and support he or she will be able to successfully accomplish most tasks that a typically developing child is able to accomplish. Views of disability have been shifting in the United States, and today there is generally a more positive perspective toward the phenomenon of disability as compared to the past, even though there is still a large variation in how different groups define and view disability in the United States. In general, the modern dominant American culture assumes that most disabilities have a biological basis, caused by assaults to the neurobiological system (Stone, 2005). As a result, we generally believe that interventions to support children with disabilities should be based on advances in medical, technological, and educational sciences.

Various societies in the world might look at disability differently in comparison to the United States (Brown & Radfore, 2007; Brown, 2007). In some ancient cultures, like Sparta, deformed infants were thrown over a precipice, while in other cultures children with disabilities were believed to have supernatural powers (Seligman & Darling, 2007). In certain African cultures, having a child with a disability is considered to be a taboo (Seligman & Darling, 1997).

Many languages in the world do not have a single equivalent word for, or a clear-cut definition of, disability or intervention for the disability (Brown, 2007). In other languages, there might be terms describing physical deformities, yet there might not be any specific terms to describe other disability types such as intellectual and cognitive disabilities (Brown & Radfore, 2007). For example, in Chinese culture, disability is viewed as the result of the person's sin in a past life or the sins of the person's parents (Liu, 2005). Shame and guilt are two common feelings that might be experienced by families of children with disabilities in the Chinese society. Chinese families, especially the head of the family, might feel shamed, and be stigmatized. As the child grows up, he or she may feel guilty for bringing shame on the family. The family might in turn feel guilty about having negative feelings about the disability and the child (Liu, 2005).

In the Mexican culture, the disability of a child is considered to be an act of God, or punishment for something one has done. Mexican mothers might feel they are to be blamed if their children are diagnosed with cognitive disabilities (Skinner, Rodriguez, & Bailey, 1999; Santana-Martin & Santana, 2005). In some Latino cultures, a strong sense of family pride makes acceptance of a child with a severe disability very hard, and a mild disability may not be recognized by the family at all (Harry, 1992).

In many cultures, physical disabilities are less stigmatizing, more accepted by the society, and are viewed in a less negative light in comparison with intellectual developmental disabilities and/or psychological disorders. In Iran, the word *ma'lul,* meaning handicapped, is used to refer to a child or adult who has a physical disability. The term *aqab-oftadeh,* meaning mentally retarded is commonly used for children with intellectual disabilities both in public and by the medical community. In the Iranian culture, while having a child with a physical disability might be tolerated and pitied, having a child with an intellectual disability is commonly considered shameful, and children with such disabilities are frequently hidden from view, or placed in institutions.

On the other hand, some cultures show a positive attitude toward intellectual disabilities, such as in the Turk Islands and Denmark (Seligmen & Darling, 1997). Native Americans have a more positive view of disability in general. To them, children are considered precious and should be accepted for themselves; therefore, a child with a disability is given all possible support to reach his or her maximum potentials (Attneave, 1982). Among some Native American tribes, some of the gods actually have disabilities. In these cultures, it is the strengths of the individuals and not the disability that is considered important (Locust, 1988).

Cultural Reciprocity

Working with families of diverse cultural backgrounds requires a respect and understanding of the family's cultural views of disability. It is also reasonable to be aware of the subcultural variations that may exist in some families with whom we work. Response to disability varies in different families regardless of how the ethnic group to which the family belongs views disabilities. The personality and characteristics of the child with the disability, the family's own unique cultural style, their spirituality or religious beliefs, the socioeconomic status of the family, and different subcultural learning all play important roles in how a child with a disability is viewed by a family. A professional's ability to understand and respect cultural variations, and be able to work with families of diverse cultural background in a nonjudgmental way, has

Steps to Establish Cultural Reciprocity between Professionals and Families of Children with Disabilities	Text Box 3.1

Step 1: The professional identifies the cultural values embedded in his or her interpretation of a child's disability, their strength, needs, and learning; as well as what his or her deems appropriate for that child to learn.

Step 2: The professional finds out whether the child's family recognizes and values these same assumptions; if they do not, the professional should uncover how the family's views differ from their own.

Step 3: The professional acknowledges and gives explicit respect to any cultural differences identified, and fully explains the cultural basis of his or her own assumptions.

Step 4: Through open communication, discussions, and collaboration, the professional determines the most effective way of adapting his or her own professional interpretations or recommendations to the value system of the family.

Source: Harry, B., Kalyanpur, M., & Day, M. (2005). *Building cultural reciprocity with families: Case studies in special education.* Baltimore: Paul H. Brookes.

been called **cultural competence** (Hanson & Lynch, 2004). Cultural competence helps break the barriers between families and teachers who might not share similar view points due to ethnic and cultural backgrounds. Cultural competence and attention to cultural family issues help optimize the opportunities to better meet the needs of children and families (Davis-McFarland, 2008).

Harry, Kalyanpur, and Day (2005) propose a model of **cultural reciprocity** in which teachers and other professionals take initiative to build a bridge between the cultures of diverse families and the culture of the school professionals by establishing a two-way process of information sharing and understanding. The model of cultural reciprocity consists of four steps in which teachers and other professionals strive to develop a true mutual understanding of each other's cultural beliefs, the child, and his or her education. This mutual understanding will, over time, build the foundations of mutual empowerment and partnership between the family and professionals (described later in this chapter). Text Box 3.1 describes steps of the model of cultural reciprocity.

POVERTY AND DISABILITY

A family's income, level of education, and the social status associated with the type of occupation the breadwinners of the family have, form the family's **socioeconomic status (SES)** (Turnbull et al., 2006). SES influences the way families fulfill their major functions. A family and its members are considered poor when the family's income is less than the income threshold set by the U.S. Census Bureau (Dalaker & Naifeh, 1998). The socioeconomic status of a family influences the quality of life of all its members, including a child's growth and development. Poverty means lack of opportunity, racial inequality, and constant struggles with social problems such as teen pregnancy, school failure, incarceration, inadequate housing, unemployment, substance abuse, and so on (Enwefa, Enwefa, & Jennings, 2006).

Over the last decade, more than one-fifth of all children living in America have lived in families with cash flow incomes below the poverty level (Enwefa et al., 2006). In 2005, about 18 percent of children (about 11.6 million) living in the United States lived in poverty (U.S. Census Bureau, 2006). As poverty has increased in the United States, so has the number of children diagnosed with disabilities (Fujiura & Yamaki, 2000). The number of children with disabilities growing up in poverty is higher as compared to the number of children without disabilities living in poverty, and about 1 in every 26 American families report that they are raising a child with a disability in poverty (U.S. Census Bureau, 2006). Research shows that families of children with disabilities experience significantly greater hardship and material shortage than other families (Parish, Rose, Grinstein-Weiss, Richman, & Andrews, 2008).

Families who live in poverty have few resources in child development, and children who grow up in poverty during their early childhood years are more likely to have lower cognitive abilities, lower rates of school success, and higher rates of behavior problems compared to other children (Brooks-Gunn & Duncan, 1997; National Research Council, Institute of Medicine, 2000). In addition, poverty puts an incredible amount of strain on the family to afford a safe and adequate diet for their children, which may lead to further risks in the health and development of the child (Enwefa et al., 2006).

African Americans and Mexican Americans are two large groups of whom significant portions live in poverty in the United States. Because a large number of African Americans are poor, the incidence of poverty-based disability resulting from poor nutrition and poor parental care is high in these families (National Research Council, Institute of Medicine, 2000; Seligman & Darling, 1997, 2007). Similarly, Mexican American children are more likely to be put in special education programs as compared with Anglo children (National Research Council, Institute of Medicine, 2000). The poor Mexican American families may not have access to consistent care for their children with special needs, and these families typically receive support from many programs and agencies that may offer inconsistent and uncoordinated care for the child (Guerra, 1980). Among families of children with disabilities, single mothers and families living in extended family structures are at higher risk for experiencing severe hardship (Parish et al., 2008).

For families of children with disabilities who live in poverty, real-life stressors that they face on a day-to-day basis are compounded by the stressors of having a child with a disability and securing disability-related services and support (Parish et al., 2008). Often, lack of financial resources becomes a barrier for these families to secure appropriate services for their children (Fujiura & Yamaki, 2000). For example, lack of transportation is a major problem for many poor families. This problem often makes educational and therapeutic services inaccessible for children with special needs who grow up in poverty.

For families who struggle to survive from day to day, achieving a developmental or academic outcome for the child might not be a priority. When we work with poverty-stricken families and families with low SES, the reality of life for these families on a day-to-day basis should be kept in mind. Early intervention and early childhood providers are usually more successful in winning the family's confidence when they bring about some immediate success for the family by securing various community services, such as public transportation or clinic appointments, etc. (Jackson, 1981).

THE CHILD WITH THE DISABILITY IN THE FAMILY

Finding out that one has become the parent of a child with a disability is perhaps the most difficult time in the life cycle of families of children with disabilities. Whether before birth, immediately after birth, or several years after birth, when a family becomes suspicious that something is wrong or receives a confirmed diagnosis, it faces a severe crisis period in which it needs the greatest support available. Families react differently to the diagnosis of their child with special needs. Many factors determine a family's reaction to the news of a disability. The severity of the disability, the age of the child at the time of identification, and the timing of the diagnosis are among factors that contribute to the reaction of parents at the time of diagnosis (Seligman & Darling, 2007).

Some disabilities such as Down syndrome and spina bifida are diagnosable before birth through some prenatal tests. In such cases, family members have time to mentally prepare—think about, discuss, seek information, secure support and services—and make adjustments and adaptations before the arrival of the infant. Often early intervention services are provided immediately after birth in the hospital for the children whose special needs are diagnosed prenatally or immediately after birth. Medical conditions, physical disabilities, and some other disorders such as cerebral palsy or spina bifida, are diagnosable before or immediately after birth. Information and support is usually provided for families during the hospital stay and shortly afterward at home.

Some neurological, regulatory, and developmental disabilities, which do not have physical characteristics, such as intellectual disabilities, autism spectrum disorders, attention hyperactivity disorders, or sensory processing disorders are not diagnosable at birth. In these cases, families are not alerted to the problem until after the first or second year of the child's life. For these parents, adjustment and adaptation might be more difficult, as up to that point they had been living with a child who to them had been completely healthy and typical.

Families and the Process of Grief

In the traditional literature on families of children with disabilities, realization that one's child has a disability is often likened to facing the death of one's child or the loss of a longed-for healthy child (Solnit & Stark, 1961). One mother has described receiving news of her child's diagnosis with developmental disabilities in the following way:

> The impact was almost physical. A fist was crashing into my chest. Immediately,
> in a reflex of self-protection, I tried to simply cancel out what the doctor was say-
> ing. If I shut my ears and eyes and then back-tracked through time, we wouldn't be

sitting here and she wouldn't be saying this anymore. Crazy thoughts tumbled over one another: . . . What a bad idea to come here . . . I turned slowly toward him [my husband]. He had the look I'd seen him wear only one other time, when he held his firstborn son, lifeless, in his arms. His face was pale, his eyes shocked, his mouth set and stiff. (Maurice, 1993, p. 25)

When given the news of a disability, parents lose all their hopes and dreams for their child. In other words, they face loss of a perfect or "normal" child. Elisabeth Kübler-Ross (1969) conceptualized five stages that characterize the reaction of people who experience loss or terminal illness. Many disability scholars have adapted and applied Ross' *stage theory* of grief and mourning to the experience of parents and family members of children with disabilities. Components of these stages are shock and denial, anger and frustration, bargaining, and acceptance (Francis & Jones, 1984; Howard, Fry-Williams, Port, & Lepper, 2001; Smith, Gartin, Murdick, & Hilton, 2006).

> **Shock and denial:** Parents might experience shock at the news of their child's disability and react in disbelief or undergo a period of denial.
> **Anger and frustration:** Parents or family members might ask "Why my child?" or "Why our family?"
> **Bargaining:** In search of an answer, parents and family members might seek information about the disability and might "shop" for a better or less severe diagnosis.
> **Acceptance:** Parents or family members might begin to see their situation in a realistic light, and come to terms with the disability of their child.

The validity of the grief stage theory for all families of children with disabilities has been questioned, and this model has been abandoned by the field since the 1990s with the advent of family-centered practices (Turnbull, Turbiville, & Turnbull, 2000; Turnbull & Turnbull, 2002).

Our attitudes regarding the families of children with disabilities have undergone a major change since the 1950s and 1960s, an era when parents of children with special needs were pathologized, and given psychotherapy and counseling in order to deal with the disability of their child. We have evidence that families of children with disabilities have different capabilities at various points in time (Walsh, 1996, 2003). Although some families might experience difficulties adjusting to multiple environmental and disability stressors in their lives at certain times, they might function in a healthy way at other times (Walsh, 1996). Many families of children with disabilities adapt and adjust to stressors, whether disability-related or not, and manage to do well and lead healthy, productive, and well-adjusted lives (Bayat, 2007; Patterson, 2002; Walsh, 2003; Scorgie & Sobsey, 2000).

Evidence of Positive Contributions of a Disability to the Family

Unlike a general assumption that having a child with a disability has a devastating impact on the family, during the last two decades research in disability has brought to attention many positive contributions that children and youth with a disability make to the growth of the family. In their work with families of children with disabilities, Summers, Behr, and Turnbull (1988) found many families with children with severe disabilities who did quite well with or without the intervention of service providers. They realized that many parents managed to make a positive adaptation to having a child with a disability. Such parents had successful marriages and emotionally well-adjusted children both with and without disabilities. Some parents found the disability of their children to be a growing experience in learning humility, patience, compassion, acceptance of, and respect for others. They even went as far as providing support to other families or service providers.

Parents and family members of children with disabilities often report life-changing experiences and transformations as a result of living with and raising a child with a disability. Many families talk about finding new perspectives or spiritual beliefs in life and gaining new strength (Scorgie & Wilgosh, 2008; Bayat, 2007; Hastings, Beck, & Hill, 2005; Taunt & Hastings, 2002; Scorgie & Sobsey, 2000).

Scorgie and Sobsey (2000) found that families of children with disabilities defined two types of transformations: personal transformation and relational transformation. *Personal transformation* means that the family members gain new roles—in the family, community, and in their careers. It also means that they acquire new traits, such as an ability to speak out and advocate for the child with a disability, or find new convictions and faith. *Relational transformation* for the families refers to changes in the ways parents and family members of children with disability relate to other people. Some parents report stronger marriages, a healthy family outcome, and acquisition of gained friendship networks with other families who have children with disabilities (Scorgie & Sobsey, 2000; Bayat, 2007).

Family Resilience

These studies and other similar works make us wonder about the processes and factors that might contribute to families responding positively to the phenomenon of disability. A family scholar, Walsh (1998) has described families who come out of adversity successfully and are strengthened as *resilient families.* She defines **family resilience** as the ability to withstand hardship and rebound from adversity, becoming more strengthened and resourceful. The concept of family resilience has been gaining attention by disability researchers and some studies are bringing to light evidence of resilience in families of children with disabilities (Vandsburger, Harrigan, & Biggerstaff, 2008; Retzlaf, 2007; Bayat, 2007; Lietz, 2006). We could say that those families who cope with disabilities of their children in positive ways, and who consider themselves stronger as a result of disability in the family, could be regarded as resilient families.

FAMILY ADJUSTMENTS AND COPING MODELS

Family adjustment and coping models have provided useful frameworks for understanding the concept of family resilience. A well-known model of coping with disabilities is that put forward by Rolland (1993). In this model, families initially go through a crisis phase—the period after the diagnosis and initial treatment and educational plan. During this period, the family's immediate tasks include learning to cope with the disability, adapting to the treatment procedures, and establishing and maintaining a relationship with the service providers or the health care personnel. In this phase, the family faces some developmental tasks, such as creating meaning for the disability, grieving the loss of the "typical" child, gradually accepting the disability, pulling together to cope with the crisis, and developing plans for the future.

The second phase for the family is the chronic phase, or "the day-to-day living" with the disability or illness. During this phase, the family usually accepts the disability psychologically and organizationally, and understands that permanent changes will have to be made in the family. What the functioning pattern of the family is (i.e., flexibility, cohesion, style) determines the way families readjust and adapt in each phase. Other models of coping with stress have also been adapted to the field of disability. The most notable among them are the Double ABCX and FAAR models.

The Double ABCX Stress Model

In 1949, Hill studied families of World War II veterans in order to understand how these families coped with the stressors that the war had brought into their homes. He designed a model known as the *ABCX stress model* (Hill, 1958). This model explained how families may cope with the normative or non-normative stressors in the family. In this model, during a crisis situation, such as the diagnosis of a child with a disability, A is the typical stressors that families face on a daily basis along with the stressors brought by a crisis. B refers to the family's resources to meet the stressors it faces, and C refers to the family's appraisal or definition of the crisis it faces. Based on Hill's model, A, B, and C interact with one another to produce X, which is the family's response to that crisis. Families might respond positively or negatively to a crisis.

In later years, McCubbin, Sussman, and Patterson (1983) in working with families of children with chronic illness advanced this model to the *Double ABCX model* (Figure 3.2). The model also takes into consideration that when a crisis occurs within a family, the family will have to deal with a new set of stressors, which would add to the normal daily stressors the family already faces. As a result, there would be a "pile-up" of stressors. Therefore, aA is the pile-up of stressors or the cumulative effect of daily stressors in addition to the stressors brought about by the disability; bB represents the previous and current resources available to families; and cC alludes to the family's perception of their stressors as well as their own appraisal of these demands against their own resources. In the Double ABCX model, the factor xX is the family's process of coping and its adaptation in response to the disability and the pile-up of demands. In other words, this model implies that the way families see themselves capable of handling the crisis influences the way they cope with the crisis.

The FAAR Model

Another useful model in understanding a family's adjustment to the demands of having a child with a disability is the *Family Adjustment and Adaptation Response model* (*FAAR*) (Patterson, 1988). In their collaborative work, Patterson and McCubbin realized that how families perceived the stressful event and how they evaluated their own capabilities to handle this event, proved to be the elemental factor in how families

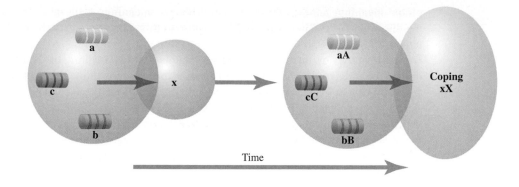

a = stressors faced by the family, including diagnosis of a child with a disability

b = existing resources of the family

c = perception of family's daily stressors ("a")

x = family's response to the stressors (crisis)

First, the way family perceives its daily stressors interacts with the family's existing resources to determine how the family might respond to stressors. This could cause a crisis (x).

aA = pile-up of daily stressors in addition to the stressors brought about by diagnosis of disability over time

bB = family's existing resources plus new resources that now exists after the diagnosis of disability (services, therapies, etc.)

cC = family's perceptions about the disability, its other stressors, and all resources the family has available

xX = coping or mal-adaptation might result from the way the family perceives its resources and overall stressors in light of the crisis (disability)

FIGURE 3.2 Double ABCX Stress Model Applied to Families of Children with Disabilities

actually dealt with the crisis situation. In the FAAR model, Patterson (1988) went further to elaborate on this process by emphasizing the family's adjustment and adaptation to the stressors rather than coping with them. She explained that when families receive the news of a disability, they begin to make meaning of this new demanding situation that has occurred; for example, asking, "What does it mean for my family to have a child with a disability?"

The FAAR model has two phases. In the first phase, the adjustment phase, when the family first encounters news of the disability, it begins to make meaning of the disability at two levels: *situational meaning* and *global meaning*. In making situational meaning, families make a subjective meaning about their definition of disability and their own capabilities to manage it (i.e., "My husband can take the baby to the doctor 1 day a week and I can do that 2 days a week."). Family members can create positive meanings or negative meanings about the situation. Attending to the positive is a cognitive coping strategy that will enable families to reduce demands and increase their capabilities (Turnbull & Turnbull, 1993). In making global meaning, families develop shared beliefs, meanings, and values regarding the disability (i.e., "There is a greater purpose to this. This is God's will" etc.) (Patterson, 1988, 1999).

Ultimately, how families make situational and global meaning of the disability in the family determines how they will balance the demands of the disability against their own psychological and material capabilities. Therefore, the second phase of this model is the adaptation phase, in which the positive way that families perceive disability and make meaning of it helps them reach equilibrium and function in a positive way (Figure 3.3). In all models of coping, a certain period of time is required for the family to come to terms with the implications of disability. Each family is unique in the amount of time it requires to adapt to the demands of a disability.

Critical Thinking Question 3.2   Referring back to the story at the beginning of this chapter, how might Maria and her husband's view of a disability in their family have contributed to their divorce?

FIGURE 3.3
The FAAR Model Applied to Families of Children with Disabilities

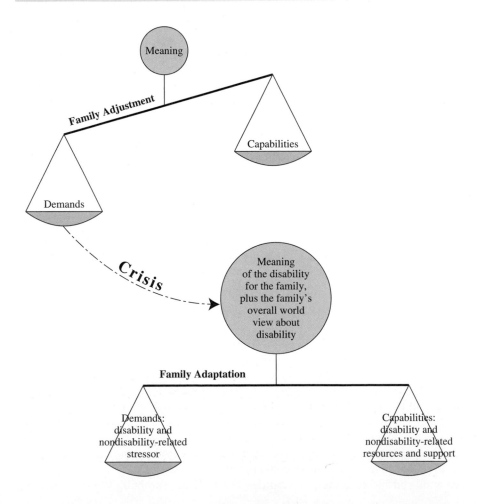

MODELS OF WORKING WITH FAMILIES

Models of coping and our understanding of a family's capabilities have provided guidelines for the U.S. policies and practices in regard to families. Models of working with families have evolved and changed throughout the past 50 to 60 years. Turnbull and her colleagues (2000, 2002) explain the evolution of intervention models, which dominated the working relationship between families and professionals in the United States. Based on Turnbull's analogy, the models of working with families have been influenced by the old paradigm in the field, which focused on "fixing" the family, and therefore "fixing" the child. The following sections describe the various parent–professional relationship models as described by Turnbull, Turbiville, and Turnbull (2000), and Turnbull and Turnbull (2002).

The Counseling/Psychotherapy Model (1950s–1960s)

This model was influenced by psychoanalysis, in that professionals believed children with disabilities created trauma, grief, and pathology in parents, and that they needed to be treated psychologically. Working mostly with mothers of young children, professionals treated parents as "cases" and provided counseling services to lead them through the stages of grief by working through the parents' own past personal experiences, which in turn would influence the parents' relationship with their child with a disability. Little attention was paid to the family environment and family system. In this model, professionals were experts and in control of treatment. The goal of treatment for the parents was to reach the final stage of grief—acceptance— by coming to terms with the disability.

Parent Training/Involvement Model (1960s–1970s)

Influenced by the political ideology of the time, which encouraged parents to increase their decision-making power, this model advocated a "parent as teacher" or "parent as therapist" philosophy. In this model, parents—primarily mothers—were trained to work with the child to provide supplemental education. Although parents participated in the planning and decision-making process, in general they were the agents or "extra hands" for the professionals. Parents' needs or roles were often ignored in this model, and parents often did not get a chance to be just "parents." This model is still practiced in certain programs across the country.

The Family-Centered Model (1980s–1990s)

Influenced by the popularity of systems theory, the family-centered practices, which are still in use in the United States, acknowledge all family members, including extended family members, as influential factors in the life of the child. The family is recognized as the final decision maker on issues related to the child and family, and therefore the decision about treatment and intervention lies within the family. Unlike the parent training model, in family-centered practices, professionals and parents share power to determine what issues should be addressed and how resources should be allocated.

Dunst, Trivette, and Deal (1988) set guidelines and principles for what in the field has become known as "empowering and enabling families." Based on their principles, professionals identify the family's needs and strength. While a family's individuality, racial, ethnic, and socioeconomic status are recognized and respected, professionals build on the strength of the family, and in collaboration with the family utilize existing resources to address the needs of both the child and the family.

Collective Empowerment or Family–Professional Partnership (1990s–2000s)

The *collective empowerment model* or *family–professional partnership* is currently promoted in the field as an ideal model of working with families. It builds on assumptions and philosophies of the family-centered model, taking the previous model one step further. The focus of this model is to:

> Access resources in a way that makes the most substantial differences to the families, so they can gain control in their lives
> Respect participation of the family at any level that is defined and determined by the family
> Change the community's ecology

This model assumes a "power-through" family–professional partnership.

Collective empowerment with families means that families are being appreciated by the professionals, and professionals are being appreciated by the families (Turnbull et al., 2000). Collaboration between the family and professionals creates a synergy that is a direct result of this mutual appreciation. This positive energy could then enhance the capacities of both parents and professionals, where both gain in competence and the ability to identify and tackle resources in the community together. In the collective empowerment model, the synergy of power and capacity building becomes a powerful resource in and of itself (Turnbull, Turnbull, & Wehmeyer, 2006).

Collective empowerment with families means that families are being appreciated by professionals, and professionals are being appreciated by the families.

The evolution of philosophies and models of working with families has long been interrelated with the changes in mandates and laws concerning the role of parents and family in early intervention and special education. In the following section, we will briefly look at laws and mandates surrounding the rights of parents and primary caregivers of children with disabilities.

Parents' Rights

The Individuals with Disabilities Education Act (IDEA) of 1990 and its amendments of 1997 and 2004 establish the system of service delivery to students with disabilities. The provisions of IDEA acknowledge parents as central to the system and the development of the child (Hanson & Lynch, 2004). Turnbull, Huerta, and Stowe (2006) in explanation of the IDEIA 2004 amendment, make the following key points:

> Part C not only enhances the family's capacity to meet the special needs of their infants and toddlers with disabilities, but also acknowledges their rights to education and treatment of their young child. Services are appropriate when they are "family-directed," and parents are included in writing the IFSP and aspects of intervention as well.

> Under principles of IDEA, parents have the right to request IEP or IFSP meetings as often as they see fit. In addition, IDEA elaborates procedural safeguards. These safeguards explain parents' rights in case of a conflict with the agency or school providing early intervention or special education. Procedural safeguards must be explained to parents in their own language. Parents have a right to:
>   > An independent educational evaluation
>   > Receive prior written notice
>   > Access to educational records
>   > Take a complaint through the due process of law
>   > Present and resolve complaints, be instructed about the time period in which to make a complaint
>   > Have the school resolve the complaint
>   > The availability of mediation
>   > Be instructed about the child's placement during the pending process of due process, and those procedures relating to it
>   > A due process hearing and all procedures relating to it

These mandates clearly imply that not only parents and their rights must be acknowledged and recognized, but parents can partner with service providers and professionals in the educational and treatment process of the child.

HOW DO WE FORM A PARTNERSHIP WITH FAMILIES?

Partnership with families is defined as a "relationship in which families and professionals collaborate with each other by capitalizing on each other's judgments and expertise in order to increase benefits for students, families, and professionals" (Turnbull et al., 2006, p. 93). In partnership, parents and early childhood educators utilize each others' resources, talents, and expertise to make a positive difference in the lives of children (Turnbull et al., 2006). When families and professionals value each other and partner together to achieve the best outcome for the child, they will both benefit by the collective power gained as a result of this partnership (Dunlap & Fox, 2007). The benefits that result from a parent–professional partnership have been described by Turnbull and colleagues (2006) as:

> ➢ Providing a trusting and safe early childhood environment to achieve the best developmental outcome for the child
> ➢ Influencing the family's quality of life by achieving gains in the child's behavior and development
> ➢ Making a difference in the lives of families on their own terms, based on the priorities they define
> ➢ Providing a fruitful educational climate for a child's learning as well as the professionals' growth

The Division for Early Childhood (DEC) of the Council of Exceptional Children has made recommendations regarding professional practices that are responsive to culture, language, and other family characteristics, and promote partnership between professionals and family members (Sandall, Hemmeter, Smith, & McLean, 2005). Table 3.2 lists some DEC recommended examples of practices to promote partnership.

Early childhood educators will inevitably benefit by working with families toward achieving a shared goal. When parents and educators partner and acknowledge their equal powers, they are able to achieve much more than when they waste their time in power struggles. The heart of any partnership is establishing a positive relationship between the teachers and other therapists and families (Blue-Banning, Summers, Frankland, Nelson, & Beegle, 2004; Dinnebeil, Hale, & Rule, 2000). Gaining trust and establishing positive relationships between families and professionals does not occur automatically, nor does it take place overnight. One of the first steps toward establishing a positive relationship with families is for the early

TABLE 3.2   DEC Council of Exceptional Children Recommended Professional Practices Which Will Promote Family–Professional Partnership

➢ Use appropriate family interviewing techniques in order to learn the priorities of the family
➢ Identify and use interpreters as needed to ensure that families have the full information about the available resources
➢ Learn at least some words and phrases in the family's preferred language
➢ Invite all family members to program activities, meetings, and special events
➢ Encourage family members to include those people they would like to have participate in meetings and other activities
➢ Honor each family's decision-making style

Source: Sandall, S., Hemmeter, M. L., Smith, B. J., & McLean, M. E. (2005). *DEC recommended practices: A comprehensive guide for practical application in early intervention/early childhood special education.* Missoula, MT: Division of Early Childhood (DEC) of the Council for Exceptional Children.

childhood educators to acknowledge parents or other primary caregivers of the child as the first experts on the child they work with.

Believing in a parent's expertise and acknowledging the family's strength are the foundations of building trust in partnership (Allen & Petr, 1996; Turnbull, Blue-Banning, Turbiville, & Park, 1999). In their studies of families of children with disabilities, Blue-Banning et al. (2004) and Turnbull et al. (2006) have suggested key principles that promote establishing a partnership and collaborative relationship between families and professionals.

Communication

Effective communication, whether verbal or nonverbal, implies that both parties listen and understand each other in a positive and respectful manner. Both families and professionals recommend several guidelines for communication (Blue-Banning et al., 2004):

> ➤ **Clarity:** Families do not appreciate jargon. They may be intimidated by professional terminology. Speaking in clear and precise sentences gets attention and promotes appreciation.
> ➤ **Honesty and openness:** Families appreciate honesty. When professionals do not have the information they are asked for, they should not hesitate to tell families this, and be willing to help them find answers.
> ➤ **Positive attitude and outlook:** Families appreciate a positive outlook during communication. A professional's positive attitude and outlook are likely to promote feelings of well-being and resilience in the family.
> ➤ **Listening:** Communication should be two-way. Early childhood educators and parents should listen carefully and nonjudgmentally to what the other has to say.
> ➤ **Frequent communication and coordination of information:** Information should be shared systematically and precisely.

Commitment

Most early childhood teachers like working with young children. Often, they strive to make a difference in the lives of children and help them grow and develop. Without a commitment to the education of young children, there is not much hope for professionals to gain competence or make a lasting change in the development of young children. When teachers are available and accessible to the child and the family, when they go above and beyond the call of duty, and when they are sensitive to the emotional needs of the child and family, they demonstrate their commitment to the family and become models of professional commitment for their team workers (Turnbull et al., 2006).

Respect

Families and professionals should regard each other with esteem, and demonstrate that they respect each other through their actions and words (Blue-Banning et al., 2004; Turnbull et al., 2006). Respecting families includes having cultural competence and honoring the family's culture, being polite and treating the child and the family with dignity, and avoiding telling the family what should and should not be done (Blue-Banning et al., 2004).

Professional Competence

Early childhood educators must have high expectations for the developmental outcome of children, and provide a high-quality education for the children with whom they work. One way to achieve this is to take advantage of various professional development opportunities in their field. A teacher's competence reassures families that the teacher is committed to the child's education and development and pursues the same goals with the families to achieve the best outcome for the child (Blue-Banning et al., 2004; Turnbull et al., 2006).

Equality

Families and educators are equal partners in both the decision making about the young child and the child's education. When families and educators work together in partnership, they feel equally powerful in working toward the best outcome for the child. One way of promoting equality between educators and family is to acknowledge and validate each other's knowledge and feelings and be willing to explore options together (Turnbull et al., 2006).

Trust

Families entrust their children into the hands of educators and therapists. To reciprocate this trust, educators and therapists should be mindful that any information regarding the child and the child's family is confidential. Professional communication should follow the appropriate code of conduct related to maintaining confidentiality and respecting the privacy of the family. Being reliable, keeping the child safe, and being discreet are practices that will lead to trust between families and educators (Turnbull et al., 2006).

Research Corner

Family Quality of Life

During the past few years, research on families of children with disabilities has focused on the area of family quality of life. In a general sense, quality of life might be defined in terms of one's happiness, health, self-esteem, self-determination, mental health, independence, and life satisfaction (Goode, 1990; Schalock, Keith, Hoffman, & Orv, 1989; Keith, 1990).

Quality-of-life researchers have been interested in understanding factors that may influence the quality of life of children and individuals with developmental disabilities. From this interest sprung further inquiries into the quality of life of families of children with disabilities. Two research teams, one from the University of Kansas's Beach Center on Disabilities (Poston et al., 2003), and the other, a group of international researchers from Australia, Canada, and Israel (Brown, Anand, Fung, Isaacs, & Baum, 2003) have done extensive work in defining the concept and factors that influence the quality of life of families of children with disabilities. Accordingly, family quality of life is defined as conditions where the family's needs are met, family members enjoy their life together as a family, and family members have the chance to do things that are important to them (Park et al., 2002).

Several aspects or dimensions influence family quality of life (Zuna, Selig, Summers, & Turnbull, 2009; Park et al., 2002; Poston et al., 2003; Turnbull et al., 2006). These are:

> **Emotional well-being:** A family's emotional well-being depends on the support it receives from friends, relatives, and the community; the availability of time and resources to pursue their members' interests; and having outside help to accommodate the needs of the child with a disability. As early childhood educators, when we provide emotional and educational support for the development of the child, we are in fact contributing to the emotional well-being of the family.

> **Parenting:** Parenting is a major task of adult members of the family. When parents know how to help their children with their developmental tasks, they are more likely to feel confident and meet the needs of their children. Early childhood educators can support parents in identifying ways to play with children, help children become independent, and learn to get along with peers.

> **Family interaction:** This dimension of family quality of life focuses on the relationship of the family members with one another. Spending time together, communicating with one another, and performing collective tasks are parts of a family's function. Members in the family, especially siblings without disability, should not feel left out or ignored.

> **Physical and material well-being:** In this chapter, we explained how poverty influences the development of the child. We should emphasize that having material and physical resources plays an important role in promoting the well-being of the whole family. When families struggle to meet their expenses and take care of their health needs, their quality of life is altered.

> **Disability-related support:** Whether they receive support from family members or others, it is important for the family to be able to take care of the special needs of the child with the disability in the family. Providing for the needs of that child depends on achieving goals at the early childhood setting, making progress at home, being able to interact with peers, and having a positive relationship with the early childhood education providers. Early childhood educators are elemental in helping families receive high-quality disability-related support.

How we work with families and children, and what goals we achieve in working with children and families, have a direct impact on at least three dimensions of quality of life of the families of children with disabilities: emotional well-being, parenting, and disability-related support.

SUMMARY

The family and its needs have become diverse in the 21st century. A family's systems model provides a useful framework in understanding families of children with disabilities. Many factors influence the functioning and well-being of a family. A family with a child with a disability faces additional challenges and stressors aside from its daily demands. Various factors, such as the family's socioeconomic status, the nature of the child's disability and the age of the child, and the family's culture and how disability is defined and viewed by the family, when mixed together determine how a family adjusts to the demands of the disability within the family. There is evidence that families of children with disabilities are capable of successfully adapting to the demands of those disabilities in the family. Different coping models such as Roland's model, Double ABCX, and FAAR explain the process of adjustment and adaptation. Families who come out of adversity strengthened are considered to be resilient families.

Influenced by popular theoretical and political ideologies, as well as mandates concerning families of children with disabilities, we have employed various models in working with families of children with disabilities in early intervention and early childhood special education. The most recent model of working with families is based on family-centered practices, with an emphasis on collective empowerment and partnership. In this model, professionals and parents share equal power, respect each other, and work together to achieve the best outcome for the child. Principles of partnership are based on communication and respect, including cultural competence, commitment, professional competence, and equality between professionals and families.

Early childhood professionals and service providers play a crucial and central role in promoting the family's well-being and enhancing the quality of life of families of children with disabilities. This awareness should prompt early childhood special educators to make every effort in forming collaborative and empowering partnerships with families of children with disabilities.

Review Questions

1. How has the definition of *family* changed over time?
2. What is a family structure and what are subsystems in a family?
3. How might a subsystem be affected when a child with a disability is born or diagnosed in the family?
4. How might a culture influence the way a family views the disability of a child?
5. What is cultural reciprocity and how might it be established?
6. What are some positive contributions of a disability to the family?
7. What is family resilience?
8. How does the FAAR model help us understand resilience in a family?
9. How does the parent training model differ from the family-centered model of working with families?
10. What is the model of collective empowerment?
11. What are some key principles that promote partnership between professionals and families?
12. What is family quality of life, and what are some dimensions?

Out-of-Class Activities

1. Design a rating survey or an interview form to research issues faced by families of children with disabilities.
   a. Conduct an interview or survey (based on your design) of three parents.
   b. Categorize general issues that parents have identified.
2. Conduct an interview of a sibling of a child with disabilities to understand various issues from the perspective of the sibling. Share the results of your interview with the class.
3. Identify five disability-related parent resource organizations and share them with the class.

Recommended Resources

Administration for Children and Family (U.S. Department of Health and Human Services)
http://www.acf.hhs.gov

Beach Center on Disabilities (University of Kansas)
http://www.beachcenter.org

Family Village (disability information for parents)
Waisman Center, University of Wisconsin
http://www.familyvillage.wisc.edu

Support for Families of Children with Disabilities
http://www.supportforfamilies.org

View the Online Resources available to accompany this text by visiting http://www.mhhe.com/bayat1e.

References

Allen, R. I., & Petr, C. G. (1996). Toward developing standards and measurement for family-centered practice in family support programs. In H. S. Singer, L. E. Powers, & A. L. Olson (Eds.), *Redefining family support: Innovations in public-private partnership* (pp. 57–86). Baltimore: Paul H. Brookes.

Attneave, C. (1982). American Indians and Alaska native families: Emigrants in their own homeland. In M. McGoldrick, J. K. Pearce, & J. Giordano (Eds.), *Ethnicity and family therapy* (pp. 55–83). New York: Guilford Press.

Baumrind, D. (1971). Current patterns of parental authority. *Developmental Psychology, 4* (1, pt. 2), 1–103.

Bayat, M. (2007). Evidence of resilience in families of children with autism. *Journal of Intellectual Disability Research, 51*(2), 702–714.

Beavers, W. R., & Hampson, R. B. (2003). Measuring family competence: The Beavers systems model. In F. Walsh (Ed.), *Normal family processes* (3rd ed.). New York: Guilford Press.

Blue-Banning, M., Summers, J. A., Frankland, H. C., Nelson, L., & Beegle, G. (2004). Dimensions of family and professional partnership: Constructive guidelines for collaboration. *Exceptional Children, 70*(2), 167–184.

Bronfenbrenner, U. (1979). *The ecology of human development: Experiments by nature and design.* Cambridge, MA: Harvard University Press.

Brooks-Gunn, J., & Duncan, G. (1997). The effects of poverty on children. *The Future of Children, 7*(2), 55–71.

Brown, I. (2007). What is meant by intellectual and developmental disabilities. In I. Brown & M. Percy (Eds.), *A comprehensive guide to intellectual and developmental disabilities* (pp. 3–15). Baltimore: Paul H. Brookes.

Brown, I., Anand, S., Fung, W. I., Isaacs, B., & Baum, N. (2003). Family quality of life: Canadian results from an international study. *Journal of Developmental and Physical Disabilities, 15*(3), 207–230.

Brown, I., & Radfore, J. P. (2007). Historical overview of intellectual and developmental disabilities. In I. Brown & M. Percy (Eds.), *A comprehensive guide to intellectual and developmental disabilities* (pp. 17–33). Baltimore: Paul H. Brookes.

Cowan, P. A., & Cowan, C. P. (2003). Normative family transitions, normal family processes, and healthy child development. In F. Walsh (Ed.), *Normal family processes: Growing diversity and complexity* (3rd ed., pp. 424–459). New York: Guilford Press.

Dalaker, J., & Naifeh, M. (1998). *U.S. Bureau of the Census: Current population reports.* Series P. 60–201. Poverty in the United States. Washington, DC: U.S. Government Printing Office.

Davis-McFarland, E. (2008). Family and cultural issues in a school swallowing and feeding program. *Language, Speech, and Hearing Services in Schools, 39,* 199–213.

Dinnebeil., L., Hale, L., & Rule, S. (2000). Early intervention program practices that support collaboration. *Topics in Early Childhood Special Education, 19*(4), 225–235.

Dunlap, G., & Fox, L. (2007). Parent–professional partnership: A valuable context for addressing challenging behaviors. *International Journal of Disability, Development, and Education, 54*(3), 273–285.

Dunst, C., Trivette, C., & Deal, A. (1988). *Enabling & empowering families: Principles for guidelines for practice.* Cambridge, MA: Brookline Books.

Enwefa, R. L., Enwefa, S. C., & Jennings, R. (2006). Special education: Examining the impact of poverty on the quality of life of families of children with disabilities. *Forum on Public Policy.* Retrieved July 8, 2010, from http://forumonpublicpolicy.com/archive06/enwefa.pdf

Fisman, S., Wolf, L., Ellison, D., Gillis, B., Freeman, T., & Szatmari, P. (1996). Risk and protective factors affecting the adjustment of siblings of children with chronic disabilities. *Journal of American Academy of Child and Adolescent Psychiatry, 35,* 1532–1541.

Francis, P. L., & Jones, F. A. (1984). Interactions of mothers and their developmentally delayed infants: Age, parity, and gender effects. *Journal of Clinical Child Psychology, 13*(3), 268–273.

Fujiura, G., & Yamaki, K. (2000). Trends in demography of childhood poverty and disability. *Exceptional Children, 66,* 187–199.

Giles-Sims, J., & Lockhart, C. (2005). Culturally shaped patterns of disciplining children. *Journal of Family Issues, 26*(2), 196–218.

Gollnick, D. M., & Chinn, P. C. (2002). *Multicultural education in a pluralistic society* (6th ed.). Upper Saddle River, NJ: Merrill/Prentice Hall.

Goode, D. A. (1990). Thinking about and discussing quality of life. In R. L. Schalock (Ed.), *Quality of life: Perspectives and issues* (pp. 41–59). Washington DC: American Association on Mental Retardation.

Gray, D. E. (2002). Ten years on: A longitudinal study of families of children with autism. *Journal of Intellectual and Developmental Disability, 27,* 215–222.

Guerra, F. A. (1980, September, October). Hispanic child health issues. *Children Today,* 18–22.

Hanson, M. J., & Lynch, E. W. (2004). *Understanding families: Approaches to diversity, disability, and risk.* Baltimore: Paul H. Brookes.

Hanson, M. J., Lynch, E. W., & Wayman, K. I. (1992). Honoring the cultural diversity of families when gathering data. *Topics in Early Childhood Special Education, 12,* 283–306.

Harry, B. (1992). *Cultural diversity, families, and the special education system: Communication and empowerment.* New York: Teachers College Press.

Harry, B., Kalyanpur, M., & Day, M. (2005). *Building cultural reciprocity with families: Case studies in special education.* Baltimore: Paul H. Brooks.

Hastings, R. P., Beck, A., & Hill, C. (2005). Positive contributions made by children with an intellectual disability in the family: Mothers' and fathers' perceptions. *Journal of Intellectual Disabilities, 9*(2), 155–165.

Hill, R. (1958). Generic features of families under stress. *Social Casework, 39,* 139–150.

Howard, V. F., Fry-Williams, B., Port, P. D., & Lepper, C. (2001). *Very young children with special needs* (2nd ed.). Upper Saddle River, NJ: Prentice Hall.

Hurd, E., Moore, C., & Rogers, R. (1995). Quiet success: Parenting strengths among African Americans. *Families in Society, 76*(7), 434–443.

Jackson, J. (1981). Urban black Americans. In A. Harwood (Ed.), *Ethnicity and medical care* (pp. 37–129). Cambridge, MA: Harvard University Press.

Kaminsky, L., & Dewey, D. (2001). Sibling relationships of children with autism. *Journal of Autism and Developmental Disorders, 31*(4), 399–410.

Keith, K. D. (1990). Quality of life: Issues in community integration. In R. L. Schalock (Ed.), *Quality of life: Perspectives and issues.* Washington DC: American Association on Mental Retardation.

Kübler-Ross, E. (1969). *On death and dying.* New York: Collier.

Lietz, C. A. (2006). Uncovering stories of family resilience: A mixed methods study of resilient families, part 1. *Families in Society, 87*(4), 575–582.

Liu, G. Z. (2005). Best practices: Developing cross-cultural competence from a Chinese Perspective. In J. H. Stone (Ed.), *Culture and disability: Providing culturally competent services* (pp. 65–85). Thousand Oaks, CA: Sage.

Locust, C. (1988). *Integration of American Indian and scientific concepts of disability: Cross-cultural perspectives.* Paper presented at the meeting of the Society for Disability Studies, Washington, DC.

Marcus, L. M., Kunce, I. J., & Schopler, E. (1997). Working with families. In D. J. Cohen & F. R. Volkmar (Eds.), *Handbook of autism and pervasive developmental disorders* (pp. 631–649). New York: Wiley.

Maurice, C. (1993). *Let me hear your voice: A family's triumph over autism.* New York: Ballentine.

McCubbin, H. I., Sussman, M., & Patterson, J. M. (1983). *Social stress and the family: Advances and development in family stress theory and research.* New York: Haworth.

McCubbin, H. I., Thompson, E. A., Thompson, A. I., & McCubbin, M. A. (1993). Family schema, paradigms, and paradigm shifts: Components and processes of appraisal in family adaptation to crisis. In A. P.

Turnbull, J. M. Patterson, S. K., Behr, D. L. Murphy, J. G. Marquiz, & M. J. Blue-Banning (Eds.), *Cognitive coping, families, and disability* (pp. 239–255). Baltimore: Paul H. Brookes.

Minuchin, S. (1974). *Families and family therapy.* Cambridge, MA: Harvard University Press.

National Research Council, Institute of Medicine. (2000). *From neurons to neighborhoods: The science of early childhood development.* Washington, DC: National Academy Press.

Park, J., Turnbull, A. P., & Turnbull, H. R. (2002). Impact of poverty on quality of life in families of children with disability. *Exceptional Children, 68*(2), 151–170.

Parish, S., Rose, R., Grinstein-Weiss, M. Richman, E., & Andrews, M. (2008). Material hardship in U.S. families raising children with disabilities. *Exceptional Children, 75*(1), 71–92.

Patterson, J. (2002). Integrating family resilience and family stress theory. *Journal of Marriage and the Family, 64,* 349–360.

Patterson, J. M. (1988). Families experiencing stress: I. The family adjustment and adaptation response model. II. Applying the FAAR model to health-related issues of intervention research. *Family Systems Medicine, 6,* 202–237.

Patterson, J. M. (1993). The role of family meanings in adaptation to chronic illness and disability. In A. P. Turnbull, J. M. Patterson, S. K. Behr, D. L. Murphy, J. G. Marquiz, & M. J. Blue-Banning (Eds.), *Cognitive coping, families, and disability.* (pp. 221–238). Baltimore: Paul H. Brookes.

Patterson, J. M. (1999). Healthy American families in a postmodern society: An ecological perspective. In H. M. Wallace, G. Green, K. Jaros, & M. Story (Eds.), *Health and welfare for families in the 21st century* (pp. 31–52). Sudbury, MA: Jones and Bartlett.

Patterson, J. M., & Garwick, A. W. (1994). Levels of meaning in family stress theory. *Family Process 33,* 287–304.

Poston, D., Turnbull, A., Park, J., Mannan, H., Marquis, J., & Wang, M. (2003). Family quality of life: A qualitative inquiry. *Mental Retardation, 41*(5), 313–328.

Retzlaf, R. (2007). Families of children with Rett syndrome: Stories of coherence and resilience. *Families, Systems, and Health, 25*(3), 246–362.

Rolland, J. S. (1993). Mastering family challenges in serious illness and disability. In F. Walsh (Ed.), *Normal family processes* (2nd ed., pp. 444–473). New York: Guilford.

Santana-Martin, S., & Santana, F. (2005). An introduction to Mexican culture of service providers. In J. H. Stone (Ed.), *Culture and disability: Providing culturally competent services* (pp. 161–186). Thousand Oaks, CA: Sage.

Sandall, S., Hemmeter, M. L., Smith, B. J., & McLean, M. E. (2005). DEC recommended practices: A comprehensive guide for practical application in early intervention/early childhood special education. Missoula, MT: Division for Early Childhood.

Satir, V. (1972). *Peoplemaking.* Palo Alto, CA: Science and Behavior Books.

Schalock, R. L., Keith, K. D., Hoffman, K. I., & Orv, K. (1989). Quality of life: Its measurement and use. *Mental Retardation, 27*(1), 25–31.

Scorgie, K., & Sobsey, D. (2000). Transformational outcomes associated with parenting children who have disabilities. *Mental Retardation, 38,* 195–206.

Scorgie, K., & Wilgosh, L. (2008). Reflections on an uncommon journey: A follow up study of life management of six mothers of children with diverse disabilities. *International Journal of Special Education, 23*(1), 103–114.

Seligman, M., & Darling, R. B. (1997). *Ordinary families, special children:* A systems *approach to childhood disability* (2nd ed.). New York: Guilford Press.

Seligman, M., & Darling, R. B. (2007). *Ordinary families, special children: A systems approach to childhood disability* (3rd ed.). New York: Guilford Press.

Skinner, D., Rodriguez, P., & Bailey, D. (1999). Qualitative analysis of Latino parents' religious interpretations of their child's disability. *Journal of Early Intervention, 22*(4), 271–285.

Smith, T. E. C., Gartin, B. C., Murdick, N. L., & Hilton, A. (2006). *Families and children with special needs: Professional and family partnerships.* Upper Saddle River, NJ: Prentice Hall.

Solnit, A. J., & Stark, M. H. (1961). Mourning and birth of a defective child. *Psychoanalytic Study of the Child, 16,* 523–537.

Stone, J. H. (Ed.) (2005). *Culture and disability: Providing culturally competent services.* Thousand Oaks, CA: Sage.

Stonik, P., & Jezewski, M. A. (2005). Culture and disability services. In J. H. Stone (Ed.), *Culture and disability: Providing culturally competent services* (pp. 15–36). Thousand Oaks, CA: Sage.

Strohm, K. (2005). *Being the other one: Growing up with a brother or sister who has special needs.* Boston: Shambhala.

Summers, J., Behr, S., & Turnbull, A. (1988). Positive adaptation and coping strength of families who have children with disabilities. In I. Irvin (Ed.), *Support for care-giving families: Enabling positive adaptation to disability* (pp. 1–17). Baltimore: Paul H. Brookes.

Taunt, H. M., & Hastings, R. P. (2002). Positive impact of children with developmental disabilities on their families: A preliminary study. *Education and Training in Mental Retardation and Developmental Disabilities, 37,* 410–420.

Turnbull, A. P., & Turnbull, H. R. (1993). Participatory research on cognitive coping: From concepts to research planning. In A. Turnbull, J. Patterson, S. Behr, D. Murphy, J. Marquiz, & M. Blue-Banning (Eds.), *Cognitive coping, families and disability* (pp. 1–14). Baltimore: Paul H. Brookes.

Turnbull, A. P., & Turnbull, H. R. (2002). From the old to the new paradigm of disability and families: Research to enhance family quality of life outcomes. In J. L. Paul, C. D. Lavely, A. Cranston-Gingras, & E. L. Taylor (Eds.), *Rethinking professional issues in special education* (pp. 83–119). Westport, CT: Ablex Publishing.

Turnbull, R., Huerta, N., & Stowe, M. (2006). The individuals with disabilities education act as amended in 2004. *Beach Center on Disability, University of Kansas, Lawrence,Kansas.* Upper Saddle River, NJ: Pearson Education Inc.

Turnbull, A. P., & Turbiville, V., & Turnbull, H. R. (2000). Evolution of family–professional partnership models: Collective empowerment is the model for the early 21st century. In J. P. Shonkoff & S. Meisels (Eds.), *The handbook of early childhood intervention* (2nd ed., pp. 630–650). New York: Cambridge University Press.

Turnbull, A., Turnbull, R., & Wehmeyer, M. (2006). *Exceptional lives: Special education in today's schools* (5th ed.). Upper Saddle River, NJ: Pearson.

Turnbull, A., Blue-Banning, M., Turbiville, V., & Park, J. (1999). From parent education to partnership education: A call for a transformed focus. *Topics in Early Childhood Special Education, 19*(3), 164–171.

Turnbull, A., Turnbull, R., Erwin, E., & Soodak, L. (2006). *Families, professionals, and exceptionality: Positive outcome through partnerships and trust* (5th ed.). Upper Saddle River, NJ: Pearson, Merrill/ Prentice Hall.

U.S. Census Bureau. (2006). *Poverty thresholds, 1998.* Washington, DC: Author. Retrieved December 19, 2009, from http://www.census.gov/hhes/www/ poverty/threshld/thresh98.html

Vandsburger, E., Harrigan, M., & Biggerstaff, M. (2008). In spite of all, we make it: Themes of stress and resiliency as told by women in families living in poverty. *Journal of Family Social Work, 11*(1), 17–35.

Walsh, F. (1996). The concept of family resilience: Crisis and challenges. *Family Process, 35*(3), 261–281.

Walsh, F. (1998). *Strengthening family resilience.* New York: Guilford Press.

Walsh, F. (2003). Changing families in a changing world: Reconstructing family normality. In F. Walsh (Ed.), *Normal family processes: Growing diversity and complexity* (3rd ed., pp. 3–26). New York: Guilford.

Wilson, J., Blacher, J., & Baker, B. (1989). Siblings of children with severe handicaps. *Mental Retardation, 27*(3), 167–173.

Zuna, N. I., Selig, J. P., Summers, J. A., & Turnbull, A. P. (2009). Confirmatory factor analysis of a family quality of life scale for families of kindergarten children without disabilities. *Journal of Early Intervention, 31*(2), 111–125.

Chapter 4

Identification and Intervention

Objectives

Upon completion of this chapter, you should be able to:

> Understand the process of identification of children who might have disabilities.
> Understand the process of evaluation.
> Discuss important factors in assessment of young children with disabilities.
> Understand service delivery, its model and components.
> Identify components of a universal curriculum model.

> Understand environmental adaptations to support inclusion.
> Identify various professional team models.
> Describe how curriculum content is developed for exceptional learners.
> Describe the concept of differentiated instruction.
> List ways to measure the progress of children with disabilities during the intervention.
> Understand program evaluation.
> Describe how to best formulate guidelines for working with families of children with disabilities.

Key Terms

alternative
   assessment (133)
assessment (115)
Child Find (111)
context of child
   development (116)
contextually based
   assessment (116)
convergent
   assessment (116)
developmental
   screening (112)
differentiated
   instruction (130)

evaluation (114)
family directed
   assessment (116)
formative
   evaluation (138)
interdisciplinary team
   model (129)
itinerant
   teachers (123)
multidisciplinary
   team (129)
norm-referenced
   tests (119)
observation (134)

performance-based
   assessment (133)
play-based
   assessment (133)
reliability (119)
service delivery
   model (122)
summative
   evaluation (138)
transdisciplinary
   team (129)
universal model of
   curriculum (124)
validity (119)

Reflection Questions

Before reading this chapter, answer the following questions to reflect upon your personal opinions and beliefs that are pertinent to early childhood special education.

1. Why is it important to have a consistent identification program in place for young children who are at risk or who have disabilities?
2. What predictions could you make for developmental and educational outcomes of children who are misidentified or not identified?
3. Why is it important to have licensed professionals conduct assessments in the evaluation process?
4. Why is it important to have an ongoing assessment of the children you work with through the intervention program?

A Child-Focused Approach

When Abed was 24 months old, his parents expressed worries to his pediatrician about Abed's lack of language abilities. The pediatrician reassured them that she could not detect any signs of hearing problems, and that every child was unique in the period in which he or she was required to develop certain skills. By 33 months of age, when Abed's vocabulary did not grow over a handful of words, his parents talked to the pediatrician again. This time, the pediatrician recommended that they take Abed to a local parent–child program that specialized in child development.

In the parent–child program, the Khalid family met other families who had similar concerns about the development of their children. Abed spent 3 hours, twice a week, in an early childhood classroom, while Renad and Ali, Abed's parents, joined a parent counseling group in which a child psychologist talked about issues related to child development and parenting. Listening to the psychologist and other parents who discussed familiar issues, such as having a daily routine at home, setting limits, and understanding developmental characteristics of their children, Renad began to feel less anxious about her son's development.

Several weeks after their enrollment in the program, the early childhood teacher, Susan, requested to meet with the Khalids to discuss Abed's development. During that meeting, Susan informed them that she had done a routine developmental screening in her classroom and was concerned because based on the screening results, Abed was behind in the areas of cognitive and language development.

The child psychologist, who had also attended the meeting, recommended that a full diagnostic evaluation be conducted to understand the extent of Abed's developmental needs. He explained that it meant Abed would be examined by licensed medical, psychological, and educational professionals and a diagnosis would be made should there be a specific condition.

During the meeting, the psychologist and the teacher provided needed information to Renad and Ali. They said an evaluation was necessary so it could be decided if Abed would be eligible to receive specialized services from available state-funded programs in their area. Describing the high costs of health and educational evaluation and interventions, they emphasized that the federal and state governments provided diagnostic evaluations as well as appropriate services for young children who were recognized as having special educational and developmental needs. Should Abed prove to be in need of specialized services, he would receive them immediately and at little cost to the parents. These services consisted of special education and other clinical supplemental services, which would help Abed develop to his full potential. They emphasized that receiving appropriate intervention was crucial in helping Abed progress and hopefully overcome his developmental problems.

Information given by Susan and the psychologist helped calm Abed's parents' anxiety, and they were able to ask specific questions about the next course of action to take. They left the meeting with a recommendation letter from the program's professionals for Abed to be fully evaluated by their State Board of Education.

(Continued)

It was explained to them that because Abed's third birthday was only a week away, he would be eligible to be evaluated under Part B of the Individuals with Disabilities Education Act, called IDEA.

Two weeks later, Abed was evaluated by a team of health and educational professionals designated by their local public school. He was diagnosed with speech and language impairment. The Khalid family was informed that Abed was eligible to receive special education and speech therapy services. With the help of the case manager appointed to coordinate the service provision for Abed, the Khalids found an inclusive public preschool program close to their home. In the new school, the family met with a team of educators and clinical professionals, and developed an Individualized Education Plan (IEP) for Abed. As Abed entered his first preschool year, he began receiving speech therapy three times a week to help him develop language skills. An early childhood special education teacher in the classroom modified activities and lessons, and worked with Abed every day to help him enhance his communication and language.

INTRODUCTION

In Chapter 1, we saw that under the Individuals with Disabilities Education Act (IDEA), children from birth to 21 years of age (22 years in some states) who have diagnosed developmental delays or specific disabilities are eligible to receive free and appropriate education services through Part B of IDEA. Part B governs special education and related services for children with disabilities between the ages of 3 and 21. Children from birth to age 3 receive services under mandates of Part C of IDEA (Part C governs early intervention services for infants and toddlers younger than the age of 3).

The responsible agency, also called the *Lead Education Agency* (*LEA*) for Part B, is the State Board of Education. The LEA for Part C is usually either the state's Department of Health and Human Services or the State Board of Education.

In this chapter's opening story, the Khalid family went through a formal process in which their child was found eligible to receive appropriate services. Although Abed ultimately received services to meet his developmental needs, the opportunity to identify him earlier than 33 months was missed when his mother originally stated her concerns around 24 months of the lack of vocabulary and language knowledge. Had Abed been referred earlier, the outcome might have been different for him. Ideally, families of children with disabilities who enter early childhood special education programs should receive timely support through the process of identification and intervention (Bailey, Scarborough, Hebbeler, Spiker, & Mallik, 2004).

Based on IDEA, identification, evaluation, assessment, and service provisions are all part of a formal process, which is funded by federal and state governments. IDEA requires that all early intervention and special education agencies provide a nondiscriminatory evaluation for any child suspected of having a disability. The implementation of this requirement varies from state to state, but in addition to having access to early intervention programs, parents can bring their child to their local school district and request an evaluation (Clair, Church, & Batshaw, 2007). In this chapter, we will learn how this process works. We will examine the different components of this process and find out how each part fits together to ensure that the needs of children are met and the rights of families and their children are respected.

> **Critical Thinking Question 4.1** What would have been a possible advantage to Abed had he been referred for evaluation at 24 months when Abed's mother first expressed concerns about his lack of vocabulary?

IDENTIFICATION

In general, there are three ways infants and toddlers with special needs might be identified. First, in the case of newborns or premature infants (as described in Chapter 2), early diagnostic tests can determine specific developmental or medical conditions (Pellegrino, 2007). In this case, early intervention services can be initiated in the hospital (Goldberg-Hamblin, Singer, Singer, & Denney, 2007). Second, a child might be identified through the state-funded process, such as **Child Find,** which screens children on a large scale for the purpose of identification. Third, parents or a friend or relative who has concerns about the child might suggest examination by one or more professionals, and eventually a diagnosis is made. Depending on the child's age, the child is then referred for early intervention services (if younger than 3 years old) or special education services (if older than 3). IDEA requires that within 45 days after referral to early intervention or special education, an IFSP should be written (Bailey et al., 2004).

There is an extreme variation between the time when young children are first identified and when the first IFSP or IEP is written. The 2003 report of the National Early Intervention Longitudinal Study indicated that, on average, the first concerns of parents are expressed at 7 months of age; the first diagnosis is made around 9 months of age; early intervention referral is made around 14 months of age; and the first IFSP is developed around 16 months of age (Bailey et al., 2004). In any event, the identification process marks the beginning of the child's entry to early childhood special education (ECSE), and is an important part of early intervention and preschool services.

Child Find

Child Find has been defined as an organized effort to identify children who might have special needs, or those who might benefit from early intervention (Jackson & Needelman, 2007). Under both Part B and Part C of IDEA, states are required to locate, identify, and evaluate children who might be at risk for or have disabilities. IDEA states:

> All children with disabilities residing in the State, including children with disabilities who are homeless or are wards of the State and children with disabilities attending private schools, regardless of the severity of their disabilities, and who are in need of special education and related services, are identified, located, and evaluated and a practical method is developed and implemented to determine which children with disabilities are currently receiving needed special education and related services. (Individuals with Disabilities, Education Improvement Act, 2004)

The Child Find program has been in place for nearly 30 years (Benner, 2003; Mindes, 2007). It is a component of IDEA that requires states to identify and refer children with disabilities for services as early as possible. IDEA requires that all states have a comprehensive Child Find program. The lead agencies responsible for carrying out Part B and Part C are in charge of providing a comprehensive Child Find program.

States have different eligibility guidelines for their early intervention and special education services. The state guidelines for the Child Find program include definition of the target population that is eligible for services. States might vary in their definitions of the population of the children to be served (Brown & Sorensen, 2007). Some states might provide early intervention services for infants and toddlers at risk for developmental delays (in addition to infants and toddlers with disabilities), while others might not. A comprehensive Child Find program provides public awareness in the community. For example, brochures and posters about children's developmental milestones might be placed in the doctors' offices or community agencies.

One of the most important components of the Child Find process is identifying infants and toddlers or preschoolers who might be experiencing developmental delays (Mindes, 2007; Benner, 2003). In proposing a model Child Find program, Jackson and Needelman (2007) describe a collaborative model between the early intervention (EI) agencies and hospital professionals in which all newborns are screened while in the hospital. In this system, during their hospital stay, the infants who are screened might be identified as low risk, moderate risk, or high risk. These groups of infants would then be referred for periodic developmental testing and monitoring based on their levels of risk until they reach 24 months of age.

Currently, the Child Find program under Part C offers well-baby checkups, or developmental screening, through local schools, community agencies, or hospitals for infants and toddlers. The Child Find program under Part B usually provides public awareness and identification services for preschool age and older children through school systems, community agencies, local clinics, rehabilitation agencies, child care centers, or other private agencies that might be cooperating with the local school system in Child Find activities (Benner, 2003).

Developmental screening might occur throughout the year in preschool or child care settings to identify children with disabilities. Screening could be part of an ongoing Child Find process or could be done separately from it. Usually kindergarten and preschool teachers conduct developmental screenings at the beginning of the school year, or toward the end of the school year to measure students' readiness for the higher grade.

Screening

Developmental screening is a way by which professionals are able to understand if a child is developing in a typical way, or if a child needs close monitoring or further assessment. A screening test is used to see if there might be any cause for concern regarding the child's development. To perform a developmental screening, a standardized and validated measure, such as the Denver Developmental Screening Test II (Frankenburg & Dodds, 1990), might be used. Developmental screening instruments are usually broad-based observational scales or checklists. The results of screening tests should never be used to establish a diagnosis or to design an intervention plan.

Screening tools do not study the child's development in any detail. Therefore, their results are sometimes *false positive*—where there is no real developmental concern— or *false negative*—where a child who has developmental delays or a specific condition is missed (Pellegrino, 2007; Benner, 2003). Having too many false positives takes time and resources away from children who actually do have disabilities, while having too many false negatives ultimately leads to under-identification (Benner, 2003).

When done appropriately, screening is a quick and cost-effective way to monitor a child's development and detect possible problems (Pellegrino, 2007). Screening tools might target a specific developmental domain or skill, such as social and emotional development, or screen for all areas of development on a broad scale (Ringwalt, 2008). They may target infants and toddlers, or be designed for preschool and older children. Some are designed for individual administration, such as the Brigance Preschool Screen (Brigance, 1998) and Brigance K & 1 Screen (Brigance, 1997), while others are for group administration, such as Developmental Indicators for the Assessment of Learning—Revised (DIAL-3) (Mardell-Czudnowski & Goldenberg, 1998).

Screening is not only beneficial during infancy as part of a periodic health checkup, but is also good for use as part of routine developmental monitoring during the preschool and kindergarten years. During primary and later school years, teachers might use academic screening in place of developmental screening at the beginning of the school year to identify children who are candidates for having learning problems or disabilities. Academic screening is part of an identification system for children with learning disabilities called Response to Intervention (RTI). Today, an RTI approach is increasingly used in most school districts around the country as an identification procedure for all children who might be at risk for disabilities (see Chapter 15 for a full discussion).

Critical Thinking Question 4.2   Referring back to the story at the beginning of the chapter, what do you think might have happened to Abed had Susan not conducted a routine developmental screening in her classroom?

EVALUATION PROCESS

The evaluation process usually begins with a referral. Referrals can be made by different parties in various ways whether through health care professionals or early childhood educators, or by parents or a concerned family member. The child is usually referred for a full evaluation under Part B or Part C, depending on the child's age. Under Part B (special education services), professionals in school districts usually conduct the evaluations. Evaluation under Part C is conducted by the professionals working for the lead agency responsible for EI services.

Some parents might decide to have their child evaluated by private professionals outside the Part B or Part C provisions. Even when parents decide to have their child evaluated by a team of privately hired professionals, they are entitled to have their child educated or receive supplemental therapy services through the public means. In this case, the lead agency responsible for the evaluation might decide to accept the results of the private evaluation, or conduct its own evaluation (Brown & Sorensen, 2007). It might also decide to conduct a partial evaluation. Accordingly, the decision of the child's eligibility would be made by the lead agency. See Figure 4.1 for a graphic representation of the evaluation process.

Critical Thinking Question 4.3   Refer to the story at the beginning of the chapter. Consider the components of the evaluation process and explain the steps that the Khalid family took in Abed's evaluation.

Evaluation vs. Assessment

The terms evaluation and assessment have frequently been used interchangeably. Although they both relate to an information gathering and testing procedure regarding a child's development and academic performance, each has a different meaning in the field. Bowe (2007) describes the difference between the evaluation and assessment in terms of the people who conduct them, their frequency, and their purpose.

Evaluation

An **evaluation** is only conducted by a team of licensed professionals and is done through a mix of tests, observations, and parent interviews. Under Part B of IDEA, evaluation is referred to as a formal process that determines if a child is eligible to

FIGURE 4.1
The Evaluation
Process

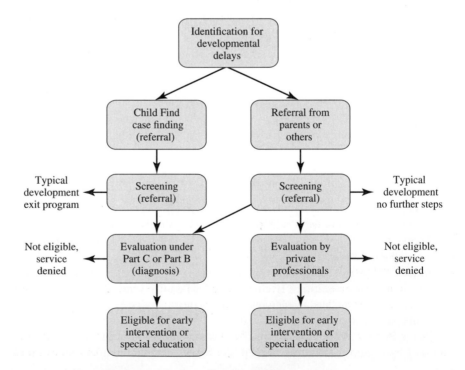

receive services. This process begins after the identification process has been completed. A diagnosis not only helps determine the specific kind of problem a child might be having, but also determines the child's eligibility to receive therapeutic, educational, and related services. After diagnosis, an evaluation is conducted periodically—usually every 3 years—to determine the child's continuous eligibility for services. An evaluation determines the child's current developmental, academic, and functioning level.

Under Part C of IDEA, an evaluation determines the eligibility for infants and toddlers to receive services by documenting the level of delays and functioning in five areas: cognitive, language, social emotional, motor, and adaptive development (Clair et al., 2007). IDEA requires that an evaluation by an EI program include an assessment of the family's needs and resources. In both the Part B and C evaluations, federal and state criteria are applied against the child's identified areas of needs so that appropriate developmental, educational, and supplemental services can be provided (Brown & Sorensen, 2007).

Assessment

Assessment is an ongoing process of gathering specific information to make decisions regarding the child (Mindes, 2007). It can be performed by a variety of educational professionals such as teachers, special educators, therapists, or others who work with children using formal or informal measures. It might occur during and/or after the child has been evaluated and deemed eligible to receive services. In assessment, the child is examined regularly to understand his or her specific and unique needs. Assessment is often based on the child's performance of everyday developmental, academic, and functional tasks.

The assessment procedure involves examining the child more deeply and purposefully to understand what kind of specific intervention is needed for that child (Mindes, 2007). The IFSP outcomes and IEP goals, as well as the lesson plans and specific activities, are designed based on the detailed assessment that educators and interventionists conduct (Clair et al., 2007).

Diagnosis

Diagnosis is a part of the evaluation procedures. It is an in-depth study of the child to understand the nature of the child's learning or developmental problem. Consider, for example, the case of Sofia, a 30-month-old girl, who has suddenly lost her ability to speak. The diagnosis procedure might include a series of medical and psychological examinations, such as hearing, vision, neurological, physical, and psychological tests.

Imagine that the results of the physical, neurological, and hearing tests indicate there are no neurological causes for Sofia's loss of speech. A thorough psychological assessment, which includes detailed interviews with family members and child observations at home at various times, reveals that Sofia's apparent loss of speech is due to an emotional trauma she suffered as a result of a car accident in which Sofia's mother lost her life. Without a comprehensive diagnostic procedure, this information might not have come to light.

Diagnosis forms one part of evaluation, which in itself consists of the assessment of several different aspects of the child's health and development. As we discussed previously in Chapter 3, because a child does not develop in a vacuum (Bronfen-brenner, 1979), an assessment of the **context of child development** is also necessary. An assessment that is contextually based takes into account a child's home environment, early childhood/school setting, and the child's community milieu as well. In a **contextually based assessment,** the child is examined within the everyday setting and activities in which he or she participates (Thurman & McGrath, 2008; Wilson, Mott, & Batman, 2004; Benner, 2003).

Although a contextually based assessment is necessary, it might not be sufficient to present an overall picture of the child's developmental capabilities. A comprehensive evaluation includes an assessment of the child in controlled/clinical settings, a contextually based assessment, and information from various people. Pulling information from different sources and people to discover whether the child can perform a predetermined skill or task is called **convergent assessment** (Torrance & Pryor, 1998; Neisworth & Bagnato, 2005).

Collecting assessment information from various sources for evaluation purposes might take place over a certain period of time, and they may involve using multiple batteries of formal and informal assessment that include health and physical examinations, as well as other sources of information. In order to understand the child's developmental level, an assessment might be conducted using either a standardized assessment instrument or carrying out an informal observation of the child during play whether at home or in the child's school or day care center. Figure 4.2 illustrates convergent assessment procedures within an evaluation process.

Assessment of Family Resources and Priorities

In general, we understand that accomplishing any goals within a program of early intervention for a child should reflect the needs and resources that exist within the family system. For children who are younger than 3 years of age, Part C of the IDEA mandates that evaluation should include a **family directed assessment,** an

FIGURE 4.2
Convergent
Assessment within
an Evaluation
Process

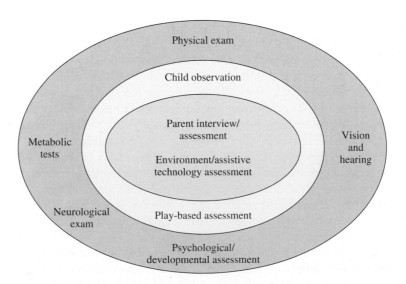

assessment of the family's resources, priorities, and concerns along with the developmental needs of the child, and identification of support and services that would enhance the family's capacity to meet the needs of the child (Benner, 2003; Brown & Sorensen, 2007).

A family directed assessment is important because even if we take meticulous care to collaborate with other professionals in conducting a comprehensive assessment of the child, but fail to consider the systemic and dynamic factors that affect the child's development, our plan of intervention might prove to be ineffective. Consider Sofia's case, for example. Let us imagine that as part of our assessment protocol, we conduct a family directed assessment that consists of a detailed interview with Sofia's father in his home.

We find out that because Sofia's father works full time, after the death of his wife, Sofia's care has been inconsistent. Every week, Sofia is cared for by different people, such as close family friends and the maternal grandmother, who has been dealing with depression after the loss of her daughter. Sofia's father tells us that the most important priority for him is not only to help Sofia begin to speak again, but to secure consistent and appropriate care for her.

Through our assessment of the family's resources, we find that Sofia's father has good financial resources, as well as a good employer who has been supportive and has agreed to the possibility of allowing Sofia's father to work from home one or two times during the week. Looking at Sofia's family's priorities and resources, we could work collaboratively with Sofia's father to draw a program plan that respects her family's priorities as well as Sofia's developmental needs. For example, our plan could begin with helping Sofia's father find more stable, consistent, and emotionally secure care for Sofia, as compared to what has so far been available to her.

One idea might be a high-quality home-based or group-based early childhood care and development program for Sofia, where she can not only enjoy consistent care, but have a chance to interact with her peers as well. We could collaborate with the early childhood educators at the center where Sofia will be enrolled to provide appropriate services for her there. Therapy services could also be provided for Sofia at her home during the time that her father is at home.

Such a plan of intervention is usually written in detail in the IFSP (Individual Family Service Plan) for the child who is served through the EI system. Detailed intervention plans for a young child (from birth to 3 years) are called the *IFSP outcomes* (refer to Chapter 5). The IFSP outcomes reflect the family's priorities and resources as well as the child's developmental needs. When children are older and are being served under Part B or a special education system, we write similar plans for the education of the child in a document called the IEP (Individualized Education Plan). Although IEP goals do not focus on the family's resources and priorities, they do reflect what visions the parents have for their child's education and learning. In addition, under Part B, social work services are available to families of children with disabilities, and such services might include a family directed assessment to identify the family's needs and help provide resource linkages to the families. Table 4.1 describes recommended practices by the Division of Early Childhood of the Council of Exceptional Children related to assessment of family resources and priorities.

TABLE 4.1   DEC Council for Exceptional Children Recommended Practices, Which Build on Family Resources and Priorities

> Resources and support are provided in ways that are flexible, individualized, and tailored to the child's family's preferences and styles, and promote well-being.
> > For example, programs move beyond a one-size-fits-all approach.

> Resources and supports match each family member's identified priorities and preferences.
> > For example, the professional talks with each family member to identify the specific needs and priorities of each member.

> Practices, supports, and resources are responsive to the cultural, ethnic, racial, language, and socioeconomic characteristics and preferences of families and their communities.
> > For example, program staff member studies the beliefs and values of families in their community in order to learn how to respect the overall family and community values in the plan of assessment and intervention.

> Family and child strengths and assets are used as a basis for engaging families in the intervention.
> > For example, the child's grandfather who used to be a librarian is asked if he would like to read to children during story time activities.

> Practices, supports, and resources build on existing parenting competence and confidence.
> > For example, information about toilet training builds on what the family is already doing with the child in that area.

Source: Sandall, S., Hemmeter, M. L., Smith, B. J., & McLean, M. E. (2005). *DEC recommended practices: A comprehensive guide for practical application in early intervention/early childhood special education.* Missoula, MT: Division of Early Childhood (DEC) of the Council for Exceptional Children.

ISSUES OF CONSIDERATION IN ASSESSMENT OF YOUNG CHILDREN WITH DISABILITIES

Since the evaluation process consists of a series of assessments conducted by different professionals at different times, it's likely a young child may not look enthusiastically upon undergoing a series of different testing sessions. Even when the child is assessed by a person she knows and in an environment she is familiar with, a variety of situational-based factors, such as the child's physical health and mood, or the specific settings, might influence the testing or the results.

Examiner Factors

Assessment of young children requires age-specific understanding and expertise in working with young children (Benner, 2003). In reality, a large number of school psychologists who perform developmental assessments of young children in special education spend the bulk of their time working with school-age children and do not necessarily have much experience working with younger children. Examiners are often required to exaggerate their tone or be playful to get a young child to participate in a testing procedure. They most certainly would need to modify their own behaviors, especially when testing a child with a disability. An examiner's expertise includes a familiarity with behavioral characteristics of different disorders so that possible atypical responses can be understood correctly (Bagnato, Neisworth, & Munson, 1997).

Private professionals or school-assigned examiners who are not familiar with the behavior characteristics of young children with disabilities are sometimes not able to obtain an accurate representation of the child's developmental level. When this is the case, the child's true abilities are neither measured nor reported. Not having a valid picture of the child's strengths and needs results in a waste of intervention time and resources (Benner, 2003).

Greenspan and Meisels (1994) recommend four basic guidelines for testing young children:

1. Avoid forcing children to be separated from their parents or other familiar caregivers at the time of testing.
2. As much as possible, have the child become familiar with the examiner before any testing takes place.
3. Do not limit assessment to the easily measured developmental skills.
4. Use formal testing as only one component among several other components of assessment.

Instrument Factors

One or more standardized instruments might be used during the evaluation process. Standardized measures are usually **norm-referenced tests.** These tests interpret a child's performance in comparison with his or her peers. Mindes (2007) makes several recommendations regarding testing instruments, such as using standardized measures that are valid and reliable, using the measures according to their purpose, following the test directions exactly, and making sure to understand the test statistics and reports.

While these recommendations are sound and should be followed by any examiner who uses the standardized testing as an ongoing assessment instrument, several issues should be kept in mind. First, most norm-referenced tests are based on the performance of typically developing children in a specific age group. It is seldom that the norm group includes children with disabilities (Benner, 2003). Therefore, some of these tests might not be valid for use with children who have severe disabilities. **Validity** of a test refers to the extent to which a test measures the targeted abilities it claims to be measuring.

Many of the batteries available are designed to measure abilities in verbal and hearing children. Administering these tests, for example, to a nonverbal, deaf, or blind child is not recommended. Finally, very few tests are culturally relevant, are translated into different languages, or are available in Braille for children who are blind. Therefore, most standardized tests are valid and reliable only for use with English speakers or children who have grown up in the United States. **Reliability** of a test refers to the dependency of a test, or the accuracy by which test items measure each specific skill for which they are designed.

Bagnato and colleagues (1997) aptly describe the inappropriateness of standardized instruments for young children in the following terms:

> Assessment of infants and preschoolers remains dominated by restrictive methods and styles that place a premium on inauthentic, contrived developmental tasks; that are administered by various professionals in separate sessions using small,

unmotivating toys from boxes or test kits; staged at a table or on the floor in an unnatural setting; observed passively by parents; interpreted by norms based solely on typical children; and used for narrow purposes of classification and eligibility determination. (p. 69)

Child Factors

Familiarity with the examiner, familiarity with the environment in which the testing takes place, time of day and duration of testing are among factors that might influence the result of the assessment. A child who gets anxious in an unfamiliar environment or in the presence of a stranger, or who gets tired during a certain time period might not be able to carry out or complete the tasks required in a test, while in reality the same child is capable of successfully performing that task under other circumstances and in a different environment. Even when the child is willing to participate in a testing session, other intrinsic factors should be kept in mind, such as the child's hunger, mood, lack of rest or sleep, or his or her physical and psychological well-being at the time of testing (Greenspan & Meisels, 1994; Benner, 2003). In an assessment's best scenario, the child is enthusiastic, interested, comfortable, and relaxed during the testing procedure.

Language and Cultural Background

Language and cultural background are other important factors to consider in assessment. IDEA requires that the assessment instruments used should be culturally and racially nondiscriminatory, (Clair et al., 2007; Espinosa, 2005). The law elaborates that the materials used to assess a child should be administered in the native language of the child, so the results are accurate in regard to what the child can and cannot do (Individuals with Disability Education Act, 2004).

Consider Najaf, a 3-year-old boy who along with his family recently moved from Pakistan and is going to be enrolled in a preschool program. Najaf's inability to speak and understand English would present a challenge to his preschool educators. Najaf would certainly have difficulties understanding rules of the classroom and following verbal directions given to him. Without any visual and augmentative communication devices, he would not be able to understand classroom rules and activities, and would probably end up guessing what to do most of the time. If he does not make the right guesses, he might get frustrated, and more than likely, he would end up acting inappropriately under certain circumstances.

Najaf's situation is not unique. Annually, hundreds of children who are not proficient in English enter public and private early childhood education settings. In many instances, teachers suspect cognitive delays, even when these children's lack of successful performance is not due to any real developmental problems—rather to their lack of English language proficiency. It is likely that if Najaf is assessed by a typical standardized instrument measure, he would fail many items in that test. And therefore, although Najaf is developing typically in all areas of development, the testing results may indicate delays in language and cognitive development.

In view of the fact that we might not find an instrument in Urdu, Najaf's native language, or an examiner who would be able to administer it in that language, we might opt to have a translator present to help Najaf understand the testing procedures

| Symptoms of a Disorder or a Cultural Norm? | Text Box 4.1 |

Cherin and her family are from Iran. They moved to the United States more than 15 years ago. Cherin credits herself with having become integrated into the general "American way of life." It wasn't until recently that she understood how culture could "color one's vision of reality."

Cherin has a 3-year-old son, Pouya, whose behaviors and development have been of concern to her and her husband. Pouya has not developed speech and throws temper tantrums frequently. A neurologist examined Pouya and did not make a specific diagnosis. She recommended that Pouya should undergo a diagnostic evaluation. During the evaluation in one of the testing sessions, the psychologist who was playing with Pouya turned to Cherin and said, "Your son does not make eye contact at all."

"Why should that be surprising?" asked Cherin, "In my culture, it is rude to make eye contact. I myself always avoided looking people in the eye, until after I had lived in the United States for several years and learned that in this country giving eye contact was valued, which is exactly opposite of what my culture values."

The psychologist explained that the presence of eye contact in children is a sign of healthy social emotional development. Cherin thought that had this not been pointed out to her, she would never have realized that lack of eye contact would be indicative of a problem, and not a cultural norm.

and tasks. Keep in mind, however, that even with a translator; the test items themselves might not be culturally relevant to the child. Imagine, for example, in one section of the test, Najaf is shown a picture of an igloo, a log, and a house. He is asked to point to items that fit in the same category. Although an igloo is commonly featured in Western cartoons, films, and books for children, this object and its concept might not be something that Najaf has learned growing up in Pakistan. Naturally, he might respond incorrectly to this item and other similar ones that are not culturally relevant to him. In addition, there might be other subtle cultural issues that need to be considered during testing. The story in Text Box 4.1 illustrates another cultural issue related to assessment.

SERVICE DELIVERY

Once the evaluation process has been completed by a team, the eligibility of the child to receive services—whether under Part B or under Part C—will be determined. After it has been determined that a child is eligible to receive services, the intervention team along with the family decide on the type and delivery of services. Type, duration, and delivery of services depend on the severity of the child's disability and the child's present level of functioning in all domains of development. The services a child receives may include:

> Specialized instruction
> Gaining free access to a variety of health and supplemental therapies (e.g., developmental, speech, and occupational therapies)

> Special and adaptive equipment and assistive technology for the child
> Group or individual counseling for parents
> Special education consultation with the general education teachers and para-professionals working with the child
> Modification and adaptation of home and classroom environments
> Transportation services

Critical Thinking Question 4.4   Referring back to the story at the beginning of the chapter, what are Abed's special educational needs, and how are the services he is receiving aligned with his developmental needs?

The Service Delivery Model

For infants and toddlers, a family's preferences, needs, and resources determine the **service delivery model,** or how and at what location services are to be provided for the child and family. IDEA requires that services be delivered to the infants and toddlers in their natural environments. Natural environment is considered synonymous with full inclusion for preschoolers and older children in school settings. Some scholars (Sylva, 2004; Bruder, 2000) believe that the definition of natural environment depends on the family's cultural views and beliefs; therefore, variables such as culture, ethnicity, and diversity of attitudes and beliefs should be considered when deciding on the natural environments. Parents and interventionists decide whether a child is to receive services at home and community settings, in a center-based setting, or in all combinations.

Preschoolers and older children receive similar services to those provided in early intervention, with the exception of family therapy and developmental therapy. They receive special education in place of developmental therapy. In addition, ECSE services are almost always provided to children in public or private school settings. Depending on the severity of the disability and the needs of the child, it is not always possible to educate a preschooler or an older child in an inclusive environment. Some severe disabilities require the child to be educated in a specially equipped and/or

Assistive technology devices are computerized devices that are designed to assist exceptional children with their daily communication needs, as well as their academic learning.

a strictly structured environment. To the degree that is possible, however, young exceptional learners are to be included with their typically developing peers, as well as in the community in which they develop.

Service Coordinators and Case Managers

A service coordinator is a professional, usually a qualified person educated in social work or a related field, who serves families and children under Part C—early intervention programs. Three mechanisms have been identified to facilitate service coordination according to IDEA (Harbin et al., 2004):

1. An individual who is responsible for service coordination
2. A document (IFSP) to guide service coordination
3. A group of policies to facilitate coordination of service delivery between various agencies and programs that might be involved

The relationship that the service coordinator forms with the family and the quality of that relationship is the cornerstone of a successful early intervention program. The service coordinator is responsible for making sure the intervention plan is implemented successfully and that all services are delivered to infants and toddlers and their families. He or she works closely with families and other professionals to ensure accurate and productive communication takes place. The service coordinator's ability to collaborate with other professionals who provide services to infants and toddlers is also an important factor in achieving positive outcomes for children and their families (Harbin et al., 2004).

A case manager in a special education program is the counterpart to the service coordinator in an early intervention program. The case manager coordinates services for preschool age and older children with disabilities (ages 3–21) in a school setting. The difference is that unlike the service coordinator who might conduct a family-centered assessment and provide direct services to the families, the case manager's responsibility solely rests on the provision and coordination of services for the child, and compliance with the provisions of IDEA within the school setting. When working with the families is necessary, the social worker is the person who carries out the responsibility of working with the families directly. In some cases, the responsibilities of the case manager and social worker are combined and carried out by one person, usually the school's counselor.

Itinerant Teachers

Some parents might decide to have their child educated in a private child care facility, preschool, or primary school. Children who are deemed eligible to receive special education and supplemental services may receive state-funded services by one or more professionals who are sent to the child's school by the State Board of Education. These professionals are often called **itinerant teachers** (Dinnebeil, McInerney, & Hale, 2006). Itinerant teachers provide consultation or direct services for the child in the school setting.

In early childhood inclusive settings, itinerant teachers might provide services in a variety of ways. For example, they might provide direct services to children, coach early childhood teachers, provide emotional support and encouragement to classroom staff, or serve as a resource for information (Dinnebeil & McInerney, 2000; Dinnebeil et al., 2006). In an inclusive early childhood classroom, the itinerant teachers help general education teachers and other classroom staff modify the environment to maximize the child's engagement in all areas of the classroom, help the child build pre-academic skills, and adapt instruction to address the IEP objectives (Sadler, 2003).

A UNIVERSAL MODEL OF CURRICULUM FOR INCLUSIVE PROGRAMS

Curriculum has been defined as organized educational experiences of children that are provided by an early childhood program and could take place inside or beyond the classroom and involve educators, family members, and other people in the community (Kostelnik, Soderman, & Whiren, 2004). The National Association for the Education of Young Children (NAEYC) details specific criteria for developmentally appropriate practices in its position statement (National Association for the Education of Young Children, 1996). Briefly, developmentally appropriate practices (DAP) refer to educational practices that are age appropriate and are based on the child's individual developmental abilities.

In general, an appropriate early childhood curriculum model is designed in such a way that it can address the needs of all students regardless of developmental needs. We call such a model a **universal model of curriculum.** This model consists of seven components: philosophical framework, environmental adaptation, professional collaboration, curriculum content, instructional adaptation, child assessment and program evaluation, and partnership with families. Figure 4.3 presents a universal model of curriculum.

Philosophical Framework

A philosophical framework is the heart of the curriculum and program planning. The philosophical framework formulates the curriculum contents, as well as the professional practice. It is the driving force in how educators work with children and

FIGURE 4.3
A Universal Model
of Curriculum

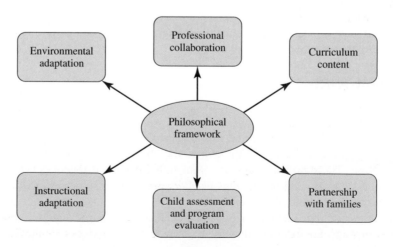

their families. As IDEA (2004) requires that evidence-based and scientific educational methods be used with children with special needs, an appropriate curriculum model is built upon sound theory and empirical evidence. In Chapter 6, philosophical ideas and various theoretical approaches in early childhood special education are described in more detail.

ENVIRONMENTAL ADAPTATION TO SUPPORT INCLUSION

Parents and caregivers of young children frequently make their children's educational placement decisions based on the physical environment of the child care, preschool, or primary school which they visit. There is no doubt that the physical environment could influence both the children's learning and the adult's performance. Furthermore, the emotional atmosphere of an environment is influenced by the way the physical space is arranged.

The physical environment for education and intervention for infants, toddlers, and older children with disabilities is not very different from that which is suitable for typically developing young children. The environment should first and foremost be warm, inviting, friendly, and safe. Children's equipment and furniture should be child-size, and materials and equipment should be at the child's eye level (Kostelnik et al., 2004).

In general, a well-organized and predictable environment is beneficial to all children with a variety of developmental needs. In addition to providing safety and enhancing opportunities for learning for the children, the arrangement of the classroom and equipment should promote inclusion. Klein, Cook, and Richardson-Gibbs (2001) recommend several guidelines for the physical environment that will promote inclusion of all children in early childhood settings:

> Arrangement of materials and the physical environment should accommodate adaptive and supportive equipments, such as wheelchairs or walkers; and furniture should be stable and secure to the floor so that children can safely maneuver and use them.

> The floor plan should minimize clutter and include clearly marked boundaries.

> Activity areas must include specific materials and toys for children with disabilities, such as toys and tools that are both appropriate and motivating for children with specific motor and sensory needs.

Uncluttered rooms are beneficial for all children. They are, however, most beneficial for children with regulatory disorders, like attention deficit hyperactivity disorder (ADHD) and children with visual impairments, since such environments reduce distraction and provide safety.

Consistent Routine

Children learn many skills and cognitive concepts through their daily routines. Infants and toddlers develop their sense of self though caregiver–child routines and interactions (Honig, 2006). It is within their daily routines that children learn about family values, parents' expectations, and cultural practices (Rogoff, 1990).

When routines are consistent and predictable, they provide a road map for the child's behavior. Consistent routines put in place clear parameters for what needs to be done, when, and how. When children have reliable routines and clearly stated expectations from adults, they understand rules that need to be followed within each schedule.

It is not surprising to discover that when a consistent routine and predictable daily schedule are provided for young children in the classroom, teachers spend less time managing and directing children's behavior and more time on instruction, while children spend more time on learning (Pianta, La Paro, & Hamre, 2004). Parents of young children similarly might find limit-setting easier when there are specific routines to be followed during the day. An additional advantage of having clear and consistent routines is that it reduces the level of anxiety in the child and promotes a feeling of emotional safety. Children regularly become fearful and anxious when they have to guess about events and activities that will be coming up during the day. This is particularly true for children with severe cognitive impairments, children with language impairments, and children with autism. Figure 4.4 illustrates a daily home routine for Elizabeth, a 2½-year-old with cerebral palsy who receives early intervention services at home.

Assistive Technology and Other Adaptive Devices

IDEA (2004) requires that the IEP team consider whether a child requires assistive technology devices and services. Assistive devices are used for children who have communication, physical, and cognitive impairments. They have the potential to increase developmental skills, and help with challenges such as behavior, attention, and communication (Parette & Stoner, 2008). Assistive technology equipment consists of a variety of specialty hardware or specialized software, which assists teachers and students in learning, as well as a range of equipment that enables children with physical disability in their mobility and daily functioning. Assistive technology devices that are associated with a child's daily activities, such as exploring the environment, learning, playing, and communicating, should be available as needed to support the child (Judge, Floyd, & Jeffs, 2008). These devices should be available as teachers anticipate the child's needs, so immediate access to meaningful experiences are allowed for children (Judge et al., 2008).

Bausch, Ault, and Hasselbring (2006) have divided the range of assistive technology devices into three categories:

> **Low-tech devices:** Non-electronic devices such as adapted spoon handles, magnifiers, pencil grips, raised line papers, and others
> **Medium-tech devices:** Noncomplicated mechanical devices such as manual wheelchairs, switch-operated toys and appliances, calculators, audio books, and others
> **High-tech devices:** Those devices that incorporate sophisticated electronics or computers, such as speech-recognition programs and electronic communication devices

A variety of educational software is available for children with disabilities. Laureate Learning Systems and Mayer-Johnson are examples of two companies that

Elizabeth's
daily routine

FIGURE 4.4
A Daily Schedule for
Elizabeth's Home
Routine

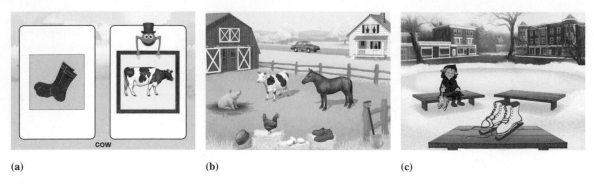

(a)   (b)   (c)

FIGURE 4.5 (a) First Words Software Helps Children with Special Needs Learn Essential Early Vocabulary, (b) Exploring Nouns Software Helps with Early Vocabulary Development in a Full-Scene Environment, (c) Language Links Software Helps with the Assessment and Intervention of Grammar and Grammatical Form

specialize in providing software and augmentative communication devices for children with disabilities (information is provided in the Recommended Resources section at the end of this chapter). Figures 4.5a through 4.5c illustrate some Laureate Learning Systems software used for language development. Boardmaker is software that produces picture symbols (Mayer-Johnson, 1992) to be used for visual schedules, labeling, and visual activities for children with communication difficulties. A variety of specially designed toys are also available for children with specific sensory needs, such as beeping balls, weighted vests, and sensory toys.

PROFESSIONAL TEAM MODELS

A team approach in both assessment and intervention has been recognized by IDEA and is valued in early childhood special education. A team has been defined as a group of people who work together in order to facilitate developmental outcomes and positive change for children and their families (Ogletree, 1999). Different team

Most team models used in special education consist of parents and a variety of professionals from different disciplines.

models are used in special education. Most teams consist of the parents and a variety of professionals from different disciplines.

Ogletree, Bull, Drew, and Lunnen (2001) describe three common team models in assessment and service delivery for children with special needs in the United States: multidisciplinary, interdisciplinary, and transdisciplinary. The major differences between these teams are not related to team membership. Rather, the differences are related to the way the teams are structured and how the team members interact with one another.

The Multidisciplinary Team Model

While the professional members of a **multidisciplinary team** might share space and work alongside each other, they conduct their assessment, intervention, and reporting separate from one another. This model has traditionally been used more often in special education. In a multidisciplinary team, there might be a lack of connection between the members of the team, which suggests that little communication or collaboration might occur between the members (Ogletree et al., 2001). Often different intervention services that are provided for the child might be fragmented and unrelated to one another.

The Interdisciplinary Team Model

In an **interdisciplinary team model,** ongoing communication is central to the interactions of the team. Although team members might provide assessment and services separately, formal channels of communication are established among all team members. Frequent meetings are usually scheduled between all members to share information and to plan and coordinate intervention for the child. In this model, team members rely on one another, and each member (including parents) are equal decision-making partners (Ogletree, 1999; Ogletree et al., 2001).

The Transdisciplinary Team Model

Similar to other teams, a **transdisciplinary team** consists of parents and professionals from a variety of disciplines. Transdisciplinary team members work together across disciplinary boundaries and train each other when needed (Ogletree et al., 2001). The focus of this team is to promote collaboration and partnership between all team members, including the parents. This model respects and recognizes the ecological view of development and acknowledges the interactive and integrated nature of child development. Aside from ongoing communication and information sharing, the model calls for a consensus among all team members on any and every intervention decision regarding the child. Team members respect and accept each other's expertise, including the family knowledge of the child, and come together to serve children and families. In this model, one or two members provide direct services, with input from other team members (Ogletree et al., 2001).

The success of any of the aforementioned models depends on the way team members collaborate with each other to achieve the best outcome for the child. The most productive and successful teams are those whose members respect one another's personal and professional knowledge and agree that each member contributes equally to the team and its accomplishment of any given task. During this process, the priorities of the family and the child take precedence over any other priority the team may deem worthy of pursuing.

IDEA requires that procedures be explained to parents and that informed parental consent must be obtained in every step of this process. Should parents decline to grant consent for some aspect of the intervention, services are provided only in regard to the aspects for which the parents have granted their consent.

CURRICULUM CONTENT

The curriculum content is based on the design of various activities and lesson plans that meet the educational needs of all children. The design of lesson plans depends on the outcomes and objectives stated in each child's IFSP and IEP. Outcomes and objectives provide guides as to what activities to design to meet specific stated goals. See Text Box 4.2 for an example of an activity designed to promote concept development in inclusive classrooms.

Lesson plans appropriate for young exceptional learners should not only address weaknesses in specific developmental domains of the child, but they should be appropriate for any young learner. The manner in which early childhood teachers provide activities, utilize materials, set up centers, and interact with their students is elemental in keeping the interest level of the young children high, keeping them engaged, and encouraging them to further explore and learn (Pianta et al., 2005).

INSTRUCTIONAL ADAPTATION

Whether in inclusive or special education classrooms, in the home or in the community, teachers and developmental therapists are responsible to make appropriate adaptations to carry out the curriculum and instruction in such a way so as to meet the needs of the child. Making appropriate adaptations and modifications based on the child's developmental needs and learning style has been referred to as **differentiated instruction.**

Tomlinson (1999, 2001, 2004) has often been credited with describing the concept of differentiated instruction and elaborating on its principles in special education. She defines differentiated instruction as:

> ensuring that what a student learns, how he/she learns it, and how the student demonstrates what he/she has learned is a match for that students' readiness level, interest, and preferred mode of learning. A readiness match maximizes the chance of appropriate challenge and growth. An interest match heightens motivation. A learning profile match increases the efficiency of learning. Effective differentiation most likely emanates from an ongoing assessment of the student's needs. (Tomlinson, 2004, p. 188)

An Activity to Promote Concept Development   Text Box 4.2

Developmental Domain: Cognitive

Objective: The child will recognize different objects in a group of similar objects.

Materials: Sets of objects or toys with six to eight similar or identical items. Examples: object with similar functions such as Fisher Price house dolls; objects with identical shapes such as blocks of different colors but identical size and shapes; toy vehicles; eating utensils; and so on. Single objects with different functions from those collected earlier for the activity, such as a Fisher Price animal, a small ball, a small musical instrument, a small piece of clothing, and others.

Play Procedure

Teacher and Child Play: Mix and put objects in three different containers. Pick up one container and begin pulling out objects and putting them on the floor. Tell the child you are sorting toys and objects and ask the child to do the same, choosing another container. You could make it fun by having a game of "which one doesn't belong" by taking turns and identifying what doesn't belong.

Small Group Activity: This game could be done in a small group of children as well. Children can play cooperatively, take turns, and identify similar and different objects.

Home Play Routine for Toddlers: Categorize and put identical items—along with one item that is different—in shoe boxes. Attach a picture of a phone and label it "phone box." When you are on the phone, give the child the box, and position yourself where you can observe the child. Watch the child playing with objects. See if the child picks up the item that is different. Watch for signs of recognition of differences. Does the child put the toy is different aside from other items? Does the child look at it or handle it longer?

Children with Visual Impairment: Choose items that have identical textures, shapes, or sounds. Mix with single objects that are different from others.

Children with Severe Motor Impairment: For children who cannot pick up and handle objects, put the identical objects in front of them one at the time. Allow time for the child to observe every item. Introduce the object that is different. Watch for facial signs. Does the child look at the item longer? Does the child look excited? Does the child look at the container you are holding for other objects that should follow?

Therefore, the concept of differentiated instruction refers to the teacher's use of a variety of methods, each addressing the learning needs and ability level of the specific student (George, 2005). For example, looking at the activity example provided in Text Box 4.3 an early childhood teacher working in a classroom with 15 students of different abilities should be able to modify the number of items, the selection of items, and the procedure for students according to their learning needs.

Similarly, the same teacher does not expect all her students to perform based on the same standard. Standards for the assessment of learning for students with special needs should be set based on their ability level and the learning objectives should be stated in the IFSP and IEP. Education scholars have argued that differentiated instruction is a needed component of education today in view of the fact that each student is unique in his or her ability, interest level, readiness level, and learning style, and therefore requires appropriate instructional and assessment strategies (Walker-Dalhouse, et al., 2009; George, 2005; Hoover & Patton, 2005).

Pianta and his colleagues (2004, 2005) have described early childhood teachers who differentiate instruction as high-quality teachers. They contend that a high-quality early childhood educator uses a variety of auditory, visual, tactile, and movement modalities to keep students engaged, and to address the different learning profiles of each child. Such a teacher spends time planning and preparing materials and activities that will help students become engaged. She actively interacts with her pupils, moves around the room to ask children questions, plays with them, provides prompts and support when needed, and, depending on the needs of the child, makes the presentation of basic information interesting to the child through facial expressions, animated movements, and communication of her own interest.

Text Box 4.3   Play-Based Assessment for Erin

Target Area of Development: To promote self-help and independent functioning.

Goal for Erin: Put on and take off her jacket independently.

What Erin Can Do Now: She can take off her jacket, but cannot put it on without an adult's help.

Play Area Setup: Provide a variety of dress-up choices—pullovers, sweaters, large jackets, tonics, and others—in the dramatic play area.

Games: Play and interact with Erin and other children to take turns putting clothes on and looking in the mirror. Ask them who they are pretending to be, and have them guess who each person is.

Providing Prompts: Provide hands-on physical prompts for Erin to put on clothes. Gradually fade prompts over time.

Assessment: Record observation every time Erin plays in the dress-up area.

CHILD ASSESSMENT DURING INTERVENTION

Based on the No Child Left Behind Act of 2001, rigorous academic standards and assessment procedures should be applied and be tied to results (Wright, Wright, & Heath, 2007). Earlier in this chapter, we discussed problems with using standardized testing for young exceptional learners. One way of measuring the progress of children who have disabilities during the intervention is by using **alternative assessment.** Alternative assessment requires the child to create a response in any way possible to indicate his ability level (Wright et al., 2007; Towles-Reeves, Kleinert, & Muhomba, 2009). Alternate assessment is a way to measure the performance of students who are unable to participate in general large-scale assessment, which is usually used by the district or state (Thompson, Quenemoen, Thurlow, & Ysseldyke, 2001; Towles-Reeves et al., 2009; Flowers, Wakeman, & Bowder, 2009). It includes authentic **performance-based assessment.**

Performance-based assessment is a systematic observation of the child's behavior and performance according to a set of previously established criteria (Benner, 2003; Mindes, 2007; Adams & Wolf, 2008). For example, we want Michael, who is nonverbal, to be able to greet the teacher and his peers every morning when he comes in. We set up specific activities for Michael to do this. We give him a greeting card before the circle time, and teach him to give this card to his friends during that activity. We devise a plan so that over time Michael can locate his greeting card every morning and hand it to people whom he would like to greet independently. For us to measure Michael's progress, we have to conduct a systematic observation of his behavior and interactions with his peers. Our criteria for measuring Michael's learning of the concept of greeting might be how Michael uses his greeting card, initiates greetings, and how he responds to his peers and teachers at the time of greeting. Observational data and a collection of the child's work sample are methods by which alternative and performance-based assessments are conducted.

Child-Centered Assessment

An authentic alternative to standardized testing for young exceptional children is a child-centered assessment. In the child-centered assessment, early childhood educators set up activities that are pleasurable and interesting, and promote positive experiences for the child. Mortimer (2004) notes, "assessment should arise naturally from familiar situations in which the child is enabled to show off his or her best as well as the level of need" (p. 171). A natural assessment is more likely to occur in play activities, which the early childhood educators set up, as opposed to during a testing procedure. A **play-based assessment** provides ample opportunity for children to demonstrate their abilities, strengths, and needs during play.

Text Box 4.3 demonstrates an example of a play-based assessment in an early childhood classroom. In a play-based assessment, the early childhood educator establishes specific learning goals and then sets up play activities through which the child will learn to perform goal-oriented tasks. The teacher later measures the child's progress over time (Thurman et al., 2008; Mortimer, 2004). Observation is the vehicle by which the early childhood educator measures and records the child's progress during a play-based assessment.

When setting up play activities, make sure the play areas are safe and adaptable to the children's needs, as well as their physical and cognitive abilities. The following guidelines are useful when preparing areas and equipment for young exceptional children (Mortimer, 2004):

> - Indoor play spaces should be safe, clean, and comfortable.
> - Indoor and outdoor play areas should provide a choice of sheltered and quiet areas, as well as busy and active areas.
> - Tables should be at adjustable heights; chairs and other play equipment should be child-size.
> - Props and puppets should be available in the book/reading area.
> - Toys and materials should be rotated on a regular basis to keep the children's interest high.
> - Open centers for activities should be switched on a weekly or biweekly basis to make sure children have a variety of opportunities for different activities.
> - All areas should be color-coded and labeled with symbols and pictures.
> - Location or containers of materials should be labeled with pictures and words.
> - Symbols and pictorial guides to use equipment or put away toys should be available in computer or other play areas.
> - Short structures should be interspersed through different play activities.
> - Opportunities for small and large group activities should be provided throughout the day.

Observation

Observation is a method by which information is gathered about the child. It is the vehicle by which the performance of the child is assessed. Nilsen (2008) describes observation as seeing each child within the context of a program, framed by the early childhood educator's knowledge of child development. During the observation, the teacher steps back and watches and listens to the children during goal-oriented activities and play. Observation should be tied to intervention (Mindes, 2007). To do so, observations should be recorded in a systematic and periodic way, and results should be studied to inform the IFSP and IEP goal planning and activities. The following outlines several types of record keeping:

> - **Anecdotal notes:** These are notes taken periodically that describe the child's behavior during specific periods of time through his or her daily activities. Teachers commonly use sticky notes, index cards, and pieces of paper attached to a clipboard kept in each play area to record anecdotes of events and the children's behavior. Anecdotal notes may contain detailed conversations among children, between children and teachers, or detailed descriptions of the child's behavior during an activity. See Figure 4.6 for an example of an anecdotal note.
> - **Checklists:** Here, lists of children's names are posted at each center, and the name of each child and duration of the time the child spends at each center is checked off on the list.

Student's name: Usha   Date: 11/4/2010   Activity: Free play

Usha was playing in the kitchen area by herself. She was holding a baby doll closely to her chest, and carrying a baby bottle and a toy pan in her other hand. Holding the baby, she put the pan on the stove, and put the bottle inside the pan. Usha was careful to keep the baby close to her chest. After a few seconds, she took the bottle out, pretended to try the temperature of the bottle's content by putting the bottle in her own mouth. She said, "It is good." Then, she went to the rocking chair, sat in the chair, and began feeding the baby with the bottle she had prepared.

FIGURE 4.6
Anecdotal Note Describing Usha's Behavior during Free Play Time

> **Time and event sampling:** In this system, the child is observed for a short period of time and at intervals, or during a specific activity that is predetermined. A prepared form is usually used by the teacher. The teacher observes the child and records occurrences of a specific behavior or skill during a specified period or activity (Mindes, 2007). Figures 4.7 and 4.8 display examples of time and event sampling.

> **Video recording, audio recording, or digital pictures:** Teachers are increasingly utilizing technology to observe and assess children's learning and progress. Video recording the children's activities and behavior at different intervals provides a productive way of documenting the progress of the children. Videos are especially useful for recording not only the child's behavior but the contextual factors in the environment that might influence a child's learning

Student's name	Date: Oct. 27–Nov. 4	Event: Lunch time
Martin	October 27	H O H
	October 28	H O H
	October 29	Prt. H O H
	November 1	Indpt.
	November 2	Indpt.
	November 3	Indpt.
	November 4	Indpt.

Notes:
H O H = Hand-over-hand prompt provided
Prt. HOH = Hand-over-hand prompt provided through part of the meal only
Indpt. = Child used a spoon independently

FIGURE 4.7
Event Sampling of Eating While Using a Spoon Independently

FIGURE 4.8
Time Sampling of
Three Behaviors
Displayed during
Morning Transition
from Circle Time
to the Small Group
Activity

Student's name: *Jerome*	Crying	Hurting self	Throwing toys
September 15 at 10:00–10:15	1 X	1 X (*Pulling hair*)	4 X
September 16 at 10:00–10:15	1 X	1 X (*Pulling hair*)	2 X
September 17 at 10:00–10:15	1 X	0 X	2 X
September 18 at 10:00–10: 15	1 X	0 X	1 X

and performance. Audio recording is frequently used to measure the children's language abilities over time. Use of digital pictures of activity products or the child at work saves space and also provides an effective way of documenting the child's work over time.

> **Flying notebooks:** Spiral notebooks are commonly used between home and school in ECSE. These notebooks contain summary anecdotes of the child's behavior during school day and at home, and are used for communication between parents and the teacher. Flying notebooks provide an effective way of understanding crucial information about the child in separate environments and under different circumstances. They provide supplemental information for the educators that can aid in their observation and assessment, and can give parents detailed information about their child's learning and progress in school.

> **Rating scales:** Rating scales can be used for measuring progress in behavior and skill learning periodically and over time. Although a number of standardized rating scales are available, simple rating scales designed by the teacher are useful in specifying and measuring the exact behavior and its rate of occurrence. An example of a rating scale is illustrated in Figure 4.9.

Documentation and Portfolios

Portfolios are effective and systematic ways of documenting a child's learning and progress, and are therefore helpful tools in understanding the effects of intervention. They are commonly used for young children and older children with or without disabilities to document alternative and authentic assessment results (Wortham, 2008; Ysseldyke & Algozzine, 2006). Portfolios contain a variety of items: a collection of a child's work samples and products, including artwork and writing samples, pictures, and audio recordings and videos, all of which provide evidence of learning and the child's progress throughout a certain time period (Ysseldyke & Algozzine, 2006). Samples of the child's work should accompany the teacher's summary explanations, anecdotal notes, a summary interview with the child when applicable, a summary interview with the parents, and other descriptive information. Electronic portfolios contain sample audios and videos of the child during both play and lesson activities, as well as digital pictures and the teacher's electronic notes. Documentation of the child's progress allows parents and educators to reflect on the child's progress and to make informed decisions regarding the child's IFSP, IEP, and further intervention planning.

Put a checkmark in the appropriate box.				
Child's behavior	**Not at all**	**Just a little**	**Pretty much**	**Very much**
Gets frustrated during every transition				
Throws tantrum when not able to do a task				
Hits, pulls, or pushes peers when angry				
Bites other children when getting frustrated				
Becomes upset when not chosen to be a line leader				
Withdraws to a corner				
When crying, has a hard time calming down				
Has difficulty sharing				

FIGURE 4.9
Sample Observation Rating Scale

Linking Assessment to Intervention

Assessment should be connected to intervention as a part of an accountability system, to ensure all students are making reasonable progress and to identify whether further improvements need to be made to the system of intervention (Flowers et al., 2009; Towles-Reeves et al., 2009; Thompson et al., 2001; Ysseldyke & Algozzine, 2006). Naturally, the results of an assessment should inform the educators if the child's educational plan and intervention have been effective. The assessment results inform the teacher whether (Ysseldyke & Algozzine, 2006):

> Lessons and activities have been effective
> The instruction and teaching techniques have been appropriate
> If other environmental factors have interfered with the intervention

The result of our assessment should inform us about how to (1) adapt or change activities when necessary; (2) improve our teaching; and (3) modify the environment if necessary (Thompson et al., 2001). When these components are not connected, children learn scattered and unrelated skills, and hence we are not able to establish solid foundations to build further learning.

PROGRAM EVALUATION

Program evaluation consists of gathering information regarding the effectiveness of intervention for an individual child as well as groups of children enrolled in the program. Program evaluation needs to be flexible in order to assess the effectiveness of intervention in a variety of service delivery models: home-based, center-based, as well as school-based programs (Bowe, 2007).

Programs might be evaluated in two ways: through **formative evaluation** or by **summative evaluation** (Mindes, 2007). In a formative evaluation, the components of a program are studied—for example, how many families and children are enrolled in the program, what kind of services are offered, how services are provided, and what evidence there is of children's progress in any given situation (Bowe, 2007). A formative evaluation occurs during the operation of a program. A summative evaluation, on the other hand, looks at the results of the intervention after a certain period of time. Summative evaluations may occur annually (Bowe, 2007). Information collected during formative assessments might be compiled to examine if children enrolled in the program have made progress, and if services have consistently and satisfactorily been delivered.

Program effectiveness is determined by examination of the outcomes of the program against the program's stated goals. Some programs cite family satisfaction as a measure of their success. Family satisfaction by itself is not an appropriate measure of program effectiveness, however, since a program might have a high parent satisfaction rate without having necessarily demonstrated that children enrolled in the program have made appropriate progress (Bowe, 2007). Therefore, a program evaluation should combine different quantitative and qualitative information, including a demonstration of the children's progress to determine the program's effectiveness.

PARTNERSHIP WITH FAMILIES

The effectiveness of family involvement depends on teachers' beliefs and the school's overall philosophy regarding the role of parents in their child's education. The teacher's beliefs about how and to what extent families should be involved in the education of their child are influenced by their own sociocultural backgrounds, personal experiences, and by the overall school culture (Souto-Manning & Swick, 2006).

Catchphrases such as "read to your child," or "supervise your child's homework," are part of an overall traditional paradigm that has dominated many schools and opinions of most teachers (Turnbull & Turnbull, 2002; Souto-Manning & Swick, 2006). This is a deficit-based paradigm in which parents are viewed as lacking in certain needed skills. In this model, involvement or partnership is defined in certain ways, and parents are supposed to follow specific points of professional advice in regard to their children.

The field of special education has consciously tried to move away from this old model by promoting the concept of family–professional partnership in its true sense (described in Chapter 3). Here we add that because partnership is a new model, a commonly used set of guidelines by schools and professionals is lacking in the field. To some degree, establishing a model of parent–professional partnership is a work in progress. The best place to start is by opening a dialogue with coworkers and team members in schools, and to begin thinking about specific guidelines regarding working with families of children with disabilities, which could be supported by the school (Nelson, Summers, & Turnbull, 2004). Any guidelines that might be set for working with parents should be driven from various informal and formal conversations with parents regarding how they define partnership and school involvement, and how schools should help them maintain their working relationship with teachers and other school professionals.

SUMMARY

A child who has a disability must have that disability identified first in order to be deemed eligible to receive early intervention and special education services. The identification process usually occurs through screening and referrals. Evaluation and service delivery are complex processes, which consist of conducting a variety of assessment procedures to establish a diagnosis and determine the specific therapeutic and educational needs of the child.

After a child is recognized as eligible to receive services by a team of professionals, the interventionists and the parents decide on an appropriate range of services, on the location where the services should be delivered, and on an educational plan for the child. An effective intervention plan for the child consists of a universal model of curriculum, which highlights the instructional adaptations and environmental modifications, the curriculum content, the assessment and program evaluation, and the professional collaboration and partnership with families.

Review Questions

1. What are the steps of identification?
2. What are the components of the evaluation process?
3. What are important factors that must be considered in the assessment of exceptional children?
4. Explain the examiner, child, and instrument factors. List areas where these factors might interact with one another.
5. What is the service delivery model?
6. What is the role of the service coordinator?
7. What is a curriculum and what are some components of a universal curriculum?
8. What is differentiated instruction?
9. What is a child-centered assessment?
10. Why is program evaluation important?

Out-of-Class Activities

1. Conduct Internet research to find what lead agency provides early intervention in your state.
2. Through your Internet search, identify the process of identification and evaluation in your state.
3. Identify and examine two preschool or infant/toddler screening tools. Write a report evaluating these two instruments.
4. Contact one early intervention program and interview a service coordinator. Request a detailed description of the service coordinator's job.
5. Contact a public school that provides ECSE, and ask for an interview with the special education case manager. Request a detailed description of the case manager's duties.
6. Compare your findings from the interviews with the case manager and service coordinator.

Recommended Resources

Child Find: U.S. Office of Special Education Programs
http://www.childfindidea.org/

National Center on Educational Outcomes—information on testing children with disabilities
http://www.education.umn.edu

National Information Dissemination Center for Children and Youth with Disabilities (NICHCY)
P.O. Box 1492
Washington, DC 20013

Phone: 800-695-0285
Fax: 202-884-8441
nichy@aed.org
http://www.nichy.org

NECTAC: National Early Childhood Technical Assistance Center
http://www.nectac.org/default.asp

Office of Special Education Programs
http://www.ed.gov/offices/OSERS/OSEP

Specialty software and assistive technology devices:

Do2Learn: Clipart for Picture Exchange Communication System
http://www.dotolearn.com/

Mayer-Johnson, LLC
2100 Wharton Street
Pittsburgh, PA 15203
Phone: 858-550-0084
Fax: 858-550-0449

Email: mayerj@mayer-johnson.com
http://www.mayer-johnson.com/

Specialty software for children with language impairments and children with autism:

Laureate Learning Systems, Inc.
110 East Spring Street
Winooski, VT 05404
http://www.laureatelearning.com

View the Online Resources available to accompany this text by visiting http://www.mhhe.com/bayat1e.

References

Adams, S., & Wolf, K. (2008). Strengthening the preparation of early childhood teacher candidates through performance-based assessment. *Journal of Early Childhood Teacher Education, 29,* 6–29.

Bagnato, S. J., Neisworth, J. T., & Munson, S. M. (1997). *LINKing: Assessment and early intervention.* Baltimore: Paul H. Brookes.

Bailey, D., Scarborough, A., Hebbeler, K., Spiker, D., & Mallik, S. (2004). *Family outcomes at the end of early intervention.* Menlo Park, CA: SRI International. Retrieved March 13, 2008, from http://www.sri.com/neils/pdfs/FamilyOutcomesReport_011405.pdf

Bausch, M. E., Ault, J. J., & Hasselbring, T. S. (2006). *Assistive technology planner: From IEP consideration to classroom implementation.* Lexington, KY: National Assistive Technology Research Institute.

Benner, S. (2003). *Assessment of young children with special needs.* Clifton Park, NY: Thomson, Delmar Learning.

Bowe, F. G. (2007). *Early childhood special education: Birth to eight.* Clifton Park, NY: Thomson, Delmar Learning.

Brigance, A. H. (1997). *Brigance K & 1 screen-revised.* North Billerica, MA: Curriculum Associates.

Brigance, A. H. (1998). *Brigance preschool screen.* North Billerica, MA: Curriculum Associates.

Bronfenbrenner, U. (1979). *The ecology of human development: Experiments by nature and design.* Cambridge: Harvard University Press.

Brown, E. J., & Sorensen, J. (2007). *An overview of early intervention.* Austin, TX: Pro-ed.

Bruder, M. B. (2000). Family-centered early intervention: Clarifying out values for the new millennium. *Topics in Early Childhood Special Education, 20*(2), 105–115.

Clair, E. B., Church, R. P., & Batshaw, M. L. (2007). Special education services. In M. L. Batshaw, L. Pellegrino, & N. J., Roizen (Eds.), *Children with disabilities* (6th ed., pp. 523–538). Baltimore: Paul H. Brookes.

Dinnebeil, L., & McInerney, W. (2000). Supporting inclusion in community-based settings: The role of the "Tuesday morning teacher." *Young Exceptional Children, 4*(1), 19–26.

Dinnebeil, L., McInerney, W., & Hale, L. (2006). Understanding the roles and responsibilities of itinerant ECSE teachers through Delphi research. *Topics in Early Childhood Special Education, 26*(3), 153–166.

Espinosa, L. (2005). Curriculum and assessment considerations for young children from culturally, linguistically, and economically diverse background. *Psychology in Schools, 42*(8), 837–853.

Flowers, C., Wakeman, S., & Bowder, D. (2009). Links for academic learning (LAL): A conceptual model for investigating alignment of alternate assessments based on alternate achievement standards. *Educational Measurement: Issues & Practice, 28*(5), 25–37.

Frankenburg, W. K., & Dodds, J. B. (1990). *Denver-II screening manual.* Denver, CO: Denver Developmental Materials.

George, P. (2005). A rationale for differentiating instruction in the regular classroom. *Theory to Practice, 44*(3), 185–193.

Goldberg-Hamblin, S., Singer, J., Singer, G. H., & Denney, M. K. (2007). Early intervention in neonatal nurseries: The promising practice of developmental care. *Infants & Young Children, 20*(2), 163–171.

Greenspan, S. I., & Meisels, S. (1994). Toward a new vision for the developmental assessment of infants and young children. *Zero to Three, 14,* 1–8.

Harbin, G. L., Burder, M. B., Adams, C., Mazzarella, C., Whitbread, K., Gabbard, G., et al. (2004). Early intervention service coordination policies: National policy infrastructure. *Topics in Early Childhood Special Education, 24*(2), 89–97.

Honig, A. S. (2006). Setting the stage for learning. *Early Childhood Today, 21*(1), 24–25.

Hoover, J. J., & Patton, J. R. (2005). Differentiating curriculum and instruction for English-language learners with special needs. *Intervention in School and Clinic, 40*(4), 231–235. Retrieved March 13, 2008, from http://www.sri.com/neils/pdfs/FamilyOutcomesReport_011405.pdf

Individuals with Disability Education Act. (2004). Retrieved June 18, 2007, from http://frwebgate .access.gpo.gov/cgi-bin/getdoc.cgi?dbname= 108_cong_public_laws&docid=f:publ446.108

Jackson, B. J., & Needelman, H. (2007). Building a system of Child Find through a 3-tiered model of follow up. *Infants and Young Children, 20*(3), 255–263.

Judge, S., Floyd, K., & Jeffs, T. (2008). Using an assistive technology toolkit to promote inclusion. *Early Childhood Education Journal, 36,* 121–126.

Klein, M. D., Cook, R. E., & Richardson-Gibbs, A. M. (2001). *Strategies for including children with special needs in early childhood settings.* Albany, NY: Thomson, Delmar Learning.

Kostelnik, M. J., Soderman, A. K., & Whiren, A. P. (2004). *Developmentally appropriate curriculum: Best practices in early childhood education.* Upper Saddle River, NJ: Pearson.

Mardell-Czudnowski, C., & Goldenberg, D. S. (1998). *Developmental indicators for the assessment of learning* (3rd ed.). Circle Pines, MN: American Guidance Service.

Mayer-Johnson, R. (1992). *The picture communication symbols (Book I–III).* Solana Beach, CA: Mayer-Johnson.

Mindes, G. (2007). *Assessing young children* (3rd ed.). Upper Saddle River, NJ: Pearson.

Mortimer, H. (2004). Hearing children's voices in the early years, *Support for Learning, 19*(4), 169–174.

National Association for the Education of Young Children. (1996). *Developmentally appropriate practices in early childhood programs serving children from birth through age 8: A position statement of the National Association for the Education of Young Children.* Washington, DC: NAYEC. Retrieved June 9, 2007, from http://www.naeyc.org/about/positions/pdf/psdap98.pdf

Neisworth, J. T., & Bagnato, S. J. (2005). DEC recommended practices: Assessment. In S. Sandall, M. L. Hemmeter, B. J. Smith, & M. E. McLean. (Eds.), *DEC Recommended practices: A comprehensive guide for practical application in early intervention/early childhood special education* (pp. 45–50). Missoula, MT: Division for Early Childhood.

Nelson, L. G. L., Summers, J. A., & Turnbull, A. P. (2004). Boundaries in family professional relationships: Implications for special education. *Remedial and Special Education, 25,* 135–165.

Nilsen, B. A. (2008). *Observation and assessment.* New York: Thomson, Delmar Learning.

Ogletree, B. T. (1999). Introduction to teaming. In B. T. Ogletree, M. A. Fischer, & J. B. Schulz (Eds.), *Bridging the family–professional gap: Facilitating interdisciplinary services for children with disabilities* (pp. 3–11). Springfield, IL: Thomas.

Ogletree, B. T., Bull, J., Drew, B., & Lunnen, K. Y. (2001). Team-based service delivery for students with disabilities: Practice options and guidelines for success. *Intervention in School and Clinic, 36*(3), 138–145.

Parette, H., & Stoner, J. (2008). Benefits of assistive technology user groups for early childhood education professionals. *Early Childhood Education Journal, 35,* 313–319.

Pellegrino, J. E. (2007). Newborn Screening: Opportunities for prevention of developmental disabilities. In M. L. Batshaw, L. Pellegrino, & N. J., Roizen (Eds.), *Children with disabilities* (6th ed., pp. 97–106). Baltimore: Paul H. Brookes.

Pianta, R. C., Howes, M., Burchinal, D., Bryant, R., Clifford, D., Early, D., et al. (2005). Features of prekindergarten programs, classrooms, and teachers: Do they predict observed classroom quality and child–teacher interactions? *Applied Developmental Science, 9*(3), 144–159.

Pianta, R. C., La Paro, K. M., & Hamre, B. K. (2004). *Classroom Assessment Scoring System [CLASS].* Unpublished measure, University of Virginia.

Ringwalt, S. (2008). *Developmental screening and assessment of instruments with an emphasis on social and emotional development for young children ages birth through 5.* Chapel Hill: The University of North Carolina, FPG Child Development Institute, National Early Childhood Technical Assistance Center.

Rogoff, B. (1990). *Apprenticeship in thinking: Cognitive development in social context.* Oxford, UK: Oxford University.

Sadler, F. H. (2003). The itinerant special education teacher in the early childhood classroom. *Teaching Exceptional Children, 35*(3), 8–15.

Sandall, S. Hemmeter, M. L., Smith, B. J., & McLean, M. E. (2005). *DEC Recommended practices: A comprehensive guide for practical application in early intervention/early childhood special education.* Missoula, MT: Division for Early Childhood.

Souto-Manning, M., & Swick, K. J. (2006). Teachers' beliefs about parent and family involvement: Rethinking our family involvement paradigm. *Early Childhood Education Journal, 34*(2), 187–193.

Sylva, J. A. (2004). Issues in early intervention: The impact of cultural diversity on service delivery in natural environments. *Multicultural education, 13*(2), 26–29.

Thompson, S. J., Quenemoen, R. F., Thurlow, M. L., & Ysseldyke, J. E. (2001). *Alternate assessments for students with disabilities.* Thousand Oaks, CA: A joint publication of the Council of Exceptional Children & Corwin Press, Inc.

Tomlinson, C. A. (1999). *Differentiated classroom: Responding to the needs of all learners.* Alexandria, VA: Association for Supervision and Curriculum Development.

Tomlinson, C. A. (2001). *The differentiated classroom: Responding to the needs of all learners.* Alexandria, VA: Association for Supervision and Curriculum Development.

Tomlinson, C. A. (2004). Sharing responsibility for differentiating instruction. *Roeper Review, 26*(4), 188–189.

Torrance, H., & Pryor, J. (1998). *Investigating formative assessment: Teaching and learning in the classroom.* Buckingham, UK: Open University Press.

Towles-Reeves, E., Kleinert, H., & Muhomba, M. (2009). Alternate assessment: Have you learned anything new? *Council for Exceptional Children, 75*(2), 233–252.

Thurman, S., & McGrath, M. (2008). Environmentally based assessment practices: Viable alternatives to standardized assessment for assessing emergent literacy skills in young children. *Reading and Writing Quarterly, 24,* 7–24.

Turnbull, A. P., & Turnbull, H. R. (2002). From the old to the new paradigm of disability and families: Research to enhance family quality of life outcomes. In J. L. Paul, C. D. Lavely, A. Cranston-Gingras, & E. L. Taylor (Eds.), *Rethinking professional issues in special education* (pp. 83–119). Westport, CT: Ablex Publishing.

Walker-Dalhouse, D., Risko, V., Esworthy, C., Grasley, E., Kaisler, G., & McIlvan, D., et al. (2009). Crossing boundaries and initiating conversations about RTI: Understanding and applying differentiated classroom instruction. *The Reading Teacher, 63*(1), 84–87.

Wilson, L. L., Mott, D. W., & Batman, D. (2004). The asset-based context matrix: A tool for assessing children's learning opportunities and participation in natural environments. *Topics in Early Childhood Special Education, 24*(2), 110–120.

Wortham, S. C. (2008). *Assessment in early childhood education* (5th ed.). Upper Saddle River, NJ: Pearson.

Wright, P. W., Wright, P. D., & Heath, S. W. (2007). *Wrights law: No child left behind.* Hartfield, VA: Harbor House Law Press.

Ysseldyke, J., & Algozzine, B. (2006). *Effective assessment for students with special needs: A practical guide for every teacher.* Thousand Oaks, CA: Corwin Press.

Chapter 5

Developing IFSP and IEP

Objectives

Upon completion of this chapter, you should be able to:

> Understand the process of family involvement in developing IEP and IFSP.
> List and describe the components and content of IFSP.
> List and describe the components and content of IEP.
> Understand issues in successful partnership among professionals.

Key Terms

annual goals (164)   measurable (165)   observable (165)

child advocate (151)   objectives (164)   paraprofessionals (171)

IFSP outcomes (152)

Reflection Questions

Before reading this chapter, answer the following questions to reflect upon your personal opinions and beliefs that are pertinent to early childhood special education.

1. In your opinion, what are some behaviors that might be indicative of cultural competence?

2. Why do you think parents are considered members of the IFSP and IEP team?

3. What are your ideas about working within a team of professionals in an early childhood inclusive classroom?

A Difficult Transition

Corey is a 4-year-old boy who was diagnosed with developmental delays 2 years ago. At the time, Ms. Vincent, Corey's teacher, had done a routine developmental screening. After talking with Corey's mother, she referred Corey to the state Birth to Three (early intervention) program for further evaluation. Corey was identified as having developmental delays and was deemed eligible to receive early intervention services that would help enhance his development.

Corey's single mother, Janet, had a positive experience with her local early intervention agency. Lisa was the early intervention service coordinator assigned to work with Janet. Lisa was herself the mother of a girl with Down syndrome. She understood Janet's fears and hopes regarding Corey's development. She was sensitive to the fact that Janet was a young single mother who had small and limited financial resources. Lisa was also mindful that Janet's family lived in Poland, and she did not have any close family members whom she could count on to provide support.

Lisa worked closely with Janet to understand the daily issues Janet and Corey faced. Together with Janet, Lisa identified what Janet considered immediate needs and priorities. She helped Janet articulate a long-term vision for Corey and herself as a family. Corey's early intervention team along with Janet wrote an Individual Family Service Plan (IFSP) for Corey, which was based on the needs and priorities that Janet felt were important.

Janet and Corey's intervention team worked successfully during the 18 months that Corey received early intervention services to achieve the outcomes stated in his IFSP. The team supported Janet in learning and discovering various ways in which she could play and interact with Corey to help him along with his development. Lisa helped Janet identify several state-funded resources in the community to help care for Corey when she needed to work extra hours. She also introduced Janet to a parent support group. Corey made notable progress in all areas of development, and Janet found a new network of friends among parents of children with special needs.

Corey transitioned into a special education preschool program in a public school close to their home after his third birthday. Janet's experience with the special education team was dissimilar to her experience with the professionals in the early intervention program. During Corey's first IEP (Individualized Education Plan) meeting, Corey's preschool teacher, Ms. Buck, seemed to be distant and formal. The school's case manager seemed mechanical and more determined to complete the paperwork than to establish a relationship with Janet. The speech therapist was rushed, and the principal, although polite and warm, left the meeting to attend to an important matter after the introductions.

In general, although the special education team focused on Corey and his educational needs, they did not discuss Janet's family resources and priorities, as had been the case in the IFSP process. Janet did not understand some of the language being used and felt intimidated during the first meeting. Her unease grew as Ms. Buck and the speech therapist outlined a series of goals that dealt with Corey performing independent tasks. Janet knew that Corey would have a difficult time learning some of the tasks mentioned on his IEP, but despite her reservations, she refrained from stating her concerns.

Janet's further encounters with Ms. Buck were not encouraging. Although Janet and Ms. Buck communicated about Corey's activities at home and in school, they seemed to be constantly at odds with each other about what types of developmental activities were appropriate for Corey. Janet felt Ms. Buck expected too much of Corey, and pushed him too hard. Ms. Buck believed that Corey was capable of learning many independent and pre-academic skills, which his mother did not see Corey capable of performing.

Corey did not seem to be happy in his new preschool, and cried most mornings, clinging to Janet before being put on the school bus. Janet called for a second IEP meeting after 6 months. At the beginning of the second meeting, Janet opposed all developmental goals that had been written by Ms. Buck previously. She explained that Corey was not happy and did not seem to have made any progress during the past months in the preschool. She believed Corey's social and emotional well-being was being ignored. Ms. Buck, on the other hand, believed Corey had made great progress, and was beginning to adjust to the structured environment of the preschool. Eventually, with the case manager's mediation, Ms. Buck and Janet came to a tentative agreement on some specific objectives, which were written in the IEP.

Eventually, Janet came to believe that Corey was beginning to make progress. However, she continued to have serious reservations about Corey's placement throughout the end of the school year. She was feeling fearful of what the future of Corey's education might look like, how she might continue to deal with a group of people who seemed to be apathetic to her views, and insensitive to Corey's needs.

INTRODUCTION

In reading the story, we could only hope that in time and given a chance, Corey's mother, Janet, and Ms. Buck would resolve their differences of opinion and would go on to work together in partnership, along with the other special education team members in Corey's preschool. Janet formed certain expectations about professionals, based on her previous positive experiences with the early intervention (EI) team, but finds her expectations unrealized as she interacts with the new special education team members. Although differences between Janet and the new special education team might be resolved in due time, her previous experience with the early intervention program will remain different as compared to her experience with the special education preschool. This is due to a fundamental difference between early intervention and special education systems. While the former puts an emphasis on working with families, the latter targets the education and academic success of the child.

Transition to special education preschool is a signal for movement to a different phase of life for children and parents. Like any transition, moving from one phase to another phase of life requires a period of adjustment and change. The child's transition from infancy and the toddler years to preschool indicates beginning a period of skill learning, which will hopefully prepare him for future academic success and independence.

In preschool, a new team with similar but separate expertise will begin working with the child and with the parents. Naturally, it takes time for the members of the special education team and parents to get to know each other and learn to work in partnership. Initial disagreements are common. When parents and the intervention team are continuously at odds with one another, there are inevitable negative consequences both emotionally and educationally for the child. On the other hand, when parents and educators partner to achieve the same goal together, the end result is always positive for the child.

> **Critical Thinking Question 5.1**   Referring to the story at the beginning of the chapter, what are some possible consequences of a conflict between parents and the special education team on the education of the child?

In the previous chapter, we examined identification, evaluation, and the intervention process. In this chapter, we will look at components of IFSPs and IEPs, and the ways that parents, therapists, and special educators can work successfully with one another to develop productive educational goals and outcomes. We will see how early childhood educators may set out to achieve these goals in partnership with parents and other family members.

FAMILY INVOLVEMENT IN THE IFSP AND THE IEP PROCESS

Family is an integral part of the educational planning for a child in EI and in special education. Families' rights and needs have been and continue to be of special interest and attention in the education of children with disabilities. The Individuals with

Disabilities Education Act (IDEA) emphasizes the active involvement of families in all aspects of the early intervention and special education processes. This includes referral, evaluation, developing IFSP or IEP for the child, annual re-evaluation, and exiting the program.

Working with Diverse Families

Based on the U.S. Census Bureau report in 2007, the minority population exceeds 100 million people in the United States, which is about one in every three residents (U.S. Census Bureau, 2007). The minority population is comprised of Hispanics, African Americans, Asians, the Inuit and Native Americans, and Native Hawaiians and other Pacific Islanders. Recall our discussions about family diversity and disability in other cultures in Chapter 3. We looked at dissimilar ways in which families from other ethnic backgrounds might view a disability from what might be considered a mainstream view. The increase in the diverse population of the United States is naturally reflected in the population of families of exceptional children in this country.

Critical Thinking Question 5.2   Referring to the story at the start of the chapter, do you consider Lisa culturally competent? Why or why not?

This same diversity, however, might not be reflected in the population of early childhood or early intervention graduates (Lynch & Hanson, 1992). When cultural backgrounds of early interventionists and special educators differ from those of the family members they work with, disagreements may occur on different aspects of intervention, including the plan of intervention and how to implement it (Stone, 2005).

As mentioned in Chapter 3, early childhood educators and interventionists must have *cultural competence* in order to work with families successfully. Cultural competence involves not only having a basic knowledge of other cultures, but being aware of one's own beliefs and cultural biases. It also includes understanding and respecting the basic values each family might hold and wish acknowledged. Cultural competence of the interventionist depends on his or her ability to reserve judgment about what is right and wrong, and to refuse to assign value to what is better or worse (Anderson & Fenichel, 1989).

Critical Thinking Question 5.3   Referring to the story at the beginning of the chapter, to what extent does Lisa's professional behavior toward Janet contribute to the success of the early intervention program for Corey?

To emphasize the importance of understanding families and working in partnership with them does not mean to downplay the role of the professionals' knowledge and child expertise. Similarly, one should be mindful of not losing sight of helping children. In fact, Hanson and Lynch (2004) mention that in the 1980s and 1990s, a great emphasis on family-centered practices frequently resulted in misunderstandings since some early intervention programs shifted their intervention focus completely from the child to the family.

Both families and the professionals should be aware that such a misunderstanding is neither beneficial to the child nor productive to the family. The central goal of early childhood intervention and special education is enhancement of the child's growth and development. The well-being of the family is important in providing the right environment for the child and other family members. Professionals and families in partnership with one another become the vehicle by which the child and the family arrive at this goal. Text Box 5.1 displays some myths and misunderstandings in early intervention as described by Hanson and Lynch (2004).

Critical Thinking Question 5.4   Referring to the story at the beginning of the chapter, what evidence suggests that a partnership existed between Janet and Corey's early intervention team?

Text Box 5.1   Myths about Families and Professionals in Early Intervention

1. **The Professionals' role is diminishing:** Professionals' knowledge of child development, their training in teaching and learning, and specific techniques should complement the family's knowledge and understanding of their own child. A partnership between families and professionals should not diminish the professionals' role. It should enhance it.
2. **Only family concerns are important:** Addressing the family's priorities does not mean that the professionals' concerns about the child should be pushed away. On the contrary, any issue of concern to the interventionist should be openly communicated to the family so the family can make an informed decision regarding their child's intervention. Open communication is the central principle of parent–professional partnership.
3. **Formal supports are bad:** Informal support—such as a friendship network, family members, or a faith community—has been known to be more effective in providing support for the family than the formal support (classes, workshops, and support groups). This, however, does not mean that families do not benefit from formal support programs. Such programs often provide information about resources in the community that might not be available through an informal support network.
4. **Only professionals must change:** For the parent–professional partnership to work, all parties involved in the intervention for the child should change when necessary. It is not realistic to expect only professionals to change. For the partnership to work, the perception of policy makers, community leaders, families, and professionals should change. Otherwise, a fragmented system will result, which provides little opportunity for collaboration.

Source: Hanson, M. J. & Lynch, E. W. (2004). *Understanding families: Approaches to diversity, disability, and risk.* Baltimore: Paul H. Brookes.

REQUIRED LEGAL DOCUMENTS (IFSP AND IEP)

IDEA requires an IFSP (Individual Family Service Plan) for infants and toddlers and their families. An IEP (Individualized Education Plan) is required by IDEA for children 3 years of age and older. Both IFSP and IEP are legal documents that are required by IDEA to be developed by teams that include special educators or general education teachers, related service providers (service coordinator, case manager, and therapists), family members (parents or legal guardians), and the child when appropriate. Both documents require that specific developmental/educational needs of the child and specific instructional adaptation and environmental/physical modifications be articulated (Valentine, 2007; Bruder, 2000). They are both designed and written annually to monitor the progress and effectiveness of intervention. Similarities and differences between the IEP and IFSP are outlined in Table 5.1.

Parents' Rights

The Individuals with Disabilities Education Act (IDEA) includes provisions for the protection of children's and parents' rights. IDEA establishes due-process rights or procedural safeguards to protect the rights of parents and children, to maximize equal educational opportunities, and to ensure parental involvement

TABLE 5.1   IFSP and IEP: Similarities and Differences

IFSP (Requirements Articulated under Part C of IDEA)	IEP (Requirements Articulated under Part B of IDEA)
➢ Addresses the developmental needs of the infants and toddlers (birth–3 years) and their families	➢ Addresses the developmental and educational needs of children (3–21)
➢ Articulates outcomes targeted for the family along with the child	➢ Articulates goals and objective targeted for the student
➢ Justification and provision of services carried out in the natural environment are articulated	➢ Justification and explanations for LRE (Least Restrictive Environment), or inclusion of the student in general education are articulated
➢ The process is carried out and supervised by a service coordinator	➢ The process is coordinated by a case manager
➢ Includes a transition plan to a preschool or a kindergarten (IDEA 2004 allows parents to have their children remain in an early intervention program until the child is ready to transition to kindergarten)	➢ Includes two transition plans, one to a high school, and one from the high school to a community employment setting
➢ Annual review is to be carried out by the service coordinator, the service providers, and the parents	➢ Annual review is to be carried out by the case manager, special educators and therapists, and the parents
➢ Includes activities undertaken with multiple agencies beyond the scope of Part C	➢ When warranted, includes a Behavior Intervention Plan (BIP)
➢ Names a service coordinator to help the family during the process of early intervention	

The IFSP and IEP require that specific developmental/ educational needs of the child and particular instructional adaptations and environmental/ physical modifications be articulated.

(Valentine, 2007; Wang, Mannan, Poston, Turnbull, & Summers, 2004). Under IDEA, parents or guardians of children with disabilities have the following rights (Wright & Wright, 2007; Ysseldyke & Algozzine, 2006):

> **The right to informed parental consent:** Parents are to be fully informed of all information (in their native language) about evaluation or intervention activities for which parental permission is sought. Parental consent is voluntary and may be withdrawn at any time without risking future participation in early intervention or special education. No activities (assessment or intervention) are to be carried out without a parent's written consent.

> **The right to a written prior notice and participation in IFSP and IEP:** Parents are to be given a written announcement (in the parents' native language) within a reasonable time in advance of any action that requires parental consent (including IFSP and IEP meetings, changes or modifications to the current intervention plan, assessments, etc.). Parents have a right to participate in IFSP and IEP meetings.

> **The right to decline services:** Parents have the right to accept or decline any early intervention or special education services.

> **The right to a multidisciplinary evaluation and an assessment of the child:** Parents have the right to a multidisciplinary evaluation of their child to determine eligibility within 45 days of the referral to an early intervention or special education program. All assessment and test results must be explained to all parents in their native language.

> **The right to review records:** Parents have the right to review their child's confidential records, to which only parents and authorized professionals may have access.

> **The right to bring a filed complaint:** Parents have the right to file a complaint with their local lead agency against the early intervention program if they believe the program has failed to provide appropriate services.

> > **The right to mediation:** Parents have the right to disagree with the services provided to their child and can petition for mediation to resolve their conflict

with the service providers. Mediation is led by an impartial party that tries to help parents and service providers resolve their conflict informally.

> **The right to a due process hearing:** Parents have the right to petition for a formal process that allows their conflict to be resolved within a formal court hearing.

Some scholars (Wang et al., 2004; Turnbull, Turbiville, & Turnbull, 2000) have articulated that federal policy relating to parents' rights establishes that not only are families affected by the service delivery system, but they are also expected to affect the system as an accountability mechanism (for example, by becoming advocates for their children and themselves).

Historically, parents who served as their children's advocates have been the ones who have laid the legislative foundations for passage of IDEA (Turnbull & Turnbull, 1996; Summers, Behr, & Turnbull, 1988). In addition, preparing parents to advocate for their children has been identified as one of the goals the early intervention programs should achieve (Bailey et al., 1988; Wang et al., 2004). Not all parents come prepared with skills to advocate for their children. When parents do not feel comfortable participating in an IFSP meeting or any other related activity alone, they have the right to bring other family members or a **child advocate** who might help them during the meeting.

EARLY INTERVENTION AND IFSP

We must emphasize that the essential difference between the IFSP and IEP is that IFSP focuses on the family along with the child, while IEP targets the child's educational needs only. The Individual Family Service Plan is a specific plan of action written with the help of parents to identify the family's and the child's needs so priorities can be set for the early intervention services and their delivery to parents and children.

As a process, IFSP begins with a family directed assessment. In the previous chapter, we described the family directed assessment as gathering information about the family's resources, priorities, concerns, and the developmental needs of the child.

Part C of IDEA clearly acknowledges the influence of the family in the child's development by mandating an assessment of the family's needs and resources as the first step in the intervention planning. Keeping in mind that every family perceives and defines its own resources and needs differently from what we as interventionists might consider strengths and needs, it is important that all aspects of assessment should involve the family members.

After the evaluation process has been completed and the child has been found eligible to receive services, families and professionals meet together to design an intervention plan for the child. The initial IFSP meeting is the first opportunity for both parents and professionals to collaborate in the IFSP development. Several individuals might participate in this meeting. Table 5.2 lists possible participants in an IFSP meeting. Individuals working together to develop an IFSP are considered to be the IFSP team members.

TABLE 5.2   Participants in the IFSP Meeting

> The parents
> Other family members, if requested by the parents
> A child advocate, if requested by the parents
> A translator, if the parents do not speak English competently
> The service coordinator who is responsible for implementing the IFSP
> At least one person directly involved in the assessment of the child
> As appropriate, early interventionists or therapists who will be working with the child and the family (e.g., developmental therapist, speech therapist, physical and occupational therapists, etc.)

IFSP Content

Although the format of the IFSP document differs from state to state, all IFSP documents have the following components in common (Bruder, 2000):

> Information about the child and the family
> Statements about the child's current developmental level, which is established based on the developmental assessment, including all domains of development:
> > Cognitive
> > Speech, language, and communication
> > Physical development including fine motor, gross motor, visual, and hearing
> > Social emotional
> > Adaptive behavior and self-help development
> Family's concerns, needs, priorities, and what resources are available for the family. Information is collected during the family directed assessment process.
> Specific outcomes, which are expected to be achieved for the child and the family.
> Specific services, which will be provided for the child based on the child's unique needs, including the intensity, frequency, and method of delivery.
> The natural environment in which the services will be delivered.
> The expected date when the intervention services will begin, and the date by which the outcome is expected to be achieved.
> The name of the service provider who will supervise and coordinate the services.
> The specific steps for transitioning to special education services.

Figure 5.1 displays an example of the portion of an IFSP related to the summary of the child's current developmental level.

IFSP Outcomes

Developing **IFSP outcomes** is at the heart of the IFSP. Family or child outcomes are a synthesis of the present level of the child's development and the family's priorities (Bruder, 2000). Outcomes indicate what needs to be achieved, with what criteria, and using which timeline. They contain both the reason for the action to be taken

FIGURE 5.1
Sample IFSP
Section: Child
Summary of Current
Developmental Level

Child's name: *Jonathan Crain*   **Date:** *June 9, 2010*

Child's age: *30 months*

CHILD'S PRESENT ABILITIES AND STRENGTHS: TEAM SUMMARY

WHAT THE CHILD CAN DO NOW—Include all developmental domains:

Adaptive self-help (how the child does things for him/herself): *Jonathan is able to hold his bottle at bedtime. He is not able to feed himself or drink independently. Currently, Mrs. Crain feeds him. Jonathan is not toilet trained. He is able to pull his pants up with assistance.*

Cognition (how the child plays and solves problems): *Jonathan seems to be aware of his surroundings. He responds to his name and plays with his toys appropriately. Jonathan is able to put a five-piece puzzle together, sort shapes in a shape sorter, and stack large blocks on top of one another. Jonathan enjoys playing with cars and trucks. He is able to load and unload a truck. Jonathan is not able to follow a play theme with more than two parts.*

Physical (how the child moves large and small muscles; oral motor development): *Jonathan has problems with his muscle coordination. He is not able to balance on a balance beam. Mrs. Crain reports that he falls down frequently when running. He slides down when sitting in a child chair. In his fine motor abilities, he seems to have problems with the pincer grasp. He is not able to pick up small objects. He is not able to hold a cup or a spoon. He seems to have difficulties holding large crayons and drawing simple lines.*

Communication (how the child expresses wants and needs): *Jonathan's receptive language is appropriate for his age. He understands simple sentences and directions. His expressive language is slightly below the norm. His vocabulary level is estimated to be about 200 to 300 words. He uses single words to express needs and wants. He has not begun putting words into simple phrases yet.*

Social emotional (how the child expresses feelings and copes with stimulations and frustrations): *Mrs. Crain reports that Jonathan has a play date with the neighbor's child once a week. He engages in parallel play when he meets with his peers. He enjoys lap games and musical games with Mrs. Crain. Jonathan does not initiate playing with other children on his own, and needs to be encouraged to respond to others in interactive simple games, or to initiate simple interactions.*

Vision and hearing: *Normal development indicated by the screening.*

Health/physical/nutrition: *Jonathan is slightly underweight. Mrs. Crain describes him as a "picky eater." Jonathan prefers starchy foods. He eats chicken and red meat, but dislikes vegetables and fruits.*

Diagnosis and other related information: *Developmental delays in all areas.*

as well as the end results for the family as a whole. Figure 5.2 displays an example of an IFSP outcome. In this example, the developmental and occupational therapists provide appropriate activities to promote fine motor and hand-eye coordination for Jonathan, a 30-month-old child. In addition, they work closely with the mother to teach her how she might implement similar activities to reinforce Jonathan's learning.

FIGURE 5.2
Sample IFSP
outcome

Child's name: *Jonathan Crain*   **Date:** *June 9, 2010*

Outcome # 1: *Jonathan will be able to drink out of a "sippy" cup and hold a spoon, scooping food out of the plate and feeding himself.*

Why is this important? *Currently, Mrs. Crain feeds Jonathan during snack and meal times. She is worried that Jonathan is not able to eat and drink independently. Mr. and Mrs. Crain believe Jonathan should learn to feed himself like other children his age usually do at this level. This is also important because Mrs. Crain is pregnant, and she is worried that she will not be able to take care of the needs of the baby and Jonathan at the same time.*

Strategies or activities to achieve outcome: (who will do what and when?) *Ms. Write (developmental therapist) will provide appropriate activities during the developmental therapy sessions. She will also model for Mrs. Crain how to provide hand-on-hand prompting for Jonathan to teach him to pick up a cup, hold a spoon, and scoop food. Mrs. Crain will follow through with this activity with Jonathan during meal times and snack times.*

Intervention type	Frequency/ length of sessions	Start date	End date	Responsible party
Developmental therapy	1 hour per week	June 11, 2010	June 11, 2011	Ms. Write

Criteria: (how will we know if we are making progress?) *Jonathan will successfully drink out of a sippy cup and scoop up macaroni and cheese using a spoon and feed himself.*

Locations: *At home and at restaurants.*

Strategies or activities to achieve outcome: (who will do what and when?) *Ms. Jones (the occupational therapist) will provide activities for Jonathan during the occupational therapy sessions for improving his pincer grasp and hand-eye coordination. She will show Mrs. Crain simple play activities that she could practice with Jonathan to improve his fine motor development.*

Intervention type	Frequency/ length of sessions	Start date	End date	Responsible party
Occupational therapy	1 hour per week	June 16, 2010	June 16, 2011	Ms. Jones

Criteria: (how will we know if we are making progress?) *Jonathan will be able to grasp and pick up small objects, successfully complete pegboard activities, place different size shapes into the shape holders, pick up Cheerios, and feed himself independently.*

Locations: *At home and during play group activities at the center.*

The IFSP outcomes should be reviewed as frequently as possible (at least every 6 months, or sooner if requested by the parents) by the interventionists who provide services to the child to make sure progress is made toward achieving the developmental outcomes. In addition, a formal IFSP review is required every 12 months (Bruder, 2000).

With the exception of the person involved in the child's initial assessment and evaluation, participants in the annual review meeting are the same as those involved in the initial IFSP meeting. During the annual review, the early intervention team discusses the child's and the family's progress and the current needs of both the family and child. In partnership with the parents, the early intervention team decides the general and specific changes that must be made to the outcomes and services for the upcoming year (Jung, 2008). At the end of each meeting, parents give their consent for the delivery of services. Although IFSP reviews are held annually, parents or other team members have the right to request a meeting as often as they deem necessary.

Writing appropriate outcomes depends on four elements: (1) statements of the present developmental level of the child in all domains of development; (2) statements of the present developmental needs of the child; (3) the resources and needs of the family; (4) the priorities of the family and what the family deems appropriate to address in regard to the child at this time (Jung, 2008; Brown & Sorensen, 2007).

A family's resources and needs are dynamic and might change at any point in time, and the IFSP outcomes should fit the family's daily routine (Jung, 2008). Accordingly, in periodic examinations of the IFSP, the early intervention team must make sure the family's priorities remain the same. Families can request re-evaluation and revision of outcomes as frequently as might be necessary. Consider the following example of a family who has recently called for an IFSP meeting. The family has stated that its new priority necessitates the revision of the IFSP outcomes.

Amy is a 2-year-old who was born prematurely. She was diagnosed with mild cerebral palsy at the time of her birth. Amy lives with her mother and father in a middle class home in the suburbs of New Jersey. Amy's father, Mr. Greer, is a successful architect working for a prominent firm. Mrs. Greer, Amy's mother, worked in a doctor's office and has not gone back to work since Amy's birth. She has cared for Amy herself since she was born. Amy began receiving early intervention services a couple of months after her birth. She has steadily gained progress in all areas of development. However, Amy continues to lag behind children her age in all areas of development. Amy's current developmental functioning is:

> **Fine and gross motor:** Physical therapy sessions have helped Amy learn to walk with the aid of an adult or using a walker. Currently, she is learning to push toy cars, stack blocks, and put simple puzzles together. Amy's occupational therapist has shown Mrs. Greer how to provide oral motor activities for Amy. Amy shows less aversion to solid food and has recently begun to eat foods like well-cooked rice and mashed potatoes. Amy continues to have problems with fine motor activities. She is able to cut a paper in two using a pair of scissors with the occupational therapist's hand-on-hand prompt.

> **Self-help:** Amy does not feed herself with her fingers yet or drink out of a cup independently.

> **Language:** A speech therapist has worked directly with Amy and with Mrs. Greer to help Amy improve in the area of communication. Amy has learned to use single words to express what she wants and needs, although she does this infrequently and continues to get frustrated and throws tantrums from time to time.

> **Social emotional:** Amy has begun to play with different toys independently. She has started to show interest in her peers. Along with her developmental therapist and her mother, Amy participates in a local "mom-and-tot" group, where she plays alongside and interacts with her peers.

> **Family's priorities:** Mrs. Greer has recently expressed an interest in going back to work after 2 years of staying home with Amy. She worries about finding appropriate child care while she is away at work. Amy's paternal and maternal grandparents have been supportive. Recently, Amy's maternal grandparents moved to a close suburb from the Greers' home to help care for Amy when needed. At this time, Mr. and Mrs. Greer are concerned that if Mrs. Greer goes back to work, there would be an interruption in Amy's intervention program. They are not convinced that Mrs. Greer's parents or other people who would be caring for Amy are able to understand Amy's needs and able to carry on the intervention program for her.

Let us put ourselves in the position of Amy's intervention team. We meet with Amy's parents in an IFSP meeting. It becomes clear that we should not only be looking at Amy's current developmental progress and needs, but Amy's family's recent priority changes as well as resources. We know that Amy's family has several resources. For example, the family has a good extended family support system and is financially secure. In addition, Amy's parents have successfully partnered with the intervention team and been actively involved in intervention planning and implementation. Our task therefore is to work with one another to explore ways to make sure Amy's intervention will be carried out successfully when Mrs. Greer goes back to work.

During the meeting, we all agree that we should write outcomes that focus on the training of, and communication with, Amy's grandparents or other caregivers who would be caring for Amy. In Figure 5.3, an intervention/lesson plan for Amy's cognitive development regarding a specific outcome is broken down into one outcome with several components. Such a plan will help us clarify different steps needed to be taken to meet each outcome. It could easily be adapted to be written in the IFSP later.

Critical Thinking Question 5.5   Referring to the story at the beginning of the chapter, in writing a language development outcome for Corey, what specific family factors should the interventionist consider?

Natural Environments

One obvious benefit of providing services for children in their natural environment is that the family becomes connected to its natural source of support, such as friends and neighbors, and therefore decreases the family's sense of isolation

FIGURE 5.3
An Intervention Plan
for Amy Addressing
Her Cognitive
Development

Outcome: *Amy will be able to participate in an interactive play theme and take turns in a simple game.*

Why is this important? *Mrs. Greer feels it necessary for Amy to have increased interaction with her peers. Amy gets frustrated when she has to wait her turn during mom-and-tot group time. Mrs. Greer is able to calm Amy down herself, but is afraid it might create problems for her mother when she takes Amy for play dates. Mrs. Greer would like Amy to develop this skill also as a preparation for a toddler program should her parents decide to enroll her in a toddler child care program.*

How do we know that we have met this outcome? *Amy will successfully take turns in a simple interactive game with two different people (an adult and a child) in two different settings (at home and in the play group).*

Routine (integration of activities during specific routines)
Meal and snack time: *Make a game out of taking turns to take a bite with the caregiver.*
Bath time: *Make a game out of taking turns for body parts to be washed.*

Skills to work on	Activities/learning opportunities ideas
• *Focus attention* • *Give eye contact* • *Interact with facial and physical gestures* • *Follow simple game rules* **What is working?** • *Amy is showing increased enjoyment when playing with others, especially other children.* **What suggestions/training do we need to give the family to work on to achieve this outcome?** • *The therapist will spend 15 minutes with Amy's caregiver each session to show him or her how to work with Amy regarding physical positioning and specific turn-taking play techniques.*	• *Music—turn-taking songs* • *In the supermarket, during grocery shopping—take turns finding items on the shelf (point)* • *During mom-and-tot games* • *During snack and meal times, when Amy is hungry* • *During touch-screen computer games with Amy, take turns touching the screen while playing computer games*

Who is involved?
Who are the members involved in helping the family achieve this goal?
• *Parents*
• *Grandparents*
• *Developmental therapist*
• *OT, PT, speech therapist*
	Location for the intervention
	• *At home*
	• *In the community*
	  o *Supermarket*
	  o *Restaurants*
	  o *Mom-and-tot group*

(Brown & Sorensen, 2007; Noonan & McCormick, 2006; Colarursso & Kana, 1991). In addition, intervention for the child along with his peers will help families focus on the child's similarities with typically developing children his age, while giving the child a chance to learn from peers. On the other hand, it would give children without disabilities an opportunity to interact with children with disabilities from an early age.

The first step in providing intervention for the child within his natural environment is to identify settings that the family considers the natural environment for the child (Noonan & McCormick, 2006; Sylva, 2005). Once these settings are identified, IFSP outcomes should be written in relation to different locations where specific activities should be carried out.

Consider the example from Figure 5.3. One of the suggested locations for Amy to learn and practice turn-taking skills is in the supermarket. A possible scenario is as follows: the developmental therapist designs the activity using a picture list of several items that are to be picked up in the supermarket. The therapist would accompany the caregiver and Amy to the supermarket and, using the list, will help Amy find specific items on the shelf that are pictured. Additionally, the interventionist models appropriate interactive language and behavior to be used with Amy for the caregiver. Table 5.3 lists guidelines for providing intervention within the child's natural environment.

In cases where the child needs to receive services in a specialized setting, a justification for why the child might need to receive services in a clinic or other restricted setting should be provided within the child's IFSP.

Transitions

IDEA requires the early intervention program to take steps in providing necessary support for families and children prior to and during the transition of the infants and toddlers to the preschool program (Malone & Gallagher, 2009). Annually, more than one million transitions between early intervention services and early

TABLE 5.3 **Providing Intervention in Natural Environments for Infants and Toddlers**

Examples of Natural Learning Environments	Recommended Steps
≽ Child's home	≽ Observe the child and family during daily routines
≽ Bathroom, kitchen, backyard, etc.	≽ Identify settings and activities in which daily routines take place
≽ Playground	
≽ Church	≽ Ask families to share with you their "outside of home" and special activities
≽ Child care facilities	
≽ Preschools	≽ Identify activities appropriate for the child within the community
≽ Neighborhoods	
≽ Stores	≽ Go along with families in community settings to model intervention for parents
≽ Restaurants	
≽ Car, train, bus rides, etc.	≽ Encourage family members to carry out intervention in different settings when you are not along

childhood programs are facilitated for infants and toddlers with special needs (Brandes, Ormsbee, & Haring, 2007). In general, children with disabilities make several transitions during intervention. Important transitions include transition from early intervention to special education, and transition from elementary special education to high school.

Transition planning from EI to the preschool program takes place when the child turns 30 to 32 months of age. One of the changes in the 2004 reauthorization of IDEA influences the transition from Part C to Part B. According to IDEIA 2004, parents whose children continue to be eligible to receive special education under Part C may choose to have their children resume receiving intervention services until the child is ready to enter kindergarten (Malone & Gallagher, 2009; Council for Exceptional Children, 2004; Mandlawitz, 2007).

Transition planning will help parents understand the differences in service provisions between early intervention and preschool or primary special education settings, so they might form realistic expectations and adjust to the changes in the service delivery model (Malone & Gallagher, 2009; Brown & Sorensen, 2007).

To begin the transition process, the Service Coordinator meets with the parents in a transition planning conference, and provides parents with detailed information regarding the process of identification, evaluation, and eligibility determination and development of the Individualized Education Plan (IEP) (Brown & Sorensen, 2007). A formal request to determine the child's eligibility signed by parents is sent to the child's school district by the service coordinator during the transition planning meeting. If an evaluation is warranted, the parents sign their consent, and the evaluation process begins. In certain states, policies are set to promote seamless eligibility and delivery of services (Illinois State Board of Education, 2001).

During the transition meeting, the intervention team and parents decide the type and amount of services, and the setting in which the child is to be educated and receive services. It is possible that the child might no longer be considered eligible to receive services under Part B. In this case, the child might be mainstreamed into a general education classroom without receiving supplemental services. The child who is found eligible to receive further services might be enrolled in an inclusive classroom, a general education classroom along with outside classroom special education services, or in a self-contained special education preschool or kindergarten classroom.

The transition process involves several steps (Malone & Gallagher, 2009; Brandes et al., 2007):

1. **Preparation of the child:** Preparing the child might include working with the child to emotionally prepare him for change, and also help the child develop skills necessary for the new settings (e.g., social behavior and self-help skills, motivation and problem-solving skills, task-oriented behavior, and communication skills).
2. **Systematic approach:** This includes arranging with various preschool and kindergartens so that families and the child can visit placement options and choose the appropriate setting.
3. **Establishing a rapport:** During the transition planning process, the parents will have a chance to be introduced to the school setting in which their child will

be enrolled and to meet with the professionals who will be working with their child. Visiting multiple inclusive and special education settings helps parents get a feel for what is entailed in the daily life of a classroom. It gives parents an opportunity to see how teachers interact with children and how they carry out the curriculum in higher grades. Parents can meet with teachers and staff, ask questions, and make notes of their observations. Observing programs in action is the best way for families to understand if and how the programs might meet the needs of their children and what changes to expect when entering the preschool or primary special education systems.

PRESCHOOL AND PRIMARY GRADE SPECIAL EDUCATION AND IEP

The Individualized Education Plan has been considered the cornerstone of the Individuals with Disabilities Education Act (IDEA) (Eason & Whitbread, 2006). IEP meetings provide the best opportunities for special and general educators and parents to form a positive relationship and devise an educational plan that is drawn according to the knowledge and expertise of both parents and the professional team regarding the child (Pierangelo & Giuliani, 2007).

Whether in an inclusive classroom or in a special education classroom, preschool special education services almost always are offered in a classroom environment. All or some activities might need to be adapted and revised to meet the needs of the child. Adaptations to the environment might also be required. These adaptations and modifications are specified and documented within the IEP. Adaptations and implementations of special education methods are usually done by an ECSE teacher or by an early childhood general education teacher who has been trained in special education methods (Eason & Whitbread, 2006).

Other supplemental services, such as speech therapy, occupational or physical therapy, etc., might be either embedded within the classroom activities, which are provided by a therapist and a teacher working in a team, or offered outside of

Preschool special education services are almost always offered in a classroom environment.

Depending on the severity of their disability, some children might be eligible to receive services for the extended school year.

the classroom within a small group or individually (McNary, Glasgow, & Hicks, 2005). In addition to the different types of services, depending on the severity of the disability, some children might be deemed eligible to receive special education services for the duration of the full year. This is called the extended school year (ESY).

Participants in the IEP meetings are similar to those in the IFSP and consist of the parents and the special education team. When appropriate, the child should also participate in the IEP meetings. Table 5.4 lists the individuals who might be present in an IEP meeting.

TABLE 5.4   Participants in the IEP Meeting

> The parents
> The child, when appropriate
> Other family members, if requested by the parents
> A child advocate, if requested by the parents
> A translator, if the parents do not speak English competently
> All professional members of either the multidisciplinary, interdisciplinary, or transdisciplinary team:
  > Case manager
  > Special education teacher—early childhood
  > General education teacher—early childhood
  > Physical, occupational, and speech therapists
  > Psychologist or diagnostician
  > Nurse as required
  > Social worker as required
> Principal/school administrator or designee as required

IEP Content

The format of the IEP document differs from state to state. All IEP documents have the following components in common (Lazara, Danaher, & Kraus, 2007):

> **Child information:** General information about the child is stated.

> **Present level of performance:** The child's present level of educational performance and developmental functioning based on the most previous evaluation or assessments available is stated. The result of the assessment should be written in a manner understandable to parents and other team members. The child's functioning level presents information about the child's strengths and needs. Based on this, the goals and objectives are written. See Figure 5.4 for a sample IEP page of a child's present level of performance.

> **Disability:** The type of disability and a statement regarding how the developmental and behavioral characteristics of the disability may impede the child's learning is included in the IEP.

> **Measurable annual goals and objectives (benchmarks):** Goals and short-term objectives, as well as the benchmarks and targeted dates for their achievement, are stated. Goals and objectives must be linked to the curriculum and activities.

> **Services:** A list of specific special education and supplemental services to be provided for the child is included in the IEP. See Table 5.5 for a breakdown of the range of services available to eligible children.

> **Adaptation of instruction and lessons:** The IEP specifies program and activity adaptations, as well as environmental modifications and support to be provided for the child to meet goals and objectives.

> **Inclusion:** Details of inclusion activities should be stated in the document. If the team and parents decide not to place the child in an inclusive classroom, a statement justifying if and why a child is not to be educated in a fully inclusive classroom should be written in the IEP.

> **Report to parents:** A statement of how the parents will be regularly informed about the child's progress (periodic report cards or other types) and how frequently this will happen is included.

> **Assessment:** The IEP team decides if the child will not participate in the state-wide assessment and a statement regarding the reason why the child will not participate in a standardized assessment is specified in the IEP.

> **Alternative testing:** The IEP specifies how the child will be tested if a standardized assessment will not be used.

> **Dates of services:** The projected date for the beginning of services and adaptations, the frequency of the program, location, and the duration of services are stated.

> **Transition:** Details about transition activities to a high school and to the community when the child turns 14 and 17 years are stated in the IEP.

> **Extended school year (ESY):** The IEP indicates whether or not the child is eligible to receive year-round schooling.

> **Behavior intervention plan:** Depending on the child's needs, a positive behavior support (PBS) plan explaining the support, intervention, and strategies necessary for the child is included in the IEP.

Name: *David*	Date of birth: *8/16/2002*	Grade level: *Pre-K*
☒ Male ☐ Female	Student ID number:	Parent/guardian:
Child/student address:		
Parent address:		
Home phone:	Work phone:	Effective IEP date from: *9/12/2006*
Meeting date: *9/12/2006*	☐ Initial IEP	☒ Periodic review

FIGURE 5.4
Sample IEP Page:
Current Level of
Developmental
Functioning and
Performance

Present level of performance and individual needs in consideration of:

- The result of the initial or most recent evaluation, the student's strengths, the concerns of the parents, the results of the student's performance on any state- or district-wide assessment programs
- The student's needs related to communication, behavior, use of Braille, assistive technology, limited English proficiency
- How the student's disability affects involvement and progress in the general curriculum
- The student's needs as they relate to transition from school to post-school activities (ages 14 and older)

Transcript information—SECONDARY STUDENTS ONLY

Diploma credit earned: **Expected date of high school completion:**

Commencement—Level state tests passed: **Expected diploma:**

ACADEMIC/EDUCATIONAL AND LEARNING CHARACTERISTICS:
Current level of knowledge and development in subjects and skill areas, including activities of daily living, level of intellectual functioning, and adaptive behavior.

Cognitive: *David's cognitive skills are in the below-average range (age 2.5) by Battle inventory at this time.*

Language: *David can follow simple two-step directions. Understands concepts of outside, in, out, and under. He scores about 2.3–2.6 year range using Preschool Language Scale (PLS). He can identify five body parts. He has a good vocabulary and has begun to put simple phrases together.*

Fine motor: *David is able to snip with scissors, use large crayons with appropriate grasp, string large beads, and manipulate a paintbrush.*

Gross motor: *David can run, hop, and jump. He has some difficulties with muscle coordination.*

Adaptive/self-help: *According to teacher's observation and parental report, David is toilet trained. He is able to put on his clothes and button his jacket. He eats independently, using utensils. He is not able to tie his shoelaces.*

Social emotional: *David enjoys peer and adult interactions. David has a difficult time sharing toys during play activities with his friends.*

The IEP is reviewed periodically by the special education and general education teachers, therapists, and other service providers. The IEP meeting takes place annually to consider whether or not the annual goals are achieved, to address any lack of progress, and to revise or write additional goals.

TABLE 5.5   Range of Services and Options Available to Children

Adaptive physical education	Itinerant services
Assistive technology	Language and speech
Audiology	Occupational therapy
Behavior management	Orientation and mobility services
Deaf- and hard-of-hearing services	Parent counseling
Education technology	Physical therapy
Group counseling	Psychological services
Health- and nursing-related services	Social work services
Individual and small group instruction	Specialized physical health care
Individual counseling	Specialized service for low-incident disabilities
Interpreter services	Transportation
	Vision services

IEP Measurable Goals and Objectives

The goals and objectives in an IEP are similar to outcomes in an IFSP. As the IEP is at the heart of the Individuals with Disabilities Act (IDEA), measurable goals and objectives are at the heart of each IEP (Luker & Luker, 2007; Bateman & Herr, 2006). In general, during early childhood years, goals and objectives address developmental needs, pre-academic, and early academic skills. Some states require that all IEP goals address standards (i.e., reading standards, listening standards, tools and technology standards, etc.) (Thompson, Quenemoen, Thurlow, & Ysseldyke, 2001). Addressing learning standards on the IEP means that all academic and non-academic skills should be taught in such a way that the child understands and is able to use them in real-life situations (Thompson et al., 2001).

Annual goals are general and broad statements in regard to what parents and educators want for the child to achieve in 1 year (Luker & Luker, 2007; Bateman & Herr, 2006). During the preprimary education years, annual goals relate to five domains of development. As children enter the primary grades, their IEP annual goals should address not only developmental goals but also different academic areas, such as reading, writing, math, social science, science, physical education, arts, and music. **Objectives** are benchmarks that describe the amount of progress each child is required to make by specific periods of time, usually each quarter (Bateman & Herr, 2006). Objectives are smaller components of each goal.

In order for goals to be written for each child, four questions must be answered (Luker & Luker, 2007; Bateman & Herr, 2006):

1. What are the child's developmental and early academic needs?
2. What curriculum activities and supplemental services are needed to achieve these goals?

3. What is the child to accomplish through activities and supplemental services as it relates to each goal?
4. How will the child's learning be assessed?

Let us answer these questions in regard to 4-year-old David, mentioned in Figure 5.4. First, according to what is stated in David's IEP, David's level of functioning is below his typically developing peers in the areas of cognitive and language development. David's problem with sharing is also an area of concern in his social emotional functioning. Second, in addition to our regular preschool curriculum, a variety of individualized language and cognitive activities should be designed to address David's needs. David also requires behavior goals to address his difficulties with sharing. Third, David should achieve all objectives specific to language, cognitive, and behavior goals that we will design. Fourth, because David is in preschool, he will be assessed using a performance-based assessment.

As we prepare to write goals and objectives for each child, we should keep in mind that they must be **measurable.** Measurability is an indispensable requirement of the goals and objectives. When goals and benchmarks are not measurable, educators will not be able to observe and assess the child's learning and progress. Measurable criteria give professionals clear indications when, or if and how, a child has achieved her goals. They will enable educators to say exactly how much progress the child has made since they started working with the child on her goals (Bateman & Herr, 2006).

Writing Measurable Goals and Objectives

A learning behavior is measurable when it can be observed. A good rule of thumb to follow is to make sure the terms used in writing goals are **observable** (Bateman & Herr, 2006). For example, a child's understanding cannot be measured since understanding is not observable on its own. On the other hand, a child's utterances are measurable, since what the child says is observable. Table 5.6 displays some observable and non-observable terms describing behaviors related to cognitive, language, and social emotional development, which can be used for writing goals and objectives.

The number of goals to be achieved should be realistic and achievable. Parental input, assessment results, and teachers' observation records and knowledge of the child provide guidelines to set realistic expectations for young children in writing goals and objectives. The criteria for the mastery of a skill is established when a child is able to perform a task with 70 percent to 80 percent accuracy. This means that a child must be 100 percent correct in performing a task 7 or 8 out of 10 times. Using percentages in writing annual goals and objectives should be done with caution. Teachers frequently use percentages to indicate mastery of a behavior, where certain behaviors are difficult to measure in terms of a percentage. For example, it is difficult to expect a child to wash his hands independently with 80 percent accuracy. It could, however, be expected of a child to wash his hands independently 80 percent of the time, or 8 out of 10 times. Three examples of annual goals, along with their objectives regarding cognitive, language, and social behaviors for David, are presented in Figures 5.5, 5.6, and 5.7, respectively.

TABLE 5.6   Terms Describing Observable and Non-Observable Behaviors
as Relating to IEP Goals and Objectives

Terms Appropriate for IEP Goals and Objectives	Terms Not Appropriate for IEP Goals and Objectives
Cognitive	**Cognitive**
➢ Identify 15 new objects	➢ Know what a body is
➢ Count from 1 to 10	➢ Understand numbers
➢ Solve a 10-piece puzzle	➢ Solve problems
➢ Identify letters	➢ Know letters
➢ Write letters of alphabet or numbers	➢ Know how to write
Language	**Language**
➢ Utter five three-word sentences	➢ Improve expressive language
➢ Follow three-step directions	➢ Improve receptive language
Social Emotional Behaviors	**Behavior**
➢ Sharing toys	➢ Being good
➢ Sitting without fidgeting	➢ Behaving
➢ Not screaming	➢ Respecting authority
➢ Raising hands	

FIGURE 5.5
Sample IEP
Measurable Goals
and Objectives:
Cognitive Domain

Objectives

Sample goals and objectives

Cognitive domain: present level of performance
    David is able to count from 1 to 3 by rote. He does not count objects or identify numbers.

Annual goal (pre-academic math concepts)
    David will count objects and identify numbers from 1 to 20. He will categorize objects in groups of 4 and 5 from 1 to 20.

Objectives/benchmarks
    1. Given a teacher's prompt, David will count by rote from 1 to 20 in 8 out of 10 teaching trials.
        a. Time frame for meeting the objective: by the end of the first quarter.
    2. David will count up to 20 objects using one-to-one correspondence in 8 out of 10 teaching trials.
        a. Time frame for meeting the objective: by the end of the second quarter.
    3. David will identify numerals from 1 to 20 in 8 out of 10 teaching trials.
        a. Time frame for meeting the objective: by the end of the third quarter.
    4. David will independently count by fives from 1 to 20, and identify numerals 1 to 20 with 100 percent accuracy in 8 out of 10 teaching trials.
        a. Time frame for meeting the objective: by the end of the fourth quarter.

Language domain: present level of performance

David is able to utter two-word phrases. He is not able to utter full sentences.

Annual goal (expressive language)

David will utter three-word sentences to express needs and wants.

Objectives/benchmarks

1. Given a PECS sentence strip "I want…," David will be able to complete the sentence strip with the teacher's prompt in 8 out of 10 teaching trials.

    a. Time frame for meeting the objective: by the end of the first quarter.

2. Given a PECS sentence strip "I want…," David will be able to complete the sentence strip independently 80 percent of the time throughout the classroom routine and in teaching trials.

    a. Time frame for meeting the objective: by the end of the second quarter.

3. David will use a variety of PECS sentence strips such as "I see…" or "I hear…" independently within structured small and large group activities in 8 out of 10 teaching trials.

    a. Time frame for meeting the objective: by the end of the third quarter.

4. David will utter three-word sentences with or without using the sentence strip to express needs or wants and in conversations 80 percent of the time throughout all classroom routines and activities.

    a. Time frame for meeting the objective: by the end of the fourth quarter.

Examples of complete and incomplete sentence strips to be used during the snack routine:

1. The child is given or picks up an incomplete sentence strip.

2. The child completes the sentence by choosing the picture from a variety of pictures on a picture board or in his or her own individual picture book. Pictures are fastened by Velcro in folders, boards, and on the picture strip.

3. The child adds the picture to the strip, while uttering the sentence.

4. The child hands in the complete sentence strip to the teacher or to another child, while uttering the sentence.

FIGURE 5.6
Sample IEP Measurable Goals and Objectives: Language Domain

FIGURE 5.7

Sample IEP
Measurable Goals
and Objectives:
Social Emotional
Domain

Social emotional domain: present level of performance

David enjoys playing with peers, but he does not share toys with his peers during play activities.

Annual goal (behavior)

David will share toys with his peers and classmates during play activities.

Objectives/benchmarks

1. Given the teacher's verbal or visual prompts, David will share toys with his classmates in three out of five consecutive play activities each day.

   a. Time frame for meeting the objective: by the end of the second quarter.

2. Given a teacher's verbal prompt, David will share toys with peers and classmates in three out of five play activities.

   a. Time frame for meeting the objective: by the end of the third quarter.

3. David will independently share toys with peers and classmates without the teacher's prompts in three out of five consecutive play activities.

   a. Time frame for meeting the objective: by the end of the fourth quarter.

Meeting Goals and Objectives through Lesson Plans and Activities

To meet goals and objectives, early childhood teachers usually design a number of activities related to every goal, which has been individualized based on the child's abilities and functioning level (Kamens, 2004). For example, David's cognitive/math goal requires several activities, each targeting prerequisite and requisite skills necessary for David to achieve his goal. First, David needs to learn counting numbers by rote from 1 to 20. This can be achieved in a variety of ways, such as using songs, music, stories, and games.

Second, David requires learning about the concept of quantity. A number of hands-on activities focusing on one-to-one correspondence could be used to establish the quantity concept. Finally, David needs to learn to group number quantities in different sets. Children learn more efficiently when a variety of hands-on activities are designed to help them understand cognitive concepts such as categorizing and grouping. Music, art, and physical motor activities should be incorporated into all activities.

Activities should be designed in large groups, small groups, and one-to-one formats. Often one-to-one teaching is required for children who have severe cognitive or physical disabilities to provide prompts and support and to make sure learning is taking place. In ECSE, usually when a small or large group activity is designed, the teacher aims to work toward achieving objectives for a number of children who have similar annual goals. As every child is unique in his or her developmental needs and learning potentials, the teacher must differentiate instructions for individual students. Text Box 5.2 displays an example of an outdoor large group activity designed to promote the grouping concept in a preschool setting.

Large Group Activity to Promote the Quantity Concept   Text Box 5.2

Developmental domain: Cognitive/pre-academic math

Location: Outdoor playground, or the gym

Objective: Children will be able to identify numbers from 1 to 5, divide objects into groups of 1, 2, 3, 4, and 5, and match numbers to each group.

Materials: Different colored sidewalk chalk.

Prerequisite skills: Children should be able to count by rote from 1 to 20.

Activity procedure: Use chalk to draw large circles on the ground. Use a different color for each circle. Circles should fit groups of children from one member to five members. Mark each circle in the middle from number 1 to 5. Match the color of circles with the color of numbers.

Categorize groups of children from one to five members, and label each group with the pertinent number. Have children race to fill in circles that belong to their group with the required number of members. Call for each number grouping individually and give time for children to run toward the pertinent circle. Those members who arrive at the pertinent circle earliest get to go inside the circle first. Help children take turns, and count the members in each circle correctly.

Routine time activity: Have children distribute one plate per child, one napkin per child, and three to five animal crackers per child during snack activity.

Modification for children with language impairments: Make picture cards for numerals 1 to 20. Use PECS (Picture Exchange Communication System— explained in Chapter 7) to establish number recognition. Make pictures of quantity groups, 1 to 20.

Modification for children with visual impairment: Use manipulative such as "bear counters" to establish the quantity concept. Cut out the numbers 1 to 20 from pieces of sand paper. Have children touch each number as they say the number out loud. Introduce the braille version after establishment of the number concepts.

Adaptation of Instruction in Inclusive and Specialized Settings

Adapting instructions to address the needs of children with physical disabilities, deafness, blindness, or those with language impairments, should be a part of all lesson planning and activity design in any early childhood special education or inclusive settings (Johnson-Martin, Jens, Attermeier, & Hacker, 1999).

Manipulative learning materials, as well as fabric and objects with various sensory textures, are not only beneficial for use with children who are blind or have visual impairment, but also to all children. In addition, the extension of activities should be carried out during different routines throughout the day (Bruder, 2000). For example, the activity in Figure 5.5 should be carried out during snack time. The advantage of this method is twofold. First, since some children with developmental disabilities have difficulties in generalizing what they have learned to a different setting, activities integrated through routines will help them carry out and apply what they have learned to a new situation. Second, children learn better when concept and skill learning is embedded in natural and daily routines and does not happen in isolation. Children show more interest when activities are meaningful and have practical implications in their daily routines.

Assessment of Goal Achievement

To ensure that all children have the opportunities to learn in an environment with high teaching standards, making improvements and changes in the intervention can be adjusted as needed. A child's assessment should be regularly tied to intervention (Pierangelo & Giuliani, 2007; Thompson et al., 2001). The No Child Left Behind Act of 2001 includes the expectations that children are assessed annually. The results of periodical assessment of all IEP goals are used to determine *accountability* (Ysseldyke & Algozzine, 2006).

Assessment of goal achievement through the use of performance-based assessment is the most common practice in ECSE (Ysseldyke & Algozzine, 2006). The organization of materials in the children's portfolios should be based on presenting evidence of learning that relates to each specific goal. Evidence of the child's learning, along with a written report (report card), should be shared with parents as frequently as possible—at least at the end of each quarter. Ultimately, this information will help early childhood educators and parents decide on the goals for the child's next IEP (Thompson et al., 2001).

SUCCESSFUL PARTNERSHIP AMONG TEAM MEMBERS

Both parents and professionals have equal rights in the design of IEP and IFSP goals, and both play crucial roles in the child's learning and progress (Pierangelo & Giuliani, 2007). In reality, professionals and parents do not always work successfully together. Disagreements are common between them, and the parties do not have to agree on every point. However, it is necessary for them to make efforts to understand each others' points of view, reasoning, and feelings.

Critical Thinking Question 5.6   Referring to the story at the beginning of the chapter, how could the behaviors of Ms. Buck and other professionals have been modified so Janet would not have been intimidated?

Critical Thinking Question 5.7   How could Janet's behavior have been modified so professionals would have been encouraged to be more collaborative?

Professional Partnership

As the traditional multidisciplinary team model has dictated, assessment and intervention of exceptional children are usually carried out in isolated units by professionals (Turnbull & Turnbull, 2002; Seligman & Darling, 2007). In Chapter 4, we described other collaborative team models and identified the transdisciplinary team model as one alternative to the most common model in use. This model promotes partnership among professionals, including a partnership between the special education teacher and general education teacher, the latter being an important member of the intervention team in an inclusive model. The mode also calls for collaboration between **paraprofessionals** and professionals.

Paraprofessionals are important members of an intervention team. Paraprofessionals often perform individual duties such as preparing, cleaning, or providing one-on-one assistance to a child in isolation from the general activities of the classroom. They often carry out individual instruction to children in inclusive classrooms. As such, they might feel isolated from the overall activities of the classroom, and feel alienated from any group teaching responsibilities. Hauge and Babkie (2006) make several recommendations regarding what special and general education teachers can do to maintain a collaborative relationship with paraprofessionals in order to better serve children in various settings. Table 5.7 lists some of these recommendations (Hauge & Babkie, 2006). Involving all team members in planning and intervention and in the classroom/environmental adaptation process can improve teaching practices and promote a collaborative community of teachers and learners. This manner of teaching and learning is also representative of the idea of inclusion in its true sense.

TABLE 5.7 Recommendations for Collaboration with Paraprofessionals

> Start the year by meeting with the paraprofessional and reviewing the roles you want the paraprofessional to take in the classroom.
> Instruct the paraprofessional on how to work effectively in inclusive environments with different teachers.
> Value and acknowledge the paraprofessional's relationship with the child.
> Ask for input from the paraprofessional regarding the child's progress and future IFSP or IEP goals.
> Discuss the paraprofessional's role with the family, and ask permission from the family to share pertinent information with the paraprofessional.
> Meet on a regular basis with the paraprofessional to discuss the upcoming schedule, lesson plans, and to address other issues.
> Teach the paraprofessional how to work effectively with the child, how to take data, and how to address various specific behavioral issues.
> Share information and materials regarding disabilities and other related issues with the paraprofessional.
> Provide ongoing and specific feedback.
> Include the paraprofessional as much as possible in all team meetings.

Source: Hauge, J., & Babkie, A. (2006). Develop collaborative special educator-paraprofessional teams: One para's view. *Intervention in School and Clinic, 41*(1), 51–53.

SUMMARY

The Individuals with Disabilities Education Act (IDEA) mandates that an IFSP, Individual Family Service Plan, and an IEP, Individualized Education Plan, be written for every child with a disability. Whereas an IFSP is developed for children from birth through 3 years of age, an IEP is developed for children 3 years and older. Both IFSP and IEP are legal documents detailing the intervention, education, and assessment plan for the child.

The basic difference between the IFSP and IEP is that the IFSP emphasizes the child's development as it relates to the child's family's needs and resources, while the IEP emphasizes the child's learning in a school setting. Outcomes and measurable goals and objectives are the central tenants of the IFSP and IEP. They describe detailed plans for what the child needs to learn in 1 year. Writing effective outcomes, goals, and objectives is a requirement for any well-developed education plan. IEP goals and objectives should be linked to classroom curriculums—lessons, activities, and assessments. To help children achieve their goals and objectives, not only should parents and professionals partner together, but professionals should also work collaboratively and in partnership with one another.

Review Questions

1. How does IDEA acknowledge the role of families in the education of children with disabilities?
2. What are some signs of cultural competence?
3. What is an IFSP?
4. What is an IEP?
5. What are differences between IFSP and IEP?
6. What are IFSP outcomes?
7. What are components of an IFSP?
8. What are the contents of an IEP?
9. Who are the members of the IEP team?
10. What are IEP annual goals and objectives?
11. What does it mean to write "measurable goals and objectives"?
12. How is assessment linked to goals and objectives?
13. How is partnership among teachers and paraprofessionals in an ECSE conducive to success?

Out-of-Class Activity

1. Download a sample IFSP or IEP from the Internet using the list of resources provided in the Recommended Resources section at the end of this chapter. Study the IFSP or the IEP and write a report explaining how components of the document work together to guarantee an appropriate education for a child with a disability.

Recommended Resources

Early Intervention Parent Leadership Project (IFSP resources for parents)
http://www.eiplp.org/home.html

Early intervention information, IFSP samples, and related information:
Waisman Center: Wisconsin Birth to Three Training and Technical Assistance

IEP-related information
University of the State of New York
http://www.nysed.gov/home.html

IEP samples
http://www.vesid.nysed.gov/specialed/publications/policy/iep/home.html

IFSP Web: Individual Family Service Program
http://ifspweb.org/

Least Restrictive Environment Coalition
Phone: 212-947-9779
http://www.lrecoalition.org

Mayer-Johnson, LLC
2100 Wharton Street
Pittsburgh, PA 15203
Phone: 858-550-0084
Fax: 858-550-0449
Email: mayerj@mayer-johnson.com
http://www.mayer-johnson.com/

National Training Center on Inclusion
Kids Included Together (KIT)
2820 Roosevelt Rd. Suite 202
San Diego, CA 92016
http://www.kitonline.org

NECTAC: National Early Childhood Technical
Assistance Center

Resources for writing good IFSP outcomes

NECTAC
Campus Box 8040
Chapel Hill, NC 27599-8040
http://www.nectac.org/topics/families/famresources.asp

Waisman Center
Wisconsin Personnel Development Project/Resource
Waisman Center—S101D
1500 Highland Avenue
Madison, WI 53705-2280
http://www.waisman.wisc.edu/cedd/ecfr.html

**View the Online Resources available to accompany
this text by visiting http://www.mhhe.com/bayat1e.**

References

Anderson, P., & Fenichel, E. (1989). *Serving culturally diverse families of infants and toddlers with disabilities.* Washington, DC: National Center for Clinical Infant Programs.

Bailey, D. B., McWilliam, R. A., Darkes, L. A., Hebbeler, K., Simeonsson, R. J., Spiker, D., et al. (1988). Family outcomes in early intervention: A framework for program evaluation and efficacy research. *Exceptional Children, 64*(3), 313–328.

Bateman, B. D., & Herr, C. M. (2006). *Writing measurable IEP goals and objectives.* Verona, WI: Attainment Publication Company Inc.

Brandes, J. A., Ormsbee, C. K., & Haring, K. A. (2007). From early intervention to early childhood programs: Timeline for early successful transition (TESTS). *Intervention in School and Clinic, 42*(4), 204–211.

Brown, E. J., & Sorensen, J. (2007). *An overview of early intervention.* Austin: Pro-ed.

Bruder, M. B. (2000). The individual family service plan (IFSP). *Eric Digest, 605.*

Colarursso, R., & Kana, T. (1991). Public Law 99-457, Part H, Infant and Toddler Programs: Status and Implications. *Focus on Exceptional Children, 23*(8), 1–12.

Council for Exceptional Children. (2004, November). *The new IDEA: CEC summary of significant issues.* Arlington: Author.

Eason, A., & Whitbread, K. (2006). *IEP and inclusion tips for parents and teachers.* Verona, WI: Attainment Co.

Hanson, M. J., & Lynch, E. W. (2004). *Understanding families: Approaches to diversity, disability, and risk.* Baltimore: Paul H. Brookes.

Hauge, J. M., & Babkie, A. M. (2006). Develop collaborative special educator–paraprofessional team: One para's view. *Intervention in School and Clinic, 42*(1), 51–53.

Illinois State Board of Education. (2001, January). *Special education policies and procedures.* Springfield: Author.

Johnson-Martin, N. M., Jens, K. G., Attermeier, S. M., & Hacker, B. J. (1999). *The Carolina curriculum for infants and toddlers with special needs* (2nd ed.). Baltimore: Paul H. Brookes.

Jung, L. (2008). Writing individualized family service plan strategies that fit into routine. *Young Exceptional Children, 10*(3), 2–9.

Kamens, M. W. (2004). Learning to write IEPS: A personalized, reflective approach for preservice teachers. *Intervention in School and Clinic, 40*(2), 76–80.

Lazara, A., Danaher, J., & Kraus, R. (2007). *Section 619 Profile* (15th ed.). Chapel Hill, NC: The University of North Carolina, FPG Child Development Institute, National Early Childhood Technical Assistance Center.

Luker, C., & Luker, T. (2007). A service is not a need. *Exceptional Parent, 37*(2), 31–32.

Lynch, E., & Hanson, M. (1992). *Developing cross-cultural competence: A guide for working with young children and their families.* Baltimore: Paul H. Brookes.

Malone, D., & Gallagher, P. (2009). Transition to preschool special education: A review of

literature. *Early Education and Development,*
20(4), 584–602.

Mandlawitz, M. (2007). *What every teacher should know*
about IDEA 2004 laws and regulations. Boston:
Allyn and Bacon.

McNary, S. J., Glasgow, N. A., & Hicks, C. D. (2005).
What successful teachers do in inclusive classrooms:
Research-based teaching strategies that help special
learners succeed. Thousand Oaks, CA: Corwin Press.

Noonan, M., & McCormick, L. (2006). *Young children*
with disabilities in natural environment: Methods
and procedures. Baltimore: Paul H. Brookes.

Pierangelo, R., & Giuliani, G. (2007). *Understanding,*
developing, and writing effective IEPs: A step-
by-step guide for educators. Thousand Oaks, CA:
Corwin Press.

Seligman, M., & Darling, R. B. (2007). *Ordinary families,*
special children: A systems approach to childhood
disability (3rd ed.). New York: Guilford Press.

Stone, J. H. (Ed.). (2005). *Culture and disability:*
Providing culturally competent services. Thousand
Oaks, CA: Sage.

Summers, J., Behr, S., & Turnbull, A. (1988). Positive
adaptation and coping strength of families who have
children with disabilities. In I. Irvin (Ed.), *Support for*
care-giving families: Enabling positive adaptation to
disability (pp. 1–17). Baltimore: Paul H. Brookes.

Sylva, J. A. (2005). Issues in early intervention: The impact
of cultural diversity on service delivery in natural
environment. *Multicultural education, 13*(2), 26–29.

Thompson, S. J., Quenemoen, R. F., Thurlow, M. L.,
& Ysseldyke, J. E. (2001). *Alternate assessments*
for students with disabilities. Thousand Oaks, CA:
A joint publication of the Council of Exceptional
Children & Corwin Press.

Turnbull, A. P., & Turbiville, V., & Turnbull, H. R.
(2000). Evolution of family–professional partnership
models: Collective empowerment is the model for
the early 21st century. In J. P. Shonkoff & S. Meisels
(Eds.), *The handbook of early childhood intervention*
(2nd ed., pp. 630–650). New York: Cambridge
University Press.

Turnbull, H. R., & Turnbull, A. P. (1996). The synchrony
of stakeholders: Lessons from the disability rights
movement. In S. L. Kagan & N. E. Cohen (Eds.),
Reinventing early care and education: A vision for
a quality system (pp. 290–305). San Francisco:
Jossey Bass.

Turnbull, A. P., & Turnbull, H. R. (2002). From the old
to the new paradigm of disability and families:
Research to enhance family quality of life outcomes.
In J. L. Paul, C. D. Lavely, A. Cranston-Gingras, &
E. L. Taylor (Eds.), *Rethinking professional issues in*
special education (pp. 83–119). Westport, CT:
Ablex Publishing.

U.S. Census Bureau News (2007, May). *Minority*
population tops 100 million. Washington, DC: U.S.
Department of Commerce. Retrieved June 14, 2007,
from http://www.census.gov/newsroom/releases/
archives/population/cb07-70.html

Valentine, J. (2007). Individualized education programs.
In A. M. Bursztyn (Ed.), *The Praeger handbook of*
special education (pp. 131–134). Santa Barbara, CA:
Praeger Publishers.

Wang, M., Mannan, H., Poston, D., Turnbull, A. P., &
Summers, J. A. (2004). Parents' perceptions of
advocacy activities and their impact on family
quality of life. *Research and Practice for Persons*
with Severe Disabilities, 29(2), 44–155.

Wright, P. W., & Wright, P. D. (2007). *Special*
education law (2nd ed.). Hartfield, VA: Harbor
House Law Press.

Ysseldyke, J., & Algozzine, B. (2006). *The legal*
foundations of special education: A practical
guide for every teacher. Thousand Oaks, CA:
Corwin Press.

Chapter 6

Theoretical Foundations in Special Education

Objectives

Upon completion of this chapter, you should be able to:

> Describe the relationship between theories of child development and the formation of a teaching philosophy and methods.

> Describe the modern constructivist and social constructive perspectives as they apply to intervention for young exceptional learners.

> Describe modern developmental theories.

> Discuss Greenspan's theory of emotional development.

> Understand sensory processing theory and how it is applied in special education.

> Understand and describe applied behavior analysis (ABA) and how it is applied in special education.
> Describe task analysis.
> Understand and discuss the modern transactional ecological model and how it is applied in special education.

Key Terms

antecedent (198)
applied behavior analysis (ABA) (198)
apprenticeship (180)
behavior (198)
circles of communication (190)
consequence (198)

developmental theories (177)
DIR model (194)
discrete trial teaching (DTT) (200)
Floortime model (194)
guided participation (180)
manipulatives (185)

prompt (200)
scaffolding (185)
self-regulation (188)
sensory integration (196)
sensory modulation (197)
sensory processing (196)
zone of proximal development (180)

Reflection Questions

Before reading this chapter, answer the following questions to reflect upon your personal opinions and beliefs that are pertinent to early childhood special education.

1. How do you think theories and philosophies of education are related to teachers' daily practices and methods of teaching?
2. In forming your philosophy of teaching, do you believe in one theory more strongly than another? Why or why not?
3. Why do you think there is a need for theories to inform teaching practices?

A Family-Focused Philosophy of Education

Chad is an early childhood special education teacher, teaching primary grade children with autism between the ages of 6 and 8. Chad has been a teacher for 18 years. His teaching philosophy is based on forming an ongoing and positive relationship with his students. He believes in understanding all aspects of development and temperament in the children he works with. Despite the school administrator's recommendation to spend the early morning hours preparing for his lessons in his classroom, Chad prefers to prepare for his lessons before arriving at school, so that he is prepared to be engaged with his students from the moment they arrive at school until they leave. He also believes in forming positive relationships with families of the children. Chad believes that making home visits is a routine part of his job, and he frequently does so.

Chad respects families and their role in their children's development and believes his teaching is only effective when it considers the family. This often makes parents comfortable in bringing their concerns or questions regarding their children to Chad. There is an ongoing communication between Chad and the parents regarding what happens in school and at home. Thus, it is not unusual for Chad to be asked to help parents modify the physical structure of their home environment or help them set up a routine at home for the child. On one of these occasions, when Chad was visiting a child in his home and helping the parents set up a routine schedule, the parents invited him to stay for dinner. During the dinner, Chad realized that his young student grabbed food from a tray that was set upon the table, without paying attention to his mother's repeated protestations. Chad asked and directed the child to sit next to him. He modeled appropriate behavior, and praised the child for "good sitting." He then prompted the child to request the food in a simple way, providing the verbal cue, and scaffolding and praising the child as the child complied. After several minutes of repeating the same procedure, both child and parent learned this behavior routine.

INTRODUCTION

Chad's philosophy of teaching and his practice of working with children and families are influenced by two different theories of child development: *ecological-transactional theory* and the *behavioral theory* of development. A philosophy of education is a set of principles and beliefs about how children learn, and therefore how they should be taught. A philosophy of education guides one's teaching and assessment methods. Teachers like Chad develop their teaching philosophies based on their theoretical knowledge.

Theories of child development provide explanations for how children learn and grow, and what possible elements might contribute to deviation in development. Having an adequate theoretical understanding of young children's learning and development will help us decide what teaching skills are necessary in our work to educate and help enhance development in typical and exceptional children. In this chapter, we will examine five major theories of development, all of which have applications in early intervention and early childhood special education. We will discuss the intervention implications of these theories in working with children with special education needs.

Critical Thinking Question 6.1   How would your philosophy of education compare with Chad's?

THEORIES AND MODELS OF CHILD DEVELOPMENT

Developmental psychologists ask questions about human development, form a hypothesis, design a research method, collect data, and interpret results to form **developmental theories.** Developmental theories consist of sets of explanations and principles that disclose a gradual process of unfolding in human growth. Theories of human development help our understanding of how children grow, develop, and learn. They help form our ideas of how children acquire knowledge, and therefore guide our practice of teaching.

Education philosophies are generally influenced by the dominating theories of development within a social and political system. Education policies are frequently influenced by prevailing theories that have gained validity through research, and have generally been accepted in education and psychology. Oftentimes, these educational and psychological theories reflect the intellectual, cultural, political, and ethical climate of the society. As such, it is not surprising to find that educational methods and ideas change and evolve over time. Neither is it surprising to see teachers dramatically differ from one another in their philosophies of teaching, in their pedagogical methods, or in their interactions with their students. It is therefore important to examine and understand major theories of child development and how educational practices relate to each theory.

In Chapter 2, we discussed factors that might lead to atypical development. We also saw how our understanding of brain development has changed and evolved since the 1990s. We have learned how important the early experiences of children are in influencing the neural pathways in every individual (Kotulak, 1996). Paired with our understanding of each disability and its characteristics, our knowledge about child development theories will form the foundations of our intervention methods with young exceptional children and their families.

Although a number of prominent developmental theories exist, in this chapter we will examine only those theories that have been applied or are likely to be applied in intervention for young exceptional learners. We will see how each theory might relate to our work with young children with disabilities and their families.

MODERN CONSTRUCTIVIST AND SOCIAL CONSTRUCTIVIST PERSPECTIVES

Constructivist and *social constructivist* perspectives are based on cognitive and social cognitive theories. Derived from the Latin word cognito, which means "to have an idea in mind" (Poole, Nunez, & Warren, 2007), the cognitive and social

Children see, hear, and interact with their environment, including peers, adults, and materials, in order to understand and construct their own knowledge.

cognitive theories are concerned with the thinking process and how children's mental processes—such as perceptions, reasoning, and memory—change and evolve as they grow.

Cognitive theory postulates that children are active learners. They see, hear, and interact with their environment, including peers, adults, and materials, in order to understand, and therefore construct, their own knowledge. These perspectives rely on ideas of two influential theorists, the Swiss psychologist Jean Piaget (1896–1980) and the Russian psychologist Lev Vygotsky (1896–1934).

Piaget's regard for children as curious and active constructivists was elemental in changing the way in which children were viewed and educated in the world. Theories of Piaget and Vygotsky counteracted the educational philosophies of the time, which regarded children as passive recipients of facts. Text Boxes 6.1 and 6.2 provide summaries of Piaget's and Vygotsky's ideas.

Piaget's Ideas: The Foundations of Constructivism   Text Box 6.1

Piaget believed that children went through four stages of development. Because Piaget made references to an age range at each stage in his reports, age has often been interpreted as a normative criterion for each stage—even though he intended for age to act as an indicator of an order for the stages. In Piaget's cognitive theory, young children first go through a *sensorimotor stage* before they enter a second stage, called *preoperational stage*. The sensorimotor stage begins in infancy and lasts about 2 years. During this stage, infants actively construct their world by seeing, hearing, touching, kicking, or putting things in their mouth, thus feeling and understanding the sensations of objects in their surroundings. In Piaget's view, children form an initial representation of the world they encounter. He called these initial representations *schemes* or *schemas*.

According to Piaget, as children begin to have more and repeated experiences in their world, they might encounter conflicting schemas, and will gradually begin to add to, refine, complement, and revise their initial schemas into categories of knowledge. He called this process *assimilation, accommodation,* and *organization*.

During the preoperational stage, which lasts about 5 years (ages 2–7), children begin to think in *symbols*. It is during this time that a child begins to ride on Daddy's back, pretending that Dad is a "horsey," or pretends to ride a car when sitting in a chair. Children will go through two more stages, *concrete operational* and *formal operational*. These stages signify a process of gradual change from young children with simple concrete cognitive mechanisms to adults with complex abstract reasoning and problem-solving skills.

Sources: Crain, W. (2005). *Theories of development: Concepts and applications* (5th ed.). Upper Saddle River, NJ: Pearson Education, Inc.; Smith, L. (2002). Piaget's model. In U. Goswami, (Ed.), *Blackwell handbook of childhood cognitive development* (pp. 515–537). Malden, MA: Blackwell; Broderick, P., & Blewitt, P. (2006). *The life span: Human development for helping professionals* (2nd ed.). Upper Saddle River, NJ: Pearson Educational Inc.; and Poole, D., Nunez, N., & Warren, A. (2007). *The story of human development.* Upper Saddle River, NJ: Pearson Education, Inc.

Text Box 6.2   Vygotsky's Ideas: Foundations of Social Constructivist Thought

Vygotsky's theory of social cognitive development is similar to Piaget's ideas in that children are active constructivists of their knowledge. However, influenced by the social Marxist values of his country, the Soviet Union, Vygotsky theorized a model in which the child's development is explained within the context and values of society, and in cooperation with other members of the child's community. He believed that a child's cognitive development could not be understood without understanding the culture in which the child lives, and without the individuals with whom the child interacts. Vygotsky believed that a culture's *symbols* or *signs,* such as the written and spoken language, influence a child's cognitive development. He agreed with Piaget that cognitive development begins within the child and through an active process. However, he theorized that after age 2, children begin to be influenced by both intrinsic forces and cultural forces in forming and constructing their own knowledge.

One of the components of Vygotsky's theory that has been frequently used in education is the concept of **zone of proximal development.** Vygotsky believed that a child's ability level would be higher when they worked with peers or adults. For example, an 8-year-old might be able to solve a problem with multiple levels of difficulties on his own, up to a specific level (e.g., up to a 9-year-old level). However, if this same child works with a peer to solve the same problem, he will be able to solve the more difficult levels of the same problem (e.g., up to a 12-year-old level). Thus, the distance between what the child is able to do on his own, and what the child will be able to do with the help of another individual, is called the zone of proximal development.

Source: Crain, W. (2005). *Theories of development: Concepts and applications* (5th ed.). Upper Saddle River, NJ: Pearson Education, Inc.

Among the more contemporary social constructivist theorists is Barbara Rogoff, an American professor of psychology, currently holding the University of California Presidential Chair. Rogoff has done extensive research investigating the teaching of, and learning processes in, children within different cultures. She has elaborated on the ideas of Vygotsky and brought forward the concepts of **apprenticeship** and **guided participation** (Rogoff, 1990).

The concept of apprenticeship explains the process of child development within the culture in which the child lives and through the interactions of the child with the caregivers. Similar to Piaget and Vygotsky's theories, in Rogoff's theory the child is an active constructivist who learns the cultural practices, social activities, and other related tasks with the ongoing support of people in his or her community.

According to this concept, children understand the rituals and routines of their family and their community and learn how to use their cultural tools through their interactions with their caregivers and other children. Cultural tools are all the concrete and abstract instruments that a society uses in order to solve daily problems.

For example, in the modern Western societies, computers and related digital technology are concrete cultural tools, and thus learning to use this technology is part of the active learning process for children (Keengwe & Onchwari, 2009). Similarly, abstract Western cultural tools consist of values such as collaboration, teamwork, or ability to delay gratification to achieve a distant goal (Mallory & New, 1994). Both concrete and abstract cultural tools are essential in young children's participation in the society, and in their development and learning.

A child's apprenticeship takes place through a guided participation in the society. Rogoff defines guided participation as "a process in which caregivers' and children's roles are entwined, with tacit as well as explicit learning opportunities in the routine arrangements and interactions between caregivers and children" (Rogoff, 1990, p. 65). Initially, young children learn from their caregivers through nonverbal and verbal communication. Early in the child's life, caregivers and other adults choose and determine the activities and materials for children.

Eventually, children will play active roles in choices of their own activities and learning. The adults' support in the child's choices, their relationship with the child, and their assistance in the child's learning are important parts in the process of guided participation. Apprenticeship and the process of guided participation are illustrated in the following example of an interaction between a mother and her 3½-year-old daughter:

> I was getting ready to leave the house, and noticed that a run had started in the foot of my stocking. My daughter volunteered to help sew the run, but I was in a hurry and tried to avoid her involvement by explaining that I did not want the needle to jab my foot. I began to sew, but could hardly see where I was sewing. Soon she suggested that *I* could put the needle into the stocking and *she* would pull it through, thus avoiding sticking my foot. I agreed, and we followed this division of labor for a number of stitches. When I absent-mindedly handed my daughter the needle rather than starting a stitch, she gently pressed my hand back toward my foot, and grinned when I glanced at her, realizing the error. (Rogoff, 1990, p. 109)

Application of Constructivist Approaches in Early Childhood Education

In early childhood education, the constructivist application can be seen in basic principles of Montessori education (Montessori, 1974), as well as in the High/Scope curriculum (Hohmann & Weikart, 1995, 2002). The Montessori principles were established by Maria Montessori (1870–1952), the first female Italian physician. Although the Montessori education is well known around the world, very few mention the fact that the Montessori education was initially and fundamentally designed for a group of children who had intellectual disabilities. Text Box 6.3 describes basic Montessori ideas in early childhood education.

Another example of the constructivist approach in early childhood is the High/Scope program, supported and funded by High/Scope Educational Research Foundation. Establishment of the High/Scope curriculum and its preschool program (Perry Preschool Project in Michigan from 1962–1967) began as a research project based on Piaget's ideas. As a part of the process of daily routine, children

| Text Box 6.3 | Montessori Ideas and the Beginning of Sensory Education for Children with Special Needs |

Montessori had become concerned with the conditions in which children labeled "insane and deficient" lived, and with the way they were treated. She was appointed the director of an asylum, where these children were confined to their rooms and deprived of any kind of interactions and stimulation. Montessori studied the work of Itard and Seguin (whom we discussed in Chapter 1), and believed that with proper stimulation, purposeful activities, and self-esteem, these children would be able to develop appropriately and succeed. Through careful observation of her students, she was able to provide appropriate environment, materials, and activities for them. Thus, her students who were previously labeled as "mentally deficient" were able to pass the standardized sixth grade test for Italy's public schools after a few years of training. Later, Montessori established a school and tried her methods with children of the poor.

Montessori regarded children as whole and unique, each deserving to be respected. Like Piaget, she believed children to be motivated to learn and active in the learning process. Montessori's educational system focuses on the use of specifically designed self-correcting sensory materials within a prepared environment. Montessori's child-centered equipment and auto-educational materials are vehicles by which children actively learn practical daily living and academic skills. In Montessori education, the teacher's role is to guide, model, and show children how to use materials and do activities. As such, the teacher is the facilitator of children's self-education. Current Montessori programs are based on the original constructivist principles and those that Maria Montessori established in early the 1900s.

Source: Stephenson, S. M. (1998). *Michael Olaf's essential Montessori, school edition, for age 3–12.* Arcata, CA: Michael Olaf Publishers.

plan the activities which they are interested to carry out, *do* a variety of chosen activities in small and large groups, and *review* by recalling and summarizing their activities throughout the day (Hohmann & Weikart, 1995, 2002). See Text Box 6.4 for more information on the High/Scope model. There are other creative curriculum approaches which utilize teachers as mediators and promote children's active learning that are also considered a constructivist-based early childhood curriculum (Bodrova & Leong, 2009).

Application of Constructivist Approaches in Special Education

In applying this model to working with children with special needs, the constructivist approach maintains its belief that children acquire knowledge through active learning, whether they are developing typically or nontypically (Bunce, 2001). The focus of working with exceptional children in such an approach is on the child's

High/Scope Curriculum Model of Early Childhood Education

Text Box 6.4

In the High/Scope curriculum model, children interact with other children, adults, materials, ideas, and events in order to construct their own knowledge. The role of the teacher in this model is to facilitate and co-direct the child's learning. The teacher interacts with, encourages, and helps the child solve problems and take further steps in learning. Observation and assessment of children takes place within a team approach on an ongoing and daily basis.

The High/Scope curriculum model resembles a wheel with active learning at its center (Figure 6.1). Within the High/Scope curriculum, adult–child interaction is guided by the children's initiative and interest. Teachers support children's learning experiences via interactions with children throughout the daily routine. Assessment of children takes place through systematic observations of children's learning experiences and interactions within their daily routine.

Source: Hohmann, M., & Weikart, D. (2002). *Educating young children: Active learning practices for preschool and child care programs* (2nd ed.). Ypsilanti, MI: High/Scope.

strengths and interests. Utilizing the child's abilities and interests, and modifying the curriculum and environment based on the child's needs, the teacher facilitates active involvement of the child in the daily routine and activities of the program (Childre, Sands, & Pope, 2009).

When adults help, support, and challenge children's thinking, all children, including those with disabilities, will become able to function within their zone of proximal development, use opportunities to solve real problems, and contribute to making new rituals and strategies (Childre et al., 2009; Bunce, 2001). As a result, they become more capable of participating in activities, increasing their abilities, and thus functioning at a more independent level (Mallory & New, 1994).

FIGURE 6.1
The High/Scope
Curriculum Wheel

The social constructivist ideas of Vygotsky and Rogoff put a special emphasis on peers and adults' roles in learning. In special education, *peer tutoring,* also known as *peer-mediated instruction,* has been gaining increasing attention (Gardner, Nobel, Hessler, Yawn, & Heron, 2007; Van Norman & Wood, 2007). With help from a more capable peer, children with both cognitive and physical disabilities often demonstrate that they are able to observe, learn, and practice new skills. (We will describe peer-mediated tutoring further in Chapter 15.)

Since the social constructivist view regards school and classroom as a community of learners, one benefit for children with disabilities is to belong and be considered as contributing members of this community (Kunc, 1992). Therefore, a social constructivist approach to education has direct implications for the *inclusion* of children with disabilities into the community of learners. See Text Box 6.5 for an example of an inclusive social constructivist program.

Some studies have indicated that children with mild disabilities such as learning disabilities or mild cognitive delays have benefited from a hands on, active learning approach in specific subjects, such as science (Childre et al., 2009; Scruggs & Mastropieri, 1993, 1994). However, research is lacking in how such activities might benefit young children with severe or multiple disabilities. In addition, with the exception of some anecdotal accounts, evidence is lacking in how model programs like Montessori, High/Scope, or Reggio Emilia have been applied for exceptional children, or whether they have been efficient for these children.

Text Box 6.5 **Reggio Emilia: An Inclusive Social Constructivist Model**

Reggio Emilia is a city in northern Italy that is known for its exemplary model of early childhood programs. The Reggio Emilia approach to education was established by talented educator Loris Malaguzzi (1920–1994) after World War II, when parents began to build new schools for their children as a part of the community effort to rebuild the city. Parents in collaboration with all the members of the community decided to build schools that promoted critical thinking to ensure a democratic society. The schools are governed by the municipality of the city. As such, parents and other community members are actively involved in the education of its young children. In this approach, children are a community of learners, in which collaboration and cooperation are central to their learning. Their education focuses on children in relation to their families, teachers, school environment, peers, and the society.

The activities of the young children in this model revolve around completing group projects that usually last 3 to 4 months. Teachers listen and ask questions to promote further thinking and problem solving. They sometimes enter into children's dialogue to prompt further reflections and discovery. They observe, record, and document children's products, and work collaboratively with other teachers and parents to further individual children's development.

Source: Loris Malaguzzi International Center. (2010). *Reggio children: The hundred languages of children.* Retrieved July 23, 2010, from http://zerosei.comune.re.it/inter/100exhibit.htm.

In examining the application of the constructivist approach in working with exceptional children, we must consider several assumptions:

> - Children are active learners.
> - Children are curious.
> - Children are internally motivated to learn.
> - Children are internally motivated to socialize.
> - Children learn best when they cooperate along with their peers.
> - Children learn best when their learning is supported by adults.

Consider one of the preceding assumptions: Children are internally motivated to learn. *Motivation* is a well-known notion in psychology. Without motivation, individuals do not have an incentive to act. Children are usually internally motivated by their own curiosity and interests. Early childhood educators do not necessarily spend much time on deciding how to motivate the young children they work with to join them in fun and playful learning activities. However, depending on the type and severity of the disability, many young exceptional learners might not have the required active motivation to learn.

When teaching young children with disabilities, we might occasionally find ourselves in need of establishing external motivations for our students so they will become active learners. Building on children's specific interests is one way of motivating children with special needs. Another is to provide positive reinforcers. Reinforcers are external incentives that motivate children with exceptionalities. (We will discuss reinforcers in a later section and in Chapter 9 in more detail.)

Additionally, in a constructivist approach to working with exceptional children, teachers have a more active role than simply facilitating learning and arranging the environment. Along with providing **manipulatives** and sensory materials to encourage children's play and hands-on learning, teachers might have to provide different kinds of scaffolding.

Scaffolding a typically developing 3-year-old might consist of asking open-ended questions, and providing verbal cues to prompt further thinking and problem solving. However, scaffolding young children with physical or intellectual disabilities can vary from hand-on-hand physical motoring of an action, to modeling an action in its entirety. For example, scaffolding a 3-year-old with motor problems in building a tower consists of holding the hand of the child with a block and leading her hand to put each block on top of the next. On the other hand, a 3-year-old with mild cognitive delays might need only to see a peer or a teacher putting the second block on top of the first one in a shared activity in order to learn how to build a tower.

Providing models of an action is an important way to scaffold a child's learning. Here, we should keep in mind that imitation is a required skill for learning from a model. Some children with intellectual disabilities lack imitation skills. In these children, therefore, scaffolding certain simple skills to build imitation is necessary before any other teaching through modeling is attempted.

Critical Thinking Question 6.2   In the opening story, Chad's knowledge of developmental theories influenced his teaching practices. What theories do you draw upon when working with children?

MODERN DEVELOPMENTAL THEORIES

Developmental and psychoanalytical perspectives are concerned with the child's emotional development and early relationships as the foundations of healthy intellectual growth. The contemporary social emotional developmental perspectives are drawn from the psychoanalytical theories of Freud and Erikson, as well as brain development research of the past three decades. For ideas of Freud and Erikson, see Text Boxes 6.6 and 6.7.

Modern developmental theories incorporate into their model the more recent findings on brain sensory processing and the regulatory systems of infants and young children. As mentioned in Chapter 2, the infant's brain grows rapidly during the first 3 years of life, and early experiences of infants with their caregivers are crucial in brain development.

Robert Emde is an American contemporary child psychiatrist and developmental psychobiologist at the University of Colorado who has conducted longitudinal

---

Text Box 6.6   The Psychoanalytic Theory of Sigmund Freud

Sigmund Freud (1856–1939) was concerned with the inner world of feelings and impulses. He believed that emotional change occurs as a result of both inner forces and maturation. Freud believed that much of human action is governed by sexual urges, or anything that causes bodily pleasure. He elaborated on the three concepts of id, ego, and superego as agents of the human mind. *Id,* a part of the unconscious mind, is dominated by seeking pleasure and acting on impulses. *Ego* is human reason and acts as the reality principle. It leads the person to make a judgment about a situation based on reality. The *superego* acts as one's conscience and consists of the person's standards of right and wrong.

Freud was a stage theorist and believed children went through four stages. The *oral stage* (birth–2 years) revolves around the infant's pleasure at sucking and eating. During the second stage, the *anal stage* (2–3 years of age), children gain pleasure from controlling their sphincter muscles and holding back their bowel movement. The *phallic stage* (3–6 years) is the period during which children become aware of their sexual organs. At this stage, children take interest in their opposite sex parent and begin to feel animosity and form negative fantasies about their parent of the same sex. Freud believed that eventually children resolve the conflicting feelings with the parent of the same sex by identifying with that parent. The *latency* period begins at about age 6 and lasts until early adolescence. Freud thought that sexual and aggressive fantasies are largely repressed during this period, and children begin to redirect their energies into socially acceptable pursuits. Finally, during the *genital stage,* the young adolescents begin to separate themselves from their parents and become independent of parental influences.

Source: Crain, W. (2005). *Theories of development: Concepts and applications* (5th ed.). Upper Saddle River, NJ: Pearson Education, Inc.

Sigmund Freud founded the psychoanalytic school of psychology.

Erik Erikson: A Pioneer in Contemporary Social Emotional Perspectives

Text Box 6.7

Erik Erikson (1902–1994) elaborated on the role of society in the development of individual emotions and identity of self, and established the foundations of modern theories of social emotional development. Erikson's theory involves eight stages of human life, of which we briefly discuss the stages pertinent to childhood. Erikson's stages are a set of encounters between the child and his world. The first stage is *basic trust versus mistrust* (age birth–2). At this stage, through interactions with their caregivers, babies learn to find predictability and reliability in their caregivers' actions. If the caregivers are responsive to the babies' needs, babies learn to depend on the caregivers and trust them. If the caregivers are not consistent in their responses and do not meet the babies' needs, babies lose confidence in them and become mistrustful.

In the second stage, *autonomy versus shame and doubt* (age 2–4), children try to exercise a choice. Toddlers who want to hold their own cup, or climb the stairs on their own, are exercising their autonomy. If a healthy balance is not maintained between the young children's exercise of autonomy and parental control, young children might develop shame about their own worth and feel doubt about their own control and power.

During the third stage, *initiative versus guilt,* which starts from age 4 and lasts for about 2 years, children become able to plan, set goals, and carry out their actions. At this stage, children learn about social rules and discover ways to channel their energy and ambitions into socially useful pursuits. Adults' encouragement into purposeful activities and valued goals are elemental in preventing

(Continued)

the child from developing a sense of guilt. The fourth stage, *industry versus infe-riority* (age 6–11), deals with children's desire to be useful and to learn skills and knowledge of how to use cultural tools. For example, children growing up in the agricultural societies learn to do farm tasks and help their parents. Conflicts might arise if the children begin to feel inferior and are unable to perform tasks adequately. Adults' attitudes toward children's successes and failures, and their scaffolding to help with more difficult tasks, are crucial in helping the children feel competence at this stage.

Source: Crain, W. (2005). *Theories of development: Concepts and applications* (5th ed.). Upper Saddle River, NJ: Pearson Education, Inc.

studies on the social emotional development of infants and young children. One of the proponents of the modern relationship-based models of development, Emde acknowledges several inborn tendencies or motives in children, such as of **self-regulation** and social fittedness. He has elaborated that these tendencies are present in infants from the earliest days after birth (Emde & Robinson, 2000; Emde, Korfmacher, & Kubicek, 2000).

Emde and Robinson (2000) elaborated on five tendencies in infants: activity, self-regulation, social fittedness, affective monitoring, and cognitive assimilation.

> **Activity:** The infants' desires to explore and understand their environment via motoric movements, such as kicking or moving their arms.
> **Self-regulation:** An inherent desire in all children to be calm and take in the world. Sleep cycles, the infant's attentiveness, and a child's later self-awareness are indicative of this motive.
> **Social fittedness:** The extent to which infants are motivated and pre-adapted to initiate and maintain interactions with their caregivers and others around them. For example, an infant's behavior, such as smiling and making baby noises, are overtures to attract a caregiver's attention, and are indicative of the infant's social fittedness.
> **Affective monitoring:** Refers to the infant's ability to monitor experiences based on what is pleasant and unpleasant. For example, infants are able to con-vey messages by crying, smiling, cooing, etc.
> **Cognitive assimilation:** Similar to an idea of Piaget's, in which from early infancy, children are motivated to explore the environment and interact with others to seek what is new in order to make it familiar. According to this view, these tendencies will remain with children and adults through life and motivate human development and growth.

A problem might arise when, due to the environment, caregivers' behaviors, or biological factors, the infant is not able to act based on these tendencies (Emde & Robinson, 2000). For example, sensory and physiological problems might make the infant sensitive to certain natural stimuli such as light and noise. In this instance, the infant might have difficulties sleeping or being calm. In another example, when a caregiver does not respond to the infant's bids for attention, the infant's motivation in interacting with the caregiver might decrease, and therefore, the infant might not be as active in trying to elicit a response from the caregiver through specific baby behaviors.

In these two examples, the biological and caregiving factors have influenced two of the infant's inborn tendencies: self-regulation and affective monitoring. These factors might influence the infant's other tendencies and motivation, and therefore such problems might eventually result in additional difficulties, such as developmental problems in the infant (Emde & Robinson, 2000; Emde et al., 2000). In addition, as the infant develops, the way family members interact with one another and with the infant (within a family's various subsystems) also influences a young child's development of emotional self-regulation (Volling, Kolak, & Blandon, 2009).

Greenspan's Stages of Emotional Development

In another relationship-based developmental theory, Stanley Greenspan, a clinical professor of psychiatry and pediatrics at George Washington University, has advanced developmental and psychoanalytical perspectives into a stage theory of relationship-based development (Greenspan, 1999; Greenspan & Weider, 2006a). According to Greenspan, children's intellectual development depends on their healthy emotional growth, and children's healthy development is dependent upon the way they as infants develop early relationships with their caregivers and other people in their environments (Greenspan, 2007).

In Greenspan's view, emotional interactions—such as a baby's smile, which might result in the caregiver's giving the baby a hug—would eventually help the baby make sense of the world and how the world works. In this instance, for example, over time the baby would realize that the act of smiling might lead to a second act like hugging. Based on this view, all emotional interactions would gradually guide the baby to understand various concepts, solve problems, and develop higher-order thinking. For example, to a young child, a quantity math concept (number sense) such as "a lot" or "a little" is only understood in the context of the child's previous early emotional experiences with quantity—"'a lot' is more than he/she wants, and 'a little' is less than he/she expects" (Greenspan, 1999, p. 10).

According to Greenspan's theory of emotional development, children construct knowledge based on their emotional interactions with others around them. Early positive relationships are not only the architects of children's social emotional and cognitive development, but are also the foundations of moral development and sense of judgment in children. Therefore, during the early years, the way infants and caregivers interact with one another results in the way children learn to relate to others and gain knowledge of people, objects, and the environments around them. Greenspan's theory takes into account the context of family and community, because it is within these contexts that interactions take place and relationships are built.

In general, Greenspan makes three assumptions that are important in understanding his theory. First, that language, cognition, and social skills are all learned through relationships that involve emotionally meaningful exchanges with the caregivers; second, that children vary in their sensory processing capabilities and might therefore react differently to various sensory stimuli; and finally, that progress in all areas of development is interrelated and connected together, and development in one domain influences development in another domain (Greenspan, 2007; Greenspan & Weider, 2006a)

Greenspan defines his eight stages of development as *functional emotional developmental capacities* (*FEDC*) (Greenspan & Weider, 2006a, 2006b). To Greenspan, mastery of each stage is necessary for the child as a foundation for further mastery in next levels. If a problem exists in one stage, it would influence development in the following stages and would eventually lead to deviation from typical development. In this chapter, we will discuss stages of this theory that relate to early childhood development as described by Greenspan and Wieder (2006a; 2006b). Later stages mark the adolescent and adult development and are thus not pertinent.

Stage I: Regulation and Interest in the World (Birth–2 Months)

During the first months of life, infants have the ability to react to sensations. Infants use all their senses to perceive and understand the world around them. When the processing of information received from infants' senses takes place in its typical fashion, infants are able to regulate themselves and remain calm.

When infants are regulated, they are able to take interest in the world and absorb information from the outside world in a typical way. For example, having regular eating and sleeping cycles, or letting themselves be soothed and calmed by caregivers, are signs of typical self-regulation in the infant. In this case, sensations from the outside world are pleasant, and infants react positively to them. However, when infants receive unpleasant sensations, they develop mechanisms to defend themselves. For example, if certain sights and sounds are overwhelming or bothersome, infants either completely tune out the outside world or become too fussy.

Stage II: Engaging and Relating (3–6 Months)

During the first months of life, babies are able to engage with their caregivers in a back-and-forth interaction. From the first months of life, infants are able to imitate their caregivers' facial expressions. Early face-to-face interaction between the infant and the caregiver is elemental in helping the infant develop an understanding of their own and others' emotions. By 5 months of age, infants have social smiles and express their own happy and sad emotions. They have learned to be a part of a relationship and are ready to begin communicating with another person. Text Box 6.8 displays some early games for the caregiver and infant at this stage.

Stage III: Intentionality and Two-Way Communication (6–9 Months)

During this stage, infants begin to use simple signals, such as making vocal sounds, smiling, crying, or kicking for communication purposes. The caregiver's ability to read the infant's cues and respond to them promptly is important in helping the baby learn to respond to the caregiver's behavior in return. When infants engage with their caregivers in an exchange of emotional signals, they have begun an intentional two-way communication. These signals take place in what Greenspan calls **circles of communication.** These circles usually begin with the infant or the caregiver providing the first signal, and the second party responding with a similar behavior. For example, when the baby makes a vocal sound, and the caregiver responds by looking

Early Games for the Baby and the Caregivers — Text Box 6.8

Maintaining Calm, Getting Focused

The "Look and Listen" Game Enjoy face-to-face games with the baby, in which you smile and talk to him about his beautiful lips, sparkly eyes, and button nose. As you slowly move your animated face to the right or left try to capture the baby's attention for a few seconds. This game can be played while you hold the baby in your arms, or you can hover near him when he's reclining in an infant seat or lying in another person's arms.

The "Soothe Me" Game Settle into a comfortable rocking chair and enjoy slow rhythmic rocking with the baby when she is fussy or tired, or during other times when you simply want to cuddle. As you soothingly touch the baby's arms, legs, tummy, back, feet, and hands and relax into the lulling back-and-forth rocking rhythm, try to gently move her little fingers and toes in a "This Little Piggy" type of game. You can move her arms and legs and fingers and toes as you change her diaper, too.

Source: Greenspan, S. (1999). *Building healthy minds: The six experiences that create intelligence and emotional growth in babies and young children.* Cambridge, MA: Perseus Books.

at the baby or saying a word, the baby has opened and the caregiver has closed a circle of communication. The caregiver might want to open a second circle by using another behavior—verbal or nonverbal—such as uttering a word or making a gesture, to which the baby might respond by vocalizing further, or performing a nonverbal action, such as clapping.

Eventually, infants learn that they can make their intentions, wants, and needs known through different communicative verbal and nonverbal behaviors. These are important foundations of language development. At this stage, infants' gaze aversion during interactions, a lack of enjoyment to respond to the caregivers' signals, or a lack of participation in opening or closing circles of communication are signs of deviation in development. See Text Box 6.9 for a circle of communication game.

Nonverbal Circles of Communication — Text Box 6.9

The Circle of Communication Game Try to see how many back and forths you can get going each time the baby touches a shiny red ball or pats your nose and you make a funny squeal or squawk in response. Or see how many times he will try to open your hand when you've hidden an intriguing object inside. Each time the baby follows his interests and takes your bait, he is closing a circle of communication.

Source: Greenspan, S. (1999). *Building healthy minds: The six experiences that create intelligence and emotional growth in babies and young children.* Cambridge, MA: Perseus Books.

Stage IV: Social Problem Solving, Mood Regulation, and Forming of a Sense of Self (9–18 Months)

During this stage, infants begin to think in symbols and use gestures to convey simple ideas. They begin to point and gesture to make their needs known and to share their object of interest with adults. They begin to recognize simple patterns and develop a simple play repertoire. They learn to solve simple problems, such as reaching for a toy up on a shelf or asking parents for help solve a similar problem.

Infants begin to read cues from adults' emotional signals at this stage and learn how to modulate their own intense emotions. For example, the way an adult responds to a 15-month-old child's screams to get a toy, gives the child cues to regulate and modulate his own emotions. At this stage, children learn to distinguish between approval and disapproval. Different exchanges between young children and adults during this time period help them form a sense of self and others. A young child who seems oblivious to the adult's emotional cues, as well as having a lack of interest to share attention with adults, might be showing some early signs of problems in language, relating, and socialization. Table 6.1 displays typical development in different areas by 18 months.

Stage V: Creating Symbols and Using Words and Ideas (18 months–2½ Years)

By 18 months of age, children have developed simple language abilities and motor skills. They are able to think in symbols and hold images in their minds. Because of children's symbolic thinking abilities at this stage, they are able to develop imaginative play. They begin to combine ideas together and put simple phrases or sentences together to communicate ideas.

Children acknowledge peers during this time period by beginning to play with other children in their simple play themes. See Text Box 6.10 for tips to play with toddlers

TABLE 6.1   Typical Development by 18 Months

Sensory	Language	Cognitive	Motor
Explore and tolerate different foods and textures	Understand simple questions	Use toys and objects as they are intended (e.g., put telephone to ear and say hello)	Able to do two-step motor actions (like throwing a ball into the air and catching it)
Tolerate loud sounds	Use single words to make needs known and refer to objects and people	Imitate behaviors seen previously	Building a tower with two or three parts
Tolerate bright lights	Imitate simple words	Play with adults or children in simple games	Remove socks
Tolerate various types of touches		Search for hidden objects in more than one place	Putting pegs in a peg board

Source: Greenspan, S. (1999). *Building healthy minds: The six experiences that create intelligence and emotional growth in babies and young children.* Cambridge, MA: Perseus Publishing.

Tips for Playing with Toddlers	**Text Box 6.10**

Dos and Don'ts of Playing with Toddlers

> Don't rely on puzzles, books, or structured games to spark the child's use of ideas.
> Do get down on the floor and become a character—such as a bear or a wizard—in a pretend drama of the child's own choosing. Ham it up, interact, talk, and emote through your character.
> Do hold long conversations about anything that interests the child, from a new toy to his favorite or most despised food. Use games, books, or stories for ideas as a basis for long back-and-forth conversations rather than as ends in their own right.

Source: Greenspan, S. (1999). *Building healthy minds: The six experiences that create intelligence and emotional growth in babies and young children.* Cambridge, MA: Perseus Publishing.

during this stage. Because by this stage, children are able to use words for communicative purposes, it is common for caregivers and adults to be alerted to a problem during this stage, when a child fails to show appropriate language development.

Stage VI: Emotional Thinking, Logic, and a Sense of Reality (2 1/2–5 Years)

During this stage, children begin to connect simple ideas in a string to tell a story. They are able to develop themes with different parts and connect them together in a logical sequence. For example, in a house play theme, children can designate roles to themselves and to their peers. They can design a going to the park story, with sequences, such as getting in the car, driving to the park, and having a picnic there. Children begin to understand the concept of time and how ideas are carried over time and space. Eventually children's ability to think in a logical sequence enables them to distinguish what is real or not real, and how their ideas might be used to create things. A preschooler's ability to draw, invent games, and play by the rules is indicative of emotional and cognitive abilities during this stage. See Text Box 6.11 for milestones in stage 6.

Developmental Milestones in Children: Checking for Milestones in Stage VI	**Text Box 6.11**

1. In pretend play, the child's two ideas are tied together, even if they are unrealistic (e.g., the mom feeds the baby before driving the car to the park).
2. Child gets his or her pretend play themes from adult's behaviors, ideas (e.g., driving the car, cooking).
3. The child's ideas in speech are connected together (e.g., I want to play, I do not want to nap).
4. The child closes two or more circles of communication (e.g., Child: "I am hungry." Adult: "What do you want to eat?" Child: "A cookie.")

(Continued)

5. The child communicates connected ideas about feelings, thoughts, and intentions.
6. The child plays motor games with rules.
7. In his or her pretend play or daily communications, the child communicates the following ideas:
   a. Closeness
   b. Pleasure and excitement
   c. Assertive curiosity
   d. Fear
   e. Limit setting

Source: Greenspan, S. & Weider, S. (1998). *Child with special needs: Encouraging intellectual and emotional growth.* Cambridge, MA: Perseus Publishing.

Stage VII: Multicausal and Triangular Thinking (5 Years–Middle Childhood)

This stage is marked by recognition of multiple causes for events. Children increasingly become aware that there is more than one cause to an event. Multicausal thinking enables children to compare different phenomena together. It also helps children begin to understand different relationships among a variety of people, such as in a family dynamic.

FLOORTIME MODEL: APPLICATION OF GREENSPAN'S THEORY IN SPECIAL EDUCATION

Application of Greenspan's theory to early intervention and special education is called the **Floortime model.** It is also called the **DIR model,** which stands for developmental, individual differences, relationship-based model (Greenspan & Weider, 1998). Floortime model or DIR can be thought of as a philosophy or as a teaching/therapy procedure. As a philosophy, it encompasses a child-centered approach that revolves around the child's interests, likes, and choices. In a Floortime approach, the child is the director of a play session, and the therapist or adult assists the child in her play. As such, the child chooses the toys and activities of her own interest and acts on materials to discover and learn, while the adult interacts with the child and facilitates this learning through establishment of a positive relationship.

As elaborated by Greenspan and Wieder (1998), Floortime consists of a one-on-one play session between the child and the therapist, the teacher, or the parent. The adult literally "gets down" so that he is at the same level with the physical and interest level of the child. The adult plays in an interactive and animated way with the child. In fact, one of the reasons that this method is referred to as "Floortime" is that the adult often has to sit down on or lay down on the floor, so that he is at eye level with the young child. Opening and closing many circles of communication and having frequent eye contact with the child are important interaction components during the Floortime.

In Floortime, the adult conveys to the child that (1) during the session, the adult is not the authority, and (2) during the session, the adult follows the lead of the child. The Floortime model is a relationship-based model, in which getting down to the child's level and following the child's interests are used as vehicles for relating to the child and establishing a positive relationship with the child on the child's own terms.

By relating to the child, the adult creates a system of interaction appropriate to the child's developmental level. The adult's knowledge of the child's developmental level should be based on knowledge of the milestones belonging to Greenspan's stages of emotional development. Therefore, through systematic developmentally appropriate interactions, the adult provides appropriate cues and prompts, helping the child to eventually overcome areas of developmental problems and meet the appropriate milestones based on each level of development.

Floortime Model Guidelines

Floortime is implemented in many early intervention and early childhood programs. Conducting Floortime requires the teachers' understanding of the DIR model and details about the milestones in Greenspan's stages of development. Some early intervention and early childhood programs provide Floortime model training for teachers and therapists. Floortime model/DIR training does not take more than 1 or 2 days, in which the training focuses on specific observational, assessment, interaction, and play techniques. Some of the basic guidelines used for conducting Floortime with children are stated next (Greenspan & Weider, 1998):

➤ Floortime should be conducted in uninterrupted 20 to 30 minute sessions when the teacher's whole attention is given to the child for that period.
➤ The teacher consciously tries to stay patient and relaxed, and therefore to encourage the child's own calmness throughout the session.
➤ The teacher should understand and empathize with the child's emotional tone, such as tiredness, excitement, sadness, happiness, and so on.
➤ The teacher ought to be aware of her own attitudes and feelings, since the adult's feelings often influence how children feel and behave.
➤ For example, if the teacher is tired or not in the mood to play, another time to play with the child should be chosen.
➤ The teacher ought to monitor his own tone of voice and gestures, since the child follows the adult's model of behavior. Sounding warm, enticing, and supportive should be a part of the teacher's behavior repertoire.
➤ The teacher must follow the child's lead and interests, and interact based on what the child wants.
  ➤ Examples: If the child wants to play with cars, the teacher could take a car and follow the child's car; if the child wants to build with blocks, the teacher could take some blocks and build a tower next to the child; if the child wants the teacher to do a specific task, the teacher should follow the child's suggestion.
➤ The teacher should be animated and playfully interactive.

> The teacher ought to understand the developmental level of the child, and use appropriate techniques, such as gestures, words, and body language, to engage and attract the child's attention to open and close many circles of communication.

> While there are no rules in Floortime, people and materials are to be respected by the child and teacher as the basic rules of Floortime (i.e., no hitting, breaking, or hurting).

SENSORY PROCESSING THEORY

Today's developmental theorists, including Emde and Greenspan, rely on the sensory processing theory. The current sensory processing theory has been derived from the information processing and sensory integration theory. In this, the human brain is likened to a computer through which information is received and processed. This process begins with receiving information through the senses and ends as the individual processes the information and converts it into knowledge and skills.

Siegler (2003) and Siegler and Alibali (2005) explain the human thinking mechanism as a complex process that begins with the sensory stimuli being perceived, received, encoded, represented, stored, and finally retrieved. In this process, learning and memory strategies are important elements of processing information.

During the past two decades, the basic concepts of neuroscience (Geva & Feldman, 2008; Coren, Ward, & Enns, 1994; Kandel, Schwartz, & Jessell, 2000) and those of information processing have been integrated to form current ideas regarding sensory processing in children's development.

The original sensory integration theory began with the ideas of Jane Ayers (1972), an occupational therapist who had come across certain learning and attention problems in children with whom she worked. When she could not attribute the learning problems of these children to any known causes, Ayers (1972, 1979) came up with the theory of **sensory integration,** which explained how the brain's difficulties in processing and integrating, that is connecting sensations from the environment to the brain, might explain the children's possible learning problems.

Ayers believed that the brain regulates sensations received from the environment by balancing and adjusting the flow of sensory input to the central nervous system (CNS). She believed that the human brain would filter out useless information and focus on important information. In addition, through a process of sensory discrimination, the brain would make the person recognize the quality, quantity, similarities, and differences between each sensation (Ayers, 1972).

Ayers' research methods have been questioned for their scientific validity. Her theory has prompted much controversy in the field. However, findings in neuroscience and brain research during the past two decades confirm many of her ideas (Geva & Feldman, 2008; Cheung & Siu, 2009). Current early intervention, special education, and occupational therapy practices constantly draw on the sensory integration theory. Widespread anecdotal evidence exists for the efficacy of sensory integration, as well as great interest in establishing an evidence base for sensory integration therapies (Schechtman, 2007).

In simple words, **sensory processing** is one's "ability to feel, understand, and organize sensory information from his body and his environment" and to make usc of thc information received (Emmons & Anderson, 2005, p. 14). This perspective states that we receive information through our sensory organs; the eyes, ears, nose, mouth, and skin. The perceptual process takes place when our brain links the received sensory information with what is stored in the memory through past experiences. Attention is directly related to the way information is processed (Talsma & Senkowsk, 2009; Fairhall & Macaluso, 2009). For example, when we pay attention, our nervous system is able to process the incoming stimuli in a balanced way, and we are able to modulate and focus our attention on different stimuli as needed. The ability to respond appropriately to ordinary levels of sensory input—rather than under- or overreacting—is called **sensory modulation** (Rosinia, 2008).

By the same token, we are able to tune out the background stimuli (such as sites and noises) that are not useful to us (Talsma & Senkowsk, 2009). This is why we are able to organize sensory information. Our ability to organize sensory information enables us to regulate our feelings and behaviors—by responding appropriately to the stimuli we receive—and therefore function well on a daily basis (Kandel et al., 2000). Therefore, from this perspective, self-regulation is the ability to regulate emotions, interact with others, focus attention, and be able to learn in a calm manner. Sensory regulation occurs as a result of sensory processing and modulation.

When the nervous system is not able to effectively process sensory information, a person's learning and behavior is influenced (Childers & Jiang, 2008; Siegler, 2003; Emmons & Anderson, 2005). For example, when the nervous system responds too quickly or too slowly to stimuli, children might appear under-responsive or over-sensitive to certain sounds, touches, images, textures, or movements. Hence, a child who covers his ears at certain sounds, gags when certain smells permeate the environment, or appears to have a high activity level, might indicate an over-responsive sensory system to sounds and smells. On the other hand, a child who appears "withdrawn" or has poor motor responses and body awareness might be indicating an under-responsive sensory processing system.

Our sensory system consists of five senses: touch, smell, taste, hearing, and seeing. These senses are organized through seven major systems (Emmons & Anderson, 2005; Rosinia, 2008): the tactile system (responsible for processing input received from the sense of touch), the olfactory system (responsible for processing input received from the sense of smell), the gustatory system (responsible for processing input received from the sense of taste), the auditory system (responsible for processing input received from the sense of hearing), the visual system (responsible for processing input received from the sense of sight), the proprioceptive system (responsible for the coordination of movement), and the vestibular system (responsible for body awareness and balance).

Application of the Sensory Processing Theory in Special Education

The evaluation and treatment of children who have sensory processing difficulties usually is done by an occupational therapist who is trained in sensory integration and processing. Occupational therapists are usually a part of the early intervention and special education interdisciplinary teams, who evaluate motor development and sensory systems and plan intervention accordingly. Occupational therapists work closely with parents and teachers to provide appropriate sensory activities that they call a sensory diet, which responds to the specific sensory needs of the child. (For a more detailed discussion of sensory motor development, see Chapter 13.)

APPLIED BEHAVIOR ANALYSIS: A MODERN BEHAVIORAL PERSPECTIVE

Earlier, we learned that constructivist theories are concerned with the cognitive learning process in children. We also saw that relationship-based models of development and current developmental and sensory processing perspectives are interested in how brain development is related to the child's behaviors, as well as early interaction quality and relationship building. Behavioral theories, on the other hand, are involved with the behaviors as observable phenomena rather than with their motives and underlying processes.

A **behavior** is anything that a human does. Behaviorists study why and how a behavior occurs. The behavioral perspectives are built on ideas of a number of 19th-century theorists, such as Pavlov (1874–1949) and Watson (1878–1958). The more modern perspectives, such as applied behavior analysis, are inspired by ideas of B. F. Skinner (1904–1990).

The modern behavioral approach, **applied behavior analysis (ABA),** first defined by Baer, Wolf, and Risley (1968), uses Skinner's behavioral principles to explain the interaction between environmental factors and behavior that will influence behaviors of children. For ideas of early behavior theorists, see Text Box 6.12.

Applied behavior analysis is one of few methods with solid scientific support (Wolery, Barton, & Hine, 2005). ABA focuses on direct measures of individual's behaviors. It uses experimental designs and procedures to manipulate an individual's behaviors as a way of establishing a framework for understanding and explaining the human behavior (Wolery, Barton, & Hine, 2005). ABA uses systematic observation and data-taking through intervention and experimental manipulation as a way of understanding changes in behaviors (Baer et al., 1968).

Central to ABA is a careful assessment or analysis of behavior. In ABA, it is not only the consequence that affects a behavior, but also the antecedent. An **antecedent** is what happens before the behavior occurs, and a **consequence** is what happens afterward. Study of antecedents and consequences of behavior are important components of a behavior analysis in ABA. Using all of these factors, ABA helps educators understand children's behaviors and predict possible future behaviors. Using such information and utilizing the principles of ABA, the teacher is able to shape and change behaviors. It might be helpful to look at the following case example to understand how ABA works:

> Joey is a preschooler with speech and language delays. He throws a violent tantrum every time the teacher, Ms. Jones, says, "It is time to go to the gym." Ms. Jones punishes Joey's behavior by putting him in "time out" during gym time. If we were to follow an ABA approach in this instance, we would look at the antecedent (teacher's announcement of gym time), the consequence ("time out"), and what

function Joey's behavior of throwing a tantrum might serve for Joey. We might surmise that for some reason Joey does not want to go to the gym. We might further decide that because Joey has problems with language, his tantrum might serve a communicative purpose for him to express that he does not want to go to the gym. The consequence of "time out" might be exactly what Joey wants to get, to escape from going to the gym.

Early Behaviorists and Their Ideas   Text Box 6.12

Pavlov: Most people are familiar with Pavlov's *classical conditioning* theory. His theory is based on his observation and experimentation with dogs' salivation. He had discovered that dogs salivated at the sight of food. His classical conditioning experiment involved pairing food with a bell tone that would normally not elicit salivation from dogs. After repeated pairing of the two stimuli, he found that a response such as salivating could be transferred to a new stimulus, such as the bell tone. Thus, the dog was conditioned to respond to the bell tone—salivate at the tone of the bell, without food being present.

Watson: Watson coined the term *behaviorism* and believed that understanding behaviors came from careful observations of behavior and the environment. He believed that the environment irrevocably influences behavior. To him, individual differences between behaviors of children did not come from genetic factors, but rather from differences in their past experiences. Watson believed that using classical conditioning principles, any child could be trained to learn and behave in specific behaviors and perform complex tasks.

Skinner: Skinner advanced theories of his predecessors in a new form of learning he called operant conditioning. Based on classical conditioning, what comes *before* the behavior, the stimulus, could cause a behavior to occur. Skinner, believed that what comes *after* the behavior, the consequence, is also important in producing or causing a behavior to re-occur, and in changing the behavior. In Skinner's view, if a consequence of a behavior is positive and pleasant to the child, the behavior is most likely to occur again. This, he called a positive reinforcement.

Receiving positive reinforcement for a behavior will guide the child to learn that behavior. On the other hand, if a child's behavior results in a negative consequence, the rate of that behavior occurring again will decrease. In behavior terms, any consequence that is unpleasant to the child is considered as a negative consequence. Skinner might pose a case as the following: imagine a toddler throwing food off his tray for the first time when he is eating independently. If the child receives some positive attention, such as a smile, the first few times he throws food on the floor, he will repeat throwing food off his tray every time he eats. If, on the other hand, he receives an unpleasant consequence, such as removal of the food, he is less likely to repeat food throwing when he eats.

Sources: Crain, W. (2005). *Theories of development: Concepts and applications* (5th ed.). Upper Saddle River, NJ: Pearson Education, Inc.

Having studied Joey's behavior, a behavior interventionist might predict, since the consequence of Joey's tantrum is rewarding to him, that Joey will continue to have a tantrum whenever it is time to go to the gym. Using experimental manipulation, the behavior interventionist might opt to change the consequences of Joey's behavior. For example, he could take Joey to the gym, and for every minute that Joey participated in the gym, he could reward him with a positive reinforcer—something that Joey really loves, which would therefore reinforce Joey's behavior of participating in the gym. Recording the intervention procedures, the interventionist could then decide how to continue with the intervention.

For example, if the behavior intervention proved successful and Joey responded appropriately to the positive reinforcer, the behaviorist would reward Joey for participating in the gym for longer periods and would systematically increase the length of time until Joey has learned to participate in the gym for the entire period. Through these procedures, the behavior interventionist has changed Joey's behavior of nonparticipation to a shaped behavior of participation in the gym regularly.

Application of ABA in Special Education

ABA has often used a discrete trial format, called **discrete trial teaching (DTT)** (Leaf & McEachin, 1999). Discrete trial teaching is a subset of ABA, which consists of intensive one-on-one sessions between the interventionist and the child. The interventionist presents a *discriminative stimulus*—usually a request for a desired response. For example, the interventionist might present several pictures of objects and ask, "Show me the picture of the red car." Through delivery of a reinforcer, the interventionist shapes the behavior of the child into the desired response. DTT could be used to teach functional life skills, communication skills, or social skills (Steege, Mace, Perry, & Longenecker, 2007).

When teachers use ABA principles to teach a new task or a new behavior to the child, we say that we have shaped a child's behavior. To do so, the teacher often provides appropriate prompts so the child can learn the new behavior. The word **prompt** in applied behavior analysis is equivalent to the words cue and scaffolding. In a way, prompts can be described as actions that help support and scaffold a child's learning. In Chapter 11, we will describe prompts and prompt hierarchy in detail.

ABA and DTT have been increasingly and widely used for children with autism (we will explain autism further in Chapter 7). Variations exist in the types of ABA being used across different programs; and although some programs use certain instructional methodologies based on ABA or the discrete trial format, they hardly use ABA in its strict and correct format (Steege et al., 2007).

Using correct ABA requires the careful training of teachers, which includes training in discrete trial teaching, meticulous behavior analysis, data gathering, and intervention assessment. In terms of personnel, ABA is costly and is seldom used in school settings, unless used for a short period of time (such as 1 hour of DTT instruction throughout the day). In the United States, certain states provide funding through their early intervention programs to deliver ABA intervention for children with autism in the child's home (5 days per week and at least for 25 hours per week, 12 months per year) (Steege et al., 2007).

In general, however, principles of behavioral approaches have been consistently used in working with children with exceptionalities in specialized and inclusive school settings. Earlier, we discussed that motivation of exceptional children is an important issue of consideration. Teachers familiar with ABA often use positive reinforcers to motivate young children to perform an activity or do a task. These positive reinforcers might vary from tangible rewards such as food items and favorite toys and activities, to repeated praises and hugs throughout the day. By this, teachers provide positive consequences for a child's behavior to promote appropriate behaviors and to teach a new task.

Some early childhood teachers are reluctant to use positive reinforcers with young children. In their opinions, applying such principles to motivate children's learning is bribing. Schloss and Smith (1998) argue that these teachers are reminded that bribery by definition involves paying someone in advance to do something that might be wrong; whereas in a behavioral approach, the positive reinforcer is used to increase the likelihood of the occurrence of a desired behavior.

Additionally, we might expect all children to learn essential behaviors and skills to be successful academically and socially. However, young children and exceptional learners require extra assistance to learn appropriate behaviors and skills (Schloss & Smith, 1998). Tangible positive reinforcers, such as a food item or a favorite toy, might help motivate these children to learn the skills they need to be successful. We should be reminded that the goal of using a behavioral approach is to eventually replace tangible reinforcers with social reinforcers, such as praises and smiles.

More recently, the principles of ABA have been integrated into an approach called positive behavior support (PBS) in special education today. In addition to the basic principles of ABA, positive behavior support attempts to understand the functions of a child's behaviors as well as the environmental antecedents, setting events, which contribute to a child's behavior. PBS has been used both as a school-wide and individual approach. In Chapter 9, we will discuss PBS in detail.

Critical Thinking Question 6.3   Referring to the story at the start of the chapter, how does Chad use behavioral approaches in teaching his student during his home visit?

Task Analysis: Another Application of Behavioral Methods in Special Education

Task analysis is another subset of ABA. Task analysis has been used for young children with and without disabilities. In special education, it has been used in teaching daily living or academic skills for tasks that involve multiple and complex steps. It has specifically been successful for children who might lack the motor sequencing abilities and cognitive abilities to learn all parts of a complex task at once. Task analysis is breaking down a task into small simple components that are manageable to teach. Using prompts, each step of a task is taught to the child separately first. For example, steps or components for washing hands might be:

1. Turn tap on.
2. Use soap.

In task analysis, each component is taught separately as a single behavior. Here, the child is taught one component, using soap, to learn to wash her hands.

3. Scrub hands.
4. Rinse hands.
5. Turn off water.
6. Dry hands.

In task analysis, each component is taught separately as a single behavior. The child will learn to perform a task through approximation and receiving a reinforcer until the desired behavior is shaped. Since complex tasks consist of a chain of components, the chain components are taught in a sequence. Learning to perform each step of a task as it is connected to the next one is called chaining (Alberto & Troutman, 2006). In the previously described task, for example, step 3 is taught after step 1 and 2 are taught, and so on. Chaining might also occur in a backward sequence. For example, step 6 might be taught first, before steps 5 and 4 are taught. A behavior chain consists of learning to perform chains of a complex behavior in its correct sequence (Alberto & Troutman, 2006). We will provide further explanations and illustrations of a task analysis in Chapter 11.

THE MODERN TRANSACTIONAL ECOLOGICAL MODEL

In Chapter 3, we discussed the ecological model of Bronfenbrenner. As we saw in that chapter, development of the child is influenced by many environmental and cultural factors. A modern ecological perspective, the transactional model, builds on Bronfenbrenner's theory (Bronfenbrenner, 1979).

This model has been elaborated by Sameroff and Fiese (2000). This view emphasizes the role of contextual factors influencing the development of the child. The development of the child is seen as an interactive process involving the child, the family, and the environment. In this view, the child has equal influence on the environment. Over time, the interplay of different factors within the child and the environment might lead to a positive or a negative outcome for the child. In an example, Sameroff and Fiese (2000) explain the transactional model while looking at an infant's first months of life after birth. In this example, the mother has gone through a complicated childbirth and is therefore worried about her child's development after release from the hospital. Sameroff and Fiese (2000) look at the mother's and the infant's behaviors:

> The mother's anxiety during the first months of life may have caused her to be uncertain and inappropriate in her interactions with the child. In response to such inconsistency, the infant may have developed some irregularities in feeding and sleeping patterns that give the appearance of difficult temperament. This difficult temperament decreases the pleasure that the mother obtains from the child, so she tends to spend less time with her child. If adults are not actively interacting with the child, and especially speaking to the child, the child may not meet the norms for language development and may score poorly on preschool language tests. (p. 142)

Based on this perspective, planning any effective intervention depends on the attention paid to the contextual factors, such as the child, the mother, the family, the physical environment, the psychological and material well-being of the parents and the child, and the culture. However, in reality, no intervention program is able to manipulate all factors contributing to development of the child. Therefore, the alternative is to understand the essential and most influential factors contributing to the child's development and to provide intervention based on the child and family's needs and the available support and resources (Sameroff & Fiese, 2000). In this model, it is necessary to understand the cultural codes, the parental behaviors, and the family's belief system, all of which form the daily practices and behaviors of the family, as well as interactions between the child and other members of the family.

Application of the Transactional Model in Special Education

An intervention based on the transactional model includes strategies to involve multiple members of the child's family and multiple disciplines in early childhood and early intervention (Sameroff & Fiese, 2000). This may involve different intervention strategies targeting both the child and other family members, and in different locations. For example, intervention for a toddler with physical developmental problems might involve not only working with the child, but working with parents and other family members to (1) educate them about the disability, (2) help facilitate optimal parenting interactions with the child, and (3) help parents provide an appropriate care to the child, utilizing community and available resources (Sameroff & Fiese, 2000).

In general, the transactional model has been roughly applied to early intervention and special education programs in the United States, because parent involvement is one of the most important dimensions of these programs and also in early childhood special education. An example of a transactional model is the Portage Project. The Portage Project is a family-guided early intervention program for children with disabilities (from birth through age 6) and their families.

Established in 1969 in Portage, Wisconsin, the program focuses on addressing outcomes for the child and family that are based on the child's developmental needs, interests, and cultural norms of the family. The IFSP and IEP goals are addressed through naturally occurring and play-based activities in the child's environment—both in the school and/or at home. The Portage team works closely with parents and all family members to help them support the healthy development of their child. This program has been replicated in various national and international locations around the world.

Head Start and Early Head Start programs are other examples of federally funded intervention programs based on ecological and transactional philosophies. Pioneered and led by Bronfenbrenner, the Head Start program was established in 1965 to give children of low-income families a "head start" in education and development.

The program aims to improve the child's physical health, cognitive, and social emotional development, improve the parent–child relationship, and enhance a sense of competence in the child. The Early Head Start program targets infants and toddlers and their families, and pregnant women. The goals of this program are to promote healthy prenatal outcome, to promote the development of very young children, and to improve family functioning and relationships. The range of services offered by these programs consist of early childhood education and development, parent education and family partnership, health and nutrition services, home visits, and other related family support services.

Final Remarks

After reading about different models of development and intervention, we might find ourselves confused as to which of the models discussed in this chapter is the most effective or viable for working with young children with special needs. We will certainly not find the field lacking in research arguments for and against each of the models discussed in this chapter.

As educators, we might find it difficult to ground our philosophy of teaching in one theory only. In addition, our experiences might have shown us that every child deserves to be understood individually and within his or her own developmental

TABLE 6.2   Modern Theoretical Approaches in Special Education

Theories	Theorists	Application to Special Education
Constructivist/social constructivist approaches	Rogoff	➤ Aspects of constructivism have been applied in special education, such as in peer-mediated instruction ➤ Integration of hands-on activities in some science and self-help skills classrooms
Relationship-based model of intervention	Emde; Greenspan and Wieder	➤ DRI/Floortime model
Modern behavioral approaches (ABA)	Baer, Wolf, and Risely	➤ Components of ABA principles have been applied in special education ➤ DTT ➤ Task analysis ➤ Positive behavior support (PBS)
Sensory processing ideas	Ayers; later research in neuroscience	➤ Occupational therapy with a focus on sensory integration therapies and sensory diet
Transactional ecological model	Bronfenbrenner; Sameroff and Fiese	➤ Roughly applied in early intervention and preschool special education (Portage Project) ➤ Compensatory programs (Head Start; Early Head Start)

context. We might have found that the intervention application of one theory has worked well with one child, but not with another. Like Chad, the teacher in the story at the beginning of this chapter, we might therefore have found that an eclectic philosophy of teaching grounded in valid theories would achieve a better outcome for the children and families we work with. No matter what philosophy informs our teaching practices, we should be careful to ground our philosophies of teaching and our practices in theories that have evidence-based interventions. Table 6.2 summarizes the major components of the modern theories we discussed in this chapter.

SUMMARY

Our philosophies and methods of working with children with disabilities, and the policies on which our education system is founded are influenced by theories of child development. The most influential theories of development in educating children with disabilities are constructivist perspectives, modern developmental and sensory processing perspectives, applied behavior analysis, and ecological/transactional models of development. Each of these theories has direct implications for those practices and methods used in working with exceptional children.

Many programs are based on specific models and theories of development. On the other hand, some programs are based on multiple theories of development. The decision about what teaching methods to use for each child must be made based on the individual child and family needs. In addition, early childhood educators ought to make their teaching decisions based on those methods that have empirical validity.

Review Questions

1. How is a philosophy of teaching related to one or more theories of child development?
2. What are the modern constructivist ideas of development?
3. In application of the constructivist and social constructivist theories in working with exceptional children, what factors should be considered?
4. What are the stages of Greenspan's relationship-based developmental model?
5. What is the influence of sensory processing on the infant's ability in self-regulation?
6. What is the Floortime model, and what are some important guidelines in conducting Floortime with children?
7. How does the sensory processing perspective account for individual differences in learning?
8. What are the important components of applied behavior analysis, and how may these components be used to teach a child a specific task or behavior?
9. What are intervention implications for the transactional ecological model?

Out-of-Class Activities

1. Design a small group lesson plan for preschool-age children or for children in primary-level classrooms.
   a. Conduct this activity using teaching practices based on the constructivist approach.
   b. Conduct this activity based on the DIR/Floortime model.
   c. Conduct this activity using behavioral principles in teaching.

Recommended Resources

High Scope Educational Research Foundation
http://www.highscope.org/

National Head Start Association
http://www.nhsa.org/

North America Reggio Emilia Alliance (NAREA)
http://www.reggioalliance.org/

Office of Head Start
Department of Health and Human Services,
Administration for Children and Families
http://www.acf.hhs.gov/programs/ohs/

Portage Project
http://www.portageproject.org/

Reggio Children
http://zerosei.comune.re.it/inter/reggiochildren.htm

Stanley Greenspan
http://www.stanleygreenspan.com/

The Interdisciplinary Council on Development and
Learning Disorders (ICDL) (Information and guidelines
on Floortime Model)
http://www.icdl.com/dirFloortime/overview/index.shtml

**View the Online Resources available to accompany
this text by visiting http://www.mhhe.com/bayat1e.**

References

Alberto, P. A., & Troutman, A. C. (2006). *Applied behavior analysis for teachers* (7th ed.). Upper Saddle River, NJ: Pearson Education, Inc.

Ayers, A. J. (1972). *Sensory integration and learning disorders.* Los Angeles: Western Psychological Services.

Ayers, A. J. (1979). *Sensory integration and the child.* Los Angeles: Western Psychological Services.

Baer, D., Wolf, M., & Risely, T. (1968). Some current dimensions of applied behavior analysis. *Journal of Applied Behavior Analysis, 1,* 91–97.

Bodrova, E., & Leong, D. (2009). Tools of the mind: A Vygotskian-based early childhood curriculum. *Early Childhood Services: An Interdisciplinary Journal of Effectiveness, 3*(3), 245–262.

Broderick, P., & Blewitt, P. (2006). *The life span: Human development for helping professionals* (2nd ed.). Upper Saddle River, NJ: Pearson Education, Inc.

Bronfenbrenner, U. (1979). *The ecology of human development: Experiments by nature and design.* Cambridge, MA: Harvard University Press.

Bunce, J. (2001). How special is special education? *High/ Scope Resource, 16,* 1. Retrieved May 22, 2007, from http://www.highscope.org/EducationalPrograms/ EarlyChildhood/HSandSpecEd.htm

Cheung, P., & Siu, A. (2009). A comparison of patterns of sensory processing in children with and

without developmental disabilities. *Research in Developmental Disabilities, 30*(6), 1468–1480.

Childers, T., & Jiang, Y. (2008). Neurobiological perspectives on the nature of visual and verbal processes. *Journal of Consumer Psychology, 18*(4), 264–269.

Childre, A., Sands, J., & Pope, S. (2009). Backward design. *Teaching Exceptional Children, 41*(5), 6–14.

Coren, S., Ward, L., & Enns, J. (1994). *Sensation and perception.* Fort Worth, TX: Harcourt Brace College Publications.

Crain, W. (2005). *Theories of development: Concepts and applications* (5th ed.). Upper Saddle River, NJ: Pearson Education, Inc.

Emde, R. N., & Robinson, J. (2000). Guiding principles for a theory of early intervention: A developmental-psychoanalytic perspective. In J. P. Shonkoff & S. J. Meisels (Eds.), *Handbook of Early Childhood Intervention* (pp. 160–178). Cambridge, UK: Cambridge University Press.

Emde, R. N., Korfmacher, J., & Kubicek, L. F. (2000). Toward a theory of early relationship-based intervention. In J. D. Osofsky & H. E. Fitzgerald (Eds.), *WAIMH handbook of infant mental health. Vol. two: Early Intervention, evaluation, and assessment* (pp. 3–32). New York: John Wiley and Sons.

Emmons, P. G., & Anderson, L. M. (2005). *Understanding sensory dysfunction: Learning, development, and sensory dysfunction in autism spectrum disorders, ADHD, learning disabilities and bipolar disorder.* Philadelphia: Jessica Kingsley Publishers.

Fairhall, S., & Macaluso, E. (2009). Spatial attention can modulate audiovisual integration at multiple cortical and subcortical sites. *European Journal of Neuroscience, 29*(6), 1247–1257.

Gardner III, R., Nobel, M., Hessler, T., Yawn, C. D., & Heron, T. (2007). Tutoring system innovations: Past practice to future prototypes. *Intervention in School and Clinic, 43*(2), 71–81.

Geva, R., & Feldman, R. (2008). A neurobiological model for the effects of early brainstem functioning on the development of behavior and emotion regulation in infants: Implications for prenatal and perinatal risk. *Journal of Child Psychology and Psychiatry, 49*(10), 1031–1041.

Greenspan, S. (1999). *Building healthy minds: The six experiences that create intelligence and emotional growth in babies and young children.* Cambridge, MA: Perseus Books.

Greenspan, S., & Wieder, S. (1998). *The child with special needs: Encouraging intellectual and emotional growth.* Reading, MA: Perseus Books.

Greenspan, S., & Wieder, S. (2006a). *Infant and early childhood mental health: A comprehensive developmental approach to assessment and intervention.* Washington, DC: American Psychiatric Publishing, Inc.

Greenspan, S., & Wieder, S. (2006b). *Engaging autism: Using the Floortime approach to help children relate, communicate, and think.* Cambridge, MA: Da Capo Lifelong Books.

Greenspan, S. (2007). Levels of infant-caregiver interactions and the DIR model: Implications for the development of signal affects, the regulation of mood and behavior, the formation of sense of self, the creation of internal representation, and the construction of defenses and character structure. *Journal of Infant, Child, & Adolescent Psychotherapy, 6*(3), 174–210.

Hohmann, M., & Weikart, D. (1995). *Educating young children: Active learning practices for preschool and child care programs.* Ypsilanti, MI: High/Scope.

Hohmann, M., & Weikart, D. (2002). *Educating young children: Active learning practices for preschool and child care programs* (2nd ed.). Ypsilanti, MI: High/Scope.

Kandel, E., Schwartz, J., & Jessell, T. (2000). *Principles of neural science* (4th ed.). New York: McGraw-Hill.

Keengwe, J., & Onchwari, G. (2009). Technology and early childhood education: A technology integration professional development model for practicing teachers. *Early Childhood Education Journal, 37*(3), 209–218.

Kotulak, R. (1996). *Inside the brain: Revolutionary discoveries of how the mind works.* Kansas City, MO: Andrews and McNeel.

Kunc, N. (1992). The need to belong: Rediscovering Maslow's hierarchy of needs. In R. A. Villa, J. S. Thousand, W. Stainback, & S. Stainback (Eds.), *Restructuring for caring and effective education* (pp. 25–39). Baltimore: Paul H. Brookes.

Leaf, R., & McEachin, J. (1999). *A work in progress: Behavior management strategies and a curriculum for intensive behavioral treatment of autism.* Austin, TX: Pro-Ed.

Loris Malaguzzi International Center. (2010). *Reggio children: The hundred languages of children.* Retrieved July 23, 2010, from http://zerosei.comune.re.it/inter/100exhibit.htm

Mallory, B., & New, R. (1994). Social constructivist theory and principles of inclusion: Challenges for early childhood special education. *The Journal of Special Education, 28*(3), 322–337.

Montessori, M. (1974). *Childhood education.* Chicago: Henry Regnery Company. Oxford: Oxford University.

Poole, D., Nunez, N., & Warren, A. (2007). *The story of human development.* Upper Saddle River, NJ: Pearson Education, Inc.

Rogoff, B. (1990). *Apprenticeship in thinking: Cognitive development in social context.*

Rosinia, J. (2008). Sensory processing. In L. Gilkerson & Klein, R. (Eds.), *Early development and the brain: Teaching resources for educators* (pp. 8.1–8.61). Washington, DC: Zero To Three.

Sameroff, A. J., & Fiese, B. H. (2000). Transactional regulation: The developmental ecology of early intervention. In J. P. Shonkoff & S. J. Meisels (Eds.), *Handbook of early childhood intervention* (pp. 135–159). Cambridge, UK: Cambridge University Press.

Schechtman, M. A. (2007). Scientifically unsupported therapies in the treatment of young children with

Autism Spectrum Disorders. *Psychiatric Annals, 37*(9), 639–645.

Schloss, P. J., & Smith, M. A. (1998). *Applied behavior analysis in the classroom.* Boston: Allyn & Bacon.

Scruggs, T., & Mastropieri, M. A. (1993). Current approaches to science education: Implications for mainstream instruction of students with disabilities. *Remedial and Special Education, 14*(1), 15–24.

Scruggs, T., & Mastropieri, M. A. (1994). The construction of scientific knowledge by students with mild disabilities. *The Journal of Special Education, 28*(3), 307–321.

Siegler, R. S. (2003). Relations between short-term and long-term cognitive development, *Psychological Science Agenda, 16,* 8–10.

Siegler, R. S., & Alibali, M. W. (2005). *Children's thinking* (4th ed.). Upper Saddle River, NJ: Prentice Hall.

Smith, L. (2002). Piaget's model. In U. Goswami (Ed.), *Blackwell handbook of childhood cognitive development* (pp. 515–537). Malden, MA: Blackwell.

Steege, M. W., Mace, F. C., Perry, L., & Longenecker, H. (2007). Applied behavior analysis: Beyond discreet trail teaching. *Psychology in Schools, 44*(1), 91–99.

Stephenson, S. M. (1998). *Michael Olaf's essential Montessori: School edition, for age 3–12.* Arcata, CA: Michael Olaf Publishers.

Talsma, D., & Senkowsk, D. (2009). Intermodal attention affects the processing of the temporal alignment of audiovisual stimuli. *Experimental Brain Research, 198*(2–3), 313–328.

Van Norman, R. K., & Wood, C. L. (2007). Innovations in peer tutoring: Introduction to the special issue. *Intervention in School and Clinic, 43*(2), 69–70.

Volling, B., Kolak, A., & Blandon, A. (2009). Family subsystems and children's self regulation. In S. L. Olson & A. J. Sameroff (Eds.), *Biopsychosocial regulatory processes in the development of childhood behavioral problems* (pp. 238–257). New York: Cambridge University Press.

Wolery, M., Barton, E. E., & Hine, J. F. (2005). Evolution of applied behavior analysis in the treatment of individuals with autism. *Exceptionality, 13*(1), 11–23.

Section 2

Disabilities and Methods

Autism Spectrum Disorders

Objectives

Upon completion of this chapter, you should be able to:

> Understand the historical context of autism, its prevalence and causal theories.
> Define and categorize disorders under Autism Spectrum Disorders.
> Identify important early signs of autism.

> Describe the developmental characteristics in autism.
> Understand sensory dysfunction and related behavioral characteristics of autism.
> Understand strategies, adaptations, and methods of working with children with autism.
> Describe the family's role in the education of children with autism.
> Understand the educator's role in working with families of children with autism.

Key Terms

causal theory (215)	parallel play (226)	self-stimulatory behaviors (231)
control sentences (241)	perspective sentences (239)	sensory diet (235)
descriptive sentences (238)	pica (230)	shared attention (224)
directive sentences (239)	Picture Exchange Communication System (PECS) (242)	social games (226)
early onset (218)	pretend play (226)	social story (238)
echolalia (225)	prevalence (213)	tactile defensiveness (230)
late onset (218)	protodeclarative pointing (222)	theory of mind (229)
matching (227)		

Reflection Questions

Before reading this chapter, answer the following questions to reflect upon your personal opinions and beliefs that are pertinent to early childhood special education.

1. In your opinion, why has the rate of autism increased during the last decades?
2. What are your personal perceptions about working with children with autism?
3. What are some issues to consider when deciding on an appropriate educational program for children with autism?
4. Why do you think collaboration with parents of children with autism is important in educating children with autism?

Earlier Is Better!

A few months ago, Tricia, a child development expert, had to inform her friend, Diana, that Diana's 9-month-old son, Kevin, displayed some early signs that might be an indication of later behavioral characteristics of young children within the Autism Spectrum Disorders. Tricia gently alerted Diana to the fact that Kevin averted his gaze when adults tried to make eye contact, did not share attention with his mother or other adults, did not respond to face-to-face interactions with enthusiasm, and displayed some signs of regulatory and sensory processing dysfunction, such as rubbing his feet on the carpet, staring at the light, or screaming when hearing certain sounds.

Tricia carefully reassured her friend that these warning signs might not amount to Kevin having a disorder. However, she advised Diana to have Kevin evaluated by a specialist. Diana was devastated to consider the possibility of autism for her son. She had seen Tricia's own son growing up with autism. Through what she had seen and through the information disseminated by the media, she had learned that autism was a serious condition with a variety of developmental problems and difficult behaviors. She could not imagine that she would have to go through the same difficulties her friend and other families of children with autism went through.

Tricia reminded Diana that children who have autism usually differ from one another in terms of the severity of their conditions and behavioral characteristics. She explained that early intensive intervention is the key to the treatment of autism. In fact, the earlier a child with ASD is diagnosed, the better the outcome would be. Therefore, it was important for Kevin to be examined in case he was seen as a candidate with certain characteristics of the disorder. Tricia added that it was seldom for an infant as young as Kevin to receive a formal diagnosis of autism, but if Kevin indicated to have specific signs, appropriate intervention was likely to help him overcome some of his early developmental difficulties.

Tricia went on to describe a variety of therapeutic options available for treatment of autism, such as ABA, Floortime, and sensory integrative therapy, all of which made amazing gains and progress possible for young children who were diagnosed early. She encouraged Diana to contact her local early intervention agency for a preliminary interview. As Tricia described the steps involved in the process of evaluation and intervention, she could not help thinking back to the time that her own son was diagnosed with autism. Receiving such news is devastating for any parent. However, recognizing a developmental problem in a child early on, and intervening as soon as possible, does make a difference in the outcome for the child.

Unfortunately, when her son was an infant, Tricia was not a child development expert, nor did she have a friend to alert her to the problem. So, her son was not diagnosed with autism until after he had turned 3 years of age. Tricia remembered that when her son was 2 years old, she expressed concerns to her son's pediatrician about his lack of language. The doctor reassured her that her own son had not spoken until well past that age. (Although today public awareness regarding Autism Spectrum Disorders has become widespread, this disorder had not been well known by the pediatricians or physicians a few years ago.)

Tricia could not help remarking to Diana that had she known of her own son's autism early on, she and her family might have been able to secure intervention for him sooner. Although Tricia's son received intervention after diagnosis and through all of his childhood and adolescence, he was never able to use language for communication, and made only modest progress throughout his school years.

As Tricia reflected upon her own experiences with autism and those which her best friend would have to face, she hoped that someday early identification tools would be available in various early care and health clinic settings so professionals would be able to identify early signs of the disorder and thus be able to provide early intervention much earlier than currently possible.

INTRODUCTION

In February 2007, the Centers for Disease Control and Prevention (CDC) issued an alarming report regarding the accelerated rate of **prevalence** of Autism Spectrum Disorders (ASD) in the United States. Prevalence is a measure of the number of individuals with a disease or a condition over a period of time. For example, the number of 3-year-old children who were diagnosed with autism in 2007 in the United States constitutes the prevalence of autism in 3-year-olds. In the 1990s, prevalence of autism was reported to be 3.3 per 10,000 children (Wing, 1993). In early 2000, this rate was reported to have increased to between 41 to 45 per 10,000 children (Yeargin-Allsopp et al., 2003), and in 2003 it had increased to between 60 to 66 in every 10,000 children (Fombonne, 2003).

The new CDC report (2007) indicated that today, the number of children who are diagnosed within the Autism Spectrum Disorder is approximately 1 in every 150 children. The CDC estimated that every year, approximately 26,670 children would be diagnosed with ASD. This report shows that compared to other disabilities, ASD is more common than disorders such as Down syndrome (1 out of every 800 births) and childhood cancer, diabetes, and AIDS put together. More recent studies have reported a higher autism prevalence of 1 in every 91 children, including 1 in every 58 boys (odds of boys having ASD being 4 times higher in comparison with girls) (Kogan et al., 2009; Baron-Cohen et al., 2009). Some investigators have gone as far as declaring an autism epidemic (Fombonne, 2001; Rimland, 1995), saying that autism could no longer be considered a low incidence disability (Simpson, 2005a), a disability that has a low prevalence rate.

Among preschool-aged children, 1 in every 125 children is diagnosed with autism (Nicolas, Carpenter, King, Jenner, & Charles, 2009). The implication of this rate increase for educators is that on average, every early childhood teacher will teach a child within the Autism Spectrum Disorders at least every 3 to 4 years. Although an early diagnosis during infancy is possible, autism is seldom diagnosed before age 2. It is therefore important that early childhood educators and health professionals understand the importance of diagnosis of ASD at the earliest age possible, because we know for certain that early intervention is one of the most effective ways of treating autism. Since early childhood educators are at the forefront of early intervention, it is especially important for them to understand the warning signs of this disorder at an early age, the behavioral characteristics of autism, as well as ways to educate children within the Autism Spectrum Disorders.

Critical Thinking Question 7.1   Referring to the story at the beginning of the chapter, and considering how Tricia informed Diana about the possibility of a developmental problem in Kevin, what do you think are some appropriate ways in which professionals can inform a parent of any warning signs that they might have observed in the development of a child with whom they work?

THE HISTORY OF AUTISM

From the early days of its discovery, autism has hardly been mentioned as a disorder separate from family influences. In 1943, Leo Kanner, a child psychiatrist at Johns Hopkins University, was the first person to describe the cases of 11 children with autism whom he had encountered. These children lacked normal communication skills, displayed repetitive behaviors, made odd noises, and seemed to be oblivious or uninterested in others around them. Kanner called this disorder autism from the Greek word *autos* meaning *self,* referring to those children's withdrawal from social life (Frith, 1989).

One year after Kanner's initial observation, the German psychologist Asperger treated a similar group of children who were lacking in social interest, yet displayed good vocabulary and language abilities. Independent of Kanner, Asperger termed the disorder of the children under his treatment as autism. Eventually, under the original classification of autism, children who displayed severe communication and autistic behavior characteristics were considered to have Kanner syndrome, and those who had good communication abilities, and yet had social relatedness problems, were labeled as having Asperger syndrome.

In his original papers, Kanner (1943, 1948) asserted that autism was partially attributed to deficits in child-rearing abilities and a lack of maternal attention. He described the parents of those 11 children under his treatment as lacking in warmth, being preoccupied by scientific or artistic interest, and lacking genuine interest in people. In general, Kanner referred to parents of children with autism as cold, bookish, formal, humorless, and detached. He raised the question whether, or to what extent, those parents might have contributed to the condition of their children.

Refrigerator Mothers

In the 1960s, Bettelheim, a German self-professed psychologist who had escaped his country during World War II, coined the term refrigerator mother to refer to mothers of children with autism. He explained infantile autism as a state of mind that developed in reaction to feeling oneself in an extreme situation, entirely without hope. According to Bettelheim (1967), during the infant's critical periods—6 to 9 months, and 18 months to 2 years—if the infant had frustrating experiences with his mother, he became passive. These frustrating experiences typically happened when the infant's overtures (smiling, kicking, making baby noises, babbling, etc.) were met with the mother's indifference and coldness. Since all of the infant's frustrated efforts to attract the mother's attention were met with irresponsiveness, the infant became convinced that nothing could be done to achieve satisfaction (love and attention) from the world or the parents. Thus, the infant withdrew to the autistic position (Bettelheim, 1967).

Bettelheim's theory, also known as the psychogenic theory, which blamed the mother's failure to form a meaningful relationship with her infant as the cause of autism, was the most popular theory in the 1950s and 1960s. Typical treatment for children with autism was to separate the child from the parents, so further damage would not be inflicted upon the child. In addition, psychotherapy was prescribed for mothers of children with autism to help them overcome their lack of love and coldness toward their children. One could only imagine the stigma and psychological trauma such a social perception imposed upon the mothers of children with autism during this period.

Autism: A Neurobiological Disorder

In 1964, Rimland, a psychologist who was also the father of a child with autism, theorized about biological causes of autism. He convincingly set forth a neural theory of autism in which the syndrome was explained as primarily a cognitive problem, an impairment in "the mode of operation of the brain mechanism which links sensation to memory" (Rimland, 1964, p. 188). His theory for the first time introduced autism as a neurobiological disorder and not a psychological one. In later years, discovery of the presence of epilepsy in one-third of individuals with autism confirmed autism as indeed a biological disorder.

Rimland's work became the foundation of rigorous scientific work in understanding autism and its causes, and it so persuasively put to rest the "parent blame" theory of autism that to this day no researcher has raised the original theory again. The discredited psychogenic concept is now only of historical value and interest. Research in the field of autism during recent years has provided evidence that autism belongs to a category of disorders that have neurobiological bases. It is interesting to note, however, that some of the original perceptions persist to this day, and in some countries causes of autism are still traced to parents, and psychotherapy is prescribed for parents of children with autism (Ferrari, 1997).

CAUSES OF AUTISM

No single explanation for the cause of autism has been determined. There is certainly no lack of causal theories providing explanation for autism and its increased rate. A **causal theory** is a theory that presents a certain rationale for causes of the disorder. Having a causal theory is important, because knowing what causes a disorder helps determine how the disorder can be treated and/or prevented in the future.

The diversity in the number and nature of causal theories in autism is due to two reasons. One is the diversity in the degree and severity of impairments in autism; the other is the differences in the intensity of behavioral characteristics of children with the ASD from one end of the spectrum to the other. The highly variable manifestations of autism range from a nonverbal child with severe cognitive impairment and aggression or self-injurious behaviors to a college student with above-average intelligence and a successful academic and work record (Muhle, Trentacoste, & Rapin, 2004).

Each of the existing causal theories of autism usually holds true only for a percentage of children within the spectrum. None of the existing theories on causes of autism have explained all cases. This lack of universality presents problems both for the diagnosis and explanation of autism, since effective educational, supplemental, and medical treatment of children with any disorder is usually based on an established or theoretical explanation of that disorder. Because there is no established cause for autism, there are numerous treatment options and claims. In the following section, we will describe some of the better-known causal theories of autism.

Genetic Factors

A number of studies have tried to find an association between specific genes and autism (Brent & Geschwind, 2009). The current genetic knowledge regarding ASD mostly comes from family and twin studies (Hyman & Towbin, 2007). For example, the risk of autism in a sibling of a child with autism is between 3 and 5 percent (Chakrabarti & Fombonne, 2001).

Some of these studies have determined that less than 10 percent of the cases of autism are associated with chromosomal abnormalities (Folstein & Rosen-Sheidley, 2001), and about 1 to 4 percent of cases indicate deletions, inversions, or duplication of a number of specific genes, such as those in the regions of chromosome 15 and chromosome 7 (Muhle et al., 2004). Chromosome X has been implicated as a cause of not only fragile X syndrome and Rett disorder but autism as well (Gilberg & Coleman, 1992). Additionally, some neurotransmitters, such as serotonin, dopamine, and acetylcholine, might be associated with autism (Gilberg & Coleman, 1992).

Immunization Theories and Controversy

In 1998, a study conducted in England instigated a great controversy within the medical community. Based on this study (Wakefield et al., 1998), a link was found between the MMR (measles, mumps, and rubella) vaccine and onset of autism in 12 children. According to the authors, the group of children they studied appeared to have normal development up until the inoculation of the MMR vaccine, which led to gastrointestinal disease in these children, eventually causing a developmental regression and autistic behaviors.

In later years, some other studies confirmed the existence of a link between the MMR vaccine and the increase in the number of children diagnosed with autism (Goldman & Yazbak, 2004). Later studies amended the earlier theory that it was thimerosal, a mercury-based preservative and additive used in the vaccines that might have been responsible for causing autism (Gier & Gier, 2003). Based on this theory, in some young children thimerosal could create instances of severe autism. These studies were later discredited for scientific inaccuracy, methodological flaw, and conflict of interest in the side of the investigators (Offit, 2008). However, the claims presented by these authors started a movement led by parents of children with autism who contested that their children had a typical development up until their immunization. Fueled by the prime-time media attention, this controversy continues to be rekindled periodically, involving politicians and Hollywood and TV celebrities alike in the public debate, and creating a general fear of the vaccine safety in children.

A number of later studies have refuted the immunization/autism link (Andrews et al., 2004; Fombonne, 2005; Offit & Jew, 2003); and to date, there is no solid conclusive evidence that mercury-based vaccines or the vaccines themselves are causes of autism (Scahill & Bearss, 2009; Offit, 2008). The intension of bringing up the immunization theory here is not to support nor repudiate this theory, but to make early childhood educators aware of one of the most publicized and controversial theories regarding the causes of autism. You are advised to examine the scientific studies and existing evidence in regard to this controversy, and decide for yourself what position you might choose to take on this issue.

Exposure to Environmental Toxins

Exposure to environmental toxins, such as maternal exposure to mercury during pregnancy, excessive use of antibiotics in children, household and environmental pesticides, and other unknown factors have been cited as possible causes of autism (Adams, Edelson, Grandin, & Rimland, 2004). Similar to the immunization theory, this theory states that exposure to toxins creates gastrointestinal problems, which cause harmful chemicals to cross over to the brain and hence lead to behavior characteristics of autism in children. A recent hypothesis proposes a complex interaction of genes and environmental exposures, possibly during a critical developmental period, involving a range of exposures in combination with one another that might contribute to autism (Berg, 2009).

CHANGES IN DIAGNOSTIC CRITERIA

Some scholars (Volkmar, Chawarska, & Klin, 2008) and professionals believe that a change in the identification and classification criteria of autism has led to a larger number of children now being identified within the Autism Spectrum Disorder. Improved diagnostic techniques have resulted in identification of many children who were not otherwise diagnosed with autism 10 or 20 years ago. Additionally, our recent diagnostic criteria include a collection of different impairments such as those belonging to Autism Spectrum Disorders. Previously, such impairments were either unidentified or diagnosed under a different disorder.

While some of the theories mentioned here, such as the thimerosal–autism link, have gained popularity among parents and some professionals, inconclusive research makes it difficult to draw any definite conclusions regarding these theories. The most plausible explanation seems to be a combination of genetic and environmental factors, as well as expansion in diagnostic criteria.

TREATMENT AND EDUCATIONAL IMPLICATIONS

Based on which causal theory of autism seems more convincing to parents, parents might choose from a variety of different treatment options available for autism. For example, the biomedical treatment of autism consists of a number of pharmacological and holistic/alternative medicines and diets (i.e., gluten-free, casein-free diet) that aim to purify the child's brain and body from any toxic substances and ensure improvements in behavioral characteristics. Claims of total recovery of autism by some parents and professionals advocating for specific treatments are aplenty. The best advice that an early childhood professional can give a parent is to study each treatment option carefully before deciding on a specific course of action. Table 7.1 displays some of the non-educational treatment options available today with their related causal theories.

TABLE 7.1   Non-educational Treatments for Autism

Treatment Categories	Causal Theories	Options
Pharmacological/ medical treatment	Neurological abnormalities, chemical deficiencies	Most prescribed rugs: ➢ Ritalin ➢ Benadryl ➢ Risperidal ➢ Zoloft/Prozac
Vitamin therapy	Chemical deficiencies	Three most used vitamins: ➢ Vitamin B_6 and magnesium ➢ DMG (dimethylglycine) ➢ Vitamin C
Biomedical	Allergy and hypersensitivity to toxins, specifically mercury and other heavy metal toxicity	➢ Chelation ➢ Hyperbaric oxygen therapy
	Gastrointestinal problems	➢ Secretin hormone therapy
Dietary nutritional	Food allergies, hypersensitivity to certain foods leading to gastrointestinal problems and toxicity	➢ Gluten-free, casein-free diet ➢ Yeast-free diet
Sensory integration training/therapy	Sensory processing dysfunction	➢ Auditory integration therapy ➢ Listening therapy ➢ Vision therapy ➢ Irlen lenses ➢ Grandin's squeeze box
Other therapies	No specific causal theory	➢ Music therapy ➢ Art therapy ➢ Hypo therapy ➢ Swimming with dolphins

Source: Autism Research Institute at http://www.autism.com.

DEFINING AUTISM

Autism Spectrum Disorders are a group of neuro-developmental disabilities that are life long. ASD affect three areas of development: communication development, social relatedness, and behavior. These three areas of deficiencies are historically known as the triad of impairments (Frith, 1989). We will discuss these three characteristics in more detail in the later sections.

Autism might manifest itself from birth in some children. This group of children is said to have **early onset.** Another group of children might show typical development up until toddler years and then exhibit some regression in the development and appearance of autistic behaviors. This group is considered to have **late onset.**

According to the *Diagnostic and Statistical Manual of Mental Disorders* of the American Psychiatric Association (2000), there are five specific autism diagnoses under pervasive developmental disorders (PDD). These five disorders are autistic disorder, Asperger disorder, Rett disorder, childhood disintegrative disorder, and pervasive developmental disorder not otherwise specified (PDD-NOS).

The child who receives the diagnosis of autistic disorder displays at least 6 of 12 symptoms of deficits in areas of reciprocal social interaction; deficits in communication; and has restricted, repetitive behaviors and narrow interests. Table 7.2 displays the categories of disorders under ASD with examples of behavior characteristics based on categories described in American Psychiatric Association (2000) and Ozonoff and Rogers (2003).

TABLE 7.2   Categories of Disorders under Autism Spectrum Disorders

Categories	Deficits and Symptoms
Autistic disorder	1. Deficits in reciprocal social communication Examples: ➤ Trouble making eye contact ➤ No interest in making friends ➤ Enjoys playing alone ➤ Does not share attention or share interest with others ➤ Not aware of others ➤ Does not notice when others are hurt or upset 2. Deficits in communication, language Examples: ➤ Very few words and no phrases by age 2 ➤ Little interest in games like peek-a-boo when young ➤ Taking adults by the hand to objects of interest, no pointing ➤ Possible echolalia (repeating what others say) ➤ Difficulty initiating conversations ➤ Little make-believe play 3. Restricted and repetitive behaviors and interests Examples: ➤ Interest in and focus on a particular activity, topic, toys ➤ Difficulty transitioning (letting go) ➤ Putting things or performing actions in certain orders ➤ Attachment to rituals and objects, becoming anxious when rituals not followed or objects taken away ➤ Severe temper tantrums, inability to calm down ➤ Repetitive hand or body movements, like flapping or rocking ➤ Walking on tiptoes, or running back and forth ➤ Interest in, or aversion of, specific sensory stimuli such as sounds, sights, tastes, movement, and touch ➤ Attachment to unusual objects

(Continued)

TABLE 7.2   (Continued)

Asperger disorder	1. Severe impairment in reciprocal social interaction Examples: ➢ Inability to interact with peers ➢ Lack of appreciation of social cues ➢ Socially and emotionally inappropriate behavior 2. All-absorbing narrow interest Examples: ➢ More rote than meaning ➢ Exclusion of other activities 3. Imposition of routine and interests
Rett disorder	1. At least a 5-month period of typical development 2. Progressive loss of speech and hand function 3. Seizure 4. Profound mental retardation 5. Progressive gait difficulties 6. No language
Childhood disintegrative disorder	1. Has 2-to-10-year period of normal development 2. Sudden and quick regression in development: a. Loss of interest in others b. Loss of language c. Severe loss of cognitive abilities d. Loss of self-help adaptive skills
PDD-NOS	1. Displays two of three deficits in the autistic disorder category: a. Impairment in social interaction b. Impairment in verbal or nonverbal communication skills c. Repetitive behavior and restrictive interests and play repertoire

Source: American Psychiatric Association. (2000). *Diagnostic and statistical manual of mental disorders,* (4th ed., Text rev.). Washington, DC: Author.

Asperger Disorder/Syndrome

Asperger disorder, named after Hans Asperger, the psychologist who first discovered children with this disorder, is known to be a milder form of autism. The major characteristic of this disorder is a lack of interest in social relationships or difficulties in forming a relationship with others. However, language is not impaired and there is no impairment in cognitive functions (Ozonoff & Rogers, 2003).

Many people confuse high functioning autism (HFA) with Asperger syndrome. Children with HFA are children who meet diagnostic criteria for autistic disorders, yet have functional language abilities and no intellectual impairments. Certainly, the two disorders share more similarities than differences (Ozonoff & Rogers, 2003). The difference is noted in the area of language, where children with

Asperger syndrome show better language abilities especially during preschool years (Ozonoff & Rogers, 2003).

Rett Disorder

Rett disorder is a condition found only in girls. Children who receive this diagnosis usually show typical growth up to 5 or 6 months of age. However, they begin to lose interest in others over time. Girls with this disorder eventually lose the use of their hands. The symptoms of this disorder include lack of language, constant hand movement—such as wringing, twisting, or rubbing the hands—severe cognitive impairment, and lack of social interaction (American Psychiatric Association, 2000).

Childhood Disintegrative Disorder

Childhood disintegrative disorder similarly constitutes a period of typical growth in the child followed by loss of developmental skills, which eventually ends in severe cognitive deficits and other abilities (American Psychiatric Association, 2000). Unlike Rett disorder, this condition occurs in either boys or girls. The child begins losing skills usually after 2 to several years of typical development in all areas, such as speech, social interaction, cognition, or self-help.

Usually after a period of typical development, the child begins a quick period of regression that lasts between 4 to 8 weeks. By the end of this regression period, the child displays all characteristics of severe autism and mental retardation. The difference between this disorder and autism is that there is little improvement in the child after intervention and the condition continues as a severe chronic disability (Ozonoff & Rogers, 2003).

Pervasive Developmental Disorders—Not Otherwise Specified: PDD-NOS

PDD-NOS is a vague diagnostic term given to children who do not display all three general impairments of autism, but usually just severe social impairment or impairment in verbal and nonverbal language development. The problem with receiving PDD-NOS as a diagnosis is that children identified under this category might not be considered in need of intensive services and therefore might not receive the variety of services and treatment options available for children with autism within the publicly funded intervention systems.

EARLY IDENTIFICATION OF AUTISM

Professionals are reluctant to give an autism diagnosis before age 2. Much of this reluctance is due to the fact that infants' developmental delays look similar in characteristics, and sometimes it is difficult to distinguish general characteristics of one disorder, such as speech delay, from another disorder, such as autism. However, autism has specific characteristics that a trained professional would be able to detect as early as 9 to 14 months.

Early intervention is the key to progress in any disability. Some available data suggests that children with autism who are identified early are less likely to be mute and more likely to improve to become independent in later years (Howlin, 2005). Although in general, progress of children with autism has seemed to be slow under different educational treatments, intense early intervention (beginning before age 3) has proven to have the highest positive outcome for children with autism.

Modified Checklist for Autism in Toddlers

Autism diagnosis is not medical. ASD is detectable through careful observations of the child's behaviors by trained professionals. As mentioned earlier, it seldom happens that autism is diagnosed before age 2. However, early identification of infants and toddlers suspected of having autism is possible through a 3-minute screening tool called the Checklist for Autism in Toddlers (CHAT) (Baron-Cohen et al., 1996).

This screening tool was first designed by a British team lead by Baron-Cohen and his colleagues (1992). CHAT was later advanced by the same team as Quantitative Checklist for Autism in Toddlers (Q-CHAT) (Allison et al., 2008). It has also been revised for use in the United States as Modified Checklist for Autism in Toddlers (M-CHAT) (Robins, Fein, Barton, & Green, 2001). We should be cautious here to note that M-CHAT is a screening tool and not a diagnostic one. As a screening tool, M-CHAT is only useful to identify children who are at risk for being diagnosed within the Autism Spectrum Disorders in later years.

M-CHAT looks for four behaviors that are universally present by the time an infant reaches 14 months of age: (1) **protodeclarative pointing:** pointing to an object of interest; (2) joint attention and gaze monitoring: the child's ability to look in the same direction that an adult is looking in; (3) imitation and pretend play; and (4) appropriate motoric and sensory behaviors (Robins, Fein, Barton, & Green, 2001; Baron-Cohen et al., 1996). Text Box 7.1 presents the M-CHAT checklist. Consistent failure in CHAT or M-CHAT at 18 months indicates a 90 percent risk of autism and at this stage expert diagnosis should be sought. The child has failed the test when two or more critical items are failed. Critical items are questions 2, 7, 9, 13, 14, and 15. Use of M-CHAT along with other developmental screening tools is advisable in early childhood education settings as a part of regular developmental screening that teachers should do on an ongoing basis with infants and toddlers.

Today, our understanding of sensory processing theory enables us to detect some motor and sensory system abnormalities early on in infants who might be later diagnosed with autism. These sensory abnormalities include, but are not limited to, lack of eye contact; aversion of or unusual attraction to certain lights, sounds, or touch feelings; difficulties with swallowing and/or certain tastes; and inability to calm down or be soothed by an adult when crying (Osterling & Dawson, 1994; Hobson & Lee, 1998).

Critical Thinking Question 7.2   Reflecting on the story at the beginning of the chapter, what other signs might Tricia have looked for that are warning signs for ASD?

Modified Checklist for Autism in Toddlers (M-CHAT)   Text Box 7.1

Please fill out the following about how your child usually is. Please try to answer every question. If the behavior is rare (e.g., you've seen it once or twice), please answer as if the child does not do it.

1. Does your child enjoy being swung, bounced on your knee, etc.? **Yes/No**
2. Does your child take an interest in other children? **Yes/No**
3. Does your child like climbing on things, such as up stairs? **Yes/No**
4. Does your child enjoy playing peek-a-boo/hide-and-seek? **Yes/No**
5. Does your child ever pretend, for example, to talk on the phone or take care of a doll or pretend other things? **Yes/No**
6. Does your child ever use his/her index finger to point, to ask for something? **Yes/No**
7. Does your child ever use his/her index finger to point, to indicate interest in something? **Yes/No**
8. Can your child play properly with small toys (e.g., cars or blocks) without just mouthing, fiddling, or dropping them? **Yes/No**
9. Does your child ever bring objects over to you (parent) to show you something? **Yes/No**
10. Does your child look you in the eye for more than a second or two? **Yes/No**
11. Does your child ever seem oversensitive to noise? (e.g., plugging ears) **Yes/No**
12. Does your child smile in response to your face or your smile? **Yes/No**
13. Does your child imitate you? (For example, if you make a face, will your child imitate it?) **Yes/No**
14. Does your child respond to his/her name when you call? **Yes/No**
15. If you point at a toy across the room, does your child look at it? **Yes/No**
16. Does your child walk? **Yes/No**
17. Does your child look at things you are looking at? **Yes/No**
18. Does your child make unusual finger movements near his/her face? **Yes/No**
19. Does your child try to attract your attention to his/her own activity? **Yes/No**
20. Have you ever wondered if your child is deaf? **Yes/No**
21. Does your child understand what people say? **Yes/No**
22. Does your child sometimes stare at nothing or wander with no purpose? **Yes/No**
23. Does your child look at your face to check your reaction when faced with something unfamiliar? **Yes/No**

Source: © 1999, Robins, Fein, & Barton. http://www2.gsu.edu/~psydlr/Diana_L._Robins,_Ph.D._files/M-CHAT_new.pdf

CHARACTERTISTICS OF AUTISM

As discussed earlier, the term triad of impairments corresponds to three areas of deficiencies found in children with autism: communication/language, behavior, and social emotional development. These three areas are core areas of development that affect all other domains of development. In this section, we will not only discuss these three areas but look at cognitive development as well, because cognitive impairment is also diagnosed in many children with autism (American Psychiatric Association, 2000).

Cognitive Impairment

Research indicates that about 75 percent of children with autism have some form of cognitive impairment (Joseph, Tager-Flusberg, & Lord, 2002). The combination of cognitive impairment and autism presents many challenges, such as aggressive behaviors, that might not be otherwise present in children with autism alone or with cognitive impairment alone (Matson & Shoemaker, 2009).

Some earlier theorists, such as Vygotsky, strongly believed that cognitive and language development were related to one another and thus difficult to separate. Perhaps it is for this reason that children with autism who have severe language impairments are usually diagnosed with having cognitive impairments as well. However, in recent years, a number of nonverbal adolescents and adults with autism have been discovered who, against their apparent cognitive impairments, demonstrated abilities in complex abstract mental tasks, such as writing poetry, creating both concrete and abstract art, and even writing and producing award-winning movies. These individuals have not only challenged theories such as those of Vygotsky, but have raised an intriguing question in regard to the complexity of the autistic brain, and the true cognitive abilities of the nonverbal individuals with autism.

We should keep in mind that professionals often use standardized intelligence tests as part of a diagnostic protocol for identifying any developmental disorders such as autism. Most typical intelligence (IQ) tests, such as Stanford Binet or Wechsler, heavily rely on the verbal language abilities of the child for intelligence performance. There is a general consensus among scholars that because many children with autism—those who are younger or are not verbal—do not have adequate verbal abilities, relying on typical intelligence test results alone do not provide a true picture of the mental abilities of children with autism (Klin, Carter, & Sparrow, 1997; National Research Council, 2001). Currently, however, there is no agreement about the most appropriate assessment instrument that would measure the true cognitive abilities of children with autism in the most accurate and reliable way (Delmolino, 2006).

Communication and Language Impairments

Although some children with autism might develop language abilities, many might not acquire any productive language, and those children who develop some language abilities usually display different language skills from that of typically developing children (Frith, 1989; Wetherby & Prizant, 2000). Language and communication problems in children with autism are usually the first signs that warn parents and other family members of the possibility of a problem in the child.

Typically developing infants begin to communicate with adults and caregivers by sharing attention. **Shared attention,** also known as joint attention, is the infant's ability to share interest with another person. For example, while the mother takes the baby out in the stroller, she may call the baby's attention to an object of interest in the street, like a cat, by saying, "Look at that cat" or "What is that?" while pointing to it. Conversely, an infant or young child frequently brings an object of interest to

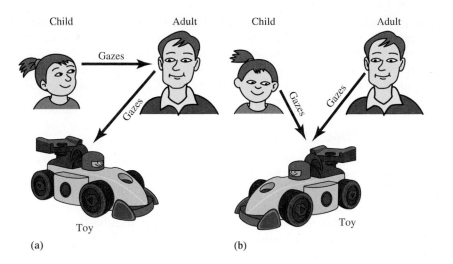

Child   Adult   Child   Adult

Gazes

Gazes   Gazes   Gazes

Toy   Toy

(a)   (b)

FIGURE 7.1
(a) Joint Attention: The Adult Is Looking at the Toy and the Child Is Looking at the Adult; (b) Joint Attention: The Child and the Adult Are Looking at the Same Object

the caregiver to show it to them. In either of these cases, when such a process occurs, both the infant and the caregiver are looking at the same object, and both are aware of their shared attention toward the object. Thus, we can say that both the infant and the adult are sharing attention or having a joint attention of that object. See Figure 7.1 for illustrations of joint attention.

This seemingly simple ability is the foundation of both language abilities and reciprocal social interaction, which infants and toddlers automatically acquire. Young children with autism do not seem to be able to form joint attention with others early on. In fact, this and some of the other early developmental signs that are foundations of communication and socialization do not seem to be present in these children (Baron-Cohen et al., 1996). For example, pointing to an object while getting the attention of the caregiver is the first sign that an infant has developed joint attention. Young children with autism do not point to objects of interest. Often, their attempt to communicate with adults is in the form of taking the adult by the hand to the objects of desire, as opposed to pointing to that object.

A typically developing child begins to utter one-word sentences as a way of communicating with others. For example, the child may say "juice" for "I want juice." Children usually have a receptive and/or expressive vocabulary of at least 50 words by about 12 months. By 2 years of age, children are usually able to put together simple phrases, like "eat cookie," or "mommy out." Children with autism usually lack this pattern of development (Bishop, Luyster, Richler, & Lord, 2008).

Although simple single words may be present in these children, the number is small, and some children with autism seldom use words for two-way communication purposes. Some children with autism might develop good language abilities as they grow older. In some of them, **echolalia** is common. Echolalia is repeating what the child hears. For example, an adult might ask a child, "Do you want a cookie?" Where a typical response would be a "yes" or a "no," a child with autism might respond, "Do you want a cookie?"

Despite the fact that some children with autism do learn to use language in a functional way, 50 percent either use language in an unconventional way or do not have any functional speech (Wetherby & Prizant, 2000). Difficulties in communication frequently result in frustration, which might lead to temper tantrums, displays of self-injurious behaviors, or aggressive behaviors toward others. One way of dealing with severe behavior of young children with autism is to empower them to communicate their needs and thoughts through the use of alternative and augmentative communication methods (described in Chapter 10).

Social Impairments

Impairments in social development constitute a major area of dysfunction in children within the Autism Spectrum Disorder. Social impairments include an inability and lack of interest in interaction with peers and adults, a lack of appreciation of social cues, difficulties relating to others, having socially inappropriate behaviors, or persisting in one's self interest. A lack of social competence in children with autism is apparent from infancy. Characteristics of social impairments during early childhood are described in the following sections.

Play in Children with Autism

Young children demonstrate their healthy social emotional development by being interested in interacting with their caregivers and adults first, and then with their peers. A toddler begins showing interest in other children by playing alongside other children, what we call **parallel play.** A common sight in an early childhood center is toddlers playing alongside each other in the sand and water area, block area, or other centers without seemingly communicating with one another. A young child playing alongside another child is considered to be engaged in parallel play. By 3 years of age, children interact with one another in a simple **pretend play** scenario by sharing toys with one another or assuming roles in different themes. For example, one child may assume the role of a mother, while another might be a child in a "house" play theme.

As they become older, children learn to play in **social games** that have rules for each player to follow and play cooperatively with each other. Typically developing children are interested in imitating their parents and those peers whom they like, and frequently use adults and other children as models for their own behaviors. Children commonly show interest in each other's interests and activities. Eventually,

In parallel play, a child begins to show interest in playing alongside other children.

peer recognition plays an important role in further social development of the young adolescents, building the foundations of social relationships as they enter adulthood.

Children with autism do not seem interested in playing with other children (Kishida & Kemp, 2009). They usually prefer to play on their own or engage in repetitive activities (Rogers & Ozonoff, 2005). They seem oblivious to and uninterested in other children's play or actions, and therefore, do not imitate others' behaviors or seek approval of grown-ups when young. Children within the autism spectrum are often interested in one or two types of toys and tend to develop attachment to specific objects (American Psychiatric Association, 2000). For example, one child with autism might only be interested in animal toys and other objects related to animals, while another child with autism might only be interested in trains and related themes. This attachment to specific objects is called a fixation. Educators often use fixations to teach children with autism specific academic and non-academic skills. For example, an interest in trains could be used to teach a child with autism numbers, colors, and shapes of different components of the train.

Unlike other 3-year-olds, the play repertoire of a 3-year-old with autism might lack the pretend play component, and the toys might not be used the way they are intended to be (Greenspan & Wieder, 1998). For example, instead of driving a car on the floor and making a car's noise, a child with autism might put a number of cars in a row, or shake or spin the car or other toys repeatedly. As children within the ASD become older, they might continue to show a lack of interest in interaction, socialization, and play with their peers as typically developing children do.

Relationship Building and Other Social Behaviors

Because autism is seldom diagnosed before age 2, our understanding of behaviors of infants with autism is based on studies of home videos of young children with autism. These home videos and other observational studies of the behaviors of infants with autism tell us that infants with autism often display a variety of avoidant behaviors during their early development (Dawson, Hill, Spencer, Galpert, & Watson, 1990; Adrien et al., 1991; Adrien et al., 1993; Osterling & Dawson, 1994; Hobson & Lee, 1998; Wimpory, Hobson, Williams, & Nash, 2000).

As we discussed in Chapter 6, some infant scholars (Greenspan & Wieder, 1998; Greenspan & Wieder, 2006a, 2006b; Emde, Korfmacher, & Kubicek, 2000) believe that children are born for the sole purpose of forming relationships with others. In fact, they believe formation of early emotional give and take with the primary caregiver builds the foundations of forming relationships as healthy adults later in life. In face-to-face interactions with a caregiver, typically developing infants are able to respond to the caregiver's facial expressions, smiles, and cooing with similar facial expressions of their own. We call this ability to respond to the caregiver's communicative expression with similar behaviors **matching.** Matching seems to be absent in infants with autism (Dawson et al., 1990; Osterling & Dawson, 1994).

Other behaviors that are indicative of a range of developmental impairments in infants with autism include an initial lack of eye contact and positive affect in face-to-face interaction with the caregivers during the first months of life, repeated failure to raise arms to be lifted up, and failing to greet parents and others or wave good-bye.

Typically developing infants are able to respond to their caregiver's facial expressions with similar facial expressions of their own.

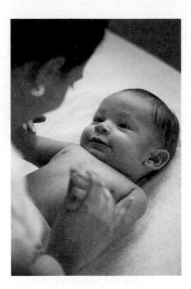

Researchers have also noticed that infants with autism seem to lack any enjoyment in lap games or interactive games with their caregivers as they become older (Osterling & Dawson, 1994; Hobson & Lee, 1998; Wimpory et al., 2000.)

During the infancy period, therefore, parents of children with autism may experience a tremendous amount of stress due to a lack of interactive behaviors in the infant, interpreting it as rejection. In explaining her face-to-face early interaction with her autistic infant, one mother described:

> In terms of actual cuddling and stimulation, I was finding it hard to give to Georgie as I had to her sister, since Georgie didn't respond . . . It was hard to give what wasn't apparently wanted, acknowledged, or appreciated, and to deal with the alarming fact that this was a baby who preferred to be left alone. She would focus on her bottle or a toy but not on me. She wouldn't look at me or make baby noises; she ignored me completely. And although she happily held objects, she wouldn't hold my finger or grab my nose or snuggle cozily against me when I rocked her. This seemingly brilliant ability to distinguish between the animate and the inanimate completely baffled me and hurt my feelings—her rejection seemed so deliberate. (Stehli, 1991, p. 15)

As the young child with autism enters the early childhood setting, it is not surprising, therefore, to find her lacking in early social emotional skills, such as interaction with peers and adults, or being interested in playing with others. Social impairment in young children with autism continues to be the major impairment in all children within the ASD.

During the elementary school years and in later years, these impairments might persist in that these children might continue to fail to initiate forming positive relationships with their peers and adults. Therefore, social emotional education of young children with autism should be an important part of any early childhood education program, where children can learn to overcome some of their difficulties in forming relationships with other children and the adults around them.

Problems with Theory of Mind

Theory of mind is a human's ability to attribute mental states to others (Frith, 1989). It is our theory of mind that enables us to understand that others can think and have opinions and beliefs, and act based on those beliefs. Theory of mind is a part of one's cognitive development and usually begins to appear in typically developing children around age 3. Development of theory of mind is related to the early development of joint attention and the development of symbols. For example, when a child holds a banana to his ear, pretending it is a phone, he is demonstrating to have acquired the prerequisite skills necessary for development of theory of mind.

Baron-Cohen (1995) noted deficiencies in the area of theory of mind in many children with autism. Based on his theory, several specific cognitive mechanisms of communication and socialization that are necessary for forming theory of mind are impaired in children with autism. For example, typical infants are able to follow the movement of objects in the environment, detect others' eye movements, and understand that others' eyes can see; therefore, they can form a mechanism called shared attention. These mechanisms work together to form one's theory of mind. By the end of the first year of life, infants can tell if they and others are looking at the same thing. Toddlers begin to pretend and play a different role rather than themselves, and by age 4 they can figure out what other people might know, think, and believe.

We know that infants with autism have difficulties holding shared attention. Their problems with this shared attention mechanism, therefore, might lead to a dysfunction in the area of theory of mind (Baron-Cohen, 1995). Problems with theory of mind create confusion for children with autism. For example, they have a difficult time interpreting facial cues of others in order to understand what others might think or do. Therefore, they can seldom adjust their behaviors based on others' reactions even when older. Their difficulties to read social cues frequently cause them to act inappropriately in social situations, or be oblivious to rules of social conduct, which young children begin to grasp during preschool and kindergarten.

In addition, certain problems with episodic memory in children with autism are coupled with theory of mind dysfunction, which makes it difficult for the children to predict what might happen in a given situation, even if they experienced the same situation in the past (Joseph et al., 2002). For example, doctors' office trips, even if conducted every month, might create the same fearful and anxious behavior in the child with autism every time. Similarly, transition to a new activity is often problematic for children with autism. Deviations from sameness or routine frequently cause violent tantrums for children with autism, since such a deviation signals change and unpredictability, which could be anxiety producing in these children.

Critical Thinking Question 7.3   From the story, we could assume that Kevin's pediatrician might not have noticed any warning signs in Kevin's development. What suggestions do you have for raising an awareness in the medical community about early signs of Autism Spectrum Disorders?

SENSORY PROCESSING DYSFUNCTION AND RELATED BEHAVIORS IN CHILDREN WITH AUTISM

Understanding and interpreting behaviors of young and nonverbal children with autism requires not only familiarity with the disorder, but experience working with a variety of children with different functioning levels within the spectrum. In Chapter 6, we discussed the sensory processing theory. Here, we will describe sensory processing deficits in children with autism.

Although there is a lack of empirical evidence regarding the sensory processing theory and sensory integration therapy, there is widespread use of sensory integration therapy for children with autism by professionals both in clinics and in schools. The importance of sensory integration therapy as a part of autism treatment has been emphasized by various scholars (Greenspan & Wieder, 1998, 2006a, 2006b; Dawson & Watling, 2000; Goldstein, 2000) because of the observed patterns of sensory processing difficulties in children with autism (Cheung & Siu, 2009).

Sensory integration therapy provided by an occupational therapist trained in sensory integration is often a part of the educational program for a child with autism. In collaboration with the therapist, early childhood educators often modify the environment and implement simple techniques that may help alleviate sensory processing difficulties in these children. In the following section, we will describe some behaviors related to sensory processing dysfunction.

Aversions to Certain Tastes, Smells, and Eating Nonfood Items

Some children with autism might react strongly to certain tastes and smells. Simple, bland, and colorless food might be better tolerated by these children. Some children with autism might show interest in eating or placing in their mouth items that are not edible. Eating nonfood items is called **pica.** This urge is usually the result of an under-responsive gustatory sensory system (Lane, Young, Baker, & Angley, 2009; Emmons & Anderson, 2005; Kranowitz, 2005). For example, the child might not be able to taste the bitter or the sour taste. As a result, the child may gravitate toward nonfood items that have strong, bitter, or sour tastes.

Aversion to, or Craving for, Certain Tactile Feelings

Many children within the ASD might display signs of problems in their tactile processing systems (Emmons & Anderson, 2005). Some children might like to walk barefoot on the gravel, rub their feet on rough surfaces, squeeze things or want to be hugged tightly, indicating signs of an under-responsive tactile processing system. Other children might be overly sensitive to certain touches and thus exhibit **tactile defensiveness.** In other words, types of touches that are otherwise ignored by others are amplified and painful to these children. A tag on the clothing, elastic on the socks, or a light touch on the shoulder could be extremely bothersome and create overwhelming and uncontrollable sensations in them. Violent temper tantrums as a result of such difficulties are common in these children.

Visual and Auditory Over-Sensitivity and Under-Responsiveness

Children who have auditory sensitivities often cover their ears when hearing specific or loud noises (Kranowitz, 2005). They might have a hard time tuning out background noises, and therefore become easily overwhelmed, resulting in aggression or temper tantrums. Some children within the ASD show similar sensory processing problems regarding visual stimuli. They might stare at the light, flicker their fingers in front of their eyes, look sideways at objects, or squint their eyes repeatedly (Rogers & Ozonoff, 2005).

SENSITIVITY TO MOVEMENT

Under- or over-sensitivity to certain movements are also common in some children within the ASD (Lane et al., 2009). They might have difficulty keeping their balance while walking on a balance beam, lack coordination in their movements, or have trouble walking in a straight line (Emmons & Anderson, 2005).

Other Behaviors

Many children with autism have self-injurious and aggressive behaviors (American Psychiatric Association, 2000). These behaviors are often dangerous to the child's own safety or the safety of peers and adults in the environment. Explosive behavior and temper tantrums are common during the early childhood years, although they might persist throughout later years as well. Self-mutilation might occur as a result of a need to satisfy an under-responsive system, while aggressive behaviors frequently occur in order to defend an overwhelmed sensory system (Kranowitz, 2005). In addition, a lack of functional language often creates feelings of frustration in these children that might lead to explosive temper tantrums.

Aside from the behaviors already discussed, children with autism often display **self-stimulatory behaviors.** Self-stimulatory behaviors, commonly referred to as *stimming* among educators, are repetitive behaviors that the child displays, such as flapping hands or rocking back and forth (American Psychiatric Association, 2000). Although self-stimulatory behaviors seem to serve no functional purpose, they are often explained as behaviors that serve in soothing the overwhelmed sensory system in the child.

STRATEGIES AND ADAPTATIONS FOR INCLUSIVE CLASSROOMS

Adaptations and modifications of the environment and curriculum for children within the ASD should be based on their sensory and behavioral needs. While certain adaptations help all children with special learning needs, they are specifically useful for children who have communication and sensory processing difficulties. Early childhood special education and inclusive classrooms will benefit from arranging the environment based on the following guidelines:

> Use of visuals in the classroom
> Specific physical arrangement of the classroom and home

> Cozy corner and sensory-oriented activities to support self-regulation
> Providing daily and weekly schedules

Use of Visuals in the Classroom

Communication is one core deficit in autism. Fifty percent of children with autism do not use words to communicate. When these children are not taught to use a functional system for communication, they tend to invent communicative behaviors and gestures that in most cases are only understood by their parents or others who work closely with them. Unfortunately, some of these inventive behaviors are not socially appropriate, nor are they understood by all.

Visuals are objects and pictures that can be used in order to enhance communication with children with autism. Visuals should be easily recognized and universally understood (Hodgdon, 1995). Pictures are symbols that represent specific objects, actions, and concepts. They are universally understood, and young children learn to associate pictures with objects early on. Although objects are sometimes used for young children with autism, pictures are easier to handle and transport, and therefore more practical for teaching young children. Visuals have become an important element of a successful intervention for children with autism in ECSE and inclusive classrooms. Picture Exchange Communication System (PECS) is an effective method of working with children with autism that enables them to communicate with peers and adults (Bondy & Frost, 1994). PECS will be described in a later section of this chapter.

Some specially designed software, like Boardmaker developed by the Mayer-Johnson (discussed in Chapter 4), are available to produce pictures for words to be used in teaching children with communication needs. See Figure 7.2 for an example of visuals representing words and concepts.

FIGURE 7.2
Example of Visuals Representing Words, Concepts, and Phrases

Thank you

Play

I don't want

Vanilla pudding

The basic recommendations for use of visuals in ECSE and inclusive classrooms with children with autism are as follows:

> Use a consistent augmentative and picture communication system in the classroom.
>> Label all areas of the classroom with visuals.
>> Modify small and large group activities, using pictures.
>> Have a Picture Exchange Communication System set up for every child.
>> Each child might have an individual binder, containing pictures specific to his or her daily communication needs and classroom activities.
>> Make pictures of every item in the classroom available for all children.
>> Produce pictures that would empower the child to hold conversations about home and school.
>> Make pictures about school activities available for the child and the family to use at home.

Specific Physical Arrangement of the Classroom and Home Environment

The classroom and home environment for children with autism should be simple in structure so as to limit clutter and chaos, and to make daily routines predictable for the child. The environment should provide specific messages in regard to where things are and what needs to be done. Visuals should be used to label tables, shelves, desks, drawers, and materials. Toys should be put in transparent bins and labeled with visuals. As much as possible, clutter should be avoided in the classroom, as it is often visually overwhelming to children with sensory processing deficits to learn in environments that are cluttered and disorganized.

These additional guidelines are useful for the physical arrangement of the classroom:

> Have materials available in established centers in the same place all the time.
> Do not change the organization of your center too frequently. If changes of organization are necessary, make changes at specific times (e.g., before holidays). Communicate upcoming changes to children via pictures and speech.
> Have items like big therapy balls and gym mattresses available in your classroom or the gym for children to use for sensory needs.

Cozy Corner and Sensory-Oriented Activities to Support Self-Regulation

Children with autism should have a cozy corner, a contained refuge that has a calming effect for children. Pillows, beanbags, and blankets should be available for children to calm down when they are having a temper tantrum as a result of a sensory overload. Sensory adaptive materials, such as a body sock and weight vest, should be available for children in order to calm their sensory system. A body sock is a sewn-up piece of clothing with an opening for the head that covers the entire body

(a)

(b)

(c)

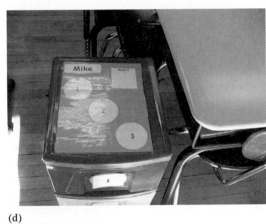

(d)

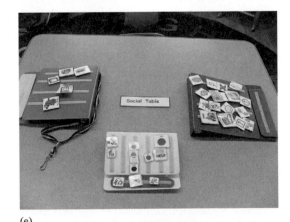

(e)

Early childhood classroom structure for children with autism: (a) small group table activity area for academic lessons; (b) calendar and weather area for morning greetings and checking the individual schedules; (c) individual work stations for individual work; (d) the work station is labeled with the child's name; (e) a social table is used for teaching social skills to children. A variety of choices of PECS pictures enables children to initiate and hold conversations with one another.

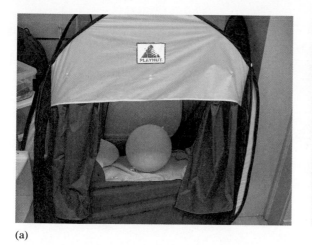

(a)

(b)

Sensory integration activities for children with autism: (a) A cozy corner provides a safe place for calming down. (b) When made available to children, sensory toys and rice and bean containers provide tactile comfort and help with sensory modulation.

to provide tactile comfort. A weight vest is a vest weighted with sewn metal inside the lining, which provides tactile comfort for children who seek tactile pressure for self-regulation.

A cozy corner and sensory equipment might be used at the beginning of the school day to promote comfort, and throughout the day as the child needs such interventions for self-regulation. Additional sensory toys and materials such as squeeze balls, light-up toys, and bins full of rice and beans should be used for children with autism to promote comfort as well as learning through senses.

All children with sensory processing difficulties, including children with autism, would benefit from activities that help them soothe and calm the nervous system. Such activities have been described to be part of a **sensory diet** (Williams & Shellenberger, 1994). A sensory diet is comprised of a plan for the day that would provide the child with a variety of sensory input that would help the child with healthy sensory processing and self-regulation.

Daily and Weekly Schedules

Children with autism benefit from a predictable routine. We discussed the benefit of consistent daily routines in Chapter 4. Visual daily schedules should be designed for individual children with autism, as it makes the day more manageable for them. The schedule can also tell the child whether there is a change in the day and when the change might occur. In a daily schedule, adults give clear messages to children about the plan of the day and what exactly will happen throughout the day. In addition to the daily schedule for each child, classrooms should have a visual weekly class schedule available for the child.

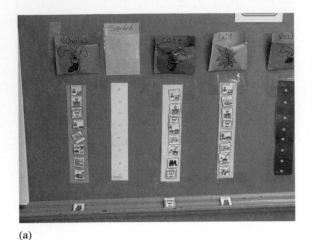

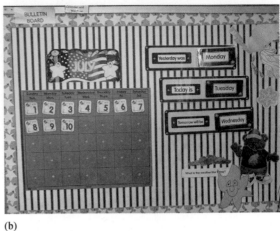

(a)   (b)

Daily and weekly schedules: (a) A child's daily schedule. The child removes each picture and puts it in the envelope on top after the specific activity on the schedule is completed. (b) A classroom's weekly schedule.

METHODS OF WORKING WITH CHILDREN WITH AUTISM

Over 40 educational and therapeutic methods for working with children with autism are available. Many of these educational interventions are considered highly controversial. Simpson (2005a) defines controversial educational treatments as those methods for which there is no scientific support, "especially when extraordinary and incomparable results are promised."

The No Child Left Behind Act (NCLB) (2001) makes it a requirement that all children, including those with disabilities, have a fair and equal opportunity to obtain a high-quality education and become proficient on state academic assessment or alternative assessment tests. Based on NCLB, all children should be educated by those education strategies that are evidenced-based (i.e., practices that are empirically validated).

Because many therapeutic and educational methods are used for children within the Autism Spectrum Disorders, and because each method has numerous claims to efficacy, it behooves us to ask three questions, which Simpson (2005b) raises when evaluating a specific educational method:

1. *What are the anticipated results of a practice, and are these outcomes in harmony with the child's needs?*

When answering this question, educators must keep in mind that because an advertisement claims a practice as "scientifically based," it does not necessarily mean it is so. A practice is considered evidenced-based when there is a good body of peer-reviewed literature that reports the efficacy of that method. Many such peer-reviewed reports are available through the Internet and can be easily accessed by educators. In addition, the intervention team should evaluate each practice based on the child's needs. For example, choosing a scientifically validated practice that focuses on developing expressive language skills is inappropriate for a child who is nonverbal.

2. *What are possible risks of a practice?*

It is often difficult to answer this question, when most methods claim benefits with very minimal or no risks to the child. In order to answer this question, however, the intervention team ought to look beyond the potential benefits of a practice for the child alone. The effects of any intervention practice on the quality of life of the family should be of primary consideration as well. Recall from our discussion in Chapter 3 that family quality of life was described as conditions in which the family's needs were met and family members enjoyed their life together and had a chance to pursue their interests. We should be careful that the intervention for the child does not adversely affect the quality of life of a family. For example, although implementation of an intensive home behavioral program might be empirically validated, doing so is time-consuming, extremely costly, and labor-intensive. This might not be an appropriate option for all children and all families. Thus, the effects of any program on the quality of life of the family should be considered carefully.

3. *How do we evaluate a method or strategy?*

In evaluating a particular method, the details of process and procedures should be considered. In other words, not only should the practice be validated by research, but also the intervention team must consider how and how frequently the practice will be evaluated; how the child will demonstrate learning; and who will carry out the evaluation. Such evaluation procedures are essential in determining the scientific validity and reliability of a method.

Some of the educational methods that are scientifically validated, some that are considered to be promising, and others that can be avoided will be discussed in the following section. As a typical program for children with autism, supplemental therapeutic services, such as speech and language therapy, and occupational therapy focusing on sensory integration, are usually recommended as part of their education.

Applied Behavior Analysis

Applied behavior analysis (ABA) is based on the behavioral theory as described in Chapter 6. Briefly, ABA is the process of applying behavioral theory principles to the improvement of certain behaviors, as well as evaluating whether or not changes in the behavior are attributed to the application of those principles (Baer, Wolf, & Risely, 1968). As such, application and evaluation or teaching and assessment take place at the same time in applied behavior analysis.

In what has been known as a discrete trial teaching (DTT) format, the teacher works one-on-one with a child, teaching sequential skills one at a time, until the child has mastery of the skills at least 80 percent of the time, in two settings, with at least two different teachers. A trial is considered to be a single teaching unit that begins with the teacher presenting a discriminative stimulus. A discriminative stimulus is the teacher's specific cue that provides information to the child about what to do. DTT is often provided in school settings for a limited portion of a day, and although it is an effective method of working with children with autism, it may not be well suited to teach the full range of skills, such as social, leisure, and functional skills to young children (Steege, Mace, Perry, &

Longenecker, 2007) since it requires long periods of one-on-one sessions with the teacher. These sessions are generally focused on isolated tasks (such as eye contact, matching colors and shapes, imitating actions, etc.). For a more detailed discussion of ABA, see Chapter 6.

Applied behavior analysis has been empirically validated. The following recommendations have been made when considering ABA as a practice to be used with children with autism (Simpson et al., 2005):

> **Qualifications of the ABA therapists:** ABA requires a proper understanding of the behavior principles as well as proper use of behavior techniques. Teachers or therapists who plan to implement this method must be well trained in principles and practices of ABA.
> **Intensity of the ABA:** Lovaas' (1987) initial study indicated that ABA is most effective when it is implemented at least 40 hours a week, and begins before the child's third birthday. Leaf and McEachin (1999) recommend at least 30 hours of therapy per week. (See Text Box 7.2 for a description of Lovaas' study.)
> **Location of the ABA therapy:** ABA could be implemented in any setting; however, it is important that there be minimal distraction when the one-on-one therapy is taking place.

Social Stories

Social stories were originally designed by Carol Gray, a social worker who worked for Jenison Public Schools in Michigan. A **social story** is a cognitive method. It describes a specific situation or concept in terms of relevant social cues, perspectives, and appropriate responses. A social story addresses the deficiencies in the children's theory of mind in that it teaches children about other people's perspectives and feelings. It can also be used as a vehicle to teach an academic skill. A social story describes a situation in a nonthreatening manner, provides insights into the feelings of the child and other individuals in the story, provides personalized instructions, teaches routines or adjustment to routines, teaches academic materials in a social setting, and addresses a range of behaviors from anxiety, to aggression, and self-injurious or aggressive behaviors (Gray, 1994).

A social story is written from a child's perspective. To write the story, the teacher must be well familiarized with the child and his typical behaviors within the specific situation the teacher is addressing. Consider the following situation:

> Every month, the school performs a fire drill. Every time the fire drill occurs, Jimmy, a kindergartner, throws a violent temper tantrum. It is difficult to soothe Jimmy when he is having one of his tantrums, and often his crying escalates. At such times, other children frequently become anxious and some begin to cry. This creates a difficult situation to handle for the teacher and her assistant. (See Figure 7.3.)

A specific format and style should be used for a social story. Gray (1994) recommends using four different sentences in a social story: descriptive, perspective, directive, and control. **Descriptive sentences** are sentences that address the what, how, when, and where of the situation. They describe the setting, subjects, and actions. For example, a descriptive sentence in a social story about being quiet in the library might state: "Every Monday, our teacher, Ms. Jones, takes us to the school library."

Ivar Lovaas and ABA in Autism   Text Box 7.2

In 1970, Ivar Lovaas, a psychologist at UCLA, began a longitudinal intervention study of 19 children with autism who were younger than 3 years of age. In his experimental design, Lovaas assigned three groups of children, all diagnosed with autism, to three conditions. Group one, the experimental group, consisted of 19 children who received more than 40 hours of intense one-on-one behavior therapy per week in their homes, community, and schools. Group two, a control group, consisted of 19 children who received 10 hours or less of one-on-one therapy each week. Group three, another control group, consisted of 21 children with autism receiving typical early intervention and special education services through local schools and community agencies. Lovaas trained his team, a number of graduate students, in methods of applied behavior analysis. In addition to providing 40 hours of one-on-one behavior therapy to the children in the experimental group, Lovaas' team trained parents to carry out behavioral techniques with their children around the clock. After 2 years of intense treatment, 9 out of 19 children in the first group had gained an average of 30 IQ points, putting them in the normal IQ range (range = 94–120).

The gain in these children was to such a degree that they no longer met the diagnostic criteria for autism. The rest of the children in the experimental group similarly gained points in their IQ level, but their gains were not as high to put them in a normal IQ range. Among the Lovass' experimental group of 19 children, 9 (47 percent) passed the normal first grade in public schools without being identified as having any special needs; 8 completed first grade in language-delayed or learning disabilities programs; and 2 were placed in programs with children with autism. The remaining children in the control groups did not show any gains in their IQ points. In a follow-up study in 1986, Lovaas reported that his subjects had retained their gains with the exception of two subjects who had been reclassified. Some scholars have challenged the scientific legitimacy of Lovaas' early intervention program, and there have been a number of criticisms raised about his behavioral method. However, today, ABA is considered to be empirically validated and among the most effective treatment options for children with autism.

Source: Lovaas, I. (1987). Behavioral treatment and normal education and intellectual functioning in young autistic children, *Journal of Consulting and Clinical Psychology, 55*(1), 3–9.

Perspective sentences are sentences that provide insights into the thoughts and feelings of the child who is the subject of the story, as well as feelings and reactions of the others in the story. A sample perspective sentence might state, "I get excited when I am in the library" or "Sometimes, when I make noises, other children in the class are bothered, and cannot do their work."

Directive sentences are sentences that give the child direction of one or more specific behaviors. They help the child have an appropriate response in place of the behaviors the child usually displays. For example, a directive sentence in our library story might be, "When I am in the library, I will use my inside voice. I will whisper, or speak very quietly, so I will not bother other people in the library who want to read."

FIGURE 7.3

The Fire Drill Social
Story

There is going to be a fire drill at school today.

Each month, we have a fire drill in our school.

The alarm will ring throughout the building so that everyone can hear.

It will be very loud, and it might hurt my ears.

My teacher will tell us to stop what we are doing… and line up at the door.

Next, we will stay in our line and all hold hands. My teacher calls this a caterpillar.

It is important that I hold hands with the two people next to me so the caterpillar doesn't break.

Then we will walk quietly down the hall…

Out the front door, and wait in front of the school. I will wait quietly in line while all the students walk outside. It is hard, but I will try to stay quiet so I do not distract my friends and my teacher.

The fire department might come to inspect the building.

I like when they come because I know they will make sure our school is safe. Once we know that the school is safe, our teacher will take us back inside to our classroom.

We have fire drills at our school so we will be prepared if there is a real fire. I do not need to be scared because my teacher will always be with me to make sure that I am safe.

Control sentences are statements that remind the child to behave in a certain way in this and other similar situations. They are usually used for older children or students who are higher functioning. Control sentences provide analogies that are related to the appropriate action and response in a child. A sample control sentence might state, "When I enter the library, I think of going 'inside' the library. Going inside reminds me that I will use my 'inside voice.'"

Relationship-Based Models of Intervention with Children with Autism

Several relationship-based intervention models are available for early childhood intervention in general, and for children within the ASD in particular. Some of these models have been extremely controversial and even have potential risks at best, such as holding therapy, in which an intense mother–child holding is the means of treatment. In this method, force is used when the child is not willing to be held (Simpson et al., 2005). Other methods have no research-based evidence behind them, such as the "Son-rise" program, where a nonjudgmental imitation of the child and play with the child is promoted.

Other models have some anecdotal and informal research evidence supporting them as well. Some of these methods are considered to be promising. Among them are guided play-based methods, in which children participate in a play group with the guidance and encouragement of able peers and teachers (Wolfberg, 1999).

As discussed in Chapter 6, Greenspan's DIR Model—developmental, individual-difference, relationship-based model, also known as Floortime—has gained popularity among early childhood educators in recent years.

Relationship development intervention (RDI) is another recent model, which focuses on developing interpersonal relationship skills in children with ASD through structured play (Gutstein & Sheely, 2002). This approach is currently awaiting peer-reviewed research. While we recommend play-based approaches of working with young children with autism, such as Floortime and guided play groups, we strongly advise against any model with no research evidence and any method in which force is used to illicit the child's participation and response.

Treatment and Education of Autistic and Related Communication-Handicapped Children

Designed by Schopler of the University of North Carolina in the late 1970s, Treatment and Education of Autistic and related Communication handicapped Children (TEACCH) is a skill-based method of intervention appropriate for young children and adults within the more severe end of the ASD. Schopler, Mesibov, and Hearsey (1995) describe four main components of this program to be: arranging physical organization, visual schedule, work system, and task organization.

The physical organization of a TEACCH classroom is based on organization of materials where specific activities take place. All irrelevant auditory stimuli and clutter is removed from such a classroom, and colored tapes and dividers organize the classroom with visuals to label each section. Individual visual schedules guide each child through the activities of the day or the period, make activities understandable through use of pictures, assist with memory, and make the day predictable for

(a)

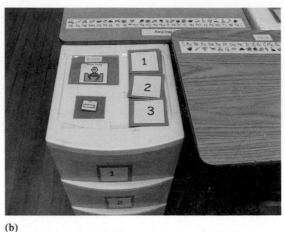

(b)

Example of a work system. (a) The work progresses from top to bottom and left to right. (b) After the child finishes all tasks, he removes the "reinforcer" picture (in this example, a Lego) from the work system and gives it to the teacher. The child receives free playtime with the desired object as a positive consequence of his accomplished task.

the child and therefore eliminate anxiety, which is common in children with autism. Work system and task organization intend to guide the child toward independence. Each work system is comprised of functional activities that the child works on and finishes independently.

In a task organization system, each task is usually placed into a container and placed in the child's work system at the child's desk. As shown in the above photographs (a) and (b), the work system is on the left-hand side of the child's desk, labeled with the child's name along with the picture of a Lego—what the child would like to receive as a reward after he has finished his work system. The work system contains numbers 1 through 3 to indicate the steps that the child needs to complete in order to finish his work system. These numbers are removable and fastened with Velcro to the top drawer.

The child begins working by removing number 1 from the top of the work system and placing it on the number 1 located on the first drawer. The child opens drawer number 1 and takes out the materials related to the task in the drawer to work with. After the child completes the first task, the completed products are put in the "finished bin" on the right-hand side, and the child begins working on step 2.

The task to be completed in each bin is divided into logical steps, and steps are often demonstrated through information provided within the visual guides that are placed on each task organizer/container. Many ECSE classrooms have been using the work system successfully around the United States. A number of studies have reported positive results on use of this model with children with autism (Lord & Venter, 1992; Mesibov, 1997; Schopler, 1991).

Picture Exchange Communication System

Picture Exchange Communication System (PECS) was designed by Bondy and Frost (1994) to enable nonverbal children with autism to communicate effectively with their peers and others. PECS uses the principles of ABA to teach children to exchange

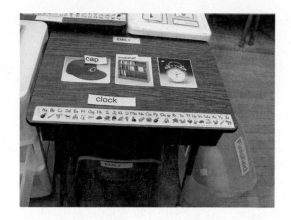

An example of a cognitive task within a work system. Here, the task of the first bin in the work system contains pictures and word strips for a matching word-to-picture activity.

pictures for communication purposes. Through six specific stages of training, children learn to first exchange one picture for a desired object, later to form sentences using pictures, and finally to answer questions and initiate conversations using picture sentence strips (see Figure 7.4). Some empirical evidence suggests PECS is an effective method of teaching communication skills to children with autism who use little or no speech (Preston & Carter, 2009). The child puts pictures on the sentence strip and hands the sentence strip to the teacher. Children are encouraged to say the sentence as they hand in the strip. A sentence strip can also be used to promote expressive language in reading activities. This strip is an example that could be used in reading *Brown Bear, Brown Bear What Do You See,* the popular children's book by Eric Carle.

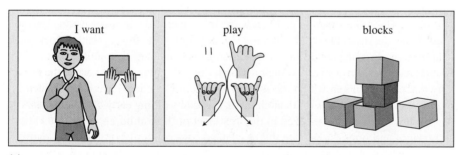

(a)

(b)

FIGURE 7.4 A sentence strip can be used to promote expressive language in basic communication.

PECS implementation requires professional training of teachers and paraprofessionals by a PECS consultant. Additionally, in order to use PECS with children, early childhood classrooms should be equipped with the Boardmaker software, a computer, printer, Velcro, and laminating equipment. PECS pictures are laminated, and Velcro is used to attach pictures to individual binders, boards, posters, equipment, objects, and other objects. Some early childhood teachers wear an apron with large pockets that are filled with a variety of PECS pictures. Pictures of objects and words should be plentiful and available to children in easy-to-reach locations. Photographs can be used for younger children who have not developed skills to associate line drawing pictures with objects.

Several studies have reported positive outcomes for children who have used PECS (Schwartz, Garfinkle, & Bauer, 1998; Bondy & Frost, 1994; Charlop-Christy, Carpenter, LeBlanc, & Kellet, 2002). Today, PECS is the hallmark of most autism early childhood and elementary-level classrooms in the United States. The use of PECS with nonverbal children with autism and young children with speech and language delays is strongly recommended.

FAMILIES AND AUTISM

Recall the historical context that we mentioned earlier in this chapter. Unlike in the early days of autism discovery, today the parental role in autism has shifted from being the cause to being the main therapist. We generally understand that the nature of autism demands more active parental involvement as compared with other disorders. Part of this understanding is based on the work of Lovaas in the 1970s. The results of his longitudinal study (1987) of a group of children with autism claimed that intensive intervention implemented early in the child's life, involving parents virtually round the clock, may lead to recovery of the child from the disorder to such a degree that autism is no longer a valid diagnosis. Lovaas' and similar research findings are probably part of the reason why parents of children within the Autism Spectrum Disorders have become increasingly involved as therapists for their children, especially during early childhood years.

Today, families get involved in the treatment of their children through a variety of services and options. Despite the movement toward family professional partnership, parents of children with autism continue to get training through an assortment of clinic-based and home-based programs (Marcus, Kunce, & Schopler, 1997). Parents might set up and supervise a home-based program, or be a part of a dual home- and clinic-based program (Marcus et al., 1997). Typically, in clinic-based programs, techniques are taught to parents, and parents are expected to carry out the intervention methods with the child at home. In home-based programs, a team of therapists might work with the child and the family members at home to carry out the treatment plan. A home-based program could vary from being behaviorally based, skill-based, or play-based to a combination of different methods (Lovaas, 1987; Williams & Wishart, 2003; Greenspan & Wieder, 1998; Marcus et al., 1997).

Working with Families

Without widespread early screening through community settings and in early childhood centers, identification of children with autism usually occurs after age 2, when abnormalities in language alert parents to the possibility that something is wrong. Because autism has usually been diagnosed during toddler or preschool years, the experiences of the parents are often different from those of parents whose child's disability is apparent earlier or at birth. Parents of children with autism might gain validation of their sense that the child's development was not typical, while conversely, the true implication of the disorder may not be initially apparent to them. It may take some time before the families come to terms with the reality of how the disorder may change their lives (Schuntermann, 2002; Bayat, 2007).

After the diagnosis, the major task of the family is establishing and maintaining a relationship with the intervention team and other service providers. One of the common early issues for families of children with autism is the stress and hardship related to navigating the intervention system to establish an appropriate educational program for the child. Parents might experience a period of intense stress, which becomes more severe as they struggle to come to terms with the disorder itself, as well as attempt to secure appropriate services for their child (Bayat, 2007; Marcus & Schopler, 1987; Marcus et al., 1997).

An important issue that families of children with autism face early on is interpreting their child's behaviors based on the sensory needs, as well as dealing with their child's aggressive behaviors. Going to outings, attending school and family functions, or taking a vacation might be impossible for some families whose children display aggressive behaviors (Bayat, 2005).

Early childhood educators can provide positive behavioral support (discussed in Chapter 9) in helping the families manage their child's inappropriate or aggressive behaviors. Consistent behavior management techniques in home and school are the key to helping families reduce the amount of stress caused by the child's inappropriate behaviors. This need is stronger in the family, especially during early childhood years, when patterns of inappropriate learned behaviors can be established without intervention.

There is evidence that when parents and family members have access to the necessary support and resources, the stress that is related to having a child with autism is reduced (Donovan, 1988). In addition, parents of children with autism have reported lower levels of stress when they have had higher levels of satisfaction with the intervention team members (Bayat, 2007; Everett, 2001). This means that family-centered behaviors in a child's early educational program often have buffering effects on parenting stress. In fact, parents who report higher levels of family-centered behaviors in early childhood providers also report higher levels of satisfaction with their child's services (Everett, 2001).

Finally, although a great number of parents of children with ASD get involved in the treatment and education of their children, it should not be assumed that all parents of children with autism do so. Considering the principles of partnership, caution is advised that in our interactions with parents, we do not imply that parental involvement in autism treatment is a requirement for treatment. It is the parents who define their degree of involvement in their child's therapy and education. Both common sense and research tell us that as early childhood educators we ought to be aware of our delicate responsibilities in relation to working with families of all children with disabilities and provide support in the way the family defines and prefers.

Research Corner

Immunization Controversy

The controversy regarding the issue of immunization in general and the effects of thimerosal-based vaccines on children in particular continues to grow. Various lawsuits have been brought by parents against pharmaceutical companies, and the debate regarding the possible adverse effects of immunization on children as it relates to autistic symptoms continues. One recent study published in January 2008 (Schechter & Grether, 2008) reported that in California, despite the exclusion of more than trace levels of thimerosal from nearly all childhood vaccines, the rate of autism in children has not decreased, therefore refuting the mercury poisoning theory of autism.

However, at the time of the writing of this text, three related studies on the safety of childhood vaccination were unveiled at the 7th Annual International Meeting for Autism Research (IMFAR), held May 15th through 17th 2008 in London, which appeared to support the possible adverse effects of MMR vaccines on children. These studies were conducted by a group of researchers in the United States who examined the effects of recommended childhood vaccines on macaque monkeys. They claimed that they had found biological changes and altered behavior in vaccinated macaques that were similar to those observed in children with autism, as compared to unvaccinated monkeys (Hewitson et al., 2008; Wakefield et al., 2008; Walker, Lobenhofer, Klein, Wakefield, & Hewitson, 2008). However, the results of these studies were withdrawn from publication while in press from the journal of *Neurotoxicology.*

Presented earlier in the chapter was the 1998 British study conducted by Wakefield and his colleagues. The study claimed a link between autism and MMR vaccine, and therefore started the autism-vaccination controversy around the world. During recent years, the accuracy of studies related to autism vaccination has continued to be repudiated by various members of the scientific community. In January 2010, the United Kingdom's General Medical Council's Fitness to Practice Panel announced that it found several specific elements of the information provided in the 1998 study were incorrect. Following the annoucement in February 2010, *The Lancet,* the journal which originally published the study, formally retracted the article from its records (The Editors of *Lancet,* 2010). Therefore, you should follow new developments related to the research publication in this area (at the time of publication of this book and later) to decide what you think about this controversial subject.

SUMMARY

Despite the recent increase in the rate of autism, and despite much publicity this disorder has received during the past decade, no specific cause has been established for this disorder. Autism Spectrum Disorders (ASD) present a range of behavior manifestations and functioning levels in children who are diagnosed within this spectrum. The most basic characteristics of autism are problems with language and/or communication, a range of atypical behaviors often caused by sensory dysfunction and communication difficulties, and lack of social relatedness.

Numerous educational and therapeutic methods are available for autism today. Implementation of those methods that are supported by research are highly recommended. A sound educational program for a child with ASD consists of evidence-based educational methods and adaptations, which are carried out through the work of a team collaborating with the family members. In addition, early childhood educators have the delicate responsibility of providing appropriate support for the families when needed so that they help alleviate the stress level in the family.

Review Questions

1. What are some viable factors that might have contributed to the autism prevalence rate?
2. What are the most likely explanations for causes of autism?
3. How relevant is the historical context of autism to our understanding of this disorder?
4. What are Autism Spectrum Disorders?
5. What are some signs of autism during infancy?
6. How is an early screening of autism possible?
7. What are the major impairments of autism?
8. What are the major sensory impairments and how might they manifest themselves in behaviors?
9. What are some ways in which early childhood educators can modify the classroom and activities for children with autism?
10. What is PECS and how might it be used in an early childhood classroom to promote communication or to teach specific lessons?
11. Why is it important to identify evidence-based practices in autism?
12. What are some educational practices that are evidence-based?
13. How can social stories help in the education of children with ASD?
14. What are some issues that families of children with autism might face?
15. What are some ways in which early childhood educators can provide support for the families of children with autism?

Out-of-Class Activities

1. Visit an autism classroom in an ECSE setting. Observe and take notes on the following components of the classroom:

   a. How are the visuals used to promote independence and positive behaviors in children?
   b. How is the physical structure arranged in this classroom?
   c. How are the daily and weekly schedules used in this class? If any, how is the work system used for individual children in the class?
   d. What kind of educational methods are used for children?
   e. What kind of sensory activities are available for children?

   Write a report about your observations. Make suggestions for improvement of the classroom.

2. Write a social story for a young child who is anxious about going to a doctor.
3. Use visuals to design a reading, math, or a social studies lesson plan to be used for children with autism.

Recommended Resources

Boardmaker and other products at Mayer-Johnson:
Mayer-Johnson, LLC
2100 Wharton Street
Pittsburgh, PA 15203
Phone: 858-550-0084
Fax: 858-550-0449

Email: mayerj@mayer-johnson.com
http://www.mayer-johnson.com/

General information and family resources:

Autism Collaboration
http://www.autism.org

AutismOne
http://www.autismone.org

Autism Society of America
http://www.autism-society.org

Autism Speaks
http://www.autismspeaks.org

National Autism Association
http://www.nationalautism.org

Research information:

Autism Autoimmunity Project
http://www.autismautoimmunityproject.org

Autism Coalition for Research and Education
http://www.autismcoalition.org

Autism Research Institute
http://www.autismresearchinstitute.com

Autism Speaks
http://www.autismspeaks.org/

Cambridge Center for Behavioral Studies
http://www.behavior.org

National Alliance for Autism Research
http://www.naar.org

Organization for Autism Research
http://www.researchautism.org

**View the Online Resources available to accompany
this text by visiting http://www.mhhe.com/bayat1e.**

References

Adams, J., Edelson, S., Grandin, T., & Rimland, B. (2004). *Advice for parents of young autistic children.* Retrieved May 10, 2007, from http://www.autismwebsite.com/ari/about/adviceforparents.htm

Adrien, J. L., Faure, M., Perrot, A., Hameury, L., Garreau, B., Barthelemy, C., et al. (1991). Autism and family home movies: Preliminary findings. *Journal of Autism and Developmental Disorders, 21,* 43–49.

Adrien, J. L., Lenoir, P., Martineau, J., Perrot, A., Hameury, L., Laramande, C., et al. (1993). Blind rating of early symptoms of autism based upon family home movies. *Journal of American Academy of Child and Adolescent Psychiatry, 32,* 617–626.

Allison, C., Baron-Cohen, S., Wheelwright, S., Charman, T., Richler, J., Pasco, G., et al., (2008). The Q-CHAT (Quantitative Checklist for Autism in Toddlers): A normally distributed quantitative measure of autistic traits at 18–24 months of age: Preliminary report. *Journal of Autism and Developmental Disorders, 38,* 1414–1425.

American Psychiatric Association. (2000). *Diagnostic and statistical manual of mental disorders* (4th ed., Text rev.). Washington, DC: Author.

Andrews, N., Miller, E., Grant, A., Stowe, J., Osborne, V., & Taylor, B. (2004). Thimerosal exposure in infants and developmental disorders: A retrospective cohort study in the United Kingdom does not support a causal association. *Pediatrics, 114*(3), 584–591.

Baer, D., Wolf, M., & Risely, T. (1968). Some current dimensions of applied behavior analysis. *Journal of Applied Behavior Analysis, 1,* 91–97.

Baron-Cohen, S. (1995). *Mindblindness: An essay on autism and theory of mind.* Cambridge, MA: MIT.

Baron-Cohen, S., Allen, J., & Gillberg, C. (1992). Can autism be detected at 18 months? The needle, the haystack, and the CHAT. *British Journal of Psychiatry, 161,* 839–843.

Baron-Cohen, S., Cox, A., Baird, G., Swettenham, J., Nightingale, N., Morgan, K., et. al. (1996). Psychological markers in the detection of autism in infancy in a large population. *British Journal of Psychiatry, 168,* 158–163.

Baron-Cohen, S., Scott, F., Allison, C., Williams, J., Bolton, P., Matthews, F., et. al. (2009). Prevalence of autism-spectrum conditions: UK school-based population studies. *British Journal of Psychiatry, 194*(6), 500–509.

Bayat, M. (2005). *How family members' perceptions of influences and causes of autism may predict assessment of their family quality of life.* (Doctoral dissertation). Available from ProQuest Dissertation and Thesis database. (UMI No. 3180946).

Bayat, M. (2007). Evidence of resilience in families of children with disabilities. *Journal of Intellectual Disability Research, 51*(9), 702–714.

Berg, R. (2009). Autism: An environmental health issue after all? *Journal of Environmental Health, 71*(10), 14–18.

Bettelheim, B. (1967). *The empty fortress.* New York: Collier Macmillan.

Bishop, S. L., Luyster, R., Richler, J., & Lord, C. (2008). Diagnostic assessment. In K. Chawarska, A. Klin, & F. R. Volkmar (Eds.), *Autism spectrum disorders in infants and toddlers: Diagnosis, assessment, and treatment* (pp. 23–49). New York: The Guilford Press.

Bondy, A., & Frost, L. (1994). The Picture Exchange Communication System. *Focus on Autistic Behavior, 9*(3), 1–19.

Brent, B., & Geschwind, D. (2009). Genetic advances in autism: Heterogeneity and convergence on shared pathways. *Current Opinion in Genetics & Development, 19*(3), 271–278.

Centers for Disease Control and Prevention (2007). *Autism Developmental Disabilities Monitoring Network.* Available at: http://www.cdc.gov/ncbddd/autism/documents/AutismCommunityReport.pdf

Chakrabarti, S., & Fombonne, E. (2001). Pervasive developmental disorders in preschool children. *Journal of the American Medical Association, 285*(24), 3093–3099.

Charlop-Christy, M., Carpenter, M., LeBlanc, L., & Kellet, K. (2002). Using the Picture Exchange Communication System (PECS) with children with autism: Assessment of PECS acquisition, speech, social-communicative behavior, and problem behavior. *Journal of Applied Behavior Analysis, 35*(3), 213–231.

Cheung, P. P., & Siu, A. M. (2009). A comparison of patterns of sensory processing in children with and without developmental disabilities. *Research in Developmental Disabilities, 30*(6), 1468–1480.

Dawson, G., & Watling, R. (2000). Intervention to facilitate auditory, visual, and motor integration in autism: A review of the evidence. *Journal of Autism and Developmental Disorders, 30*, 415–421.

Dawson, G., Hill, D., Spencer, A., Galpert, L., & Watson, L. (1990). Affective exchange between young autistic children and their mothers. *Journal of Autism and Developmental Disorders, 18*, 335–345.

Delmolino, L. (2006). Brief report: Use of DQ for estimating cognitive ability in young children with autism. *Journal of Autism and Developmental Disorders, 36*(7), 959–963.

Donovan, A. M. (1988). Family stress and ways of coping with adolescents who have handicaps: Maternal perceptions. *American Journal on Mental Retardation, 92*, 502–509.

Emde, R. N., Korfmacher, J., & Kubicek, L. F. (2000). Toward a theory of early relationship-based intervention. In J. D. Osofsky & H. E. Fitzgerald (Eds.), *WAIMH Handbook of infant mental health. Vol. Two: Early Intervention, evaluation, and assessment* (pp. 3–32). New York: John Wiley and Sons.

Emmons, P. G., & Anderson, L. M. (2005). *Understanding sensory dysfunction: Learning, development and sensory dysfunction in autism spectrum disorders, ADHD, learning disabilities and bipolar disorder.* Philadelphia: Jessica Kingsley Publishers.

Everett, J. R. (2001). The role of child, family, and intervention characteristics in predicting stress in parents of children with autism spectrum disorders. *Dissertation Abstracts International, 62(B-6),* 2972. (University Microfilms International).

Ferrari, P. (1997). Conceptualization of autism and intervention practices: International perspectives. In D. J. Cohen & F. R. Volkmar (Eds.), *Handbook of autism and pervasive developmental disorders* (pp. 961–967). New York: John Wiley.

Folstein, S. E., & Rosen-Sheidley, B. (2001). Genetics of autism: Complex aetiology for a heterogeneous disorder. *Nature Reviews Genetics, 2,* 943–955.

Frith, U. (1989). *Autism: Explaining the enigma.* Oxford: Blackwell.

Fombonne, E. (2001). Is there an epidemic of autism? *Pediatrics, 107,* 411–412.

Fombonne, E. (2003). The prevalence of autism. *Journal of American Medical Association, 289*(1), 87–89.

Fombonne, E. (2005). Epidemiology of autistic disorder and other pervasive developmental disorders. *Journal of Clinical Psychiatry, 6,* 3–8.

Gier, M., & Gier, D. (2003). Thimerosal in childhood vaccines, neurodevelopmental disorders, and heart disease in the United States. *Journal of American Physicians and Surgeons, 8,* 6–10.

Gilberg, C., & Coleman, M. (1992). *The biology of the autistic syndromes.* Oxford, UK: McKeith.

Goldman, G., & Yazbak, F. (2004). An investigation of the association between MMR vaccination and autism in Denmark. *Journal of American Physicians and Surgeons, 9*(3), 70–75.

Goldstein, H. (2000). Commentary: Interventions to facilitate auditory, visual, and motor integration in autism: "Show me the data." *Journal of Autism and Developmental Disorders, 30,* 423–425.

Gray, C. (1994). *Comic strip conversations: Colorful, illustrated interactions with students with autism and related disorders.* Jenison, MI: Jenison Public Schools.

Greenspan, S. I., & Wieder, S. (1998). *The child with special needs: Encouraging intellectual and emotional growth.* Reading, MA: Perseus.

Greenspan, S., & Wieder, S. (2006a). *Engaging autism: Using the Floortime approach to help children relate, communicate, and think.* Cambridge, MA: Da Capo Lifelong Books.

Greenspan, S., & Wieder, S. (2006b). *Infant and early childhood mental health: A comprehensive developmental approach to assessment and intervention.* Washington, DC: American Psychiatric Publishing, Inc.

Gutstein, S. E., & Sheely, R. (2002). *Relationship development intervention with young children: Social and emotional development activities for Asperger syndrome, autism, PDD and NLD.* London: Jessica Kingsley Publishers Ltd.

Hewitson, L., Lopresti, B., Stott, C., Tomko, J., Houser, L., Klein, E. et al. (2008). *Pediatric vaccines influence primate behavior and amygdala growth and opioid ligand binding.* Study presented at the 7th Annual International Meeting for Autism Research 2008 (IMFAR), London. Retrieved June 11, 2008, from http://www.safeminds.org/research/pediatric-vaccines-influence-primat-behavior.html

Hobson, R. P., & Lee, A. (1998). Hello and goodbye: A study of social engagement in autism. *Journal of Autism and Developmental Disorders, 28,* 117–127.

Hodgdon, L. A. (1995). *Visual strategies for improving communication: Practical supports for school and home.* Troy, MI: Quirk Roberts Publishing.

Howlin, P. (2005). Outcomes in autism spectrum disorders. In F. R. Volkmar, R. Paul, A. Klin, & D. J. Cohen (Eds.), *Handbook of autism and pervasive developmental disorders* (3rd ed., Vol. 1, pp. 201–222). Hoboken, NJ: Wiley.

Hyman, S. L., & Towbin, K. E. (2007). Autism spectrum disorders. In M. L. Batshaw, L. Pellegrino, & N. J. Roizen (Eds.), *Children with disabilities* (6th ed., pp. 325–343). Baltimore: Paul H. Brookes.

Joseph, R., Tager-Flusberg, H., & Lord, C. (2002). Cognitive profiles and social-communicative functioning in children with autism spectrum disorder. *Journal of Child Psychology and Psychiatry, 43*(6), 807–821.

Kanner, L. (1943). Autistic disturbances of affective contact. *Nervous Child, 2,* 217–250.

Kanner, L. (1948). Problems of nosology and psychodynamics of early infantile autism. *American Journal of Psychiatry, 56,* 701–707.

Kishida, Y., & Kemp, C. (2009). The engagement and interaction of children with autism in segregated and inclusive early childhood center-based settings. *Topics in Early Childhood Special Education, 29*(2), 105–118.

Klin, A., Carter, A., & Sparrow, S. (1997). Psychological assessment. In D. Cohen & F. Volkmar (Eds.), *Handbook of autism and pervasive developmental disorders* (pp. 418–427). New York: John Wiley & Sons.

Kogan, M., Blumberg, S., Schieve, L., Perrin, J., Singh, G., Trevathan, E., et al. (2009). Prevalence of parent-reported diagnosis of autism spectrum disorder among children in the U.S., 2007. *Pediatrics, 124*(5), 1395–1403.

Kranowitz, C. S. (2005). *The out-of-sync child: Recognizing and coping with Sensory Processing Dysfunction.* New York: The Berkley Publishing Group.

Lane, A., Young, R., Baker, A., & Angley, M. (2010). Sensory processing subtypes in autism: Association with adaptive behavior. *Journal of Autism and Developmental Disorders, 40,* 112–122.

Leaf, R., & McEachin, J. (1999). *A work in progress: Behavior management strategies and a curriculum for intensive behavioral treatment of autism.* New York, NY: DRL Books.

Lord, C., & Venter, A. (1992). Outcome and follow-up studies of high-functioning autistic individuals. In E. Schopler & G. Mesibov (Eds.), *High-functioning individuals with autism* (pp. 187–199). New York: Plenum.

Lovaas, O. I. (1987). Behavioral treatment and normal education and intellectual functioning in young autistic children. *Journal of Consulting and Clinical Psychology, 55*(1), 3–9.

Marcus, L. M., & Schopler, E. (1987). Working with families: A developmental perspective. In D. Cohen, A. Donnellan, & R. Paul (Eds.), *Handbook of autism and pervasive developmental disorders* (pp. 499–512). New York: John Wiley and Sons.

Marcus, L. M., Kunce, L. J., & Schopler, E. (1997). Working with families. In D. Cohen & F. Volkmar (Eds.), *Handbook of autism and pervasive developmental disorders* (2nd ed., pp. 631–649). New York: John Wiley and Sons.

Matson, J., & Shoemaker, M. (2009). Intellectual disability and its relationship to autism spectrum disorder. *Research in Developmental Disabilities, 30*(6), 1107–1114.

Mesibov, G. (1997). Formal and informal measures on the effectiveness of the TEACCH program. *Autism: The International Journal of Research and Practice, 1,* 25–35.

Muhle, R., Trentacoste, S., & Rapin, I. (2004). The genetics of autism. *Pediatrics, 113*(5), 472–486.

National Research Council. (2001). *Educating children with autism.* Washington, DC: National Academy Press.

Nicolas, J., Carpenter, L., King, L., Jenner, W., & Charles, J. (2009). Autism Spectrum Disorders in preschool-aged children: Prevalence and comparison to a school-aged population. *Annals of Epidemiology, 19*(1), 808–814.

No Child Left Behind Act of 2001. 20 U.S.C.70 § 6301 *et seq.* (2001).

Offit, P. (2008). *Autism's false prophets: Bad science, risky medicine, and a search for a cure.* New York: Colombia University Press.

Offit, P. A., & Jew, R. K. (2003). Addressing parents' concerns: Do vaccines contain harmful preservatives, adjuvants, additives, or residuals? *Pediatrics, 112*(6), 1394–1401.

Osterling, J., & Dawson, G. (1994). Early recognition of children with autism: A study of first birthday home videotapes. *Journal of Autism and Developmental Disorders, 24,* 247–257.

Ozonoff, S., & Rogers, S. (2003). From Kanner to the millennium: Scientific advances that have shaped clinical practice. In S. Ozonoff, S. Rogers, & R. Hendren (Eds.), *Autism Spectrum Disorders: A research review for practitioners* (pp. 3–33). Washington, DC: American Psychiatric Publishing, Inc.

Ozonoff, S., Rogers, S., & Hendren, R. (2003). *Autism Spectrum Disorders: A research review for practitioners.* Washington, DC: American Psychiatric Publishing, Inc.

Preston, D., & Carter, M. (2009). A review of the efficacy of the picture exchange communication system intervention. *Journal of Autism and Developmental Disorders, 39,* 1471–1486.

Rimland, B. (1964). *Infantile Autism,* New York: Meredith.

Rimland, B. (1995). Is there an autism epidemic? *Autism Research Review, 9*(3), 3.

Robins, D., Fein, D., Barton, M., & Green, J. (2001). Modified checklist for autism in toddlers (M-CHAT). *Journal of Autism and Developmental Disorders, 31*(2), 131–144.

Rogers, S. J., & Ozonoff, S. (2005). Annotation: What do we know about sensory dysfunction in autism?: A critical review of the empirical evidence. *Journal of Child Psychology and Psychiatry, 46*(12), 1255–1268.

Scahill, L., & Bearss, K. (2009). The rise in autism and the mercury myth. *Psyhopharmacology, 22*(1), 51–53.

Schechter, R., & Grether, J. K. (2008). Continuing increases in autism reported to California's developmental services system: Mercury in retrograde. *Archives of General Psychiatry, 65*(1), 19–24.

Schopler, E. (1991). *Current and past research on autistic children and their families.* TEACCH Research Report. Chapel Hill, NC: Conducted by Division TEACCH.

Schopler, E., Mesibov, G., & Hearsey, K. (1995). Structured teaching in the TEACCH system. In E. Schopler & G. Mesibov (Eds.), *Learning and cognition in autism* (pp. 243–267). New York: Plenum.

Schuntermann, P. (2002). Pervasive developmental disorder and parental adaptation: Previewing and reviewing atypical development with parents in child psychiatric consultation. *President and Fellows of Harvard College, 10,* 16–27.

Schwartz, I. S., Garfinkle, A. N., & Bauer, J. (1998). The picture exchange communication system: Communicative outcomes for young children with disabilities. *Topics in Early Childhood Special Education, 18*(3), 144–159.

Simpson, R. (2005a). Evidence-based practices and students with autism spectrum disorders. *Focus on Autism and Other Developmental Disabilities, 20*(3), 140–149.

Simpson, R. L. (2005b). *Autism Spectrum Disorders: Interventions and treatments for children and youth.* Thousand Oaks, CA: Corwin Press.

Simpson, R., De Boer-Ott, S., Griswold, D., Myles, B., Byrd, S., Ganz, J. et al. (2005). *Autism Spectrum Disorders: Interventions and treatments for children and youth.* Thousand Oaks, CA: Sage.

Steege, M., Mace, C., Perry, L., & Longenecker, H. (2007). Applied behavior analysis: Beyond discrete trial teaching. *Psychology in School, 44*(1), 91–99.

Stehli, A. (1991). *The Sound of a Miracle: A child's triumph over autism.* New York: Doubleday.

The Editors of Lancet (Eds.). (2010, February). Retraction: Ileal-lymphoid-nodular hyperplasia, non-specific colitis, and pervasive developmental disorder in children. *The Lancet, 375*(9713), 445.

Volkmar, F. R., Chawarska, K., & Klin, A. (2008). Autism Spectrum Disorders in infants and toddlers: An introduction. In K. Chawarska, A. Klin, & F. R. Volkmar (Eds.), *Autism Spectrum Disorders in infants and toddlers: Diagnosis, assessment, and treatment* (pp. 1–22). New York: The Guilford Press.

Wakefield, A., Lopresti, B., Tomko, J., Houser, L, Sackett, G., & Hewitson, L. (2008). *Pediatric vaccines influence primate behavior, and brain stem volume and opioid ligand binding.* Study presented at the 7th Annual International Meeting for Autism Research 2008 (IMFAR), London. Retrieved June 11, 2008, from http://www .safeminds.org/research/pediatric-vaccines-influence-primat-behavior.html

Wakefield, A. J., Murch, S. H., Anthony, A., Linnell, J., Casson, D., Malik, M., et al. (1998). Ileal-lymphoid-nodular hyperplasia, non-specific colitis, and pervasive developmental disorder in children. *The Lancet, 351,* 637–641.

Walker, S. J., Lobenhofer, E. K., Klein, E., Wakefield, A., & Hewitson, L. (2008). *Microarray analysis of GI tissue in a macaque model of the effects of infant vaccination.* Study presented at the 7th Annual International Meeting for Autism Research 2008 (IMFAR), London. Retrieved June 11, 2008, from http://www.safeminds.org/research/pediatric-vaccines-influence-primat-behavior.html

Wetherby, A. M., & Prizant, B. M. (2000). *Autism Spectrum Disorders: A transactional developmental perspective* (Vol. 9). Baltimore: Paul H. Brookes.

Williams, K. R., & Wishart, J. G. (2003). The Son-Rise program intervention for autism: An investigation into family experiences. *Journal of Intellectual Disability Research, 47,* 291–299.

Williams, M. S., & Shellenberger, S. (1994). *How does your engine run? A leader's guide to the alert program for self-regulation.* Albuquerque, NM: Therapy Works.

Wimpory, D. C., Hobson, R. P., Williams, J. M. G., & Nash, S. (2000). Are infants with autism socially engaged? A study of recent retrospective parental reports. *Journal of Autism and Developmental Disorders, 30,* 525–536.

Wing, L. (1993). The definition and prevalence of autism: A review. *European Journal of Child and Adolescent Psychiatry, 2,* 61–74.

Wolfberg, P. J. (1999). *Play and imagination in children with autism.* New York: Teachers College Press.

Yeargin-Allsopp, M., Rice, C., Karapurkar, T., Doerngerg, N., Boyle, C., & Murphy, C. (2003). Prevalence of autism in a U.S. metropolitan area. *Journal of American Medical Association, 289*(1), 49–55.

Chapter 8

Children with Attention Deficit Hyperactivity Disorder

Objectives

Upon completion of this chapter, you should be able to:

> Understand the history of ADHD.
> Understand characteristic symptoms of ADHD.

> Identify subtype categories diagnosed under ADHD.
> Understand the etiology of ADHD.
> Identify and describe other disorders associated with ADHD.
> Identify the range of treatments available for children with ADHD.
> Understand strategies and adaptations necessary for working with children with ADHD in inclusive classrooms.

Key Terms

combined type (260)
comorbidity (267)
executive function (264)
hyperactivity (259)
impulsivity (259)

inattention (259)
neurotransmitters (266)
predominantly
  hyperactive-
  impulsive type (260)

predominantly
  inattentive type (260)
register (276)
tics (269)

Reflection Questions

Before reading this chapter, answer the following questions to reflect upon your personal opinions and beliefs that are pertinent to early childhood special education.

1. What are your perceptions of a child who has ADHD?
2. In your opinion, how important is the role of teachers in managing the behaviors of a child who has ADHD?
3. In your opinion, how could an early childhood educator detect signs of inattention and learning problems in a young child?
4. In your opinion, what are the pros and cons of the use of medication for young children who have ADHD?

The Faces of ADHD

Six-year-old Jordan and eight-year-old Amy are both diagnosed with ADHD. Although both are identified as having the same disorder, their behavior characteristics are very different from one another. Jordan's mother, Suzie, can barely recall any peaceful moments since Jordan began to walk:

> I would have to watch Jordan 24/7. If he was out of my sight for one minute, I knew that he had gotten himself into some sort of trouble. He was constantly "on the go." I had to keep him entertained so that he would not get into a scrape. We had boxes of toys on hand and my husband and I took turns playing with him. If we did not keep him busy, he would do silly things. Once, when he was 4 years old, I was on the phone for two or three minutes. After I got off the phone, I found Jordan in the bathroom. He had taken the paper hole-puncher from my husband's study and somehow had managed to punch holes in the toothpaste tube.

He would do things like that all the time. We tried different diets with Jordan, but nothing helped. We could hardly ever get together with friends or do things with the family because Jordan managed to do something disruptive or destructive.

One time our new neighbors, who had a boy Jordan's age, invited Jordan for their son's third birthday so that both the kids and adults could get to know each other. Not ten minutes after we got into their living room, Jordan launched both his hands into the cake that was put on the table. Needless to say, we had to leave with much embarrassment. Neither Jordan nor we were ever invited to their home again.

Amy's mother's description of Amy is very different from Suzie's story. Unlike Jordan, Amy had always been a quiet child, who seemed to enjoy being in her own world. Amy's mother, Sheila, describes Amy as a well-behaved child:

We had no problems with her, until after she finished kindergarten and got into the first grade. Amy would forget almost everything that the teacher taught her in the class. At home, she would have trouble remembering what I told her to do. For example, I would tell her to bring her backpack from upstairs. She would go upstairs and not come back downstairs again. I would go up and find her sitting in the middle of the floor cutting paper. She had already forgotten what I had told her to do. Ironically, Amy could remember the smallest details of events that happened when she was 3 or 4 years old, but not what I or the teacher had told her just a few hours before.

Amy's first grade teacher and I worked hard to communicate with each other on a daily basis to help Amy with her school and homework. Her teachers often said that Amy was smart, if she'd only focus on her work. When she was interested in a project, she did a great job, but she seemed to have a hard time sitting at her desk and doing her daily homework assignments. She tried hard, but her attention wandered, or she got up after five minutes to do something else. I would sit with her every time to make her focus on her work. Lately, she seems to be daydreaming a lot more. So, it is not just a matter of sitting her down, but to find a way to keep her attention from wandering.

When Jordan was 5 and when Amy entered third grade, each of them received a diagnosis of ADHD. Jordan and Amy were seen by different pediatricians who each recommended that Jordan and Amy be put on some stimulant medications. Jordan's family agreed to put Jordan on medication.

Since Jordan was put on medication, his pediatrician has changed the prescription two times, because with each medication Jordan developed some kind of side effect, such as an excessive amount of anxiety, irritability, and lack of sleep. The last change was to a stimulant medication called Concerta. Although he seemed to be a bit less on the move, he threw frequent temper tantrums and cried over every small matter.

Sheila and her husband were more skeptical about putting Amy on medication. They read up on the subject and participated in chat rooms and Internet blogs on ADHD. Their concerns were about the long-term effects of drugs on their daughter. On the other hand, they also had serious doubts if their daughter would be able to succeed in anything without some sort of help.

INTRODUCTION

Children who display signs of hyperactivity and impulsivity (such as Jordan), or indicate signs of inattentiveness (such as Amy), usually receive a diagnosis of ADHD. Diagnosis of ADHD in children like Jordan commonly occurs during preschool, kindergarten, or early primary years, where children are required to follow specific classroom rules and structures. On the other hand, children like Amy, who do not display any signs of hyperactivity or impulsive behaviors, may not be identified until later grades, as problems with their academic performance might come to the surface gradually. These children might not be noticed until years into their elementary or even secondary school experiences.

During the last 20 years, the rise in the diagnosis rate of ADHD has caused an interest in the research of this topic to the degree that ADHD has been known to be one of the most researched childhood disorders in history (Selikowitz, 2004; National Institute of Mental Health, 2004). The estimated prevalence of ADHD among school age children is estimated to be between 3 to 7 percent of the total number of school age children in the United States (Humphries, 2007). Although much is known about ADHD and its characteristics, educators continue to search for answers on how best to work with children with this disorder.

Early childhood educators are especially concerned, because typically developing young children usually have some degree of hyperactivity and inattention. They are concerned with questions like: (1) Exactly how much hyperactivity and impulsivity might indicate ADHD in a child?; (2) What are similarities between children like Amy and Jordan that make them identified under the same disorder?; and (3) How can early childhood teachers help young children with ADHD?

In this chapter, we will provide answers to these questions. Because attention deficit hyperactivity disorder is sometimes presented in children along with other disorders, we will briefly discuss related disorders to ADHD as well. In addition, we will provide guidelines as to how to work with young children with ADHD in early childhood classrooms.

ATTENTION DEFICIT HYPERACTIVITY DISORDER

Among young children, the number of those diagnosed with ADHD has drastically risen during the past two decades (LeFever, Arcona, & Anonuccio, 2003), and currently, ADHD is among the most prevalent childhood disorders (Glanzman & Blum, 2007). At present, the prevalence rate of ADHD ranges from 3 to 7 percent in all children ages 6 to 12. (Brown et al., 2001; National Institute of Mental Health, 2004). Boys are more likely to be diagnosed with attention deficit hyperactivity disorder (ADHD), but it is not a new disorder. In 1845, Heinrich Hoffmann, a German physician in his book of children's poetry, *Der Struwwelpeter* or *Slovenly Peter,* described what is today known as the symptoms of different types of ADHD. His poem "Fidgety Phillip" describes the characteristics of a child with a hyperactive and impulsive type of ADHD. In another poem, "The Story of Johnny Head-in-Air," Hoffmann portrays features of a child with the inattentive type of ADHD. See Figures 8.1 and 8.2 for Hoffmann's poems from 1845.

Like the portrayal of Phillip and Johnny in Hoffmann's poetry, in the past, a child with symptoms of ADHD was regarded as an unruly, rude, or mischievous child. Historically, the general public has not been too sympathetic to the plight of the child with ADHD, who in reality might not have much control over his behavior or thought

The Story of Johnny Head-in-the-Air

As he trudg'd along to school
It was always Johnny's rule
To be looking at the sky
And the clouds that floated by;
But what just before him lay,
In his way
Johnny never thought about;
So that everyone cried out-
"Look at little Johnny there,
Little Johnny Head-in-Air"
Running just in Johnny's way,
Came a little dog one day;
Johnny's eyes were still astray
Up on high, in the sky;

And he never heard them cry—
"Johnny, mind, the dog in nigh!"
Bump!
Dump:
Down they fall, with such a thump,
Dog and Johnny in a lump!
Once with head as high as ever,
Johnny walk'd beside the river.
Johnny watch'd the swallows trying
Which was cleverest at flying.
Oh! What fun!

Johnny watch'd the bright round sun
Going in and coming out:
This was all he thought about.
To the rivers very brink,
Where the band was high and steep,
And the water very deep;
And the fishes in a row
Started to see him coming so.
One step more! Oh! Sad to tell!
Headlong in poor Johnny fell.
And the fishes, in dismay,
Wagg'd their tails and ran away.
There lay Johnny on his face,
With his nice red writing-case;
But, as they were passing by,
Two strong men heard him cry;

And, with sticks, these two strong men
Hook'd poor Johnny out again.
Oh! You should have seen him shiver
When they pull'd him from the river
He was in a sorry plight!
Dripping wet, and such a fright!
Wet all over, everywhere,
Clothes, and arms, and face, and hair
Johnny never will forget
What it is to be so wet.
And the fishes, one, two, three,
Are come back gain, you see;
Up they came the moment after,
To enjoy the fun and laughter.
Each popp'd out his little head,
And to tease poor Johnny said,
"Silly little Johnny, look,
You have lost your writing-book!"

FIGURE 8.1

Description of a Child with the Inattentive Type of ADHD by Heinrich Hoffmann, Written in 1845

Source: Der Struwwelpeter, available online: at http://www.fln.vcu.edu/struwwel/struwwel.html.

FIGURE 8.2

Description of ADHD in Heinrich Hoffmann's Poetry, Written in 1845

Source: Der Struwwelpeter, available online at http://www.fln.vcu.edu/struwwel/struwwel.html.

Fidgety Phillip

"Let me see if Philip can
Be a little gentleman;
Let me see if he is able
To sit still for once at table."
Thus spoke, in earnest tone,
The father to his son;
And the mother looked very grave
To see Philip so misbehave.
But Philip he did not mind
His father who was so kind.
He wriggled
And giggled,
And then, I declare,
Swung backward and forward
And tilted his chair,
Just like any rocking horse;—
"Philip! I am getting cross!"

See the naughty, restless child,
Growing still more rude and wild,
Till his chair falls over quite.
Philip screams with all his might,
Catches at the cloth, but then
That makes matters worse again.
Down upon the ground they fall,
Glasses, bread, knives, forks and all.
How Mamma did fret and frown,
When she saw them tumbling down!
And Papa made such a face!
Philip is in sad disgrace.

Where is Philip? Where is he?
Fairly cover'd up, you see!
Cloth and all are lying on him;
He has pull'd down all upon him!
What a terrible to-do!
Dishes, glasses, snapt in two!
Here a knife, and there fork!
Philip, this is naughty work.
Table all so bare, and ah!
Poor Papa and poor Mamma
Look quite cross, and wonder how
They shall make their dinner now.

processes. In fact, children who are today considered as having ADHD were in the past considered to lack moral restraint (Rafalovich, 2008).

In the past, the cause of ADHD was considered to be bad parenting or bad child-rearing practices. Punishment and fear inducement were recommended methods by which these children were treated in order to control their behaviors. In fact, whether or not Hoffmann had observed children with ADHD in his medical practice, he created his stories in order to scare children who behaved inappropriately or broke rules into acting properly. Unfortunately, the idea of lack of discipline as the cause, and fear inducement as the treatment for children with ADHD, continues to be believed in many parts of the world.

In 1902, George Still, a British physician, after working with a group of 20 children who likely had ADHD, described them as aggressive, passionate, lawless, inattentive, impulsive, and overactive children. He defined his patients as having a deficit in volitional inhibition or those who had a defect of moral control (Still, 1902). In 1917 and 1918, an outbreak of encephalitis in America led scientists to discover the brain damage that would come to be associated with ADHD (Barkley, 1997; Baeyens, Roeyers, & Walle, 2006; Heward, 2006). Eventually, interest in ADHD began to revolve around understanding specific hyperactive and impulsive behaviors of children with this disorder, and therefore symptom-oriented terms such as *restless syndrome* and *hyperactive child syndrome* were employed to refer to ADHD (Baeyens et al., 2006).

In the 1970s and 1980s, the disorder was associated with problems of sustained attention in addition to impulse control and hyperactivity, and hence the label attention deficit disorder (ADD) was used. This emphasized both the cognitive and developmental nature of this disorder (Barkley, 1997). ADD was known to be of two types, with or without hyperactivity. In the late 1980s and early 1990s, sensory processing researchers found that children with ADHD had problems with motor control and response inhibition, and that problems with impulsivity and hyperactivity were related in these children. Thus, the term ADD was renamed attention deficit hyperactivity disorder (ADHD), the disorder's symptoms being inattention, hyperactivity, and impulsivity. Today, the term ADD is considered outdated (National Institute of Mental Health, 2004).

Symptoms of ADHD

The main symptoms of ADHD are hyperactivity, impulsivity, and inattention. **Hyperactivity** can be described as a condition in which the child is easily excitable, over-active, or exuberant (Krummel, Seligson, & Guthrie, 1996). **Impulsivity** refers to the child's inability to think first before resorting to an action (American Academy of Child and Adolescent Psychiatry, 2008). Impulsive children might not think of the consequences of their behaviors. **Inattention** generally indicates that the child might have a short attention span, or have difficulties in sustaining his or her attention for more than a brief period of time.

Hyperactivity and impulsivity usually appear during early childhood years. However, symptoms of inattention might not be detected until later years, since it is children who are disruptive to the classroom or have hard-to-control and inappropriate behaviors that are immediately noticed and deemed to be in need of help and intervention. In fact, children who are quiet yet have serious learning difficulties are seldom noticed or thought of as those who might need intervention.

It is for this reason that children with attention problems or learning disabilities who might have developed certain strategies to survive from one grade to the next have repeatedly fallen through the gaps in our school system. It is not until serious learning, behavioral, or psychological issues have come to the attention of teachers and other educators who work with them that they are noticed. (We will discuss this topic further in Chapter 14.)

Critical Thinking Question 8.1   Recall the story at the beginning of this chapter. Amy and Jordan are both diagnosed with ADHD, yet their behavior characteristics and their needs seem to be very different from one another. How can we reconcile these two very different pictures and explain their difficulties under one disorder?

SUBTYPES OF ADHD

The *Diagnostic and Statistical Manual of Mental Disorders* (American Psychiatric Association, 2000) categorizes three types of behaviors that fall under ADHD. These three subtypes of ADHD are **predominantly hyperactive-impulsive type, predominantly inattentive type,** and the **combined type.** Children who are identified as the hyperactive-impulsive type usually do not display signs of inattention. Children who are diagnosed with the inattentive type do not show any symptoms of hyperactivity and impulsivity. Finally, children who are diagnosed with the combined type of ADHD display all three symptoms of ADHD.

More recent studies on ADHD classification indicate that the subtypes of ADHD are not consistent over time, and as children grow older, they might be identified with a different subtype than the one they had initially been identified with in early childhood (Rawland et al., 2008; Lahey, Pelham, Loney, Lee, & Willcutt, 2005). Rawland and his colleagues (2008) explain that one reason for this variability is that the ADHD classification studies have used varied and multiple sources of information to establish diagnosis of ADHD in the children they have studied. For example, where one study has used one source of symptoms report (i.e., the parental report), others might have used multiple sources of reports (i.e., the parental, teacher, and child reports), which in turn could have influenced the accurate diagnosis of the child with a specific subtype (Rawland et al., 2008).

Inattention

Children who are inattentive have a hard time focusing on a single task. They get bored with a task shortly after starting it. During early childhood years typically, they go from one play activity or game to the next before finishing the previous one. They are frequently forgetful about what they are told and about their daily tasks and activities (Baeyens et al., 2006; Barkley, 1997).

Children with ADHD might be easily distracted by irrelevant stimuli in the environment, like a car going by or a sound coming from outside. As they get older, these children do not pay close attention to details, make careless mistakes in their schoolwork, and are disorganized. They might lose their school supplies or things that are necessary for completing a task (Glanzman & Blum, 2007; Barkley, 1998).

Children who are considered to have the predominant inattentive type of ADHD might look "spacey" (National Institute of Mental Health, 2004). They might process information slower than their typically developing peers, and when teachers give them instruction, they might not fully understand what they are supposed to do, even though they might appear to be sitting quietly and attending to the teacher (National Institute of Mental Health, 2004). Children with ADHD who have inattention symptoms might have sustained attention during the time they are engaged in activities that they really enjoy. However, they might avoid any task that requires sustained mental effort (Brown, 2005).

In terms of play activities, preschoolers with ADHD are not easily distinguished from their peers during free play. The behavioral differences of these children, however, become apparent during structured play, where they might become frustrated (such as in cases of waiting their turn) and possibly act aggressively toward their peers (Lougy, DeRuvo, & Rosenthal, 2007).

Hyperactivity

Young children who have symptoms of hyperactivity are usually described as children who are "on the go." They often fidget or squirm while seated and have a hard time sitting for more than a few minutes. For example, in preschool and kindergarten they usually have a hard time participating during circle time without moving or without doing something that might be distracting to others (National Institute of Mental Health, 2004).

Although most young children have a certain level of high activity, the activity level of children with ADHD differs significantly from their typically developing peers (Glanzman & Blum, 2007). For example, they may get up from their seat if required to remain seated for a while. They might run about, climb, or jump when it is inappropriate to do so. During free play, they usually have a hard time playing quietly.

Impulsivity

Children who are impulsive have difficulties waiting in line or waiting for their turn. They might interrupt others frequently or utter inappropriate comments. They might blurt out answers before a question is completely asked. These children seem unable to think before they act. They appear to be concerned with immediate gratification, and even when they are older, they commonly fail to consider the consequences of their actions (National Institute of Mental Health, 2004). Young children with ADHD might display "intense" temperament and cognitive inflexibility, and when frustrated, they might hit, push, or hurt other children (Glanzman & Blum, 2007).

The activity level of children with ADHD differs significantly from their typically developing peers.

Other Possible Behaviors in Children with ADHD

Children with ADHD, especially those with hyperactivity and impulsivity, might display other behaviors in addition to those described earlier. Lougy, DeRuvo, and Rosenthal (2007) categorize other behaviors of children with ADHD as:

> **Risk-taking behaviors:** Children with ADHD often seek behaviors that are highly stimulating and risky, without regard for consequences. For this reason, they are often considered accident-prone.
> **Emotionally volatile behaviors:** Children with ADHD often experience unpredictable moods, showing little control for their behaviors. They seem to have a low tolerance for frustration and often become irritable and upset quickly.
> **Self-centeredness:** Although most preschool and younger children are self-centered, children with ADHD are especially affected. They seem to lack awareness of how their behaviors impact others and often do not accept responsibility for what might go wrong as a result of their action.

Diagnosis

During preschool years, many young children have different levels of symptoms of ADHD without having the disorder (Connor, 2002). Sometimes young children might display ADHD-like behaviors due to other causes. For example, there might be a sudden change in the child's life, or there might be an undetected medical condition present that may affect brain functions (National Institute of Mental Health, 2004). Therefore, in young children, the appearance of the symptoms alone does not necessarily suggest that a child might have ADHD (Connor, 2002). Although identification of ADHD in young children is difficult, the early identification and treatment of ADHD is important, since ADHD has been known to affect a child's functioning through adolescence and adulthood (Barkley, 2003).

Because diagnosis of ADHD is difficult during early childhood, it should be conducted by a licensed professional—usually a psychiatrist, a psychologist, or a physician. Smith and Corkum (2007) have identified four methods that are usually incorporated into the diagnosis of ADHD:

> Behavioral rating scales, such as the Preschool Behavior Questionnaire (Behar, 1977), completed by parents and early childhood teachers to indicate a variety of behaviors or symptoms in the child.
> Structured interviews of the child (when applicable) and parents to obtain family background and additional child information, such as medication and health history.
> Structured observation of the child to monitor, classify, and analyze the child's behavior.
> A test of attention, hyperactivity, and impulsivity, which is usually conducted using specific measures such as the Conners' Continuous Performance Test (Conners, 2001).

Additionally, evaluating a child with ADHD should not only focus on symptoms of ADHD alone, but on the possible coexisting conditions and associated medical, psychosocial, and learning issues, which can influence the treatment plan for the child (Glanzman & Blum, 2007).

In general, in order to diagnose ADHD, the professionals must make sure the child has shown any one or more symptoms of ADHD before age 7 and that the child continues to display these symptoms for over 6 months (American Psychiatric Association, 2000). In addition, the behavior characteristics should be present in at least two areas of the child's life. For example, a child who is hyperactive and impulsive should show these symptoms both at home and in school.

ETIOLOGY OF ADHD

Over the years, there have been a number of causal theories regarding ADHD. To date, no specific cause has been pinpointed for the disorder. A number of studies (Martin, Levy, Pieka, & Hay, 2006; Nigg, Willcut, Doyle, & Sonuga-Barke, 2005; Biederman, 2005) have associated certain genetic and brain impairments with ADHD. In the following sections, we will briefly describe the causal theories of ADHD.

Early Causal Theories of ADHD

One early theory stated that ADHD was a result of minimal brain damage, injury, or dysfunction (National Institute of Mental Health, 2004). This theory was rejected since not all children with ADHD have a history of brain trauma. A second more popular theory was that refined sugars and food additives caused children to be hyperactive. This theory encouraged some parents to try sugar-free and natural diets to help their children with ADHD during the 1980s. The theory, however, was rejected based on a number of biomedical and scientific research studies on this topic, which found no evidence that sugar or other food substances cause ADHD (Matthews, 2002; Wolraich, Millich, Stumbo, & Schultz, 1985). However, some studies suggest that a healthy diet might improve the behaviors of a small percentage (about 5 percent) of children with ADHD (Matthews, 2002). A similar theory postulates that ADHD in some children is a result of an allergic reaction to environmental allergens (Pelsser, Buitelaar, & Huub, 2009). This theory has not been tested yet.

Prenatal and Environmental Factors and ADHD

Although no conclusive evidence has been found, a number of small and large studies have found a link between maternal smoking during pregnancy and ADHD in the child (Milberger, Biederman, Faraone, & Jones, 1998; Linnet et al., 2003; Linnet et al., 2005; Altink et al., 2009). These studies suggest that mothers who smoke during pregnancy are at increased risk for having children with ADHD or ADHD-symptoms compared with nonsmokers.

Other environmental factors, such as lead poisoning, have also been associated with the possibility of ADHD (National Institute of Mental Health, 2004; Braun, Kahn, Froehlich, Auinger, & Lanphear, 2006; Wang et al., 2008). Braun and his colleagues (2006) studied over 4,704 children between the ages of 4 and 15 years. They found that environmental lead exposure, measured in the children's blood accounted for about 290,000 excess cases of ADHD in U.S. children. Although materials used in modern buildings do not contain lead any longer, an occurrence of lead poisoning is still a possibility with today's children, who might be exposed to lead through their environment (i.e, lead is found in some imported toys, and also in cleaning supplies, paint, and some old buildings).

Genetics and ADHD

Genetics play an important role in ADHD. Research has shown that children with ADHD are likely to have other family members with the disorder (Sharp, McQuillin, & Gurling, 2009; Lifford, Harold, & Thapar, 2009; Wilens, Faraone, & Biederman, 2004). Some studies (Biederman, Faraone, Keenan, Knee, & Tsuang, 1990; Biederman, 2005) indicate that there is a 29 percent chance that parents of children with ADHD might have ADHD themselves. Roughly 57 percent of children who have parents with ADHD are diagnosed with this disorder. In addition, there is a 30 to 35 percent chance that siblings of children with ADHD may also have this disorder. Many adults with ADHD are not diagnosed until another family member, usually their child, is diagnosed.

Most children do not outgrow their ADHD. ADHD genetic studies reveal that up to 80 percent of children diagnosed with ADHD will continue to have symptoms in adulthood (August, Stewart, & Holmes, 1983; Barkley, Fischer, Smallish, & Fletcher, 2002; Claude & Firestone, 1995). However, some evidence exists that genetic influences of ADHD might vary with age and development (Hay, Bennett, McStephen, Rooney, & Levey, 2004; Levy, Hay, & Bennett, 2006). This means that the influence of ADHD-related genes decreases in a small number of children as they become older. Therefore, there is a possibility that in some families, children might recover from their ADHD as they enter adulthood. While this might be true for some children, it is not the same for all children with ADHD (Levy et al., 2006; Hay et al., 2004). Therefore, we ought to be cautious not to generalize these findings as pertinent to all children.

Developmental Impairment of the Executive Function

The neurobiological causes of ADHD have received the most research support during the past decade (Tripp & Wickens, 2009). Various methods of brain studies, such as functional magnetic resonance imaging (fMRI), positron emission tomography (PET), and single photon emission computed tomography (SPECT), have been employed to study ADHD.

The human brain is a complex organ, with amazing information processing capabilities. The brain organizes and processes all information received from outside of the human body, as well as those received from inside, such as emotions and thoughts. After all of the information is processed, the brain sends a variety of responses to the body. The tasks of the brain are organized from simple, such as moving muscles, to complex, such as self-regulation. These complex tasks are carried out by what is called the **executive function** of the brain (Barkley, 1997; Brown, 2006). See Figure 8.3.

The executive function of the brain is responsible for goal-oriented behaviors and actions. The executive function is the main mechanism responsible for self-control and self-regulation in an individual. It is also in charge of abilities such as: self-appraisal, self-organization, sustained attention, reflection, compliance, working memory, and coordination of movement (Selikowitz, 2004). Those skills that are carried out by the executive function are mediated by the frontal cortex,

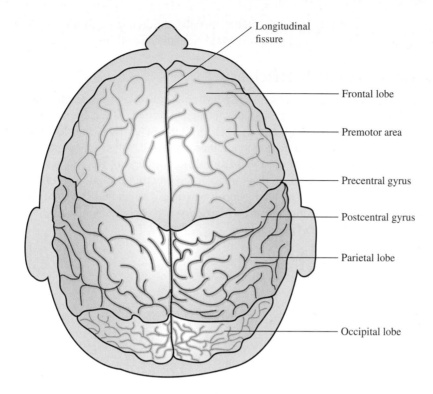

Longitudinal
fissure

Frontal lobe

Premotor area

Precentral gyrus

Postcentral gyrus

Parietal lobe

Occipital lobe

FIGURE 8.3
The Executive
Function of the
Brain Is Responsible
for Goal-Oriented
Behaviors and
Actions

especially the prefrontal lobe, of the brain. The frontal lobe communicates messages to other parts of the brain via a rich network of nerve pathways while it integrates and coordinates works of all other parts of the brain (Tripp & Wickens, 2009;
Brown, 2006; Selikowitz, 2004).

In many children with ADHD, the connecting pathways to and from the frontal
lobe do not function adequately (Tripp & Wickens, 2009; Selikowitz, 2004; National
Institute of Mental Health, 2004), and therefore, children with ADHD are considered to have specific impairments in executive functioning of their brain (Barkley,
1997; Welsh, 2002; Nigg et al., 2005; Brown, 2006). The difficulties of children with
ADHD that are related to the executive functioning of their brain include problems
with (Barkley, 1997; Selikowitz, 2004; Lougy et al., 2007):

> Motor sequencing and coordination of movement
> Mental computation of facts or events
> Planning and anticipation
> Verbal fluency and communication of feelings
> Effort allocation to do a task
> Applying organizational strategies and planning to solve a problem
> Internalization of self-directed speech to describe or reflect on an event before
  responding to it
> Adhering to restrictive instructions
> Self-regulation of emotional arousal so as not to react purely on emotions, but
  evaluate events rationally and respond

Therefore, when the executive function fails, children react to the world in an unfocused, disorganized, and impulsive way (Selikowitz, 2004).

Neurotransmitter Inefficiency

The human brain contains over a billion nerve cells called *neurons*. Each neuron has a number of branch-like long projections located at its end, called *axons*. Individual nerve cells communicate with one another through low-current electrical impulses traveling from axons of one neuron to another nerve cell. These electrical impulses contain information being sent to and from different parts of the brain. Axons do not touch the neuron to which they are sending electrical impulses. Information from one neuron flows to another neuron across a gap, called the *synapse*. The impulses are carried out through the synapse by a group of chemical messengers called **neurotransmitters** (Figure 8.4).

FIGURE 8.4
Neurotransmitters Facilitate a Smooth Transmission of Information between Neurons

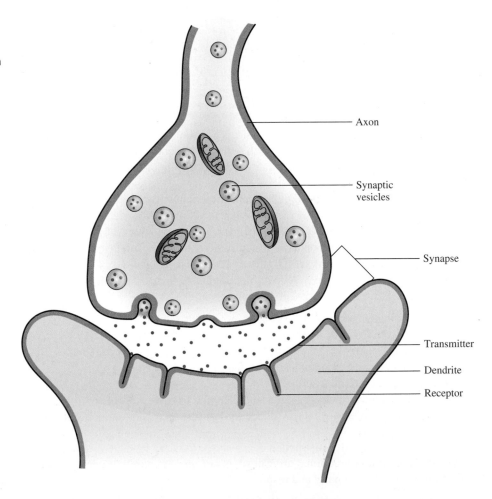

Axon

Synaptic vesicles

Synapse

Transmitter

Dendrite

Receptor

Neurotransmitters are released by the tip of axons. *Dopamine* and *norepineph-rine* are two important neurotransmitters that carry messages among the network of cells to and from the frontal lobe. One causal theory of ADHD indicates that children with ADHD have a basic defect in the metabolism of dopamine and norepinephrine at the synapses, which leads to poor transmission and communication among that part of their brain (Tripp & Wickens, 2009; Selikowitz, 2004; Biederman, 2005).

OTHER DISORDERS ASSOCIATED WITH ADHD

Several other disorders have been found to be present along with ADHD in some children. When two conditions commonly co-occur with one another, they are considered to be *comorbid*. Some disorders are more likely to be comorbid with ADHD inattentive types. Others are more likely to have **comorbidity** with other types of ADHD. For example, learning disabilities (LD) are more likely to be comorbid with the ADHD inattentive type, while oppositional defiant disorder (ODD) is more likely to be comorbid with the ADHD hyperactive-impulsive or combined type (Jong et al., 2009; Mayes, Calhoun, & Crowell, 2000).

Reading or Learning Disabilities

About 70 percent of children with ADHD have some kind of learning difficulty (Mayes et al., 2000). Of this group of children with ADHD, reading disabilities occur in about 31 percent (Martin et al., 2006). During the preschool years, these children might have trouble in receptive and expressive language, such as a problem with phonetic knowledge—understanding certain sounds or words—or expressing themselves through language. As children enter primary grades, their struggles might show in their spelling and reading (National Institute of Mental Health, 2004).

It is difficult to distinguish between a child who has ADHD and a child who only has a learning disability (LD). School-age children who have a learning disability might show symptoms similar to ADHD without actually having the disorder (U.S. Department of Education, 2006a). For example, many children with learning disabilities get frustrated when trying to learn. They might act up in school, not pay attention, or fall into a pattern of daydreaming (Matthews, 2002). Careful testing is required to determine whether a child has a comorbid condition, or just one disorder.

Oppositional Defiant Disorder

About one-third to one-half of children diagnosed with ADHD have a condition called oppositional defiant disorder (ODD) (U.S. Department of Education, 2006a; Spencer, 2009). ODD is usually present during early childhood years in children who have the hyperactive-impulsive type or the combined type of ADHD (Spencer, 2009). Young children with ODD may argue, talk back, and defy parents, teachers, and others. They might be openly uncooperative and hostile toward other individuals. Patterns of contrary and antagonistic behaviors in these children are usually to such a degree that it might interfere with their daily functioning (National Institute of Mental Health, 2004). Text Box 8.1 describes a typical day in the life of a 4-year-old girl with ODD.

Text Box 8.1   The Face of Oppositional Defiant Disorder
Does Briana Ever Behave Appropriately?

Briana is 4 years old. She lives with her parents in a suburban home in Detroit. Briana's parents both work full time. Briana goes to her grandparents' house in the mornings and to a preschool in the afternoons. She has a large extended family, so her paternal grandparents ask their other children to help care for Briana some mornings during the week. Briana's aunt and uncle believe that Briana never outgrew her terrible twos. They secretly call her the little monster, and dread the time that they have to babysit her.

Briana begins every morning by whining for 30 minutes until her parents are woken up. Briana's mother is an organized person and has frequently told Briana to put her things in their proper places. So every morning, after Briana finishes her whining, the first thing she does is to throw her bedding on the floor. She then pulls out all her clothes from her drawer and scatters them around the room. During breakfast, she goes through a ritual of refusing to eat for the first 10 minutes, until her parents are sufficiently flustered, at which point, Briana gets up and is ready to go to Grandma's. After she is dropped off at her grandparents' home, Briana usually has a lot to tell her grandmother about the ways in which she was punished by her mother in the morning or the previous night, much of which are gross exaggerations. This usually sets arguments between her grandparents and her father when he arrives at lunchtime to pick up Briana for preschool. Briana seems to enjoy setting such fights between adults.

At preschool, Briana bosses other children around and constantly tells everyone what to do. If she does not get her way, she becomes angry and tends to attempt to retaliate. Although she does a good job with all of her preschool activities, she does the activities only the way she wants to, not the way the teacher asked her to do them. When it is not her turn to be the line leader, she gets very angry and throws a tantrum, which sometimes takes about 15 minutes. At these times, the teacher puts Briana in time out. However, time out does not seem to deter her. Briana tells the teacher and children that she hates them. Sometimes when she gets angry, she throws the toys and supply bins on the floor.

When Briana goes home after school, she demands that her mother play with her. If her mother is busy making dinner and can't play with her, she bangs the furniture around and screams at her mother. Most nights she refuses to eat dinner, until her mom and dad sit down and play with her, and do exactly what she tells them to do during the play. Because they want to have some peace and quiet, Briana's parents comply, but their play usually ends in Briana screaming at them, because they "don't do things right." Briana's bedtime routine takes over 2 hours, because she goes through a pattern of refusing to be bathed and to brush her teeth.

Every night, after Briana is finally put to bed, Briana's parents are exhausted and stressed. Briana's grandparents and aunts and uncles are glad that each of them doesn't have to take care of her every morning. Briana's teacher is similarly glad that the preschool program in which Briana is enrolled is only 2.5 hours. Does Briana ever behave appropriately? Well, yes! She could be an angel, when she has everyone's undivided attention!

Conduct Disorder

Between 25 and 50 percent of children with ADHD might eventually develop conduct disorder (CD) (Harada et al., 2009; Spencer, 2009; Rathouz, 2007; National Institute of Mental Health, 2004). Conduct disorder is a serious pattern of antisocial behaviors. Oppositional defiant disorder and conduct disorder have many similarities. However, conduct disorder is a more dangerous form of ODD. Children who have CD are aggressive toward people and animals. They might deliberately destroy or set fire to property, bully others, or be aggressive and fight with peers (Rathouz, 2007). These children might be deceitful or steal others' possessions, and seriously violate major rules. Although conduct disorder is different from oppositional defiant disorder, a child with severe ODD might develop CD as he or she gets older (Rathouz, 2007). Children with CD are at great risk for substance abuse and getting into trouble at school or with authorities during adolescence (National Institute of Mental Health, 2004).

Anxiety Disorder

Showing anxiety in certain situations is typical for young children. For example, during late infancy and the toddler years, when separated from parents, being in new places or situations, or meeting a stranger, children commonly become anxious. However, as children become older, if anxiety persists to such a degree that it becomes difficult for a child to function well in various environments, medical intervention might be necessary to help the child. Children with ADHD are considered to be at risk for having anxiety; and anxiety is present in about 25 percent of children with ADHD (Lavigne, LeBailly, Hopkins, Gouze, & Binns, 2009; Matthews, 2002).

Depression

About 18 percent of children with ADHD deal with depression (Matthews, 2002; National Institute of Mental Health, 2004; Lavigne et al., 2009). When depression is recognized and treated in a child with ADHD, the child will be able to handle symptoms of ADHD better. It is important that a child is clinically diagnosed as having depression, because medication prescribed for depression for a child who has both depression and ADHD might be different from that prescribed for a child with only depression (National Institute of Mental Health, 2004).

Tourette's Syndrome

Named after a French physician, Georges Gilles de la Tourette, who first described this disorder, Tourette's syndrome is a neurological disorder that is characterized by nervous **tics.** Tics are repetitive and involuntary movements such as eye blinks or facial twitches; or vocalizations such as snorts or sniffs (Gaze, Kepley, & Walkup, 2006). The early symptoms of Tourette's are usually seen in children between 7 and 10 years of age. Although a small percentage of children with ADHD have Tourette's syndrome, about 60 percent of all children who are diagnosed with Tourette's syndrome also have ADHD (O'Rourke, Scharf, Yu, & Pauls, 2009; Gaze et al., 2006).

TREATMENT OF ADHD

ADHD is a serious public health problem, and therefore identifying effective treatment is crucial. Research on the treatment of ADHD shows that a combination approach consisting of therapeutic intervention, parent–professional collaboration and partnership, and medication has been the most effective way to address symptoms of ADHD in children who are 6 years old and older. For younger children, using positive behavioral support in collaboration with parents is considered to be the most effective way of addressing behavioral characteristics of ADHD.

The *multimodal treatment* study done by NIMH is the largest-scale and most comprehensive study conducted on the treatment of ADHD to date. The results of this study, along with the treatments available for ADHD, are presented in the following sections.

The Multimodal Treatment Study

The Multimodal Treatment Study of Children with ADHD (Edwards, 2002; National Institute of Mental Health, 2004) was a major effort that examined the efficacy of different treatments, including drugs, for ADHD. Schools and families, including teachers and parents, cooperated in this research. The study involved 579 children with ADHD in multiple sites over a 14-month period. Children were assigned to four different treatment programs: (1) medication only; (2) behavior treatment only; (3) a combination of both with parent collaboration; and (4) routine community care.

The results of this study suggested that children receiving the combined treatment showed a significantly superior improvement compared with children in the behavior treatment–only, medication only, and routine community care groups. Children who received the combination of medication and behavior treatment showed superior gains in the areas of academic performance, opposition, parent–child relationship, social skills, and anxiety. In addition, children in the combined treatment group required lower doses of medication compared to children who were in the medication-only group (Edwards, 2002; National Institute of Mental Health, 2004).

The study results suggested that an effective treatment program for children with ADHD included a combination approach consisting of collaboration with parents, behavioral intervention, social skills training, educational adaptation, and medication (Glanzman & Blum, 2007; Edwards, 2002; National Institute of Mental Health, 2004).

Pharmacological Treatment

Pharmacological treatment of ADHD includes use of psychostimulants, antidepressants, antianxiety, antipsychotic, and mood stabilizer medications (Glanzman & Blum, 2007; U.S. Department of Education, 2006a; National Institute of Mental Health, 2004). All drugs prescribed for ADHD increase the amount of one or both neurotransmitters, dopamine and norepinephrine (Selikowitz, 2004). The appropriate medications will produce an adequate amount of neurotransmitters, which in turn increases the child's level of attention and decreases hyperactivity and impulsivity. The most common drugs prescribed for children 3 years old and older are listed in Table 8.1.

TABLE 8.1 Most Common Medications Used in ADHD, Their Approved Age, and Possible Side Effects

Medication	Common Name	Approved Age	Some Possible Side Effects
Methylphenidate	Ritalin Concerta Metadate	6 years and older	➤ Lack of sleep ➤ Low appetite ➤ Headache
Amphetamine	Adderall	3 years and older	➤ Palpitation of heart ➤ Raised blood pressure ➤ Dizziness or insomnia ➤ Exacerbation of symptoms of Tourette's Syndrome, such as tics
Atomoxetine	Strattera	6 years and older	➤ Gastrointestinal problems ➤ Decrease in appetite ➤ Headache or dizziness ➤ Irritability
Dexamphetamine	Dexedrine Dextrostat Facoline	3 years and older	➤ Palpitation of heart ➤ Raised blood pressure ➤ Restlessness, dizziness, or insomnia ➤ Headache ➤ Gastrointestinal problems
Clonidine	Catapres	6 years and older	➤ Weakness or fatigue ➤ Insomnia ➤ Dry mouth ➤ Gastrointestinal problems ➤ Palpitation of heart ➤ Headache ➤ Nervousness and agitation
Impiramine	Tofranil	6 years and older	➤ Dizziness ➤ Drowsiness ➤ Dry mouth ➤ Headache ➤ Increased appetite ➤ Nausea ➤ Tiredness or weakness

(Continued)

TABLE 8.1   (Continued)

Risperidone	Risperdal	18 years and older	➢ Coughing
			➢ Constipation or diarrhea
			➢ Drowsiness
			➢ Dry mouth
			➢ Headache
			➢ Increased sleep or increased dream activity
			➢ Unusual tiredness or weakness
			➢ Weight gain

Source: National Institute of Mental Health, available at http://www.nimh.nih.gov.

Medications have been found to be effective in 75 to 90 percent of children with ADHD (U.S. Department of Education, 2006a; Edwards, 2002). The effects of some medication used for ADHD are temporary. Therefore, if medication is chosen as a mode of treatment, it must be given to the child on a consistent basis (National Institute of Mental Health, 2004).

During the past decade there has been a great public controversy in the media in regard to use of medications for children with ADHD. The number of children taking medication for ADHD has steadily risen during recent years. It is estimated that annually about 5 to 6 million children in the United States receive medication for ADHD (Sinha, 2001). Conflicting views among parents, medical professionals, and educators regarding the use of drugs in children who are diagnosed with ADHD continue. In general, parents are concerned about the drug's unknown safety factors, and possible long-term effects of medication use on their children. Teachers and educators are likewise anxious about the behavior management of children with ADHD. Teachers are uneasy about providing an equitable education to all children in their classroom while their attention might be monopolized by the child with ADHD.

No matter what the reasoning, educators in general and early childhood educators in particular should be aware that the decision to recommend or consider use of medication for children with ADHD is the responsibility of the medical and mental health professionals in partnership with parents. Recommendation for medication use requires an in-depth study of all dimensions of the child's life and well-being, including physical, neurological, cognitive, and social emotional development, as they relate to the family's belief, which is outside the scope of the teacher's knowledge and skills (U.S. Department of Education, 2006a).

Collaboration with Parents

Although every family is different in the way they respond to the unique or special learning needs of their child, it is expected that parents of children with ADHD might experience some levels of stress or frustration due to possible learning and behavioral difficulties, which are characteristics of ADHD (Rathouz, 2007). Hyperactive, impulsive, or oppositional behavioral issues, as well as academic problems associated with ADHD, could put an excessive amount of stress on parents.

Providing information on ADHD and its available treatment resources is the first step toward partnership with families of children with the disability. Parents (and children themselves when appropriate) would benefit from learning about ADHD as much as possible so they can be effective decision makers and advocates (Glanzman & Blum, 2007). In addition, providing positive behavioral support (discussed in Chapter 9) for children in collaboration with parents is the cornerstone of ADHD treatment (Ford, Olmi, Edwards, & Tingstrom, 2001).

It is therefore necessary that professionals partner with parents and work closely with them to (1) identify the child's behavioral areas that need to be addressed; (2) identify positive strategies to be used both by parents and teachers at home and in early childhood settings; (3) help the young child choose to act appropriately in different situations; and (4) set up the child for academic success. A parent–professional collaboration would lead to creating consistent and calming environments both at home and in school for the child in which learning is maximized.

Because children with ADHD might display oppositional and defiant behaviors, the relationship between adults and the child with ADHD is frequently at jeopardy at home, in the community, and at schools (Rathouz, 2007). Therefore, part of the collaboration between parents and professionals should include a discussion of possible ways in which parents and professionals might enhance and maintain positive relationships with children with ADHD in view of their oppositional behaviors. Table 8.2 displays some suggestions for building positive relationships with children in the early childhood classrooms, and specifically with children who have oppositional behaviors.

TABLE 8.2 Suggestions for Building Positive Relationships with Children in Early Childhood Inclusive Classrooms

Building a Positive Adult–Child Relationship	Support the Child's Appropriate Behaviors
Observe the child to better understand the child's interests and behaviors.	Set clear limits for behaviors for each situation, place, and circumstance.
Take a genuine interest in what the child does by looking, listening, and paying attention.	Set clear and explicit daily routines, and follow consistently.
Interact with the child in a playful manner and follow the child's lead during play.	State explicit and clear expectations for each behavior, and follow consistently.
Withhold criticism and judgment at all costs; when the child displays any feelings, validate those feelings.	Provide consistent and immediate positive consequences for every appropriate behavior that the child does.
Be attentive to what the child is doing.	Provide a variety of positive reinforcers to encourage appropriate behaviors.
Describe the child's behaviors and play repertoire.	Withhold reinforcement when the child commits an inappropriate behavior.
Have frequent physical contact.	Praise the child for appropriate behaviors throughout the daily routines.

STRATEGIES AND ADAPTATIONS FOR INCLUSIVE CLASSROOMS

Although under IDEA there is no specific category for ADHD, this disorder is usually considered under *other health impairments,* since ADHD results in the child's limited alertness with regard to the educational environment. Children with ADHD might also be eligible for services under *specific learning disability,* or *emotional disturbance,* or, if the child has a comorbid condition, under other categories.

Receiving a diagnosis of ADHD is not enough to determine eligibility of a child for special education services. An eligibility evaluation should be conducted as a second step to determine if the child requires special education and related services in order to be successful academically. Because of the least restrictive environment (LRE) criteria, almost all children with ADHD are educated in general education classrooms or in inclusive classrooms.

In general, young children with ADHD benefit from classroom and curriculum adaptations and modifications as discussed in Chapters 5 and 7. The U.S. Department of Education (2006b, 2008) recommends integration of the following four components for education of children with ADHD:

> Behavior management/positive behavior support
> Environmental organization
> Instructional adaptation
> Reinforcing social skills

Behavior Management/Positive Behavior Support

A well-planned behavior management program has been found to be one of the most effective and crucial parts of a comprehensive education plan for children who have ADHD. Behavior management has been defined as the actions that "teachers and parents engage in to enhance the probability that others will develop effective behaviors that are personally fulfilling, productive and socially acceptable" (Walker, Shea, & Bauer, 2004). Positive behavior support (PBS) is a behavior management strategy that consists of positive approaches that support a child learning appropriate behaviors that are likely to promote his or her success in the classroom, at home, and in the community. (We will focus on this topic further in Chapter 9.)

A teachers' ability to provide effective behavior management lies in his or her philosophy concerning it. Teachers ought to be clear about their beliefs regarding their expectations of children's behaviors, classroom rules, and consequences that would follow appropriate and inappropriate behaviors (Walker et al., 2004). The following strategies have been recommended (Walker et al., 2004; U.S. Department of Education, 2006b, 2008) for children with ADHD to be used in inclusive early childhood classrooms:

1. **Set up clear expectations and consistent limits:** Teachers and parents of young children frequently assume that children understand what they are and are not supposed to do. In reality, however, not all children automatically and naturally

learn what is appropriate and what is not just by observing adults' behaviors. Expectation on how to behave in any specific situation should be explicitly and clearly defined and explained to children. The adult's expectations of children must be realistic and according to the child's developmental level. For example, it may not be realistic to expect any 2- or 3-year-old to sit in one place for more than 5 to 10 minutes.

2. **Classroom rules for sitting, talking, and interacting should be clearly articulated:** Rules should be brief and clear. Early childhood teachers can review rules before beginning an activity and during transition. In addition, teachers should be careful to be consistent in regard to reinforcing the rules they set up. For example, to reinforce the rules at certain times and not do so at others conveys mixed messages to children, which result in children's disregard of rules. Visual cues for appropriate behaviors posted in the classroom are good reminders of rules. Figure 8.5 displays some examples of classroom rules.

3. **Use visual and nonverbal cues to redirect a child's behavior during teaching:** Redirection of a child's behavior can occur as the teacher is talking, reading a story, or interacting with the child. This can be done through the use of hand gestures, physical cues, or by using a picture or word card that illustrates the appropriate behavior for the child to follow (Dillon & Osborne, 2006).

FIGURE 8.5
Examples of Classroom Rules

No hitting, instead use your words

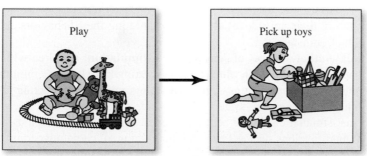

After play, pick up toys

4. **Provide immediate consequences for children's behaviors:** As much as it is important to manipulate antecedents to a behavior to prevent a behavior from occurring, it is important that children receive a clear message that their behaviors will have consequences once they have been committed. For children with ADHD, consequences of behaviors should be delivered more immediately than might be done for other children, since these children act on impulses.

5. **Use a variety of positive reinforcers:** A range of activities and objects that are reinforcing to the child should be available so that reinforcers do not become predictable. In addition, praise should be used with all children and very frequently throughout each activity and during the routine tasks.

Critical Thinking Question 8.2 Consider Jordan from the opening story. Come up with ideas for teachers and family members to help him change his behavior.

Environmental Organization

Children with ADHD benefit from a well-structured classroom that offers the least amount of distraction to them. The following simple adjustments in the classroom will help children with ADHD or other related disorders to self-regulate and be prepared to learn (U.S. Department of Education, 2006b, 2008):

> **Have uncluttered and organized centers:** It is important that centers are tidy and free of clutter and confusion. Busy and disorganized environments cause distractions and over-stimulation for children with ADHD.

> **Keep the noise level to a minimum:** The same way that visual clutter is distracting to a child with ADHD, a high noise level might also be overwhelming to some children (Rosinia, 2008). Some educators believe that early childhood classrooms are by nature noisy places. This common misconception has often led to many mismanaged early childhood classrooms in which learning could not take place. Part of a healthy social emotional development is for children to learn appropriate behaviors and **register** for each situation, circumstance, and place. Young children are well capable of modulating their noise level as well as regulating their behaviors according to each circumstance.

> **Modulate other sources of sensory over-stimulation:** Children with ADHD respond to environments in which all sensory stimuli are kept to a minimum. For example, fluorescent lightings and vivid colors might be distracting and overwhelming to the sensory system (Emmons & Anderson, 2005). Such sources of visual stimulation should be eliminated or minimized as much as possible. Small modifications such as changing the lighting, or carpeting certain areas of the classroom, will help muffle sounds and sights that might be distracting.

Instructional Adaptation

The following strategies are specifically useful when working with young children with ADHD (U.S. Department of Education, 2006b, 2008; Lougy et al., 2007):

1. **Differentiate content and activities based on children's needs:** Because many children with ADHD also have specific learning disabilities, it is important that the curriculum content be adapted based on their specific learning needs. For example, children with ADHD might need:

   a. Task analysis
   b. To be allowed more time to complete each step
   c. Immediate feedback when completing each step
   d. Frequent breaks between tasks

2. **Make group and individual schedules available for each child:** Posters, planners, charts, class, and individual schedules are options that outline daily routines and activities for children. Children with ADHD need to have clear visual schedules of the upcoming activities and events in- and outside of the classroom. Stormont (2008) suggests the use of colorful sticky notes and high-lighters to attract the attention of the child to specific items on the schedule or worksheets as to what to attend to first, second, and so on.

3. **Move among children, interact with them, and provide support when needed:** Early childhood educators should be on their feet as much as children are to keep them engaged throughout all aspects of their classroom activities. When an educator keeps instructions and lessons engaging, and thus children active, it helps focus the attention of all children, especially children with ADHD. It also prevents inappropriate behaviors from occurring.

4. **Use proximity control:** Children show an increase in their attention to a task when the teacher is in close physical proximity (Ford et al., 2001; Gettinger & Seibert, 2002). Standing close to the child, or sitting next to the child during small and large group activities, helps the child focus his or her attention and improve compliance.

> **Critical Thinking Question 8.3**   Referring to the story presented at the beginning of the chapter, what suggestions can you make in regard to Amy's classroom and instruction to help her be more successful in her learning?

Reinforcing Social Skills in Children with ADHD

Social skill training is an important component of early childhood special education and inclusive classrooms. Early childhood classrooms are like early laboratories in which children try out and develop their repertoire in which social skills are learned (Lavoie, 2005). Rothenberg (2005) categorizes social skills into four components:

> **Input:** Understanding verbal and nonverbal social cues and body language.
> **Organization:** Organizing the social information received into specific categories. For example, whether or not to act or react in a certain situation, based on what is observed or heard.
> **Output:** Deciding on the best course of action or reaction and committing to it based on the given information organization.
> **Self-monitoring:** Concluding whether or not an action has been appropriate or inappropriate.

Although most children naturally learn these social skills' components through their interactions and interpersonal relationships with other children and adults, children with ADHD and other children with special needs might not necessarily learn these skills without explicit instruction. Teaching self-monitoring, self-evaluation, and self-regulation strategies has been shown to be effective with children with ADHD (Westby & Cutler, 1994). Teachers can teach self-monitoring and self-regulation by modeling "self talk"—talking out loud about their thought processes, about decision making, and their reflection on the consequences of their actions during their interactions with children (Rothenberg, 2005).

Teachers can influence and reinforce children's social behaviors by directly teaching them how to begin a conversation, how to join and play in groups, how to establish and maintain friendship, how to solve problems and resolve conflicts, and how to "tune in" to social skills of other children around them (Lougy et al., 2007).

Teaching friendship skills is especially imperative for children with ADHD because they often have a hard time making friends and maintaining friendship due to their impulsive or possibly aggressive behaviors. Social stories (described in Chapter 7) have been used successfully for children with ADHD to teach them appropriate social skills (Lougy et al., 2007). Using children's literature, role play, and modeling are other common ways in which teachers can teach children friendship skills, such as smiling and approaching another child, greeting, introducing oneself, asking open-ended questions to get information about the child, and suggesting to play together (Lougy et al., 2007). Text Box 8.2 provides examples of two social skill activities appropriate for early childhood classrooms.

Text Box 8.2   Activities to Promote Social Skills in Children Preschool Age and Beyond

Developmental Domain: Social emotional

Activity 1

Objective: Children will be able to perform affective, physical, and verbal behaviors necessary for greetings.

Materials: None

Social skills training procedures

This activity can be done by having children sit around in a circle, or in small groups if children have a hard time sitting in one place.

The teacher models greetings by physical demonstration and saying:

1. "Turn your body"
2. "Look your friend in the eye"
3. "Say hello"

Children practice in paired groups, or in the circle by each child turning toward the next child in the circle and saying hello.

Modifications for Nonverbal Children: Make a PECS or a teacher-made greeting card with the word hello on it. Have children exchange "hello" cards in the morning, following three steps, "turn your body," "look your friend in the eye," "give the greeting card to your friend."

Developmental Domain: Social emotional

Activity 2

Objective: Children will be able to take conversational turns during a simple conversation.

Materials: One or more stop signs. Stop signs can be made by children as a previous art activity, using poster board and paint.

Social skills training procedures

The skills could be practiced in a circle/large group activity or in small groups of three.

Circle Time: The teacher chooses a child to be the "stop sign holder." The child stands in the middle of the circle, holding the stop sign. The teacher gives students a "share and tell" topic. For example, "What we did during free play today" or "The places we have seen." The teacher designates a "speaker" from the children sitting in the circle. The "speaker" begins talking about the topic. All other children are "listeners." The rule is that no one says anything while the "speaker" is talking. The teacher gives a signal to the "sign holder" to raise the stop sign when appropriate. When the stop sign is raised, the "speaker" should finish his or her sentence and stop speaking. The procedure is repeated for all children. Children should take turns being the "stop sign holder" and "speaker." The goal is that children take turns speaking and give each other a chance to speak and listen.

Small Group: The procedure can be done in groups of three consisting of a "stop sign holder," a "speaker," and a "listener."

Research Corner

The Preschool ADHD Treatment Study

In 2001, the National Institute of Mental Health funded a multi-site longitudinal study of preschool children with ADHD conducted by the New York State Psychiatric Institute, Duke University, Johns Hopkins University, New York University, the University of California at Los Angeles, and the University of California at Irvine. Because a major public concern has been the safety of prescribed medication for young children with ADHD, the Preschool ADHD Treatment Study (PATS) was the first major research to examine the safety and efficacy of methylphenidate, a stimulant medication frequently prescribed for young children. The PATS study involved 303 children from 3 to 5 years of age who had been diagnosed with ADHD. It used a randomized placebo-controlled double-blind design and was initiated in 2001 and completed in 2004. In a double-blind placebo-controlled experimental design, neither the individuals under study nor the researchers know who belongs to the control group and the experimental group. This design is used to eliminate subjective bias on the part of both the subjects and the experimenters. Currently, the PATS research team is tracking the children participating in the study for 5 years to study the long-term outcomes.

The early findings of these studies suggested that side effects of stimulant medications seemed to be stronger and larger in number in the preschool age children who took the medication (Wigal et al., 2006). For example, when taking medication, younger children tended to have more emotional outbursts, repetitive behaviors, difficulties falling sleep, a decreased appetite, and were more irritable and anxious compared with older children who take similar medications. In general, young children seem to be less tolerant of the effects of stimulant medications. Other findings related to this study showed that young children who are on stimulant medications might have a reduction in growth rate while they are on the medication (Swanson et al., 2006).

These findings are clear indications that prescription medications for young children should only be considered when all other educational and behavioral methods have consistently failed. The preliminary results of the PATS study indicate that negative side effects of medication in 3- to 5-year-olds may far outweigh their benefits.

Critical Thinking Question 8.4   Referring back to the opening story, what is your opinion about using medication for Amy, as compared to using it for Jordan?

SUMMARY

ADHD is one of the most serious and prevalent disorders in children, affecting between 3 and 7 percent of preschool- and school-age children. ADHD was identified in the late 19th century and has historically been defined as a disorder of the brain. The major symptoms of ADHD consist of hyperactivity, impulsivity, and inattention. Children with ADHD might fall under three general categories: inattentive type, hyperactive-impulsive type, or combined hyperactive-impulsive and inattentive type. Children who have the hyperactive-impulsive and the combined type of ADHD are more easily identified during early childhood years. However, those who are inattentive might not be identified until years later when they might have problems in academic performance. The causes of ADHD are unknown. Current research points to a dysfunction in the executive function of the brain.

ADHD is sometimes associated with other serious disorders, such as oppositional defiant disorder, learning disabilities, or depression. A number of treatment options are available for ADHD. The most effective treatment has been found to be a combination of medication, positive behavior support, and parent–professional collaboration. Strategies for working with children with ADHD in inclusive classrooms consist of positive behavior support, environmental organization, instructional adaptations, and reinforcing social skills. The most current research in ADHD indicates that the use of medication in young and preschool-age children with ADHD might have a variety of severe side effects. Therefore, it might be best to consider using medication as a last alternative for young and preschool-age children with ADHD.

Review Questions

1. Why is ADHD a serious public health concern?
2. How has the definition of ADHD and its related terminology changed over the past century?
3. What are the major symptoms of ADHD?
4. What are the major subtypes of ADHD according to the *DSM-IV?*
5. What is the theory of executive function regarding ADHD?
6. How do medications try to correct the impairments in ADHD?
7. What is the best treatment option for children with ADHD?
8. What are some instructional and classroom adaptations that would benefit inclusive classrooms?
9. What does current research tell us about the issues of consideration in the use of medication for preschool-age children with ADHD?

Out-of-Class Activities

1. Interview a parent of a young child with ADHD:
   a. Examine helpful strategies that parents use on a daily basis with their children.
   b. Write a report summarizing your findings.
2. Interview at least two early childhood teachers who have successfully worked with children with ADHD:
   a. Find out the specific adaptations these teachers have made to their environment and to their instructions.
   b. Find out the method by which they have communicated and collaborated with families.
   c. Write a report about your findings.
3. Interview at least five early childhood teachers to examine their opinion about the use of medication with preschool-age or younger children with ADHD. Write a report of your findings.

Recommended Resources

ADHD medicine Concerta guide
http://www.concerta.net/index.html

A.D.D. Warehouse
Books, videos, and audios on ADHD:
http://www.addwarehouse.com

Attention Deficit Disorder Association (ADDA)
P.O. Box 543
Pottstown, PA 19464
Phone: 484-945-2101
http://www.add.org

Children and Adults with Attention Deficit Hyperactivity
Disorder (CHADD) & Parent Support Groups
8181 Professional Place, Suite 150
Landover, MD 20785
Phone: 301-306-7070
http://www.chadd.org

Learning Disabilities Association of America
4156 Library Road
Pittsburg, PA 15234
Phone: 412-341-1515
http://www.ldanatl.org

U.S. Department of Education
Information and resources on ADHD:
http://www.ed.gov/rschstat/research/pubs/adhd/
adhd-identifying.html

General information and parent support:

About.com: ADHD
http://www.add.about.com

ADDITUDE
http://www.additudemag.com

ADHD support in the UK:
ADDISS, The National Attention Deficit Disorder
Information and Support Service
http://www.addiss.co.uk

Attention Deficit Disorder Association
http://www.add.org/

Children and Adults with Attention Deficit Hyperactivity
Disorder (CHADD)
http://www.chadd.org/

**View the Online Resources available to accompany
this text by visiting http://www.mhhe.com/bayat1e.**

References

Altink, M., Slaats-Willemse, D., Rommelse, N.,
    Buschgens, C., Fliers, E., Arias-Vaasquez, A., et al.
    (2009). Effects of maternal and paternal smoking
    on attention control in children with and without
    ADHD. *European Child & Adolescent Psychiatry,
    18*(8), 465–475.

American Academy of Child and Adolescent Psychiatry
    (2008). *ADHD: A guide for families.* Retrieved
    February 12, 2008, from http://www.aacap.org/cs/
    adhd_a_guide_for_families/what_is_adhd

American Psychiatric Association. (2000). *Diagnostic and
    statistical manual of mental disorders: DSM-IV-TR*
    (4th ed., text rev.). Washington, DC: Author.

August, G. J., Stewart, M. A., & Holmes, C. S. (1983).
    A four-year follow up of hyperactive boys with
    and without conduct disorder. *British Journal of
    Psychiatry, 143,* 192–198.

Baeyens, D., Roeyers, H., & Walle, J. V. (2006). Subtypes
    of attention deficit hyperactivity disorder (ADHD):

Distinct or related disorders across measurement
    levels? *Child Psychiatry and Human Development,
    36,* 403–417.

Barkley, R. A. (1997). *ADHD and the nature of self-
    control.* New York: Guilford Press.

Barkley, R. A. (1998). Primary symptoms, diagnostics
    criteria, prevalence, and gender differences. In R. A.
    Barkley (Ed.), *Attention-deficit hyperactivity
    disorder: A handbook for diagnosis and treatment*
    (pp. 56–96). New York: Guilford Press.

Barkley, R. A. (2003). Attention deficit/hyperactivity
    disorder. In E. J. Mash & R. A. Barkley (Eds.),
    Child psychopathology (2nd ed., pp. 75–143).
    New York: Guilford Press.

Barkley, R. A., Fischer, M., Smallish, L., & Fletcher, K.
    (2002). The persistence of attention-deficit/
    hyperactivity disorder into young adulthood as a
    function of reporting source and definition of disorder.
    Journal of Abnormal Psychology, 111(2), 279–289.

Behar, L. B. (1977). Preschool behavior questionnaire. *Journal of Abnormal Child Psychology, 5*(3), 265–275.

Biederman, J. (2005). Attention deficit hyperactivity disorder: A selective overview. *Biological Psychiatry, 57*(11), 1215–1220.

Biederman, J., Faraone, S., Keenan, K., Knee, D., & Tsuang, M. (1990). Family genetic and psychosocial risk factors in DSM-III attention deficit disorder. *Journal of the American Academy of Child and Adolescent Psychiatry, 29*(4), 526–533.

Braun, J. M., Kahn, R. S., Froehlich, T., Auinger, P., & Lanphear, B. P. (2006). Exposures to environmental toxicants and attention deficit hyperactivity disorder in U.S. children. *Environmental Health Perspectives, 114*(12), 1904–1909.

Brown, R., Freeman, W., Perrin, J., Stein, M., Amler, R., Feldman, H., et al. (2001). Prevalence and assessment of attention deficit hyperactivity disorder in primary care settings. *Pediatrics, 107*(3). Retrieved June 8, 2007, from http://www.pediatrics.org

Brown, T. E. (2005). *Attention deficit disorder: The unfocused mind in children and adults.* New Haven, CT: Yale University Press.

Brown, T. E. (2006). Executive functions and attention deficit hyperactivity disorder: Implications of two conflicting views. *International Journal of Disability, Development, and Education, 53*(1), 35–46.

Claude, D., & Firestone, P. (1995). The development of ADHD boys: A 12-year follow up. *Canadian Journal of Behavioural Science, 27,* 226–249.

Conners, C. K. (2001). *Conners' kiddie continuous performance test.* Toronto: Multi-Health Systems.

Connor, D. F. (2002). Preschool attention deficit hyperactivity disorder: A review of prevalence, diagnosis, neurobiology, and stimulant treatment. *Developmental and Behavioral Pediatrics, 23*(1S), S1–S9.

Dillon, R. F., & Osborne S. S. (2006). Intelligence and behavior among individuals identified with attention deficit disorders. *Exceptionality, 14*(1), 3–18.

Edwards, J. H. (2002). Evidenced-based treatment for child ADHD: "Real world" practice implications. *Journal of Mental Health Counseling, 24*(2), 126–139.

Emmons, P. G., & Anderson, L. M. (2005). *Understanding sensory dysfunction: Learning, development, and sensory dysfunction in Autism Spectrum Disorders, ADHD, learning disabilities, and bipolar disorder.* Philadelphia: Jessica Kingsley Publishers.

Ford, A. D., Olmi, D. J., Edwards, R. P., & Tingstrom, D. H. (2001). The sequential introduction of compliance training components with elementary-aged children in general education classroom settings. *School Psychology Quarterly, 16,* 142–157.

Gaze, C., Kepley, H., & Walkup, J. (2006). Co-occurring psychiatric disorders in children and adolescents with Tourette Syndrome. *Journal of Child Neurology, 21,* 657–664.

Gettinger, M., & Seibert, J. K. (2002). Best practices in increasing academic learning time. In A. Thomas (Ed.), *Best practices in school psychology IV: Volume I* (4th ed., pp. 773–787). Bethesda, MD: National Association of School Psychologists.

Glanzman, M., & Blum, N. (2007). Attention deficits and hyperactivity. In M. L. Batshaw, L. Pellegrino & N. J. Roizen (Eds.), *Children with disabilities* (6th ed., pp. 349–369). Baltimore: Paul H. Brookes.

Harada, Y., Hayashida, A., Hikita, S., Imai, J., Sasayama, D., Masutani, S., et al. (2009). Impact of behavioral/developmental disorders comorbid with conduct disorder. *Psychiatry & Clinical Neurosciences, 63*(6), 762–768.

Hay, D., Bennett, K., McStephen, M., Rooney, R., & Levey, F. (2004). Attention deficit hyperactivity disorder in twins: A developmental genetic analysis. *Australian Journal of Psychology, 56*(2), 99–107.

Heward, W. L. (2006). *Exceptional children: An introduction to special education* (8th ed.). Upper Saddle River, NJ: Pearson Education, Inc.

Humphries, T. (2007). Attention-deficit/hyperactivity disorder. In I. Brown & M. Percy (Eds.), *A comprehensive guide to intellectual and developmental disabilities* (pp. 295–307). Baltimore: Paul H. Brookes.

Jong, C., Van de Voorde, S., Roeyers, H., Raymaekers, R., Ooster Laan, J., & Sergeant, J. (2009). How distinctive are ADHD and RD? Results of a double dissociation study. *Journal of Abnormal Child Psychology, 37*(7), 1007–1017.

Krummel, D. A., Seligson, F. H., & Guthrie, H. A. (1996). Hyperactivity: Is candy causal? *Critical Review in Food Science & Nutrition, 36*(1-2), 31–47.

Lahey, B., Pelham, W., Loney, J., Lee, S., & Willcutt, E. (2005). Instability of DSM-IV subtypes of ADHD from preschool through elementary school. *Archives of General Psychiatry, 62,* 896–902.

Lavigne, J., LeBailly, S., Hopkins, J., Gouze, K., & Binns, H. (2009). The prevalence of ADHD, ODD, depression, and anxiety in a community sample of

4-year-olds. *Journal of Clinical Child & Adolescent Psychology, 38*(3), 315–328.

Lavoie, R. (2005). *It's so much work to be your friend: Helping the child with learning disabilities find social success.* New York: Touchstone Press.

LeFever, G., Arcona, A., & Antonuccio, D. (2003). ADHD among American school children: Evidence of over-diagnosis and overuse of medication. *The Scientific Review of Mental Health Practice, 2*(1). Retrieved June 8, 2007, from http://www.srmph.org/0201/adhd.html

Levy, F., Hay, D., & Bennett, K. (2006). Genetics of attention deficit hyperactivity disorder: A current review and future prospects. *International Journal of Disability, Development, and Education, 53*(1), 5–20.

Lifford, K., Harold, G., & Thapar, A. (2009). Parent–child hostility and child ADHD symptoms: A genetically sensitive and longitudinal analysis. *Journal of Child Psychology & Psychiatry, 50*(12), 1468–1476.

Linnet, K. M., Dalsgaard, S., Obel, C., Wisborg, K., Henriksen, T. B., Rodriquez, A., et al. (2003). Maternal lifestyle factors in pregnancy risk of attention deficit hyperactivity disorder and associated behaviors: Review of the current evidence. *American Journal of Psychiatry, 160*(6), 1028–1040.

Linnet, K. M., Wisborg, K., Obel, C., Secher, N. J., Thomsen, P. H., Agerbo, E., et al. (2005). Smoking during pregnancy and the risk for hyperkinetic disorder in offspring. *Pediatrics, 116*(2), 462–467.

Lougy, R., DeRuvo, S., & Rosenthal, D. (2007). *Teaching young children with ADHD: Successful strategies and practical interventions for pre-k-3.* Thousand Oaks, CA: Corwin Press.

Martin, N., Levy, F., Pieka, J., & Hay, D. (2006). A genetic study of attention deficit hyperactivity disorder, conduct disorder, oppositional defiant disorder and reading disability: Aetiological overlaps and implications. *International Journal of Disability, Development, and Education, 53*(1) 21–34.

Matthews, D. (2002). *Attention deficit disorder sourcebook.* Detroit, MI: Omnigraphics.

Mayes, S. D., Calhoun, S. L., & Crowell, E. (2000). Learning disabilities and ADHD: Overlapping spectrum disorder. *Journal of Learning Disabilities, 33,* 417–424.

Milberger, S., Biederman, J., Faraone, S. B., & Jones, J. (1998). Further evidence of an association between maternal smoking during pregnancy and attention deficit hyperactivity disorder: Findings from a high-risk sample of siblings. *Journal of Clincial Child Psychology, 27,* 352–358.

National Institute of Mental Health. (2004). *Attention Deficit Hyperactivity Disorder.* Bethesda, MD: National Institute of Mental Health, National Institute of Mental Health, U.S. Department of Health and Human Services; [electronic version]. Retrieved July 2, 2007, from http://www.nimh.nih.gov

Nigg, J. T., Willcut, E. G., Doyle, A. E., & Sonuga-Barke, E. J. (2005). Causal heterogeneity in attention deficit hyperactivity disorder: Do we need neuropsychologically impaired subtypes? *Biological Psychiatry, 57,* 1224–1230.

O'Rourke, J., Scharf, J., Yu, D., & Pauls, D. (2009). The genetics of Tourette syndrome: A review. *Journal of Psychosomatic Research, 67*(6), 533–545.

Pelsser, L., Buitelaar, J., & Huub, F. (2009). ADHD as a (non) allergic hypersensitivity disorder: A hypothesis. *Pediatric Allergy and Immunology, 20*(2), 107–112.

Rafalovich, A. (2008). *Framing ADHD children: A critical examination of the history, discourse, and everyday experience of attention deficit/hyperactivity disorder.* Lanham, MD: Lexington Books.

Rathouz, P. J. (2007). Maternal depression and early positive parenting predict future conduct problems in young children with attention deficit hyperactivity disorder. *Developmental Psychology, 43*(1), 70–82.

Rawland, A., Skipper, B., Rabiner, D., Umbach, D., Stallone, L., Campbell, R. et al. (2008). The shifting subtypes of ADHD: Classification depends on how symptom reports are combined. *Journal of Abnormal Child Psychology, 36*(5), 731–743.

Rosinia, J. (2008). Sensory processing. In L. Gilkerson & R. Klein. (Eds.), *Early development and the brain: Teaching resources for educators* (pp. 8.1–8.61). Washington, DC: Zero To Three.

Rothenberg, S. (2005). *Playing with self esteem: The importance of social skills.* Retrieved June 17, 2008, from http://www.nldline.com/dr.htm

Selikowitz, M. (2004). *ADHD: The facts.* Oxford: Oxford University Press.

Sharp, S., McQuillin, A., & Gurling, H. (2009). Genetics of attention-deficit hyperactivity disorder (ADHD). *Neuropharmacology, 57*(7/8), 590–600.

Sinha, G. (2001, June). New evidence about Ritalin: What every parent should know. *Popular Science,* 58–52.

Smith, K. G., & Corkum, P. (2007). Systematic review of measures used to diagnose attention-deficit/hyperactivity disorder in research on preschool children. *Topics in Early Childhood Special Education, 27*(3), 164–173.

Spencer, T. (2009). Issues in management of patients with complex attention-deficit-hyperactivity disorder symptoms. *CNS Drugs, 23,* 9–20.

Still, G. F. (1902). Some abnormal psychical conditions in children. *Lancet, 1,* 1008–1012, 1077–1082, 1163–1168.

Stormont, M. A. (2008). Increase academic success for children with ADHD using sticky notes and highlighters. *Intervention in School and Clinic, 43*(5), 305–308.

Swanson, J., Greenhill, L., Wigal, T., Kollins, S., Stehli, A., Davies, M., et al. (2006). Stimulant-related reductions of growth rates in the PATS. *Journal of American Academy of Child and Adolescent Psychiatry, 45*(11), 1304–1313.

Tripp, G., & Wickens, J. (2009). Neurobiology of ADHD. *Neuropharmacology, 57*(7/8), 579–589.

U.S. Department of Education. (2006a). *Identifying and treating attention deficit hyperactivity disorder: A resource for school and home.* Retrieved July 18, 2007, from http://www.ed.gov/rschstat/research/pubs/adhd/adhd-identifying.html

U.S. Department of Education. (2006b). *Teaching children with attention deficit hyperactivity disorder: instructional strategies and practices.* Retrieved July 16, 2007, from http://www.ed.gov/rschstat/research/pubs/adhd/adhd-teaching-2006.pdf

U.S. Department of Education. (2008). *Teaching children with attention deficit hyperactivity disorder: Instructional strategies and practices.* Washington, DC: Office of Special Education Programs (ED/OSERS).

Walker, J. E., Shea, T. M., & Bauer, A. M. (2004). *Behavior management: A practical approach for educators.* Upper Saddle River, NJ: Pearson Education, Inc.

Wang, H., Chen, X., Yang, B., Ma, F., Wang, S., Tang, M., et al. (2009). Case-control study of blood lead levels and attention deficit hyperactivity disorder in Chinese children. *Environmental health perspectives, 116*(10), 1401–1406.

Welsh, M. C. (2002). A meta-analytic examination of comorbid hyperactive-impulsive attention problems and conduct problems. *Psychological Bulletin, 128,* 118–150.

Westby, C. E., & Cutler, S. K. (1994). Language and ADHD: Understanding the bases and treatment of self-regulatory deficits. *Topics in Language Disorders, 14*(4), 58–76.

Wigal, T., Greenhill, L., Chuang, S., McGough, J., Vitiello, B., Skrobala, A., et al. (2006). Safety and tolerability of methylphenidate in preschool children with ADHD. *Journal of American Academy of Child and Adolescent Psychiatry, 45*(11), 1249–1303.

Wilens, T., Faraone, S., & Biederman, J. (2004). Attention deficit hyperactivity disorder in adults. *Journal of American Medical Association, 292,* 619–623.

Wolraich, M., Millich, R., Stumbo, P., & Schultz, F. (1985). The effects of sucrose ingestion on the behavior of hyperactive boys. *Pediatrics, 106,* 657–682.

Young Children with Behavioral and Social Emotional Needs

Objectives

Upon completion of this chapter, you should be able to:

> Understand factors contributing to social and emotional competencies in children.
> Identify the internalizing and externalizing behavior problem categories.
> Understand emotional and behavioral problems in children.
> Identify the environmental and other risk factors contributing to behavior problems.
> Understand strategies and adaptations necessary for working with children with behavioral and social emotional needs in inclusive classrooms, including positive behavior support (PBS) strategies.

> Describe how to assess the individual behavioral needs of children.
> Describe functional behavior analysis and its components.
> Understand the importance of the adult's attention in promoting positive behaviors in children.

Key Terms

affect attunement (290)

contingent praise (312)

differential attention (DA) (317)

emotional competence (290)

externalizing behaviors (291)

functional behavior analysis (FBA) (305)

functional behavioral assessment (FBA) (303)

internalizing behaviors (291)

negative attention (317)

negative reinforcement (314)

neurobiological risk factors (290)

planned ignoring (317)

positive behavior support (PBS) (300)

positive reinforcers (312)

problem or challenging behaviors (304)

reinforcements (310)

setting events (307)

social competence (289)

specific praise (312)

Reflection Questions

Before reading this chapter, answer the following questions to reflect upon your personal opinions and beliefs that are pertinent to early childhood special education.

1. Why do you think some children engage in inappropriate and challenging behaviors?
2. In your opinion, how might home environmental factors contribute to children's lack of social and emotional competencies?
3. In your opinion, what percentage of children's challenging behaviors might be due to biological factors?
4. In your opinion, could reactions of adults and other children contribute to children's challenging behaviors? If so, how?

Whose Fault Is It?

Steve is a behavior consultant working with the State Board of Education. Every day, he visits one early childhood or elementary-level classroom to observe the behaviors of children who have been identified as challenging. He usually spends the entire day observing one child in his or her classroom environment. During his observations, he prepares many pages of careful notes.

After his initial observation, Steve spends the following days interviewing the teachers and other school personnel. He makes phone calls to the child's parents to set up phone or in-person interviews. When possible, he meets with parents to discuss the child's behavior at home and to get the parental perspectives regarding the child's behavior. Steve also spends some time interacting and playing with the child. After he completes his interviews and child observations, he organizes his notes into narratives and creates tables and charts depicting the frequency and intensity of the child's behavior in a described situation. He studies his data and draws some preliminary conclusions.

Thereafter, Steve meets with other special education team members to discuss his findings, to get additional insights, and to collaborate with teachers and other school professionals to design an intervention plan for the child. After Steve and other education team members have discussed an initial plan, they call for a conference with the child's parents. By the end of the conference, the education team and parents have agreed on a behavioral intervention plan for the child to be followed in the school and at home.

Today, a Monday morning in October, Steve is visiting Ruth's state pre-k inclusive classroom. Ruth is an early childhood educator with 20 students in her classroom. Mrs. Brown is Ruth's assistant in the classroom. Ruth has called for Steve's expertise for help with Mathew's behavior. Mathew is 5 years old and has been attending pre-kindergarten since September.

Ruth describes Mathew's behaviors as hard to control, aggressive, and annoying. Ruth explains that Mathew demands her attention most of the time during the school day. She tells Steve,

> Mathew constantly asks to be the center of attention. He always wants to be the line leader or the classroom helper of the day. When he does not get what he wants, he throws toys around and topples the furniture. During large group activities, when children are supposed to be sitting peacefully next to one another, he teases and bothers other children by pushing those who are sitting next to him or touching their hair or clothing.

Steve observes Mathew and other children throughout the day. He takes careful notes of his observations. He notices that Ruth repeatedly becomes irritated if Mathew displays any small infraction, like fidgeting while sitting, or moving out of the line. Steve studies his notes later in the day. Based on his data, Ruth called on Mathew to sit up, keep his hands to himself, or be quiet 38 times during the 2.5 hours of the morning period. At one point, Ruth called for children to line up to go to the washroom. Mathew asked if he could be the line leader. Ruth said no to this request, and Mathew began crying. Ruth told Mathew to go to the time out chair until he learned to behave himself. Mathew seemed to get frustrated, and began toppling furniture on his way to the time out chair. Ruth asked Mrs. Brown to stop Mathew and take him to the chair.

In another episode, when Mathew's request to be the classroom helper received a negative response from Ruth, he threw a temper tantrum, which ended in Ruth taking away the stars that he had earned a few minutes earlier for his artwork. Mathew's behavior seemed to make Ruth frustrated repeatedly. In one instance, Ruth became angry with Mathew to the extent that she had to have Mrs. Brown watch the classroom, as she left the room to calm herself down. During circle time, when Mathew pushed the child sitting next to him, Ruth could not help herself but to scream at Mathew to stop.

Steve conducted an interview with Ruth after the school day. Ruth told him that she was aware that her attitude toward Mathew was not a positive one, but she believed she was not to be blamed for that. Ruth explained that Mathew's behavior required her constant attention, which took away valuable teaching time from other children in the classroom. This often made her feel frustrated and inadequate at her job. She confessed that she frequently wished for Mathew's absence so she could get on with her job of teaching children.

INTRODUCTION

Children's challenging behaviors are usually recognized during the preschool years since some children might show difficulties in negotiating different social situations and forming positive relationships with their peers and adults. Some estimates suggest that about 10 percent of preschoolers exhibit noticeable problem behaviors, with 4 to 6 percent of this population exhibiting serious behavior difficulties (Raver & Knitzer, 2002). Gilliam (2005) presented a sobering report regarding behavior problems in preschool programs in 40 states. His report indicated that pre-kindergarten children are expelled at a rate that is three times that of the older children in K–12 grades.

Many teachers are concerned that children with behavior difficulties continuously disrupt the classroom and take the attention of the teacher away from other children. In addition, a child's social emotional difficulties often result in stunted relationships between that child and his peers and the teacher. Whether the challenging behaviors in a child are due to a diagnosable condition or because of environmental factors, the child more than likely will continue to have problems with peers, teachers, and other adults unless a positive approach is used to support the young child to develop social and emotional competencies.

In this chapter, we examine children's behaviors in their social contexts. We will discuss various types of neurological problems that contribute to a lack of social and emotional competencies in young children. We will also look at factors that contribute to children's behavioral difficulties, and positive ways of addressing their emotional and behavioral needs in inclusive and special education classrooms.

THE BEHAVIOR AND DEVELOPMENT OF SOCIAL AND EMOTIONAL COMPETENCIES

The appropriateness of a child's behavior is generally judged within certain developmental expectations based on the child's age. For example, by the time a child enters preschool, he or she is expected to have both a social and an emotional competence.

Social competence has been defined differently in the field. For example, it has been defined as having a set of social-cognitive skills and such knowledge that the child will exhibit appropriate behaviors in various situations and contexts (Yates & Selman, 1989). The social-cognitive skills necessary for social competence include a variety of capabilities such as helpfulness, self-reliance, empathy, and self-assertiveness (Waters, Noyes, Vaughn, & Ricks, 1985).

Because peer rejection is often associated with the child's later school difficulties (Rose-Krasnor, 1997), a child's ability to be well liked by peers is also considered to be indicative of having a social competence (Rose-Krasnor & Denham, 2009; Putallaz & Sheppard, 1992; Dodge, 1985; Gresham, 1986). Finally, a child's ability to initiate positive relationships with others and form friendships with peers is considered to be a developmental indication of social competence (Rose-Krasnor & Denham, 2009; Lindsey, 2002).

For the purpose of this book, we use the definition of social competence presented by Denham and colleagues (2003) and Rose-Krasnor (1997). Accordingly, social competence in a child (3 years old and older) is defined as the child's ability to have effective interactions with peers and others, and to have positive engagement and self-regulation during those interactions (Rose-Krasnor & Denham, 2009; Denham et al., 2003; Rose-Krasnor, 1997).

For a child to be able to interact with others and form positive relationships, the child should also have an **emotional competence** (Saarni, 1990; Parke, 1994). An emotionally competent child (1) is emotionally expressive, (2) has knowledge of emotions and feelings of self and others, and (3) has *emotional regulation,* meaning he or she is generally able to monitor, evaluate, and modify her emotional reactions (Rose-Krasnor & Denham, 2009; Denham et al., 2003; Parke, 1994). Social and emotional competencies are intertwined and related to one another. Thus, for a child to be socially competent, the child needs to be emotionally competent as well.

Neurobiological Risk Factors and Social and Emotional Competencies

The nervous system in the brain is responsible for sensory processing in a child. It allows the child to receive stimuli and react to the environment. A developing infant learns early on to regulate his reactions to the sensory stimuli received from the environment (Rosinia, 2008; National Research Council & Institute of Medicine, 2000). As discussed in Chapter 6, the child's ability to manage arousal, emotion, attention, and all other behaviors appropriately for a task or a situation is called self-regulation (Als, Gilkerson, & Klein, 2008; Emde, Korfmacher, & Jubicek, 2000).

Self-regulation in an infant is a developmental task and relates to the maturity of various brain areas related to sensory processing and executive function. Self-regulation is not only essential for the development of social and emotional competencies, but also for learning and cognitive development (Als et al., 2008). Self-regulation is an important predictor of successful relationships with peers and family members, and positive academic outcome in the child (Trentacosta & Shaw, 2009; McCleelan & Tominey, 2009). Other various environmental conditions, such as **affect attunement** and responsiveness of the caregiver to the infant's bio-behavioral cues, help the infant learn how to self-regulate as she develops (see Chapter 2 for a discussion of developmental care and Chapter 6 for a discussion of self regulation). Affect attunement is a pattern of reciprocal behaviors and emotional harmony that the caregiver and infant share that enable the infant to develop and sustain an appropriate level of self-regulation (Stern, 2000).

Neurobiological risk factors might contribute to a lack of self-regulation in children. Some neurobiological risk factors are genetic, while other factors might denote a diagnosable condition in the child before, during, or after birth (Percy, Lewkis, & Brown, 2007; Delfos, 2004). For example, dysfunctions in sensory processing often cause a lack of self-regulation, where the child might act out in aggression or frustration as a way of dealing with the overwhelming sensations. Problems with the executive function might result in the child having less self-control and more impulsive and dangerous behaviors. Impairments in language inherent in cognitive disabilities and communication disorders have also been associated with poor social competence and problem behaviors in children (Ford & Milosky, 2008; McCabe, 2005; McCabe & Marshall, 2006).

As children with self-regulatory problems grow up, they might not develop the skills needed for social competence. Therefore, they might display a range of behaviors that are usually described as inappropriate or "problem." These behaviors are also known as externalizing or internalizing behaviors.

EXTERNALIZING AND INTERNALIZING BEHAVIORS

In general, what many observers of behavior consider as challenging or "problem" behaviors fall into two groups of **internalizing** and **externalizing behaviors** (Achenbach & Edelbrock, 1978). Externalizing behaviors are those inappropriate behaviors that are visible, such as physical and verbal aggression, temper tantrums, or defiance. Internalizing behaviors, on the other hand, are not easily detectable or visible. These are behaviors such as depression or anxiety that are just as serious but not necessarily observable. Aside from these two types of behaviors, young children might experience other emotional or behavioral difficulties, such as eating and sleeping problems, or difficulties with being toilet trained (Gimpel & Holland, 2003; Porter, Kaplan, Homeier, & Beers, 2005).

At any time, children with behavior difficulties might display either or both externalizing and internalizing behavioral symptoms. Because young children on occasion might act out using behaviors that fall under externalizing or internalizing

Children with behavior difficulties might display externalizing behaviors, such as physical and verbal aggression, temper tantrums, or defiance.

Internalizing behaviors, such as depression or anxiety, are not easily detectable or visible.

problem behaviors, displaying these behaviors is not necessarily indicative of a specific neurological problem. In general, a behavior is serious if it persists over a period of time, and if it impedes the child's ability to learn, or prevents the child from negotiating positive interactions and forming relationships with peers and adults (Campbell, 2002).

Neurological Impairments Associated with Externalizing Behaviors

Several disorders have been associated with externalizing behaviors. In the previous chapters, we discussed a number of these disorders: attention deficit hyperactivity disorders (ADHD), pervasive developmental disorders (PDD), Autism Spectrum Disorders (ASD), oppositional defiant disorder (ODD), and conduct disorder (CD) (Gimpel & Holland, 2003; Emond, Ormel, Veenstra, & Oldehinkel, 2007). Some externalizing behaviors have also been associated with language impairments and intellectual disability (Ford & Milosky, 2008; McCabe, 2005; McCabe & Marshall, 2006).

Neurological Impairments Associated with Internalizing Behaviors

It is not common for preschool- and kindergarten-age children to display a range of internalizing behaviors. However, during recent years, there has been an awareness that internalizing behavior symptoms do exist in some very young children (Pavuluri, Janicak, Naylor, & Sweeney, 2003). Since internalizing behaviors are not as easily observable, they are not usually identified as other challenging behaviors in children. Disorders which are associated with internalizing behavior symptoms include depression, generalized anxiety disorder, separation anxiety disorder, and obsessive compulsive disorder (OCD) (Robb & Reber, 2007; Percy, Brown, & Lewkis, 2007).

Depression is not common among young children. In general, for a child to be diagnosed with depression, the episodes of depressive moods should occur frequently with at least two-month intervals between them (Robb & Reber, 2007).

Young children with depression might show irritability or display social withdrawal.

The American Psychiatric Association (2000) indicates that signs of depression in young children might not include having a depressed mood. Rather, the young child might show irritability. Young children with depression might also display social withdrawal. Difficult temperament and low parental self-efficacy have been found to be two risk factors for depression in young children (Cote et al., 2009).

Generalized anxiety disorder refers to extreme anxiety in various situations, such as during play, in school, and at home (Robb & Reber, 2007). Children who display signs of generalized anxiety disorder usually show exaggerated anxiety, sometimes accompanied with physical symptoms like headaches or stomach aches (Percy et al., 2007).

Separation anxiety disorder involves extreme anxiety about being separated from home or from people to whom the child is attached (Eisen & Shaefer, 2005). Some young children might show varying levels of separation anxiety, up to age 6. However, when the degree of anxiety is more severe than those typically expected from a young child, it might be indicative of a separation anxiety disorder. Children with separation anxiety disorder are excessively fearful of being abandoned, or being alone. They might believe that some calamitous event might occur or some harm might come to them or to their caregiver or parents (Eisen & Shaefer, 2005). Separation anxiety disorder usually co-occurs with other disorders, such as generalized anxiety, depression, or obsessive compulsive disorder (OCD) (Gimpel & Holland, 2003).

Obsessive compulsive disorder (OCD) is marked by the child's recurrent obsessions and compulsions to think, say, or do a certain action in a specific way. *Obsessions* are uncontrollable impulses, thoughts or images that might occur at inappropriate times and that are usually intrusive and persistent (Robb & Reber, 2007). For example, the child might have repeated doubtful thoughts about something. *Compulsions* are uncontrollable desires to perform and repeat a behavior or a mental act in a certain way (Robb & Reber, 2007). For example, a child might want to wash his hands frequently, put things in a specific order, walk at a specific pace, or repeat certain words.

TABLE 9.1   Conditions Associated with Internalizing and Externalizing Behaviors

Disorders with Externalizing Behavior Symptoms	Disorders with Internalizing Behavior Symptoms
Attention deficit	Depression
Hyperactivity disorder	Generalized anxiety disorder
Oppositional defiant disorder	Separation anxiety disorder
Conduct disorder	Obsessive compulsive disorder
Pervasive developmental disorders	Phobias
Autism spectrum disorders	Panic disorder
Language impairments	
Intellectual and developmental disabilities	

Panic disorder and *phobias* are other problems that are considered to be associated with internalizing behaviors (Percy et al., 2007; Robb & Reber, 2007). Children with panic disorder usually have repeated occurrences of short, yet intense periods of fear and discomfort (Robb & Reber, 2007). Children with phobias might have an inordinate amount of fear of certain objects or situations that they actively avoid. Some children might have a social phobia, in which they typically avoid interaction with peers or avoid joining social situations. Table 9.1 displays conditions that have been associated with internalizing and externalizing problem behaviors.

EMOTIONAL AND BEHAVIORAL DISORDERS IN CHILDREN

Under the disability categories of IDEA, the term emotional disturbance refers to any condition that would have behavioral or emotional symptoms over a long period of time that would adversely affect a child's educational performance. Table 9.2 displays characteristics of emotional disturbance under IDEA.

Aside from the disorders mentioned earlier, young children might experience a number of other conditions, such as feeding and eating disorders, toileting difficulties, and selective mutism. Table 9.3 provides brief explanations of these disorders.

Some children who present a range of internalizing and externalizing behaviors together might have serious conditions, such as bipolar disorder, posttraumatic stress disorder, and schizophrenia. Generally, these conditions occur rarely during early childhood years, and diagnoses of these disorders are seldom given to young children. However, during the past decade, there have been a growing number of diagnoses of these disorders in preschool-age children. Therefore, general definitions and symptoms of these conditions are brought here so you might become familiar with them.

TABLE 9.2   Characteristics of Emotional Disturbance under IDEA

Emotional Disturbance Is a Condition Exhibiting One or More of the Following Characteristics over a Long Period of Time and to a Marked Degree That Adversely Affects a Child's Educational Performance:

a. An inability to learn that cannot be explained by intellectual, sensory, or health factors.

b. An inability to build or maintain satisfactory interpersonal relationships with peers and teachers.

c. Inappropriate types of behavior or feelings under normal circumstances.

d. A general pervasive mood of unhappiness or depression.

e. A tendency to develop physical symptoms or fears associated with personal or school problems.

The term includes schizophrenia. However, it does not apply to children who are socially maladjusted, unless it is determined that they have an emotional disturbance.

TABLE 9.3   Other Childhood Behavior Problems

Other Behavior Problems Diagnosed during Early Childhood	
Feeding and eating problems	Problems of eating that are not due to a medical condition or cultural practices
Pica	Eating nonnutritive or nonfood substances
Rumination disorder	Repeated regurgitation and rechewing of food
Feeding disorder of infancy or early childhood	Failure to eat and gain weight
Elimination problems	Problems of toileting that are not due to physiological condition; the child is over 4 years of age, and the problem occurs frequently
Encopresis	Repeated passage of feces into inappropriate places (like on the floor or in clothing), whether involuntary or intentional that is not attributed to an illness or medical condition
Enuresis	Repeated voiding of urine into bed or clothes, whether involuntary or intentional that is not attributed to an illness or medical condition
Selective mutism	Consistent failure to speak in specific social situations in which there is an expectation for speaking, despite speaking in other situations
Childhood schizophrenia	Presence of delusions, hallucinations, disorganized speech or behaviors, or manic-depressive episodes for a significant period of time
Bipolar disorder	Presence of recurrent manic mood episodes that are not contributed to other disorders, such as schizophrenia
Posttraumatic stress disorder	Child has been exposed to (experienced or witnessed) a traumatic event involving actual or threat of death or serious injury of self or others; and the child expresses intense fear through agitated or disorganized behaviors

Source: American Psychiatric Association. (2000). *Diagnostic and Statistical Manual of Mental Disorders* (4th ed., text revision). Washington, DC: Author.

Childhood Schizophrenia

Pediatric schizophrenia is extremely rare in young children. Because schizophrenia is uncommon, it is seldom diagnosed at an early age. In rare occasions when mental health and medical professionals are faced with the possibility of this disorder, they are reluctant to give a child this diagnosis before he or she reaches adolescence (Pavuluri et al., 2003). In addition, it is often difficult to differentiate between symptoms of this disorder and bipolar disorder in young children because of the similarities between manic behavioral characteristics of these conditions in young children (Robb & Reber, 2007).

Bipolar Disorder

Bipolar disorder is commonly known as manic depression. Similar to schizophrenia, a diagnosis of bipolar disorder is rare and not usually given to a young child. Symptoms of this disorder in children consist of episodes of alternating manic behaviors such as extreme rage, aggression, and dangerous behaviors to experiencing depression and sadness (Porter et al., 2005). Young children with this disorder frequently react in uncontrollable anger when they are disagreed with. These children might also experience periods of hyperactivity and giddiness at one time, or feel sleepy and lack energy at another time (Percy et al., 2007).

Posttraumatic Stress Disorder

Posttraumatic stress disorder (*PTSD*) usually develops as a result of the child being exposed to a catastrophic experience or to a series of extremely traumatic and stressful events (Vasterling & Verfaellie, 2009; Porter et al., 2005). Such stressful situations usually involve conditions where someone's life has been threatened or a serious injury has occurred. Traumatic situations might include being a victim or witness of physical or sexual abuse, domestic violence, natural disaster, an automobile accident, a serious illness, or living in a war zone. The severity of PTSD depends on the seriousness of the trauma, the number of times the child has been exposed to the trauma, and the child's level of social emotional development. Children with intellectual disability are especially at risk for PTSD, because they have limited coping abilities and therefore might experience severe trauma when faced with a stressful event (Robb & Reber, 2007).

Natural disasters and wars are often sources of PTSD. The 2004 tsunami in Indonesia and Louisiana's Hurricane Katrina in 2005 left in its wake thousands of victimized children at risk for posttraumatic stress disorder. Children who live through wars and natural disasters unquestionably experience PTSD for many years after the event (Weems & Overstreet, 2008). During the past 20 years, the possibility of young children experiencing PTSD as a result of living in areas of war and violence has increased. See Text Box 9.1 for the statistics on children living in war zones today.

Considering the staggering statistics regarding children living in wars and through natural disasters, or those who witness or experience domestic violence, there is an increased likelihood that early childhood and other educators around the

Armed Conflicts and Children's Social Emotional Well-Being

Text Box 9.1

The past decades have been known as the most violent years in the history of the world. The impact of armed conflicts—whether due to a war or terrorism—has been tremendous on children. In 2000, the United Nations published a report by the expert Secretary General of the United Nations on the impact of armed conflict on children around the world. This report indicated that throughout the 1980s and 1990s, as a result of armed conflict around the world, 2 million children had been killed; between 4 to 5 million had been disabled; 12 million had been left homeless; 1 million had been orphaned or separated from their parents; and 10 million had been psychologically traumatized. Today, many war refugees seek homes in industrial or safer countries. About 50 percent of all refugee populations around the world consist of children.

Alan and Susan Raymond, documentary filmmakers, interviewed hundreds of children living in different wars around the world in 2000. In documenting the psychological effects of war on children, they demonstrated that the repeated experience of trauma, which is typical of wars, damages children's sense of identity and outlook of life more severely than physical wounds. Their documentary film, *Children in War,* illustrates the devastating effects of war on children who are exploited as soldiers, starved and exposed to extreme brutality, or are maimed and raped during the modern armed conflicts around the world today.

Sources: United Nations report on the impact of armed conflict on children. Available at http://www.unicef.org/graca/; and Raymond, A., & Raymond, S. (2000). *Children in war.* New York: TV Books.

world might be working with children experiencing PTSD at some point in their professional life. Therefore, awareness of this phenomenon and understanding the symptoms of PTSD is necessary for teachers. See Table 9.4 to become familiar with some possible symptoms of PTSD.

TABLE 9.4   Possible Symptoms of Posttraumatic Stress Disorder

Posttraumatic Stress Disorder Symptoms in Young Children
> Having frequent memories of the event
> Play in which some or all of the trauma is repeated over and over
> Having upsetting and frightening dreams
> Acting or feeling like the experience is happening again
> Developing repeated physical or emotional symptoms when reminded of the event
> Worry about dying
> Having problems falling or staying asleep

Source: Porter, R. S., Kaplan, J. L., Homeier, B. P., & Beers, M. H. (Eds.). (2005). *The Merck manual for healthcare professionals.* White House Station, NJ: Merck Research Laboratories. Available at http://www.merck.com.

DIAGNOSIS OF EMOTIONAL AND BEHAVIORAL DISORDERS

Children having any of the disorders mentioned in this chapter might display various internalizing or externalizing behaviors—depressive, anxious, aggressive, oppositional, noncompliant, hyperactive, impulsive, and even self-injurious in some cases. As we have seen, causes of these behaviors vary and might be different in nature for each child. Diagnosis of any disorders that have characteristics of behavioral or emotional disorders requires careful examination and evaluation of the child by one or a group of licensed mental health professionals (Robb & Reber, 2007).

ENVIRONMENTAL AND OTHER RISK FACTORS

So far, we have described neurobiological risk factors and disorders that might lead to a lack of social and emotional competencies and a variety of externalizing and internalizing behaviors in children. Environmental factors might also contribute to a lack of self-regulation, or specific emotional and behavioral disorders in children (O'Brien & Yule, 1995). Environmental risk factors include family-related risk factors, such as poverty, parental mental health, and abuse and neglect.

School-related risk factors, such as lack of classroom management and lack of high-quality instruction, might also contribute to problems with self-regulation in children. We will describe family-related and school-related risk factors in detail in Chapter 14. In the following section, we will look at early relationships, attachment, and other factors that might influence children's self-regulation and their healthy social emotional development. (See Table 9.5 for family and other risk factors that might influence a child's healthy social emotional development.)

Early Relationships and Attachment

In Chapter 2, we described attachment and its implications for child development. As a reminder, our understanding of attachment in children is based on the ideas of John Bowlby, Mary Ainsworth, and other attachment scholars. Bowlby (1982)

TABLE 9.5   Factors Predicting Lack of Self-Regulation and Developmental Problems in Children

Environmental Risk Factors	Other Factors
Early relationship and attachment difficulties	Neurobiological influences
Child rearing and parenting style	Gender differences
Parental stress and depression	Child's temperament
Neglect and abuse	
Socio-economic and demographic factors (poverty)	
School related factors	

described attachment as a bond between the infant and a primary caregiver. The quality of attachment evolves over time as the infant and caregiver interact with one another and form a relationship. Bowlby believed that early relationships are vital in reducing or preventing problems with emotional and behavioral competencies in children.

Ainsworth (1984) categorized different patterns of attachment in children that would develop as a result of their caregivers' response to the child's needs and bids for care and attention. In a typical and healthy attachment situation, infants would form a secure attachment to their caregivers, because their caregivers had been responsive and available to them. These infants are able to explore their environments knowing that supportive care would be available if they need it. If distressed, they are able to self-regulate and settle their emotions based on this security.

Later attachment researchers, such as Sroufe (1995), believed that the quality of attachment is vital for the infant's emotional regulation. In other words, through dyadic interactions with the caregivers, infants learn to regulate their own emotions and arousal level; how infants ultimately regulate their emotions depends on the behaviors of the caregiver. Thus, a mutual regulation or *co-regulation* is a by-product of attachment (Tronick, 1989; Als et al., 2008).

The implications of these studies indicate that when an infant receives inconsistent, chaotic, and neglectful care, or at worst is rejected or abused, the child is at risk to develop problems with emotional and social competencies, especially with interpersonal relationships. Therefore, the quality of attachment and early relationship between a child and the caregiver might influence a child's future relationships with other adults and peers.

Other Factors

Some studies suggest that males are biologically more predisposed to develop problem behaviors and psychological and medical conditions (Magee & Roy, 2008; Delfos, 2004). Disorders such as autism and ADHD occur in boys in a higher percentage as compared to girls. There is some evidence that the hormone testosterone influences thinking and emotions, as well as aggression and sexual feelings (Slabbekoorn, 1999). Some studies suggest that the influence of testosterone in a male can result in diminished abilities to put thoughts into words, an increased ability to act out, and inclinations to become physically aggressive (Delfos, 2004). Additionally, where boys show more externalizing behavior problems, girls show more internalizing behavior problems (Verhulst & Akkerhuis, 1986).

Finally, child temperament is often considered an explanation for a lack of social competence and behavioral difficulties in children (Magee & Roy, 2008; Rothbart, Ahadi, & Evans, 2000; Carey & McDevitt, 1995; Kegan & Snidman, 1999). Temperament generally refers to an individual's way of experiencing and reacting to the environment (Carey & McDevitt, 1995).

In their classic work, Thomas, Chess, Birch, Hertzig, and Korn (1963) categorized children's temperament in three major clusters: (1) the *difficult child,* who is slow to approach and to adapt to the environment; (2) the *easy child,* who is approachable, adaptable, and generally positive in mood; and (3) the *slow-to-warm-up child,* who is usually shy and withdrawn and slow to adapt to environments. Most studies on temperament indicate that temperamental characteristics, such as those of a difficult child, may predispose a child to subsequent development of externalizing problem behaviors during the preschool period (Earls & Jung, 1987; Fagan, 1990).

STRATEGIES AND ADAPTATIONS FOR INCLUSIVE CLASSROOMS

Most young children respond to general behavioral guidance in their home or in the classroom. However, children with specific social emotional and behavioral needs require a well-designed plan to help them overcome their behavioral difficulties and learn new behavior repertoires that are accepted and appropriate within their social settings.

Positive Behavior Support

In 1999, the amendment to IDEA identified **positive behavior support (PBS)** as an intervention approach to be used for all children who might have emotional and behavioral needs. Since 1999, PBS has been employed either individually to help a child directly or to be used school-wide to support children in learning appropriate social behaviors in their classroom, school, and community. IDEA requires that the IEP team consider designing a positive behavior support plan for the child when the child's behavior impedes his own learning or the learning of others and when an IEP needs to be amended to address problem behaviors (Turnbull, Wilcox, Stowe, & Turnbull, 2001).

Because positive behavior support is IDEA's preferred strategy to deal with children's problem behaviors, it is imperative that all teachers who work with children with special needs have sufficient knowledge and understanding of PBS to ensure an adequate design and implementation of a plan that supports the child's behavioral and emotional needs (Turnbull et al., 2001).

Positive behavior support has been defined as the "application of positive behavioral interventions and systems to achieve socially important behavior changes" (Sugai et al., 1999). PBS is an evidence-based approach that uses educational methods to expand on a child's behavior repertoire, and to implement a systems change. A systems change consists of changes in relationships and components of the systems in which the child lives in such a way as to enhance the child's quality of life and to minimize the child's problem behavior (Carr et al., 2002).

Positive behavior support differs from applied behavior analysis in three important ways: (1) it recognizes the child's enhanced quality of life as the desired outcome for the intervention; (2) it seeks proactive ways of approaching the child's behavior to prevent the problem behavior from occurring; and (3) it requires that the behavioral intervention is implemented across multiple settings for the child (Carr et al., 2002). Unlike ABA, which focuses on manipulation of consequences of behavior for behavioral change, positive behavior support uses multiple approaches, such as altering environments, modifying others' reactions to the child's behaviors, improving teaching skills, and appreciating positive behaviors in order to support the behavioral needs of a child (Ruef, Poston, & Humphrey, 2004). PBS is a systematic

Teachers should be clear about their expectations regarding children's behavior, classroom rules, and the consequences that follow inappropriate behavior.

approach to behavior that involves collaboration of many people—including teachers and parents—and within different settings in order to support the child in learning new socially appropriate behaviors, as opposed to ABA, which could be done individually. PBS is an appropriate framework to be used in preschool settings (Fox & Hemmeter, 2009). In addition, working with parents to provide positive support at home can indirectly foster school readiness and behavioral health in young children (Lukenheimer et al., 2008).

School-Wide Positive Behavior Support

Positive behavior support has been successfully used both as a school-wide strategy and as an intervention to be used for a child. As a school-wide approach, positive behavior support seeks to provide support in inclusive schools for children with disabilities, since problem behaviors have been known to be the most common reason why a student with a disability is removed from a regular classroom or school (Lewis & Sugai, 1999). School-wide positive behavior support (SWPBS) establishes support systems to promote both academic success and pro-social behaviors in all children (Blonigen et al., 2008). In such an approach, all school personnel are provided with training in areas of systems change principles and the application of research-based behavioral approaches both at a group and individual level, so as to increase the school's capacity to address effectively and efficiently the behavioral support needs of all students and staff (Lewis & Sugai, 1999).

School-wide positive behavior support has three components: (1) universal support, (2) group support, and (3) individual support (Horner, 2000; Lewis & Sugai, 1999). While the universal support is less intensified and provided to all students, the individual and group support are the more intense intervention and support, which are provided to a smaller number of children (Turnbull et al., 2002).

In providing a blueprint for school-wide positive behavior support, Turnbull and her colleagues (2002) recommend the following components as features of implementation:

> Identify problem behaviors in school and develop a plan for adopting PBS.
> Become familiar with current resources, and devote time and funds to professional development.
> Identify and communicate common expectations of positive behavior standards for the entire school.
> Provide opportunities for practicing both acceptable and non-acceptable behaviors, and establish procedures for rewarding and recognizing positive and acceptable behaviors.
> Institute appropriate scope and intensity for positive behavior support for children according to their needs, including more intensive support for children who require individual intervention plans.

Class-Wide Strategies to Promote Social Competence

Creating a positive classroom climate is the key to promoting behavior and social competence in children. A positive and safe classroom environment creates opportunities for celebrating diversity, fosters a sense of belonging by reinforcing respectful dialogue among children, as well as between children and the teacher, and builds opportunities for social interactions (Meadan & Monda-Amaya, 2008; Cihak, Kirk, & Boon, 2009). Conroy and her colleagues (2008) recommend several important class-wide intervention strategies for teachers, which can be used in inclusive and special education early childhood classrooms as a way of fostering social competence:

> Use close supervision and monitoring of all children at all times by scanning, moving frequently, initiating, and reciprocating purposeful interactions.
> Establish and teach classroom rules, which detail expected behaviors at the beginning of each year, and systematically teach the rules to children throughout the school year. Make sure to monitor and reward children's compliance with the rules all the time.
> Provide opportunities for children to respond by questioning, providing visual and verbal prompts, and incorporating corrective feedback and wait time to allow children to process and respond.
> Increase use of contingent and specific praise by frequently acknowledging children's appropriate behaviors in a descriptive way.
> Provide feedback and help children learn the correct response in a timely fashion.

Core Principles of Positive Behavior Support

Positive behavior support, whether implemented at the individual level, at the classroom level, or at the school level, it follows several values and assumptions at its core. Ruef and colleagues (2004) describe these assumptions and values as the following:

> Behavior serves a function.
> The cause and purpose of the behavior should be understood.

> A child who displays problem behaviors is not the problem. Rather, it is the environment, settings, and developmental or learning deficiencies that cause the challenging behavior.
> Instead of "fixing the child," the environment and learning systems should be fixed.
> New relationships should be established for the child:
> > Positive relationships should be established between the child and his peers, among the team members, and between the child and adults.
> It takes not one person, but a collaborative team to support a child to learn appropriate behaviors.
> New skills should be taught to the child.
> Only positive approaches should be used for changing behaviors, teaching new skills, and establishing relationships.
> It takes time to establish and maintain a system that consists of appropriate and responsive environments and appropriate behaviors in the child.
> The learning environment, home, methods, and people involved in the plan need to be flexible.
> The inclusion of children in all aspects of their home, school, and community is central to this process.

Family Involvement

PBS must involve and engage parents and other family members in both school-wide and individual plans. Schools could develop a variety of engagement activities related to parenting and learning at home that are delivered at open houses or other school-sponsored events (Muscott et al., 2008). For example, one typical activity could be helping parents design a behavioral matrix according to home routines that is consistent with the school-wide behavioral expectations (Muscott et al., 2008).

Shared decision making with parents is another way of engaging them in PBS. This not only involves having families share their vision for the child's future behaviors, but having family representation in the school-wide positive behavior support leadership team at all times and during the decision-making process (Muscott et al., 2008).

ADDRESSING INDIVIDUAL BEHAVIORAL NEEDS OF CHILDREN

Any behavioral intervention plan begins with assessing the child's behavior. Assessment of a child's behavior is a complex task. **Functional behavioral assessment (FBA)** is a process that determines why a child engages in a specific behavior and how the child's behavior relates to his or her environment (Chandler & Dahlquist, 2006). It gathers data from multiple sources to identify the antecedent and consequent events that predict and maintain problem behaviors (Crone, Hawken, & Bergstrom, 2007). FBA offers a good understanding of what purpose might lie behind a child's behavior. Usually the reason behind a child's behavior is appropriate, but the behavior itself is deemed inappropriate.

A functional behavioral assessment involves:

> Analysis of the child's behavior
> The conditions that might contribute to the child's behavior
> Forming a hypothesis regarding the reason for the behavior
> Identifying consequences that might contribute to the prevention, or reoccurrence of, the behavior in the future

Defining Problem Behaviors

The first step is to decide whether a child's behavior merits functional behavior assessment, or if it can be modified and changed through implementing general guidance and classroom management techniques (Chandler & Dahlquist, 2006). Because children generally respond to a well-structured and well-managed classroom, some children who are considered as having problem behaviors or challenging behaviors might actually learn to change their behaviors when teachers modify their own responses, instructions, materials, and activities (Pianta, Hamre, & Stuhlman, 2001). In addition, when teachers implement clear limits and behavior guidelines, children are prompted to behave accordingly in those set limitations. Therefore, the question to ask is, "Is this child's behavior really challenging?"

We are interested to identify those problem behaviors in children that are serious and severe enough that they merit behavioral intervention. We might consider **problem** or **challenging behaviors** as those behaviors that: (1) interfere with the child's learning or the learning of other children, (2) hinder positive social interactions and relationships, and (3) harm the child, peers, adults, or family members (Chandler & Dahlquist, 2006). Problem behaviors are often disruptive, dangerous, or destructive.

Consider for example the case of Mrs. Parker, a kindergarten teacher who believes that young children should learn to sit quietly and with little motion during small or large group time. Lately, she has decided to ask the special education team in her school for advice to set up a behavior plan for Sharon. Sharon, is a 5-year-old who has just transitioned into Mrs. Parker's kindergarten class from her previous preschool. She rocks back and forth when she sits in her seat. She fidgets frequently, and shakes her hands from time to time. During unstructured time, Sharon has a tendency to run around in the classroom. Although Sharon follows Mrs. Parker's directions well, and completes her in-class and homework assignments correctly, Mrs. Parker believes that Sharon needs to have a behavior plan to learn to sit and behave appropriately.

Another early childhood educator might not agree with Mrs. Parker, and consider Sharon's behavior appropriate for her age and developmental level. We could see that determining what behaviors might be challenging enough to target for intervention is a subjective decision. However, several strategies (recommended by Chandler & Dahlquist, 2006) can help us make an appropriate decision regarding a child's behavior.

First, examine the impact of the behavior on the child's learning and development, as well as on other children (Chandler & Dahlquist, 2006). For example, does Sharon's fidgety behavior have an adverse effect on her development or learning? Does rocking back and forth prevent Sharon from doing her work or interacting appropriately with other children and adults? Does Sharon's occasional running around the classroom and her fidgetiness present a danger or harm to other children and adults in the classroom? If the answers to these questions are no, then Sharon's behaviors should not be considered a problem.

Second, the frequency of the behavior is important (Chandler & Dahlquist, 2006). For example, if a child has a tendency to push other children every once in a while only during group activities, this behavior might not need to be addressed using a behavioral plan. Rather, it might be addressed through some simple rules for maintaining an individual space, and setting a group behavior structure during large group activities and interactions.

Third, we should be mindful that our expectations of children to behave in a certain way should be developmentally and age appropriate for each child (Chandler & Dahlquist, 2006). Not being able to sit still or fidgeting in a chair for more than 15 minutes is both developmentally and age appropriate for a child in kindergarten. Being messy or forgetful is also typical of a young child. To expect behaviors from children that may not be appropriate for their developmental level means that we are automatically setting them up for failure in meeting our expectations.

Fourth, challenging and problem behaviors should not be confused with annoying and pesky behaviors (Chandler & Dahlquist, 2006). For example, nagging and whining are annoying behaviors that young children might typically display at various times. Although these behaviors are bothersome, they are neither impediments to development and learning nor harmful to the child and others. Such behaviors are usually displayed when children want to get attention from adults. These behaviors are easily controlled and could be replaced with appropriate behaviors through positive attention and redirection.

FUNCTIONAL BEHAVIOR ANAYLSIS: COLLECTING INFORMATION AND RECORDING DATA

Functional behavior analysis is the second stage of functional assessment in which the function of the behavior is examined so that a *replacement behavior* that could serve the same purpose can be taught to the child (Maag & Kemp, 2003). It helps us understand not only what function the behavior serves for the child, but what reinforces it and what environmental circumstances are most likely to stimulate it (Christensen, Young, & Marchant, 2004; Gresham, Watson, & Skinner, 2001). Functional analysis is the central tool of the functional behavioral assessment and provides detailed analysis of components contributing to the occurrence of the behavior.

Functional behavior analysis deals with the ABC of the behavior, where (A) = the antecedent, what occurs before the behavior; (B) = the behavior; and (C) = the consequence, what occurs after the behavior. Direct observations of the child's behavior, the environment, and the behavior of other people around the child provide information that can help us understand the ABC of behavior intervention.

Drawing a simple ABC diagram or creating an ABC data chart are useful ways of collecting data. An ABC baseline chart is a good way of documenting what happens throughout the day. A baseline chart is the first set of observational notes

Text Box 9.2   **Simple ABC Analysis Diagram Describing Two Consecutive Challenging Behavior Episodes (Baseline Data)**

Antecedent → Behavior → Consequence
A   →   B   →   C

A => Teacher: "Playtime is over. Joey, please put the blocks in their bin."
B => Joey begins throwing the blocks around.
C => Teacher: "No. Stop throwing bocks! Go to the time out chair right now!"
A => Teacher approaches Joey and takes him by the arm to the time out chair.
B => Joey begins screaming. He throws himself on the ground and begins kicking.
C => Teacher calls her assistant for help to restrain Joey and to take him outside of the classroom so he is not disturbing other children.

taken of the child's problem behavior before any positive behavioral intervention is planned and implemented. It would inform us of the kind and range of problem behaviors, the frequency of the behavior, and circumstances around the behavior. See Text Box 9.2 and Table 9.6 for examples of the ABC diagrams and charts.

Critical Thinking Question 9.1   Referring to the story at the beginning of the chapter, what are some classroom factors that could contribute to Mathew's inappropriate behaviors?

The ABC baseline chart could help us identify one or two target behaviors to work with first. A target behavior is the behavior that is considered a problem which needs to be replaced. A baseline behavior chart could also help us decide on how we might prevent the behavior from reoccurring by providing the correct response and environment for the child and what kind of replacement behavior the child might need to learn (Scheuermann & Hall, 2008).

A good analysis should incorporate information gathered from other sources, such as parents, the child, and the environment (Scheuermann & Hall, 2008). Information from other sources could be collected through interviews with parents or other adults involved with the child (such as therapists or teachers), interviews with the child, and examining the child's medical and developmental history. If a child has an IFSP or an IEP, some of this information, such as medical or developmental history, would already be available through the documented reports.

Parent Interview

Parents are the best sources of information about the history of their children's behaviors. They could provide valuable information about possible current difficulties that their child might have outside of the school environment. Similarly,

TABLE 9.6   A Sample ABC Analysis Chart (Baseline Data)

Time	Antecedent	Behavior	Consequence
9:30 a.m.	Told children that playtime was over. Told them to clean up. Everyone began cleaning up except for Joey, who was playing in the block area. I told him to put the blocks in the bin.	Joey began throwing blocks.	I told him "no" and to stop throwing.
9:35–9:50 a.m.	I took Joey by the arm to the time out chair.	He began kicking me, dropped on floor, screamed and kicked in the air.	I called Mrs. Brown to help restrain Joey. She took him outside of the room and stayed with him until he calmed down.
11:00 a.m.	I told students to line up to go wash their hands. It was time for lunch.	Joey was playing in the housekeeping area. He began screaming "no."	I reminded him it was time to get ready for lunch.
11:05 a.m.	I went to the housekeeping area to help Joey put the toys away and line up for the bathroom.	Joey began throwing the toys around. He toppled the toy stove. Two children who were around him got scared and went to another corner. When I went to take his hand to lead him to the line, Joey became mad at me. He wanted to hurt me. He scratched my face and tried to kick me.	I yelled at him "no" and held his hands down to his side, so he could not scratch me. I called for Mrs. Brown to come and help.

they could describe the setting events that might contribute to the child's behavior. **Setting events** are events and factors that might not be immediately noticeable but that contribute to a child's behavior (Scheuermann & Hall, 2008; Chandler & Dahlquist, 2006). For example, a death in the family, birth of a child, a recent move, or a divorce could influence the child's emotional well-being and behavior in the classroom and at home.

Teachers could use their already established communication channels with parents to discuss issues related to the child's behavior, and set up a behavioral support plan that would work both at home and in school (Gimpel & Holland, 2003). A positive and ongoing channel of communication between the teachers and parents could be established via newsletters, daily notes, phone calls, and home visits when possible.

When meeting with parents for an interview or to design a behavior plan for the child, teachers could reiterate their supportive role for both parents and children. As educators and parents work together, an agreement could be made between the parents and professionals that they both would adhere to a common goal of supporting the child's appropriate behaviors through positive means

Text Box 9.3	Useful Information to Gather during a Parent–Teacher Conference

1. Challenging behaviors that occur at home, if any
2. Times the behavior is most likely to occur
3. Circumstance under which the behavior is most likely to occur
4. Reactions of parents or other family members to the child when the behavior occurs
5. Other events concerning the child and others in the family that might take place following the occurrence of the behavior
6. Things that the child really enjoys doing
7. Child's special interests
8. Food items that the child likes to eat
9. Child's favorite toys and objects
10. Child's special talents
11. Child's relationship with parents and other family members
12. Child's relationship with other children outside school
13. General patterns of relationship among the family members
14. Recent unusual and typical events that might have occurred in the family
15. Any medical or health condition that the child might have that the family has not communicated to school
16. Any medication the child is taking that the parents might have forgotten to tell the school about

(Chandler & Dahlquist, 2006). Text Box 9.3 displays some useful information to gather during a parent interview.

Child Interview

It is difficult to imagine that a young child, especially one with cognitive problems, might be capable of participating in a meaningful interview process (Gimpel & Holland, 2003). However, children are able to give us important information that might be valuable in understanding causes of their behaviors. For example, information such as the child's feelings, interests and dislikes, thinking process, as well as the child's mental state could be important underlying causes of a child's behavior. This type of information could be obtained during a child interview. A personal interview with the child might also set the stage for establishing a positive teacher/child relationship, which could support the child's positive behavior (Scheuermann & Hall, 2008).

When children are nonverbal and not able to express their feelings or thoughts through words, pictures and visual cues might help educators obtain basic information regarding the child's feelings and thoughts (Scheuermann & Hall, 2008). Figure 9.1 illustrates an example of a visual interview. Child interviews should never be relied upon as the only source of information.

Today I am feeling:

FIGURE 9.1
Visual Interview Form

Sad Yes   No

Happy Yes   No

Tired Yes   No

Mad  Yes   No

Noises bother me Yes   No

I hurt  Yes   No

I am having a bad day Yes   No

I am having a good day Yes   No

Antecedent

Antecedent is the event that takes place before the behavior occurs. It might contribute to the occurrence and reoccurrence of a behavior. In Table 9.6, the ABC baseline analysis indicates that the antecedent to Joey's behavior of throwing blocks (one possible target behavior) around and at other children was the teacher's statement that the playtime was over and her instruction to children to clean up. In the second analysis of the same example, the antecedent to Joey's screaming and kicking behavior (other possible target behaviors) was the teacher's taking him by the arm to lead him to the time out chair. When we look at Table 9.6, we can see that Joey threw toys around again on the same day the teacher told children it was time to line up to go wash their hands.

Behavior

A positive behavioral support plan may be applied to a range of similar behaviors, since a child might need intervention for a variety of problem behaviors at once, such as behaviors that are distracting, like screaming and throwing violent tantrums; behaviors that are hurtful to self and others, like hitting or kicking; or behaviors that are destructive, like damaging equipments or toys. Once we have identified the range of target behavior for change, we should be careful to identify and record the antecedent and consequences related to that specific behavior.

When we observe behaviors and record them, we ought to take care to be objective and record only the behaviors that we can observe. Therefore, we must avoid recording anything we cannot see. In the ABC analysis in Table 9.6, for example, the teacher recorded, "He wanted to hurt me." Here the teacher had no way of knowing if Joey in fact was intentionally trying to hurt her. Intentions are not something that we can observe. Joey's act of aggression might have occurred as a result of frustration and anger.

In addition, instead of making absolute statements like, "Joey became mad," an objective observer would make tentative remarks like, "Joey seemed to have become mad." We might record statements like, "The child *seemed* frustrated by the expression on his face." This last statement tells us that we are not sure of the feelings of the child, but this is what it *looked like* at the time. Table 9.7 displays examples of statements of non-observable behaviors versus statements describing observable behaviors.

Consequence

Consequence is what occurs after a behavior has taken place. Consequences can either reinforce a behavior to occur in the future again or prevent the behavior from reoccurring. When the consequence to a behavior is positive, the behavior is reinforced, or is more likely to occur again. **Reinforcements** are events or experiences that are rewarding, and therefore increase the likelihood of a behavior occurring in the future (Alberto & Troutman, 2006).

When the consequence to a behavior is negative, the behavior is less likely to occur. A *punishment* is a negative consequence to a behavior. Punishment is used

TABLE 9.7   Recording Observable Behaviors

Avoid Making Judgmental Statements	Instead, Record Observable Events
He is mean and malicious.	He makes hurtful remarks to his friends, such as "You are so stupid."
He intended to hurt other children.	He began hurling himself at children who were sitting nearby.
She does not like Sammy.	She pushed Sammy away when he got too close to her.
She is deceitful.	She told her mother that I had punished her on Monday when all I did was to ask her to keep her hands to herself during the circle time.
He is slow.	He required that I repeat instructions several times before he understood what I meant.

in ABA to decrease a rate of behavior (Figure 9.2). In positive behavioral support (PBS), punishment and other negative approaches to controlling behaviors are not used (McEvoy & Reichle, 2000)

To apply a positive behavior approach to our previous example: Joey's behavior (see Table 9.6) tells us that he usually displays a range of problem behaviors during transition time. A study of other factors and settings in the environment could give us similar information about Joey's behavior. For example, an interview with Joey's mother may inform us that Joey has similar difficulties during transition to meal time and bedtime. Joey also has a hard time expressing his feelings verbally. When he gets frustrated, he usually throws things. At home, a typical consequence following his screaming or throwing behavior is to allow him to play longer, until he is ready, which means Joey might miss the family meal time, or go to bed very late.

This consequence, which is, incidentally, what Joey wants, has reinforced his throwing behavior to get more time to finish his play. In school, the typical consequences following Joey's behavior are the teacher's saying "no," physically

FIGURE 9.2
ABC Diagram: Influences of Antecedent and Consequence on Behavior

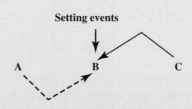

Setting events

A   B   C

A = Antecedent, B = Behavior, C = Positive consequence

Consequence determines occurrences of a behavior in the future. If a consequence is positive, the behavior is more likely to occur again in the future.

Antecedent might inform us of the function of the behavior. Manipulation of the antecedent could predict occurrence of a behavior in the future.

Setting events are conditions or factors that might change how the child responds to a consequence or to an antecedent, thus influencing the behavior of the child.

intervening with him, or sending Joey to the time out chair. These negative consequences are often antecedents to more aggressive behaviors in Joey. Neither type of consequence following Joey's behavior at home and in school has been working.

The main question to ask here is, "What is the function of Joey's behavior?" Looking at our ABC baseline chart, interview notes, and other observational notes, it becomes obvious that Joey's behavior occurs because he has a difficult time tearing himself apart from the play activity that he is doing during transition times. It might be helpful for Joey to have some advanced notice so he can cognitively prepare to finish what he is doing.

Joey might not understand his own need for a transition notice. His language difficulties do not help matters. Therefore, he gets frustrated and begins throwing toys and other objects around. It is clear that the function of Joey's behavior is communication. He is telling us, "I need time to finish what I am doing." Understanding the purpose of Joey's behavior also tells us he would benefit from some support to learn appropriate language to use when he is frustrated.

Critical Thinking Question 9.2   Considering Mathew's behavior in the opening story, what information do you need to consider to determine the function of his behavior?

A behavioral plan could be designed to include giving Joey transition notices before changing from one activity to the next, incorporating language activities that focus on expression of feelings, and using positive reinforcers every time Joey successfully goes through a transition time. Text Box 9.4 displays some transition notice activities that might be used in early childhood classrooms.

Positive and Negative Reinforcers

Positive reinforcers are objects, events, or activities that are rewarding to the child and make the behavior more likely to occur again (Alberto & Troutman, 2006). Positive reinforcers can be tangible rewards like food items or toys. They can be specific activities that a child might like, such as playing with blocks. Positive reinforcers can also be social emotional rewards, like acknowledgment, positive feedback, praise, or hugs.

Praise is a powerful positive reinforcer for children's appropriate behaviors. Effective praise is contingent and specific (Sutherland, 2000). **Specific praise** describes the behavior that the teacher targets to occur. For example, instead of saying "Good boy" to Charlie who is reading quietly, the teacher would say, "Good job, you have been reading quietly, Charlie." In this way, the teacher clearly articulates expectations for reading behaviors during the reading time, as well as positively reinforcing the appropriate target behavior. For some examples of descriptive and specific praise, see Table 9.8. **Contingent praise** is a specific praise that is given only contingent upon the occurrence of the appropriate and targeted behavior. So, for example, the teacher praises Charlie only when Charlie performs a certain task, like reading quietly.

| **Transition Notices** | **Text Box 9.4** |

Transition notices help children understand that a change will be taking place soon so they can cognitively make adjustments and get ready for this change.

1. **Use a kitchen timer:**
   a. About 5 to 7 minutes before it is time for transition, put a timer in the area where the children are playing. Tell the children, "We are getting ready to move to another activity. You need to finish your play soon. When this timer rings, it is time for you to finish what you are doing and start putting the toys away."
2. **Give verbal notices:**
   a. Let children know that a change is coming. Give a verbal notice every other minute and at the transition time. Begin 5 minutes before the transition:

   > "In 5 minutes you should finish your game and line up for the bathroom."
   > "In 3 minutes you should finish your game and line up for the bathroom."
   > "In 1 minute you should finish your game and line up for the bathroom."
   > "Now, it is time for you to put the toys away and line up for the bathroom."

3. **Provide visual cues for children with language difficulties:**
   a. Use picture cues for 5-, 3-, and 1-minute notices. Pictures should be large. Pictures can be glued to large rulers and raised up for children to see when you are giving verbal transition notices.

Praise and other forms of positive reinforcers should be used consistently following a desired behavior and every time a child engages in the replacement behavior that he or she has been redirected to do. They should also be used when the child learns a new or difficult skill. If the teacher decides to use tangible positive reinforcers with a child, the teacher might first need to identify the objects or activities that the child likes. This can be done through systematic observations of the child and through parent interviews. Table 9.9 displays a sample list for positive reinforcers.

TABLE 9.8   Use of Specific Praise Models Appropriate Behaviors

Avoid General Praise	**Instead, Praise the Behavior, and Be Specific**
Good job!	Good job putting the toys in the basket.
Good girl!	I like the way you are playing so quietly.
Excellent!	Excellent job sharing your toy with your friend.
Way to go!	Way to go with painting this beautiful picture.

TABLE 9.9   Sample List of Positive Reinforcers

Positive Reinforcer List

Child's name: Suzie
Date: October 6, 2012

Child's Favorite Foods/Snacks

1. M&Ms
2. Froot Loops cereal
3. Cheerios
4. Ritz crackers
5. Chicken nuggets
6. French fries

Child's Favorite Toys

1. Squeeze balls
2. Pokemon
3. Barbie
4. Disney toys
5. "Princess" dress-up items

Child's Favorite Activities

1. Playground swing
2. Books
3. Play-Doh
4. Dress-up activities
5. Art activities: especially coloring and anything to do with paint

Child's Favorite Social Reinforcers

1. Praise
2. High-fives
3. Stickers, stars, and other similar rewards
4. Name being put on the chart of the "Classroom Stars of the Day"
5. Telling parents that she has done a good job for the day

A negative reinforcer is not the same as punishment. **Negative reinforcement** is removal of a negative and undesirable stimulus from the child (Alberto & Troutman, 2006). These are things that might be physiologically or cognitively bothersome to the child, such as loud noises, or painful conditions. When such a stimulus is removed, the experience would become rewarding for the child. Negative reinforcement is a form of reward (Alberto & Troutman, 2006). Since a rewarding experience makes a desired behavior more likely to occur again, a negative reinforcer also prompts a behavior to occur, when presented immediately after the appropriate replacement behavior.

To use an example, Connor, who has learning disabilities, has a hard time paying attention to teacher's verbal directions when there is too much noise or activity in the classroom. The teacher's behavioral goal for Connor is to increase his rate of attention to the teacher's verbal instructions and directions. One way to help Connor achieve this goal is to present him with a negative reinforcer. By this, the teacher can take Connor to a quiet area and give him clear instructions. Removing extra noise and visual stimuli is a negative reinforcer for Connor's attention, and therefore it will increase the likelihood for him to pay attention in an environment with the least amount of sensory stimulation.

Setting Events

Setting events might influence how a child might respond to an antecedent or to a consequence (Chandler & Dahlquist, 2006; Scheuermann & Hall, 2008). Setting events might change the relationship between antecedent and behavior. They might also change the nature of consequences from positive to negative (Chandler & Dahlquist, 2006). For example, a child who is hungry and tired would respond negatively to having to participate in activities that require focus or movement. Let us imagine that a typical positive reinforcer for this child is to put his name on the chart of classroom stars. Under normal circumstance, this consequence might be positive and reinforcing. However, this is not necessarily rewarding when the child is tired and hungry. In this case, the setting events of hunger and physical fatigue in this child have changed the effects of antecedent and the positive consequence.

The teacher's behavior and reactions to the child's problem behaviors are among the most important setting events. Throughout this chapter and in the story we have seen cases where some teachers' responses to children's behavior have been punitive or marked by anger. Emotional reactions to children are often antecedents to further aggressive and problem behaviors in children. A good rule to follow is to treat the child's behavior, not the child.

Setting events may occur before or during the behavior, or have a removed temporal distance to the behavior. Arrangements of the environment, noise level, or physical space are examples of setting events that have a close temporal distance to the behavior. Biological factors such as pain or sensory processing difficulties, or an event that has occurred earlier in the day, are considered removed setting events (Chandler & Dahlquist, 2006).

Punishment

Use of physical or emotional punishment in children is not only unethical, but might result in negative physical, emotional, or psychological consequences for the child (Brazelton & Greenspan, 2000). Children who are physically punished are more likely to learn to use aggressive behaviors toward others in conflict situations (Brazelton & Greenspan, 2000). Punishment is more likely to create fear of, or resentment toward, the authority figure. This fear is usually situational, where it prevents the child from engaging in an inappropriate behavior only when the authority figure is around. Fear and resentment in children are impediments to forming positive relationships and might interfere with their learning abilities (Brazelton & Greenspan, 2000).

In addition, punishment, whether physical or emotional, has no educational value. Although it might prevent a child from engaging in a specific behavior, it does not teach the child any alternative appropriate behavior. In other words, punishment teaches a child what the child *should not do* as opposed to what he or she *should do* (Maag, 2004). A positive approach to behavior intervention is always a teaching approach, which enables the child to replace her inappropriate behavior with an appropriate one.

Critical Thinking Question 9.3   In the opening story, Ruth punishes Mathew by taking away the stars that he has earned for his other activities. What is wrong with this approach of behavior management?

Critical Thinking Question 9.4   What are some alternative positive approaches that Ruth could use with Mathew?

Use of Time Outs

Time out is a set of strategies designed to reduce a child's inappropriate behavior by removing the child from a reinforcing environment (Ryan, Sanders, Katsiyannis, & Yell, 2007). A number of time out procedures are used:

> **Inclusion time out:** Involves removing reinforcement from the child, rather than removing the child from the reinforcing environment (Cooper, Heron, & Heward, 1987). For example, the child continues to observe the classroom but is not allowed to participate in the activities or be acknowledged by other children or the teacher.
> **Exclusion time out:** Consists of positioning the child away from other children and classroom activities, such as sitting in the corner of the classroom and facing the wall (Ryan et al., 2007).
> **Seclusion time out:** Involves removing the child from the classroom and placing her in a room or area from where she cannot leave (Busch & Shore, 2000).
> **Restraint time out:** Is usually used for young children and consists of placing the child in a position and maintaining that position by physically restraining the child (Busch & Shore, 2000).

In early childhood classrooms, teachers use a variety of time out procedures as a negative consequence for problem behaviors or other infractions. In most situations, the effectiveness of time out procedures is compromised when several mistakes are made (Ryan et al., 2007). For example, when time out is used very frequently and for any minor infraction, it can become ineffective. Time out might also become a desirable option when the emotional atmosphere of the classroom is not pleasant or the activities are not engaging and interesting. For example, giving time outs to children with autism who often prefer to be on their own and not interact with other children might not be an appropriate procedure to use.

Typically, in a positive approach to behavior support, we avoid using time outs unless a child is a threat to self and others. In this case, a seclusion or restraint time out could be used for the child to support her to calm herself. When a child is put in a time out, whether or not the child needs to be physically and safely restrained,

An *exclusion time out* consists of positioning the child away from other children and classroom activities.

an adult should always be present with the child to make sure the child will not hurt herself. Finally, if time out procedures are to be used in the classrooms, teachers benefit from establishing a time out policy that clearly states what type of time out is to be used in their classroom and under what circumstances those procedures are to be implemented (Ryan et al., 2007).

THE IMPORTANCE OF ADULT ATTENTION

A majority of children's behavior categorized under "problem" behaviors are usually intended to get the adults' or peers' attention, even if that attention is negative (Maag & Kemp, 2003). **Negative attention** is making negative or restraining remarks, or reacting in a punitive way, which usually occurs when a child is engaged in an inappropriate behavior. When we give negative attention, we use words such as "no," "stop," or "don't." Many educators pay negative attention to children's behaviors more frequently than giving positive attention to children's appropriate behaviors. Attention, whether negative or positive, is always reinforcing to a child's behavior.

Planned Ignoring and Differential Attention

One way of teaching children to use appropriate behavior to get an adult's attention is **planned ignoring** (Ryan et al., 2007). Planned ignoring involves withdrawing social attention for a predetermined period of time upon occurrence of a problem behavior, and returning the attention to the child at the end of that period (Knoster, Wells, & McDowell, 2003).

Another type of approach similar to planned ignoring is called **differential attention (DA)** (Lavigne, n.d.). The difference between differential attention and planned ignoring is that in DA the adult withdraws his attention from the child only when the behavior is inappropriate and immediately pays attention to the child when the child displays appropriate behaviors. In other words, the adult turns his attention off or ignores the child when the child engages in bothersome or irritating behaviors. The adult turns

Text Box 9.5   Use of Differential Attention

Four-year-old Bella and her mother are shopping in a supermarket

Bella whines, "I want to go to the park." Mother ignores Bella's whining.

Bella continues to whine with a louder voice, "I don't want to come shopping. I want to go to the park." Mother continues looking at the shelves, ignoring Bella, as if she does not hear her.

Bella pulls mother's hand and whines again, "I want to go to the park." Mother acts as if she did not hear Bella. She pulls her hand away to pick up a can from the shelf. She puts the can in the cart, and without looking at Bella, goes around her to reach for another item on the shelf.

Bella suddenly stops whining and asks, "Can I get a box of Oreo cookies?"

Mother looks at Bella. She smiles and says, "Of course, you can. I like the way you are using your voice so nicely to ask for cookies." Bella smiles back and goes to the shelf to pick up her cookie box.

his attention on the moment the child starts acting appropriately. This strategy conveys this message to the child, "I pay attention to you only when you use appropriate behavior to get my attention." Text Box 9.5 describes a typical use of DA for a child.

Differential attention should not be used for harmful, dangerous, or aggressive behaviors. It should be used only for behaviors such as whining, nagging, crying, making inappropriate noises, using inappropriate or rude language, or other similar behaviors that are likely to irritate or distract other adults or children, but not harm them.

Differential attention or planned ignoring work in the classroom only if all children and teachers present in the classroom ignore the child who is displaying inappropriate behaviors. Either one of the procedures could be modeled to all children in the classroom to be used as one of the standard rules among other classroom rules in response to inappropriate behaviors for all to follow.

Banking Time is a special time devoted to relationship building, not teaching.

Research Corner

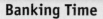

Banking Time

Research has shown that the same way that a good relationship between the caregiver and child will result in a positive social emotional outcome for a child, a supportive relationship between the teacher and child during early childhood years would result in various positive academic and social outcomes for children (Birch & Ladd; 1997; Pianta, Hamre, & Stuhlman, 2001; Hamre & Pianta, 2001). To promote a positive relationship between young children and early childhood teachers, Hamre and Pianta (2001) at the University of Virginia have developed an approach called Banking Time that enables teachers to establish and maintain supportive relationships with children.

Banking Time has been designed to improve the quality of teacher–child relationships. The approach is called Banking Time to emphasize that relationships are capitals for children. Early childhood teachers invest in these capitals during the one-on-one time they spend with children. They may draw on these banked resources at times of conflicts to help them maintain a positive attitude while solving behavioral problems of children (Driscoll, Mashburn, & Pianta, 2007).

Banking Time is similar to Greenspan's Floortime. The difference is that where in Floortime establishing a positive relationship has a set of developmental and therapeutic goals for language and social emotional development in the child, the sole goal of Banking Time is to improve the quality of the relationship between the child and the teacher.

Banking Time (My Teaching Partner, 2005) consists of a set of one-on-one meetings between the early childhood teacher and the child. These sessions should take place in an allocated time regularly, such as once a week, and as often as it is practical in a general and inclusive early childhood classroom. During Banking Time, the teacher devotes the entire session to giving her undivided attention to the child. The teacher follows the child's lead in an activity of the child's choice. The teacher does not teach during this time since Banking Time is a special time devoted to relationship building, not teaching.

During the session, the teacher observes the child and does not initiate any interactions. Banking Time's techniques consist of a series of simple observational techniques that the teacher implements during the session. For example, the teacher follows the child's lead, observes the child's actions, and describes what the child is doing. The teacher might listen and repeat what the child says, label the emotions that the child displays during the play, and imitate the child's play and actions to show that she is interested in what the child does and will follow the child's lead.

Because Banking Time is in its experimental phase, no study has been published yet on its efficacy. One unpublished study (Driscoll et al., 2007) has found Banking Time to be an effective tool for building close relationships between teachers and children during preschool years, which may offer lasting benefits to a child's academic future and social emotional development. For more information on Banking Time, visit http://www.myteachingpartner.net.

SUMMARY

The appropriateness of a child's behavior depends on the development of social and emotional competencies in her. A lack of social and emotional competencies might lead to behaviors deemed challenging. Children with challenging behaviors might display a range of externalizing and internalizing behaviors. Behavior problems in children might be due to some diagnosable condition, such as autism, ADHD, depression, or anxiety. They might also be due to some environmental risk factors. Environmental and biological risk factors can predict challenging and inappropriate behaviors in children. Success in working with children with behavioral and social emotional problems depends on the teacher's level of understanding of many internal and external factors that influence a child's behavior. An important strategy to use in inclusive settings is positive behavior support (PBS). PBS is an intervention approach to working with children's difficult behaviors. Via functional behavioral assessment, an early childhood teacher can analyze a child's behavior and understand factors that contribute to the challenging behaviors in that child. Antecedents, consequences, and setting events are three important factors that influence a child's behavior. By providing appropriate positive consequences and by manipulating antecedents and setting events, teachers can devise positive intervention plans that help the child change her behavior. Ignoring harmless inappropriate behaviors of children, providing positive attention to children throughout the day, and using effective praise for appropriate behaviors are some simple and effective ways of changing inappropriate behaviors in children.

Review Questions

1. What are social and emotional competencies?
2. What is self-regulation, and what might contribute to a lack of self-regulation in children?
3. What are internalizing behaviors?
4. What are some disorders associated with externalizing and internalizing problem behaviors?
5. Describe how problems in the adult–child relationship might be a risk factor for a lack of self-regulation.
6. What is positive behavior support (PBS)?
7. What is a school-wide positive behavior support?
8. What is functional behavioral assessment (FBA)?
9. What are some components of functional behavior analysis?
10. What are setting events?
11. What are positive and negative reinforcers?
12. List and describe the various types of time outs.
13. When should planned ignoring or DA be used?

Out-of-Class Activities

1. Ask permission to visit an early childhood classroom for the day. Assume the role of a behavior specialist and measure and record the following:
   a. Measure the frequency of the time the teacher provides negative attention to the children's behavior.
   b. Measure the frequency of the time the teacher praises children.
   c. Choose a child and draw a general ABC diagram for different behaviors of that child that are worthy of recording and that occur throughout the day.
   d. Record antecedent, behaviors, and consequences carefully.
   e. Record possible setting events that are observable, such as the arrangement of environment

and materials, the lights, the teachers' and children's behaviors, and so on.

2. Analyze the data you have collected in the following way:

   a. Compare the rate of the teacher's negative to positive attention, and draw a conclusion regarding the teacher's attention to children.

   b. List some of the teacher's specific behaviors that are setting events to different behaviors in the children you observed.

   c. List some positive consequences that this teacher uses for the children's behaviors.

   d. List some negative consequences that the teacher uses for the children's behaviors.

Recommended Resources

Anxiety Disorder Association of America
http://www.adaa.org/
8730 Georgia Avenue Suite 600
Silver Spring, MD 20910

Attachment Research at Stony Brook Institute
http://www.psychology.sunysb.edu/attachment/

Center for Evidence-Based Practice: Young Children with Challenging Behaviors
http://challengingbehavior.fmhi.usf.edu/

Center on the Social and Emotional Foundations for Early Learning
http://www.vanderbilt.edu/csefel/

Mayer-Johnson, LLC
2100 Wharton Street
Pittsburgh, PA 15203

Phone: 858-550-0084
Fax: 858-550-0449
Email: mayerj@mayer-johnson.com
http://www.mayer-johnson.com/

PACER Center
Parents Advocacy Coalition for Education Rights
http://www.pacer.org

Technical Assistance Center for Positive Behavioral Intervention and Support
http://www.pbis.org

United Nations report on the impact of armed conflict on children
http://www.unicef.org/graca/

View the Online Resources available to accompany this text by visiting http://www.mhhe.com/bayat1e. "

References

Achenbach, T. M., & Edelbrock, C. S. (1978). The classification of child psychopathology: A review and analysis of empirical efforts. *Psychological Bulleting, 85,* 1275–1301.

Ainsworth, M. D. S. (1984). Attachment. In N. S. Endler & J. McVicker Hunt (Eds.), *Personality and behavioral disorders* (Vol. 1, pp. 559–602). New York: Wiley.

Alberto, P. A., & Troutman, A. C. (2006). *Applied behavior analysis for teachers* (7th ed.). Upper Saddle River, NJ: Pearson Education, Inc.

Als, H., Gilkerson, L., & Klein, R. (2008). Neurobehavioral observation. In L. Gilkerson & R. Klein (Eds.), *Early development and the brain: Teaching resources for educators* (pp. 3.1–3.59). Washington, DC: Zero to Three.

American Psychiatric Association. (2000). *Diagnostic and statistical manual of mental disorders: DSM-IV-TR* (4th ed., text revision). Washington, DC: Author.

Birch, S. H., & Ladd, G. W. (1997). The teacher–child relationship and children's early school adjustment. *Journal of School Psychology, 35,* 61–79.

Blonigen, B. A., Harbaugh, W. T., Singell, L. D., Horner, R. H., Irvin, L. K., & Smolkowski, K. S. (2008). Application of economic analysis to school-wide positive behavior support (SWPBS) programs. *Journal of Positive Behavior Interventions, 10*(1), 5–19.

Bowlby, J. (1982). *Attachment and loss: Vol. 1. Attachment.* New York: Basic Books.

Brazelton, T. B., & Greenspan, S. I. (2000). *The irreducible needs of children: What every child must have to grow, learn, and flourish.* Cambridge, MA: Perseus Publishing.

Busch, A., & Shore, M. (2000). Seclusion and restraint: A review of recent literature. *Harvard Review, 8*(5), 261–270.

Campbell, S. B. (2002). *Behavior problems in preschool children: Clinical and developmental issues.* New York: Guilford Press.

Carey, W. B., & McDevitt, S. C. (1995). *Coping with children's temperament: A guide for professionals.* New York: Basic Books.

Carr, E. G., Dunlap, G., Koegel, R. L., Turnbull, A. P., Sailor, W., Anderson, J. L., et al. (2002). Positive behavior support: Evolution of an applied science. *Journal of Positive Behavior Intervention, 4*(1), 4–16.

Chandler, L. K., & Dahlquist, C. M. (2006). *Functional assessment: Strategies to prevent and remediate challenging behavior in school settings.* Upper Saddle River, NJ: Prentice Hall.

Christensen, L., Young, K., & Marchant, M. (2004). The effects of a peer-mediated positive behavior support program on socially appropriate classroom behavior. *Education and Treatment of Children, 27*(3), 199–234.

Cihak, D., Kirk, E., & Boon, R. (2009). Effects of classwide positive peer "tootling" to reduce the disruptive classroom behaviors of elementary students with and without disabilities. *Journal of Behavioral Education, 18*(4), 267–278.

Conroy, M. A., Sutherland, K. S., Snyder, A. L., & Marsh, S. (2008). Classwide interventions: Effective instruction makes a difference. *Teaching Exceptional Children, 40*(6), 24–30.

Cooper, J. O., Heron, T. E., & Heward, W. L. (1987). *Applied behavior analysis.* Upper Saddle River, NJ: Prentice Hall.

Cote, D., Boivin, M., Liu, X., Nagin, D., Zoccolillo, M., & Tremblay, R. (2009). Depression and anxiety symptoms: Onset, developmental course and risk factors during early childhood. *Journal of Child Psychology and Psychiatry, 50*(10), 1201–1208.

Crone, D. A., Hawken, L. S., & Bergstrom, M. K. (2007). A demonstration of training, implementing, and using functional behavioral assessment in 10 elementary and middle school settings. *Journal of Positive Behavior Interventions, 9*(1), 15–29.

Delfos, M. F. (2004). *Children and behavioral problems: Anxiety, aggression, depression and ADHD—a biopsychological model with guidelines for diagnosis and treatment.* London: Jessica Kingsley Publishers.

Denham, S. A., Blair, K. A., DeMulder, E., Levitas, J., Sawyer, K., Auerback-Major, S., et al. (2003). Preschool emotional competence: Pathway to social competence. *Child Development, 74*(1), 238–256.

Dodge, K. A. (1985). Facets of social interaction and the assessment of social competence in children. In B. Schneider, K. H. Rubin, & J. Ledingham (Eds.), *Children's peer relations: Issues in assessment and intervention* (pp. 3–22). New York: Springer-Verlag.

Driscoll, K. C., Mashburn, A. J., & Pianta, R. C. (2007). *Fostering supportive teacher–child relationships: Intervention implementation in a state-funded preschool program.* Unpublished paper, University of Virginia.

Earls, F., & Jung, K. G. (1987). Temperament and home environment characteristics as causal factors in the early development of childhood psychopathology. *Journal of the American Academy of Child and Adolescent Psychiatry, 26,* 491–498.

Eisen, A. R., & Shaefer, C. E. (2005). *Separation anxiety in children and adolescents.* New York: Guilford Press.

Emde, R. N., Korfmacher, J., & Jubicek, L. F. (2000). Toward a theory of early relationship-based intervention. In J. D. Osofsky & H. E. Fitzgerald (Eds.), *WAIMH handbook of infant mental health. Vol. 2: Early intervention, evaluation, and assessment* (pp. 3–32). New York: John Wiley and Sons.

Emond, A., Ormel, J., Veenstra, R., & Oldehinkel, A. (2007). Preschool behavioral and social-cognitive problems as predictors of (pre)adolescent disruptive behavior. *Child Psychiatry and Human Development, 28,* 221–236.

Fagan, J. (1990). The interaction between child sex and temperament in predicting behavior problems of preschool-age children in day care. *Early Child Development and Care, 59,* 97–111.

Ford, J. A., & Milosky, L. M. (2008). Influence generation during discourse and its relation to social competence: An online investigation of abilities of children with and without language impairment. *Journal of Speech, Language, and Hearing Research, 51,* 367–380.

Fox, L., & Hemmeter, M. L. (2009). A program-wide model for supporting social emotional development and addressing challenging behavior in early childhood settings. In W. Sailor, G. Dunlap, G. Sugai, & R. Horner (Eds.), *Handbook of Positive Behavior Support* (pp. 177–202). New York: Springer.

Gilliam, W. S. (2005). Prekindergarteners left behind: Expulsion rates in state prekindergarten programs. *Foundation for Child Development: FCD policy brief series No. 3.* New Haven, CT: Yale University Child Development Center. Retrieved July 10, 2009, from http://www.challengingbehavior.org/explore/policy_docs/prek_expulsion.pdf

Gimpel, G. A., & Holland, M. L. (2003). *Emotional behavioral problems of young children: Effective interventions in the preschool and kindergarten years.* New York: Guilford Press.

Gresham, F. (1986). Conceptual and definitional issues in the assessment of children's social skills: Implications for classification and training. *Journal of Clinical Child Psychology, 15,* 13–15.

Gresham, F. M., Watson, T. S., & Skinner, C. H. (2001). Functional behavior assessment: Principles, procedures, and future directions. *School Psychology Review, 30*(2), 156–172.

Hamre, B. K., & Pianta, R. C. (2001). Early teacher–child relationships and the trajectory of children's school outcomes through eighth grade. *Child Development, 72*(2), 625–638.

Horner, R. H. (2000). Positive behavior supports. *Focus on Autism and Other Developmental Disabilities, 15*(2), 97–105.

Kegan, J., & Snidman, N. (1999). Early childhood predictors of adult psychopathology. *Harvard Review of Psychiatry, 3,* 341–350.

Knoster, T., Wells, T., & McDowell, K. C. (2003). *Using time out in an effective and ethical manner.* Des Moines, IA: Iowa Department of Education.

Lavigne, V. (n.d.). *Tuesday's child parent training manual.* Chicago: Tuesday's Child.

Lewis, T. J., & Sugai, G. (1999). Effective behavior support: A systems approach to proactive schoolwide management. *Focus on Exceptional Children, 31*(6), 1–24.

Lindsey, E. W. (2002). Preschool children's friendships and peer acceptance: Links to social competence. *Child Study Journal, 32*(3), 145–156.

Lukenheimer, E., Dishion, T., Shaw, D., Connell, A., Gardner, F., Wilson M., et al. (2009). Collateral benefits of the family check-up on early childhood school readiness: Indirect effects of parents' positive behavior support. *Developmental Psychology, 44*(6), 1737–1752.

Maag, J. (2004). *Behavior management: From theoretical implications to practical applications.* San Diego, CA: Singular Publishing Group Inc.

Maag, J. W., & Kemp, Su. E. (2003). Behavioral intent of power and affiliation: Implications for functional analysis. *Remedial and Special Education, 24*(1), 57–64.

Magee, T., & Roy, S. C. (2008). Predicting school-age behavior problems: The role of early childhood risk factors. *Pediatric Nursing, 34*(1), 37–44.

McCabe, P. (2005). Social and behavioral correlates of preschoolers with specific language impairment. *Psychology in Schools, 42*(4), 373–387.

McCabe, P. C., & Marshall, D. J. (2006). Measuring the social competence of preschool children with specific language impairment: Correspondence among informant ratings and behavioral observations. *Topics in Early Childhood Special Education, 26*(4), 234–246.

McCleelan, M., & Tominey, S. (2009). Self-regulation in early childhood: Assessment and educational implications. *Early Education and Development, 20*(3), 563–564.

McEvoy, M. A., & Reichle, J. (2000). Further consideration of the role of the environment on stereotypic and self-injurious behavior. *Journal of Early Intervention, 23*(1), 22–23.

Meadan, H., & Monda-Amaya, L. (2008). Collaboration to promote social competence for students with mild disabilities in general classroom: A structure for providing school social support. *Intervention in School and Clinic, 43*(3), 158–167.

Muscott, H. S., Szczesiul, S., Berk, B., Staub, K., Hoover, J., & Perry-Chisholm, P. (2008). Creating home-school partnerships by engaging families in schoolwide positive behavior support. *Teaching Exceptional Children, 40*(6), 7–14.

My Teaching Partner. (2005). *Banking Time Manual.* Retrieved February 20, 2007, from http://www.myteachingpartner.net/activities/soc_relat/bankingtime/index.php

National Research Council & Institute of Medicine. (2000). *From neurons to neighborhoods: The science of early childhood development.* Washington, DC: National Academy Press.

O'Brien, G., & Yule, W. (1995). *Behavioral phenotypes.* London: Mac Keith Press.

Parke, R. B. (1994). Progress, paradigms, and unresolved problems: A commentary on recent advances in our understanding of children's emotions. *Merrill-Palmer Quarterly, 40,* 157–169.

Pavuluri, M., Janicak, P., Naylor, M., & Sweeney, J. (2003). Early recognition and differentiation of pediatric schizophrenia and bipolar disorder. *Adolescent Psychiatry, 27,* 117–134.

Percy, M., Brown, I., & Lewkis, S. (2007). Abnormal behavior. In I. Brown & M. Percy (Eds.), *A comprehensive guide to intellectual and developmental disabilities* (pp. 309–331). Baltimore: Paul H. Brookes.

Percy, M., Lewkis, S. Z., & Brown, I. (2007). Introduction to genetics and development. In I. Brown & M. Percy (Eds.), *A comprehensive guide to intellectual and developmental disabilities* (pp. 87–108). Baltimore: Paul H. Brookes.

Pianta, R. C., Hamre, B., & Stuhlman (2001). Relationships between teachers and children. In W. Reynolds & G. Miller (Eds.), *Comprehensive handbook of psychology: (Vol. 7) Educational psychology* (pp. 199–234). New York, NY: John Wiley and Son.

Porter, R. S., Kaplan, J. L., Homeier, B. P., & Beers, M. H. (Eds.). (2005). *The Merck manual for healthcare professionals.* White House Station, NJ: Merck Research Laboratories. Retrieved June 18, 2008, from http://www.merck.com/mmpe/sec19/ch300/ch300d.html

Putallaz, M., & Sheppard, B. (1992). Conflict management and social competence. In C. Shantz & W. W. Hartup (Eds.), *Conflict in child and adolescent development* (pp. 330–355). New York: Cambridge University Press.

Raver, C. C., & Knitzer, J. (2002). *Ready to enter: What research tells policymakers about strategies to promote social and emotional school readiness among three- and four-year-old children* (NCCP Policy paper No. 3). New York: Columbia University Mailman School of Public Health.

Raymond, A., & Raymond, S. (2000). *Children in war.* New York: TV Books.

Robb, A., & Reber, M. (2007). Behavioral and psychiatric disorders in children with disabilities. In M. L. Batshaw, L. Pellegrino, & N. J., Roizen (Eds.), *Children with disabilities* (6th ed., pp. 297–311). Baltimore: Paul H. Brookes.

Rose-Krasnor, L. (1997). The nature of social competence: A theoretical review. *Social Development, 6*(1), 111–133.

Rose-Krasnor, L., & Denham, S. (2009). Social-emotional competence in early childhood. In K. Rubin, W. Bukowski, & L. Brett (Eds.), *Handbook of peer interactions, relationships, and groups* (pp. 162–179). New York, NY: Guilford Press.

Rosinia, J. (2008). Sensory processing. In L. Gilkerson & R. Klein (Eds.), *Early development and the brain: Teaching resources for educators* (pp. 8.1–8.61). Washington, DC: Zero To Three.

Rothbart, M. K., Ahadi, S. A., & Evans, D. E. (2000). Temperament and personality: Origins and outcomes. *Journal of Personality and Social Psychology, 78,* 122–135.

Ruef, M., Poston, D., & Humphrey, K. (2004). *PBS putting the "positive" into behavioral support: An introductory training packet* (2nd ed.). Lawrence, KS: Beach Center on Disability, The University of Kansas. Retrieved August 6, 2007, from http://www.beachcenter.org/Books/Chapters/PDF/PuttingPositivePart1.pdf

Ryan, J. B., Sanders, S., Katsiyannis, A., & Yell, M. L. (2007). Using time out effectively in the classroom. *Teaching Exceptional Children, 39*(4), 60–67.

Saarni, C. (1990). Emotional competence. In Ross Thompson (Ed.), *Nebraska symposium: Socioemotional development* (pp. 115–161). Lincoln, NE: University of Nebraska Press.

Scheuermann, B. K., & Hall, J. A. (2008). *Positive behavioral supports for the classroom.* Upper Saddle River, NJ: Pearson Education, Inc.

Slabbekoorn, D. (1999). *Effects of sex hormones on cognition and emotion.* Utrecht: Proefschrift.

Sroufe, L. A. (1995). *Emotional development: The organization of emotional life in the early years.* New York: Cambridge University Press.

Stern, D. N. (2000). *The interpersonal world of the infant: A view from psychoanalysis and developmental psychoanalysis.* New York: Basic Books.

Sugai, G., Horner, R. H., Dunlap, G., Hieneman, M., Lewis, T. J., Nelson, C. M., et al. (1999). *Applying positive behavioral support and functional behavioral assessment in schools.* Eugene, OR: University of Oregon, OSEP Center on Positive Behavioral Intervention and Support.

Sutherland, K. S. (2000). Promoting positive interactions between teachers and students with emotional/behavioral disorder. *Preventing school failure, 44,* 110–115.

Thomas, A., Chess, S., Birch, H. G., Hertzig, M. E., & Korn, S. (1963). *Behavioral individuality in early childhood.* New York: Guilford Press.

Trentacosta, C., & Shaw, D. (2009). Emotional self-regulation, peer rejection, and antisocial behavior: Developmental associations from early childhood to early adolescence. *Journal of Applied Developmental Psychology, 30*(3), 356–365.

Tronick, E. (1989). Emotions and emotional communication in infants, *American Psychologist, 44,* 112–119.

Turnbull, A. P., Edmondson, H., Griggs, P., Wickham, D., Sailor, W., Beech, S., et al. (2002). A blueprint for schoolwide positive behavioral support: Full implementation of three components. *Exceptional Children, 68*(3), 337–402.

Turnbull, H. R., Wilcox, B. L., Stowe, M. J., & Turnbull, A. P. (2001). IDEA requirements for use of PBS: Guidelines for responsible agencies. *Journal of Positive Behavior Intervention, 3*(1), 11–18.

U.S. Office of Special Education Programs, National Technical Assistance Center on Positive Behavioral Supports and Intervention. (2004). *School wide positive behavior support: Implementer's blueprint and self assessment.* Center on Positive Behavioral Interventions and Supports: University of Oregon. Retrieved June 19, 2008, from http://www.pbis.org/files/Blueprint%20draft%20v3%209-13-04.doc

Vasterling, J., & Verfaellie, M. (2009). Posttraumatic stress disorder: A neurocognitive perspective. *Journal of the International Neuropsychological Society, 15*(6), 826–829.

Verhulst, F. C., & Akkerhuis, G. W. (1986). *Mental health in Dutch children: An epidemiological study.* Meppel, Netherlands: Krips Repro.

Waters, E., Noyes, D., Vaughn, B., & Ricks, M. (1985). Q-sort definitions of social competence and self-esteem: Discriminant validity and related constructs in theory and data. *Developmental Psychology, 21,* 508–522.

Weems, C., & Overstreet, S. (2008). Child and adolescent mental health research in the context of hurricane Katrina: An ecological needs-based perspective and introduction to the special section. *Journal of Clinical Child and Adolescent Psychology, 37*(3), 487–494.

Werner, E. E., & Smith, R. S. (1982). Vulnerable but invincible: A study of resilient children. New York: McGraw Hill.

Yates, K. O., & Selman, R. L. (1989). Social competence in the schools: Toward an integrative developmental model of intervention. *Developmental Review, 9,* 64–100.

Children with Communication Difficulties: Speech and Language Impairments

Objectives

Upon completion of this chapter, you should be able to:

> Understand communication impairments and related factors.

> List and describe various types of speech disorders.

> List and describe various types of language disorders.

> Understand factors related to diagnosis of speech and language disorders in children.

> Understand strategies and adaptations necessary for working with children with communication difficulties in inclusive classrooms.

> Identify and understand various strategies to enhance language development in inclusive classrooms.

> Understand and identify the types and uses of augmentative communication and assistive technology devices.

Key Terms

augmentative and
  alternative
  communication
  (AAC) (351)
comments (346)
communication (330)
critical period
  hypothesis (333)
expansion (350)
extension (350)
incidental teaching (344)
indirect language
  stimulation (346)

labeling (345)
language (330)
language
  disorder (332)
language
  modeling (347)
mean length utterance
  (MLU) (342)
morpheme (341)
parallel talk (347)
phonological
  awareness (336)
phonology (336)

prelinguistic foundations
  of language
  development (344)
prelinguistic milieu
  teaching
  (PMT) (344)
repetition (350)
self-talk (346)
speech (330)
speech and language
  delay (331)
speech disorder (331)
stuttering (337)

Reflection Questions

Before reading this chapter, answer the following questions to reflect upon your personal opinions and beliefs that are pertinent to early childhood special education.

1. Do you attribute children's language development to a natural process or do you think environment plays a role in the development of language in children?

2. What are some problems that young second language learners might encounter in early childhood education settings?

3. How do you think the environment contributes to, or impedes, a child's language development?

4. How important do you think technology is in teaching language and literacy to children who have communication and language disorders? Why?

"Can We Talk and Play Together?"

It is the second week of Austine's student teaching in Ms. Bailey's preschool classroom. Austine is an undergraduate student working toward her degree in early childhood education. To receive a teaching certificate in early childhood education, she has to complete 150 hours of student teaching in an early childhood inclusive classroom. Austine spent her first week in Ms. Bailey's classroom trying to get to know individual students and understand the classroom schedule and activities. She studied children's portfolios and work samples, and interacted with them during their play routines and activities. This morning, Ms. Bailey asked Austine to make observational notes of three students, Mason, Gianna, and Hanna, in small group activities and dramatic play.

Austine observed Mason and Gianna during a reading activity and interacted with Hanna through dramatic play. She made detailed notes regarding their physical and verbal behaviors. She also made audio recordings of the children's conversations during their play interactions to get a good idea of their language development. At the end of the day, Austine was amazed at the differences in levels of language development among these three children. As she listened to the recordings of two separate conversations, one with Mason and Gianna, and the other with Hanna, Austine noted the particular differences between Hanna's, Gianna's, and Mason's receptive and expressive language abilities, even though the three were around the same age.

Austine's recorded conversations with Mason and Gianna while reading the book *How Big Is a Pig* is as follows:

Austine:	Okay, let's look at this picture here. See these hens? Why are these hens outside of the house? What do you think they are doing?
Mason:	Cuz they want to eat worms.
Austine:	They want to eat some worms. Do you think they like to eat worms? Would you like to eat some worms?
Mason and Gianna:	EW! No! EW! No!
Austine:	Gianna, what are these hens doing inside of the house?
Mason:	They are resting, I think.
Gianna:	Well, they don't wanna eat some worms.
Austine:	They don't want to eat some worms. So, what would they do inside?
Mason:	I think they are resting.
Austine:	They're resting. Okay, so they're getting some sleep inside the house maybe.
Gianna:	Frogs!
Austine:	Frogs. You are right.
Mason:	Look at that pig!
Austine:	Yes, let us look at that pig and the frogs. Some frogs are "jumpy" and that means "they are moving around a lot."
Gianna:	But, but, but, it . . . it's green.

Austine compared this recording with the one of a conversation she had with Hanna. Austine and Hanna had been playing in the house area. Hanna had pointed at a doll:

Hanna: Me get.
Hanna: Get.
Austine: You get what?
Hanna: That.
Hanna: Get.
Hanna: Doll.
Austine: You want to get the doll?
Hanna: Doll, doll.
Austine: Do you want me to get the doll from Jason and give it to you?
Hanna: [silence]
Austine (modeling): Say, "Can I have the doll?"
Hanna: Have doll?
Austine: Good job trying to say the words!
Austine: Jason is playing with the doll. Let's see if he would give it to us when he is finished. [Austine turns to Jason who is playing in the corner.] Jason, when you are finished playing with the doll, could you give it to Hanna, please?
Jason: [Puts the doll down.] I am done! [Jason goes to the block area.]
Austine: Here you are. [Gives the doll to Hanna.]
Hanna: [Takes the doll and turns her back to Austine to go to the corner of the house area.]
Austine: Can I play with you?
Hanna: [Turns around, thinks a moment, and nods, yes.]
Austine: Okay, what should we do with the baby doll?
Hanna: Eat!
Austine: Oh, you want to feed the baby. What do we need to feed the baby with?
Hanna: Bottle.
Austine: That's right! We need the bottle to feed the baby . . .

As Austine listened to her conversations with the children, she made the following notes:

Mason (3 years old): During the interaction, Mason listened and comprehended what was said. He spoke in full sentences with at least three to four words. He was able to ask and answer questions during the interaction. He was enthusiastic to respond and initiated language on his own. He seemed to have difficulties understanding some complex concepts.

Gianna (3 years old): Gianna listened carefully. She was hesitant to answer questions and required encouragement to respond. She was able to make full sentences but seemed to prefer to respond in single words or phrases. Gianna had difficulties following simple themes and related concepts.

Hanna (3½ years old): During our play session, Hanna comprehended simple questions and directions well. This seems to be the area of Hanna's strength in language development. However, as compared to her peers (Mason and Gianna) she seemed to be behind in expressive language. Hanna had difficulty speaking in full sentences. She made her requests by uttering single words. When modeling for her to make a full sentence, Hanna made very good efforts, but she was only able to utter the last two words in the modeled sentences.

It was apparent to Austine that both Gianna and Mason would be able to understand concepts and follow themes if they received appropriate language scaffolding. While Gianna's language development did not seem to be completely on par with that of Mason's, she was within the range of typical language development for her age. However, Hanna's difficulties in putting sentences together and holding simple conversations indicated to Austine that she might have some language delays. With this knowledge, Austine decided to take her summary of anecdotal notes to Ms. Bailey and ask for ideas to help all three children enhance their language knowledge and development.

INTRODUCTION

Communication is an important area of development. It involves a process of sending and receiving messages and ideas about a person's needs, desires, perceptions, knowledge, or affective states (McCormick, Loeb, & Scheifelbusch, 2003; National Joint Committee for the Communication Needs of Persons with Severe Disabilities, 2003). Communication can take place using various modalities, such as gestures, signs, symbols, expressions, eye contact, or body movement. Because communication allows one a sense of belonging and participating in social activities, impairment in communication can negatively affect a person's quality of life (Schlosser, Sigafoos, Rothschild, Burke, & Palace, 2007).

Many sensory and cognitive processes interact with one another to enable a person to communicate. Communication involves mastery of visual, social, and behavioral skills in addition to verbal ones (Grizzle & Simms, 2005). Vision provides contextual cues for sounds in the environment and helps children make meaning of sounds. Social emotional development provides environmental cues for children regarding the use of language to make things happen through communication. Therefore, skills such as interpreting physical cues, engaging, responding, and maintaining reciprocal interactions with others depend on the social emotional development of children (Grizzle & Simms, 2005). Finally, cognitive development is related to understanding concepts and expressions of thought through the use of **language.**

Language is the code through which communication may take place. Language is defined as a "socially shared code that uses a conventional system of arbitrary symbols to represent ideas about the world that are meaningful to others who know the same code" (Nelson, 1998). In simpler terms, it is a system of rules for sounds, signs, or written symbols among a group of people to communicate with one another. Language is complex and socially shared, and the rules in language differ from one community to the next.

Speech is an oral manner by which language can be used and exchanged. Speech is a voluntary and complex neuromotor behavior (Pence & Justice, 2008).

It includes neuromuscular coordination of respiration (breathing), phonation (production of sounds by the larynx), articulation (production of speech sounds), resonance (vibratory response, which controls the quality of the sound wave), and fluency (production of smooth speech sounds) (McCormick et al., 2003; Schlosser et al., 2007). Although speech would be a series of meaningless sounds and noises without language, language and speech have their own separate processes (Pence & Justice, 2008). For example, one might not be able to speak due to a speech disorder. This, however, does not necessarily mean the same person does not know any language and cannot communicate via other linguistic means, such as signs or written words.

Since speech and language are ways in which communication takes place, a problem with either or both can impede a person's way of communicating. In this chapter, we discuss impairment in communication, including speech and language disorders, and ways of working with children who might have language difficulties. Although problems with hearing are related to difficulties with speech development, we will cover hearing loss in another chapter.

COMMUNICATION IMPAIRMENTS

Communication is possible through various brain mechanisms that support different processes involved in communication. Communication has four components (Stuart, 2007):

1. **Hearing:** For perceiving and processing speech sounds.
2. **Speech:** For using voice and articulation to speak.
3. **Language:** Consists of language form (grammar), language content (meaning of words), and language use (manipulating language in a social context) to be used for the purpose of communication.
4. **Fluency:** Consists of joining sounds, syllables, and words using specific rhythms, rates, and emphasis while speaking (McCormick & Loeb, 2003).

The cerebellum contains many functions related to hearing, speech, and language; the frontal lobe of the cerebrum holds Broca's speech production area; and the temporal lobe contains the primary auditory area and Wernick's language comprehension area (Stuart, 2007). (See Figure 10.1.) The brain formulates, regulates, and integrates messages through these communication components that underlie the process of listening and speaking.

Communication impairment can result from (1) problems in the neurological processes used for cognition and/or communication, and (2) problems in one or more components of communication (hearing, speech, or language). The terms communication delays, communication impairments, and communication disorders are used interchangeably to refer to a delay or a problem in a child's speech and language development.

A **speech and language delay** usually refers to a lateness in emergence of speech and aspects of language use, or a slower than typical pace of language development (Grizzle & Simms, 2005; Zigler & Bella, 1982). A **speech disorder** is an

FIGURE 10.1
Diagram of the
Brain Specifying the
Cerebellum and Parts
Related to Speech
and Language
Development

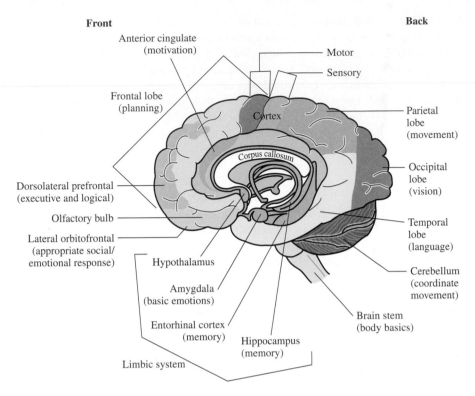

inability to produce speech sounds correctly or fluently or to have problems with one's voice (American Speech-Language-Hearing Association, 2008a). A **language disorder** refers to problems with understanding others (receptive language), or sharing thoughts, ideas, and feelings completely (expressive language), or both (American Speech-Language-Hearing Association, 2008a).

· Speech and language disorders are the most common forms of disabilities among children in the United States, affecting more than one million children in special education programs (National Dissemination Center for Children with Disabilities, 2004). Speech and language disorders range from simple sound substitutions to the inability to understand or use language or use the oral-motor mechanism for functional speech and feeding (National Dissemination Center for Children with Disabilities, 2004). The prevalence of speech and language disorders is reported to be anywhere between 3 to 15 percent in the preschool age population (Downey et al., 2002).

Communication Impairments Related to Developmental Disabilities

Because communication and cognition are highly related, an intellectual or developmental disability often involves some form of speech and language disorder (Schlosser et al., 2007). Many speech and language disorders are associated with neurological disabilities such as autism and intellectual disabilities such as Down syndrome, fragile X syndrome, cerebral palsy, and others. For example, about 65.5 percent of children with cognitive impairments and 50 percent of children with autism are estimated to have some type of speech and language problems (McQueen, Spence, Garner, Pereira, & Winsor, 1987).

The severity of the disability does not always predict the extent or type of speech and language problems in children. For example, some children with developmental disabilities might experience speech disorders (e.g., stuttering) that might not be related to their cognitive impairments (Schlosser et al., 2007; McQueen et al., 1987). The problems of speech and language in children with intellectual disability range from a mild delay in the emergence of syntax or conversational skills to severe problems with little or no functional speech that can result in serious communication difficulties (Zigler & Bella, 1982; Schlosser et al., 2007).

Communication Impairments Related to Problem Behaviors

Children with speech and language problems often have difficulties comprehending what occurs in the environment or have problems expressing their thoughts, desires, and needs. This frequently results in frustrations and various externalizing or internalizing behaviors, such as tantrums, impulsiveness, aggression, or depression and withdrawal (Burke-Brassem & Palace, 2003). The development of friendship and social skills is naturally affected by problems in communication. In addition, children with communication difficulties might resort to other problem behaviors, such as self-injurious behaviors, as a way of expressing their need for attention (Schlosser et al., 2007).

Physiological and Sensory Factors Related to Speech and Language Problems

Physiological factors related to speech and language consist of auditory, visual, or tactile acuity, oromuscular capabilities, and speech transmission mechanisms (McCormick et al., 2003). Any impairment in visual, hearing, tactile, olfactory, or gustatory senses will prevent the child from receiving critical information from his or her environment. For example, with hearing loss, a lack of auditory input impedes a child from understanding speech sounds and from developing speech. Similarly, children with visual impairment or blindness usually experience a delay in cognitive functioning because of their mobility problems that restricts their experience with materials in the environment. Additionally, visual impairments prevent the child from receiving information such as facial expressions and gestures that are essential for communication purposes (McCormick & Loeb, 2003). Therefore, a visual and hearing assessment is the first step in the evaluation process when a speech and language problem is suspected.

The Relationship between Environmental Factors and Speech and Language Delays and Disorders

The cases of feral children have often been used as the evidence of the **critical period hypothesis.** This hypothesis supports the idea that the first few years of life is the crucial time during which a child can acquire language, provided that the child is presented with adequate language and social stimuli. If language input and social stimuli are not presented to the child during the first few years of life, the child will never achieve a full command of language. Specifically, the child will never learn the grammatical structure of language. The documented cases of feral children, such as Victor of Aveyron described in Chapter 1, is a clear testimony to this fact. See Text Box 10.1 for other cases of feral children.

Text Box 10.1   Feral Children and the Nature of Language Acquisition

The Story of Kamala and Amala, "The Wolf Girls of Midnapore"

In 1920, two girls aged 5 and 3 were found in India's Midnapore in the Bengal jungle. The two girls lived in a wolf pack, walked on four legs, and seemed to have no traces of human behavior. These girls were assumed not to be biologically related to one another, but to have been abandoned by their parents at different times and then found and raised by wolves. The girls were rescued and taken in by an Indian priest who named them Kamala and Amala. The priest attempted to rehabilitate them. Amala, the younger girl, died shortly after she was found. The priest worked with Kamala to teach her language and human social behavior for the next 9 years. He managed to teach Kamala to utter partial words. However, after 9 years of teaching, by age 16, Kamala only had the cognitive abilities of a 3-year-old. Although she had learned a small vocabulary, she was never able to utter more than those words. Kamala died in 1929 of typhoid.

The Story of Genie, "The Modern Wild Child"

The story of Genie, a modern day wild child after Victor of Avyron, has gained much attention in the linguistic circles and the scientific community. Genie was discovered in her home in Temple City, California by a social worker and was rescued in 1970. Aside from being fed and cleaned by her elderly parents, Genie had been locked in a room alone with no human contact and sensory stimulation for all her life. At the time of her discovery, Genie was 13 years old. She had been tied to a potty chair in a bare room during the day and at nights was tied and restrained in a sleeping bag. When Genie was found, she weighed 59 pounds.

Genie could not walk properly, was not able to chew food or swallow properly, was not toilet trained, and had virtually no language abilities. After being admitted to Children's Hospital in Los Angeles, she triggered the interest of a variety of developmental psychologists and educators. A group of scientists began experimenting with her to understand the process of cognitive and language learning. Genie was an enthusiastic learner and showed a remarkable recovery and development in a short span of time. She learned to function independently and interact and play with others. She formed a vast amount of vocabulary in a very short period of time. However, Genie never learned to put words together to make simple or complex sentences. Scientists were not certain that Genie had a cognitive impairment. They were not able to come to a clear conclusion as to why Genie, despite her apparent intelligence and hundreds of hours of language intervention, was never able to learn to speak.

Due to loss of funding, research with Genie ended after 5 years. Genie was put in different foster homes and Genie's mother brought a lawsuit against the scientific team that had worked with Genie, saying they manipulated Genie for their own ends. As a result, the research team was forbidden to have further contact with Genie. Sadly, Genie never learned to speak, and today lives in a group home affiliated with an institution that cares for children and adults with developmental disabilities.

In spite of what has been learned from studies of feral children, scientists continue to disagree on a specific conclusion regarding the exact nature of language acquisition and development in humans.

Source: www.feralchildren.com.

Social/cultural variables, such as socioeconomic status, second-language learning in light of the home language and culture of the child, and the quality of adult/child linguistic experience also influence language development (Otto, 2006). The groundbreaking study done by Hart and Risley (1995) is a testament to the influence of environment and early adult/child linguistic interactions on a child's language development. Over a period of 2 years, Hart and Risley studied three groups of children: children growing up in professional families, those being raised in working families, and those growing up in families receiving public assistance.

They found that children who were raised in working families or families on public assistance had the least exposure to a positive linguistic input and interactions. Children in these groups were more likely to hear punitive language or prohibitions, such as "no" or "don't do this," as opposed to the children in professional families. Children in the professional families by far had the largest number and more frequent exposure to positive language and verbal interactions as compared with the two other groups. They also found that by the time children in their study were 3 years old, those in professional families had a vocabulary that was equal in size (e.g., number of words) to the vocabularies of the parents on public assistance.

The study done by Hart and Risley is more complex in nature than to be summarized in a few words, and it has clear implications for intervention. However, this study should make clear the case that the development of language in children might vary among different groups due to environmental factors, quality of linguistic interactions between adults and children, family stress and resources, and the socioeconomic status of families. Therefore, while a delay in language development in one child might be due to neurological and developmental causes, a similar delay in another child might be a result of environmental and demographic conditions.

SPEECH DISORDERS

Speech disorders are usually related to problems with sound production that might be related to articulation problems, resonance, or phonological processing difficulties (Stuart, 2007). Articulation difficulties are generally related to oral mechanisms, such as tongue, lips, teeth, or jaw. Articulation problems are often connected to neurological problems, such as neuromotor dysfunction, in which there are impairments in motor programming (Beach, 2007; Schlosser et al., 2007).

Resonance relates to the amount of nasality. If someone has a structural abnormality, such as a cleft palate, there might be too much nasal resonance (hypernasality); if someone's nose is congested, there will be little nasal resonance (hyponasality) (Schlosser et al., 2007).

Developmental Phonological Disorder

Phonological processes concern distinguishing and understanding the sounds of one's language, producing those sounds, and combining sounds to make words and sentences. **Phonology** governs how sounds are produced and combined. A *phoneme* is the smallest meaningful unit of sound in a language combined together to form words. For example, the /b/ in the word "bat," the /p/ in the word "pat," and the *a* in the word "apple" are some phonemes in the English language. The standard English American language has 39 phonemes consisting of 15 vowels and 24 consonants (Pence & Justice, 2008).

Phonological processes in children are developed over time, up to 6 years of age (Goldman & Fristoe, 2000). All children have unintelligible speech when they are very young. For example, only 25 percent of the speech of 18-month-old infants is intelligible (Bowen, 1998). Young children frequently mispronounce words. They might pronounce "tiss" for "kiss," or "nanna" for "banana." Such deviations are typical of phonological process and development in children, and are usually eliminated by age 5 (McCormick & Loeb, 2003). However, when such deviations are not dissolved in children as they get older, a *developmental phonological disorder* might be suspected (Bowen, 1998).

A developmental phonological disorder might occur due to hearing loss, such as that resulting from ear infections (also known as otitis media), or a congenital hearing loss (Bowen, 1998; Beach, 2007; Preston & Edwards, 2007). In these cases, the child does not hear the speech sounds correctly, and therefore utters the sounds incorrectly. Children with phonological disorders have difficulty organizing their speech sounds into a coherent sound pattern. Children's problems with phonological processes and articulation might range from mispronunciation of the "s" sound to multiple sound impairments, which can result in unintelligible speech.

Children's conscious awareness of different speech sounds in their language is called **phonological awareness** (also called phonetic knowledge). Children's phonetic knowledge contributes to their verbal abilities and is elemental in their literacy learning as they begin experimenting with speech and print.

Childhood Apraxia/Dyspraxia of Speech

Apraxia, also known as *dyspraxia of speech,* is a disorder related to motor planning in children (Beate & Stoel-Gammon, 2005; Nelson, 1998). Children with apraxia often appear to struggle to talk. They may have very few words or have difficulties initiating speech. These children might have a hard time uttering syllables or voluntarily beginning and sustaining conversations. Some children with apraxia may not be able to produce long or complex words. For example, they may utter the word car, but a word such as caravan might be more difficult. In addition, these children might misplace sounds, such as *pasghetti* versus *spaghetti* (Beach, 2007).

The exact nature and causes of apraxia are not known. It is certain that children with apraxia do not have any problems with the biological mechanisms required for speech, such as larynx, lips, tongue, or palate (Beach, 2007; Nelson, 1998). Instead, the difficulty lies within the brain processes that communicate with these mechanisms to move and produce speech, as well as difficulties in processes that enable the brain to retrieve speech sounds and patterns.

Dysarthia

Dysarthia is a class of speech disorders that affect structures of the oral tract resulting in the dysfunction of larynx, palate, tongue, or lips, which can create slowness and slurring of speech (Beach, 2007). Dysarthia is caused by a problem in the nervous system that can occur due to trauma or a degenerative neurological condition (Duffy, 2005). In dysarthia, the severity and type of speech problem differs depending on the area of nerve damage.

Problems with Fluency

Fluency problems might exist when a child's speech lacks rhythm. **Stuttering** is the disruption in the production of speech sounds, also called disfluencies (American Speech-Language-Hearing Association, 2008b). Children might hesitate, repeat certain sounds or words, prolong sounds, or use interjections throughout their speech. Stuttering usually begins during early childhood, between ages 2 and 4 (Scott, 2009). Stuttering could persist throughout the lifespan. The causes of stuttering are unknown, but it is likely that a combination of factors, such as genetics, family dynamics, and neurophysiology are involved (Scott, 2009). Specific techniques and exercises designed by a speech-language pathologist can help children overcome certain stuttering problems.

LANGUAGE DISORDERS

All types of language disorders relate to specific problems in receptive or expressive language, and might have a variety of neurological or physiological causes. Characteristics of language disorders might differ from one child to the next, depending on the causes and the nature of the problem. They might include improper use of words and their meanings, an inability to express ideas, inappropriate grammatical patterns, reduced vocabulary, an inability to follow directions, or a combination of these characteristics (National Dissemination Center for Children with Disabilities, 2004). Table 10.1 displays characteristics of speech and language difficulties associated with certain disabilities.

Certain warning signs may indicate a delay or a language disorder in the young child. During infancy and the early toddler years, these warning signs are generally related to cognitive-prelinguistic areas of development. As children grow, other signs of possible speech and language problems become directly related to receptive and expressive areas of language development. Table 10.2 displays selected warning signs related to language development in children.

Longitudinal studies of children diagnosed with language disorders indicate that young children with language and communication problems are at risk for a
• variety of learning and psychological problems later in life (Snowling, Bishop, Stothard, Chipchase, & Kaplan, 2006; Delgado, Vagi, & Scott, 2005; Beitchman,

TABLE 10.1   Characteristics of Speech and Language Problems in Some Disabilities

Autism Spectrum Disorders

➢ Functional language abilities totally absent (occurs in roughly 50 percent of children with an ASD)
➢ Has difficulty modulating tone
➢ Confuses pronouns
➢ Uses simple sentences
➢ Has difficulty initiating and maintaining conversations
➢ Uses few gestures
➢ Doesn't make eye contact when communicating
➢ Focuses only on one topic

Intellectual and Developmental Disabilities (e.g., Down Syndrome, Cerebral Palsy, Fragile X Syndrome)

➢ Has problems producing speech
➢ Uses simple sentences
➢ Has a slow rate of vocabulary acquisition
➢ Has difficulty initiating and maintaining conversation

Traumatic Brain Injury

➢ Has difficulty with speech production (e.g., slurred speech)
➢ Has difficulty with pitch and loudness of speech
➢ Uses fragmented sentences
➢ Has a small vocabulary
➢ Has problems finding words
➢ Uses socially inappropriate topics

TABLE 10.2   Warning Signs for Language Problems in Children

Age Range	Receptive Language	Expressive Language
By 9 months	➤ Does not give eye contact or hold eye gaze	➤ Does not babble or use voice to get attention ➤ Does not turn to sounds that are heard
By 15 months	➤ Does not point to objects of interest ➤ Does not share interest with another ➤ Does not respond to name ➤ Does not shake head "yes" or "no" ➤ Does not recognize picture of familiar objects when asked to identify a picture ➤ Does not follow one-step directions	➤ Does not use single words to communicate ➤ Does not repeat words ➤ Does not have a vocabulary of 10 to 50 words
By 2 years	➤ Does not respond to "yes" or "no" questions ➤ Does not follow two-step directions	➤ Does not put two words together such as, "want cookie," or "all gone" ➤ Does not have a vocabulary of 100 to 200 words ➤ Does not say "me," "mine," or "my"
By 3 years	➤ Does not recognize and put objects in appropriate categories ➤ Does not identify at least five colors, five numbers, and five letters ➤ Does not understand simple concepts	➤ Does not speak in full sentences ➤ Does not name colors and shapes ➤ Does not talk to peers
By 5 years	➤ Does not follow multistep directions ➤ Does not understand abstract concepts such as time, friendship, or family ➤ Does not recognize most letters and numbers ➤ Unable to listen to and follow long stories	➤ Does not speak in narrative ➤ Not able to narrate a story with one or more themes with beginning, middle, and end ➤ Does not make complex (4–6 word) sentences ➤ Does not use different tenses correctly

Cohen, Konstantareas, & Tannock, 1996). About 50 to 80 percent of preschoolers who have language impairments without cognitive problems continue to show language problems for up to 20 years beyond the initial diagnosis (Grizzle & Simms, 2005). Other children who have language disorders with cognitive disabilities are at risk for psychological and psychiatric problems (Snowling et al., 2006; Baker & Cantwell, 1982).

Specific Language Impairment

Specific Language Impairment (SLI), also called developmental language disorder, is characterized by poor expressive and receptive language abilities that are not associated with any medical causes, intellectual disability, hearing loss, or neuro-developmental disorders (Rinaldi, Rogers-Adkinson, & Arora, 2009; Tomblin, Records, & Zhang, 1996). SLI is usually diagnosed during preschool years, and its prevalence has been estimated to be approximately 7 to 8 percent of all preschool-age children (Grizzle & Simms, 2005; O'Brien, Xuyang, Nishimura, Tomblin, & Murray, 2003). Although the exact causes of SLI are not clear, familial studies have linked the occurrence of this disorder to genetic factors (O'Brien et al., 2003; Monaco, 2007).

SLI has been associated with a lack of social competence and the frequent occurrence of problem behaviors (Rinaldi, et al., 2009; McCabe & Marshall, 2006; McCabe, 2005). A number of studies suggest that, compared with their peers, pre-school children with SLI do not readily join in with their peers, tend to verbally address children much less, have problems managing conflict, respond inappropriately to peers, and rely much more on adults as conversation partners than on peers (Scott, 2009; McCabe & Marshall, 2006; Craig, 1993). Children with SLI are also at risk for further language difficulties and learning problems (Montgomery & Windsor, 2007).

Central Auditory Processing Disorder

Central auditory processing disorder (CAPD), also known as auditory processing disorder, is the inability of the central nervous system to process incoming auditory information (American Speech-Language Hearing Association, 2005). Children with CAPD have problems understanding the sounds they hear in their environment. It is often difficult for them to distinguish between words that sound similar to one another, or understand what is heard in noisy places. For example, a child might hear "hair" instead of "chair." Auditory processing disorder often coexists with ADHD, dyslexia, learning disabilities, autism, and social emotional problems (Nelson, 1998). Children who have an auditory processing disorder might have a hard time following long conversations, focusing on one activity when there are other sounds in the environment, remembering what was heard, or following directions with multiple steps (McCormick & Loeb, 2003).

Hyperlexia

Hyperlexia is a developmental disorder characterized by advanced word recognition skills, while the child simultaneously has oral language and social competence difficulties (Siegel, 1984; Glosser, Grugan, & Friedman, 1997). Children with hyperlexia show precocious reading skills early on—far above what is expected of their age. In fact, between 18 and 24 months of age, these children usually have learned to decode printed words without being taught by parents or teachers (American Hyperlexia Association, 1997). Regardless of their reading abilities, children with hyperlexia might have problems with expressive language, social skills, or both (Lee, Hwang, Nam, & Yi, 2008). Children with hyperlexia might be diagnosed as having a disability such as Autism Spectrum Disorder, another language disorder, or learning difficulties.

Aphasia

Aphasia is another language disorder that is usually acquired as a result of a brain injury that might have occurred because of an accident, stroke, or other medical condition (Beach, 2007). Aphasia affects all aspects of language and speech, specifically conversation, listening comprehension, repetition, word retrieval, and reading and writing. The type of language problem depends on the area of the brain in which damage might have occurred (Beach, 2007).

THE DIAGNOSIS OF SPEECH AND LANGUAGE DISORDERS

The diagnosis of a speech or language disorder takes into consideration different physiological, environmental, and cultural factors that might influence a child's language development. Such diagnoses should be done by a certified professional, such as a speech and language pathologist (SLP) (Downey et al., 2002). Accurate identification of speech and language disorders in children, especially bilingual and very young children who have receptive language comprehension deficits, is difficult. Using multiple accurate measures, including instruments that measure speech comprehension and expressive language abilities, is recommended for accurate diagnoses (Skarakis-Doyle, Dempsey, & Lee, 2008; Fernald, 2002). See Text Box 10.2 for an example of one way in which professionals assess a child's expressive language development.

> **Critical Thinking Question 10.1**   Referring to the story at the beginning of this chapter, does Hanna's apparent language delay warrant evaluation by a specialist?

Intervention strategies designed in collaboration with a speech language pathologist and that are integrated within the daily classroom and home routines of the child are likely to be most beneficial for the child.

Calculating Mean Length Utterance	**Text Box 10.2**

The complexity of the word structure or the number of morphemes contained in words used in the language of a young child is one indication of the level of language development in that child. A **morpheme** is the smallest unit of meaning in a word. Words can be manipulated in such a way that a single word can contain more than one morpheme. For example, the word "fair" has one meaning or one morpheme. We could add a prefix or suffix or both to give more morphemes to the word. If we add the prefix "un" to our original word, we will have the word "unfair," which is still one word, but now has two morphemes: the morpheme "un," meaning "not," and the morpheme "fair," meaning "just."

(Continued)

Like all other aspects of language, morpheme development depends on the development of vocabulary (semantics) and grammar (syntax) as well as the sound system of language (phonology), and social usage of language (pragmatics). Because the complexity of morpheme and syntax development in children is a good indication of the level of language development in children, professionals often measure an **mean length utterance (MLU)** of a child to assess the child's language development. A mean length utterance is an average numeric value that is calculated by dividing the total number of morphemes contained in a child's utterances by the total number of the child's utterances.

Brown (1973) described different stages of language development for children. He designated an MLU range for each stage:

Stage I	Children 15–30 months old	MLU range: 1.5–2.0
Stage II	Children 28–36 months old	MLU range: 2.0–2.5
Stage III	Children 36–42 months old	MLU range: 2.5–3.0
Stage IV	Children 40–46 months old	MLU range: 3.0–3.7
Stage V	Children 42–52 months and older	MLU range: 3.7–4.5

Of course, as children acquire more language, the number value for MLU will increase. To get an accurate value for a child's MLU, a language sample from the child should be obtained, consisting of at least 100 utterances.

Example: Obtaining MLU for Anna

A conversation between Anna, a 2½-year-old girl, and her mother:

Mother: Let's play together.
Anna: Play ball.
Mother: Which ball do you want to play with?
Anna: Blue ball.
Mother: Where is it?
Anna: Under table.
Mother: [Gets the ball from under the table.] Looks like someone has put something *yucky* all around it.
Anna: [giggles] Ball *chocolaty*.

Number of morphemes in Anna's utterances:

Utterances	Number of Morphemes
Play ball	2
Blue ball	2
Under table	2
Ball chocolaty	3

Total number of morphemes in Anna's utterances: 9

Anna's total number of utterances: 4
Anna's MLU: 9/4 = 2.24

➢ Anna's MLU = 2.2
➢ MLU range based on Brown's stages of language development:
   15 to 30 months: MLU 1.5 to 2.0
➢ Anna's MLU is above average for her age

Source: Brown, R. (1973). *A first language: The early stages.* Cambridge, MA: Harvard University Press.

Diagnosis of Bilingual Children with Speech and Language Disorders

Children who are second language learners are frequently misdiagnosed as having a disability. Preschool children who are in the process of learning English are usually less fluent and cohesive in their language use (Otto, 2006). Therefore, it is often difficult to distinguish between children who have a temporary limited English proficiency (LEP) due to second-language learning and those who do have language disorders (Stein, Flores, Graham, Magana, & Willies-Jacobo, 2004).

In order for a young English language learner (ELL) to be diagnosed with communication impairment, the problems in speech and language should exist in both
• languages. The assessment of bilingual children should follow nondiscriminatory guidelines outlined by IDEA (2004) (Chapter 4). These necessitate the use of multiple procedures, a variety of empirically derived testing batteries, and direct that the assessment take place in the child's native language (Gutierrez-Clellen & Simon-Cereijido, 2009; Clair, Church, & Batshaw, 2007; Oetting, Cleveland, & Cope, 2008; Stein et al., 2004).

STRATEGIES AND ADAPTATIONS FOR INCLUSIVE CLASSROOMS

Any early childhood classroom that has a language-rich curriculum will be beneficial for both children with exceptional needs and those with typical development. A language-focused curriculum is not necessarily related to the availability of specific structural features, such as books, toys, or equipment, in the learning environment (Pianta et al., 2005). On the contrary, a curriculum that focuses on language and literacy development in young children mainly relies on the quality of interaction between the early childhood teacher and the children, and the amount of language modeling and scaffolding an early childhood educator uses in the classroom.

Indeed, there has been growing evidence that the language development of young children, including their further academic success, depends on the quality of interaction between the teacher and students (NICHD Early Child Care Research Network, 2000; Early et al., 2006; FPG Child Development Institute, 2005; Pianta et al., 2005). The extent to which early childhood educators model language for children, the way they promote children's conversations among their peers and with the adults in the classroom, the number of times they expand on children's language, and the extent to which they encourage children to use language for logical reasoning and concept development are critical in further language development of both typically developing children and children with special needs.

Evidence shows, however, regardless of what we know about the importance of a language-rich curriculum in early childhood education, that most early childhood education teachers fail to engage children in conversations or language-based activities (Pianta, La Paro, & Hamre, 2004). In fact, research indicates that early childhood educators do not typically expand on children's utterances and rarely ask open-ended questions, which invite children to engage in linguistic interactions (Dickinson & Smith, 1991; Wittmer & Honig, 1991). When a child has a communication impairment, it might be especially difficult to engage the child in language-rich activities. Specific strategies to help all children with and without communication difficulties to participate in language activities should be used in order to encourage and scaffold children's verbal interactions.

Prelinguistic Milieu Teaching

Several communicative skills are necessary prerequisites for language development. These skills form the **prelinguistic foundations of language development** (Abbeduto, Brady, & Kover, 2007). Prelinguistic skills include eye contact, joint attention, pointing, gestures, vocalizations, and single words. While it is important to enhance children's receptive and expressive language, simultaneously teaching prelinguistic skills will help children learn effective ways of communicating.

One method that has gained empirical validation during the past 10 years is **prelinguistic milieu teaching (PMT),** milieu meaning environment. This method, described by Fey, Warren, Brady, Finestack, Bredin-Oja, Fairchild, Sokol, and Yoder (2006), is used for young children with language and communication disorders, children with intellectual disabilities, and children who are deaf-blind. The goal of PMT is to teach the child important prelinguistic skills such as gesturing, vocalization, or making eye contact during naturally occurring activities and routines. In PMT, early childhood educators follow several important steps while following the child's lead and interest to teach them these foundation skills (Thiemann & Warren, 2004). Incidental teaching is a necessary prerequisite teaching technique for PMT.

Incidental Teaching

Incidental teaching is an approach that provides structured learning opportunities in the natural environment of the child by using the child's interests and motivations. In this approach, parents or interventionists take advantage of naturally occurring situations to teach the child a specific skill. Through incidental teaching, PMT focuses on teaching preverbal skills to young children. Several steps are followed in prelinguistic milieu teaching (Thiemann & Warren, 2004; Turnbull, Turnbull, & Wehmeyer, 2006). These are:

1. The teacher observes the child to identify child's interests and to follow the child's lead.

2. The teacher arranges the environment (like placing the snack items or toys out of reach) to prompt the child with explicit verbal directions:

    a. The teacher prompts the child to communicate. For example, teacher asks, "What do you want?"
    b. The teacher prompts the child to give her eye contact by putting her hand under the child's chin and lifting her chin gently to look at her.
    c. The teacher models appropriate verbal behavior, "Say Play-Doh."
    d. The teacher imitates and then expands on what the child says. For example, the child says, "pay." The teacher says, "play." The child says, "pay." The teacher says, "Play-Doh!"
    e. The teacher complies with the child's request.

3. The teacher provides natural consequences to the child's behavior. For example, the child receives the Play-Doh.
4. The teacher acknowledges the child's communicative behavior. For example, the teacher says, "You asked for Play-Doh!"
5. The teacher continues interacting with the child while providing praise and encouragement. For example, the teacher says, "Good job asking for the Play-Doh."

STRATEGIES TO ENHANCE RECEPTIVE LANGUAGE DEVELOPMENT

In order for children to use language to communicate and develop social relationships, they need to comprehend language. The ability to comprehend what is known as receptive language is the foundation of becoming a listener (Otto, 2006). The ability to listen to and understand what is being said are the building blocks for becoming a speaker (Otto, 2006). Strategies to enhance receptive language development are appropriate to be used as early as infancy, and as long as children require language intervention to improve and expand their language abilities.

Labeling

Labeling is the strategy by which a very young child begins to comprehend the name of objects, persons, and actions in their environments. When caregivers, parents, and educators constantly point to different objects and label them, when they name their own actions and actions of others, and when they repeatedly call attention to objects throughout the day, an infant begins to comprehend and develop a receptive vocabulary (Pianta et al., 2005).

Verbal labeling of objects and actions should continue to take place in early childhood general, inclusive, and special education classrooms at all times. In addition, as we have noted in Chapter 7, toys, materials, and equipment should also be labeled by words and pictures. For example, the children's cabinets, desks, and drawers should be labeled with both their names and pictures. This type of labeling is one way to build the receptive vocabulary of children. An advanced form of labeling is description (Vigil, Hodges, & Klee, 2000). In description, a short sentence or a phrase is used to describe an object. For example, the teacher might say, "This is a big ball!" or "The toy truck is broken."

Self-Talk

Self-talk is a strategy employed to enhance comprehension in toddlers and older children (Girolametto, Weitzman, Van Lieshout, & Duff, 2000). Self-talk indirectly stimulates spoken language in children, and therefore has been referred to as a form of **indirect language stimulation** (Girolametto et al., 2000). Unlike direct language modeling, in which the child is encouraged to imitate a specific verbal model, in indirect language stimulation, techniques and strategies are embedded within the daily routine to help with language comprehension (Girolametto et al., 2000).

In self-talk, the caregiver or early childhood educator describes his or her own action as the action that is taking place. It is an effective strategy that works well when it is used during simple daily routines such as washing hands or setting the table, or during adult/child interactive play (Bingham & Pennington, 2007). Text Box 10.3 provides an example of self-talk.

Making **comments** is another indirect language stimulation strategy similar to self-talk. Comments are the teachers' or caregivers' remarks on events, activities, and things that provide additional information to the child (Girolametto, Weitzman, & Greenberg, 2006; Girolametto et al., 2000). For example, in Text Box 10.3, Mr. Chad's self-talk provides explanations for his behaviors as he is getting ready during transition time before story reading. When he describes his action as he puts the puppet in front of him, he could comment by adding, "This puppet, Mr. Mouse, happens to be the first character in our story." Comments can be spread throughout different activities and interactions with children to provide additional information.

Text Box 10.3	**Example of Self-Talk during Transition Time**

Mr. Chad has just asked all children to sit down on the carpet in the book area so he can read everyone a big book. As children sit around on the carpet, Mr. Chad sits on the floor and arranges the props and puppets he has brought with him on the carpet. As children begin sitting in a circle, Mr. Chad begins to speak.

Mr. Chad: Okay! I am organizing all the toys here so that I won't get confused. [He points to one of the puppets.]
Let me put this puppet here. I am putting it close to me so I can pick it up when I need it as I read the story. [Mr. Chad puts the puppet in front of him.]
Let me look around. [Mr. Chad looks around and notices that all the children are seated on the floor and are looking at him expectantly. He picks up the big book and shows it to the class.]
Okay, I am going to begin the story now. Here we go! The title of our book is, *If You Give a Mouse a Cookie.*

Example of Parallel Talk (Narrating) during Play — Text Box 10.4

Andy and Ms. Brown are playing with cars and trains in the dramatic play area of a preschool classroom. Andy is 3 years old. He has cerebral palsy and language delays. Andy has very limited receptive and expressive vocabulary. Ms. Brown, the preschool teacher, has been working with him to help him improve his receptive language. Today, Ms. Brown is sitting in front of Andy. A number of cars and trains are arranged on the floor. Andy picks up a truck and begins driving it back and forth on the carpet.

Ms. Brown: I see you are picking up the red truck.
You are driving the truck BACK and FORTH. [Ms. Brown imitates Andy's action, moving a car on the carpet back and forth, as she repeats the words "BACK and FORTH."]
[Andy picks up speed and drives his truck faster.]

Ms. Brown: Wow! You are driving very FAST. [Ms. Brown shows a fast motion with her hand.]
[Andy stops the truck and turns around. He looks at a small train and reaches for it.]

Ms. Brown: Oh, you just STOPPED. [She slaps her hands together as she says STOPPED.]
I see you are going to pick up *Thomas the Tank Engine.*

Parallel Talk

Parallel talk is similar to self-talk. The difference between self-talk and parallel talk is that in parallel talk instead of describing his or her own actions, the teacher describes the child's behaviors, matching words to the child's action (Bingham & Pennington, 2007). Parallel talk has often been described as sports casting. Use of parallel talk is appropriate as soon as toddlers begin to move freely and act on objects and events. The teacher and caregiver describe everything that is taking place in much the same way that a sports caster describes a game. Parallel talk is also known as *narrating.* In Text Box 10.4, Ms. Brown demonstrates parallel talk with one of her students during play.

STRATEGIES TO ENHANCE EXPRESSIVE LANGUAGE

In addition to the methods described earlier, several direct and indirect strategies can help enhance oral language in children. Expressive language strategies can be used with children when they begin uttering single words around their first birthday.

Language modeling is a strategy used to elicit language from children (Pianta et al., 2004). Modeling has been used with children with speech and language disorders both with and without the aid of technology, such as graphic symbols and voice output (Girolametto et al., 2006; Schlosser, Belfiore, Nigram, Blischak, & Hetzroni,

1995; Harris & Reichle, 2004). Language modeling is also used for typically developing children to enhance their oral language development.

In young children with language problems, modeling and language stimulation need to be direct, explicit, and systematic. Depending on the verbal abilities of the children, the teacher might model sound utterances, called *phonological cueing,* before a complete word utterance is modeled. For example, the goal for a child might be to utter the isolated sounds in a word by following the model of a specific phoneme. The teacher might model uttering the sound /b/ in book saying "bbbb" first before modeling the word "book." Success is measured when children vocalize targeted sounds in an attempt to utter a word, or when children are able to produce an approximation of the word by uttering most sounds in that word. For instance, in the previous example the child might respond by uttering "booo."

Children with language impairments produce a smaller variety of words compared to their typically developing peers, usually as a result of problems with phonological and semantic processing (Gray, 2005). Therefore, it is important to provide both semantic and phonological cues to these children to promote word learning. Gray (2005) outlines a procedure for word learning using phonological and semantic cues that consist of the following steps:

1. Present an object or a picture of a common object to the child while naming it: "This is a [target word]" and provide meaning of the word (semantic cueing) to enhance semantic development—for example, "It is used for [contextual cue for the word]."
2. Provide a comprehension prompt for each of the target objects: "Hand me [the target word]."
3. Ask the child to produce the word by saying "What is this?" or "What are you holding?" Additionally, provide language/phonological modeling to elicit word production.

As children show progress in expressive language, the teacher might decide to gradually add to the complexity of modeling by uttering short phrases and sentences for the child to repeat. The more elaborate form of language modeling in early childhood classrooms includes modeling complex vocabulary and the pragmatic use of language among children throughout their social interactions and activities; and asking open-ended questions (e.g., "What are you doing?" or "How did you do that?") to promote conversational skills. Text Box 10.5 provides two examples of word and pragmatic language modeling.

Text Box 10.5 | **Examples of Language Modeling in Two Early Childhood Inclusive Classrooms**

Language Modeling during Snack Time

Juanita has just prepared the children for snack time. The children are sitting around a table. A few minutes earlier, the children had helped set up the table by passing out the cups, napkins, and snack plates to each other. Juanita brings around two boxes, one containing cookies, and the other containing crackers. Today is Julie's turn to pass the snacks. She hands Julie the boxes. Julie approaches each child. She calls the child by the name and asks, "What would you like to have today?"

Each child responds by saying, "I would like a cookie please," or "I would like a cracker please." Julie holds the appropriate box to the child, as the child reaches in for the snack.

As Julie approaches Molly, she asks, "Molly, what would you like?" Molly looks at the cookie box, but remains quiet. Although Molly understands most things that are said to her, she is not yet able to produce more than a handful of words. Juanita has been working with Molly to help her utter single words to state her needs. Juanita approaches Julie and Molly. She asks Julie for a cookie. Julie reaches in the box and hands a cookie to Juanita. Juanita kneels down to be at eye level with Molly, showing the cookie to her, Juanita loudly and clearly says, "COOKIE!"

Molly tries, "cccooookkkkiii."

Juanita smiles and says, "Nice job asking for cookie!" She hands the cookie to Molly, "Here you are!" Julie follows Juanita's cue, getting closer to Molly, she asks, "Would you like another cookie?"

Molly repeats, "Cookie."

Julie smiles excitedly, "Nice job. Here you are!"

Language Modeling during Social Interactions

Fran usually sets up different centers for children in such a way that there are opportunities for interaction between children. For example, in the writing center, chairs face each other around tables. In the sensory area, there is plenty of room around the sand, beans, or water tables, so children can stand across from one another and play. In the art center, the easels are placed next to each other so children can converse and show each other their work as they paint. The block center is a large area, providing room for at least three children to play together.

As the children engage in their activities, they talk with each other and share toys and materials. Fran joins the children in their activities from group to group. She listens to their conversations, occasionally asks them questions to encourage problem solving and more conversations, and from time to time makes suggestions so the children can cooperate and interact with one another. As Fran approaches Max and Jane in the art center, she notices that Jane is standing in front of her easel, looking at Max, who is busy drawing a picture.

Jane has a diagnosis of ASD. Although she is able to make sentences, she often seems unable to initiate conversations unless she is asked a question. Fran pulls up a chair and sits close to Jane, asking, "Jane, would you like to ask Max to share some of his paint with you?"

Jane nods her head and says, "I like the green color."

Fran smiles and says, "That's simple. Just ask Max, 'Max, can I borrow the green paint, please?'"

Jane turns toward Max and says, "Max, can I borrow the green paint please?"

Repetition

Repetition is a language stimulation technique that helps the child learn the correct articulation of words and the formation of sentences (Pianta et al., 2004; Bingham & Pennington, 2007). In repetition, the teacher repeats or imitates exactly what the child says, using the correct articulation (Vigil et al., 2000). For example, the child might say, "Wed wagon." The teacher would repeat, "Red wagon."

Expansion

Expansion is an important oral language stimulation technique that provides a good model for the child to revise and complete his or her speech (Girolametto, Pearce, & Weitzman, 1996). Expansion has been successfully used for toddlers and older children with language delays as well as typically developing children (Girolametto et al., 1996; Girolametto, Weitzman, Wiigs, & Pearce, 1999). Expansion can be used when a child makes an utterance that might not be syntactically correct. In expansion, the adult *recasts* the child's utterance into a correct form. The following exchange provides an example of expansion.

> **Child:** Doggy run!
> **Adult:** Yes, the dog is running.
> **Child:** Big doggy.
> **Adult:** It is a big dog!

In this example, the adult introduces more correct and mature structures for the child's sentences. Expansion should be used to complete and recast the child's speech, providing a model for the correct use of pronouns, questions, gerunds, plurals, and other grammatical structures.

Extension

Extension is an advanced form of expansion. In **extension,** the teacher not only expands the child's utterance into its correct form, but also extends it by adding more information to the child's statement (Bingham & Pennington, 2007; Vigil et al., 2000). Using the preceding example, the teacher could extend the child's utterances in the following ways:

> **Child:**   Doggy run!
> **Teacher:** Yes, the dog is running. The dog is running fast!
> **Child:**   Big doggy.
> **Teacher:** It is a big dog. It is a brown furry dog.

Critical Thinking Question 10.2   Refer back to the story presented at the beginning of the chapter. Using the short dialogue between Hanna and Austine, think about the ways Austine could have elicited expressive language from Hanna. What kind of indirect and direct language stimulation and modeling strategies could Austine use with Hanna?

AUGMENTATIVE COMMUNICATION AND ASSISTIVE TECHNOLOGY

No matter what the nature of a child's language delays, with appropriate intervention, all children with language disorders are able to learn to use some effective form of communication. Children who have developmental or neurological disorders often learn to use **augmentative and alternative communication (AAC)** methods to help them communicate with adults and their peers. AAC refers to "approaches that add to (hence, the term *augmentative*) or replace (thus, the word *alternative*) a person's natural speech and/or writing abilities to communicate" (Schlosser et al., 2007).

Augmentative and alternative communication is an intervention that incorporates the use of manual and electronic technology (such as sign language), picture and symbol boards, and computerized electronic devices, along with the child's existing language abilities, to help the child communicate effectively within his or her environment (Romski, 2005). In augmentative communication, the child's own abilities are utilized along with one or multiple media, like a mixture of spoken words, gestures, pictures, or electronic devices. For example, a child may point to a picture communication symbol (Mayer-Johnson, 1992) to request something he wants, or use a talking computer to convey a message. These approaches are commonly referred to as *aided approaches* and include various modes and ways to empower an individual to communicate (Lloyd, Fuller, & Arvidson, 1997). Assistive technology includes a variety of devices that can aid a child with communication difficulties, allowing them to better engage in both social and learning experiences at home and in school.

Sign Language

As an augmentative communication method or an assistive device, sign language is not usually used as a primary mode of communication for children who have

Augmentative communication devices include simple teacher-designed picture boards or communication books to sophisticated computers with gaze detectors and touch screens which help children communicate with peers and adults.

language and communication problems. Rather, children are taught a limited number of signs, usually names of favorite foods, activities, or toys, as well as common words and phrases such as "I want," "more," "my turn," "no," "stop," and so on (Skau & Cascella, 2006). These signs help children communicate about the relevant daily situations in which they are involved. The approximation of signs is acceptable when children might have fine motor difficulties but not be able to sign the exact words. To empower children to communicate with other adults and children in their home environment, early childhood educators work closely with parents and family members to teach those specific signs that the child has learned to use at home (Skau & Cascella, 2006).

Use of Graphic Symbols and Other Visual Strategies

We have previously discussed the importance of the use of visual cues in early childhood classrooms (Chapter 7). Graphic symbols (Mayer-Johnson, 1992) and pictures are low-tech assistive technology devices that have become practical and useful in early childhood inclusive and special education classrooms to help children with or without special learning needs communicate effectively. Graphic symbols and pictures are often used to replace words (Smith, 2006).

Communication boards are poster boards that contain graphic symbols in a child's environment related to activities, play, daily routine, and the needs of the child (Romski, 2005; Skau & Cascella, 2006). Children use symbols and pictures to communicate their meaning to teachers and caregivers. Pointing to or exchanging pictures are common ways in which picture communication boards are used.

PECS (Picture Exchange Communication System) books (Bondy & Frost, 1994) are individual customized books belonging to children, which, similar to communication boards, contain pictures that describe events, objects, activities, and actions particular to that child's activities, interests, and environment. PECS has been predominantly used for children with autism, but the system is also appropriate for all children with communication difficulties. (See the discussion pertinent to PECS in Chapter 7.) Pictures are fastened with Velcro to pages of the book and are removed by the child and handed to the person the child intends to communicate with. The difference between a communication board and a PECS book is that the PECS book provides a portable communication system for the child. For example, the child could bring the PECS book with them for use at home, in the community, and at recreational places. As described in Chapter 7, use of PECS requires professional training by a PECS consultant.

Visual lessons consist of activities that contain the visual representations of concepts, vocabulary, or questions to be used for teaching specific lessons or performing targeted activities (Jaime & Knowlton, 2007). A variety of lesson plans can be converted into a visual format for an individual child or for small and large groups so children with communication problems can understand their teachers' verbal instructions and at the same time be able to answer questions nonverbally. Figures 10.2 through 10.4 illustrate several visual lessons and activities.

Story and song boards are similar devices that are used to aid in language and communication during language and literacy activities (Jaime & Knowlton, 2007).

(a)

(b)

(c)

(d)

FIGURE 10.2
Matching Word
to Picture Book

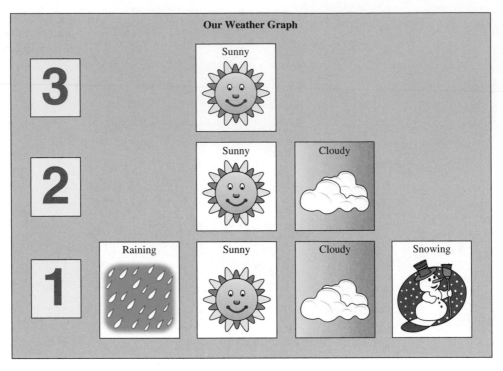

FIGURE 10.3 The Weather Graph

Teachers can use story or song boards during interactive read-aloud reading and music activities. These boards contain pictures of major characters and events of the story or the song. As the teacher reads the story or sings the song, he or she points to the picture or graphic symbol corresponding to the word. The specific pictures chosen to be used for each sentence are usually the ones that carry the most weight in the meaning of that sentence (Skau & Cascella, 2006).

Electronic Vocal Output Devices

Electronic vocal output devices are computerized systems that help children communicate. These devices usually contain prerecorded messages or words which the child has difficulty uttering (Skau & Cascella, 2006). The devices have buttons or switches that the child can push, causing the device to speak. Most devices have illustrated buttons so the child can see the picture representation of a word (Bausch, Ault, & Hasselbring, 2006). One creative way of using these electronic devices is to program into them vocabulary words that the teacher intends to teach during the week or program in lines of the story that the teacher intends to read to the class. By utilizing vocal output devices for teaching lessons, children can participate in small and large group activities such as storybook reading, and answer teachers' questions by pushing the appropriate buttons (Bellon-Harn & Harn, 2008; Skau & Cascella, 2006).

FIGURE 10.4
Matching Word
to Picture Puzzle

Research Corner

The National Center for Research in Early Childhood Education

The National Center for Research in Early Childhood Education (NCRECE) is a research organization established in 2006 to conduct research in the area of early childhood education. The NCRECE researchers from the University of Virginia, University of North Carolina, Chapel Hill, and University of California, Los Angeles, in collaboration with 2- and 4-year colleges in the United States, have been conducting research on professional development approaches designed to improve the quality of teaching in early childhood professionals, with a focus on methods to enhance early language development in children.

This center has designed a preservice college course for students in early childhood education, based on a strong body of previous research (such as NICHD Early Child Care Research Network, 2000; Early et al., 2006; FPG Child Development Institute, 2005; Pianta et al., 2005; and Pianta et al. 2004), consisting of a series of effective strategies that will support language development in preschool children in early childhood general and inclusive classrooms.

The NCRECE course is based on several important philosophical elements: (1) the teacher–child relationship is a platform for children's engagement and language learning, and a basis for children's social and academic development; (2) high-quality teaching is based on a teacher's skills in providing emotional support, well-organized and managed classrooms, and instructional methods that support children's active involvement and engagement in their own learning; and (3) language and early literacy learning are the foundations of academic growth and success in children.

Currently the center is collaborating with a number of 2- and 4-year colleges in the United States to examine the efficacy of this course in a longitudinal study. It is hypothesized that the course, along with ongoing consultation support, will provide future early childhood educators with strong and high-quality teaching skills to support language development in young children. More information is available at http://www.ncrece.org.

SUMMARY

Communication, language, and speech are three separate yet related processes. Language is one vehicle by which communication takes place. Speech is an oral means of communication, while language is divided into two main areas of receptive speaking: listening and expressive. A variety of speech and language disorders are possible during early childhood years. Problems in speech and language in children might be due to neurological factors, environmental factors, and physiological problems related to neurobiological and behavioral components of communication. The diagnosis of speech and language disorders is done by a professional clinician, such as a speech and language pathologist.

Children with or without a language disorder can benefit from an early childhood curriculum that focuses on the promotion of language development in children. Different strategies to enhance receptive and expressive language development consists of indirect and direct language stimulation and modeling techniques, such as self-talk, parallel talk, expansion, extension, and open-ended questions.

Augmentative and alternative communication (AAC) is an intervention strategy that utilizes the child's ability along with manual and assistive technology devices to empower children with language and communication disorders to communicate with adults and peers, and participate in different classroom, home, and community activities.

Review Questions

1. Describe the difference between communication, language, and speech.
2. What are the components of communication?
3. What are the differences between speech and language delays and speech and language disorders?
4. What are some factors that might contribute to speech and language disorders?
5. How important is environmental and social stimuli in the development of language in children, and why?
6. Name and describe one articulation problem.
7. What is central auditory processing disorder?
8. What is Specific Language Impairment and how does it differ from other language disorders?
9. Name and describe two strategies to promote receptive language abilities.
10. Name and describe three strategies to promote expressive language abilities.
11. What is augmentative and alternative communication?

Out-of-Class Activities

1. Spend at least 45 minutes interacting with three children, one between 2 and 3 years of age, one between 4 and 5 years of age, and one between 6 and 8 years of age. Obtain permission from teachers and parents or guardians for this activity, as you will be required to make a digital recording of your interaction with the child.
   a. Make a digital recording (audio or video) of your interaction with each child.
   b. Transcribe your conversations with each child.
   c. Based on your transcription, evaluate the following areas in each child:

   i. What is the child's MLU?
   ii. How does each child's language development differ from the other?
   iii. Write a report describing each child's general language development.

2. Design a picture board for a reading activity with a child with communication impairment.
3. Conduct an Internet search to find out which assistive technology devices are most recently being used for communication enhancement. Share your findings with your class.

Recommended Resources

Statistics on communication problems:
American Speech-Language-Hearing Association (ASHA)
http://www.asha.org/default.htm

Augmentative Communication, Inc. (ACI)
(Augmentative communication resources)
http://www.augcominc.com/index.html

Enabling Devices
(Assistive technology devices)
http://enablingdevices.com/catalog

Gateway: Guidance for Assistive Technology in
Education and Workplace Advancing Young People with
Disabilities
http://www.gateway2at.org/index.php

Mayer-Johnson, LLC
(Assistive technology software and hardware)
2100 Wharton Street
Pittsburgh, PA 15203
Phone: 858-550-0084
Fax: 858-550-0449
Email: mayerj@mayer-johnson.com
http://www.mayer-johnson.com/

National Institute on Deafness and Other Communication
Disorders
(Information about auditory processing disorder)
http://www.nidcd.nih.gov/health/voice/auditory.htm

National Early Intervention Longitudinal Study
http://www.sri.com/neils/

Speechville
(Information available on communication impairments)
http://www.speechville.com/communication-
impairments.html

The Stuttering Foundation
(Information about stuttering in children)
http://www.stutteringhelp.org/

Zero to Three
(Enhancing language development and literacy skills in
children during infancy and the toddler years)
http://www.zerotothree.org/site/PageServer?pagename=
key_language

**View the Online Resources available to accompany
this text by visiting http://www.mhhe.com/bayat1e.**

References

Abbeduto, L., Brady, N., & Kover, S. T. (2007).
Language development and fragile X syndrome:
Profiles, syndrome-specificity and within-syndrome
differences. *Mental Retardation and Developmental
Disabilities Research Reviews, 13,* 36–46.

American Hyperlexia Association. (1997). *Hyperlexia
handbook: A guide to intervention strategies and
resources.* Elmhurst, Illinois: American Hyperlexia
Association.

American Speech-Language-Hearing Association. (2005).
*Technical report: (Central) auditory processing
disorders.* Rockville, MD: Author.

American Speech-Language-Hearing Association.
(2008a). *Speech and Language Disorders and
Diseases.* Retrieved June 24, 2008, from http://www
.asha.org/public/speech/disorders/

American Speech-Language-Hearing Association.
(2008b). *Stuttering.* Retrieved June 24, 2008, from
http://www.asha.org/public/speech/disorders/
stuttering.htm

Arnold, D. S., & Whitehurst, G. J. (1994). Accelerating
language development through picture book reading:
A summary of dialogic reading and its effects. In
D. K. Dickinson (Ed.), *Bridges to literacy: Children,*

families, and schools (pp. 103–128). Oxford, UK:
Blackwell.

Baker, L., & Cantwell, D. P. (1982). Psychiatric disorder
in children with different types of communication
disorder. *Journal of Communication Disorders, 15,*
113–126.

Bausch, M. E., Ault, J. J., & Hasselbring, T. S. (2006).
*Assistive technology planner: From IEP
consideration to classroom implementation.*
Lexington, KY: National Assistive Technology
Research Institute.

Beach, W. A. (2007). Disorders of communication: Why
do they talk like that? *American Journal of Electro-
neurodiagnostic Technology, 47*(1), 29–46.

Beate, P., & Stoel-Gammon, C. (2005). Timing errors in
two children with suspected childhood apraxia of
speech (sCAS) during speech and music-related tasks.
Clinical Linguistics and Phonetics, 19(2), 67–87.

Beitchman, J. H., Cohen, M., Konstantareas, M., &
Tannock, R. (Eds.). (1996). *Language learning and
behavior disorders.* Cambridge, UK: Cambridge
University Press.

Bellon-Harn, M. L., & Harn, W. E. (2008). Scaffolding
strategies during repeated storybook reading: An

extension using a voice output communication aid. *Focus on Autism and Other Developmental Disabilities, 23*(2), 112–124.

Bingham, A., & Pennington, J. (2007). As easy as ABC: Facilitating early literacy enrichment experiences. *Young Exceptional Children, 10*(2), 17–29.

Bondy, A., & Frost, L. (1994). The Picture Exchange Communication System. *Focus on Autistic Behavior, 9*(3), 1–19.

Bowen, C. (1998). *Developmental phonological disorders: A practical guide for families and teachers.* Melbourne: The Australian Council for Educational Research Ltd.

Brown, R. W. (1973). *A first language: The early stages.* Cambridge, MA: Harvard University Press.

Burke-Brassem, M., & Palace, L. (2003). Communication considerations associated with developmental disabilities. In I. Brown & M. Percy (Eds.), *Developmental disabilities in Ontario* (2nd ed., pp. 453–464). Toronto: Ontario Association on Developmental Disabilities.

Clair, E. B., Church, R. P., & Batshaw, M. L. (2007). Special education services. In M. L. Batshaw, L. Pellegrino, & N. J. Roizen (Eds.), *Children with disabilities* (6th ed., pp. 523–538). Baltimore: Paul H. Brookes.

Craig, H. K. (1993). Social skills of children with specific language impairment: Peer relationships. *Language, Speech, and Hearing Services in Schools, 24,* 206–215.

Curtis, M. E. (1987). Vocabulary testing and instruction. In M. G. McKeown & M. E. Curtis (Eds.), *The nature of vocabulary acquisition* (pp. 37–51). Hillsdale, NJ: Erlbaum.

Delgado, C. E. F., Vagi, S. J., & Scott, K. G. (2005). Early risk factors for speech and language impairments. *Exceptionality, 13*(3), 173–191.

Dickinson, D., & Smith, M. (1991). Preschool talk: Patterns of teacher–child interaction in early childhood classrooms. *Journal of Research in Childhood Education, 6*(1), 1–11.

Downey, D., Mraz, R., Knott, J., Knuston, C., Holte, L., & Van Dyke, D. (2002). Diagnosis and evaluation of children who are not talking. *Infant and Young Children, 15*(2), 38–48.

Duffy, J. (2005). *Motor speech disorders* (2nd ed.). St. Louis: Elsevier Mosby.

Early, D., Bryant, D., Pianta, R., Clifford, B., Burchinal, S., Ritchie, C., et al. (2006). Are teachers' education,

major, and credentials related to classroom quality and children's academic gains in pre-kindergarten? *Early Childhood Research Quarterly, 21,* 174–195.

Fernald, A. (2002). Understanding understanding: Historical origins of current questions about the early development of receptive language competence. In W. H. Hartup & R. A. Weinberg (Vol. Eds.), *Child psychology in retrospect and prospect: In celebration of the 75th anniversary of the institute of child development: Vol. 32. The Minnesota symposia on child psychology* (pp. 103–129). Mahwah, NJ: Erlbaum.

Fey, M. E., Warren, S. F., Brady, N., Finestack, L. H., Bredin-Oja, S., Fairchild, M., et al. (2006). Early effects of responsivity education/prelinguistic milieu teaching for children with developmental delays and their parents. *Journal of Speech, Language, and Hearing Research, 49,* 526–547.

FPG Child Development Institute: The University of North Carolina at Chapel Hill. (2005). NCLD pre-kindergarten study. *Early Developments, 9*(1).

Girolametto, L., Weitzman, E., Wiigs, M., & Pearce, P. (1999). The relationship between maternal language measures and language development in toddlers with expressive vocabulary delays. *American Journal of Speech-Language Pathology, 8,* 364–374.

Girolametto, L., Pearce, P. S., & Weitzman, E. (1996). Interactive focused stimulation for toddlers with expressive vocabulary delays. *Journal of Speech and Hearing Research, 39,* 1274–1283.

Girolametto, L. E., Weitzman, E., van Lieshout, R., & Duff, D. (2000). Directiveness in teachers' language input to toddlers and preschoolers in day care. *Journal of Speech-Language-Hearing Research, 43,* 1101–1114.

Girolametto, L. E., Weitzman, E., & Greenberg, J. (2006). Facilitating language skills. *Infants and Young Children: An Interdisciplinary Journal of Special Care Practices, 19*(1), 36–49.

Glosser, G., Grugan, P., & Friedman, P. (1997). Semantic memory impairment does not impact on phonological and orthographic processing in a case of developmental hyperlexia. *Brain and Language, 56,* 234–247.

Goldman, R., & Fristoe, M. (2000). *Goldman-Fristoe test of articulation—2(GFTA-2).* Circle Pines, MN: AGS Publishing.

Gray, S. (2005). Word learning by preschoolers with specific language impairment: Effects of phonological or semantic cues. *Journal of Speech, Language, and Hearing Research, 48,* 1452–1467.

Grizzle, K. L., & Simms, M. C. (2005). Early language development and language learning disabilities. *Pediatrics in Review, 26*(8), 274–283.

Gutierrez-Clellen, V., & Simon-Cereijido, G. (2009). Using language sampling in clinical assessments with bilingual children: Challenges and future directions. *Seminars in Speech and Language, 30*(4), 234–245.

Harris, M. D., & Reichle, J. (2004). The impact of aided language stimulation on symbol comprehension and production in children with moderate cognitive disabilities. *American Journal of Speech-Language Pathology, 13,* 155–167.

Hart, B., & Risley, T. R. (1995). *Meaningful differences in the everyday experience of young American children.* Baltimore: Paul H. Brookes.

Jaime, K., & Knowlton, E. (2007). Visual supports for students with behavior and cognitive challenges. *Intervention in Schools and Clinic, 42*(5), 259–270.

Lee, S. H., Hwang, M., Nam, M., & Yi, K. (2008). On-line processing of word and non-word reading in children with hyperlexia. Retrieved June 25, 2009, from http://www.asha.org/NR/rdonlyres/6641CE82-17E5-4B7E-B641-50BB40C89EE7/0/567Handout.doc

Lloyd, L., Fuller, D., & Arvidson, H. (1997). *Augmentative and alternative communication: A handbook of principles and practices.* Boston: Allyn & Bacon.

Mayer-Johnson, R. (1992). *The picture communication symbols (Book I–III).* Solana Beach, CA: Mayer-Johnson.

McCabe, P. C. (2005). Social and behavioral correlates of preschoolers with specific language impairment. *Psychology in the Schools, 42*(4), 373–387.

McCabe, P. C., & Marshall, D. J. (2006). Measuring the social competence of preschool children with specific language impairment: Correspondence among informant ratings and behavioral observations. *Topics in Early Childhood Special Education, 26*(4), 234–246.

McCormick, L., & Loeb, D. F. (2003). Characteristics of students with language and communication difficulties. In L. McCormick, D. F. Loeb, & R. Schiefelbusch (Eds.), *Supporting children with communication difficulties in inclusive settings: School based language intervention* (2nd ed., pp. 71–108). Needham Heights, MA: Allyn & Bacon.

McCormick, L., Loeb, D. F., & Schiefelbusch, R. L. (2003). *Supporting children with communication difficulties in inclusive settings: School based language intervention* (2nd ed.). Needham Heights, MA: Allyn & Bacon.

McQueen, P. C., Spence, M. W., Garner, J. B., Pereira, L., & Winsor, E. J. (1987). Prevalence of major mental retardation and associated disabilities in the Canadian Maritime provinces. *American Journal of Mental Deficiency, 91,* 460–466.

Monaco, S. P. (2007). Multivariate linkage analysis of specific language impairment (SLI). *Annals of Human Genetics, 71,* 660–673.

Montgomery, J. W., & Windsor, J. (2007). Examining the language performances of children with and without specific language impairment: Contributions of phonological short-term memory and speed of processing. *Journal of Speech, Language, and Hearing Research, 50,* 778–797.

National Dissemination Center for Children with Disabilities. (2004). *Speech and language impairments* (NICHCY Fact Sheet No. 11). Retrieved June 24, 2008, from http://nichcy.org/pubs/factshe/fs11.pdf

National Joint Committee for the Communication Needs of Persons with Severe Disabilities. (2003). Position statement on access to communication services and supports: Concerns regarding the application of restrictive "eligibility" policies. *ASHA Supplement, 23,* 19–20.

Nelson, N. W. (1998). *Childhood language disorders.* Boston: Allyn & Bacon.

NICHD Early Child Care Research Network. (2000). Characteristic and quality of child care for toddlers and preschoolers. *Applied Developmental Science, 4,* 116–135.

O'Brien, E. K., Xuyang, Z., Nishimura, C., Tomblin, B., & Murray, J. C. (2003). Association of specific language impairment (SLI) to the region of 7q31. *American Journal of Human Genetics, 72,* 1536–1543.

Oetting, J. B., Cleveland, L. H., & Cope, R. F. (2008). Empirically derived combinations of tools and clinical cutoffs: An illustrative case with a sample of culturally/linguistically diverse children. *Language, Speech, and Hearing Services in Schools, 39,* 44–53.

Otto, B. (2006). *Language development in early childhood.* Upper Saddle River, NJ: Merrill Prentice Hall.

Pence, K. L., & Justice, L. M. (2008). *Language development from theory to practice.* Upper Saddle River, NJ: Merrill Prentice Hall.

Pianta, R. C., Howes, M., Burchinal, D., Bryant, R., Clifford, D., Early D., et al. (2005). Features of prekindergarten programs, classrooms, and teachers: Do they predict observed classroom quality and child–teacher interactions? *Applied Developmental Science, 9*(3), 144–159.

Pianta, R. C., La Paro, K. M., & Hamre, B. K. (2004). *Classroom Assessment Scoring System [CLASS].* Unpublished measure, University of Virginia.

Preston, J. L., & Edwards, M. L. (2007). Phonological processing skills in adolescents with residual speech sound errors. *Language, Speech, and Hearing Services in Schools, 38,* 297–308.

Rinaldi, C., Rogers-Adkinson, D., & Arora, A. (2009). An exploratory study of the oral language and behavior skills of children with identified language and emotional disabilities in preschool. *International Journal of Early Childhood Special Education, 1*(1), 32–45.

Romski, M. A. (2005). Augmentative communication and early intervention. *Young Children, 18*(3), 174–185.

Schlosser, R. W., Belfiore, P. J., Nigam, R., Blischak, D., & Hetzroni, O. (1995). The effects of speech output technology in the learning of graphic symbols. *Journal of Applied Behavior Analysis, 28,* 537–549.

Schlosser, R. W., Sigafoos, J., Rothschild, N., Burke, M., & Palace, L. M. (2007). Speech and language disorders. In I. Brown & M. Percy (Eds.), *A comprehensive guide to intellectual and developmental disabilities* (pp. 383–401). Baltimore: Paul H. Brookes.

Scott, L. (2009). Helping stutterers. *Education Digest: Essential Readings Condensed for Quick Review, 74*(8), 59–62.

Siegel, L. (1984) A longitudinal study of a hyperlexic child: Hyperlexia as a language disorder. *Neuropsychologia, 22,* 577–585.

Skarakis-Doyle, E., Dempsey, L., & Lee, C. (2008). Identifying language comprehension impairment in preschool children. *Language, Speech, and Hearing Services in Schools, 39,* 54–65.

Skau, L., & Cascella, P. (2006). Using assistive technology to foster speech and language skills at home and in preschool. *Teaching Exceptional Children, 38*(6), 12–17.

Smith, M. (2006). Speech, language, and aided communication: Connections and questions in a developmental context. *Disability and Rehabilitation, 28*(3), 151–157.

Snowling, M. J., Bishop, D. V. M., Stothard, S. E., Chipchase, B., & Kaplan, C. (2006). Psychosocial outcomes at 15 years of children with preschool history of speech-language impairment. *Journal of Child Psychology and Psychiatry, 47*(8), 759–765.

Stein, M. T., Flores, G., Graham, E. A., Magana, L., & Willies-Jacobo, L. (2004). Cultural and linguistic determinants in the diagnosis and management of developmental delay in a 4-year-old. *Pediatrics, 114*(5), 1442–1447.

Stuart, S. (2007). Communication disorders. In M. L. Batshaw, L. Pellegrino, & N. J. Roizen (Eds.), *Children with disabilities* (6th ed., pp. 313–323). Baltimore: Paul H. Brookes.

Thiemann, K., & Warren, S. F. (2004). Programs supporting young children's language development, *Encyclopedia on Early Childhood Development.* Retrieved October 25, 2007, from http://www.excellence-earlychildhood.ca/documents/Thiemann-WarrenANGxp.pdf

Tomblin, J. B., Records, N. L., & Zhang, X. (1996). A system for the diagnosis of specific language impairment in kindergarten children. *Journal of Speech and Hearing Research, 39,* 1284–1295.

Turnbull, A., Turnbull, R., & Wehmeyer, M. L. (2006). *Exceptional lives: Special education in today's schools* (5th ed.). Upper Saddle River, NJ: Pearson Education, Inc.

Vigil, D. C., Hodges, J., & Klee, T. (2000). Quantity and quality of parental language input to late-talking toddlers during play. *Child Language Teaching and Therapy, 21*(2), 107–122.

Wittmer, D. S., & Honig, A. S. (1991). Convergent or divergent? Teacher questions to three-year-old children in day care. *Early Child Development and Care, 68,* 141–147.

Zigler E., & Bella, D. (Eds.). (1982). *Mental retardation: The developmental-difference controversy.* Mahwah, NJ: Erlbaum.

Children with Intellectual Disabilities

Objectives

Upon completion of this chapter, you should be able to:

> Provide various definitions of intellectual disability.
> Understand the history of intellectual disability.
> List and describe the classifications of intellectual disability.
> Understand causes of intellectual disability.
> Understand issues related to the diagnosis of intellectual disability.
> Identify disorders associated with intellectual disabilities.

➢ Understand strategies and adaptations related to working with children with intellectual disabilities.

➢ Describe how to teach early academic and literacy skills to children with intellectual disabilities.

Key Terms

American eugenics movement (368)	learned helplessness (392)	prompt hierarchy (387)
deinstitutionalization (371)	logo reading (390)	responsive teaching (386)
intellectual disability (365)	mental retardation (365)	self-determination (394)
intelligence (377)	picture fading (390)	sensory-kinesthetic approach to phonics (390)
intelligence quotient (IQ) (368)	prompt (387)	
	prompt dependency (387)	
	prompt fading (387)	

Reflection Questions

Before reading this chapter, answer the following questions to reflect upon your personal opinions and beliefs that are pertinent to early childhood special education.

1. What are your ideas about children with intellectual disabilities (for example, how do you think they learn)?

2. Reflect on your past experiences in your home and school environment. How did other people—relatives, friends, and peers—regard a child with intellectual disabilities?

3. How do you think the attitudes of people in your environment and community influenced your own perceptions and attitudes toward individuals with intellectual disabilities?

Then and Now

Flora Gibson is a grandmother to five children ranging in age from 2 to 14. One of her grandchildren, Roy, is a 4-year-old who was born with Down syndrome. Flora takes care of Roy in her home after preschool 2 days a week. On those days, Roy is picked up by his parents later in the evening. Roy reminds Flora of her own brother, Peter. Caring for Roy a few hours every day has convinced Flora that Peter's life might have been different had he survived pneumonia over 40 years ago. Peter was Flora's older brother who had been born with Down syndrome in 1947. At that time, children with Down syndrome were called mongols. Flora's parents had regarded Peter's birth as an inescapable tragedy. Doctors caring for Flora's mother in the hospital had explained to her that Peter would benefit from being put in an institution for mentally deficient children.

Flora's parents looked for help but they were told by the hospital professionals that having a mentally deficient child in the family was stressful, and to deal   *(Continued)* with the stress was almost impossible. One doctor told Flora's mother that Peter would never be normal. And unless she faced the truth and gave up hope, she would destroy both herself and her family. He had suggested that committing Peter to an institution and being silent about him was probably the best course of action for both the parents and the family. Flora's parents were eventually persuaded that Peter should be cared for and trained by doctors and nurses who knew how to help children like Peter. They put Peter in a special training school for "retarded children" before Peter reached his 11th birthday.

Along with her parents, Flora visited Peter once a month in his training school, which was about a hundred miles from their small home town in New York. Flora vividly remembered Peter's crying and clinging to their parents during parting time at the end of every visit. The sadness was overwhelming for Flora and her parents as they witnessed the school staff pulling Peter away. Peter became ill with pneumonia 3 years after living in the institution and passed away a few weeks after contracting the illness.

Roy's story was very different from Peter's. When Roy's mother, Catherine, was pregnant, she had undergone a chorionic villus sampling (CVS) through which it was detected that Catherine's baby had Down syndrome. Catherine, her husband, and their family members talked about the baby and what it would entail to have a child with Down syndrome. Roy's parents consulted with professionals and other family members, and together they mentally and practically prepared for their son's birth. After he was born, Roy began receiving early intervention services in the hospital and continued to receive services at home for the next 3 years. Roy's parents, and Flora who would care for Roy, had worked closely with professionals to help Roy learn and develop. Although Roy's development did not progress at a typical rate, he had made great progress in all areas of development. He participated in typical activities for a young child his age and was included in all family and community events.

Roy began going to a Montessori preschool last year, where he made several friends, and looked forward to going to school every day. Currently, a special education teacher works directly with Roy and consults with his teacher several hours a week. Roy seems very happy in his preschool environment, and his parents hope that he will continue to thrive in an inclusive classroom throughout his future school years. As Flora thinks about the differences between Roy's care and that of Peter's, she cannot help thinking that Peter's life could have turned out so differently had he survived his illness and were alive today.

INTRODUCTION

When we hear the term intellectual disability or mental retardation, we seldom think of a very young child. In fact, early intervention professionals are reluctant to use these terms for young children who have no established genetic condition that might be associated with an intellectual disability. Instead, our early intervention system prefers to use a general category specified under IDEA, as developmental delay (DD), to describe young children who demonstrate significant delays in one or more domains of development and who are eligible to receive services (Delgado, Vagi, & Scott, 2007). (For further details on developmental delay, see Chapter 1.)

The term mental retardation and intellectual disability have been used interchangeably to refer to children and individuals who have problems in the area of cognitive development and adaptive skills to the degree to which their day-to-day functioning is adversely influenced. In the most recent report from the Centers for Disease Control and Prevention, the prevalence of intellectual disability is reported to be about 12 in every 1,000 children (Morbidity and Mortality Weekly Report, 2006).

In this chapter, our focus is on understanding disorders associated with intellectual disability and the specific behavioral and developmental characteristics of children with these disorders. Along with its history, we will examine changes in the ways we have defined children with intellectual disabilities. Finally, we will explore methods of working with children with intellectual disabilities in inclusive and specialized settings.

WHAT IS AN INTELLECTUAL DISABILITY?

The definition and terminology used to describe an intellectual disability has changed many times over the past two centuries as a result of changes in that field and in public views regarding individuals with cognitive or intellectual disabilities. The term **mental retardation** has increasingly fallen out of favor, since mental retardation has been commonly viewed as a condition that likely would not improve over time.

In more recent years, the term **intellectual disability** has been increasingly adopted over mental retardation by scholars and organizations such as the American Association on Intellectual and Developmental Disabilities (AAIDD) formerly known as American Association on Mental Retardation (AAMR), International Association for the Scientific Study of Intellectual Disabilities, and the President's Committee for People with Intellectual Disabilities (Shogren et al., 2009; Schalock et al., 2007). The preference over the use of the term intellectual disability is due to two factors. First, advanced knowledge in the area of neuroscience has helped professionals to gain a better understanding of the different causes of a variety of intellectual disabilities and ways to support children and adults with intellectual disabilities. Second, educators, parents, and more importantly individuals with disability themselves have increasingly informed us of the stigma that is attached to the term mental retardation (Brown, 2007). Indeed, where mental retardation refers to a static condition that cannot be improved over time, intellectual disability emphasizes a more positive view which focuses on the child and the fact that through interactions with the environment and with people, and through appropriate support and education, the development and functioning level of the child can in fact be enhanced (Schalock et al., 2007).

The American Association on Intellectual Disability defines intellectual disability as "a disability characterized by significant limitations both in intellectual functioning and in adaptive behavior as expressed in conceptual, social, and practical adaptive skills. This disability originates before age 18" (American Association on Intellectual and Developmental Disabilities, 2010; Switzky & Greenspan, 2006). An intellectual disability is a dynamic condition and can change over time. The degree of change depends on the causes and severity of the intellectual disability and on the type of environmental support and education that the child receives (American Association on Mental Retardation, 2002). The American Association on Intellectual and Developmental Disabilities (2010) considers five assumptions as essential in defining intellectual disabilities:

1. Limitations in present functioning must be considered within the context of community environments typical of the individual's age, peers, and culture.
2. Valid assessment considers cultural and linguistic diversity as well as differences in communication, sensory, motor, and behavioral factors.
3. Within an individual, limitations often coexist with strengths.
4. An important purpose of describing limitations is to develop a profile of needed supports.
5. With appropriate personalized supports over a sustained period, the life functioning of the person with an intellectual disability generally will improve.

In IDEA, the definition of an intellectual disability is provided under the category of mental retardation. It is defined as "significantly sub-average general intellectual functioning, existing concurrently with a deficit in adaptive behavior, and manifested during the developmental period that adversely affects a child's educational performance [34 code of Federal Regulations § 300.7 (c) (6)]."

To further clarify the field terminology, we utilize the categorization employed by Brown (2007) to define basic terminologies that are used interchangeably for all children with disorders associated with intellectual disability. Brown distinguishes the meaning of these terms in the following way:

> **Intellectual disabilities:** Term used to refer to a group of disorders, those associated with intellectual impairments, that might be present with or without other disability conditions and characteristics, such as cerebral palsy, Down syndrome, fragile X syndrome, and ASD. It is also used to refer to a field of study or service.
> **Intellectual disability:** General term used to describe a disorder characterized by limitations in intellectual functioning; also used as an adjective for an individual child or an adult.
> **Developmental disabilities:** Term used for a group of disabilities related to development of abilities. It also refers to a field of study or service.
> **Developmental disability:** General term used to describe a disorder; or used as an adjective for an individual child or adult.
> **Developmental delay:** Used to refer to a group of children, as related to the education of children with developmental delay; also used an adjective for an individual child.

Although the term mental retardation as a diagnosis is less likely to disappear, since it has been written into laws (Batshaw, Shapiro, & Farber, 2007), throughout this book and in this chapter, we use the terms intellectual disability or intellectual disabilities instead of mental retardation. This is done to avoid negative connotations associated with the old term and to emphasize that an intellectual disability need not be handicapping to a child, and that with appropriate intervention and support, children with intellectual disabilities can improve and function independently within their environment and community.

THE HISTORY OF INTELLECTUAL DISABILITY

Throughout history, children and individuals with intellectual disabilities have played various roles, such as being considered subhuman, menaces, diseased organisms, holy innocents, objects of ridicule, or eternal children (Wolfenberger, 1972). For the most part, individuals with intellectual disabilities were excluded from their societies throughout the world (Radford & Park, 2003; Hamilton & Atkinson, 2009). Over time, with the rise of science and advances made in the industrial societies, large institutions were built for people who did not fit into mainstream society (Brown & Radford, 2007). During the 19th century, children with intellectual disabilities were placed in those institutions that had been established to serve children and individuals with all kinds of disabilities, such as deafness, blindness, and intellectual disability (Trent, 1994; Harris, 2006).

In Europe and the United States, the issue of educating children with intellectual disabilities was brought into the public's consciousness by efforts of the early interventionist, Jean-Marc-Gaspard Itard in the 1800s. As described in Chapter 1, Itard spent 5 years educating Victor, the "wild boy of Aveyron." In 1866, Seguin, Itard's student, advocated a specific training methodology called the physiological method, which he had used successfully in working with a child with an intellectual disability. Seguin advocated institutionalization of children with intellectual disabilities where they could profit from a special classroom education. Samuel Gridley Howe, a friend of Seguin, persuaded states to establish specialized schools for children with intellectual disabilities in the United States (Trent, 1994; Harris, 2006).

By the mid-1800s, asylums, institutions, and training schools for children and individuals with intellectual disabilities had grown in size and number both in Europe and the United States (Harris, 2006). Though at first these institutions were established to educate and train children, soon they became the dumping grounds for those children and adults who were at that time called morons, imbeciles, idiots, feeble minded, or mentally deficient, and were considered a burden to the society (Trent, 1994). The care and living conditions of individuals in these institutions were at best suboptimal.

Over the next hundred years, many changes occurred in the form and operation of these institutions. During the first half of the 20th century, children and individuals living in such institutions began to be called inmates (Trent, 1994; Harris, 2006). They were taught job skills and were assigned specific work throughout the day. The type of work they did depended on their gender and functioning abilities. For example, higher-functioning women inmates were often put in charge of lower-functioning persons and young children who entered the institution (Trent, 1994). Males learned farm skills and other labor-intensive jobs. In later years, two other developments—the establishment of intelligence testing by Alfred Binet and the Eugenics movement—influenced the treatment of children and individuals with intellectual disabilities further.

Binet's Intelligence Test

In 1921, Henry Goddard introduced the Binet test for use with individuals with intellectual disabilities. It was at this time that the idea of **intelligence quotient (IQ)** was championed as the measure of intelligence (Brown & Radford, 2007; Harris, 2006). The intelligence quotient takes into account the child's mental age over the child's chronological or physical age. Traditionally, IQ is calculated as:

$$\text{IQ score} = \text{Mental Age/Chronological age} \times 100$$

When the child's chronological age is equal to his or her mental age, the IQ score is 100. A score of 100 indicates that a child or individual has an average intelligence. If the chronological age is above the mental age, the IQ score falls below 100. So, for example, Malcolm is a 7-year-old child whose mental age shows to be at 3 years of age according to the Stanford Binet test. Malcolm's IQ score is calculated in the following way: $3/7 \times 100 = 43$. Malcolm's IQ, 43, is significantly below average.

The Eugenics Movement

Around the same time as the introduction of the Binet test, the **American eugenics movement** was founded in the 1920s by Charles Davenport, a Harvard zoologist. The eugenicists believed certain behaviors and mental conditions, such as criminal behaviors or feeblemindedness were the result of an inferior trait. They thought intelligence, as well as feeblemindedness, was genetically hereditary, and advocated that bad genes were the root of social problems, and thus were a serious threat to American society (Noll & Trent, 2004). The main concern of the eugenics movement was to curb the overproduction of those who were in the lower social classes and to promote procreation among those considered more socially desirable and worthy (Brown & Radford, 2007). From the eugenicists' perspective, the solution to all social problems was to eradicate from society all those who were of an inferior type. See Text Box 11.1 for more information about the eugenic ideology.

Text Box 11.1   Popularity of the Eugenics Ideology

The American eugenics movement originates from the ideas of the British eugenicist, Sir Francis Galton, who had coined the term *eugenics* in 1883 and believed inferior and superior breeds existed that genetically transmitted specific characteristics from one generation to the next. During the 1920s and 1930s, the American Eugenics Society, an organization formed to advocate the eugenics ideology, devoted its activity to popularization of the eugenic philosophy. Movies supporting sterilization were made, Sunday church sermons focused on encouraging the eugenic beliefs, high school science textbooks were written to teach children the basic eugenic ideas, and university courses on eugenics were offered in many leading American universities such as Harvard, Cornell, and Brown.

The American Eugenics Society organized "Fitter Families Contests" in different cities around the United States. In these contests, adults and children received physical examinations, where the families' "pedigrees" were recorded, and "high–grade" families were encouraged to reproduce. A typical exhibit sign might state, "Some Americans are born to be a burden on the rest." Around the country, popular authors lectured on the threat of the increase in feeblemindedness.

According to the eugenicists, the ills of the society were caused by those of inferior birth. This included immigrants. Aside from institutionalizing the feebleminded and sterilizing them to prevent a possible increase in feeblemindedness in the population, restrictions were put on immigration to the United States. An intelligence test was conducted on all immigrants at the time of entry to Ellis Island. Test results determined if permission to enter would be granted.

Source: American Archives on Eugenics movement: http://www.eugenicsarchives.org.

The scientists of that time agreed that children who were feebleminded should be institutionalized and sterilized on a large scale to reduce the incidence of mental illness. As a result of this movement, between 1907 and 1949 more than 47,000 individuals in the United States were sterilized without their consent (Cullen, 2007; Braddock & Parish, 2002; Harris, 2006). See Text Box 11.2 for the U.S. Supreme Court decision that lead to the large scale sterilizations in the United States.

Buck v. Bell	**Text Box 11.2**

In May 1927, the U.S. Supreme Court upheld the concept of eugenic sterilization for people who were considered genetically "unfit." The case concerned a 17-year-old girl, Carrie Buck, her infant daughter Vivian, and her mother, Emma. Emma Buck was a widowed mother of three young children, whom she supported through prostitution. Seven years earlier, Emma was brought before the justice of the peace and committed to an institution: the Virginia Colony for Epileptics and Feebleminded in Lynchburg.

Emma's daughter, Carrie, lived with a family called Dobbs, and after going to school for several years, she assumed housekeeping responsibilities. Carrie claimed to have been raped by the Dobbs' son and became pregnant. The Dobbs family committed Carrie to the Virginia Colony institution and raised Carrie's infant.

The superintendent of the Virginia Colony institution, Dr. Albert Priddy, who was a eugenicist and known to have sterilized more than 75 women in his institution, brought suit against Carrie to a U.S. circuit court to declare Carrie Buck feebleminded and suitable for compulsory sterilization. Sterilization laws had previously been passed by the Virginia legislation.

In May 1925, the district court upheld the Virginia sterilization law and ordered for Carrie Buck to be sterilized. The case was appealed before the Virginia Court of Appeals, and the appeals court similarly upheld the circuit court decision. *(Continued)*

The case was brought before the U.S. Supreme Court. In 1927, the U.S. Supreme Court upheld the state of Virginia's right to forcibly sterilize "feebleminded" individuals. Justice Oliver Wendell Holmes, Jr. wrote the majority's opinion, "It is better for all the world if instead of waiting to execute degenerate offspring for crime, or to let them starve for their imbecility, society can prevent those who are manifestly unfit from continuing their kind. . . . Three generations of imbeciles is enough."

The decision led to numerous sterilizations around the country. By 1935, 30 states had statutes for sterilization, and more than 21,000 individuals declared to have been feebleminded had been sterilized without their consent. Carrie and her sister were among those sterilized soon after the court's decision.

Sources: Ethics and American Democracy, available at http://www.eppc.org; American Archives on Eugenics Movement, available at http://www.eugenicsarchive.org and http://law.jrank.org.

Critical Thinking Question 11.1   Refer back to the story that began this chapter. How do you think the education and treatment of Peter would have been influenced by the ideas and attitudes of professionals regarding intellectual disability at that time?

Disability Organization and Policies

Beginning in the late 1930s, parents and other family members began to mobilize and form different organizations, such as the United Cerebral Palsy Association founded in 1949 and the National Association for Retarded Citizens (later called ARC) founded in the 1950s, to support children with intellectual and other disabilities (Turnbull, Turnbull, Erwin, & Soodak, 2006). It was due to parents' incessant efforts that policies regarding children and individuals with intellectual disabilities began to change.

In the 1960s, the Kennedy family made it its mission to make intellectual disabilities its main charitable cause. President Kennedy, at the urging of his sister, Eunice Kennedy Shriver (1921–2009), a staunch advocate for individuals with intellectual disabilities, appointed the President's Panel on Mental Retardation. Among many recommendations of this panel were: (1) the expansion of community services to integrate individuals with intellectual disabilities in the community, and (2) the downsizing of institutions (Nirje, 1969).

The subsequent public laws such as PL 88-156, the Maternal and Child Health and Mental Retardation Planning Law and its amendments, provided funding for state programs to establish a number of community mental health centers to help and provide services for individuals and children with intellectual disabilities and other mental health needs.

Along with President Kennedy's efforts came a series of public laws on education (PL 89-10, The Elementary and Secondary Education Act of 1969, and its consequent amendments), which eventually led to the first mandated law for free and appropriate public education for all children with disabilities (PL 94-142, The Education for All Handicapped Children Act).

Finally, advances in the medical science, which had begun in the 1950s, in addition to changes in public policy, eventually resulted in a **deinstitutionalization** movement, whereby over time fewer children and adults with disabilities resided in institutions and hospitals, and more children and adults with disabilities were integrated and included within their family, home, and community environments (Braddock & Parish, 2002; Brown & Radford, 2007). Today, the prospect of living in special training schools or institutions is no longer a norm for children with intellectual disabilities, as they are typically educated in their natural environments, in inclusive and general education settings, and in specialized settings integrated within and among their communities.

Critical Thinking Question 11.2   Referring to the story that opened the chapter, why do you think Flora believes Peter's life would have been different had he survived the pneumonia and survived until today?

CLASSIFICATION OF INTELLECTUAL DISABILITIES

The classification of intellectual disabilities is necessary so that various types of disabilities can be identified and studied, and so appropriate services can be secured for children according to their needs (American Association on Mental Retardation, 2002). The American Association on Intellectual and Developmental Disabilities in a classification published in 2010 described five dimensions that must be closely considered when diagnosing an intellectual disability (American Association on Intellectual and Developmental Disabilities, 2010). These five dimensions consist of:

1. **Intellectual abilities (Dimension I):** Such as a child's reasoning, planning, abstract thinking, and their understanding of complex ideas.
2. **Adaptive behavior (Dimension II):** Such as social skills (interpersonal relationships and following rules), conceptual skills (concepts of money, self-direction), practical skills (eating, toileting, dressing, and other independent skills).
3. **Health (Dimension III):** Physical and psychological (mental well-being).
4. **Participation (Dimension IV):** Engagement in school, at home, in the community, and in society. This includes the child's daily interactions with peers and family members, and roles that the child might take later as an adult in the community and society.
5. **Context (Dimension V):** Environment and culture, including the child's immediate family, ethnic culture, language, religion, neighborhood, and sociopolitical environment.

Systems of support for children with intellectual disabilities should be provided based on these five dimensions. For example, a health support system (considering Dimension III) should consist of a comprehensive health care system that addresses the emotional, mental, and physical well-being of a child. This system should take into consideration factors such as nutrition, medication, physical exercise, and a positive behavior support system to enable the child to function successfully both at home and in the school and community (American Association on Intellectual and Developmental Disabilities, 2010).

The American Psychological Association specifies that three conditions must be present for a child to be diagnosed with an intellectual disability. These conditions consist of (1) an intellect functioning significantly below average (an IQ of approximately 70 or below, based on an accurate intelligence test), (2) impairments in adaptive functioning, and (3) the onset of the condition before the child is 18 years old (American Psychiatric Association, 2000). Based on the American Psychological Association's classification, the severity of intellectual disability is classified into four categories of mild, moderate, severe, and profound. (See Table 11.1 for the American Psychiatric Association's *Diagnostic and Statistical Manual* definition and classification.)

TABLE 11.1   The American Psychiatric Association's Classification of Intellectual Disability

Conditions Required for the Diagnosis of an Intellectual Disability

1. A significant below-average intellectual functioning: an IQ of approximately 70 or below on an individually administered IQ test.
   a. For infants, a clinical judgment of significantly below-average intellectual functioning is required.

2. Concurrent impairments in present adaptive skills functioning in at least two of the following areas:
   a. Communication
   b. Self-care
   c. Home living
   d. Social/interpersonal skills
   e. Use of community resources
   f. Self-direction
   g. Functional academic skills
   h. Work
   i. Leisure
   j. Health
   k. Safety

3. The onset is before the age of 18.

Classification of Intellectual Impairment

1. Mild mental retardation	IQ level 50 to approximately 70
2. Moderate mental retardation	IQ level 35 to 49
3. Severe mental retardation	IQ level 20 to 34
4. Profound mental retardation	IQ level below 20

Source: Adapted with permission from the American Psychiatric Association. (2000). *Diagnostic and statistical manual of mental disorders* (4th ed., text revision). Washington, DC: Author.

Children with a Mild Intellectual Disability

Between 75 to 85 percent of all children with an intellectual disability are considered to have a mild intellectual disability (Harris, 2006). These are children whose IQs range from 50 to 69 when assessed using a valid standardized intelligence instrument, such as the Binet test (American Psychiatric Association, 2000). With the exception of certain disorders associated with intellectual disability, such as fragile X syndrome or Down syndrome, children with mild intellectual disabilities do not have any distinctive physical characteristics and may not be identified early on. It is usually after age 2 that their difficulties with speech and language development might cause concern in parents or early educators. Language problems in these children might limit their abilities in different areas of development. However, with appropriate intervention, children with a mild intellectual disability are capable of learning social and academic skills, and can learn to function independently.

In Europe, some scholars and educators (McMillan, Gresham, & Siperstein, 1993) have questioned the use of the category of mild intellectual disability, because in most European countries, as a child with a mild intellectual disability enters school, he or she usually receives a diagnosis of a learning disability as opposed to an intellectual disability to avoid the stigma attached to the latter diagnosis. In the United States, however, diagnoses of learning disabilities are applied to children who have an average or above-average intelligence range, but have difficulties in specific academic areas.

Children with a Moderate Intellectual Disability

Children with a moderate intellectual disability have an IQ range of 35 to 49 and make up about 10 percent of the population of all children with intellectual disabilities (American Psychiatric Association, 2000). The level of language impairments varies among different children in this group. Where some children might acquire speech and be able to carry on simple conversations, other children might have to use augmentative communication devices or sign language to communicate. Some children in this group might develop good social skills, where other children in this group might have social impairments due to Autism Spectrum and related disorders (Harris, 2006). With appropriate intervention and support, young children with a moderate intellectual disability are able to learn basic academic skills and independent adaptive skills.

Children with a Severe Intellectual Disability

Children with a severe intellectual disability have an IQ range of 20 to 34. This group makes up about 3 to 4 percent of children with an intellectual disability (American Psychiatric Association, 2000). The majority of these children have severe language and communication impairments. Motor problems, seizures, and other physical disabilities might also be present and be severe, so that specialized care is necessary for some of these children (Harris, 2006). During early childhood years, children with a severe intellectual disability are readily identified because of their lack of motor coordination and language development. As they develop, these children are likely to require continued support through adulthood.

Children with a Profound Intellectual Disability

The IQ for children with a profound intellectual disability is below 20 (American Psychiatric Association, 2000). This population makes up about 1 to 2 percent of the total number of children with an intellectual disability (Harris, 2006). The neurological impairments in these children often create severe motor and mobility problems. Language understanding and communication are very limited in children with profound intellectual disabilities. Early intervention and appropriate support for such children focus on functional self-help skills, the enhancement of motor abilities, coordination, mobility, and functional communication skills. These children will require continued support throughout adulthood.

CAUSES OF INTELLECTUAL DISABILITIES

Understanding the cause or *etiology* of intellectual disabilities is necessary for the assessment, diagnosis, and classification of children with an intellectual disability. In addition, understanding the causes of an intellectual disability will help in the design of interventions and the provision of appropriate services. Four aspects to consider could help professionals pinpoint the causes of an intellectual disability as described by Percy (2007):

1. **The severity of the intellectual impairment:** The more severe the impairment, the more likely that the cause is genetic or biomedical.
2. **The severity of sensory impairments associated with an intellectual disability:** Children with known causes of an intellectual disability often have hearing, speech, and language impairments, cerebral palsy, seizures, and so on.
3. **The gender of the child with an intellectual disability:** More boys are found to have intellectual disabilities as compared with girls.
4. **Scientific technology:** Advances in molecular biology, brain imaging technologies, and genetics have helped with the identification of a variety of developmental and intellectual disabilities that have a genetic basis.

Intellectual disabilities have two general categories of causal factors: biological and environmental factors. Environmental factors consist of social, behavioral, and educational risk factors (American Association on Mental Retardation, 2002). A mild intellectual disability has often been associated with environmental factors, whereas a more severe intellectual disability is frequently associated with neurobiological causes (Batshaw et al., 2007; Noble, Tottenham, & Casey, 2005; Percy, 2007).

Social Risk Factors

Social factors are specific, socially driven risks that children might face from birth (for a more detailed discussion of children at risk, see Chapter 13). Poverty, for example, is a social risk factor that might lead to a lack of good nutrition, and a lack of medical care for both the parent and the child. Lack of access to prenatal care and good nutrition during pregnancy are important risk factors which might cause damage to the central nervous system in the fetus and put the child at risk for an intellectual disability (Centers for Disease Control, 2006). Postnatal environmental factors, such as malnutrition (e.g., protein and vitamin deficiencies) and a lack of appropriate stimulation for a child with an initial biological insult (e.g., intrauterine growth restriction), can compound the problem and put the child at risk for an intellectual disability (Batshaw et al., 2007; Percy, 2007; National Research Council Institute of Medicine, 2000).

Behavioral Risk Factors

Inappropriate parental behaviors frequently put children at risk for developmental problems. For example, parental drug and alcohol use and smoking are established risk conditions that might cause cognitive impairment and other developmental problems in children (National Research Council Institute of Medicine, 2000) (see Chapter 2 for a further discussion). Child abuse and neglect, domestic violence, and inadequate safety measures also present serious risks for children's cognitive, social-emotional, and physical development (American Association on Mental Retardation, 2002).

Educational Risk Factors

Lack of parental knowledge on how to take care of the mother during pregnancy pose an important risk to the development of the fetus. On the other hand, parents who are emotionally and mentally unprepared for the birth of their baby might not be able to provide appropriate nurturance, care, and stimulation, which the child needs in order to have a healthy development (National Research Council Institute of Medicine, 2000; American Association on Mental Retardation, 2002). An unawareness of the importance of appropriate medical care for the child after birth and during early childhood might cause a delayed diagnosis when a serious health or developmental problem threatens the child. Because early intervention is a key to a positive child developmental outcome, a delayed diagnosis will certainly deprive the child of appropriate early intervention. Deprivation of appropriate early intervention and special education services might inevitably prevent the child from having valuable chances for progress and possible recovery (American Association on Mental Retardation, 2002).

Considering the ecological view of development, these categories of risk factors often interact with one another. The interaction of these factors might exacerbate the possibility of an intellectual disability in the child, even when one single factor is not strong enough to create such a condition by itself. For example, an infant might be born with an inborn error of metabolism, such as phenylketonuria (PKU). PKU is a metabolic disorder in which the body is unable to utilize the amino acid phynelalanine (see Chapter 2 for more on the topic). Without appropriate treatment, PKU can result in brain damage (an intellectual disability) in the child (Batshaw, 2007). Screening for PKU is done for all infants in hospitals in most countries of the world.

Where with an appropriate diet and monitoring by professionals an intellectual disability in the child can be averted, many infants with this disorder who are born in poverty-stricken regions of the world usually go undiagnosed and untreated. Even if diagnoses were possible for some of these infants, lack of access to appropriate nutrition in families of these children would make it less likely for these infants to have an appropriate diet.

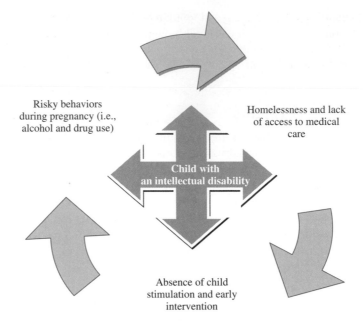

The interactions of risk factors contributing to an intellectual disability are exhibited in Figure 11.1. In this illustration, homelessness, a lack of access to appropriate prenatal and postnatal care, risky behaviors during pregnancy, and the absence of appropriate child stimulation are conditions that might occur because of poverty and lack of parental education. Interactions of different risk factors with one another might cause an intellectual disability in the young child, even when the child would have not been biologically predisposed to have an intellectual disability.

DIAGNOSIS OF INTELLECTUAL DISABILITIES

The diagnosis of children with intellectual disabilities is conducted by a number of professionals, such as psychologists, neurologists, and other health care professionals when a genetic or biological condition is present. The intellectual functioning of these children is usually measured using a valid standardized psychological test conducted by a trained professional who is familiar with children with intellectual disabilities. The most commonly used psychological tests for children older than 3 years of age are the Wechsler scales, such as WPPSI-III and WISC-IV (Wechsler, 1991, 2002, 2003). One word of caution about use of IQ tests in children with intellectual disabilities is that some children might have a range of cognitive abilities in different areas. For example, they might have strong visual motor abilities, but have severe language impairments. This type of variability is often not measured via typical intelligence testing (Switzky & Greenspan, 2006). Therefore, an IQ score alone might not be an accurate representation of the range of intellectual abilities in these children.

Intelligence in Intellectual Disabilities

Intelligence is an overall mental capacity, which includes the ability to reason, solve problems, think abstractly, plan, learn from experience, and understand one's surroundings (American Association on Mental Retardation, 2002). Great controversy has arisen among scholars about measuring intelligence. Where some scholars believe that intelligence is a unilateral trait that can be measured and represented by an IQ score, others believe that intelligence is not a single entity and therefore cannot be measured and certainly not represented by a single score. Howard Gardner, for example, believes that there are eight distinct intelligences, each of which is independent of one another (Walters & Gardner, 1986).

Gardner devised his theory of multiple intelligences (MI) from his observation of typically and atypically developing children. Gardner believes that an IQ test does not capture a child's full range of intelligence. His theory recognizes many different facets of cognition, attesting that people have different cognitive strengths and styles (Gardner, 2006). Gardner's initial model consisted of seven different intelligences to which he later added an eighth intelligence. These intelligences consist of linguistic, logical-mathematical, spatial, musical, bodily-kinesthetic, interpersonal, intrapersonal, and naturalistic intelligence. Table 11.2 describes each of these intelligences.

Gardner defines intelligence as one's capacity to solve problems or create things that are valued in a specific culture (Gardner, 2006). From this point of view, a child with an intellectual disability might have one or more specific intelligences that are not measured through traditional IQ tests. The traditional intelligence tests measure only three types of intelligence: linguistic (i.e., the ability to use oral and written

TABLE 11.2   Gardner's Eight Intelligences in the Theory of Multiple Intelligences

Musical intelligence	Musical abilities, such as understanding pitch, sounds, and playing an instrument
Bodily-kinesthetic intelligence	Abilities to control bodily movements, as demonstrated by athletes and dancers
Logical-mathematical intelligence	Problem-solving and logical reasoning abilities, as demonstrated by scientists and lawyers
Linguistic intelligence	Abilities in the use of language for different expressions, such as that of poets, writers, and public speakers
Spatial intelligence	Abilities in visualization and understanding space, size, angles, and objects to solve problems or create things, such as that found in sea navigators, artists, or architects
Interpersonal intelligence	The ability to understand emotional and mental distinctions among others, such as differences in moods, temperament, motivations, and intention, as demonstrated in social leaders, teachers, salespersons, or therapists
Intrapersonal intelligence	Knowledge of one's own internal aspect; for example, feelings, emotional range, and thinking, and to be able to guide one's behavior based on that knowledge
Naturalistic intelligence	Ability in identifying and distinguishing between diverse plants, animals, mountains, or cloud configurations in their ecological niches

Source: Gardner, H. (2006). *Multiple intelligence: New horizons, completely revised and updated.* New York: Basic Books.

language), logical-mathematical (i.e., problem-solving ability), and spatial intelligences (i.e., understanding space, size, shapes, and their properties) (Davidson & Downing, 2000). Consider, for example, the case of Malcolm, the 7-year-old-child whose IQ score we earlier calculated to be 43. Malcolm is identified as having a moderate intellectual disability. Malcolm has a strong musical ability. He is able to play the piano, and has a nice singing voice. Malcolm's musical intelligence is undetected through use of a typical IQ test, such as the Wechsler Intelligence Scale for Children, WISC-IV, a standardized instrument that measures cognitive strengths and weaknesses in children (Wechsler, 2003).

Despite the efforts of numerous scholars to change views of intelligence, with the exception of its educational application, Gardner's theory of multiple intelligences and other similar theories remain theoretical (American Association on Mental Retardation, 2002). Although, some newly developed instruments are available, such as the Cognitive Assessment Instrument (Naglieri & Das, 1997) and the Wide Range Intelligence Test (Glutting, Adams, & Sheslow, 2000), which provide the full range of intellectual functioning, these measurement instruments are not commonly known or used broadly.

Adaptive Skills

Children who are diagnosed with an intellectual disability not only must have a limitation in intellectual functioning, but must show impairments in their ability to adapt and function in daily life (Ditterline & Oakland, 2009; Batshaw et al., 2007). Adaptive skills refer to the children's abilities to perform age-appropriate behaviors in relation to self-care, hygienic needs, and other areas that let them adapt to their environment and different circumstances (American Association on Mental Retardation, 2002). Adaptive skills usually consist of a combination of skills in different areas of development. For example, putting shoes on and tying the shoe laces independently before going outside are a set of adaptive skills. For a child to demonstrate mastery of this skill, he or she needs to have several other developmental skills: (1) appropriate fine and gross motor abilities to tie the shoe laces, (2) good coordination, and (3) a general knowledge and awareness (cognition) to put his shoes on and tie the laces before going outside.

Assessment of adaptive skills in early childhood is usually accomplished by parent interviews and the teacher's observation of the child's independent and self-help skills in the classroom. Several adaptive behavior standardized scales can be used for assessing adaptive behaviors in children. Vineland Adaptive Behavior Scales, Second Edition (Vineland II) is an adaptive skills measurement instrument in a survey interview format completed by parents, caregivers, or teachers, which is frequently used for young children as well as older children (Sparrow, Balla, & Cicchetti, 2005).

DISORDERS ASSOCIATED WITH INTELLECUTAL DISABILITIES

The knowledge regarding the disorders associated with an intellectual disability is changing rapidly (Percy et al., 2007). Advances in genetics have resulted in the identification of over 1000 different genetic causes of intellectual disabilities, which contribute to 55 percent of cases of children with moderate to severe intellectual disabilities and 10 to 15 percent of children with mild intellectual disabilities (Tartaglia, Hansen, & Hagerman, 2007). A description and discussion of all disorders associated with intellectual disability is beyond the scope of this book. In this section, we will only examine those disorders that are relatively more common or are better known.

Down Syndrome

Down syndrome is the most commonly known genetic intellectual disability. The prevalence of Down syndrome is approximately 1 in every 733 individuals according to a report released by the Centers for Disease Control in 2006 (Centers for Disease Control, 2006). This disorder was discovered by a British physician, John Langdon Down in 1866 (Lovering & Percy, 2007). Originally known as *mongolism,* the disorder was renamed as Down's syndrome in the 1970s, and later as simply Down syndrome. Down syndrome is a chromosomal abnormality with genetic causes.

Human cells normally have 46 chromosomes, which are arranged in 23 pairs. Cell divisions occur by mitosis (where one cell becomes two and each cell has the exact number and type of chromosome) or by meiosis (when one cell splits into two, resulting in each cell having half the number of chromosomes of the original parent cell). When cells divide, an error might occur. In the majority of cases of Down syndrome, there is an extra number of chromosome 21. This is known as trisomy 21 ("tri" means three and "somy" refers to chromosome). Although most cases of Down syndrome are caused by trisomy 21, approximately 4 percent are caused by an extra part of the chromosome 21 being attached to another chromosome (Lovering & Percy, 2007). In other children with Down syndrome, the cause might be an extra whole chromosome 21 in only a proportion of their body's cells (Selikowitz, 1997; Batshaw, 2007).

Down syndrome can be identified through prenatal screening and diagnostic tests. The screening might consist of an initial blood test, which seeks to identify high levels of certain chemical markers typical of Down syndrome. A fetal ultrasound analysis can also be done to screen for this disorder (Lovering & Percy, 2007).

Down syndrome is the most commonly known genetic intellectual disability.

The screening results might direct the medical professionals to conduct further diagnostic tests. Prenatal diagnostic procedures might include the following:

> **Amniocentesis between 14 to 18 weeks of pregnancy:** In amniocentesis, a needle is inserted below the umbilical cord through the abdominal and uterine walls to collect 1 to 2 ounces of amniotic fluid, something which is usually reproduced within 24 hours (Schonberg & Tifft, 2007).
> **Chorionic villus sampling (CVS) between 9 and 11 weeks of pregnancy:** CVS is a biopsy of the chorion, the outermost membrane surrounding the embryo (Schonberg & Tifft, 2007).
> **Percutaneous umbilical blood sampling (PUBS) between 18 to 22 weeks:** In PUBS, a needle is inserted through the abdominal walls and directed to the umbilical vein to get a small sample of fetal blood. This procedure is done under ultrasound guidance (Schonberg & Tifft, 2007; Batshaw, 2007; Harris, 2006).

Physical and Developmental/Behavioral Characteristics of Down Syndrome

Down syndrome has specific physical characteristics known to professionals, which makes a diagnosis possible immediately after birth, even if a prenatal diagnosis had not been made earlier. Down syndrome's physical anomalies include, but might not be limited to, upturned outward slanting eyes, a low hair line, a smaller than typical head size, relatively short upper arms, a large cleft between the first and second toes, short fingers, broad hands, folded skin in the upper eyelids, flat nasal bridge, and short stature (Batshaw, 2007; Lovering & Percy, 2007).

Children with Down syndrome most commonly have a moderate to severe intellectual disability (Harris, 2006). Although they vary in rate of development, in general they develop at a slower rate than typically developing children in all developmental domains (Selikowitz, 1997). For example, the muscle control abilities in infants with Down syndrome might be slower. They might begin to sit, crawl, and walk later than typically developing children. Children with Down syndrome might not learn basic cognitive concepts such as shapes or colors as quickly as other children typically would. The slow rate of growth for these children seems to hold from before birth to adolescence (Lovering & Percy, 2007).

Sensory impairments such as vision and hearing problems are frequent, occurring in about 60 percent of children with Down syndrome (Roizen, 2007). Hearing loss is present in about two-thirds of children with Down syndrome, which frequently leads to specific deficits in speech and language production in many of these children (Lovering & Percy, 2007; Roizen, 2007). In addition to sensory issues, the auditory or verbal short-term memory present in these children frequently leads to problems in listening comprehension and in expressive language by the time they enter preschool (Chapman & Hesketh, 2001; Camarata, Yoder, & Camarata, 2006). Recent research has found a specific molecular mechanism that might account for problems in learning in children with Down syndrome (Glue & Patterson, 2009). The implication of this finding raises the possibility that drug treatments might be developed to target this mechanism and therefore enhance learning in children with Down syndrome (Glue et al., 2009).

Fragile X Syndrome

Intellectual disabilities that are related to X-linked disorders are collectively referred to as "X-linked mental retardation (XLMR)" by medical professionals. Fragile X syndrome is the most common of X-linked disorders and the most common inherited cause of intellectual disability around the world (Meyer, 2007). In 1991, it was discovered that fragile X syndrome is caused by the mutation of a single gene called the fragile X mental retardation 1 (FMR1) gene (Tartaglia et al., 2007). This gene is located on the long arm of the X chromosome. The FMR1 gene is not able to produce the protein that the gene would normally make. About 1 in 130 females and 1 in 800 males carry the FMR1 gene with a small defect (Finestack, Richmond, & Abbeduto, 2009; Tartaglia et al., 2007). The condition of a gene with a small defect is called permutation. In individuals with permutation, the region of DNA is stretched longer than it normally would be. The carriers of fragile X permutation do not show any symptoms of fragile X. Although children with permutation fragile X might not have any typical symptoms of the disorder, they might develop ADHD or social emotional difficulties during adolescence and adulthood (Tartaglia et al., 2007).

When the fragile X permutation is passed from a woman to her children, the DNA stretch might grow longer to become a full mutation, called fragile X syndrome. A male child who inherits the full mutation exhibits all symptoms of fragile X, while the female child might not exhibit all symptoms because females have two X chromosomes, while males have only one X chromosome. Accordingly, each female cell needs only one X chromosome that it randomly selects, while deactivating the other X chromosome (Fragile X Research Foundation, 2007).

About 85 percent of boys and 25 percent of girls with fragile X syndrome have an intellectual disability, while others might have learning disabilities or autism (Tartaglia et al., 2007). Approximately 1 in every 4,000 males and 1 in every 6,000 females of all ethnic backgrounds are affected by fragile X syndrome (Crawford, 2001). Many children with fragile X syndrome might have a decline in their cognitive functioning over time, the reason of which might be related to molecular variables (Tartaglia et al., 2007).

The Physical and Developmental/Behavioral Characteristics of Fragile X Syndrome

The most common physical features associated with fragile X in males are long face, prominent jaw and forehead, and large protruding ears (Tartaglia et al., 2007; Meyer, 2007). Depending on the severity of the symptoms in girls, they might display some or all physical characteristics. These features might not be readily detectable in infants, but might become more noticeable during middle and late childhood.

In terms of development, children with fragile X syndrome have a variety of developmental characteristics. Young children with fragile X syndrome usually have an intellectual disability by age 4 (Baily et al., 1998). The severity of the intellectual disability can range from mild cognitive difficulties and learning disabilities to a severe intellectual disability (Mazzocco & Holden, 2007). Problems in speech and language development are common during early childhood, and some children might require augmentative communication methods in order to communicate with others (Finestack et al., 2009; Meyer, 2007).

Many young children with fragile X syndrome display symptoms of sensory overreactivity (Fragile X Research Foundation, 2007). These are especially noticeable in the areas of tactile (sense of touch) and vestibular (movement and balance) systems. Tantrums might be common during early childhood years due to significant problems with sensory processing (Tartaglia et al., 2007). These might appear in the form of anxiety or challenging behaviors in environments that are noisy or otherwise overstimulating. Repetitive behaviors such as hand flapping and self-injurious behaviors might also be common in some children with fragile X syndrome (Moss, Oliver, Arron, Burbidge, & Berg, 2009; Baily et al., 1998).

As mentioned earlier, some children with fragile X syndrome receive a secondary diagnosis of autism, or have social relatedness difficulties and aggressive behaviors (Murphy & Abbeduto, 2005). A majority of boys have significant hyperactivity, or impulsiveness, and might also receive a secondary diagnosis of ADHD (Tartaglia et al., 2007).

Velocardiofacial Syndrome (22q11.2 Deletion)

Velocardiofacial syndrome (VCFS) was discovered in 1981. This disorder results from a deletion in a small piece of the long arm of chromosome 22 (Percy et al., 2007). VCFS along with other disorders such as Pierre Robin syndrome and DiGeorge syndrome are rare syndromes that have a deletion in chromosome 22. These are collectively called 22q11.2 deletion disorders (Harris, 2006; Gothelf & Lombroso, 2001). VCFS is the second most common genetic disorder after Down syndrome, affecting 1 in every 4,000 children (Gothelf & Lombroso, 2001). The diagnosis of VCFS is done using a technology called *fluorescence in situ hybridization* (*FISH*). This technology allows for detection of any gene deletion, which is otherwise not detectable under a standard microscope (Tartaglia et al., 2007). Prenatal testing, such as amniocentesis and CVS are available for fetuses that are at risk for this disorder as a result of their family's genetic history.

Physical and Developmental/Behavioral Characteristics of Velocardiofacial Syndrome (22q11.2 Deletion)

More than 180 developmental and behavioral characteristics are associated with VCFS (Goldberg, Motzkin, Marion, Scambler, & Shprintzen, 1993). A majority of children with this disorder, about 75 percent, have congenital heart disease, and about 83 percent have palatal abnormalities, such as a cleft palate (Gothelf & Lombroso, 2001; Harris, 2006). Typical physical features are a narrow face, a prominent tubular nose, and a bulbous nasal tip (Harris, 2006).

The most common developmental characteristics of children with VCFS are mild intellectual impairments and learning disabilities, which occur in almost all children with this disorder (Gothelf, Frisch, Michaelovsky, Weizman, & Shprintzen, 2009; Harris, 2006). Psychiatric problems are also common in these children as they grow up (Gothelf & Lombroso, 2001). Two developmental weaknesses in these children are problems with visual spatial abilities and abstract reasoning. Preschool children with VCFS might have poor memory and delays in language development. Difficulties with language are more pronounced in expressive language. The majority of children with VCFC have social-emotional competency issues. They might be shy or withdrawn or look disinterested in and unconcerned about other children and adults (Tartaglia et al., 2007; Harris, 2006).

Fetal Alcohol Spectrum Disorders

Fetal alcohol spectrum disorders (FASD) is a term that was recommended by Barr and Streissguth (2001) to describe a range of disorders caused by the mother's alcohol consumption during pregnancy. FASD includes fetal alcohol syndrome (FAS). Fetal alcohol syndrome is the most common nonhereditary cause of an intellectual disability in children. The prevalence of fetal alcohol spectrum disorders in general is about 1 in every 100 live births in the United States (Burbacher & Grant, 2006) and about 0.5 to 2 children in every 1,000 births are affected by fetal alcohol syndrome (May & Gossage, 2001).

The severity of FASD in children depends on the frequency and amount of alcohol consumed by the mother during pregnancy. As little as one drink per day might result in problems with the fetus' growth (May & Gossage, 2001). Alcohol can affect most areas of brain development and might cause a variety of developmental problems after birth (Arzumanyan, Anni, Rubin, & Rubin, 2009; Nulman, Ickowicz, Koren, & Knittel-Keren, 2007).

The most common physical characteristics of fetal alcohol syndrome include low birth weight, small head size, and small eye openings (Harris, 2006). Infants with FAS might have problems with sleeping and sucking. Mild to severe intellectual disabilities and poor motor coordination are common in children with FAS (Tartaglia et al., 2007). Inattention, hyperactivity, poor memory, problems with abstract reasoning, speech and language delays, and reading and math learning disabilities in school-age children with fetal alcohol syndrome are also common (Burbacher & Grant, 2006). Young children with FAS might have problems in the areas of social emotional development. In particular, some children with FAS are prone to conducting inappropriate behaviors without understanding the consequences (Nulman et al., 2007).

Other Disorders

A number of other disorders are known to be associated with intellectual disabilities. These disorders are less common in children than those just described.

Smith-Magenis Syndrome

Smith-Magenis syndrome is a genetic disorder affecting about 1 in every 15,000 to 25,000 children (Greenburg et al., 1991). This disorder is caused by deletion of genetic material on chromosome 17p11.2. Smith-Magenis syndrome is diagnosed via FISH testing. In FISH testing, the presence of specific chromosomes or chromosomal regions are identified under fluorescent lighting via fluorescently labeled DNA probes (Tartaglia et al., 2007). General physical characteristics include a broad square-shaped face, prominent jaw, and down-turned mouth (Percy et al., 2007). During infancy, children with this disorder might have sleep problems. Other developmental problems include intellectual disabilities; language delays; and a range of problem behaviors, such as self-injurious behaviors, attention-seeking behaviors, mood shifts, anger bouts, and hyperactivity (Harris, 2006).

Turner Syndrome

Turner syndrome is a disorder occurring in girls, and results from absence of an X chromosome. Although Turner syndrome is genetic, it is not hereditary, because the loss of the X chromosome could occur during conception (Percy et al., 2007). Physical features include short stature and failure in sexual maturation during puberty. Five percent of girls with Turner syndrome may have an intellectual disability (Harris, 2006). Anxiety and problems with social relatedness might be present in young girls with Turner syndrome.

Lesch-Nyhan Syndrome

This disorder is inherited in an X-linked recessive manner and is passed on by the mother to the son. Lesch-Nyhan is caused by an inborn metabolic error, which causes the buildup of uric acid in body fluids (Percy et al., 2007). This eventually leads to intellectual disability, poor muscle control, and severe gout in children (Tartaglia et al., 2007). The major behavioral characteristic of this disorder is severe self-injurious behaviors initially beginning with self-biting in early childhood years and progressing to more severe self-mutilating behaviors (Harris, 2006).

Prader-Willi Syndrome

Prader-Willi syndrome is a genetic disorder of chromosome 15, which affects 1 in every 10,000 to 22,000 children (Percy et al., 2007; Harris, 2006). Children with Prader-Willi syndrome are usually overweight. Although during infancy, poor weight gain due to feeding problems is an issue, between age 1 and 6 these children begin to gain weight rapidly (Harris, 2006). Children with Prader-Willi have a range of cognitive abilities. Most of them have a mild to moderate intellectual disability. School-age children with Prader-Willi might have learning disabilities in the areas of math and reading (Tartaglia et al., 2007). Young children with this disorder have unusual food-related behaviors, such as compulsive eating, food seeking, and hording. They might also display challenging behaviors, such as opposition, temper tantrums, anxiety, and depression (Oliver, Woodcock, & Humphreys, 2009).

Angelman Syndrome

Similar to Prader-Willi, Angelman syndrome is a genetic disorder related to a deficiency in chromosome 15 (Percy et al., 2007). This disorder might go undetected during infancy because there is no developmental delay evident during a child's first months. Developmental delays in these children are often detectable around 6 to 12 months of age (Percy et al., 2007). Impairments consist of severe speech and language problems, and a severe to profound intellectual disability. Children with Angelman syndrome are sociable and laugh frequently and inappropriately (Tartaglia et al., 2007).

Williams Syndrome

Williams syndrome is a rare genetic disorder causing mild to moderate intellectual disability. Children with this disorder have an unusual facial appearance, consisting of a broad forehead, medial eyebrow flare, depressed nasal bridge, widely spaced teeth, full lips, wide mouth, and prominent cheeks (Percy et al., 2007). Children with Williams syndrome might have cardiovascular problems caused by narrowed arteries (Tartaglia et al., 2007). Developmentally, although they have some level of cognitive impairment, their expressive language abilities are strong. Children with Williams syndrome are often characterized as extremely sociable and friendly, and showing excessive empathy even to strangers (Harris, 2006).

STRATEGIES AND ADAPTATIONS FOR INCLUSIVE CLASSROOMS

The term *best practices* is frequently used in fields of early intervention and intellectual and developmental disabilities to refer to diagnostic and intervention methodologies that through research and experience have proven to be reliable and effective (Sandall, Hemmeter, Smith, & McLean, 2005; Percy et al., 2007). Best practices are likely to ensure all children's developmental and educational success. Using best practices with children with intellectual disabilities in particular requires a commitment to use all the reliable knowledge and technologies available to ensure their progress (Percy, 2007).

In Chapter 4, we described the concept of differentiated instruction. In other chapters, we discussed and recommended different methods of working with children of various abilities and with different needs. In an inclusive early childhood classroom where children with intellectual disabilities are educated, best practices include appropriate differentiated instruction using various methods and techniques

In an inclusive early childhood classroom where children with intellectual disabilities are educated, best practices include appropriate differentiated instruction so as to promote the success of children with intellectual disabilities and their typical peers in their learning and living communities.

that we have previously discussed. These are combined and adapted so as to promote the success of children with intellectual disabilities and their typical peers in their learning and living communities. Here we will discuss how some of these methods can be used to help children with intellectual disabilities in inclusive environments in addition to other strategies.

Responsive Teaching

Responsive teaching is an early intervention curriculum and teaching strategy that was developed by Gerald Mahoney beginning in the 1980s. This curriculum is appropriate for toddlers and preschool children, and has been successfully used with young children with intellectual disabilities, such as Down syndrome and other developmental disabilities (Mahoney, Fingers, & Powell, 1985; Mahoney, 1988; Mahoney & McDonald, 2007).

Responsive teaching was designed to be implemented by parents and professionals who spend a significant amount of time caring for young children. It focuses on helping children develop important early skills that are foundations of development and learning, such as joint attention, social play, problem solving, cooperation, and feelings of competence (Mahoney, Perales, Wiggers, & Herman, 2006). In particular, responsive teaching promotes three domains of developmental functioning (Mahoney et al., 2006):

1. **Cognitive function:** Focusing on the child's ability to think, reason, solve problems, and learn new information
2. **Communication function:** Focusing on the child's ability to convey feelings, observations, and intentions and respond to the feelings and actions of others through nonverbal, symbolic, and expressive language
3. **Social-emotional function:** Focusing on the ability of the child to engage in and enjoy developmentally appropriate interactions with peers and adults, and to comply with reasonable rules and expectations

In this method, parents and professionals join the child's activity and support the child's learning by saying and doing things that are similar to what their children are doing (Mahoney et al., 2007). Professionals and parents who use responsive teaching primarily focus on encouraging young children to build on those skills that children already have, instead of teaching them new skills. In fact, responsive teaching builds on a class of behaviors (such as attention, persistence, imitation, initiation, and affect) that are pivotal to early learning. These are skills that infants and young children must themselves demonstrate in order to be ready to learn more complex developmental behaviors (Mahoney et al., 2006). Responsive teaching strategies consist of five interactive dimensions (Mahoney et al., 2006):

1. **Reciprocity:** Engage the child. Keep a balance between the child's actions and your own actions. Join the child during games, routines, and other naturally occurring activities.
2. **Contingency:** Observe and be aware of the child's behaviors. Have accurate timing in responding to the child's signals and behaviors. Understand the child's

intent through the child's nonverbal actions. Frequently examine your own responsiveness and behaviors.

3. **Shared control:** Use moderate direction by communicating with the child without asking questions; imitating the child's actions and communicative behaviors; and giving the child choices. Facilitate the child's learning by playing with a purpose; expanding on the child's play to show the child the next developmental step; expanding on the child's intention to help the child develop topics. Change the environment when needed to keep the child interested.

4. **Affect:** Be animated, playful, and interesting to the child. Use gestures and nonverbal communication when needed. Take enjoyment in the child's play. Be warm and gentle. Accept the child by valuing what the child does and by praising the child.

5. **Match:** Have interactions that developmentally match what the child does. Have interactions that match the interest level of the child. Have interactions that match the behavioral style of the child by being sensitive to the child's behavioral cues.

Appropriate Use of Prompts to Promote Independent Task Learning

In Chapter 6, we briefly described applied behavior analysis and methods of prompting children in order to promote independent task learning. Tasks are specific learning units that the child is required to learn in order to successfully perform academic as well as adaptive skills independently (Alberto & Troutman, 2006). All children require assistance at one time or another. Children with intellectual disabilities and physical motor problems require teachers' assistance more frequently in order to complete academic and adaptive tasks. Assistance and scaffolding are called prompts. Prompts are routinely provided to all children in early childhood classrooms to maximize learning.

A **prompt** is a specific teacher's scaffolding and assistance, which might be done through physical, gestural, or verbal means (Kauffman & Snell, 1977; Alberto & Troutman, 2006). Prompts should be provided for all young children as long as they are unable to complete a task independently. However, teachers must be careful so that children do not become prompt dependent. **Prompt dependency** occurs when teachers and parents routinely provide assistance during a task, whether or not the child has developed the appropriate skills to perform that task independently (Alberto & Troutman, 2006; Lionello-Denolf, Barros, & McIlvane, 2008). In such situations, children learn that an adult will always be at hand to help. Therefore, they might fail to develop a sense of initiative and independence. Our goal should be to fade prompts as soon as possible, so that children do not depend on peers or adults for continuous assistance. **Prompt fading** should be done as soon as children have learned to perform a task, so that independent functioning is promoted (Lionello-Denolf et al., 2008). Prompt fading is done gradually and as the child begins to demonstrate learning. In order to implement and fade prompts when needed, we first should understand different types of prompts in a **prompt hierarchy** (Parson & Reid, 1999; Kauffman & Snell, 1977; Wilder & Atwell, 2006). A prompt hierarchy contains different types of prompts in a system of most to least, or from a least to most intrusive type of scaffolding (Alberto & Troutman, 2006; Bondy, 1996).

Levels of Decreasing Prompts

In academic and adaptive task learning, prompt fading is done by decreasing the prompts from the most intrusive to the least intrusive type of assistance for children (McDonnell & Furguson, 1989). Academic and adaptive skills are tasks that children should learn to perform independently, such as putting on an item of clothing, washing hands, picking up toy items, playing appropriately with toys, putting a puzzle together, writing, or coloring. Levels of decreasing prompts are done gradually as the child has become familiar with the task and physically and cognitively demonstrated abilities to perform that task independently. The hierarchy of prompt from most to least restrictive consists of (Bondy, 1996):

> ➤ **Full physical prompt:** Full physical assistance such as a hand-over-hand prompt is usually done when the targeted task is physical in nature. Hand-over-hand prompt is a form of physical prompt in which the teacher guides the student by physically moving his or her hands in order to accomplish a task. For example, the adult might put his hand on the child's and move the child's hand to pick up a piece of puzzle and put it in the right place on the puzzle board; or the adult physically helps the child jump up and down by lifting the child from the floor. Full physical assistance should always be done from behind, so that the child does not visually expect assistance every time the task performance is expected. Assisting the child from behind also makes it easier for the adult to fade the prompt gradually.

> ➤ **Partial physical prompt:** A partial physical prompt is less intrusive. For example, as the child learns to grasp the puzzle piece, the adult might touch the child's hand to move and put the puzzle piece to the appropriate place. Or as the child learns to jump up and down, the teacher might encourage jumping by touching the child's arms.

> ➤ **Modeling:** In modeling, the teacher shows the child how to do a task without providing any kind of assistance. This is usually done when the child has learned to perform different motor acts and knows how to imitate others.

> ➤ **Gestural prompt:** A gestural prompt is accomplished by pointing to a specific object, touching the general area of a target object, or using body language or facial expressions to communicate what is expected of the child.

> ➤ **Direct verbal prompt:** A direct verbal prompt is making a statement of what the child would be required to do. For example, the teacher would say, "Make the puzzle," or "Jump up and down."

> ➤ **Indirect verbal prompt:** An indirect verbal prompt is a cue for the child to figure out what is expected. An indirect verbal prompt is usually in the form of a question. For example, the teacher puts the puzzle on the table and asks, "What do you need to do?" or points to an object and asks, "What is this?"

> ➤ Finally, a child's independence is achieved when the child has learned to perform a task without any need for assistance and scaffolding.

See Figure 11.2 for examples of prompts.

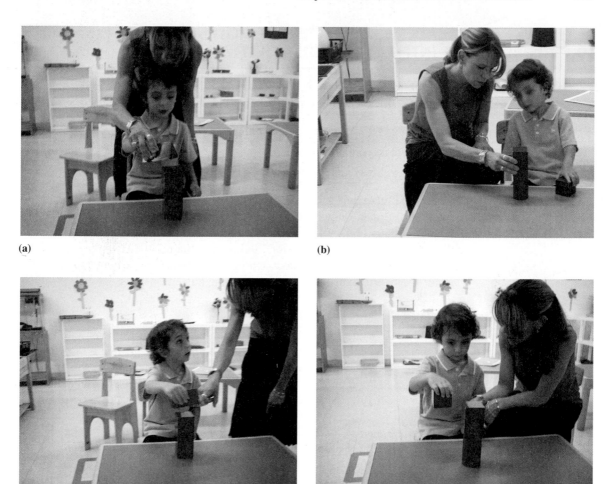

FIGURE 11.2 Examples of Prompts: (a) Full Physical Prompt, (b) Modeling, (c) Gestural Prompt, and (d) Indirect Verbal Prompt

Task Analysis

Recall our discussion of task analysis in Chapter 6. Task analysis is breaking a task into small achievable steps for the child and teaching the child each step individually (Bondy, 1996). With what we have learned about levels of prompts, it should be relatively easy to understand when and how to provide the appropriate prompt for the child to perform individual steps of a task. Decisions on how many steps a task should be broken into and what kind of prompts might be appropriate for a child to complete every step should always be made after we have done a thorough assessment of the child's developmental and functioning level, and have set specific IFSP and IEP goals. A task should be broken into realistic steps, and appropriate prompts should be provided based on the child's skills level. Prompt fading should occur as the child learns each step.

TEACHING EARLY ACADEMIC AND LITERACY SKILLS TO CHILDREN WITH INTELLECTUAL DISABILITIES

Early learning experiences for young children with intellectual disabilities usually revolve around learning basic physical, health, and cognitive skills to build awareness and independence (Downing, 2006). Children with intellectual disabilities might have limited life experiences due to their cognitive and communication impairments or other health issues (Arthur, 2003; Downing, 2006). In addition, they might receive partial or inadequate visual and auditory information from their environment as a result of their impairments (Lewis & Tolla, 2003).

Learning functional academic skills begins in preschool. Early functional academics consist of meaningful early literacy and numeracy skills that can help the child develop later literacy and math skills she will need to function successfully on a daily basis in the community (Taylor, Smiley, & Richards, 2009). In this section, we will describe some teaching methods appropriate for teaching early literacy skills. In Chapter 15, we will explain methods of teaching numeracy skills.

Teaching Early Literacy Skills

Several phonetic strategies are useful in facilitating the identification of letter–sound correspondence in children with intellectual disabilities. One method is the **sensory-kinesthetic approach to phonics** (Thiemann & Warren, 2004). In this strategy, which is used to build phonemic awareness in children, the teacher has children use their index fingers to trace letters made of sandpaper while the teacher says the word. Children who are able to vocalize repeat the sounds of each letter, and eventually the word, after the teacher's model.

Picture fading is another approach to literacy, in which the teacher presents a child with a picture card that carries its corresponding word printed on it. The teacher reads the word while handing the picture to the child. The child interacts with these pictures during their free play and instructed activities. The teacher gradually fades the picture on the card, leaving only the word in place, as the child learns to recognize the words. **Logo reading** (Tartaglia et al., 2007) is an example of the picture fading approach. In this approach, signs and logos that are in the daily environments of the child are used. Over time, logos are faded, while the describing words remain. For an example of logo teaching, see Figure 11.3. In this example, the logo picture can be used during play and in simple games. After the child has had repeated opportunities to interact and work with the picture, the picture is removed. Repeated exposures to the logo and hearing the sounds representing the logo, the

FIGURE 11.3
Logo Reading for Literacy

child learns to associate the picture with the letters and sounds of the words in the logo. She learns to recognize letters in these words and associate them with their appropriate sounds. By the time the picture is removed, the child has learned to read the word without its respective picture.

In addition to these strategies, assistive technology instruction in which specially designed hardware and software are utilized are also effective for working with children with intellectual disabilities. Assistive technology consists of a range of supports that help young children with disabilities increase, maintain, and improve their functioning capabilities (Mistrett, 2004). A range of assistive technology devices used to promote academic skills in children with disabilities is listed in Table 11.3.

Empowering Children with Intellectual Disabilities to Communicate and Conduct Appropriate Behaviors

In Chapter 9, we described the use of behavioral principles and the application of positive behavioral support in managing the behavior of children. Use of behavioral

TABLE 11.3   Assistive Technology and Computer Devices for Children with Disabilities to Enhance Early Academic Learning

Assistive Technology for Computer Use	Assistive Technology for Interaction with Books and Prints	Assistive Technology for Early Writing	Assistive Technology for Early Math
Keyboard: pointing aid, key guard, key labels (large braille letters), alternate and customized keyboard, keyboard overlay with object/pictures/words, switch + switch interface	Switch-operated recordable devices with repetitive storyline, comments	Adaptive writing tool (grip weights)	Adapted measuring tool
Mouse: adapted mouse, touch screen, trackball, and joystick	BookWorm Literacy Tool (AbleNet) with prerecorded pages of favorite book with switch use	Hand wrap/universal cuff for holding, arm support	Large button/display talking calculator
Large computer monitor, speakers, microphone, color printer, graphic/braille embosser, child and computer positioning aid	Book adapted with page turner, text label/symbols electronic reading systems (e.g., PowerTouch books)	Adaptive paper/outlines (raised, color lines)	Computer play set: Kitchen, construction
Digital microscope	Portable touch-activated reading and learning system	Software: "Word + Picture," "Create Books"	Software: building, sorting, counting

Sources: Technology Fan: Supports For Young Children; Technology and media division of the Council of Exceptional Children, available at www.tamcec.org; and Mistrett, S. (2004). Assistive technology helps young children with disabilities participate in daily activities. *Technology in Action, 1*(4).

principles, such as positive reinforcers, is extremely effective in working with children with intellectual disabilities. This is the case because motivation is a problem in some children with intellectual disabilities (Gilmore & Cuskelly, 2009). In fact, the term **learned helplessness** has frequently been used to describe the learning experiences of many children with intellectual and learning disabilities. The concept of learned helplessness was first introduced by Saligman and Maier in 1967, as a result of an experiment they were conducting in conditioning dogs. Later psychological experiments established this concept as a psychological condition that many individuals might experience when faced with repeated failures. Accordingly, learned helplessness is a condition in which one has learned to behave helpless in a particular situation, even if in reality the situation can easily be overcome. Learned helplessness usually occurs when a person has had repeated negative experiences in a situation and the person has come to believe that he has no control over the outcome of that specific situation.

Many older children with intellectual or learning disabilities, who have had unsuccessful or negative learning experiences early on, might eventually develop an attitude of learned helplessness. This attitude is marked by a lack of persistence or interest in doing tasks that realistically could be mastered (Gilmore & Cuskelly, 2009; Luchow, Crowl, & Kahn, 2001). Often, an extrinsic motivating factor such as a positive reinforcer is needed to encourage these children to learn.

Behavioral techniques when combined with visual strategies and support can successfully teach children with intellectual disabilities what to do and how to be successful. In addition, appropriate visual support helps increase the children's comprehension and communication, and therefore prevents or reduces frustration and behavioral outbursts (Jaime & Knowlton, 2007).

Social Stories

Although social stories are thought to be exclusively used for children within the Autism Spectrum Disorder, they have been effectively used for children with other disabilities, such as ADHD and children with intellectual disabilities, to increase the comprehension of functional academics and promote appropriate behaviors (Lougy, DeRuvo, & Rosenthal, 2007).

Choice Boards

Choice boards (Jaime & Knowlton, 2007) help children understand what may or may not be available in their environment. Choices for activities, food items during snack time, and toys or other materials might be presented by using photographs of the items, actual objects, or picture symbols. Choice boards have been used with children with intellectual disabilities to promote awareness and empower their choice making (Stafford, 2005).

The best way to use a choice board is to create individual small boards carrying the choices for a specific scheduled time (Jaime & Knowlton, 2007). For example, when it is time for small group activities, the teacher could present an *activity choice board,* containing pictures of the activities available in the open centers. During snack time, a *snack choice board* of food items available might be presented so that

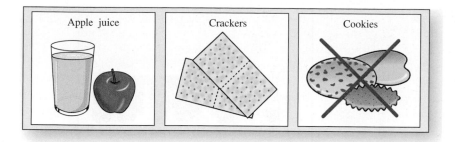

FIGURE 11.4
Example of a Snack Choice Board

the child can make appropriate choices. To prevent confusion and possible behavioral outbursts, only choices that are available should be presented (Hodgdon, 1998). If an item is not available for the time being, either the pertinent picture should be removed, or the unavailability of that item should be clearly specified. See Figure 11.4 for an example of a snack choice board. In this example, the board communicates to the child that cookies are not available today. Pictures can be photographs, hand-drawn, or computer-generated, such as the ones on this board. Pictures might be glued or fastened by Velcro. Removable pictures fastened with Velcro make it possible for the board to be used for different purposes and with a variety of pictures.

Token Boards

A token board is part of a token economy system. In a behavioral approach, a token economy system is used as a way of dispensing positive reinforcements in a systematic way (Kazdin, 1977; Lavigne et al., 1998; Alberto & Troutman, 2006). In this system, earned tokens are exchanged for a desired and reinforcing object or activity (Kazdin, 1994). Token economy systems have been widely used for children of all ages and with various disabilities, such as autism, ADHD, and intellectual disabilities (Tarbox, Ghezzi, & Wilson, 2006; Miltenberger, 2001; Kazdin, 1994) to encourage them to focus, increase compliance, or to complete academic and nonacademic tasks. For example, in such a system the teacher might want to have a child sit quietly during story time. The teacher decides that for every 2 to 3 minutes that the child is quiet, the child will receive a token. When the child has acquired a number of desired tokens, the child will receive a reward. A reward is a reinforcing object or activity that the child has previously chosen. Real coins, cut up pictures of objects of the child's interest, stars, or any other symbols that represent the child's accomplishment might be used as a token and posted on a token board. See Figure 11.5 for an example of a token board. In this example, the token board might be used during a teacher-directed activity, or for an independent activity that the teacher has assigned for the child (such as completing a puzzle or working with a peg board). The child has previously chosen a reinforcing object (toy train). Every time that the child completes a portion of the activity, the child receives a token. Once the child has received all the tokens required, the child is given the reward. The number of tokens to be received should be realistically achievable. This number can increase as the child learns to focus and complete activities more independently. The ultimate goal is that eventually the child will not need a token board for targeted behaviors or activities.

FIGURE 11.5
Example of a Token
Board

I am working for

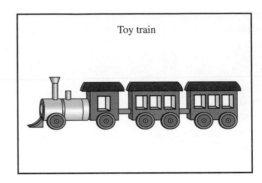

Toy train

Token # 1	Token # 2	Token # 3	Token # 4

Research Corner

Self-Determination

The goal of any educational system is to teach children to eventually become self-sufficient and productive citizens of their societies. Achieving this goal, as far as children with moderate to severe intellectual disabilities are concerned, has been far reaching in most special education systems of the world. Throughout the 1990s, a new area of study called **self-determination** has emerged in the special education field and disabilities studies. Self-determination has been recognized as an educational outcome for all students with disabilities. The concept of self-determination as described by Martin and Marshall (1995) refers to educating children so that they can choose "what they want and how to get it. From an awareness of personal needs, self-determined individuals choose goals, and then doggedly pursue them. This involves asserting an individual's presence, making his or her needs known, evaluating progress toward meeting goals, adjusting performance, and creating unique approaches to solve problems" (p.147). In other words, self-determined children are able to make things happen as they relate to their own lives (Wehmeyer, Abery, Mithuag, & Stancliffe, 2003). To do so, children ought to be able to make choices, solve problems, and set goals (Wehmeyer, 2001).

Strong evidence exists that during the early childhood years, teachers and parents can implement a self-determined learning model of instruction in the classroom and at home for children with a variety of disabilities (Erwin et al., 2009; Palmer & Wehmeyer, 2003). To implement such a learning model in an early childhood classroom, the following guidelines have been suggested (Holverstott, 2005):

> Find out what motivates your young students.
> Prioritize children's preferences and interests.
> Make children's activities meaningful and real.
> Allow children to be "causal agents" (e.g., give them space so they can make choices without any interference; and have their desires fulfilled by themselves or by someone else).
> Teach children how to make effective choices.
> Embed choice into every part of the school day and classroom activities.
> Give children an active role in deciding what they will learn.
> Process emotions associated with the decision-making process (e.g., regrets, sadness, anger, etc.).
> Enable children to emotionally self-regulate.
> Allow children to participate in goal setting (e.g., allow children to select a simple goal and help them learn how to achieve that goal).
> Allow children to earn a reward, no matter what.
> Build strategies, such as visual support, to promote self-determination and help them function independently.
> Learn with children.
> Listen actively to children.
> Remember that behaviors are communicative, no matter how unconventional they may seem.
> Build on pre-existing skills rather than targeting deficits.
> Enlist peers to help support students in becoming self-determined.
> Accept and value every child.

SUMMARY

The concept of intellectual disability has undergone a tremendous amount of change during the past two hundred years, from considering children and individuals with intellectual disabilities as feebleminded in the 19th century to advocating for them to receive educational and support services so they can become self-determined in the 21st century. Definitions and classifications of the term intellectual disability have evolved over the years. In general, an intellectual disability refers to limitations in intellectual functioning and daily adaptive skills that prevent the child from performing the day-to-day tasks required within his or her environment. A number of disorders have been associated with intellectual disabilities, many of which have genetic causes, such as Down syndrome and fragile X syndrome. These disorders may exhibit various physical, behavioral, and developmental characteristics.

Working with children with intellectual disabilities requires an in-depth understanding of the child's developmental level and characteristics, as well as differentiated instructions to help these children develop appropriate developmental skills and independence. Self-determination, the ability to make appropriate goals autonomously and follow those goals, should be the aim of any educational and supportive services for young children with intellectual disabilities.

Review Questions

1. What are two major societal developments in the early 20th century and how did they influence the professional treatment of intellectual disability?
2. Explain the difference between the terms *mental retardation* and *intellectual disability.*
3. Define *intellectual disability.*
4. Describe the classification of intellectual disability based on the APA classification system.
5. Name at least four disorders associated with intellectual disability.

6. Describe how genetics might contribute to intellectual disability. Provide one or more examples as needed to illustrate your reasoning.
7. What is a prompt?
8. What is a prompt hierarchy?
9. What is an example of task analysis and how might a system with a prompt hierarchy be used in a task analysis?
10. What are some ways of promoting self-determination in young children?

Out-of-Class Activities

1. Using the Recommended Resources list at the end of this chapter, conduct research on the eugenics movement in America and Europe, and write a paper describing the influences of this movement throughout history on the treatment of intellectual disability.
2. Conduct case studies of four young children with intellectual disabilities, each with different disorders. Observe each student in their learning and home environments (if possible), and make detailed notes of the way they interact socially and perform different learning activities through their play and structured time. Write a paper describing each case. Outline similarities and differences among these

children's developmental and learning characteristics. (Note that before you complete this activity, you should obtain permission from parents/guardians and the school/teachers to observe the children.)
3. Design a task analysis for an adaptive skill. Outline in detail a schedule of a prompt hierarchy and how you might use different prompts at each step of this task.
4. Write a lesson plan for logo teaching within a thematic play unit.
5. Make a token board for a structured small group activity. How often do you reinforce the child and why?

Recommended Resources

American Association of Intellectual and Developmental Disabilities
http://www.aamr.org/

Angelman Syndrome Foundation, Inc.
http://www.angelman.org

FRAZA—The Fragile X Research Foundation
http://www.fraxa.org

Image Archive on the American Archives on Eugenics Movement
http://www.eugenicsarchive.org

Mayer-Johnson, LLC
2100 Wharton Street

Pittsburgh, PA 15203
Phone: 858-550-0084
Fax: 858-550-0449
Email: mayerj@mayer-johnson.com
http://www.mayer-johnson.com/

National Down Syndrome Society
http://www.ndss.org

National Organization on Fetal Alcohol Syndrome
http://www.nofas.org

Parents and Researches Interested in Smith-Magenis Syndrome
http://www.prisms.org/start.htm

Prader-Willi Syndrome Association
http://www.pwsausa.org

The National Fragile X Foundation
http://www.nfxf.org

The Williams Syndrome Association
http://www.williams-syndrome.org

Velocardiofacial Educational Foundation, Inc.
http://www.vcfsef.org

**View the Online Resources available to accompany
this text by visiting http://www.mhhe.com/bayat1e.**

References

Alberto, P. A., & Troutman, A. C. (2006). *Applied behavior analysis for teachers* (7th ed.). Upper Saddle River, NJ: Pearson Education, Inc.

American Association on Intellectual and Developmental Disabilities. (2010). *Intellectual disability— Definition, classification, and systems of supports: The 11th edition of the AAIDD definition manual.* Washington, DC: Author.

American Association on Mental Retardation. (2002). *Mental retardation: Definition, classification, and systems of supports* (10th ed.). Washington, DC: Author.

American Psychiatric Association. (2000). *Diagnostic and statistical manual of mental disorders* (4th ed., text revision). Washington, DC: Author.

Arthur, M. (2003). Socio-communicative variables and behavior states in students with profound and multiple disabilities: Descriptive data from school settings. *Education and Training in Developmental Disabilities, 38,* 200–219.

Arzumanyan, A., Anni, H., Rubin, R., & Rubin, E. (2009). Effects of ethanol on mouse embryonic stem cells. *Alcoholism: Clinical & Experimental Research, 33*(2), 2172–2179.

Baily, D. B., Jr., Mesibov, G. B., Hatton, D. D., Clark, R. D., Roberts, J. E., & Mayhew, L. (1998). Autistic behavior in young boys with fragile X syndrome. *Journal of Autism and Developmental Disorders, 28*(6), 499–508.

Barr, H. M., & Streissguth, A. P. (2001). Identifying maternal self-reported alcohol use associated with fetal alcohol spectrum disorders. *Alcoholism: Clinical and Experimental Research, 25*(2), 283–287.

Batshaw, M. L. (2007). Genetics and developmental disabilities. In M. L. Batshaw, L. Pellegrino, & N. J. Roizen (Eds.), *Children with disabilities* (6th ed., pp. 3–21). Baltimore: Paul H. Brookes.

Batshaw, M. L., Shapiro, B., & Farber, M. L. (2007). Developmental delay and intellectual disability. In M. L. Batshaw, L. Pellegrino, & N. J. Roizen (Eds.), *Children with disabilities* (6th ed., pp. 245–261). Baltimore: Paul H. Brookes.

Bondy, A. (1996). *The pyramid approach to education: An integrative approach to teaching children and adults with autism* (1st ed.). Newark, DE: Pyramid Educational Consultants, Inc.

Braddock, D., & Parish, S. L. (2002). An institutional history of disability. In Braddock (Ed.), *Disability at the dawn of the 21st century and the state of the states* (pp. 3–61). Washington, DC: American Association on Mental Retardation.

Brown, I. (2007). What is meant by intellectual and developmental disabilities. In I. Brown & M. Percy (Eds.), *A comprehensive guide to intellectual and developmental disabilities* (pp. 3–15). Baltimore: Paul H. Brookes.

Brown, I., & Radford, J. P. (2007). Historical overview of intellectual and developmental disabilities. In I. Brown & M. Percy (Eds.), *A comprehensive guide to intellectual and developmental disabilities* (pp. 17–33). Baltimore: Paul H. Brookes.

Burbacher, T. M., & Grant, K. S. (2006). Neurodevelopmental effects of alcohol. In P. W. Davidson, G. J. Myers, & B. Weiss (Eds.), *International review of mental retardation research: Vol. 30. Neurotoxicity and developmental disabilities* (pp. 1–46). San Diego: Elsevier Academic Press.

Camarata, S., Yoder, P., & Camarata, M. (2006). Simultaneous treatment of grammatical and speech comprehensibility deficits in children with Down syndrome. *Down Syndrome Research and Practice, 11*(1), 9–17.

Centers for Disease Control. (2006). *Progress made in estimating frequency of birth defects: New numbers provide improved national estimates for 18 birth defects.* Retrieved October 18, 2009, from http://www.cdc.gov/od/oc/media/pressrel/r060105.htm

Chapman, R. S., & Hesketh, L. J. (2001). Language, cognition, and short-term memory in individuals with Down syndrome. *Down Syndrome Research and Practice, 7*(1), 1–7.

Crawford, D. C. (2001). *FMR1 and fragile X syndrome.* National Office of Public Health Genomics. Retrieved October 18, 2007, from http://www.cdc.gov/genomics/hugenet/factsheets/FS_FragileX.htm

Cullen, D. (2007). Back to the future: Eugenics: A bibliographic essay. *Public Historian, 29*(3), 163–175.

Davidson, J. E., & Downing, C. L. (2000). Contemporary models of intelligence. In R. J. Sternberg (Ed.), *Handbook of intelligence* (pp. 34–49). Cambridge, UK: Cambridge University Press.

Delgado, C. E., Vagi, S. J., & Scott, K. G. (2007). Identification of early risk factors for developmental delay. *Exceptionality, 15*(2), 119–136.

Ditterline, J., & Oakland, T. (2009). Relationship between adaptive behavior and impairment. In S. Goldstein & J. Naglieri (Eds.), *Assessing impairment: From theory to practice* (pp. 31–48). New York: Springer.

Downing, J. E. (2006). Building literacy for students at the presymbolic and early symbolic level. In D. M. Browder & F. Spooner (Eds.), *Teaching language arts, math, & science to students with significant cognitive disabilities* (pp. 39–61). Baltimore: Paul H. Brooks.

Erwin E., Brotherson, M., Palmer, S., Cook, C., Wiegel, C., & Summers, J. (2009). How to promote self-determination for young children with disabilities: Evidence-based strategies for early childhood practitioners and families. *Young Exceptional Children, 12*(2), 27–37.

Finestack, L., Richmond, E., & Abbeduto, L. (2009). Language development in individuals with fragile X syndrome. *Topics in Language Disorders, 29*(2), 133–148.

Fragile X Research Foundation. *Fragile X is caused by just one gene.* Retrieved October 18, 2007, from http://www.fraxa.org/aboutFX_cause.aspx

Gardner, H. (2006). *Multiple intelligences: New horizons, completely revised and updated.* New York: Basic Books.

Gilmore, L., & Cuskelly, M. (2009). A longitudinal study of motivation and competence in children with Down syndrome: Early childhood to early adolescence. *Journal of Intellectual Disability Research, 53*(5), 489–492.

Glue, P., & Patterson, T. (2009). Can drug treatments enhance learning in subjects with intellectual disability? *Australian and New Zealand Journal of Psychiatry, 43*(10), 899–904.

Glutting, J., Adams, W., & Sheslow, D. (2000). *Wide range intelligence test: Manual.* Wilmington, DE: Wide Range.

Goldberg, R., Motzkin, B., Marion, R., Scambler, P. J., & Shprintzen, R. J. (1993). Velocardiofacial syndrome: A review of 120 patients. *American Journal of Medical Genetics, 45*(3), 313–319.

Gothelf, D., Frisch, A., Michaelovsky, E., Weizman, A., & Shprintzen, R. (2009). Velocardiofacial syndrome. *Journal of Mental Health Research in Intellectual Disabilities, 2*(2), 149–167.

Gothelf, D., & Lombroso, P. J. (2001). Genetics of childhood disorders: XXV velocardiofacial syndrome. *Journal of the American Academy of Child and Adolescent Psychiatry, 40*(4), 481–491.

Hamilton, C., & Atkinson, D. (2009). "A story to tell": Learning from the life-stories of older people with intellectual disabilities in Ireland. *British Journal of Learning Disabilities, 37*(4), 316–322.

Harris, J. C. (2006). *Intellectual disability: Understanding its development, causes, classification, evaluation, and treatment.* Oxford, UK: Oxford University Press.

Hodgdon, L. A. (1998). *Visual strategies for improving communication: Practical supports for school and home* (Vol. 1). Troy, MI: Quirk-Roberts Publishing.

Holverstott, J. (2005). Promote self-determination in students. *Intervention in School and Clinic, 41*(1), 39–41.

Jaime, K., & Knowlton, E. (2007). Visual support for students with behavior and cognitive challenges. *Intervention in School and Clinics, 42*(5), 259–270.

Kauffman, J. M., & Snell, M. E. (1977). Managing the behavior of severely handicapped persons. In E. Sontag (Ed.), *Educational programming for the severely and profoundly handicapped* (pp. 203–220). Reston, VA: Council for Exceptional Children.

Kazdin, A. E. (1977). *The token economy: A review and evaluation.* New York: Plenum.

Kazdin, A. E. (1994). *Behavior modification in applied settings.* Pacific Grove, CA: Brookes/Cole.

Lewis, S., & Tolla, J. (2003). Creating and using tactile experience books for young children with visual impairments. *Teaching Exceptional Children, 35*(3), 22–28.

Lionello-DeNolf, K. M., Barros, R. D., & McIlvane, W. J. (2008). A novel method for teaching the first instances of simple discrimination to nonverbal children with autism in a laboratory environment. *The Psychological Record, 58,* 229–244.

Lougy, R., DeRuvo, S., & Rosenthal, D. (2007). *Teaching young children with ADHD: Successful strategies and practical interventions for pre-k-3.* Thousand Oaks, CA: Corwin Press.

Lovering, J. S., & Percy, M. (2007). Down syndrome. In I. Brown & M. Percy (Eds.), *A comprehensive guide to intellectual and developmental disabilities* (pp. 149–172). Baltimore: Paul H. Brookes.

Luchow, J. P., Crowl, T. K., & Kahn, J. P. (2001). Learned helplessness: Perceived effects of ability and effort on academic performance among EH and LD/EH children. *Journal of Learning Disabilities, 18*(8), 470–474.

Mahoney G., Perales, F., Wiggers, B., & Herman, B. (2006). Responsive teaching: Early intervention for children with Down syndrome and other disabilities. *Down Syndrome Research and Practice, 11*(1), 18–28.

Mahoney, G. J. (1988). Communication patterns between mothers and developmental delayed infants. *First Language, 8,* 157–172.

Mahoney, G. J., Fingers, I., & Powell, A. (1985). The relationship between maternal behavioral style to the developmental status of mentally retarded infants. *American Journal of Mental Deficiency, 90,* 296–302.

Mahoney, G., & MacDonald, J. (2007). *Autism and developmental delays in young children: The responsive teaching curriculum for parents and professionals.* Austin, TX: PRO-ED.

Martin, J. E., & Marshall, L. H. (1995). ChoiceMaker: A comprehensive self-determination transition program. *Intervention in School and Clinics, 30,* 147–156.

May, P. A., & Gossage, J. P. (2001). *Estimating the prevalence of fetal alcohol syndrome: A summary.* National Institute of Alcohol Abuse and Alcoholism of the National Institute of Health. Retrieved October 18, 2007, from http://pubs.niaaa.nih.gov/publications/arh25-3/159-167.htm

Mazzocco, M. M., & Holden, J. J. A. (2007). Fragile X syndrome. In I. Brown & M. Percy (Eds.), *A comprehensive guide to intellectual and developmental disabilities* (pp. 173–187). Baltimore: Paul H. Brookes.

McDonnell, J., & Furguson, B. (1989). A comparison of time delay and decreasing prompt hierarchy strategies in teaching banking skills to students with moderate handicaps. *Journal of Applied Behavior Analysis, 22*(1), 85–91.

McMillan, D. L., Gresham, F. M., & Siperstein, G. N. (1993). Conceptual and psychometric concerns about the 1992 AAMR definition of mental retardation. *American Journal of Mental Retardation, 98,* 325–335.

Meyer, G. A. (2007). X-linked syndromes causing intellectual disability. In M. L. Batshaw, L. Pellegrino, & N. J. Roizen (Eds.), *Children with disabilities* (6th ed., pp. 275–283). Baltimore: Paul H. Brookes.

Miltenberger, R. G. (2001). *Behavior modification: Principles and procedures.* Belmont, CA: Wadsworth.

Mistrett, S. (2004). Assistive technology helps young children with disabilities participate in daily activities. *Technology in Action, 1*(4), 1–8.

Morbidity and Mortality Weekly Report. (2006). *Prevalence of four developmental disabilities among children aged 8 years—Metropolitan Atlanta developmental disabilities surveillance program, 1996 and 2000.* Department of Health and Human Services, Centers for Disease Control and Prevention. Retrieved October 8, 2007, from http://www.cdc.gov/mmwr

Moss, J., Oliver, C., Arron, K., Burbidge, C., & Berg, K. (2009). The prevalence and phenomenology of repetitive behavior in genetic syndromes. *Journal of Autism and Developmental Disorders, 39*(4), 572–588.

Murphy, M. M., & Abbeduto, L. (2005). Indirect genetic effects and the early language development of children with genetic mental retardation syndromes: The role of joint attention. *Infants and Young Children, 18,* 47–59.

Naglieri, J. A., & Das, J. P. (1997). *Cognitive Assessment System: Interpretive hand book.* Itasca, IL: Riverside.

National Research Council, Institute of Medicine. (2000). *From neurons to neighborhoods: The science of early childhood development.* Washington, DC: National Academy Press.

Nirje, B. (1969). The normalization principle and its human management implications. In W. Wolfensberger & R. Kugel (Eds.), *Changing patterns in residential services for the mentally retarded,* (pp. 181–195).Washington, DC: President's Committee on Mental Retardation.

Noble, K. G., Tottenham, N., & Casey, G. J. (2005). Neuroscience perspectives on disparities in school readiness and cognitive achievement. In C. Rouse, J. Gooks-Gunn, & S. McLanahan, *The future of the children: School readiness, 15*(1), 71–89.

Noll, S., & Trent, J. W. (Eds.). (2004). *Mental retardation in America: A historical reader.* New York: New York University Press.

Nulman, I., Ickowicz, A., Koren, G., & Knittle-Keren, D. (2007). Fetal alcohol spectrum disorder. In I. Brown & M. Percy (Eds.), *A comprehensive guide to intellectual and developmental disabilities* (pp. 213–227). Baltimore: Paul H. Brookes.

Oliver, C., Woodcock, K., & Humphreys, G. (2009). The relationship between components of the behavioral phenotype in Prader-Willi syndrome. *Journal of Applied Research in Intellectual Disabilities, 22*(4), 403–407.

Palmer, S. B., & Wehmeyer, M. L. (2003). Promoting self-determination in early elementary school: Teaching self-regulated problem-solving and goal-setting skills. *Remedial and Special Education, 24,* 115–126.

Parson, M. B., & Reid, D. H. (1999). Training basic teaching skills to paraeducators of students with severe disabilities: A one-day program. *Teaching Exceptional Children, 31*(4), 48–54.

Percy, M. (2007). Factors that cause or contribute to intellectual and developmental disabilities. In I. Brown & M. Percy (Eds.), *A comprehensive guide to intellectual and developmental disabilities* (pp. 125–148). Baltimore: Paul H. Brookes.

Percy, M., Cheetham, T., Gitta, M., Morrison, B., Machalek, K., Bega, S., et al. (2007). Other syndromes and disorders associated with intellectual and developmental disabilities. In I. Brown & M. Percy (Eds.), *A comprehensive guide to intellectual and developmental disabilities* (pp. 229–267). Baltimore: Paul H. Brookes.

Radford, J. P., & Park, D. C. (2003). Historical overview of developmental disabilities in Ontario. In I. Brown & M. Percy (Eds.), *Developmental disabilities in Ontario* (2nd ed., pp. 3–18). Toronto: Ontario Association on Developmental Disabilities.

Roizen, N. (2007). Down syndrome. In M. L. Batshaw, L. Pellegrino, & N. J. Roizen (Eds.), *Children with disabilities* (6th ed., pp. 263–283). Baltimore: Paul H. Brookes.

Saligman, M., & Maier, S. (1967). Failure to escape traumatic shock. *Journal of Personality, 44,* 38–51.

Sandall, S., Hemmeter, M. L., Smith, B. J., & McLean, M. E. (2005). *DEC Recommended practices: A comprehensive guide for practical application in early intervention/early childhood special education.* Missoula, MT: Division for Early Childhood.

Schalock, R. L., Luckasson, R. A., Shogren, K. A., Borthwick-Duffy, S., Bradley, V., Buntinz, W., et al. (2007). The renaming of mental retardation: Understanding the change to the term intellectual disability. *Intellectual and Developmental Disabilities, 45*(2), 116–124.

Schonberg, R. L., & Tifft, C. (2007). Birth defects and prenatal diagnosis. In M. L. Batshaw, L. Pellegrino, & N. J. Roizen (Eds.), *Children with disabilities* (6th ed., pp. 83–96). Baltimore: Paul H. Brookes.

Shogren, K., Bradley, V., Gomez, S., Yeager, M., Schalock, R., Borthwick-Duffy, S., et al. (2009). Public policy and the enhancement of desired outcomes for persons with intellectual disability. *Intellectual and Developmental Disabilities, 47*(4), 307–319.

Selikowitz, M. (1997). *Down syndrome: The facts.* Oxford, UK: Oxford University Press.

Sparrow, S. S., Balla, D. A., & Cicchetti, D. V. (2005). *Vineland Adaptive Behavior Scales (2nd edition): Vineland II.* Shoreview, MN: AGS Publishing.

Stafford, A. M. (2005). Choice making: A strategy for students with severe disabilities. *Teaching Exceptional Children, 37*(6), 12–17.

Switzky, H. N., & Greenspan, S. (2006). *What is mental retardation? Ideas for an evolving disability in the 21st century.* Washington, DC: American Association on Mental Retardation.

Tarbox, R. S., Ghezzi, P. M., & Wilson, G. (2006). The effects of token reinforcement on attending in a young child with autism. *Behavioral Intervention, 21,* 155–164.

Tartaglia, N., Hansen, R. L., & Hagerman, R. J. (2007). Advances in genetics. In S. L. Odom, R. H. Horner, M. E. Snell, & J. Blacher (Eds.), *Handbook of developmental disabilities.* New York: Guilford Press.

Taylor, R. L., Smiley, L. R., & Richards, S. B. (2009). *Exceptional students: Preparing teachers for the 21st century.* Boston: McGraw-Hill Higher Education.

Theimann, K., & Warren, S. F. (2004). Program supporting young children's language development. In R. E. Tremblay, R. G. Barr, & R. Peters (Eds.), *Encyclopedia on Early Childhood Development* (pp. 1–11). Montreal, Quebec: Centre of Excellence for Early Childhood Development.

Trent, J. W. (1994). *Inventing the feeble mind: A history of mental retardation in the United States.* Berkeley, CA: University of California Press.

Turnbull, A., Turnbull, R., Erwin, E., & Soodak, L. (2006). *Families, professionals, and exceptionalitiy: Positive outcome through partnerships and trust* (5th ed.). Upper Saddle River, NJ: Pearson, Merrill/Prentice Hall.

Walters, E., & Gardner, H. (1986). The theory of multiple intelligences: Some issues and answers. In R. J. Sternberg & R. K. Wagner (Eds.), *Practical intelligence.* Cambridge, UK: Cambridge University Press.

Wechsler, D. (1975). Intelligence defined and undefined. *American Psychologist, 30,* 135–139.

Wechsler, D. (1991). *Wechsler intelligence scale for children* (3rd ed.). San Antonio, TX: Psychological Corp., Harcourt Brace.

Wechsler, D. (2002). *Wechsler preschool and primary scale of intelligence* (3rd ed.). San Antonio, TX: Harcourt Assessment.

Wechsler, D. (2003). *Wechsler intelligence scale for children* (4th ed.). San Antonio, TX: Harcourt Assessment.

Wehmeyer, M. L. (2001). Self-determination and mental retardation. In L. M. Glidden (Ed.), *International review of research in mental retardation* (Vol. 24, pp. 1–48). San Diego, CA: Academic Press.

Wehmeyer, M. L., Abery, B., Mithaug, D. E., & Stancliffe, R. J. (2003). *Theory in self-determination: Foundations for educational practice.* Springield, IL: Thomas.

Wilder, D., & Atwell, J. (2006). Evaluation of a guided compliance procedure to reduce noncompliance among preschool children. *Behavioral Interventions, 21*(4), 265–272.

Wolfenberger, W. (1972). *The principle of normalization in human services.* Toronto: National Institute on Mental Retardation.

Children with Deafness, Hearing Loss, Blindness, and Visual Impairment

Objectives

Upon completion of this chapter, you should be able to:

> List and describe various low-incidence disabilities.
> Understand the history of deaf education.
> Understand the possible causes of hearing loss.
> List and describe the types and degrees of hearing loss and their diagnoses.
> List and describe the types of assistive and medical technology used to help children with hearing loss.
> Understand the developmental characteristics of children who are deaf or have hearing loss.
> Understand strategies, methods, and adaptations related to working with children with hearing loss.
> Understand types of visual impairments.
> Understand the history of education of children with visual impairments.
> Identify developmental characteristics of children with visual impairment.
> Define the causes of visual impairments and their diagnoses.
> Understand strategies and adaptations used for children with visual impairments in inclusive classrooms.

Key Terms

acquired deafness (409)
American Sign Language (ASL) (406)
assistive listening devices (411)
conductive hearing loss (409)
congenital blindness (422)
congenital deafness (408)
Deaf (406)
deaf (406)
Deaf community (406)
decibels (dB) (410)
field of vision (417)

functional vision assessment (FVA) (422)
hard of hearing (406)
hearing impairment (406)
hearing loss (406)
hertz (HZ) (410)
implants (411)
legally blind (417)
low-incidence disabilities (405)
low vision (417)
manual/hand babbling (413)

mixed hearing loss (410)
mobility (425)
orientation (425)
orientation and mobility specialists (425)
partially sighted (417)
perception (405)
sensation (405)
sensorineural hearing loss (SN hearing loss) (409)
totally blind (418)
visual acuity (417)
visual impairment (417)

Reflection Questions

Before reading this chapter, answer the following questions to reflect upon your personal opinions and beliefs that are pertinent to early childhood special education.

1. Do you think a child who is deaf should learn a sign language, or should the child learn to read speech and speak to communicate? Why?

2. What is your opinion about considering individuals who are deaf belonging to a community of their own (i.e., the Deaf community)?

3. What do you think the appropriate age is for a child who is blind to learn to read braille?

Sign Language or Oral Language: Which One Is Better?

Habib is 2 years old and his parents are from Pakistan. They have been living in the United States for the past 3 years. Nadia, Habib's mother, has been working in a bakery close to their apartment in the city of Pittsburg. Her husband, Hamid, is a construction worker who works all day, and does not get home until 7 p.m. Nadia cares for Habib during the day and works from midnight to early morning in the bakery. Habib began to babble and make baby sounds when he was 6 months old, but as he grew older, he babbled less and eventually became quiet. Habib seems to be a content baby, who quietly plays on his cot most of the day. This has worked out to Nadia's advantage because she gets to rest a couple of hours when Habib plays quietly in his crib.

Nadia's aunt, Cherin, who lives in England, visited with Nadia and Hamid several months ago. During her visit one day, she noticed that Habib did not respond to his name when she called him. Habib was sitting on the floor playing with some blocks. Cherin came behind Habib and began clapping, but Habib did not turn around. She made a toy squeak. Habib did not respond to that noise either.

When Nadia came home, Cherin expressed her concerns regarding Habib's hearing. However, Nadia and Hamid said that Habib did hear, and was able to respond to his name on other occasions. To demonstrate, Nadia called Habib's name loudly, and Habib turned his head around to look at her.

Habib continued to be a quiet child. When he did not begin to use words and speak after he had passed his second birthday, Nadia began to think about her aunt's concerns. Nadia expressed her worries to her husband, and they decided to take Habib to a children's hospital nearby. After several tests and examinations, an audiologist informed the family that except for very loud sounds, Habib could not hear anything and was considered deaf. This was a sad day for the family.

Nadia and Hamid asked many questions, and the audiologist provided information regarding the treatment options that might be available. He explained that for the type of congenital deafness—deafness present from birth—that Habib had, amplification would not be helpful. However, there were a number of therapeutic and educational services that could help Habib learn to communicate.

A hospital social worker met with Nadia and Hamid and explained the early intervention services that were available for Habib. She put Nadia in contact with one of the EI Service Coordinators in the hospital to begin the process of evaluation and intervention for Habib. During the family directed assessment process, the service coordinator asked Nadia and Hamid if they would be interested in learning

American Sign Language. Hamid did not like the idea of his son speaking in sign language. He told the service coordinator that he wanted Habib to be like every other child. He expressed his wish for Habib to be able to communicate with everyone: "Not everyone knows how to sign. What if he wants to go to a restaurant, or shopping? Is everyone going to understand what he is saying? He should learn to speak."

Hamid remembered that the father of one of his friends was deaf, but was able to understand speech by looking at people's lips and speak like everyone else. Couldn't Habib learn to read speech and talk, too? Nadia did not agree with Hamid. She wanted her son to have every chance to learn and be successful in life, and she said as much, "So what if Habib uses signs instead of words? Isn't signing just like speaking a different language? People who speak different languages learn to communicate with one another. I am sure he can, too."

Hamid and Nadia have not agreed on what might be the best educational approach for their son. The early intervention team will meet to discuss how they might help this family make a decision regarding the best educational options for their son.

INTRODUCTION

Children's development depends on the way they process information through their sensations and perceptions. **Sensation** is picking up information from sensory receptors in the ears, eyes, skin, tongue, and nose, such as touching a rough surface or looking at a bright light. **Perception** is the interpretation of the information that has been picked up by the sensory receptors. In other words, perception is the interpretation of what has been sensed, such as perceiving something as hot, cold, bright, loud, or sweet. When one sense does not work well, or is lacking, the integration of information that is received from all sensory areas are affected, and thus the perception of the information is altered. Children who are deprived of one sense have to rely on other senses in order to make meaning of their surroundings, to develop knowledge, and to learn. A sensory deprivation, such as in a child with deafness or blindness, alters the way that the child senses and perceives things, and therefore influences the way the child learns.

In this chapter, we will learn about a collection of disorders called **low-incidence disabilities.** IDEA defines low-incidence disabilities as "a visual or hearing impairment, or simultaneous visual and hearing impairments; a significant cognitive impairment; or any impairments for which a small number of personnel with highly specialized skill and knowledge are needed in order for children with the impairment to receive early intervention services and a free appropriate public education" (20 U.S.C. 1400 § 673(a)(3). Blindness and deafness are considered low incidence because these disabilities do not affect a large number of children and individuals in the world. Children who are blind, visually impaired, deaf, or hard of hearing are estimated to comprise about 2 percent of all school-age children (U.S. Department of Education, 2000). Other categories of conditions that are considered to be low incidence include moderate, severe, and multiple disabilities, and physical, medical, and health conditions.

Here we will examine the effects of hearing loss and visual impairment on children's learning and development. We will also briefly explore other severe disabilities and health impairments in children. Working with children with low-incidence disabilities requires specialized, intensive training and preparation related to the education of children with vision impairments, hearing loss, and other severe disabilities (Ludlow, Conner, & Schechter, 2005). Therefore, we will only discuss issues of general consideration in relationship to the education of children with low-incidence disabilities.

CHILDREN WHO ARE DEAF OR HAVE HEARING LOSS

Before we begin our discussion about young children who are deaf or have a hearing loss, we must define several related terminologies. The term **Deaf**—with a capital *D*—refers to children and individuals who use **American Sign Language (ASL)** as their primary mode of communication and share common cultural values (Raver, 1999). These individuals consider themselves members of the **Deaf community,** which defines itself as a minority group with its own distinct language and culture. American Sign Language is a visual or manual/gestural language system that is used by the majority of children and adults who are deaf.

A child or an adult who is considered **deaf**—with a lower case "d"—has severe hearing loss and cannot utilize hearing, with or without a hearing aid, to use language (Herer, Knightly, & Steinberg, 2007). These individuals and children may or may not use ASL as the primary mode of communication, and may or may not consider themselves part of the Deaf community. A child or person who is considered **hard of hearing** has some residual (leftover) hearing, which can be utilized for learning. Children who are hard of hearing are usually able to speak and benefit from amplification (Herer et al., 2007).

Hearing loss refers to any degree, range, or type of difficulties in hearing. Degrees of hearing loss include slight, mild, moderate, severe, and profound (Herer et al., 2007; Northern & Downs, 2002). IDEA uses the term **hearing impairment** to describe children who have various degrees of hearing loss. The Deaf community is against the use of this terminology because the members of this community do not view themselves as having a condition or impairment that needs to be corrected or repaired. Instead, they consider themselves members of a distinct linguistic and cultural group (Lane, Hoffmeister, & Bahan, 1996). They prefer to use such terms as *deaf child* or *deaf person* to refer to individuals with hearing loss. In this book, as is the custom of special educators, we prefer to use a language that is child- or individual-first, and so refer to this group of children as *children who are deaf,* or *children with hearing loss.*

THE HISTORY OF DEAF EDUCATION

Aristotle, the Greek philosopher, believed that people who were deaf could not be educated. For many centuries, this belief dominated the public perceptions throughout the different cultures of the world. Children who were born with deafness or lost their sense of hearing through an illness or accident were treated much the same way as those who were considered to be imbeciles.

Individuals who were deaf did not have many legal rights, such as rights to own property, to inherit, or to make a will. It was not until the 16th century in Spain when a Benedictine monk, Pedro Ponce De Leon (1529–1584), began educating deaf children that public opinion began to change regarding deaf individuals (Braddock & Parish, 2002). De Leon was able to teach his students to read, write, speak, calculate, and learn other languages such as Greek, Latin, and Italian, thus demonstrating the various intellectual abilities of people who were deaf (Plann, 1997).

It is not clear exactly when and where the first sign language began to develop. It is understood, however, that certain manual signs had instinctively begun to appear in different parts of the world, originated by the deaf as a way to communicate with others around them. The first book on the manual alphabet was published in 1620, written by Juan Martin Bonet, called *Simplifications of the Letters of the Alphabet and Method of Teaching Deaf Mutes to Speak.* This method was a one-handed manual alphabet which formed the foundations of the sign alphabets used in different languages around the world today (Gannon, 1981).

The first school for children who were deaf was opened in 1755 in Paris by Abbe de l'Epee. Abbe de l'Epee believed that children who were deaf could learn to use language. His school was the first free school for the deaf in the world. Around the same time (in 1760), in Britain, Thomas Braidwood taught children who were deaf using the combined method of natural gestures and speech (Gannon, 1981). Braidwood had established the first British school in Edinburgh, Scotland (Minski, 1957). Similarly, in Germany in 1778, Samuel Heinicke established the first public school with government funding for children who were deaf. Heinicke did not employ manual signs to teach children. Instead, children were taught speech and speech-reading (Braddock & Parish, 2002). Following Abbe de l'Epee's tradition in France, Abbe Roch Sicard taught children who were deaf by using manual signs. He opened the school for the deaf in Bordeaux in 1782, and wrote the elaborate dictionary *Theory of Signs* (Gannon, 1981).

Fingerspelling the letter X.

In 1815, Thomas Hopkins Gallaudet, a Congregational American minister, became interested in educating children who were deaf. He traveled to Europe to study different methods of educating these children. In England, he tried to study the method that Thomas Braidwood had established earlier (Minski, 1957). Gallaudet was unsuccessful in learning the Braidwood method, because the Braidwood educators were unwilling to share it. Abbe Sicard invited Gallaudet to visit his school for the deaf in Paris. Gallaudet traveled to France and studied sign language. He brought back Laurent Clerc, a deaf sign language teacher, to the United States to teach children who were deaf in America (Braddock & Parish, 2002; Zapien, 1998).

Gallaudet established a school in Hartford, later to be known as the American School for the Deaf in 1817. Following this development, in 1864 the U.S. Congress established the first college for individuals who were deaf. Today, this college is known as Gallaudet University, and is the world's only university specifically designed for individuals who are deaf or hard of hearing (Gallaudet University, 2008). In the United States, the 1800s were the years during which sign language flourished. During this time, over half of the teachers educating children in U.S. schools for the deaf were deaf themselves, and thus the 19th-century United States might be considered the "golden era of signed deaf education" (Zapien, 1998). In other countries, however, oral methods of speech and speech-reading were used to educate children who were deaf (Braddock & Parish, 2002).

In 1880, an international conference of deaf education was held in Milan. The focus of the Milan conference was on evaluating two different instructional methods of sign and oral education for children who were deaf. The conclusion of the conference was that the oral methods were superior to sign language (Zapien, 1998). This conclusion influenced the methods of educating deaf children around the world. Within the next few years, sign language became forbidden in schools for children who were deaf, because educators believed that if children signed, they would never learn to speak. The number of deaf teachers teaching deaf children dropped drastically during this time (Zapien, 1998). To this day, the controversy continues over which one of these methods is more appropriate for children who are deaf.

In 1960, a Gallaudet professor, William Stokoe, wrote *Sign Language Structure.* In his book, he argued that American Sign Language (ASL) meets the full criteria of linguistic phonology, semantics, morphology, syntax, and pragmatics to be classified as a language (De Clerck, 2007). Stokoe's argument reversed the assessment of sign language in the world and established the formation of what is today known as the *Deaf culture.* Over the last 30 years, deaf individuals have begun to perceive themselves as a minority group with their own culture and their own language (De Clerck, 2007).

CAUSES OF HEARING LOSS

The most common causes of hearing loss in young children are hereditary. Genetic factors are responsible for about half of those born deaf, although only 1 out of 10 parents of children who are deaf are deaf themselves (Cohen et al., 1999; Marschark, 1993). In some children, hearing loss might be present at birth, which is often referred to as **congenital deafness,** which can occur as a result of hereditary factors, an event or injury in-utero, or perinatal circumstances (Smith, Bale, & White, 2005). Maternal rubella, for example, which might occur during pregnancy, can result in the child's deafness (Bell, 2007). However, if hearing loss occurs sometime after birth as a result of an illness or a condition, it is referred to as **acquired deafness** (Herer et al., 2007). Exposure to different viruses and environmental toxins before and after birth can also result in deafness or hearing loss. For example, cytomegalovirus (CMV), a viral infection occurring prenatally, is one of the most common causes of deafness and hearing loss in children (Bell, 2007; Turnbull, Turnbull, & Wehmeyer, 2007). Other factors include mother–child blood incompatibility, meningitis, and complications in premature infants (Moores, 1997).

One of the most common postnatal causes of hearing loss in children is otitis media with effusion (OME) (Herer et al., 2007). OME is the medical term for ear infection. An ear infection occurs when fluid collects in the middle ear (Herer et al., 2007). Ear infections are common in young children, partly because a child's immune system is at a developing stage, and it is harder for children to fight infections as compared to adults. When fluid is present in the child's ear, the child has trouble hearing because the eardrum and middle ear bones cannot move freely. Repeated ear infections (defined as more than 6 episodes within a 12-month period) during infancy and the toddler years prevent young children from hearing speech sounds at a crucial time for language development (Campbell et al., 2003). Although otitis media in itself does not lead to a hearing problem, if the infection goes undetected for a long period of time it can lead to permanent hearing loss (Campbell et al., 2003; Herer et al., 2007).

TYPES OF HEARING LOSS

Sensorineural hearing loss (SN hearing loss) occurs because of damage to the sensory cells within the cochlea (Herer et al., 2007). The cochlea is a snail shell–like structure in the inner ear. It is divided into three fluid-filled parts. Two are canals that transmit pressure, and the third is the actual organ of hearing called the organ of corti, which detects pressure impulses and responds with electrical impulses that travel along the auditory nerve to the brain (Herer et al., 2007).

If the cochlea or auditory nerves are damaged, hearing loss occurs. SN hearing loss might occur as a result of an inherited genetic problem (Nance, 2003). Some drugs, such as chemotherapy drugs used for cancer, can cause a SN hearing loss as well (Li, Womer, & Silber, 2004). SN hearing loss cannot be fixed medically or surgically, which means that the hearing loss is significant or permanent. A child with it has a decreased sensitivity to sounds and a lack of clarity in speech and environmental sounds (Herer et al., 2007). Hearing aids, other amplification devices, and cochlear implants have often been recommended and used for children with sensorineural hearing loss to better help them hear sounds (Li et al., 2004).

Conductive hearing loss occurs due to problems in the outer or middle ear. In this case, sound is not successfully and efficiently conducted through the outer ear canal to the eardrum and the small bones of the middle ear (Herer et al., 2007). Children with conductive hearing loss have a difficult time hearing faint sounds in the environment. Fluid in the middle ear and earwax might also cause this. This type of hearing loss might be corrected by surgery or by medication (American Speech-Language-Hearing Association, 2007).

Mixed hearing loss is when conductive and SN hearing loss occur in combination with one another (Herer et al., 2007). In this case, the damage might be in all areas: outer, middle, and inner ear, or in the auditory nerve.

THE SEVERITY OF HEARING LOSS

The severity and degree of hearing loss varies from child to child. The hearing range in a child is determined by measuring how loud a sound is at different pitches before the child can hear it (Northern & Downs, 2002). Sounds are measured in terms of their frequency (high or low) or in terms of their intensity (soft or loud). Frequency is measured in **hertz (HZ),** while loudness is measured in **decibels (dB).** In normal hearing, the range of frequencies is from 20 to 20,000 HZ. The typical range of loudness is between 0 to 120 dB. Individuals with various degrees of hearing loss can hear only specific frequencies and intensities (American Speech-Language-Hearing Association, 2007). Table 12.1 displays the range of hearing loss in different categories of hearing problems.

DIAGNOSIS

The National Institute on Deafness and other Communication Disorders (2001) recommends that all newborns be screened for hearing loss prior to being discharged from the hospital. By observing an infant's reactions to different pitches and frequencies, professionals are able to detect possible hearing loss in infants. In a *universal newborn hearing screening* model (Gallagher, Easterbrooks, & Malone, 2006), infants are screened for hearing loss after birth in the hospital. If they fail this initial hearing screening, they are referred for full diagnostic evaluation, including examination by a behavioral audiologist (White, 2008; Gallagher et al., 2006; White, Vohr, & Behrens, 1993; American Academy of Pediatrics, 1999). In this model, collaborative efforts are made to track children and link them with intervention processes to ensure the best possible outcome (White, 2008; Gallagher et al., 2006).

A diagnosis of hearing loss is conducted by a group of professionals, including (1) the child's pediatrician, (2) an *otologist,* a specialist in diseases of the ear, and (3) an *audiologist,* a trained professional in the testing and measurement of hearing.

TABLE 12.1   Categories of Hearing Loss

Mild loss	20 to 40 dB
Moderate loss	40 to 60 dB
Severe loss	60 to 80 dB
Profound loss	80 dB or more

Source: American Speech-Language-Hearing Association, available at http://www.asha.org.

An audiologist administers a hearing test to a young child.

Physical examinations and a case history study are parts of the diagnostic process. Early infant diagnosis enables professionals to provide appropriate early intervention services for infants before they reach 6 months of age (American Academy of Pediatrics, 1999).

The identification of hearing loss during the toddler and preschool years requires parents and early childhood educators to pay close attention to the child's behavioral cues, such as following simple verbal directions or locating the speaker in a group (American Speech-Language-Hearing Association, 2007). Some warning signs in young children include difficulties in hearing and articulating specific phonemes, having frequent articulation errors, and having an unusual voice quality. Parents and early childhood educators should also be cognizant of repeated or persistent colds and ear infections, which can influence the child's hearing (American Speech-Language-Hearing Association, 2007).

HEARING AIDS, ASSISTIVE DEVICES, AND IMPLANTS

A hearing aid is a small electronic device worn in or behind the ear. Although advances in technology have produced a number of sophisticated hearing aids, in general hearing aids amplify all sounds, including any background noise in the environment (Scollie & Seewald, 2001). Therefore, it might not be productive for children to wear hearing aids when they are in very noisy environments.

Several **assistive listening devices** can help children function better in the classroom. A listening device might be connected to the hearing aid or be separate from the hearing aid to help isolate and amplify specific sounds (Scollie & Seewald, 2001). A personal frequency modulation (FM) system is a listening device consisting of a transmitter microphone and a receiver. The wireless microphone could be worn by the teacher, while the transmitter could be connected to the child's hearing aid or to a headset. The FM system amplifies the teacher's voice above the background and other classroom noises so the child can understand the teacher more clearly (Scollie & Seewald, 2001).

Implants came into practice starting in the 1980s as a major breakthrough in the education and treatment of deaf children (Bat-Chava, Martin, & Kosciw, 2005).

Hearing aids are small electronic devices worn in or behind the ear.

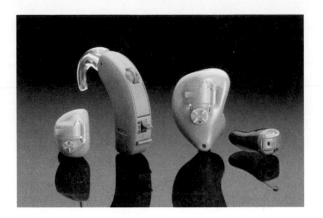

Implants are used for children and individuals who have severe-to-profound hearing loss. They are small electronic devices that are surgically inserted underneath the skin (Bat-Chava et al., 2005; Herer et al., 2007). A cochlear implant provides a sensation of hearing for individuals who have severe hearing loss (Herer et al., 2007). A bone-anchored implant is used for individuals with conductive or mixed hearing loss. The bone-anchored implant conducts sounds from the implant in the skull behind the ear to the inner ear (Cohen, 2004). An auditory brain implant is used with individuals who have auditory nerve damage. The implant contains electrodes placed in the part of the brain that processes the auditory signals carried from the ear to the brain (Cohen, 2004). A middle ear implant is a small microphone that carries sounds from the middle to inner ear. Studies of the efficacy of implants have shown that they improve the oral language abilities of profoundly deaf children significantly (Moog & Geers, 1999). Children who receive an implant before the age of 5 are more likely to progress at rates close or equal to that of hearing children (Schraer-Joiner & Chen-Hafteck, 2009; Svirsky, Robbins, Kirk, Pisoni, & Miyamoto, 2000).

Critical Thinking Question 12.1 Refer to the story at the beginning of this chapter. If you were a member of the early intervention team, how would you help Habib's family make a decision regarding the best educational options for their son?

DEVELOPMENTAL CHARACTERISTICS OF CHILDREN WITH DEAFNESS

Children who are deaf develop typically in most areas except for communication and cognitive and social development. Because language and cognition are interconnected, children who are hard of hearing usually have delays in understanding concepts and forming a general knowledge of what is in their environment. In addition, because they are deprived of sociolinguistic information through auditory input, young children who are deaf usually have social emotional difficulties early on (Compton, 1994).

Cognitive and Language Development in Children Who Are Deaf

Sounds in the environment play a vital role in causing a general awareness of the events that occur in children's surroundings. Children who have hearing loss or who are deaf receive minimal or no information from their auditory system. Therefore, they might develop a very limited awareness and knowledge of their environment through their auditory sense. Until these children have developed communication skills, their cognitive development may progress at a slower rate compared to their typically developing peers (Marschark, 1993). In addition, because these children are unable to predict an event based on its sounds, they may frequently feel confused or powerless (Raver, 1999).

The most obvious result of an auditory sensory deprivation is that children with severe hearing loss do not readily learn to use speech for communication (Campbell et al., 2003). Much like typically developing children, children who are deaf begin to babble sometime around 6 months of age. However, without a speech input from their environment, their babbling patterns fail to resemble speech patterns, and it eventually stops around 9 months of age (Campbell et al., 2003).

Depending on how early hearing loss is identified, children who are deaf and have hearing parents might not have a specific channel of communication available to them during infancy, especially if the parents are not aware of the problem immediately (Eleweke, Gilbert, Bays, & Austin, 2008; Marschark, 1993). These children may struggle until they are diagnosed and early intervention services are secured for them. Without exposure to sign language or an Alternative and Augmentative Communication (AAC) system, they seldom develop a useful system of communication with other young children and adults by the time they enter preschool. In addition, some studies have found that the play abilities of children who are hard of hearing are related to their language abilities. Also, those children with hearing loss who have better language abilities spend more time in imaginative play with specific themes and story lines (Marschark, 1993).

Children who are deaf and have deaf parents, on the other hand, can learn sign language from their parents early on (Bailes, Erting, Thumann-Prezioso, & Erting, 2009). Infants who are exposed to sign language are able to babble through gestures, which is called **manual** or **hand babbling** (Petitto, Holowka, Sergio, & Ostry, 2001). Manual babbling is a sequence of hand gestures that resembles signs and that will develop into signs as the infant continues to be exposed to sign language by people in her surroundings (Petitto et al., 2001).

The Social Emotional Development of Children with Deafness

A typical fetus responds to the sounds it hears in the womb. It is especially responsive to human speech and more particularly its mother's voice (Klein, Gilkerson, & Davis, 2008). Research has shown that a newborn recognizes and responds to his mother's voice from his early memories in the womb (Haffner, 2007; Klein et al., 2008).

During infancy, the caregivers and infants establish a routine pattern of interaction, much of which is based on vocalization and expressions of feelings and affection (Bailes et al., 2009; Compton, 1994). Deaf infants do not receive any auditory cues that might soothe or calm them, nor do they interact with these sounds, so the parents' attention to eye gaze and eye contact, and their effort to initiate interactions with the infants are crucial in the social emotional development of the child (Bailes et al., 2009; Moores, 1997). The children may miss expressions of affection and other sociolinguistic information that are necessary in helping them form crucial behaviors they will need in order to have successful social interactions later with their peers and adults (McGinnis, Orr, & Freutel, 1980; Compton, 1994). Therefore, deaf children may not readily participate in group activities or in games that require cooperation and teamwork by the time they reach preschool age.

STRATEGIES AND ADAPTATIONS FOR CHILDREN WITH DEAFNESS OR HEARING LOSS IN INCLUSIVE CLASSROOMS

As we noted in the history of deaf education, methods of education and training of deaf children continues to evolve and be debated. During the past two decades, in the United States, there have been some qualitative and quantitative changes in the field that have raised the expectations of families as well as standards by which deaf children are being educated (Luckner, Muir, Howell, Sebald, & Young III, 2005). Some of these changes are as follows (Luckner et al., 2005):

> Extensive use of newborn hearing screening has resulted in earlier identification and intervention for infants and young children who are deaf or are hard of hearing.
> Advancement in implant technologies have resulted in:
>> A widespread use of cochlear implants in infants, toddlers, and young children who have profound hearing losses
>> An increase in the number of deaf children who are deemed appropriate to be included in general education classrooms
> The number of children with severe and profound hearing loss has decreased.
> More families use sign language with their young hearing children so as to empower them to communicate more effectively.
> Higher standards and greater accountability now exist partly due to the No Child Left Behind Act of 2001.

Regardless of these changes, educating children who are deaf requires specialized training. Programs that prepare teachers for children who are deaf or have hearing loss are usually connected to programs in speech and language therapy and audiology, because it is not only required for teachers working with deaf children to learn sign language, but it is usually necessary for them to learn techniques for teaching speech-reading and speech production (Jones & Ewing, 2002). In addition to these components, teacher preparation in the area of deaf education includes behavioral methods related to the psychology of deaf children as well as the adaptation of general education curriculum methods to the special needs of children who are deaf or hard of hearing (Luckner et al., 2005).

The quality and intensity of programs designed for the education of young children who are deaf or hard of hearing are drastically different from general and inclusive early childhood education programs. In general, educational programs for deaf children use two types of training approaches: (1) an oral approach and (2) a manual communication approach, using signing of some kind, such as the ASL (Humphries & Allen, 2008).

Oral Communication Methods

An oral communication method is usually used along with implant technologies or other forms of assistive devices to help children use their residual hearing. *Auditory communication* is one method of oral communication in which children are encouraged to use both their listening and visual skills to understand what they hear and see (Baker, 2008). Using visual skills to read and understand people's utterances is called *speech-reading.*

In another form of oral communication, auditory verbal training, children are taught to solely rely on their residual hearing—with or without the help of assistive devices—to develop speech and to communicate. They are not allowed to use their visual skills to read speech. In both methods, children are taught to develop speech and communicate verbally and orally (Baker, 2008). Some evidence exists that children with hearing loss, who use auditory verbal methods, make similar progress in language development and speech production as compared to their hearing peers (Dornan, Hickson, Murdoch, & Houston, 2007).

Manual Communication

Manual communication stresses the use of sign language. In this approach, students' visual abilities are utilized; hands, body, facial expressions, gestures, and movements are used to communicate (Schembri & Johnson, 2007). Fingerspelling might be used in a sign language. *Fingerspelling* involves the use of hand configurations to represent letters of written words (Schembri & Johnson, 2007). The alphabet that is represented by fingerspelling is called the *manual alphabet.*

American Sign Language (ASL) is a visual language used by the Deaf community in the United States and Canada (Schembri & Johnson, 2007; National Association of the Deaf, 2008). (See Figure 12.1.) Young children without any hearing problems whether born into deaf or hearing families may also use sign language. (Luckner et al., 2005). Strong evidence exists that fluency in ASL is associated with reading achievement. When children learn ASL early in life, they are more likely to not only learn the English language faster and with more ease, but also to progress in literacy development (Bailes et al., 2009; Padden & Ramsey, 1998; Commission of Education of the Deaf, 1988). In addition, the use of computers to teach spelling and reading to young deaf children has shown to be an effective strategy in early childhood classrooms (Reitsma, 2009).

ASL is a complex system that relies on facial features, such as the movement of lips, mouth, and eyebrows, as well as body movement and hand gestures. There is no

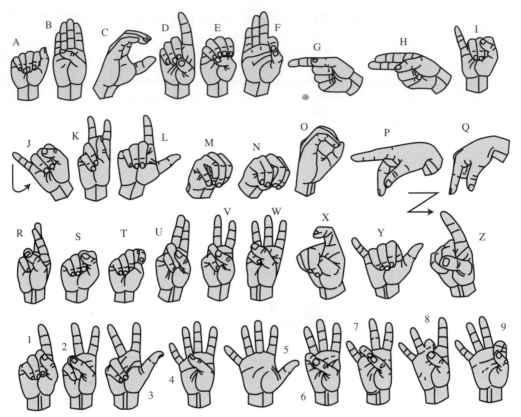

FIGURE 12.1 American Sign Language (ASL) Is a Visual Language Used by the Deaf Community in the United States and Canada

universal sign language. *British Sign Language,* for example, differs from American Sign Language, even though both languages are English (Baker, 2008). ASL also differs from *Signed Exact English* (*SEE*). SEE is an English manual language that uses some ASL signs in addition to certain special signs—such as for plurals and pronouns—that allows English to be signed exactly as it is spoken. Other sign languages used in the United States are *Conceptually Accurate Signed English, Seeing Essential English*, and *Pidgin Sign English.*

The Education of Deaf Children and the Value of the Deaf Community

Both oral and manual methods of deaf education focus on the development of speech and language in English, and both seldom focus on the child's assimilation into the culture of Deaf people (Humphries & Allen, 2008). The Deaf community values the natural rights of deaf persons to exercise the right to preserve their very character and language (i.e., to communicate using ASL) (Baker, 2008; Pribanic, 2006). The education of young deaf children, therefore, should acknowledge an existing cultural

ASL relies on facial features, such as the movement of lips, mouth, and eyebrows, as well as body movement and hand gestures.

approach to deafness and respect the values of the Deaf community in regards to education (Pribanic, 2006). To establish a cultural reciprocity (discussed in Chapter 3) between professionals and families of children who are deaf or hard of hearing, professionals need to work closely with families to understand and honor the family's wishes in regards to the assimilation of their child into the Deaf culture.

CHILDREN WITH VISUAL IMPAIRMENT AND BLINDNESS

The term **visual impairment** refers to a functional loss of vision and includes children who are **partially sighted,** those who have **low vision,** and children who are **legally blind** (National Dissemination Center for Children with Disabilities, 2004). These terms are defined as follows (National Dissemination Center for Children with Disabilities, 2004):

> Partially sighted children are those who have some type of visual problems and need special education.
> Children with low vision have severe visual impairments and are unable to read even with the aid of eyeglasses or contact lenses. They might require adaptations in lighting, the size of print, and the use of braille (a special alphabet system that enables a blind person to read and write).
> Children who are legally blind have less than 20/200 visual acuity in the better eye, or have a very limited field of vision. **Visual acuity** refers to the child's accuracy of vision in far and close distances and is measured by having a child read an eye chart from a distance of 20 feet (Holladay, 1997). A 20/200 vision means that when a child stands 20 feet away from a vision chart, the child can see what a typical person sees standing 200 feet away from the same chart. In other words, a child with 20/200 vision can only read the top line, which has a print size of 200, when standing 20 feet away (Holladay, 1997).

Children whose field of vision is 20 degrees or less are also considered legally blind. **Field of vision** refers to the surrounding area a person can see when looking ahead. A child with normal vision has a visual field of 160 degrees (Turnbull et al., 2007).

Children with visual loss have varying degrees of abilities. Children who are **totally blind** are those whose visual sensory impairment deprives them from receiving any meaningful visual input from their environment (Holladay, 1997). These children would have to utilize other senses, such as tactile or auditory, or their sense of smell and taste, to learn about their environment.

THE HISTORY OF EDUCATING CHILDREN WITH VISUAL IMPAIRMENTS

Prior to the Middle Ages, children who were blind might have been killed or abandoned. After the Middle Ages, blind children and adults often begged for food in public and lived in almshouses for the poor or in institutions (Oliphant, 2006). In the 17th and 18th centuries, hospices were established in some European countries to care for children and individuals who were blind (Braddock & Parish, 2002). Despite their poor treatment, however, many individuals with visual impairments have gained remarkable literary, artistic, musical, or scientific recognition in various societies (persons such as Louis Braille, Helen Keller, John Milton, Claude Monet, and Ray Charles, to name but a few).

It is difficult to know exactly when, where, and by whom the first educational methods for children with visual impairments were devised. Valentin Haüy (1745–1822) has often been credited with having devised the first formal method for the education of children and individuals who were blind (Braddock & Parish, 2002). Haüy was a French linguist who established the first school for blind children, The Royal Institution for Blind Youth, and designed a system of reading and writing through raised letters of the alphabet for children who had visual disabilities. He advocated for the education of children with visual impairments for most of his life and his ideas about a system of reading and writing for the blind formed the foundation of the braille system, which today is the most widely used system of educating children who are blind (Oliphant, 2006).

The braille system was designed by the French-born Louis Braille (1809–1852), who was the son of a saddler. When he was 3 years old, Braille poked his eye while playing with one of his father's working tools. This led to an infection in one eye and later in the other eye, resulting in the loss of vision in both his eyes. Through the efforts of his parents and the local teacher, Louis was provided with early opportunities to learn. He was allowed to attend the local school and learn by listening. As a young boy, he learned to read by means of upholstery studs hammered into pieces of wood in the shapes of letters and numbers (Oliphant, 2006). He continued to further his education in Paris at The Royal Institution for Blind Youth.

When he was 15, Braille advanced on an already designed system called Sonography, which had been invented earlier to help soldiers read and write at night without light. Braille changed Sonography into a system of the alphabet, which is known today as the braille system (Cavendish, 2002). The braille characters are different *cells,* each having a six-dot position arranged in a rectangle with two columns with three dots each. A dot may be raised at any position, or in any combination to correspond to a letter of the alphabet or a number.

Throughout the next several years, numerous institutions were established around the world to educate children who were blind. In the United States, the New England

A child reading braille.

Asylum for the Blind in 1829, the New York Institution for the Blind in 1831, the Pennsylvania Institution for the Blind in 1832, and The Wilberforce Memorial School for the Blind in 1833 were among the notable schools established to educate children with visual impairments (Bergen, 2007). These schools used braille, invented their own dot systems, or used other raised alphabet systems such as embossed English or Roman letters to educate their students.

In the 19th century, technologies such as the Kleidograph, a machine for embossing, were designed to enable blind children to write as well as read (Hernandez, 2007). Technology to educate children with visual impairments has continued to evolve over the past century. Over the last 50 years, a variety of assistive technology devices have been designed to enable children with visual impairments to read, write, listen, and function efficiently and quickly in their schools and communities. Digital books and readers, computer braille devices, and digital video magnifiers are examples of the types of devices used today to help educate children and youths who are blind (Hernandez, 2007).

DEVELOPMENTAL CHARACTERISTICS OF CHILDREN WITH VISUAL IMPAIRMENT

Children with visual impairments develop typically, although their rate of development might lag when compared to their typical peers (Hatton, Baily, Burchinal, & Ferrell, 1997; Warren, 1994). Seeing things and imitating adults and peers are natural ways by which children develop and learn. Typical children use their vision to move around, play with objects and toys, and see how things work and what others do. When children are not able to use their sense of vision, their rate of development is influenced (Hatton et al, 1997).

Motor Development

Vision is crucial to motor development (Warren, 1994). During the first months of life, visual input encourages infants to move their arms and legs. Early in development infants begin to reach for the object of their interest and as they develop their fine muscles they learn to grasp it. Later, as infants continue to see things and move their muscles, they begin to crawl toward their goal. Children who do not see tend to move less. In general, infants with visual impairments have a delay in developing motor milestones and fine motor skills (Brown & Bour, 1986). They may hold up their head, crawl, and sit at a later date compared to their typically developing peers.

Because infants with visual impairments do not have the natural opportunities that other children have to learn and move, it is important for the parents and caregivers to help infants use their other senses, such as hearing and touch, to develop the appropriate skills (Warren, 1994). Learning how to move safely is an important part of the education of children with visual impairment.

Cognitive Development

Although children with visual impairments are healthy intellectually, their cognitive development might be slower as a result of the visual sensory deprivation (Kesiktas, 2009; Hatton et al., 1997). Infants and children form their general knowledge and awareness of the physical world by seeing. They develop early problem-solving skills by touching, mouthing, and looking at objects and toys. For example, they learn to pull a string in a toy, shake a rattle, put simple round objects through holes, or stack toy cups on top of one another. Unless opportunities for interaction and playing with toys, objects, and people are provided for infants and young children with visual impairments, the rate of their cognitive development becomes slower compared with their typical peers (Warren, 1994).

Language Development

Infants begin communicating with their caregivers through face-to-face interactions. Smiles are early communicative messages that infants and caregivers send to one another. Infants who cannot see their caregivers' faces and smiles do not receive the messages that are intended for them. If the caregivers do not communicate to them through touching, caressing, tickling, and talking, infants with visual impairments will have delays in developing appropriate early communication skills (Warren, 1994).

For children who cannot see, skills like pointing, joint attention, and using gestures to communicate should be taught through tactile interactions (Holladay, 1997). In addition, various opportunities to interact with adults and children should be provided for them so they have an opportunity to learn other social skills. Because much of communication in early childhood and later years depends on observing the behaviors of others, children who cannot receive nonverbal cues might show *echolalia* (repeating what they hear), use pronouns incorrectly, or may not turn toward the person who is talking (Perez-Pereira & Conti-Ramsden, 1999).

Stereotypical Behaviors

Children with visual impairment display a wide variety of stereotypical and repetitive behaviors similar to those that some children within Autism Spectrum Disorders display. These behavior mannerisms have been termed *blindisms* (Holladay, 1997).

Blindisms might include eye pressing, body rocking, blinking forcefully, gazing at lights, waving fingers in front of the face, rolling the head, and rocking the body (Good & Hoyt, 1989). These behaviors might occur because of a lack of visual sensory stimulation, or may be an attempt to increase sensory stimulation in other areas, such as in the vestibular system (Warren, 1994). Blindisms seem to decrease with age (Holladay, 1997).

Social Emotional Development

Because early interactive behaviors of caregivers and infants are essential in the development of the infants' attachment, if parents of blind infants do not utilize different tactile and auditory stimulations to help their infants interact with them and relate to their surroundings, the quality of parent–infant social emotional relationships might be altered (Hatton et al., 1997). During preschool years, children with visual impairments show a pattern of social emotional development similar to their peers (Holladay, 1997). By the time they reach school age, however, they might show some social competence issues related to a poor self-image and isolation (Holladay, 1997). It is, therefore, important to address skills that are important in socialization and friendship early on in these children.

THE CAUSES OF VISUAL IMPAIRMENT

Several problems can lead to visual impairment in children. Some causes of blindness might be genetic, while others may be related to diseases and infections. In general, the three leading causes of visual impairment in children are: (1) cortical visual impairment (CVI), (2) retinopathy of prematurity (ROP), and (3) optic nerve hypoplasia (Hatton, 2001).

1. **Cortical visual impairment:** Is a lack or reduction of vision when eyes appear to be normal. CVI is caused by abnormalities in the visual cortex (Hatton, 2001).
2. **Retinopathy of prematurity:** Is a condition primarily found in premature infants. ROP results from vascular damage to the retina. In premature infants, the retinal blood vessel growth is incomplete. During the process of growth, a ridge can develop with some blood vessels growing toward the center of the eye. Although the abnormal blood vessels eventually die, the resultant scar tissue can pull on the retina and lead to a retinal detachment and loss of vision (Holladay, 1997).
3. **Optic nerve hypoplasia:** Occurs when the optic nerve does not function appropriately. In hypoplasia, a small optic nerve transmits impaired information to the brain (Holladay, 1997).

Some genetic conditions are associated with visual impairment, such as Down syndrome and albinism. Children with Down syndrome are likely to have certain visual problems such as cataracts, glaucoma, or myopia (Roizen, 2007). Children with albinism may be sensitive to light and require dark lenses in order to see well. Infections are also common causes of visual impairment. Infection in a pregnant woman, for example, can affect the fetus (see a more detailed discussion of this topic in Chapter 2). When a child is born blind, we consider that child to have **congenital blindness.** Other causes of visual impairment in children are as follows (Holladay, 1997):

> ➤ **Strabismus:** A muscle problem that causes one or both eyes to be out of alignment. Depending on which muscle is affected, the misalignment can be outward, inward, upward, or downward.
> ➤ **Nystagmus:** A muscle problem that causes involuntary "jerky" or "jumpy" eye movements. Sensory nystagmus indicates that the sensory input from the eye to the brain is impaired.
> ➤ **Retinal disorders as a result of injuries, infections, or other conditions:** Nonaccidental injuries such as shaken baby syndrome can cause retinal hemorrhages, scarring, and detachment of the retina that can lead to visual impairment. Certain congenital infections and inborn conditions such as Tay-Sachs disease and retinal tumors can lead to blindness in the infected eye.

The incidence of blindness among children with developmental delays or other disabilities is higher (about 200 times) compared to typically developing children (Warburg, Frederiksen, & Rattleff, 1979; Flett & Saunders, 1993; McQuaid & Arvidsson, 1992). Some studies suggest that the high prevalence of visual impairment in children with developmental disability is related to their low level of cognitive functioning (Nielsen, Skov, & Jensen, 2007).

Diagnosis of Visual Impairment

Vision tests are done using direct observation of the eyes and the use of eye charts or high-tech equipment (Holladay, 1997). The success of using eye charts depends on the child's verbal responses and can be done beginning around age 3 (Broderick, 1998). In younger children or children who are nonverbal, certain nonverbal technologies can be used, such as optokinetic nystagmus (OKN), preferential looking (PL), and electrophysiological testing (Jackson & Saunders, 1999).

In OKN testing, the child's response is determined by rotating a black-and-white vertically striped drum in front of the child's eyes while examining the child's eye movements. The child's eyes should involuntarily move back and forth as they follow the movement of one stripe and then quickly jerk back to fixate on another (Holladay, 1997). In PL testing, the child is shown a series of cards with patterns of black-and-white stripes on one side and a blank gray target on the other side. The patterns become thinner on successive cards that require better visual resolution. The examiner presents the cards at a specific distance and watches the child's fixation through a peephole in the center of each card, looking for the child's ability to reliably look at the finer patterns (Holladay, 1997). Finally, in electrophysiological testing the examiner determines whether the vision problems are primarily related to the eyes or the brain (Weleber & Palmer, 1991). During the diagnostic process, the cause of visual impairment is identified, and the medical team determines whether or not vision might be corrected via medical means.

Aside from the medical evaluation and diagnosis, the early intervention or the special education team might perform a **functional vision assessment (FVA)** of the child. A functional vision assessment helps in understanding how the child can use his vision in different situations. The early intervention or early childhood special education team usually examines the child within his natural environment to determine if and how the child utilizes his residual vision in order to do things (Turnbull et al., 2007). Residual vision is any visual ability that the child might possess. FVA helps educators understand whether or not the child is able to see certain objects in specific lightings and environments—such as in the playground, at home, or in the classroom—or whether and to what extent the child can see small and large objects.

STRATEGIES AND ADAPTATIONS FOR CHILDREN WITH VISUAL IMPAIRMENTS IN INCLUSIVE CLASSROOMS

Children who are blind or have various degrees of visual impairment are able to learn and develop along with their typical peers if they receive appropriate early intervention. These children need to learn how to move safely in their environment, utilize other senses, and use technology and assistive devices that will help them learn and stay safe in their environment (Holladay, 1997). The outcome for children with visual impairment who do not receive appropriate early intervention may be very different from those who do (see Text Box 12.1 for an illustration).

What Happens If We Don't Intervene?	**Text Box 12.1**

Nasrin's Story

Nasrin is a 7-year-old girl who lives with her parents in a village in Iran. When Nasrin was 6 months old, her parents were told by a doctor that she could not see. Nasrin was a quiet baby who did not move a lot. She would stay in one corner and not reach for things nearby. Because Nasrin's mother had to work all day long weaving carpets, she secured Nasrin with a rope nearby while she wove carpets. Her husband worked on the farm. As a result, Nasrin's parents were often unable to play with her. Nasrin had two older siblings who did play with her, sometimes carrying her to places with them. But because she could not see, they were afraid she would hurt herself. So they preferred to keep her at home and played with her there. When Nasrin was 5, her mother took her to the school in the village. Nasrin did not like the classroom. She cried all the time because she did not know the other children and the teacher. Nasrin's mother took her out of school after a few days and allowed her to spend her days at home, or close to her in the weaving shed. Nasrin sat quietly most of the day, playing with small objects around her. Her siblings and parents took care of her needs and did most things for her. They took her places and helped her move about. By the time she was 7, Nasrin had not learned to move about without help from a sibling or a parent. Although she had learned to feed herself, she was unable to dress or take care of her hygiene needs independently.

(Continued)

The Difference—Javad's Story

Javad is an 8-year-old boy who grew up in another village in Iran. His mother, Fatmeh, realized that Javad could not see when he was very young. Fatmeh's father had lost his vision when he was old, and Fatmeh remembered how he had to learn to find his way around and do things for himself. Having seen her father, Fatmeh knew that Javad could also learn. From the time Javad was very young, Fatmeh talked and played with him. For example, she would shake things that made sound near him and encourage him to move toward the sound to grasp the shaking object. When she worked on the farm, she would take Javad with her. She secured Javad on her back with a sling and explained everything to him as she worked. She made Javad touch and feel things around the farm and told him what they were. As soon as Javad began to crawl, she let him crawl in safe places. When he was able to walk, she described to him where things were, so that he could move about safely and find his way with a cane. Javad learned to play with animals and explore objects safely. Javad had many friends amongst the children in the village and participated in their games and play. By the time he was 5, Javad had learned to move about and go to different places in the village with the help of a cane. People in the village knew Javad, and stopped to talk to him when he walked by. He learned to go to school by himself and sit in a first grade class. The schoolteacher wrote to the education ministry, and a teacher was sent from the city nearby to train Javad and his teacher to read and write using the Persian braille system. By the time Javad was 8, he was in the third grade. In the evenings, when he was done with his homework, he wove small baskets for his mother to sell in the city market.

Adaptations and Environmental Modifications for Children with Visual Impairment

Adjustment of and use of appropriate lighting at home and in early childhood classrooms is elemental in enhancing the vision of children with visual impairment. Understanding what kind of lighting is appropriate for the child with a visual impairment depends on that child's FVA and should be decided in consultation with experts. Some children with low vision have a sensitivity to light. In such cases, it might be better to keep the area dimly lit, while placing target objects under spotlights (Klein, Cook, & Richardson-Gibbs, 2001). Other children with low vision may not be sensitive to light. In those cases, such children might benefit from bright classrooms. While children with low vision benefit from the illumination of specific toys and other educational materials, direct light or glare on the child's face should be avoided as much as possible (Klein et al., 2001). The positioning of objects with colors that contrast one another will also provide optimal visual input for young children and infants with visual impairment. For example, dark objects can be placed on top of lighter objects, or vice versa.

For children whose field of vision is restricted, choosing the appropriate size and positioning of objects and materials is important. For example, children whose field of vision is restricted to the middle—that is, children with *tunnel vision*—should have objects put in front and further away from them. They might also benefit from viewing smaller objects compared to bigger ones (Klein et al., 2001). Classroom and home furniture must be secured to the floor and should be placed in such a way that movement and mobility is safe for children with visual impairment.

Promoting Orientation and Mobility

In order for infants and young children to learn to become independent, they first need to learn to move on their own in their environment. **Orientation** refers to a child's ability to figure out where they are, while **mobility** describes skills that help the child move about (Matsuba & Graham, 2008; Sonksen, Petrie, & Drew, 1991). Orientation and mobility (O&M) skills help children with visual impairment find their way around and move about within their environment. **Orientation and mobility specialists** are educators who are trained to help children with visual disabilities to develop a sense of direction and body awareness, discover and understand environmental sounds, and learn to move safely in their environment. When appropriate, they also teach children how to utilize toys, such as push toys, and use an assistive device, such as a cane, to move about (Matsuba & Graham, 2008; Emerson & Corn, 2006). Orientation and mobility services are part of the supplementary services mandated by IDEA for children with visual impairment.

Orientation and mobility training in infants begins with teaching infants their body parts and their positions, and how to locate things in their environment (Matsuba & Graham, 2008). Learning to listen to and understand environmental sounds is another component of O&M skills. Specifically, distinguishing dangerous sounds is the key to moving about safely and staying away from dangerous events (Warren, 1994). Text Box 12.2 provides some tips for providing orientation and mobility training for infants and toddlers.

Tips for Orientation and Mobility Training for Infants and Toddlers	Text Box 12.2

> Provide hand-on-hand prompts for the infant in order to help him touch different parts of his face and body. Name the body parts as the infant touches them.
> Provide hand-on-hand prompts for the infant to help her touch different parts of your face and body. Name the body parts as the infant explores them.
> Describe the position of the child's body parts.
> Shake a sounding toy, or rattle, and encourage the infant to crawl toward the direction of the sound.
> Have the toddler touch different objects located in various places and call out different positional directions: top, bottom, left, right, above, under, and so on.
> Describe the direction of objects and toys to the toddler: "The doll is next to your left foot."
> Describe the location of furniture and structural features: "The door is coming up just in front of you."

(Continued)

> Point out far away and muffled sounds to encourage listening skills.
> Describe what sounds mean: "The beep-beep sound means that a truck is backing up."

Source: Warren, D. (1994). *Blindness and children: An individual differences approach.* New York: Cambridge University Press.

Promoting Play and Exploration

Objects and toys that make a noise are appropriate for infants and very young children with visual impairment. Caregivers and educators should describe different items in simple words and short sentences. It is important to use real objects in place of their representational toys. For example, using a real telephone or a real cat is more meaningful than using a toy phone or a stuffed cat, since the child with visual impairment needs to understand what the object is first, before realizing its representations (Warren, 1994). It is also important to provide appropriate physical prompts so that children with visual impairment learn how to explore those objects appropriately (McAllister & Gray, 2007). Providing appropriate verbal cues by using self- and parallel talk when guiding children to explore and play with objects is especially important.

Language and Literacy Skills

Adults' verbal input and use of language with children with visual impairment is elemental in teaching them communication and literacy skills (Ferrell, 2006). Just as it is important for all children to be exposed to print and books during early childhood, it is imperative for young children with visual impairment to have an environment that is rich in braille labels and books as early as possible (Emerson, Holbrook, & D'Andrea, 2009; Ferrell, 2006). Toys and objects in the environment could be labeled in braille. In addition, talking or audio books should be plentiful and accessible to these children. Making available the braille and audio versions of the same book at the same time helps these children connect braille print to the words they hear. Many children's books are available in both braille and print. Such books are good vehicles for read-a-loud and shared book reading activities where all children can participate. The parents' participation in various tactile activities provided in the early childhood classroom is an effective way of supporting parents in helping them provide similar activities at home (Ryles & Bell, 2009).

FINAL REMARKS ON SENSORY DEPRIVATION AND LEARNING

The efforts of early educators in exposing children with sensory deprivation to a variety of experiences are crucial for the children's developmental and future academic success. As illustrated in Text Box 12.3, Anne Sullivan, Helen Keller's teacher, wanted Helen to be exposed to every kind of experience. Because Helen did not have the typical use of her sense of hearing and vision, Sullivan capitalized

Helen Keller and her teacher, Anne Sullivan.

on Helen's other senses. For example, to teach Helen about wild animals, she went as far as having Helen feel a lion (albeit a well-fed young lion), shake hands with a circus bear, and be lifted up to touch the ears of a giraffe (Brooks, 1954). Much as Anne Sullivan did, the education of children who have sensory impairments depends on utilizing those senses that do work well.

In this approach, called *family centered functional therapy,* the family and the therapists (and when appropriate, the child) will identify movement goals for the child to achieve. The emphasis is placed on success in accomplishing a task rather than attaining "normal" patterns of movement. This intervention approach is heavily guided by the family's goals, input, and its success depends on the successful partnership between the intervention team and the family.

Helen Keller and the Use of Language   Text Box 12.3

Helen Keller was a famous author who was deaf and blind. When she was 19 months old, she contracted a fever that left her with no sense of hearing or vision. For most of Helen's early childhood, she was a child who lived in silence and darkness. When Helen was 7, Anne Sullivan, a special educator who had a visual impairment herself, took on the task of educating Helen. In the following passage, Helen describes how she was first taught the function of words.

> We walked down the path to the well-house, attracted by the fragrance of the honeysuckle with which it was covered. Someone was drawing water and my teacher placed my hand under the spout. As the cool stream gushed over one hand, she spelled into the other [hand] the word *water,* first slowly, then rapidly. I stood still, my whole attention fixed upon the motions of her fingers. Suddenly I felt a misty consciousness as if something forgotten—a thrill of returning

(Continued)

thought; and somehow the mystery of language was revealed to me. I knew then that "w-a-t-e-r" meant the wonderful cool something that was flowing over my hand...I learned a great many words that day...*mother, father, sister, teacher* were among them—words that were to make the world blossom for me (Keller, 1902, pp. 23–24).

Because Helen could not hear, she had no idea how words and things in her surroundings sounded, and because she could not see, she did not know what people's speech looked like when they spoke. Helen learned most things by using her sense of touch. Helen touched her teacher's lips and throat to feel the words and the vibration of sounds. She relied on Anne Sullivan's assistance constantly to articulate each sound in hundreds of ways, while Helen felt Sullivan's lips and throat.

Helen's first language was sign language. She learned the manual alphabet before she learned to speak. Helen felt each letter by touching the hand of the manual speaker. With constant practice, Helen learned to understand what others said, and learned to spell words manually rapidly. Being mentored and educated by Anne Sullivan, Helen received a degree from Radcliffe College and wrote several books. She became a public speaker and an advocate for the blind until the day she died in 1968.

Source: Keller, H. (1902). *The story of my life.* New York: Grosset & Dunlap.

Research Corner

The Importance of Early Identification of Infants with Permanent Hearing Loss

Vohr and her colleagues (2008) at Brown University conducted a longitudinal study of 30 infants who had mild to severe congenital hearing loss at birth, comparing their development with 96 children with typical development. Their study, published in 2008, reported that infants who have permanent hearing loss benefit in their language development if they are enrolled in early intervention programs before age 3 months (Vohr, Jodoin-Krauzyk, Tucker, Johnson, & Topol, 2008). Previous research had indicated that, in general, children with hearing loss lag behind their typically developing peers in language development.

Vohr and her colleagues (2008) have found that children with hearing loss when enrolled in early intervention very early (before age 3 months) have a significantly higher level of language development (i.e., the number of words understood, words produced, and gestures) compared with infants with hearing loss who were enrolled at 3 months and older. Their study has serious implications for the early identification of infants with congenital hearing loss and very early intervention.

SUMMARY

Low-incidence disabilities refer to a group of disabilities that do not affect a large number of children within schools. These disorders include, but are not limited to: deafness and hearing loss, blindness and visual impairment, and other physical and health impairments (such as chronic illness and degenerative diseases).

Historically, children who are deaf and blind have been treated poorly in different societies. However, within the last couple of centuries educators have devoted effort in designing a variety of methods to educate these children. Advances in technology and medical science have enabled children with

deafness and blindness to participate in schools and communities along with their typical peers and achieve goals similar to those of their peers. Educating children with deafness requires specific training in deaf education and also various methods (such as sign language) of working with children with hearing loss. Working with deaf children also requires sensitivity to values within the Deaf community.

Children with visual impairment are often educated in inclusive classrooms. Working with children with visual impairment requires knowledge of specific methods, the braille system, and specific adaptations of the environment to promote mobility.

Review Questions

1. Define the term *low-incidence* disabilities.
2. What is the difference between the terms *Deaf* and *deaf*?
3. What are some possible causes of hearing loss?
4. What is the difference between acquired and congenital deafness?
5. What are assistive listening devices?
6. What are implants?
7. What is manual babbling?
8. Describe two methods of oral and manual communication.

9. What is American Sign Language (ASL) and how does it differ from Signed Exact English (SEE)?
10. What is visual acuity?
11. What are the types of visual impairment?
12. Who might be considered legally blind?
13. How does the development of children with visual impairment differ from their typically developing peers?
14. What are orientation and mobility (O&M) skills?

Out-of-Class Activities

1. Interview a member of the Deaf community regarding sign language and other issues of importance to their community. Research arguments against the issues raised by the Deaf community. Use your findings to participate in a class debate on sign language versus oral language and other related issues.

2. Record a 15-minute segment of a TV newscast. Watch the recorded segment without any volume. Watch the movement of the reporters' lips. Try to identify and write down as many words as you can just by watching the movement of their lips. Try to guess what the news story was about. Listen to the segment and compare your notes to what the news was actually about.

Recommended Resources

Alexander Graham Bell Association for the Deaf and
Hard of Hearing
http://www.agbell.org

American Foundation for the Blind
http://www.afb.org

American Sign Language (ASL) University
http://www.lifeprint.com

American Speech-Language-Hearing Association (ASHA)
http://www.asha.org

Blind Childrens Center
http://www.blindchildrenscenter.org

Blind Children's Fund
http://www.blindchildrensfund.org

Braille Plus Inc. (resources on braille for individuals with
visual impairments)
http://www.brailleplus.net

Laurent Clerc National Deaf Education Center: Gallaudet
University
http://clerccenter.gallaudet.edu

Raising Deaf Kids
http://www.raisingdeafkids.org

The American Foundation for the Blind
http://www.afb.org

**View the Online Resources available to accompany
this text by visiting http://www.mhhe.com/bayat1e.**

References

American Academy of Pediatrics. (1999). Newborn and
   infant hearing loss: Detection and intervention.
   Pediatrics, 103(2), 527–530.

American Speech-Language-Hearing Association. (2007).
   Types, degrees, and configuration of hearing loss.
   Retrieved November 29, 2007, from http://www.
   asha.org/public/hearing/disorders/types.htm

Bailes, C., Erting, L., Thumann-Prezioso, C., & Erting C.
   (2009). Language and literacy acquisition through
   parental mediation in American Sign Language. *Sign
   Language Studies, 9*(4), 417–456.

Baker, K. (2008). *Oral communication versus American
   Sign Language.* Retrieved July 5, 2008, from http://
   www.drury.edu/multinl/story.cfm?ID=9901&
   NLID=166

Bat-Chava, Y., Martin, D., & Kosciw, J. G. (2005).
   Longitudinal improvements in communication and
   socialization of deaf children with cochlear implants
   and hearing aids: Evidence from parental reports.
   Journal of Child Psychology and Psychiatry, 46(12),
   1287–1296.

Bell, M. J. (2007). Infections and the fetus. In
   M. L. Batshaw, L. Pellegrino, & N. J. Roizen (Eds.),
   Children with disabilities (6th ed., pp. 71–82).
   Baltimore: Paul H. Brookes.

Bergen, A. (2007). A philosophical experiment: The
   Wilberforce School for the Blind c.1833–1870.
   European Review of History, 12(2), 147–162.

Braddock, D., & Parish, S. L. (2002). An institutional
   history of disability. In D. Braddock (Ed.), *Disability
   at the dawn of the 21st century and the state of
   the states* (pp. 3–61). Washington, DC: American
   Association on Mental Retardation.

Broderick, P. (1998). Pediatric vision screening for the
   family physician. *American Family Physician, 58,*
   691–700, 703–704.

Brooks, V. W. (1954). *Helen Keller: Sketch for a portrait.*
   New York: Dutton & Co., INC.

Brown C., & Bower, B. (1986). *Movement analysis and
   curriculum for visually impaired preschoolers:
   A resource manual for the development and evaluation
   of special programs for exceptional students.*
   Tallahassee, FL: Florida Department of Education,
   Bureau of Education for Exceptional Students.

Campbell, T. F., Dollaghan, C. A., Rockette, H. E.,
   Paradise, J. L., Feldman, H. M., Shriberg, L. D.,
   et al. (2003). Risk factors for speech delay of
   unknown origin in 3-year-old children. *Child
   Development, 74*(2), 346–357.

Cavendish, R. (2002). Death of Louis Braille. *History
   Today.* 52(1), 54.

Cohen, N. (2004). CI candidacy and surgical considerations.
   Audiology & Neuro-otology, 9, 197–202.

Cohen, E. S., Kelley, P. M., Fowler, T. W., Gorga, M. P.,
   Lefkowitz, D. M., Kuehn, H. J., et al. (1999).
   Clinical studies of families with hearing loss

attributable to mutations in the connexin 26 Gene (GJB2/DFNB1). *Pediatrics, 103*(2), 546–550.

Commission on Education of the Deaf. (1988). *Toward equality: Education of the deaf.* Washington, DC: U.S. Government Printing Office.

Compton, M. V. (1994). Expression of affection in young children with sensory impairments: A research agenda. Education & Treatment of Children, *17*(1), 68–86.

De Clerck, G. A. M. (2007). Meeting global deaf peers, visiting ideal deaf places: Deaf ways of education leading to empowerment, an exploratory case study. *American Annals of the Deaf, 152*(1), 5–15.

Dornan, D., Hickson, L., Murdoch, B., & Houston, T. (2007). Outcomes of an auditory-verbal program for children with hearing loss: A comparative study with a matched group of children with normal hearing. *The Volta Review, 107*(1), 37–54.

Eleweke, C., Gilbert, S., Bays, D., & Austin, E. (2008). Information about support services for families of young children with hearing loss: A review of some useful outcomes and challenges. *Deafness & Education International, 10*(4), 190–212.

Emerson, R. S. W., & Corn, A. L. (2006). Orientation and mobility content for children and youth: A Delphi approach pilot study. *Journal of Visual Impairment and Blindness, 100*(6), 331–342.

Emerson, R., Holbrook, M., & D'Andrea, F. (2009). Acquisition of literacy skills by young children who are blind: Results from ABC braille study. *Journal of Visual Impairment & Blindness, 103*(10), 610–624.

Ferrell, K. A. (2006). Evidence-based practices for students with visual disabilities. *Communication Disorders Quarterly, 28*(1), 42–48.

Flett, P., & Saunders, B. (1993). Ophthalmic assessment of physically disabled children attending a rehabilitation school. *Journal of Pediatric Child Health, 29,* 132–135.

Gallagher, P. A., Easterbrooks, S., & Malone, D. G. (2006). Universal newborn hearing screening and intervention: Assessing the current collaborative environment in service provision. *Infants and Young Children, 19*(1), 59–71.

Gallaudet University. (2008). *Gallaudet history: The first 50 years.* Retrieved July 3, 2008, from http://www .gallaudet.edu/x228.xml

Gannon, J. R. (1981). *Deaf heritage: A narrative history of deaf America.* Silver Spring, MD: National Association of the Deaf.

Good, W. V., & Hoyt, C. S. (1989). Behavioral correlates of poor vision in children. *International Ophthalmology Clinics, 38,* 251–264.

Haffner, W. H. J. (2007). Development before birth. In M. L. Batshaw, L. Pellegrino, & N. J. Roizen (Eds.), *Children with disabilities* (6th ed., pp. 23–33). Baltimore: Paul H. Brookes.

Hatton, D. D. (2001). Model registry of early childhood visual impaired collaborative group: First year results. J*ournal of Blindness and Visual Impairments, 95,* 418–433.

Hatton, D. D., Bailey, D. B., Burchinal, M. R., & Ferrell, K. A. (1997). Developmental growth curves of preschool children with visual impairments. *Child Development, 68*(5), 788–806.

Herer, G. R., Knightly, C. A., & Steinberg, A. G. (2007). Hearing: Sounds and silences. In M. L. Batshaw, L. Pellegrino, & N. J. Roizen (Eds.), *Children with disabilities* (6th ed., pp. 157–183). Baltimore: Paul H. Brookes.

Hernandez, J. (2007, November). *The history of technology for the blind,* paper presented at the Overbrook School for the Blind's 175 Anniversary Technology Seminar. Retrieved November, 26, 2007, from http://www.nyise .org/osb175/index_files/frame.html

Holladay, J. T. (1997). Proper method for calculating average visual acuity. *Journal of Retractive Surgery, 13,* 388–391.

Humphries, T., & Allen, B. M. (2008). Reorganizing teacher preparation in deaf education. *Sign Language Studies, 8*(2), 160–180.

Jackson, A. J., & Saunders, K. J. (1999). The optometric assessment of the visually impaired infant and child. *Ophthalmic and Physiological Optics, 2,* 49–62.

Jones, T. W., & Ewing, K. M. (2002). An analysis of teacher preparation in deaf education: Programs approved by the Council of Education of the Deaf. *American Annals of the Deaf, 147*(5), 71–79.

Keller, H. (1902). *The story of my life.* New York: Grosset & Dunlap.

Kesiktas, A. (2009). Early childhood special education for children with visual impairments: Problems and solutions. *Educational Sciences: Theory & Practice, 9*(2), 823–832.

Klein, M. D., Cook, R. E., & Richardson-Gibbs, A. M. (2001). *Strategies for including children with special needs in early childhood settings.* Clifton Park, NY: Delmar, Thomson Learning.

Klein, R., Gilkerson, L., & Davis, E. (2008). Prenatal development. In L. Gilkerson & R. Klein (Eds.), *Early development and the brain: Teaching resources for educators,* (pp. 2.9–2.50). Washington, DC: Zero To Three.

Lane, H., Hoffmeister, R., & Bahan, B. (1996). *A journey into the Deaf-world.* San Diego: Dawn Sign Press.

Li, Y., Womer, R., & Silber, J. (2004). Predicting cisplatin ototoxicity in children: The influence of age and the cumulative dose. *European Journal of Cancer, 40,* 2445–2451.

Luckner, J. L., Muir, S. G., Howell, J. J., Sebald, A. M., & Young III, J. (2005). An examination of the research and training needs in the field of deaf education. *American Association of the Deaf, 150*(4), 358–368.

Ludlow, B. L., Conner, D., & Schechter, J. (2005). Low incidence disabilities and personnel preparation for rural areas: Current status and future trends. *Rural Special Education Quarterly, 24*(3), 15–24.

Marschark, M. (1993). *Psychological development of deaf children.* New York: Oxford University Press.

Matsuba, C., & Graham, M. (2008). MM:5 Orientation and mobility-moving towards independence: The early years. *Developmental Medicine & Child Neurology, 40*(sup.4), 82.

McAllister, R., & Gray, C. (2007). Low vision: Mobility and independence training for the early years child. *Early Child Development and Care, 177*(8), 839–852.

McGinnis, M., Orr, C., & Freutel, J. (1980). Becoming a social being. *The Volta Review, 80,* 370–379.

McQuaid, R. D., & Arvidsson, J. (1992). Vision examination of children in Riyadh's handicapped children house. *Journal of American Optometric Association, 63,* 262–265.

Minski, L. (1957). *Deafness, mutism, and mental deficiency in children.* New York: Philosophical Library.

Moog, J. S., & Geers, A. E. (1999). Speech and language acquisition in young children after cochlear implantation. *Otolaryngologic Clinics of North American, 32,* 1127–1141.

Moores, D. (1997). *Educating the deaf: Psychology, principles and practices* (4th ed.). Boston: Houghton Mifflin.

Nance, W. (2003). The genetics of deafness. *Mental Retardation and Disabilities Research Review, 9,* 109–119.

National Association of the Deaf. (2008). *American Sign Language.* Retrieved July 5, 2008, from http://www.nad.org/site/pp.asp?c=foINKQMBF&b=99566

National Dissemination Center for Children with Disabilities. (2004). *Visual impairments* (NICHCY Fact Sheet No. 13). Retrieved July 5, 2008, from http://www.nichcy.org/pubs/factshe/fs13.pdf

National Institute of Deafness and other Communication Disorders. (2001). *Has your baby's hearing been screened?* Retrieved July 3, 2008, from http://www.nidcd.nih.gov/health/hearing/screened.asp

Nielsen, L. S., Skov, L., & Jensen, H. (2007). Visual dysfunctions and ocular disorders in children with developmental delay. II. Aspects of refractive errors, strabismus and contrast sensitivity. *Acta Ophthalmologica Scandinavica, 85,* 419–426.

Northern, J. L., & Downs, M. P. (2002). *Hearing in children* (5th ed.). Philadelphia: Lippincott, Williams & Wilkins.

Oliphant, J. (2006). Empowerment and debilitation in the educational experience of the blind in nineteenth-century England and Scotland. *History of Education, 35*(1), 47–68.

Padden, C., & Ramsey, C. (1998). Reading ability in signing deaf children. *Topics in Language Disorders, 18*(4), 30–46.

Perez-Pereira, M., & Conti-Ramsden, G. (1999). *Language development and social interaction in blind children.* Philadelphia: Psychology Press.

Petitto, L. A., Holowka, S., Sergio, L. E., & Ostry, D. (2001). Language rhythms in baby hand movements. *Nature, 413,* 35.

Plann, S. (1997). A *silent minority: Deaf education in Spain, 1550–1835.* Berkeley, CA: University of California Press.

Pribanic, L. (2006). Sign language and deaf education: A new tradition. *Sign Language and Linguistics, 9*(1), 233–254.

Raver, S. (1999). *Intervention strategies for infants and toddlers with special needs: A team approach,* (2nd ed.). Upper Saddle River, NJ: Prentice Hall.

Reitsma, P. (2009). Computer-based exercises for learning to read and spell by deaf children. *Journal of Deaf Studies & Deaf Education, 14*(2), 178–189.

Roizen, N. (2007). Down syndrome. In M. L. Batshaw, L. Pellegrino, & N. J. Roizen (Eds.), *Children with disabilities* (6th ed., pp. 263–283). Baltimore: Paul H. Brookes.

Ryles, R., & Bell, E. (2009). Participation of parents in the early exploration of tactile graphics by children who are visually impaired. *Journal of Visual Impairment & Blindness, 103*(10), 625–634.

Schembri, A., & Johnson, T. (2007). Sociolinguistic variation in the use of fingerspelling in Australian sign language: A pilot study. *Sign Language Studies, 7*(3), 319–347.

Schraer-Joiner, L., & Chen-Hafteck, L. (2009). The response of preschoolers with cochlear implants to musical activities: A multiple case study. *Early Child Development & Care, 179*(6), 785–798.

Scollie, S., & Seewald, R. (2001). Hearing aid selection and verification in children. In J. Katz (Ed.), *Handbook of clinical audiology* (pp. 687–706). Philadelphia: Lippincott, Williams & Wilkins.

Smith, R., Bale, J. J., & White, K. (2005). SN hearing loss in children. *The lancet, 365*(9462), 879–890.

Sonksen, P. M., Petrie, A., & Drew, K. J. (1991). Promotion of visual development of severely visually impaired babies: Evaluation of a developmentally based programme. *Developmental Medicine and Child Neurology, 33,* 320–335.

Svirsky, M. A., Robbins, A. M., Kirk, K. I., Pisoni, D. B., & Miyamoto, R. T. (2000). Language development in profoundly deaf children with cochlear implants. *Psychological Science, 11,* 153–158.

Turnbull, A., Turnbull, R., & Wehmeyer, M. (2007). *Exceptional lives: Special education in today's schools* (5th ed.). Upper Saddle River, NJ: Prentice Hall.

U.S. Department of Education. (2000). *Twenty-second annual report to Congress on the implementation of the Individuals with Disabilities Education Act.* Washington, DC: Author.

Vohr, B., Jodoin-Krauzyk, J., Tucker, R., Johnson, M., & Topol, D. (2008). Early language outcomes for early-identified infants with permanent hearing loss at 12 to 16 months of age. *Pediatrics, 122*(3), 535–544.

Warburg, M., Frederiksen, P., & Rattleff, J. (1979). Blindness among 7,720 mentally retarded children in Denmark. *Clinics in Developmental Medicine, 73,* 56–67.

Warren, D. H. (1994). *Blindness and children: An individual differences approach.* Cambridge, UK: Cambridge University Press.

Weleber, R., & Palmer, R. (1991). Electrophysiological evaluation of children with visual impairment. *Seminars in Ophthalmology, 6*(4), 161–168.

White, K. R., Vohr, B. R., & Behrens, T. R. (1993). Newborn hearing screening using transient evoked otoacoustic emissions: Results of the Rhode Island hearing assessment project. *Seminars in Hearing, 14*(1), 18–29.

White, K. (2008). Screening. *Seminars in Hearing, 29*(2), 149–158.

Zapien, C. (1998). *Options in deaf education: history, methodologies, and strategies for surviving the system.* Retrieved November 2, 2007, from http://www.listen-up.org/edu/options1.htm

Chapter 13

Children with Motor Problems and Other Health Impairments

Objectives

Upon completion of this chapter, you should be able to:

> Understand theoretical foundations and issues related to motor development in children.

> Describe gross and fine motor development in infancy.

> Describe gross and fine motor development in preschool-age children and those in their early primary years.

> Understand the influences of motor development on the development of adaptive skills.

> Understand and describe types of neuromotor problems, gross motor problems, and oral motor problems in children.
> Understand strategies and adaptations related to working with and supporting children with motor problems in inclusive classrooms.
> Understand important childhood degenerative diseases and chronic illnesses.
> Describe ways in which early childhood educators help children with chronic health impairments achieve the maximum benefits from their school community.

Key Terms

acquired
  immunodeficiency
  syndrome (462)
adaptive skills (440)
auditory system (447)
cephalocaudal (449)
dynamic systems
  model (439)
fine motor (439)
graphomotor (445)
grasping (441)
gross motor (439)
gustatory system (447)
handedness (445)
human immunodeficiency
  virus (462)

hypertonia (450)
hypotonia (450)
locomotion (441)
motor or movement
  planning (448)
musculoskeletal (MSK)
  system (449)
neuromuscular (NM)
  system (449)
olfactory system (447)
oral motor (439)
perceptual motor
  skills (440)
postural and balance
  control (441)
praxis (448)

proprioceptive
  system (447)
proximodistal (449)
reaching (441)
sensory integration (439)
sensory motor (439)
sensory processing
  dysfunction (449)
spasticity (450)
tactile system (447)
universal health
  precautions (462)
vestibular system (447)
visual system (447)

Reflection Questions

Before reading this chapter, answer the following questions to reflect upon your personal opinions and beliefs that are pertinent to early childhood special education.

1. In your opinion, how might the development of motor skills be related to other areas of development, such as cognitive or adaptive skills?
2. In your opinion, how important is it for a preschool-age child to learn self-care skills?
3. In your opinion, what are some issues you should be aware of when working with a child who has severe motor problems?
4. What are some issues you would like to address if you work with a child who is HIV positive?
5. What are some supports that you think are important to have if you work with a child who has a chronic health problem?

Penny's Success

Penny is an 8-year-old girl who has cerebral palsy. She lives with her parents in a small town in Missouri. When Penny was an infant, her mother Grace noticed that Penny frequently arched her back and her arms, and her legs became very stiff. Grace also noticed that as an infant Penny had problems with suckling and feeding. Grace and her husband became increasingly concerned about their daughter's problems and discussed it with their child's pediatrician. The doctor recommended a series of medical tests that eventually showed Penny had spastic quadriplegia cerebral palsy. This meant that Penny's entire body was affected by cerebral palsy, including the muscles involved in her eating.

Penny began to receive early intervention, consisting of physical therapy in the hospital and nursing support at home. Grace and her husband learned to care for Penny at home. Penny made very slow but steady progress in her motor development. By age 1, she continued to have difficulty moving her legs and arms. However, by the time Penny was 22 months old, she had learned to sit with support, walk using a walker, and lift herself into her wheelchair with support. Often she had jerky and out of control movements. Despite her motor development, at 24 months, Penny was only slightly behind her peers in cognitive development.

When Penny was 2½ years old, she began attending an early care program that was established and funded by the company in which Penny's father worked. None of the early childhood personnel at the center had worked with children with special needs prior to Penny's enrollment in the program. At first, they felt nervous about working with Penny. The director of the center decided that the best way for her staff to learn about Penny and her needs was to work and partner with Penny's parents.

Because eating was difficult for Penny, as she frequently coughed and vomited during eating, Penny had a gastrostomy tube (G-tube) inserted for feeding when she was 3 years old. Grace and her husband were more than happy to work with teachers. Every day they took turns stopping at the center and showing staff how to feed Penny with the G-tube. They brought in Penny's physical therapist and nutritionist from the hospital to speak about Penny's specific care and needs. They showed staff how to work with Penny's stander, gait trainer, and wheelchair. The director of the center, along with Penny's parents, worked with a local public school to develop an IEP for Penny and have an occupational therapist and an itinerant special educator come to the program to work with Penny toward meeting her IEP goals.

When Penny was 4½ years old, the doctors recommended that Grace and her husband consider Intrathecal Baclofen (ITB) therapy for Penny. ITB therapy involves surgically inserting a pump under the skin of the abdomen. The pump is programmable and connected to a catheter that delivers a liquid form of Baclofen (a medicine used to treat spasticity [increased muscle tone]) into the body and around the spinal cord. Penny made remarkable improvements with the ITB therapy. It helped her move her arms and legs with more ease. Through the therapy and the concerted efforts of her parents, educators, and therapists, Penny made remarkable gains in all areas of development. A year later, Penny no longer required a G-tube and had begun to move and do self-care tasks independently.

When she was 6 years old, Penny was enrolled in a public school and received her first grade education in an inclusive classroom. Today, Penny is educated in a third grade general education classroom. Although she has some difficulties with specific movements and daily activities, Penny is now able to do all tasks independently, and participate in all aspects of school and community life along with her peers.

INTRODUCTION

In the opening story, Penny's cerebral palsy adversely affected her physical and cognitive development. Fortunately for Penny, well-coordinated teamwork and intervention helped her overcome many of her initial movement and motor problems. Although a similar sequence of events is what is hoped for for all children with motor development problems, not all children with orthopedic impairments or other health conditions have the same outcome. The type and severity of motor problems and health issues in children are varied, and thus intervention and outcomes are also varied.

Children who have orthopedic impairments or have health conditions that impede their learning are eligible to receive special education services under IDEA. In this chapter, we focus on these two groups of children. To understand issues related to the physical development of children, we will first examine gross and fine motor development and their characteristics in infants and young children in light of the most recent theoretical framework in motor development. We will then look at a number of the most common motor impairments in children, along with strategies for inclusive classrooms. Finally, we will examine a number of chronic health problems in young children and their related issues.

THE THEORETICAL FOUNDATIONS OF MOTOR DEVELOPMENT

Our understanding of the process of motor development in children has undergone dramatic changes during the past three decades. In traditional views of motor development, articulated by Arnold Gesell and Myrtle McGraw in the 1920s through the 1940s (Gesell & Thompson, 1938; McGraw, 1943), motor development was seen as a rigid and gradual unfolding of posture and movement milestones that took place as a result of the maturation of the central nervous system. This view, called the *maturational* or *hierarchical model* of development, emphasized that the regularities seen in motor development reflected regularities in brain development and maturation in all infants, and therefore any deviation in milestones indicated a deviation or problem in brain development in the infant.

In the 1980s and 1990s, the traditional views of motor development began to shift with a series of sophisticated infant experiments done by Thelen and her colleagues (Lockman & Thelen, 1993). Thelen explained an infant's motor development through a general theory that incorporated action, perception, and cognition (Thelen & Smith, 1994). This view of motor development is known as the **dynamic systems model** of development. According to Thelen, although the central nervous system plays a role, other factors also play crucial roles in motor development. She characterized development not as a process of gradual change, but as a process marked by variability, discontinuities, jumps, regressions, and instabilities (Savelsbergh, Van Hof, Caljouw, Ledebt, & Van Der Kamp, 2006).

According to the dynamic systems model, motor development is not only influenced by the maturation of the brain, but it occurs as a result of an interaction between the biomechanical and energetic properties of the body (such as leg and arm muscles), environmental support (such as gravity), and the specific or changing demands of the particular task (such as body position and object size) (Savelsbergh et al., 2006; Thelen & Smith, 1994; Thelen, 1995). In this model, perception is not separated from motor action. Rather, sensory processing works in tandem with motor movement, and are in fact interconnected (Thelen, 1995).

The dynamic systems model is influenced by the discoveries in the field of infant brain research and neuroscience of the last two or three decades that state: (1) there is no predetermined point-to-point wiring of the brain; brain development depends on the experiences of the infant through interactions with the environment and other people, and (2) all areas of the brain are interconnected with one another and changes in one brain network influence development in other networks of the brain. Therefore, all sensory and motor areas of the brain are integrated together with other parts of the brain to create a coordinated response across the body (Thelen, 1995). Using this dynamic systems model as our framework, we will now explain motor development in children in the following sections.

ISSUES OF CONSIDERATION IN MOTOR DEVELOPMENT

Motor development is divided into two general sets of skills: **gross motor** and **fine motor** skills. Gross motor skills consist of the movement and coordination of the large muscles of the limbs and trunk, including posture and locomotion, while fine motor skills are those related to the use of small muscles in the arms and hands, required in the handling and manipulation of small and large objects (Eliot, 2000).

The development of fine and gross motor skills include **oral motor** development and **sensory motor** development. Oral motor abilities include skills such as swallowing, suckling, sucking, munching, and chewing (Eicher, 2007). The development of oral motor skills depends on the growth of oral motor structures, such as the tongue, soft palate, the jaw, the larynx (voice box), and the pharynx (throat), as well as the functioning of the oral and nasal cavity (Eicher, 2007).

Sensory motor development encompasses the physiological and sensory processing mechanisms that reside within the nervous system. The process of **sensory integration** is central to coordination and to the execution of all motor skills. Sensory integration is the process of organizing sensations from the body and environment (Ayers, 1979; Williamson & Anzalone, 2001). (For a more detailed discussion of the sensory integration theory, see Chapter 6.) Sensory integration is key to the development of **perceptual motor skills.** Perceptual motor skills are the ability to mentally organize, interpret, and respond motorically to what one sees, such as visually understanding shapes and letters and being able to draw and write them on paper. Perceptual motor abilities require appropriate sensory integration, hand-eye coordination, movement coordination, and the development of gross and fine muscles (Bushnell & Boudreau, 1993).

All motor abilities—gross, fine, oral motor, and sensory motor—are necessary for a child to develop **adaptive skills** so she can master and control her environment. Adaptive skills are those skills necessary for the independent functioning of a child, including self-care, feeding, dressing, and play when the child is young (Campbell, 2006), and encompass daily living skills and problem solving as she gets older.

The Principles of Motor Development

Motor development in children takes place in a predictive way in relationship to their overall physical growth, which takes place rapidly after birth. During the first year of life, an infant's weight and height grow dramatically. Four major principles are involved in motor development (DeHart, Sroufe, & Cooper, 2000):

> **Differentiation:** An infant's poorly defined motor skills develop into a set of distinguished skills; each has a different function.
> **Cephalocaudal motor development:** Control over motor skills progresses from the head downward toward the lower portions of the body.
> **Proximodistal motor development:** Control over motor skills progresses from the center of the body to the limbs and fingers.
> **Role of multiple factors:** The development of motor skills is influenced by multiple factors, such as brain development, biomechanical and physical growth, sensory processing, and the child's cognitive development and motivation.

The Relationship between Cognitive Processes and Motor Development

Throughout this book, the relationship between all areas of development, has been emphasized. In understanding a child's motor development, the relationship between cognition and motor functioning is particularly important because specific cognitive processes influence motor skills directly. These processes include attention, perception, concept formation, memory, and task learning (Rao, 2006):

> **Attention:** Is the foundation of perception and memory. By attending to an object or a stimulus, the infant perceives and stores the information in his memory. Later, when he attends to an object, he matches his perception to the information in his memory storage (Rao, 2006). Attention also enables a child to give preference to an object or a stimulus (or motivates them to reach for that object), which is fundamental to performing a motor action.
> **Perception:** Occurs through workings of the various sensory systems—auditory, visual, tactile, and so on. The perceptual system works in collaboration with the

motor system to utilize information received from the environment and perform an action. Movement and motor actions are constantly adapted in response to the information received from the perceptual system (Rao, 2006).

> **Concept formation:** Is a higher-order thinking that requires differentiation and categorization of perceived information into the memory system. A child understands a concept before she forms specific goals related to that concept. It is this goal orientation that motivates the child to move and act in response to a specific goal.

> **Memory:** Is formed after information is perceived, attended to, differentiated and categorized, and stored for further use. Motor acts involve both short- and long-term memory systems. Specifically, a working memory system holds information for a short period of time while an action is being performed. For example, when a child is writing numbers from 1 to 10, the child's working memory is being employed to help him retrieve information from his short-term memory, use that information to perform the act of writing, and ultimately send the information to his long-term memory storage for later use. (For a more detailed discussion of working memory, see Chapter 15.)

> **Skill learning:** Depends on the functioning of all cognitive processes discussed in the preceding paragraphs. As the information is processed, a child learns to perform a task through practice. All motoric acts and movements are therefore refined by repetition and practice.

The Components of Motor Acquisition in Children

Several areas are critical in motor control and in the acquisition of skills in children. These areas consist of **postural and balance control, locomotion, reaching,** and **grasping.** Campbell (2006) defines these components as follows:

> **Postural and balance control:** Refers to the efficiency of all kinds of movement such as standing, twisting, sitting, reclining, bending, swinging, and stretching (Arnheim & Pestolesi, 1973). Posture and balance control enable the child to be in charge of his static and dynamic postures, and be able to balance, adapt, and adjust his posture as needed (Sveistrup, Schneiberg, McKinley, McFadyen, & Levin, 2008; Campbell, 2006). To make this possible, sensory, motor, and musculoskeletal systems work in cooperation with one another to help the child achieve control of both her static and dynamic posture.

> **Locomotion:** Refers to movements that move the child from one location to another (Harrow, 1972). It requires the evolution of motor control in a child so he can move from reflexes to a natural, spontaneous, and rhythmic motor movement and behavior (Sveistrup et al., 2008; Campbell, 2006).

> **Reaching:** Requires the development of hand-eye coordination that enables the child to track a static or moving object and make contact with that object using their arms and hands (Jones & Lederman, 2006; Campbell, 2006).

> **Grasping:** Is part of a child's hand function that involves the development of fine muscles and control in the fingers, enabling the child to grasp, hold, and pick up objects (Jones & Lederman, 2006). Reaching and grasping skills are closely related to one another.

GROSS AND FINE MOTOR DEVELOPMENT IN INFANCY

Gross and fine motor skills develop in tandem. Like other areas of development, children master specific motor milestones at particular times in their development (Frankenburg & Dodds, 1967). While 50 percent of children achieve motor milestones at a specific median age, the other 50 percent achieve these milestones after that specified period (Eliot, 2000). Campbell (2006) describes five early stages of gross and fine motor development: functional head control, upright trunk control, lower trunk control in the upright position, fine lower extremity control in the upright position, and object manipulation.

Functional Head Control

The newborn is able to right her head from either full flexion or full extension when she is supported in an upright position. An infant cannot hold her head upright for more than 1 or 2 seconds; however, by the end of 3 or 4 months of age, she is able to hold her head steady in space (Sveistrup et al., 2008; Campbell, 2006). This is necessary for independent sitting and also so the infant can develop eye-head-hand control. In addition, by about 3 months of age, the infant is able to swat or swipe with his legs and arms. For example, when held upright, the infant can keep his leg extended and pound the supporting surface, or make large arm-swiping motions when excited (Campbell, 2006). The absence of these abilities or the presence of tight range muscle activities in some infants might indicate problems in the central nervous system, such as cerebral palsy. In terms of fine motor abilities, at this time the infant is able to open and close her fingers in a kneading pattern and bring a clutched object that is typically held in one hand to the mouth or to the midline (Bushnell & Boudreau, 1993).

Upright Trunk Control

By 6 months of age, an infant can sit independently and manipulate an object with one hand, while holding it with the other. At this time, the infant is not able to turn around independently, or move in and out of the sitting position freely. However, this stage marks the beginning of object manipulation for the child. Although manipulation might not be easy, the child's ability to grasp and feel an object allows him to perceive the object's characteristics and begin understanding its depth (Bushnell & Boudreau, 1993).

Control of Lower Extremities in the Upright Position

By 8 months of age, a child can creep, crawl, and pull himself up to stand up (Eliot, 2000). He can also lower himself from the standing position, flex his hips, and extend his knees partially. Gradually, these abilities enable the child to move while standing up, first with support, and later independently. As the child becomes older, the strides become longer and faster (Campbell, 2006). By about age 2½, the child's foot locomotion has moved from walking to running to jumping, bouncing, and galloping (Robertson & Halverson, 1984).

Object Manipulation

A newborn is capable of automatic grasping reflexes immediately after birth. She is able to flex her fingers when her palm contacts a stimulus. As the infant grows older, her grasping becomes more sophisticated and purposeful. Wallace and Whishaw (2003) classified the evolution of grasping and finger movements in infants (from birth to 5 months of age) into three phases: (1) the formation of fists, preprecision grips (e.g., sideways grasps in which the thumb contacts the side of other fingers), (2) self-directed precision grips (such as the pincer grasp), and (3) object-directed power grips. As the infant develops, her grasping and finger movements become more visually and goal-oriented.

Hand movement and language development seem to be synchronized together (Caulfield, 2001). Vocalization begins somewhere between 2 and 4 months and hand-babbling (described in Chapter 12) begins around the same time (Wallace & Whishaw, 2003).

By 9 months of age, the infant is not only able to rip, bend, squeeze, or pull apart objects, but has learned a coordinated use of her hands, such as opening a box with one hand and pulling its contents out with the other (Campbell, 2006). During the first year of life, the experience of the infant with various objects is especially important, because it is through object manipulation that the infant learns to control objects in the environment and understand cause and effect and object permanence (Karniol, 1989).

Mastery of Oral Motor Skills

The mastery of oral motor skills occurs in stages, with each mastered skill providing the foundation for the next. Oral motor skills consist of the following (Eicher, 2007):

> **Swallowing:** Requires the coordination of muscles in the head, neck, respiratory and gastrointestinal tracts, and input from the nervous system. Swallowing is a complex motor process. When one swallows, respiration ceases as the soft palate elevates to close off the airway at the back of the mouth. Swallowing begins during weeks 12 to 14 of fetal development.
> **Suckling:** Begins around weeks 12 to 14 of fetal development. Suckling and swallowing work in tandem. Suckling is a reflexive action, but gradually (with brain maturation) the infant learns to initiate and control suckling.
> **Sucking:** Requires the tongue to be raised and lowered independently of the jaw.
> **Munching:** Consists of a rhythmical bite-and-release pattern generated by the jaw's opening and closing, while *chewing* is the process of grinding food into smaller pieces.

The development of oral motor skills depends on the growth and maturation of the oral structure involved in swallowing and also on a child's respiration and digestive system health (Eicher, 2007). Any medical condition, such as cerebral palsy, that impairs digestion or respiration can influence the feeding and swallowing process in the child and affect oral motor functioning (Erasmus et al., 2009). Other factors influencing oral motor development and functioning include sensory motor processing difficulties that influence the efficiency of sensory input in the feeding process, and also high or low muscle tone (present in cerebral palsy) that can interfere with trunk, neck, and head alignment, which ultimately influence feeding (Eicher, 2007).

> **Critical Thinking Question 13.1**   In the opening story of this chapter, Penny's mother Grace noticed that Penny had problems with suckling. How do you think Penny's cerebral palsy prevented her from suckling?

MOTOR DEVELOPMENT DURING A CHILD'S PRESCHOOL AND EARLY PRIMARY YEARS

Fine and gross motor development proceeds at a rapid pace in toddlers and pre-schoolers and becomes more refined as children enter school. During the early childhood years, motor development is especially influenced by the pace of sensory development, physical growth, strength, nutrition, motivation, and daily practice (Eliot, 2000).

Environmental factors or daily practices with motor abilities are especially important. To illustrate the importance of environment in motor development, it helps to consider the phenomenon of *African infant precocity*. This term was coined by Leiderman and his colleagues as a result of their 1973 seminal study. They found that in their motor and cognitive development, babies in African cultures are usually many weeks ahead of their counterparts in industrial countries. And although genetic factors might be responsible for some of the differences, about 25 percent of the difference in motor performance in the African children is due to the environmental factors and child-rearing practices of their cultures. For example, it is a necessity for African mothers to teach their young children to sit and walk independently as soon as possible, so that mothers can carry out their daily chores (Eliot, 2000).

Looking at the expanding world of infants and young children, we can therefore surmise that much of the motor development in preschool-age and older children depends on the play and exploration activities that engage all motor components in the child.

Gross Motor Development

Beginning at around age 2, children gain about 5 pounds in weight and 2.5 inches in height every year (Campbell, 2006). Early experiences that encourage toddlers to walk, climb, and hop are extremely important at this age. By age 3, a child's locomotion, posture, and balance control evolve drastically. At this age, children are able to run, catch and throw a ball, alternate feet up and down stairs, stand on one foot for several seconds, walk backward, slide, hop, climb, and gallop (Robertson & Konczak, 2001; Wang, 2004).

Even when the development of motor abilities is restricted due to special needs, gross motor skills can be improved by practicing sequences of motor acts (Gallahue & Ozmun, 1995; Wang, 2004). In 2004, Wang recommended a movement program

Motor development in the early childhood years is especially influenced by the pace of sensory development, physical growth, strength, nutrition, motivation, and daily practice.

for preschoolers that focuses on introducing, developing, and practicing basic loco-motor skills, such as walking backward, forward, sideways, faster, hopping, skipping, and so on.

Fine Motor Development

By preschool age, a child's hand functions have begun to become complex and sophisticated. From age 3 to 6, children gain increasing control over the movement of their hands. Preschoolers generally can employ isolated movements of their fingers, have control over the release of objects, and have developed complex skills that require a complementary coordination between two hands (Henderson & Pehoski, 2006; Pehoski, 2006). Around age 3, children begin enjoying fine motor activities such as scissor cutting, bead stringing, and pasting. Development of fine motor muscles during the preschool years allows young children to begin writing and learning adaptive skills such as pulling pants up and down, putting socks on, buttoning coats, tying shoelaces, holding a glass, and feeding one's self. Fine motor development includes **graphomotor** skills and **handedness.**

Graphomotor Skills

Graphomotor skills refer to abilities that are necessary for drawing and handwriting (Ziviani & Wallen, 2006). While *drawing* involves the creation of a picture with various drawing utensils and on various surfaces, *handwriting* is concerned with the formation of letters and symbols on paper. In young children, graphomotor development begins with their early experiences with finger paint, crayon, and pencil. Both handwriting and drawing are motor tasks that children learn and their efficiency depends on the development of their sense of vision, the development of grasp, the coordination of movement, the manipulation of writing and drawing implements, and utilization of their perceptual motor skills (Ziviani & Wallen, 2006).

This latter consideration is especially important, because young children draw and write what they perceive—or in case of drawing from memory, they draw from what they have held in their working memory from their previous perceptions—rather than what a shape or object might actually look like (Freeman, 1980). As children become more efficient in the integration of sensory information, their drawing and handwriting improves. For example, children integrate the visual sensory information they receive in a progressive manner, from first observing vertical and horizontal lines, to recognizing circles, crosses, squares, oblique lines, triangles, and others (Beery, 1989).

Drawing doesn't always involve precision in grasping. It depends on what kind of drawing implement a child uses and what a child is drawing. Even then, children go through a range of grips before they develop skills to hold a drawing or writing implement using what is called a *tripod grip,* which is developed by around age 6 (Dennis & Swinth, 2001).

Handwriting development is an important component of motor development. It is a vehicle for communication and although its importance has lessened with the advent of technology, it continues to be one of the child's first encounters with literacy (Dobbie & Askov, 1995). Handwriting quality and precision depends on the child's age, language development, working memory, sensory processing and perceptual abilities, the maturity of pencil control, the quality of handwriting instruction, and the child's practice (Ziviani & Wallen, 2006). A child's performance in handwriting legibility and speed evolves qualitatively and quantitatively over time (Ziviani & Wallen, 2006).

Handedness

Handedness includes hand preference and hand performance (Kraus, 2006). *Hand preference* is the person's preference to do the majority of tasks with one hand instead of the other, while *hand performance* refers to one hand's superior proficiency over another hand (Kraus, 2006). Therefore, handedness is defined as a consistent and more proficient use of the preferred hand, compared with the non-preferred hand, and in performing skilled tasks, such as drawing, writing, or object manipulation (Annett, 1985). Handedness occurs as a result of the specialization of motoric, cognitive, language, and social emotional tasks in two brain hemispheres, and is crucial to the healthy development of the child (Mori, Iteya, & Gabbard, 2007). When handedness is not established in a child, it is often indicative of developmental delays or other conditions (Coren, 1992). In addition, an absence of established handedness might result in a lack of proficiency in doing skilled tasks (Kraus, 2006).

Some evidence exists that suggests handedness is hereditary and linked genetically to the X chromosome (McKeever, 2000), and that humans are genetically predisposed to be right-handed (Kraus, 2006). Other evidence indicates that prenatal, perinatal, and postnatal factors such as birth weight, prematurity, difficult delivery, induced birth, the mother's age, and smoking during pregnancy might contribute to left-handedness as opposed to right-handedness (Coren, 1992; Baken, 1991).

Kraus (2006) categorizes handedness in the following way:

> **Right- or left-handed:** A child who clearly prefers to use either the right or left hand, and when the hand also demonstrates superior performance over the other hand.
> **Unestablished handedness:** When a child switches hands during and across tasks. This might mean that the child is in the process of developing handedness.
> **Mixed handers:** An adult or an older child who continues to switch hands during and across tasks.
> **Switched handers:** A child who is inherently left-handed, but learns to draw and write with the right hand.
> **Pathologic handedness:** When there is prenatal, perinatal, and postnatal evidence of trauma in the child that has caused a significant weakness in one hand over the other, while at the same time the child shows a preference for using the weak hand over the stronger one.
> **Ambidextrous:** A child or an adult who is able to draw, write, and perform skilled tasks with both hands in the average to above average normative range.

Sensory Motor and Sensory Integration

Sensory integration describes the various modalities through which a child receives sensory information from his surroundings and his body and organizes this information for use in all tasks. Sensory integration controls the level of arousal (alertness and wakefulness and the transition between the two), attention, affect, and action (Williamson & Anzalone, 2001). The child uses seven sensory systems to integrate and process information: (1) the **auditory system,** (2) **visual system,** (3) **tactile system,** (4) **olfactory system,** (5) **gustatory system,** (6) **vestibular system,** and (7) **proprioceptive system** (Emmons & Anderson, 2005; Kranowitz, 2005; Rosinia, 2008).

> **Auditory system:** Is responsible for sound perception and the processing of the auditory sensory input.
> **Visual system:** Is responsible for visual perception and processing of the visual sensory input.
> **Tactile system:** Allows one to feel the different sensations of hot, cold, sharp, dull, rough, and smooth. It helps one understand four sensations or tactile input: touch and texture, pain, deep and light pressure, and temperature.
> **Olfactory system:** Is responsible for detecting and processing smell.
> **Gustatory system:** Is responsible for detecting and processing taste input.
> **Vestibular system:** Coordinates the movement of eyes, body, and head through space, and helps with the body's movement. It is the vestibular system that allows one to walk while balancing the two sides of one's body and catch oneself when falling.
> **Proprioceptive system:** Uses information from various muscles and joints, and helps one be aware of the body's position in space. It is this system that allows one to know which body part is moving, where one is, and where one is going.

A child with typical sensory motor development not only manages reactions to different sensations she receives from these systems, called *sensory modulation* (for further details see Chapter 6), but is also able to use sensory input to formulate goals, and to plan, sequence, and execute motoric and nonmotoric actions (Savion-Lemieux, Bailey, & Penhune, 2009; Williamson & Anzalone, 2001). This latter aspect, the sensory system's ability to design goals for action is called **praxis.** Praxis controls a great deal of **motor** or **movement planning,** the process of figuring out how to accomplish a goal that involves a sequence of actions, like reaching for and grasping an object or climbing stairs (Williamson & Anzalone, 2001).

Motor planning enables the child to receive sensory information from the tactile and vestibular systems and also from his body's previous movement, and then use this information to plan and execute the action. This is evident in the act of catching a ball. To be able to catch the ball, the child must predict the direction of the moving object (ball) and reach for it at the appropriate time (Rösblad, 2006).

Sensory integration plays a key role in all areas of development, but especially in motor development. For example, a child's feeding and eating is influenced by workings of the oral motor and the gustatory system; his performance in fine motor tasks such as writing, drawing, or cutting with scissors depends on the input received and processed through the visual perceptual system and through motor planning. Or his efficiency in gross motor tasks such as walking, sitting, running, climbing, and balancing depends on the integration and processing of sensory information through the vestibular system, and on the child's motor planning.

THE DEVELOPMENT OF ADAPTIVE SKILLS

Almost all adaptive skills are motor acts and require the development of many components of motor development, such as small and large muscles, sensory and perceptual motor processing, hand-eye coordination, control, and balance. Earlier in this chapter and in Chapter 11, we defined adaptive skills to be daily living skills that are necessary to the independent functioning of the child. Adaptive skills such as eating, dressing, toileting, and bathing are critical to the overall health and well-being of a child, and are tied into the general physical, mental, and social emotional development of the child (Henderson & Pehoski, 2006). In addition, a child's mastery of self-care skills signals independence and a control over the environment that is elemental in the promotion of self-determination in a young child early on. (For a full discussion of self-determination, see Chapter 11.)

In the United States, the acquisition of daily living skills early on is of utmost importance to mainstream culture. For example, all preschool general education programs require that children in their programs be toilet trained. However, many children with special needs have difficulties with achieving adaptive skills, which might become a barrier to their functioning in home and school (Henderson & Pehoski, 2006).

Competency in adaptive skills depends on the development of all motor abilities in conjunction with cognitive development in the child. As a result, any problem with self-care skills in children with special needs might vary depending on the severity of motor or cognitive functioning in those children. For example, performing a daily living task requires that a child recognize what, how, and when to perform a task, and be able to do simple problem solving when needed. Furthermore, a child's motivation is also important, since it helps the child with goal orientation and task performance. For example, toddlers usually say, "Me do it," or "I do it," when grown-ups try to help them with self-care or dressing tasks.

Motor skills required for daily living skills are complex and varied. For example, dressing requires that a child is able to reach above their head and behind their back; buttoning requires bilateral development, efficient use of the two hands together, and the ability to differentiate the movement of individual fingers (Pehoski, 2006); and feeding requires that the child has developed oral motor muscles in addition to head control, and has learned to use tools such as a spoon, fork, or cup (Henderson & Pehoski, 2006).

Perceptual motor abilities are also important in the achievement of adaptive skills, since the child should not only understand the various functions of tools used in self-care, such as a toothbrush, spoon, or zippers and fasteners, but be able to use his or her visual skills to determine the correct order of things, such as whether a shirt is inside out or backward (Henderson & Pehoski, 2006).

CHILDREN WITH NEUROMOTOR PROBLEMS

Muscles, bones, and joints are connected by ligaments and tendons. Together, they form the **musculoskeletal (MSK) system.** The musculoskeletal system is connected to the brain through the **neuromuscular (NM) system,** which consists of a network of nerves from the brain to the different members of the body (Escolar, Tosi, Rocha, & Kennedy, 2007). The neuromuscular system transfers messages from the brain to the musculoskeletal system to perform a movement. The sensory system sends messages from the various members of the body to the brain, providing information regarding the body position and specific sensations. When MSK and NM systems do not operate properly, motor and physical problems occur. Children might show signs of neuromuscular or musculoskeletal disorder immediately after birth or later as they get older. Other problems and abnormalities in the motoric system might also result from disorders in the MSK and NM systems.

As explained earlier, the physical development of infants takes place from the center out **(proximodistal)** and from head to toe **(cephalocaudal),** so the infants are first able to lift their heads before they are able to lift their shoulders, or they are able to move their arms before they are able to hold an object (Santrock, 2006). When infants do not show patterns of proximodistal and cephalocaudal development, parents and professionals become concerned that a possible physical or motor problem might exist.

Different types of motor problems in children have various etiologies (causes) in children. These disorders might be divided into four large categories of disorders: **sensory processing dysfunction,** problems of posture and tone, disorders of gross motor, and oral motor and feeding problems (Escolar et al., 2007).

Sensory Processing Dysfunction

Sensory processing dysfunction includes problems with sensory integration, which may involve oversensitivity or underreactivity of the child to specific sensations in the areas of touch, sight, movement, sound, taste, or smell (Emmons & Anderson, 2005). These problems are most prevalent among children with Autism Spectrum Disorder and in some children with ADHD. (For a detailed discussion of sensory problems in children with ASD, see Chapter 7.)

Disorders of Tone and Posture

A number of disorders affect muscle tone. Muscle tone is the degree of tension that exists in the muscle when it is at rest (Escolar et al., 2007). Although not all children with gross motor problems display problems of muscle tone, some of them have variations of muscle and postural tone problems. Children diagnosed with certain neuromotoric or genetic disorders, such as cerebral palsy and Down syndrome, might have variations in their muscle tone.

Hypotonia is a condition in infants or young children that is marked by a lack of muscle tone. Infants or children who have hypotonia appear to be floppy and are not able to control their muscles. Hypotonia might be caused by premature birth or be a characteristic of cerebral palsy (Hooper & Warren, 2004). Children who have hypotonicity might put more effort into moving their arms and legs, or have a hard time sitting straight in a chair.

The opposite condition of hypotonia is **hypertonia.** Hypertonia refers to the increased tightness of muscles. It is also called **spasticity** (Escolar et al., 2007). When muscles are spastic or hypertonic, they have little ability to stretch. Children with hypertonia appear "rigid" in posture. They might have uncontrollable muscle spasms, have a stiffening or straitening out of muscles, or have shocklike contractions of all or part of a group of muscles. Depending on the severity of hypertonia and the distribution of muscle spasticity in the body, children might appear rigid in one extremity, or in parts of or all extremities. Children with hypertonia might have movement difficulties, which may or may not lead to further problems and deformities in the future.

Muscular Dystrophy

Muscular dystrophy (MD) is a group of genetic disorders marked by progressive weakness and *atrophy*—degeneration—of the body's muscles that control movement (Bushby, Lochmuller, Lynn, & Straub, 2009). The most common form of muscular dystrophy is Duchenne muscular dystrophy, which affects only boys (Escolar et al., 2007). Muscular dystrophy is usually detected between ages 3 and 5, and progresses rapidly. Some children, by the time they are 12 years old, lose their ability to walk.

As the disorder progresses, respiratory problems might become prevalent, and some children may need respirators to breathe. Some drugs, such as corticosteroids, have been used to slow down the progression of MD (Escolar et al., 2007). However, no treatment has been found that can cure it. Physical, occupational, and respiratory therapies help children manage MD (Bushby et al., 2009). In addition,

TABLE 13.1   Disorders of the MSK and NM Systems

Disorders of the Musculoskeletal System	Disorders of the Neuromuscular System
Skeletal dysplasia	**Spinal muscular atrophy**
Conditions characterized by abnormalities in the development, growth, and maintenance of the skeleton, such as short stature	A condition caused by a congenital and progressive loss of neurons, which results in muscle weakness and atrophy
Connective tissue disorder	**Disorders of muscles**
Conditions marked by joint hypermobility or brittle bones, caused by mechanical failure of collagen, which connects tissues	Such as Duchenne muscular dystrophy (DMD), which is a common form of muscular dystrophy in childhood. It is a progressive muscle disorder that is caused by a genetic mutation in the X-linked dystrophin gene, which results in the absence of a critical protein
Joint disorders	**Disorders of the peripheral nerves**
Conditions caused by limitation of normal joint motion during fetal growth. These can be caused by abnormalities in muscle function, abnormalities in the nerves that connect the muscles, abnormalities in connective tissue, a limitation of space within the uterus, vascular compromise leading to the loss of neurons, or maternal illness	These conditions lead to paralysis of the muscles

Source: Escolar, D., Tosi, L., Rocha, A., & Kennedy, A. (2007). Muscles, bones, and nerves. In M. Batshaw, L. Pellegrino, & N. R. Roizen (Eds.), *Children with disabilities* (6th ed.). Baltimore: Paul H. Brookes.

various new medications are also currently under investigation for the management of MD (Bushby et al., 2009). Orthopedic equipment and appliances, such as braces, crutches, and wheelchairs, help children with MD become mobile. Assistive technology for fine motor skills, such as switching and pointing devices, can help these children perform fine motor tasks independently. See Table 13.1 for a list of other disorders related to the MSK and NM systems disorders.

DISORDERS OF GROSS MOTOR

Several disorders of gross motor affect children. In this section, we will discuss the most common disorders. Some, like cerebral palsy, might also be classified under orthopedic impairments. In addition, some conditions, like Down syndrome (discussed in Chapter 11), might commonly have gross muscle and muscle tone problems associated with them.

Cerebral Palsy

Cerebral palsy is an umbrella term referring to a group of disorders that affect the voluntary control of movement and muscles (Fehlings, Hunt, & Rosenbaum, 2007). The term *cerebral* refers to the motor area of the outer layer of the two hemispheres of the brain called the cerebral cortex; the term *palsy* refers to the loss or impairment of motor function (National Institute of Neurological Disorders and Stroke, 2007). Cerebral palsy appears at birth, during infancy, or in early childhood years (Fehlings et al., 2007; Pellegrino, 2007). Although most children are born with it, the disorder might not be identified until months after birth, when some of these infants begin to show delays in motor development or show abnormal muscle tones. Cerebral palsy is caused by certain abnormalities in those parts of the brain that control muscle movement. However, its exact etiologies continue to be unknown.

The main features of cerebral palsy are (Fehlings et al., 2007):

➢ Motor problems caused by brain impairment
➢ Abnormal muscle tone and the impaired control of movements, poor motor coordination and balance, problems with movement and posture, or a combination of these features
➢ Permanent disability that is nonprogressive; however, its manifestations might change over time
➢ Often accompanied by one or more of the following: intellectual disability, speech and language disorders, problem behaviors, visual impairments, hearing loss, perceptual issues, and seizure disorders.

Cerebral palsy might occur prenatally, perinatally, or postnatally (Fehlings et al., 2007). Four possible causes have been identified for cerebral palsy: (1) damage to the white matter of the brain, (2) genetically based problems with brain development, (3) bleeding in the brain, and (4) brain damage caused by a lack of oxygen to the brain, sometimes occurring as a result of premature birth (Pellegrino, 2007). There are several risk factors for cerebral palsy, such as low birth weight or premature birth, multiple births, infections during pregnancy, blood type incompatibility, maternal drug use or exposure to toxic substances, fetus breech presentation, complication during labor, small for gestational age, a low Apgar score in the infant, and infant jaundice and seizures (National Institute of Neurological Disorders and Stroke, 2007).

Children with cerebral palsy might have varying degrees of abilities or problems. Some children may only have mild problems in muscle control and movement. These children will benefit from various types of physical therapy before age 4 (Mattern-Baxter, Bellamy, & Mansoor, 2009). Others may have very limited control of their muscles. There are five different types of cerebral palsy (Pellegrino, 2007):

➢ **Spastic cerebral palsy:** The most common type of cerebral palsy, marked by tightness of the muscles.
  ➢ **Spastic hemiplegia:** One side of the body is more affected than the other.
  ➢ **Spastic diplegia:** The legs are more affected than the arms.
  ➢ **Spastic quadriplegia:** All four limbs and usually the trunk and muscles that control the mouth, tongue, and pharynx are affected (Erasmus et al., 2009).
➢ **Dyskinetic cerebral palsy:** Also known as extrapyramidal cerebral palsy, it's characterized by abnormalities in muscle tone that involve the whole body. The patterns of muscle tone might change from day to day or hour to hour.
➢ **Athetoid cerebral palsy:** Involuntary and jerky movements of the head or other extremities.

> **Ataxic cerebral palsy:** Involves a lack of coordination and balance.
> **Mixed cerebral palsy:** A mixture of more than one type of motor pattern, creating a mix of stiffness or floppiness.

Diagnosis of cerebral palsy is done via specific medical testing, such as brain imaging, ultrasonography during fetal or neonatal development, computed tomography (CT), and magnetic resonance imaging (MRI). Newer technologies such as positron emission tomography (PET), functional magnetic resonance imaging (fMRI), single photon emission computed tomography (SPECT), and diffusion tensor imaging (DTI) provide information about brain metabolic function, which in some cases might be abnormal even when the brain structure appears to be normal (Pellegrino, 2007).

Critical Thinking Question 13.2   Consider the opening story in this chapter. Examine the relationship between Penny's parents and professionals in the story as well as the type of intervention and methods by which the intervention was carried out for Penny. What do you think contributed to Penny's eventual success in the school and community?

Traumatic Brain Injury

Traumatic brain injury (TBI) is another term for head injury, which occurs when a sudden trauma causes damage to the brain. Sports and motor vehicle accidents are common causes of TBI. Each year, more than 500,000 children receive care for head trauma (Michaud et al., 2007). TBI is more common in adolescents than young children and more common in boys than in girls (Bowe, 2007). Depending on the severity and location of the brain damage, the degree of abilities and disabilities in children with TBI might vary from one child to the next (Anderson, Catroppa, Morse, Haritou, & Rosenfeld, 2009; Michaud et al., 2007). Problems can vary in the areas of physical and motor; feeding; cognition, such as in thinking, problem solving, and memory; behavior, such as aggression, anxiety, or depression; sensory processing; and language and communication (Anderson et al., 2009; Michaud et al., 2007).

Spina Bifida

Second to Down syndrome, spina bifida is one of the most common birth defects in the world. Spina bifida, which means cleft spine, is a type of neural tube defect. Spina bifida refers to an incomplete development of the brain, spinal cord, and meninges—the protective covering around the spinal cord and brain (Liptak, 2007). The four types of spina bifida are (Liptak, 2007):

> **Occulta:** One or more vertebrae are malformed. The opening of the spine is covered by a layer of skin. This type of spina bifida is mild and rarely causes any symptoms.
> **Closed neural tube defects:** The spinal cord is marked by a malformation of fat, bone, or membranes. The symptoms may be mild, cause an incomplete paralysis, or constitute urinary and bowel control problems.

> ➤ **Meningocele:** The meninges protrude from the spinal opening, or may not be covered by a layer of skin. Some children may not have any symptoms, while others might have levels of paralysis, bowel, and urinary dysfunction.
>
> ➤ **Myelomeningocele:** The spinal cord is exposed through the opening in the spine. This can result in a partial or complete paralysis of the parts of the body below the spinal opening. The paralysis can be very severe in some children, so severe they may not be able to walk.

Although most children with spina bifida have typical cognitive development, depending on the size and location of the malformation, some children with this disorder may have intellectual and learning disabilities (Barnes, Dennis, & Hetherington, 2004). Most types of spina bifida are detectable before birth through prenatal screening tests; such as, amniocentesis and alpha-fetoprotein screening (AFP). (AFP is a blood test that measures the level of alpha-fetoprotein in the mother's blood during pregnancy.) Some mild forms might go undetected until after birth. For other disorders of movement and the brain, see Table 13.2.

TABLE 13.2   Other Brain Impairments Associated with Muscle and Movement Problems

Movement Disorders	
Stereotypies	Rapid and repetitive movements, such as hand waving or body rocking
Choreoathetosis	Rapid, random, and abrupt movements that usually affect all parts of the body
Dystonia	Distorted posture of the face, limbs, or trunk
Tremor	Rhythmic regular oscillation of one or more body parts
Myclonus	Sudden brief muscle contractions that produce quick jerks
Neural Tube Defect	
Hydrocephalus	Excessive accumulation of fluid in the brain
Pediatric Epileptic Disorders	
Primarily generalized seizures:	Large areas of the brain are affected simultaneously. The child might have a decrease in motor activities, or reversely, have vigorous motor behaviors
Absence seizures	Previously known as petit mal seizures, this type of seizure is a brief behavioral arrest, usually lasting less than 3 minutes
Partial seizures	An abrupt and unprovoked alteration in behavior
Myoclonic seizures	Motor attacks, marked with sudden flexion or the bending backward of the upper torso and head
Atonic seizures	Involves loss of muscle tone or lack of posture control

TABLE 13.2

Tonic-clonic seizures	Commonly known as grand mal seizure, is a behavioral arrest that usually entails repetitive jerking movements that occur at a regular rate, and with sustained stiffening, both taking place within the same seizure
Febrile seizures	Convulsions that occur as a result of fever—temperature above 102 degrees Fahrenheit
Sleep disorders	Random jerks of extremities or eyes occurring during sleep when the child is dreaming; it is more common in newborns

Source: Batshaw, M., Pellegrino, L., & Roizen, N. (2007). *Children with disabilities* (6th ed.). Baltimore: Paul H. Brookes.

ORAL MOTOR AND FEEDING PROBLEMS

Oral motor problems might occur because of problems in muscle tone, respiratory or gastrointestinal problems, and problems with oral motor structure and patterns (Barbosa et al., 2009; Eicher, 2007). As a result, eating might become associated with pain and feeding problems may occur. A number of feeding difficulties that might be associated with oral motor problems include (Eicher, 2007):

> **Oral loss of food:** Food is exhaled from the mouth, or falls out of the mouth
> **Prolonged feeding time:** Due to weak oral muscles, or needing more time for breathing between bites, the feeding time for the child is very slow
> **Food pocketing:** The child holds the food in the cheeks or front of the mouth for a long period as a result of difficulties with the oral motor structure that prevents him from swallowing the food
> **Coughing, gagging, or choking:** Problems with swallowing sometimes lead to the child's coughing or gagging during the meal. Sensory sensitivities toward different textures of the food also lead to gagging or choking. A child whose chewing is inadequate might also cough or choke on large pieces of soft solid food
> **Aspiration:** Food enters into the airway, which can occur before, during, or after swallowing
> **Food refusal:** The child does not accept enough food to be adequate for growth and development
> **Food selectivity:** The child eats only certain foods. This is common among children with sensory processing problems, such as autism. Children with cerebral palsy also show food selectivity due to their oral motor problems.
> **Vomiting:** Common in children with digestive problems, it occurs as a result of gastric intolerance
> **Failure to thrive:** This is a term used to describe a growth that deviates from the normal growth rate in a child. It usually results from an inadequate caloric intake, or the body's inability to use calories appropriately. Food selectivity, food refusal, or other oral motor problems can lead to a failure to thrive

Cleft Lip and Palate

Clefts of the lip, palate, or both can occur as a result of an interruption in the formation of the roof and upper front of the mouth during weeks 6 through 13 of fetal development when these structures of the mouth are formed (Blackman, 1997). Front lips and hard and soft palates are necessary for speech production and eating. The latter by controlling liquids and foods during eating, moving food to the back of the mouth for swallowing, and helping with suckling and suction. Because infants and children with cleft lips have problems with sucking and swallowing, liquid and food is often forced into the nasal cavity (Blackman, 1997). A child with a cleft lip or palate also has problems with speech production (i.e., his voice might be nasal, or the utterance of sounds might be difficult). A cleft lip and palate might cause hearing problems, dental problems, or upper respiratory infections (Blackman, 1997).

THE DIAGNOSIS OF MOTOR PROBLEMS IN CHILDREN

Whenever concern arises over a child's progress in any area of motor development, such as problems with posture and movement, or in sensory processing, the child should be referred for a diagnostic evaluation. The diagnosis of motor impairments is conducted by an occupational or physical therapist, or a medical specialist such as a neurologist or orthopedic specialist. Similar to the diagnosis of other disabilities, the assessment of motor problems includes a review of background and medical information, an interview with the parents and professionals working with the child, and observation of the child during play and daily activities in her natural environment. In addition, the therapist or specialist carefully examines muscle tone and strength, the joint range of motion, and the child's sensory responses and perceptions (Kurtz, 2007).

Therapists and medical personnel use a variety of standardized tests and measurements for assessing a child's motor function. For example, the Alberta Infant Motor Scale (AIMS) (Piper & Darrah, 1994) is used to assess motor development from birth through 18 months; the Mullen Scale for Early Learning: AGS Edition (MSEL:A) (Mullen, 1995) is used to assess motor and perceptual abilities from birth to 3 years; the Peabody Developmental Motor Scales (2nd ed.) (PDMS-2) (Folio & Fewell, 2000) are used to assess the children's motor skills from birth through age 5; and the Bruininks-Oseretsky Test of Motor Proficiency (BOT 2, 2nd ed.) (Bruininks, 2006) is used to assess fine and gross motor balance and coordination in children ages 4 through 21.

STRATEGIES AND ADAPTATIONS FOR CHILDREN WITH MOTOR PROBLEMS IN INCLUSIVE CLASSROOMS

Working with children with motor impairments requires a close and ongoing collaboration of early childhood and special educators with parents and other health professionals who might be working with the child outside of school. Because appropriate positioning of some children with motor problems is important and because some children might need to use assistive devices, teachers should work closely with physical and occupational therapists to learn appropriate positioning, as well as how to use assistive devices in and outside of the classroom.

Many children with motor impairments have cognitive, language, and social emotional difficulties as well. Therefore, aside from utilizing assistive devices and technologies to enable children in movement and mobility, working with children who have motor impairments also involves those methods employed for children with cognitive, language, or social emotional issues, which have been discussed in previous chapters (i.e., task analysis, responsive teaching, appropriate use of prompts, and strategies to promote receptive and expressive language development).

Assistive Technology Devices

A wide variety of devices are used to help with the mobility and positioning of children with motor and muscle problems. Useful devices for classrooms have been listed in Table 13.3.

A number of devices are used for bracing to help the child in standing, walking, and for correct alignment of the joints (Blackman, 1997). A child's need for braces (also known as *orthotics*) is determined and prescribed by an orthopedic specialist in consultation with a physical therapist. Helping a child with his orthotic management means to help him use splints or braces to improve or maintain his motor functioning, which is an important aspect of intervention for that child (Kurtz, 2007).

Splints and braces used to help children with motor problems are either static (rigid) or dynamic (with moveable parts) (Kurtz, 2007). They support weak muscles,

TABLE 13.3   Assistive Devices Used for Children with Motor Problems

Assistive Devices Used for Positioning	Assistive Devices Used for Mobility
On back: mat, wedge, Boppy, beanbag chair	Crawling: padded, textured flooring; crawling support frame
On stomach: wedge, cylindrical pillows	Walking: walkers or gait device, wheeled stander, weighted vest, ankle–foot brace
On side: wedge, Side-Lyer	Riding: supportive collapsible stroller, manual and motorized wheelchair with joystick control, adaptive bicycle; switch-adapted scooter
Sitting up: Boppy, booster chair, adaptive chair, tilting chair with lateral insert and head supports, custom-fitting chair	
Standing up: Stander and prone standing devices	
Adjustable aids: neck and head rest, lap belt, foot strap, chest harness	

Source: Technology and Media Division of the Council for Exceptional Children. Technology fan: Supports for young children. Available at www.tamcec.org.

increase muscle length needed for mobility, control involuntary movements, or serve as a base for support (Kurtz, 2007). Some commonly used braces are listed next (Blackman, 1997; Kurtz, 2007):

> **Swivel walker:** Is a rigid body brace mounted on swiveling feet. It is used to encourage standing and walking without crutches or a walker.
> **Parapodium:** Is a body brace mounted on a platform base. It is used for standing and walking with the help of crutches or a walker.
> **Reciprocating gate orthesis (RGO):** Is a plastic molded brace that provides support for the child's legs to have independent movement and motions.
> **Knee–ankle foot orthoses:** Are long leg braces that help the child stand, walk, or stretch.
> **Ankle–foot orthoses:** Are short leg braces designed to allow better joint motion and muscle control at the ankle level.
> **Foot ortheses:** Help children have control over their feet for sideways motions at the ankle or foot.
> **Body shell:** Is a plastic shell fastened at the sides, which helps keep the body steady.
> **Resting hand splint:** Prevents deformity of the hand and keeps the hand in a functional position.

Other simple and complex assistive technology devices might be used to help children with motor problems to participate in all aspects of classroom and community activities. These devices may range from simple devices to more complex computer technologies to help children with motor problems function at ease and with increased independence. For example:

> Adaptive scissors, spoons, or pens that have especially designed handles are used to help children have better grasps.
> Specifically designed standers (like supine, prone, floor, and box standers) are used to help with correct alignment, movement, and better positioning of the child.

Braces are used to help children with motor problems and are either static (rigid) or dynamic (with moveable parts).

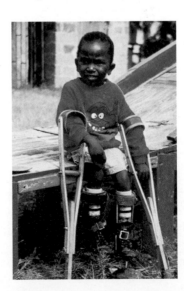

a) Appropriate equipment help children who have weak muscle strength and minimal muscle tone, to be held upright, so that they could have mobility and movement.
b) Powered or manual assisted-wheelchairs help children move around and participate in school and community activities along with their peers.

(a)   (b)

> Various walkers and motorized wheelchairs are used to enhance the child's mobility. Computerized technology devices, such as neural stimulators, are also used to increase mobility. Treadmills with support frames might be used to increase strength in the leg muscles (Desch, 2007; Kurtz, 2007).
> Modifications are generally made to seats and high chairs with straps, harnesses, and padding to enhance fine motor functioning and better positioning during feeding.
> Adaptive computer devices like touchscreens are used to enable children to use a computer for various cognitive tasks.

Supporting Children to Learn Self-Care and Adaptive Skills

Most simple self-care and adaptive skills are learned in preschool and kindergarten. The acquisition of all adaptive skills, such as eating, dressing, toilet learning, and self-grooming, occurs in specific stages, and through specific sequences of skills that begin to be acquired sometime after 6 months of age. To support children with motor problems so they can learn these skills, an early childhood educator should be aware of the appropriate sequences of skills for each task (Henderson & Pehoski, 2006).

Teaching adaptive skills should also be considered in the context of the child's family and cultural values, because every culture has specific rules and values regarding eating, dressing, and hygiene activities. It is important to note that any single component of a self-care task might involve learning a set of skills on its own. For example, eating with a spoon requires the child to learn a sequence of skills such as grasping a spoon, filling the spoon, lifting the spoon, carrying it to the mouth without spilling the food, putting the food in the mouth, and removing the spoon. This may require the use of adaptive utensils, as well as the design of a task analysis. (For a more detailed discussion of task analysis, see Chapters 6 and 11.) In the following section, we describe sequences of skills in eating, dressing, and hygiene tasks. Understanding the sequences of skills helps early childhood educators in task analysis and in the design of strategies to teach each step accordingly.

Eating Skills

Eating independently not only depends on oral motor health and abilities, but on the acquisition of certain skills such as using utensils and observing cultural standards regarding eating manners (Henderson & Pehoski, 2006). Children begin to use their fingers to eat sometime after 6 months of age and progress to mastering all skills involved in self-feeding by 3 years of age. Other behaviors related to eating, like setting a table, observing table manners, and being able to prepare a simple meal (such as making a sandwich) are learned gradually and are mastered by the child by around 7 to 9 years of age (Henderson & Pehoski, 2006).

Dressing Skills

Somewhere around 18 to 24 months of age, children begin to learn the simple components of dressing skills. Dressing skills depend on the development of fine motor abilities such as grasping and object manipulation. Children's dressing skills begin when they first initiate cooperation with grown ups in getting dressed, such as lifting the feet to put on pants and shoes, or raising the arms for shirts (Henderson & Pehoski, 2006). Children first learn to undress themselves, such as by pulling off items of clothing, such as hat, socks, or shoes, by about 9 to 10 months of age and proceed to learn to put on clothing items independently. Fastening buttons, zippers, snaps, and ties are the last skills to be learned, since they require fine motor control and object manipulation, which is developed around age 3.

Hygiene and Grooming Skills

Most grooming and hygiene tasks like rubbing hands together to wash, combing hair, or brushing teeth require bilateral development, good posture, movement control, and balance. Many hygiene tasks, such as toileting, bathing, washing the face and hands, brushing teeth, caring for the nose, and so on, do not begin until after 2½ to 3 years of age, and children are often able to perform some of these tasks before they are willing to take responsibility for them (Henderson & Pehoski, 2006).

Supporting Children with Sensory Integration Problems

An appropriate sensory diet is helpful to children with sensory processing dysfunction and can be incorporated and individualized in the classroom and home routines. A *sensory diet* is comprised of a collection of activities and intervention strategies that are designed to respond to the various sensory needs of a child with sensory processing problems. It is usually designed after a careful assessment of

TABLE 13.4   Promoting Healthy Sensory Motor Development

Activities for the tactile system	**Rub-a-dub-dub:** Provide a variety of textures for the child to rub against her skin (sponges, thick washcloths, plastic brushes, creams, lotions, soap, etc.).
	Hot dog game: Have the child lie down on the mattress (the plate). The child is the hot dog. Use heavy pillows and blankets for tomatoes, lettuce, and pickles. Roll the covered hot dog gently on the plate, providing firm, calming pressure.
Activities for the vestibular system	**Rocking:** Have a rocking chair in your classroom's cozy corner. Let children take turns sitting and rocking in the chair several times throughout the day. This will help them organize and energize.
	Balancing on a large therapy ball: Have a large therapy ball available on the patio or in the gym. Allow children to lie on their stomach and back and then sit and bounce on the ball.
Activities for the proprioceptive system	**Hermit crab:** Put a large bag of rice or beans on the child's back and let him carry the "heavy shell" around on his back.
	Bulldozer: Have a child sit inside a large cardboard box or atop a folded gym mat. Have another child push the load across the floor using their head, shoulders, back, or feet to make it move. Have children take turns.
Activities for the visual system	**Maze:** Use tape to draw mazes on the classroom floor or carpet. Have children drive car toys through the maze.
	Tracking: Hide small objects inside a big bowl of Froot Loops cereal. Without using their hands, have children look into the bowl and try to find the hidden objects.
Activities for movement and motor planning	**Walking like animals:** Encourage children to lumber like a bear, on all fours; to be a turtle creeping; a snake crawling; an inchworm, by stretching flat and pulling knees toward the chest; an ostrich, while grasping ankles, etc.
	Ribbon dancing: Attach ribbon, streamers, or scarves to a dowel. Holding the dowel with both hands, the child swirls the dowel overhead, from side to side, and up and down to the music.

Source: Kranowitz, C. S. (2005). *The out-of-sync child: Recognizing and coping with sensory processing disorder.* New York: Perigree.

the child's sensory processing needs so as to understand the nature of the child's possible sensory processing dysfunction. Assessment of sensory needs and the design of a sensory diet are done by an occupational therapist trained in sensory integration therapy.

Early childhood educators, however, can utilize a variety of sensory-focused activities to help promote healthy sensory motor development in all children. Table 13.4 displays some activities that promote healthy sensory processing in children.

CHILDREN WITH DEGENERATIVE CONDITIONS AND CHRONIC HEALTH IMPAIRMENTS

Degenerative conditions are those that cause progressive weakness and increasing disability over time. Degenerative disorders may include HIV and AIDS, muscular dystrophy, seizure disorders, and diabetes. Children with degenerative disorders and those with chronic health conditions might require the use of specific medical or technological support so that further disability is prevented. Some children might need 24-hour care that may necessitate the use of specific machines for ventilation or feeding.

IDEA considers children with *other health impairments* as those who have limited strength or varying degrees of alertness due to chronic or acute health problems that could adversely affect their educational performance. Some of these conditions include motor problems, which have already been described in this chapter. In the following section, other health impairments that might be common during early childhood years are described.

HIV and AIDS

A great number of children around the world are infected with HIV every year. UNICEF (2005) has reported that in 2005, 380,000 children died of AIDS, and 540,000 were newly infected. At the end of 2007, about 2.5 million children lived with HIV in the world (Avert, 2007). AIDS stands for **acquired immunodeficiency syndrome.** It is a disease that prevents the body from fighting infections. The **human immunodeficiency virus,** which is known as HIV, infects and damages parts of the body's defenses against infections (Renwick, Goldie, & King, 2007). HIV can be transmitted through direct contact with blood or other body fluids. Children commonly contract HIV during fetal development in the mother's uterus, at the time of birth, or during breastfeeding (Alvarez & Rathore, 2007).

An accurate diagnosis of HIV infection in infancy is only possible through specific medical tests. Not all infants born to HIV-positive mothers will have the HIV infection. However, the most common way children contract HIV is through mother-to-baby transmission (Renwick et al., 2007). The spread of HIV in child care or early childhood settings has not been documented. Early childhood educators and care providers are required to practice **universal health precautions** as recommended by the Office of Environmental Health and Safety (1998) to prevent the spread of diseases and viruses, including HIV.

Universal health precautions consist of a set of routine practices to be used in order to prevent the transmission of diseases from one person to the next. Recommendations for early childhood educators and professionals consist of (Office of Environmental Health and Safety, 1998):

> Wearing gloves when changing the infant's diaper, or touching blood or nonintact skin during a child's injury. This includes wearing gloves when touching body fluids, mucous, or handling items or surfaces soiled with blood and body fluids.
> Gloves should be changed after contact with each child.

Universal precautions, including wearing gloves when changing an infant's diaper, prevent the transmission of disease from one person to the next.

> When a child has an injury, hands and other skin surfaces should be washed immediately and thoroughly if contaminated with blood and other body fluids.
> Hands should be washed immediately before and after gloves are removed.
> Soiled diapers or other materials that might be contaminated with blood and body fluid should be put in a well-constructed container with a secure lid.
> All surfaces should be cleaned and decontaminated if soiled by blood and body fluids.
> All professionals should wash their hands frequently, especially before and after changing an infant's diapers.
> All children should wash their hands frequently throughout the day.

Many schools have policies and guidelines regarding the inclusion of children with HIV in general education classes, especially in regards to confidentiality and disclosure (Renwick et al., 2007). When working with young children with HIV, it is important to consider how the individual children might be affected by this condition. The emotional, psychological, and physical needs of a child with HIV depend on a variety of factors, such as the child's age, general awareness, and overall health. Some children may miss many days during the school year. Other children might deal with depression and anxiety. Collaboration with families and health professionals is important in providing the appropriate educational and emotional environment for the child, which is appropriate and responsive to the child's needs (Renwick et al., 2007).

Diabetes

Diabetes is one of the most common childhood diseases. It is a disorder of metabolism that has tripled since 1985 around the world (Bloomgarden, 2004). The Centers for Disease Control and Prevention (CDC) reports that about 1 in every 400 to 600 children have type 1 diabetes (National Diabetes Information Clearing House, 2005). Although type 1 diabetes is the most common diabetes in children, in recent years the number of children with type 2 diabetes has also increased (Phillips & Phillips, 2009). Type 1 diabetes is the condition in which the body has insufficient insulin, a hormone produced by the pancreas that metabolizes glucose, the blood sugar produced from food. Most children with type 1 diabetes need to have insulin injected regularly. Children with type 2 diabetes are generally overweight (Phillips & Phillips, 2009). Obesity is a growing problem in young children in the United States. Physical activity and appropriate diet are important in the management and care of diabetes in children. Diabetes in children can occur as early as infancy. Causes of neonatal diabetes are unknown. Some recent studies have found genetic links for pediatric diabetes (Colombo et al., 2008)

Asthma

Asthma is a chronic lung disease that is common in children (Mark, 2009). It is an inflammatory condition of the bronchial airways. The inflammation causes airways to overreact, and therefore produce more mucus, which leads to chest tightness, wheezing, and coughing. The episodes of wheezing are common in infants and young children (Weiss, 2008). The American Lung Association (2007) reported that in the United States over 6.5 million children suffered from asthma. Colds and allergic reactions to pollen and smoking might trigger an asthma attack episode in a child. Environmental pollutions have also been linked to asthma in children (Mark, 2009; Delfino et al., 2008). Treatment for asthma in young children begins with efforts to identify environmental triggers and their elimination. Asthma can be controlled in children by medication and control of exposure to allergens.

THE EDUCATION AND CARE OF CHILDREN WITH CHRONIC HEALTH IMPAIRMENTS

Intervention for children with chronic health impairments requires a collaborative effort between professionals and families. Ongoing communication and consultation with physicians, rehabilitative consultants, and nurses to ensure provision of related medical and physical care for these children on a daily basis is necessary. Collaboration with the school social worker is especially important, because children with chronic health impairments require additional emotional support both at home and in school to better deal with their ongoing health issues. In addition, in order to help children with chronic health impairments achieve the maximum benefit from their school community, educators should consider a program of partnership with parents to explore the merits of a possible class and school-wide program of health awareness that will target educational activities around specific conditions such as HIV, diabetes, or asthma. Such a program helps children understand issues related to growing up with, and caring for, a chronic health condition, as well as helps to promote a spirit of community among all children.

Research Corner

Family Centered Functional Therapy

During the past 40 years, the therapeutic methods available to children with physical and motor dysfunction, particularly cerebral palsy, have been dominated by theories that have influenced the neurodevelopmental treatment of children. Neurodevelopmental treatments focus on inhibiting the involuntary and abnormal movements in children with cerebral palsy and improving their quality of movements. Recently, however, scholars and educators have suggested a different approach to the physical therapy of young children with physical and motor problems.

This approach, called family centered functional therapy, proposed by Darrah, Law, and Pollock (2001), suggests a shift in thinking from an emphasis on a purely orthopedic treatment to a therapy approach that emphasizes the functional independence of the child. In other words, in this treatment model, it is not important to correct an involuntary movement of a child with cerebral palsy, but rather to empower the child to accomplish a task successfully in any movement pattern that might be possible for the child.

In this approach, the family and the therapists (and when appropriate, the child) will identify movement goals for the child to achieve. The emphasis is placed on success in accomplishing a task rather than attaining "normal" patterns of movement. This intervention approach is heavily guided by the family's goals and input, and its success depends on the successful partnership between the intervention team and the family.

SUMMARY

Motor development in children is a complex dynamic system that is influenced by many factors, such as biomechanical and physical development, environmental factors, demands of the task, and cognitive and sensory processing in the brain. Motor development includes gross motor, fine motor, oral motor, and sensory motor development. Motor development occurs in predictive stages. For example, children's motor development occurs from top to bottom (head to toe), and from the center to the sides and the lower extremities. During the preschool and early primary years, all areas of motor development become refined and sophisticated, and children learn to perform many self-care tasks, such as dressing, grooming, and bathing independently.

Children with special needs might have a variety of motor problems, such as gross motor problems, problems with tone and posture, sensory processing difficulties, and oral motor problems. The diagnosis of motor problems is done by health professionals, such as orthopedic specialists, and physical and occupational therapists. Strategies of working with children with motor problems should be designed through collaboration with parents and the child's therapists to incorporate the use of assistive technologies, appropriate positioning and moving of the child, and supporting the child to learn adaptive skills in their correct sequences. In addition, appropriate sensory activities should be designed in consultation with an occupational therapist trained in sensory integration therapy.

Children with a variety of chronic illnesses and degenerative diseases can be educated in inclusive and general education classrooms through the collaboration of educators, family members, and medical professionals. The treatment and education of children with chronic health impairments require observation of universal health precautions and familiarity with the medical and emotional needs of these children to help and encourage them to participate in all aspects of their school and community lives.

Review Questions

1. What is the dynamic systems model of motor development?
2. What are the major areas of motor development?
3. What are principles of motor development?
4. What is the relationship between cognitive processing and motor development?
5. How do gross and fine motor development occur in infants?
6. What are major changes in motor development during preschool and early elementary school years?
7. How is adaptive skills development influenced by motor development?
8. Name and define two types of neuromotor problems in children.
9. Name and define two types of gross motor problems in children.
10. What are some issues related to oral motor or feeding problems in children?
11. How do assistive technology devices help children with various motor problems?
12. What are some considerations for supporting children to learn adaptive skills?
13. What are some sensory integration activities that can help support children with sensory dysfunction?
14. What are some important considerations for early childhood educators who work with children with chronic health impairments, such as children who are HIV positive?

Out-of-Class Activities

1. Using Internet resources, research and find a variety of low- and high-tech devices available for children with gross motor and fine motor problems. Write a report describing different categories of devices used to support fine motor, gross motor, or movement and posture development. Share your report with your class.
2. Interview parents of a child (ages 3 through 8 years) with a motor problem, such as cerebral palsy, oral motor and feeding problems, or a sensory processing dysfunction. Find out about the child's daily routines at home, and how the parents help their child participate in various aspects of their home and community.
3. With the permission of the parent or guardian, interview an older child who has a motor problem or a chronic illness, and write a report regarding the experiences of this child in his or her educational setting.
4. Interview a teacher who has worked, or is currently working with, a child with a chronic illness. Write a report regarding the experiences of this educator.

Recommended Resources

Asthma and Allergy Foundation of America
http://www.aafa.org/

American Diabetes Association, Youth Zone
http://www.diabetes.org/youthzone/youth-zone.jsp

Muscular Dystrophy Association
http://www.mdausa.org/

National Institute of Neurological Disorders and Stroke
http://www.ninds.nih.gov/

Resources for Growth and Feeding Issues of Children
http://www.childrensdisabilities.info/feeding/resources.html

Spina Bifida Association
http://www.sbaa.org

United Cerebral Palsy
http://www.ucp.org/

Women, Children, and HIV: Resources for Prevention and Treatment
http://www.womenchildrenhiv.org/

View the Online Resources available to accompany this text by visiting http://www.mhhe.com/bayat1e.

References

Alvarez, A. M., & Rathore, M. H. (2007). Hot topics in pediatric HIV/AIDS. *Pediatrics Annals, 36*(7), 423–432.

American Lung Association. (2007). *Asthma fact sheet.* Retrieved November 29, 2007, from http://www.lungusa.org/site/apps/nl/content3.asp?c=dvLUK9O0E&b=2058817&content_id={05C5FA0A-A953-4BB6-BB74-F07C2ECCABA9}&notoc=1

Anderson, V., Catroppa, C., Morse, S., Haritou, F., & Rosenfeld, J. (2009). Intellectual outcome from preschool traumatic brain injury: A 5-year prospective, longitudinal study. *Pediatrics, 124*(6), e1064–e1071.

Annett, M. (1985). *Left, right, hand and brain: The right shift theory.* Hillsdale, NJ: LEA.

Arnheim, D. D., & Pestolesi, R. A. (1973). *Developing motor behavior in children: A balanced approach to elementary physical education.* St. Louis, MO: The C. V. Mosby Company.

Avert. (2007). *Children, HIV & AIDS.* Retrieved November 28, 2007, from http://www.avert.org/children.htm

Ayers, J. (1979). *Sensory integration and the child.* Los Angeles: Western Psychological Corporation.

Baken, P. (1991). Handedness and maternal smoking during pregnancy. *International Journal of Neuropsychologia, 11,* 363–366.

Barbosa, C., Vasquez, S., Parada, M., Gonzalez, J., Jackson, C., Yanez, D., et al. (2009). The relationship of bottle feeding and other sucking behaviors with speech disorder in Patagonian preschoolers. *BMC Pediatrics, 9, 66.* doi:10.1186/1471-2431-9-66.

Barnes, M., Dennis, M., & Hetherington, R. (2004). Reading and writing skills in young adults with spina bifida and hydrocephalus. *Journal of the International Neuropsychological Society,10,* 655–663.

Beery, K.E., (1989). *The VMI developmental test of visual-motor integration: Administration, scoring, and teaching manual.* Cleveland, OH: Modern Curriculum Press.

Blackman, J. A. (1997). *Medical aspects of developmental disabilities in children birth to three* (3rd ed.). Gaithersburg, MD: Aspen Publishers Inc.

Bloomgarden, Z. (2004). Type 2 diabetes in the young. *Diabetes Care, 27*(4), 998–1010.

Bowe, F. G. (2007). *Early childhood special education: Birth to eight.* Clifton Park, NY: Thomson, Delmar Learning.

Bruininks, R. H. (2006). *Bruininks-Oseretsky test of motor proficiency (BOT 2: 2nd ed.).* Upper Saddle River, NJ: Pearson Education, Inc.

Bushby, K., Lochmuller, H., Lynn, S., & Straub, V. (2009). Interventions for muscular dystrophy: Molecular medicines entering the clinic. *Lancet, 374*(9704), 1849–1856.

Bushnell, E. W., & Boudreau, J. P. (1993). Motor development and the mind: The potential role of motor abilities as a determinant of aspects of perceptual development. *Child Development, 64*(4), 1005–1021.

Campbell, S. K. (2006). The child's development of functional movement. In S. K. Campbell, D. Vander Linden, & R. Palisano (Eds.), *Physical Therapy for children* (3rd ed., pp. 76–130). St. Louis, MO: Saunders, Elsevier.

Caulfield, R. A. (2001). *Infants and Toddlers.* Upper Saddle River, NJ: Prentice Hall.

Colombo, C., Porzio, O., Liu, M., Massa, O., Vasta, M., Salardi, S., et al. (2008). Seven mutations in the human insulin gene linked to permanent neonatal/infancy-onset diabetes mellitus. *Journal of Clinical Investigation, 118*(6), 2148–2156.

Coren, S. (1992). *The left-hander syndrome: The causes and consequences of left-handedness.* New York: Free Press.

Darrah, J., Law, M., & Pollock, N. (2001). Family-centered functional therapy: A choice for children with motor dysfunction. *Infants and Young Children, 13(4),* 79–87.

DeHart, G. B., Sroufe, L. A., & Cooper, R. G. (2000). *Child development: Its nature and course* (4th ed.). Boston: McGraw-Hill Higher Education.

Delfino, R. J., Staimer, N., Tjoa, T., Gillen, D., Kleinman, M. T., Sioutas, C., et al. (2008). Personal and ambient air pollution exposures and lung function decrements in children with asthma. *Environmental Health Perspectives, 116*(4), 550–558.

Dennis, J. L., & Swinth, Y. (2001). Pencil grasp and children's handwriting legibility during different-length writing tasks. *American Journal of Occupational Therapy, 55*(2), 175–183.

Desch, L. W. (2007). Technological assistance. In M. L. Batshaw, L. Pellegrino, & N. J. Roizen (Eds.), *Children with disabilities* (6th ed., pp. 557–569). Baltimore: Paul H. Brookes.

Dobbie, L., & Askov, E. (1995). Progress of handwriting research in the 1980s and future prospects. *Journal of Educational Research, 88*(6), 339–351.

Eicher, P. (2007). Feeding. In M. L. Batshaw, L. Pellegrino, & N. J. Roizen (Eds.), *Children with disabilities* (6th ed., pp. 479–497). Baltimore: Paul H. Brookes.

Eliot, L. (2000). *What is going on in there? How the brain and mind develop in the first five years of life.* New York: Bantam Book.

Emmons, P. G., & Anderson, L. M. (2005). *Understanding sensory dysfunction: Learning, development and sensory dysfunction in autism spectrum disorders, ADHD, learning disabilities and bipolar disorder.* Philadelphia: Jessica Kingsley Publishers.

Erasmus, C., Van Hulst, K., Rotteveel, L., Jongerius, P., Van Den Hoogen, F., Roeleveld, N., et al. (2009). Drooling in cerebral palsy: Hypersalivation or dysfunctional oral motor control? *Developmental Medicine & Child Neurology, 51*(6), 454–459.

Escolar, D. M., Tosi, L. L., Rocha, A. C., & Kennedy, A. (2007). Muscles, bones, and nerves. In M. L. Batshaw, L. Pellegrino, & N. J. Roizen (Eds.), *Children with disabilities* (6th ed., pp. 203–215). Baltimore: Paul H. Brookes.

Fehlings, D., Hunt, C., & Rosenbaum, P. (2007). Cerebral palsy. In I. Brown & M. Percy (Eds.), *A comprehensive guide to intellectual and developmental disabilities* (pp. 279–285). Baltimore: Paul H. Brookes.

Folio, M. R., & Fewell, R. F. (2000). *The Peabody development motor scales* (2nd ed.). Austin: TX: PRO-ED.

Frankenburg, W. K., & Dodds, H. J. B. (1967). The Denver developmental screening test. *Journal of Pediatrics, 71,* 181–185.

Freeman, N. H. (1980). *Strategies for representation in young children.* London: Academic Press.

Gallahue, D. L., & Ozmun, J. C. (1995). *Understanding motor development: Infants, children, adolescents, and adults* (3rd ed.). Madison, WI: Brown & Benchmark.

Gesell, A., & Thompson, H. (1938). *The psychology of early growth including norms of infant behavior and a method of genetic analysis.* New York: McMillan.

Harrow, A. J. (1972). *A taxonomy of the psychomotor domain: A guide for developing behavior objectives.* New York: David McKay.

Henderson, A., & Pehoski, C. (2006). *Hand function in the child: Foundations for remediation* (2nd ed.). St. Louis, MO: Mosby, Elsevier.

Hooper, S. R., & Warren, U. (2004). *Young children with special needs* (4th ed.). Upper Saddle River, NJ: Pearson Education, Inc.

Jones, L. A., & Lederman, S. J. (2006). *Human hand function.* Oxford, UK: Oxford University Press.

Karniol, R. (1989). The role of manual manipulative stages in the infant's acquisition of perceived control over objects. *Developmental Review, 9,* 205–233.

Kranowitz, C. S. (2005). *The out-of-sync child: Recognizing and coping with Sensory Processing Dysfunction.* New York: The Berkley Publishing Group.

Kraus, E. H. (2006). Handedness in children. In A. Henderson & C. Pehoski. *Hand function in the child: Foundations for remediation* (2nd ed., pp. 161–191). St. Louis, MO: Mosby, Elsevier.

Kurtz, L. A. (2007). Physical therapy and occupational therapy. In M. L. Batshaw, L. Pellegrino, & N. J. Roizen (Eds.), *Children with disabilities* (6th ed., pp. 571–579). Baltimore: Paul H. Brookes.

Leiderman, P. H., Babu, B., Kagia, J., Kraemer, H. C., & Leiderman, G. (1973). African infant precocity and some social influences during the first year. *Nature, 242,* 247–249.

Liptak, G. S. (2007). Neural tube defects. In M. L. Batshaw, L. Pellegrino, & N. J. Roizen (Eds.), *Children with disabilities* (6th ed., pp. 419–438). Baltimore: Paul H. Brookes.

Lockman, J. J., & Thelen, E. (1993). Developmental biodynamics: Brain, body, behavior connections. *Child Development, 64,* 953–959.

Mark, J. (2009). Pediatric asthma: An integrative approach to care. *Nutrition in Clinical Practice: Official Publication of American Society for Parenteral and Enteral Nutrition, 24*(5), 578–588.

Mattern-Baxter, K., Bellamy, S., & Mansoor, J. (2009). Effects of intensive locomotor treadmill training on young children with cerebral palsy. *Pediatric Physical Therapy, 21*(4), 3018–3318.

McGraw, M. G. (1943). *The neuromuscular maturation of the human infant.* New York: Columbia University Press.

McKeever, W. F. (2000). A new family handedness sample with findings consistent with X-linked transmission. *British Journal of Psychology, 91,* 21–39.

Michaud, L. J., Duhaime, A. C., Wade, S., Rabin, J. P., Jones, D. O., & Lazar, M. F. (2007). Traumatic brain injury. In M. L. Batshaw, L. Pellegrino, & N. J. Roizen (Eds.), *Children with disabilities* (6th ed., pp. 461–476). Baltimore: Paul H. Brookes.

Mori, S., Iteya, M., & Gabbard, C. (2007). Hand preference consistency and simple rhythmic bimanual coordination in preschool children. *Perceptual & Motor Skills, 104*(3), 792–798.

Mullen, E. M. (1995). *Mullen scales of early learning: AGS edition.* Circle Pines, MN: American Guidance Service.

National Diabetes Information Clearing House. (2005). *National diabetes statistics.* Retrieved November 29, 2007, from http://diabetes.niddk.nih.gov/dm/pubs/statistics/#8.

National Institute of Neurological Disorders and Stroke. (2007). *Cerebral palsy: Hope through research.* Retrieved November 28, 2007, from http://www.ninds.nih.gov/disorders/cerebral_palsy/detail_cerabral_palsy.htm

Office of Environmental Health and Safety (1998). *Info Sheet: Universal precautions.* Retrieved November, 2008, from http://www.utexas.edu/safety/ehs/resources/info.universal.pdf

Pehoski, C. (2006). Object manipulation in infants and children. In A. Henderson & C. Pehoski (Eds.), *Hand function in the child: Foundations for remediation* (2nd ed., pp. 143–160). St Louis, MO: Mosby, Elsevier.

Pellegrino, L. (2007). Cerebral palsy. In M. L. Batshaw, L. Pellegrino, & N. J. Roizen (Eds.), *Children with*

disabilities (6th ed., pp. 387–408). Baltimore: Paul H. Brookes.

Phillips, J., & Phillips, P. (2009). Children get type 2 diabetes too. *Australian Family Physician, 38*(9), 699–703.

Piper, C., & Darrah, J. (1994). *Alberta infant motor scale (AIMS).* Philadelphia: WB Saunders, Elsevier.

Rao, A. K. (2006). Cognition and motor skills. In A. Henderson & C. Pehoski (Eds.), *Hand function in the child: Foundations for remediation* (2nd ed., pp. 101–113). St. Louis, MO: Mosby, Elsevier.

Renwick, R., Goldie, R. S., & King, S. (2007). Children, families, and HIV infection. In I. Brown & M. Percy (Eds.), *A comprehensive guide to intellectual and developmental disabilities* (pp. 269–278). Baltimore: Paul H. Brookes.

Robertson, M. A., & Halverson, L. E. (1984). *Developing children—Their changing movement: A guide for teachers.* Philadelphia: Lea & Febiger.

Robertson, M. A., & Konczak, J. (2001). Predicting children's overarm throw ball velocities from their developmental levels in throwing. *Research Quarterly for Exercise and Sport, 72*(2), 91–103.

Rösblad, B. (2006). Reaching and eye-hand coordination. In A Henderson & C. Pehoski (Eds.), *Hand function in the child: Foundations for remediation* (2nd ed., pp. 89–99). St. Louis, MO: Mosby, Elsevier.

Rosinia, J. (2008). Sensory processing. In L. Gilkerson & Klein, R. (Eds.), *Early development and the brain: Teaching resources for educators* (pp. 8.1–8.61). Washington, DC: Zero To Three.

Santrock, J. W. (2006). *Life-span development* (10th ed.). Boston: McGraw-Hill.

Savelsbergh, G. J., Van Hof, P., Caljouw, S. R., Ledebt, A., & Van Der Kamp, J. (2006). No single factor has priority in action development: A tribute to Esther Helen's legacy. *Journal of Integrative Neuroscience, 5*(4), 493–504.

Savion-Lemieux, T., Bailey, J., & Penhune, V. (2009). Developmental contributions to motor sequence learning. *Experimental Brain Research, 195*(2), 293–306.

Sveistrup, H., Schneiberg, S., McKinley, P., McFadyen, B., & Levin, M. (2008). Head, arm, and trunk coordination during reaching in children. *Experimental Brain Research, 188*(2), 237–247.

Thelen, E. (1995). Motor development: A new synthesis. *American Psychologist, 50*(2), 79–95.

Thelen, E., & Smith, L. B. (1994). *A dynamic systems approach to the development of cognition and action.* Cambridge, MA: MIT Press.

UNICEF. (2005). *HIV/AIDS and children.* Retrieved November 28, 2007, from http://www.unicef.org/aids/

Wallace, P. S., & Whishaw, I. Q. (2003). Independent digit movements and precision grip patterns in 1–5-months-old human infants: Hand babbling, including vacuous then self-directed hand and digit movements, precedes targeted reaching. *Neuropsychologia, 41,* 1912–1918.

Wang, J. H. (2004). A study on gross motor skills of preschool children. *Journal of Research in Childhood Education, 19*(1), 32–43.

Weiss, L. N. (2008). The diagnosis of wheezing in children. *American Family Physician, 77*(8), 1109–1114.

Williamson, G. G., & Anzalone, M. E. (2001). *Sensory integration and self-regulation in infants and toddlers: Helping very young children interact with their environment.* Washington, DC: Zero To Three.

Ziviani, J., & Wallen, M. (2006). The development of graphomotor skills. In A. Henderson & C. Pehoski (Eds.), *Hand function in the child: Foundations for remediation* (2nd ed., pp. 217–236). St. Louis, MO: Mosby, Elsevier.

Chapter 14

Children at Risk and Gifted Children

Objectives

Upon completion of this chapter, you should be able to:

> Understand the definition of at-risk children.
> Identify and understand various categories of risk factors.

> Understand types of child maltreatment and related issues.
> Understand the concept of resilient children.
> Identify risk and protective factors related to resiliency in children.
> Identify types of intervention programs available for at-risk children.
> Discuss ways to enhance the teacher–child relationship.
> Understand the concept of giftedness in children.
> Understand the characteristics of gifted children.
> Understand appropriate strategies and adaptations for working with gifted children in inclusive classrooms.

Key Terms

acceleration (500)

asynchronous development (499)

child abuse (481)

child neglect (480)

enrichment (500)

internal dyssynchrony (499)

protective factors (487)

readiness skills (485)

resilient children (486)

risk factors (474)

socialization mismatched hypothesis (484)

three-ring model of giftedness (497)

twice exceptional children (500)

Reflection Questions

Before reading this chapter, answer the following questions to reflect upon your personal opinions and beliefs that are pertinent to early childhood special education.

1. How do you think at-risk children might be able to have a healthy development and succeed academically?
2. What kind of strategies do you think might help at-risk children become successful?
3. Do you think gifted children need to have specialized education services? Why or why not?
4. Do you think gifted children might be at risk for underachievement? Why or why not?

A Teacher's Attitude Makes a Difference

Pedro and Miguel are cousins. When they were both 4 years old, they moved to Chicago from Mexico along with their parents. Pedro and Miguel lived with their parents, grandparents, uncle, and their siblings—a total of 13 family members—in a two-bedroom apartment. Shortly after their families' arrival in Chicago, Miguel and Pedro attended their neighborhood elementary school and were placed in two different preschool classrooms.

Miguel recalls his preschool and kindergarten years with fondness. His teacher, Ms. Martin, was a young teacher who made Miguel feel welcome in her classroom.

Miguel did not speak or understand English. But this was not an impediment to his participation in all classroom activities, because Ms. Martin spent every opportunity to work one-on-one with him to help him understand the classroom routine and academic activities.

During snack and lunch time, when Ms. Martin's assistant worked with other children, Ms. Martin sat down with Miguel to teach him new words. Every morning, as Miguel came in, she asked Miguel to teach her and the other children a Spanish word. Ms. Martin visited Miguel's family at their home to learn more about Miguel's culture and his family. She invited Miguel's grandmother to come to preschool and show children how to make some Mexican snacks. During the morning routine, children said hello in English and Spanish, and listened and danced to music from different parts of the world, including Mexican music. Ms. Martin encouraged other children to learn Spanish from Miguel as much as possible during both structured and free play time. In her class, both teachers and students quickly learned simple sentences in Spanish and used them in the classroom to communicate with Miguel if they needed to.

Ms. Martin was Miguel's teacher for preschool and kindergarten. Miguel loved going to school every day. He was a successful student through elementary school and entered high school with good grades. After finishing high school, Miguel was admitted to a local community college and transferred to a 4-year university in the city a year later. Next year, Miguel will be graduating with a degree in early childhood education and a teaching certificate in early childhood, with a bilingual endorsement. Miguel believes Ms. Martin was responsible for creating a love of school and learning in him. His fond memories of Ms. Martin and his early childhood years were the reason Miguel decided to become an early childhood teacher.

Pedro's story is very different from Miguel's. Pedro's preschool and kindergarten teacher, Ms. Hock, believed that for Pedro to learn English as soon as possible he should be exposed only to English. Ms. Hock was not particularly interested in learning Spanish. She frequently became frustrated when Pedro was not able to communicate. When Pedro mispronounced a word other children laughed and Ms. Hock seldom used the opportunity to take corrective action, or to use it as a teaching moment. So Pedro did not like to speak English, even when he knew the words, for fear of being ridiculed. He thought himself stupid and was afraid to answer the teacher's questions.

Ms. Hock called Pedro's parents to school frequently to tell them about Pedro's problems with language and learning. Pedro did not like to go to school. He did not like to participate in group activities, especially when Ms. Hock called on him to answer a question. Pedro had problems with reading in later grades. In third grade, his teacher recommended that Pedro be evaluated for learning disabilities. He was evaluated, diagnosed with a reading disability, and began to receive remedial special education in a resource room. Although his reading improved, he continued to dislike school.

Pedro enjoyed working with his hands and fixing electrical and mechanical objects. His uncle, who was an auto mechanic, allowed him to come to his shop on the weekends and learn what he could. Pedro struggled through elementary school and the first 2 years of high school. In the end, his family decided to let him drop out of high school when he was a junior to work full time in his uncle's auto shop.

INTRODUCTION

Many children grow up to become healthy and successful adolescents and adults who eventually become contributing members of their communities. Like Pedro, however, some children face certain risk factors that can become obstacles to their healthy development and learning. Pedro faced an important risk factor, a negative school experience. His earliest classroom experiences may have been critical in causing his lack of self-esteem and enthusiasm about learning and may have eventually led to his subsequent problems in school.

Children who have to overcome various risks and problems on their way to adulthood are considered to be children at risk. Children at risk are threatened by risk factors that may exist in their family, community, school, or in their biological makeup. In this chapter, we will look at this group of children. We will examine different risk factors, as well as factors that will buffer risk and might contribute to a child's health and success in school.

Additionally, we will look at another group of exceptional children: children who are gifted. Gifted children are exceptional learners with unique educational needs. Early childhood educators are likely to have gifted children in their inclusive classrooms. Without the identification of gifted children, their educational needs might be overlooked, which can in turn put them at risk for underachievement and an unsuccessful school experience.

CHILDREN AT RISK

The term *risk* refers to linking the probability of a certain factor to the occurrence of a negative outcome (Pianta, 1999). For example, it is probable that a child who does not receive appropriate nutrition (risk) will develop some physical health or cognitive health problems (outcome). Risk is relative and not all risk conditions will result in negative outcomes. The probability of a negative outcome often depends on the level of risk and its possible interactions with other risk conditions.

Who Are Children at Risk?

As we mentioned in Chapter 1, generally the term children at risk has been used to refer to children who, because of risk factors in their environment or their biological makeup, might not be able to develop to their fullest potential, or succeed in school and the community as they reach adolescence and adulthood (Stormont, 2007; Anthony, Alter, & Jenson, 2009). Some children at risk might have problems making friends and adjusting to social demands, or may struggle academically.

Many factors can impede a child's development and learning. These are considered **risk factors.** For example, lack of access to appropriate health care might put a young child who has repeated colds at risk for more serious illnesses, such as strep throat or ear infections. Stormont (2007) categorizes risk factors into three general groups:

> Risk factors that are embedded within the child due to biological or neurological causes

FIGURE 14.1
Risk Factors
Associated with
Developmental
Problems and School
Failure in Children

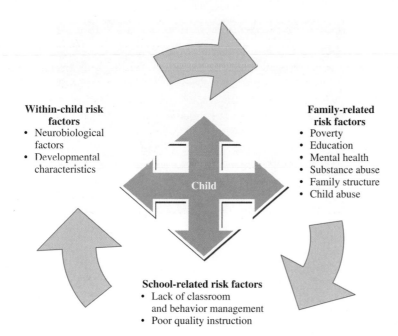

Within-child risk factors
- Neurobiological factors
- Developmental characteristics

Child

Family-related risk factors
- Poverty
- Education
- Mental health
- Substance abuse
- Family structure
- Child abuse

School-related risk factors
- Lack of classroom and behavior management
- Poor quality instruction

> Risk factors that are related to the family and parental behaviors
> Risk factors that are related to school and the learning environment

Figure 14.1 presents categories of risk conditions that might contribute to developmental and learning problems in young children. Although each of these factors could be a risk to a child's healthy development, often it is the interaction or combination of some of these factors that might eventually lead to problems of learning and development, especially because these factors hardly work in isolation from one another.

FAMILY-RELATED RISK FACTORS

Negative factors existing within the family are considered the most serious risks to the healthy development of a child (Magee & Roy, 2008; Patterson & Albers, 2001; Barry, Dunlap, Cotten, Lochman, & Wells, 2005; Gimpel & Holland, 2003). Six types of family-related risk factors can result in negative developmental and learning outcomes for children (Rouse & Fantuzzo, 2009; Weissbourd, 2009; National Research Council, Institute of Medicine, 2000; Stormont, 2007). One of these risk factors is related to the socioeconomic status of the family; the remaining risk factors are related to qualities that concern the parents' and caregivers' status and behaviors (Figure 14.2). These factors consist of poverty, parental education, parental mental health, parental substance abuse, parental maltreatment of children, and family structure (Weissbourd, 2009; Stormont, 2007; Gimpel & Holland, 2003; National Research Council, Institute of Medicine, 2000; Barry et al., 2005).

Poverty and hunger are family-related risk factors associated with developmental problems and school failure in children.

Poverty

Poverty is the most threatening risk factor to all children around the world (National Research Council, Institute of Medicine, 2000). There is no question that poverty is especially detrimental during the early childhood years (Patterson & Albers, 2001; Brooks-Gunn & Duncan, 1997). Families who have access to resources, such as money and time, are able to provide a variety of learning opportunities for their children and therefore influence their child's development through their resources, as compared to those families who do not have the same resources (National Research Council, Institute of Medicine, 2000). In 2003, 4.7 million children younger than age 6 lived below the poverty line ($18,660 annual income for a family of four, or $14,824 for a single parent family of three). Of this number, 39 percent were African American children, and 32 percent were Hispanic (RAND, 2005).

FIGURE 14.2
Family-Related Risk Factors Are among the Most Serious Risk Factors Threatening Healthy Child Development

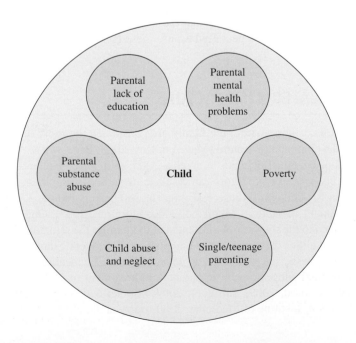

Children who live in poverty have fewer opportunities for appropriate social interactions. They might lack positive role models, appropriate learning materials such as toys and books, access to good nutrition and health care, adequate child care, and access to environments such as parks, playgrounds, and libraries (Weissbourd, 2009; Enwefa, Enwefa, & Jennings, 2006; National Research Council, Institute of Medicine, 2000). Although many children who grow up in poverty might become productive adults, these are important conditions that contribute to the healthy physical, emotional, and intellectual growth of children.

In 2000, the National Research Council, Institute of Medicine reported that the United States had more poor, and more affluent, children than most other Western countries in the world. During the past 25 years, young children in the United States have become the poorest age group in society. More African American, Hispanic, and immigrant children grow up in poverty than Caucasian children (Hernandez, Denton, & Macartney, 2009; National Research Council, Institute of Medicine, 2000; Seligman & Darling, 2007). Young children raised in poverty have been falling behind developmentally and educationally compared with their more affluent peers (Rouse & Fantuzzo, 2009; Kyunghee, 2009; National Research Council, Institute of Medicine, 2000; Brooks-Gunn & Duncan, 1997).

Home Learning Environment and Safety

Children who grow up in unsafe homes and neighborhoods, where they are in constant fear for their safety, are less likely to be autonomous, to explore, and be curious (Brooks-Gunn & Duncan, 1997; Molnar, Cerda, Roberts, & Buca, 2008; Enwefa et al., 2006). Warm and positive home learning environments contribute to a child's motivation, as well as her cognitive and emotional growth. In fact, an unsafe home environment and neighborhood for some of these children may provide negative learning experiences, where children can be exposed to violence and abusive language and behavior from which they are likely to model their own behaviors (Graham-Bermann & Seng, 2005; Molnar et al., 2008).

Parental Education

Lack of education in parents often leads to a lack of income. Parents who have a college education are less likely to be unemployed, have very low incomes, or live in unsafe and poor neighborhoods (National Research Council, Institute of Medicine, 2000). In addition, parents who are educated are more likely to provide appropriate health care and nutrition for their children, play and interact with them, read books to them, and stimulate their language and cognitive growth through positive verbal interactions and conversations (Hart & Brassard, 1987; Otto, 2006). Research shows that 31 percent of children in the United States have mothers who did not finish high school (RAND, 2005). These children are at a disadvantage and are likely to enter kindergarten or first grade lagging behind their peers (National Research Council, Institute of Medicine, 2000).

Parental Mental Health

By some estimates, mental health problems are as high as 60 percent in parents of children younger than 5 years of age (Oats, 1997). Depression is one of the most prevalent mental health problems among parents, affecting more mothers than fathers (Weissbourd, 2009; Barry et al., 2005). Depression is known to be associated with social and economic status, and is more prevalent in families with low income—about 35 percent of low-income mothers of young children suffer from depression (Smith, 2004).

Throughout this book, we have emphasized the importance of early attachment patterns, as well as positive caregiver and child interactions in promoting healthy emotional growth in children. Mental health problems impair parenting abilities. For example, a parent or caregiver who is dealing with a mental problem, such as depression, might not be able to interact with and respond to the child in an enthusiastic way (Patterson & Albers, 2001). Symptoms of self-preoccupation, disorganization, and an impaired parent–child relationship are likely to be common in these parents (Smith, 2004). Many such parents express self-doubt about their ability to care for their children, or consider their child as being difficult (National Research Council, Institute of Medicine, 2000).

Studies that have examined the effect of maternal depression on a child's development (Campbell & Ramey, 1995; Cummings & Davis, 1994; Oats, 1997; Smith, 2004; Patterson & Albers, 2001; Barry et al., 2005) have found that children who have depressed mothers are likely to have special education needs. It is estimated that about 40 percent of children who have parents with depression develop problem behaviors (Smith, 2004). In general, these children are two to five times more likely to develop internalizing and externalizing behaviors, as compared with children whose parents do not deal with depression. Additionally, children whose parents have depression are more likely to have persistent cognitive problems, low self-esteem, and suffer from major depression (Campbell & Ramey, 1995; Smith, 2004; Barry et al., 2005).

We should keep in mind that not all parents who deal with mental health issues become risks to their children's development. Many parents who deal with depression and anxiety raise healthy well-developed children. However, when poor parental mental health is coupled with other factors, such as low socioeconomic status, stress, or substance abuse, it is more likely to lead to developmental problems in children.

Parental Substance Abuse

The number of children living with parents who indulge in substance abuse has risen alarmingly during the past decades. It is estimated that one in every four children in the United States is exposed to parents or another family member who engage in substance abuse (Grant, 2000). In addition to the risks that parental substance abuse poses to the unborn child (discussed in Chapter 2), parents who use drugs and alcohol are more likely to resort to violence against their children (Kilpatrick, Saunders, & Smith, 2003).

Parental substance abuse might result in a variety of negative psychological outcomes for children. For example, emotional deprivation, attachment problems, lack of self-esteem, and loss of childhood are amongst the various emotional problems in children of parents who abuse drugs or alcohol (Kroll, 2004; VanDeMark, et al., 2005). The negative effects of parental substance abuse on children are exacerbated when the family has a low socioeconomic status (Jacobson & Jacobson, 2001).

Family Structure

As explained in Chapter 3, family structure refers to the members and their relationships in the family. For example, a household might consist of a two-parent family structure, a single-parent family structure, or an extended membership family structure. Studies show that children growing up in single family households or living with people other than their own parents are more likely to be at risk for developmental problems, behavior problems, academic failure, and low self-esteem compared with children who grow up in two-parent family households (Logsdon, Birkimer, Ratterman, Cahil, & Cahil, 2002; Hetherington, Bridges, & Isabella, 1998; Amato & Keith, 1991).

During the past two decades, the proportion of children who live with one parent, who live in homes with neither parent, and who live in step-family households has risen steadily. Today in the United States, more African American and Latino children live in single-parent households (National Research Council, Institute of Medicine, 2000). Because of the high divorce rate and the increase in the number of unmarried mothers, almost one-third of all American children live with only one parent, or with step-families (Fields, 2003). Children living in single-parent households are often affected by their lower socioeconomic status, and on average, children living with only a single parent have lower social emotional and academic levels compared to those who live with both parents (Turner, Finkelhor, & Ormrod, 2007; National Research Council, Institute of Medicine, 2000). Many children who grow up in single family homes have unwed mothers, of whom an increasing number are teenagers (Logsdon et al., 2002; U.S. Department of Commerce, Bureau of the Census, 1997).

Teenage parenthood is associated with a number of negative outcomes, such as behavior problems for young children and emotional problems in older children (Mittendorfer-Rutz, Rasmussen, & Wasserman, 2004; Logsdon et al., 2002). Research shows that teenage mothers have less appropriate developmental expectations, demonstrate less sensitivity to their children, seem to be less responsive verbally and emotionally to their children, and are considered to be more punitive as compared with other parents (Conger, McCarty, Yang, Lahey, & Burgess, 1984; Christ et al., 1990). In regard to children who live with stepfamilies, there is some evidence that these children are at risk for being abused and victimized by either parents or siblings (Turner et al., 2007).

CHILD MALTREATMENT

Child maltreatment results from different parental (or caregivers') behaviors, which can have profound long-term psychological and physical effects on the child (Kaplow & Widom, 2007). Children whose parents are single and very young, or have learning problems, are at risk for maltreatment (McDaniel & Dillenburger, 2007). Child maltreatment has enduring and persistent harmful effects on the child's physical health, as well as their social and emotional development (De Bellis, 2005; Thomlison, 2003). The most common form of child maltreatment is child neglect.

Child Neglect

Neglect is the most prevalent form of child maltreatment and leads to significant poor psychological and educational outcomes for children in the short and long term (De Bellis, 2005; Stevenson, 2004). Neglect often co-exists with other forms of abuse (Daniel, 2004). There is no agreed upon definition for neglect. The definition of neglect is not a statement of what are unacceptable acts in regard to children, rather it is a statement of what children need to have based on the standards of care in the society in which the child lives (Gough, 2004). Therefore, in general, **child neglect** is defined as a form of maltreatment consisting of a failure to provide a minimal of age appropriate and socially or culturally expected standards of care for the child (De Bellis, 2005; Gough, 2004).

In the United States, the key federal legislation addressing child abuse and neglect is the Child Abuse Prevention and Treatment Act (CAPTA), which was originally enacted in 1974 (PL. 93-257). It has been amended several times and was most recently amended and reauthorized in 2003 by the Keeping Families and Children Safe Act of 2003 (PL. 108-36). The Federal Child Abuse Prevention and Treatment Act (CAPTA) (1996) defines four different types of neglect: physical, medical, educational, and emotional.

Physical Neglect

The majority of children who are maltreated suffer from physical neglect. Physical neglect is child abandonment and the caregiver's refusal or extreme delay in providing necessary and needed safety for the child, adequate physical care, appropriate clothing, basic hygiene, and good nutrition (De Bellis, 2005). Signs of physical neglect in young children might include chronic diaper rash, infected sores, dirty bodies, nails, and clothes, matted or thin hair, chronic infestation, and immature motor skills (Lewin & Herron, 2007).

Medical Neglect

Medical neglect is withholding medical care when the child is in need of treatment, even though parents or caregivers are actually able to do so (De Bellis, 2005). Signs of medical neglect might include refusal to attend regular developmental and medical check-ups or immunizations, and noncompliance with therapy or health care appointments (Lewin & Herron, 2007).

Educational Neglect

Educational neglect consists of the parents' or caregivers' failure to provide adequate supervision for the child, resulting in the child's lack of engagement in learning activities (De Bellis, 2005). Young children who lack adequate supervision and are not encouraged to participate in school and home learning activities, are likely to develop chronic truancy during their school years. These children tend to have low achievement or fail academically.

Emotional Neglect

Emotional neglect might occur when parents and caregivers fail to provide emotional care and affection to children (De Bellis, 2005). As we have discussed in previous chapters, an attachment problem in the child is a typical result of emotional neglect during infancy when the parent fails to respond to the infant's bids for attention. Children who are neglected emotionally are at risk for further behavioral or academic problems. Child emotional maltreatment might lead to serious problems such as behavior and conduct disorders, violence and aggression, and substance abuse in adolescence (Carleton, 2006). Table 14.1 summarizes the types of child neglect.

Child Abuse

Child abuse is another form of child maltreatment and exposes the child to repeated trauma. It has been defined as an act that endangers the safety of a child and causes (a) any unnecessary physical pain, suffering, or injury, (b) any emotional injury, or (c) any injury to the child's health or development (Chan, Elliott, Chow, & Thomas, 2002). Based on this definition, child abuse can be physical, sexual, or emotional.

All forms of child abuse have significant psychological and emotional consequences for children, such as depression, extreme anxiety, aggression, violence, and conduct problems (Kaplow & Widom, 2007; McDaniel & Dillenburger, 2007). Globally, children experience trauma and abuse in various settings and from different sources; such as in homes (from parents and caregivers), in orphanages and

TABLE 14.1   Types of Child Neglect

Types of Neglect	Examples
Physical neglect	Abandonment
	Lack of provision of safety
	Lack of provision of appropriate nutrition
	Lack of provision of appropriate clothing
	Lack of provision of adequate care
Medical neglect	Lack of provision of health care
	Lack of provision of medical care when needed
Educational neglect	Lack of supervision
	Lack of provision of adequate stimulation
	Lack of provision of adequate learning experiences
Emotional neglect	Lack of provision of emotional nurturance
	Lack of adequate response to a child's bids for attention
	Lack of affection

group care settings (from caregivers and other professionals), in wars from combatants, and through prostitution, exploitation, and pornography. Research has shown that the earlier the child is exposed to abuse, the more profound its effects will be later in life (Kaplow & Widom, 2007).

Physical Abuse

Physical abuse or violence has serious implications for a child's development. It affects the child's health, their ability to learn, and their willingness to go to school (Westby, 2007). Many children who are physically abused might be afraid to report that abuse, or may think they have deserved the punishment. A child's speech and language, as well as his cognitive development, might also be affected because of physical and emotional abuse. Young children, especially those who have an intellectual disability, are at risk for being abused because they usually fail to meet adults' unrealistic expectations (Westby, 2007).

Emotional Abuse

Emotional abuse is not easily definable and is often viewed as the least serious form of abuse (Carleton, 2006). However, all forms of abuse are considered emotional in nature, even when the abuse is physical or sexual, since the act of abuse itself results in psychological or mental problems in children (Hart & Brassard, 1987). Emotional abuse can be defined as a pattern of behavior that might corrupt the child and thus prompt inappropriate behavior; that ignores the child by withholding affection or emotional nurturance from the child; that isolates the child from appropriate stimulations and interactions; that rejects the child by expressing that the child is unwanted or worthless; or that terrorizes the child through punishment, threats, or different forms of physical abuse (Garbarino, Gottmann, & Seeley, 1987). Table 14.2 displays the types of emotional abuse. The effects of emotional abuse are not as easily detectable and visible as physical abuse might be since the results of emotional abuse are psychological and behavioral as opposed to physical (Carleton, 2006).

Sexual Abuse

The sexual abuse of infants and children occurs around the world every day. Sexual abuse happens when an adult or older person is in a position of power and interacts with a child in a sexual way for the gratification of the older person (Bayley & King, 1990). Sexual abuse can occur within a family by a family member, or from outside the family by people who interact with children frequently. Sexual abuse interferes with a child's healthy emotional and physical development, and has both short- and long-term psychological effects on children (Fitzgerald et al., 2008).

Children who are abused sexually experience severe emotional disturbances, including feelings of confusion, guilt, and shame. Young children who are abused sexually might display symptoms of posttraumatic stress disorder (PTSD) (Raghaven & Kingston, 2006). These children may exhibit such behaviors as bedwetting, compulsive masturbation, excessive curiosity about sex, phobias and fears, separation

TABLE 14.2   Categories of Emotional Abuse

Types	Examples
Corrupting	Teaching the child to witness or to have antisocial or inappropriate behaviors (e.g., criminal behaviors, sexual acts, etc.)
	Encouraging or permitting the child to perform abusive behaviors toward animals or other children
Ignoring	Lack of interest in the child
	Ignoring the child's presence
	Lack of affection and affectionate behaviors
	Extreme inconsistency in caregiving, affection, and in responding to the child
Isolating	Keeping the child in his or her room
	Preventing the child from participating in age-appropriate activities with peers
	Preventing the child from being exposed to appropriate stimulation
	Preventing the child from interacting with others
Rejecting	Telling the child he is unwanted or not liked
	Degrading or devaluing the child by calling her names or telling the child she is worthless
	Refusing to talk to and interact with the child
	Blaming the child for things that go wrong
Terrorizing and Harassment	Singling out the child for punishment
	Ridiculing the child for typical emotions and behaviors
	Threatening to harm or abandon the child
	Having expectations beyond the child's normal abilities

anxiety, or learning problems (Raghaven & Kingston, 2006). In addition, they might have social adjustment problems as they grow up (Fitzgerald et al., 2008).

Reporting Child Maltreatment

In the United States under the Child Abuse Prevention and Treatment Act (CAPTA), all states have statutes designating professions whose members are required to report, should they witness any child maltreatment. These professions are generally those that have frequent contact with children, such as teachers, early intervention providers, other school personnel, child care providers, physicians and health care providers, mental health professionals, medical examiners, social workers, and law enforcement personnel (Asawa, Hansen, & Flood, 2008; Child Welfare Information Gateway, 2008). Most states allow for any person to report child maltreatment voluntarily that is called permissive reporting. In addition to a National Child Abuse Hotline, every state has a toll-free telephone number or a child abuse hotline—usually provided by the Department of Health and Human Services—for receiving suspected reports of abuse or neglect.

WITHIN-CHILD RISK FACTORS

A number of risk factors may be inherent within the child's biological makeup, or may be acquired due to accidents, infections, illnesses, or environmental factors. Throughout this book, we have described a variety of genetic and biological conditions, such as Autism Spectrum Disorders, attention deficit hyperactivity disorder, and emotional behavioral disorders in young children that are considered within-child risk factors. Because these topics have already been examined in detail, we will not discuss them further in this chapter. Limited second language (English) proficiency is a within-child risk factor discussed in this chapter.

Limited English Proficiency

Bilingualism in itself is not a risk factor. However, young bilingual children who have limited English proficiency (LEP), where English is the language used in school and the community, are another group of children who are at risk for developmental and learning problems (Rodriguez & Higgins, 2005). Lack of English proficiency often puts bilingual children at risk for learning problems, specifically reading difficulties, low achievement, and school failure (Espinosa, 2007).

Critical Thinking Question 14.1   Refer back to the story at the beginning of this chapter. How might Pedro's limited English proficiency have contributed to his problems with learning?

As we mentioned in Chapter 10, Hart and Risely (1995, 1999) found that family members' talkativeness and verbal interactions with the child are the most elemental factors in language acquisition in young children. Children who grow up in families where parents or other family members converse with them frequently and regularly develop better vocabulary and expressive language. Similarly, these children are more likely to succeed in school by the time they reach age 9.

These findings help us understand why children who grow up in families who do not use the dominant language in the society at home might be at risk for learning problems at school. This idea forms the foundation of a hypothesis called the **socialization mismatched hypothesis** (Faltis, 1998). This hypothesis states that children are more likely to succeed in school if the language used at home and the socialization patterns dominant at home are similar to those used and valued in mainstream society (Faltis, 1998). Patterns of socialization and language interaction include the ways that young children are spoken to and conversed with; the way they are expected to respond verbally and behaviorally; and the way they are given opportunities to explore, think, and speak.

Language acquisition and learning is a complex process for all children. Children who enter preschool and have a different home language from that spoken in society are faced with an additional challenge of learning a new language, which might have very different features from that used at home (Otto, 2006). These children have a difficult task of acquiring a second language, given that the basis for the first language has already been established (Spinosa, 2007).

Young children who enter school with limited English proficiency face a difficult task of learning the particular sounds, grammar, and vocabulary of a new language, in addition to learning a different culture and socialization patterns (Spinosa, 2007). These differences might pose risks for language, cognitive, and social emotional development in these children.

Critical Thinking Question 14.2   Referring to the story at the beginning of the chapter, how do you think Ms. Martin's cultural responsiveness contributed to Miguel's love of learning and success in school?

SCHOOL-RELATED RISK FACTORS

School-related risk factors have to do with variables related to the classroom that are embedded in the daily interactions of children with teachers and school personnel (Stormont, 2007). These factors include teachers' attitudes, such as classroom and behavior management, the quality of instruction, and a negative teacher–child relationship. Depending on how early these factors are present and how they interact with other risk factors, these variables can pose a threat to the child's learning and future academic success.

Lack of Appropriate Classroom and Behavior Management

In general, classrooms provide the best opportunities for learning. Well-managed classroom environments, in which children are engaged and interested in learning activities, are more likely to promote success in children (Pianta, La Paro, & Hamre, 2004). The teacher's ability to monitor individual children, prevent negative behavior, and redirect the children's behaviors appropriately contributes to the general management of the classroom (Pianta et al., 2004).

Lack of appropriate teacher's guidance and consistent classroom guidelines and structure create a learning environment in which behavioral expectations are unclear, limitations are not set, boundaries are not observed, and finally, inappropriate behaviors are encouraged. Given an unmanaged classroom condition in preschool, children might enter kindergarten without having appropriate **readiness skills** (Stormont, 2007). Readiness skills are those social emotional, cognitive, and behavioral skills that are essential to learning. They include, but are not limited to, the child's ability to be seated for an appropriate length of time necessary for an activity; the child's ability to express emotions, thoughts, and needs; to follow directions; to abide by classroom rules; to take turns; and to finish tasks (Stormont, 2007). When children enter kindergarten and first grade without readiness skills, they are at risk for learning problems and a negative school experience, which might ultimately lead to academic failure.

Poor Quality of Instruction

A teacher's quality of instruction depends on their ability to maximize the children's learning by keeping them engaged and interested; utilizing appropriate learning materials; fostering language development; and providing learning activities in such a way that the maximum amount of time is spent on learning activities (Pianta et al., 2004). The teacher's responsiveness to the children's cultural backgrounds, including support of their family values and home language, is another aspect of high-quality instruction. Finally, teachers with strong instructional quality have high expectations for children and are able to differentiate instruction, modify the curriculum, and adapt learning materials and activities based on an ongoing and appropriate assessment of the children's learning (Stormont, 2007).

Teachers who fail to maximize the children's learning or who don't hold high expectations for them provide a poor and suboptimal quality of instruction. Children who are educated in mediocre or poorly instructed early childhood classrooms will have a hard time developing the foundational academic and social skills necessary for school success in later years. Unfortunately, most urban schools in the United States face the problem of having transient administrators, and lack the will to recruit and retain high-quality teachers (Stormont, 2007). Such schools are ones in which the majority of children who are already at risk, usually children from poor, immigrant, or single- or teenage-parent households, are educated. These children grow up in both home and school environments that are ridden with a variety of risk conditions.

Critical Thinking Question 14.3   Considering the story at the beginning of this chapter and the experiences of Pedro and Miguel, to what extent do you think a teacher's attitude and behavior might put a child at risk for school failure?

RISK AND RESILIENCE: WHO ARE RESILIENT CHILDREN?

Children who are exposed to risk factors do not necessarily develop problems in social emotional development or learning. In fact, an important body of research (Seidman & Pedersen, 2003; Wyman, 2003; Werner, 1993, 1995; Masten, Best, & Garmezy, 1991; Anthony & Cohler, 1987; Rutter & Quinton, 1984) has shown that a great number of at-risk children, despite growing up in adverse conditions, become caring, successful, and competent members of their communities.

You might recall our discussion regarding the topic of family resilience in Chapter 3, where we explained that many families of children with disabilities manage to be productive and well functioning regardless of the number of stressors they deal with. We called these families *resilient families*. Similar to those families, at-risk children who overcome adversity and become productive adults are considered to be **resilient children.**

Resilient Children

Despite their high-risk status, resilient children have positive developmental outcomes (Horning & Gordon-Rouse, 2009). One of the most influential and well-known studies of resilient children, The Kauai Longitudinal Study (KLS), was conducted by Werner and Smith (1992; Werner, 1993, 1995, 2000). They studied a group of children in Garden Island, Hawaii for more than three decades. Thirty percent of the children they studied were considered to be at-risk children. They were born in chronic poverty, had experienced prenatal stress, lived in unsafe home environments, were raised in divorced or single-parent families, or had parents who dealt with mental health issues.

Werner and her colleagues studied these children at ages 1, 2, 10, 18, 32, and 40. They found that two-thirds of those children who experienced four or more risk factors during early childhood had learning, behavioral, or developmental problems by age 10; or had conduct problems, teenage pregnancy, or mental health problems by age 18. However, one-third of the children experiencing four or more risk factors became competent and caring adults (Werner, 1995, 2000).

This and other similar longitudinal studies have prompted a number of scholars to investigate why such a disparity exists between these two groups of children: those who come out of adversity with a positive outcome and those who do not. Resilience research has found that under any risk conditions, there might be **protective factors** or mechanisms that can moderate or buffer the child from the affects of risk factors (Rutter & Quinton, 1984).

Protective mechanisms or factors might interact with risk factors in such a way that the child will react to the risk factors in a more adaptive and successful way than would be the case if the protective factors were not present (Rutter, 2000). For example, an easygoing personality and temperament can be a protective factor against the effects of poverty (Werner, 2000). Protective factors do not eliminate risks and stressors; instead, they allow the child to deal with risks effectively.

FACTORS THAT PROMOTE RESILIENCE IN YOUNG CHILDREN

Studies that examine resilience in children vary in nature and methodology. However, they point to a number of common protective factors that might buffer children from the negative effects of multiple risk factors. Werner (1995, 2000) categorizes these common protective factors into three groups: (1) factors within the child; (2) factors within the family; and (3) factors within the school or community. Table 14.3 displays these factors.

Werner (2000) points to certain child and maternal factors that can act as buffers against particular risk factors:

> A child's low distress level may buffer against poverty, abuse and neglect, other risks in school, and within the family.
> A child's being active may buffer against poverty and multiple risks.
> A child's alertness may buffer against multiple risks.
> A child's sociability, easygoing personality, and cuddliness may buffer against parental mental illness, divorce, poverty, and multiple risks.
> A child's problem-solving skills and good language abilities may buffer against poverty, multiple family and school risks, parental mental health problems, and parental substance abuse.

TABLE 14.3 Categories of Protective Factors in Children

Factors within the Child	Factors within the Family	Factors within the School and Community
> Infancy	> Positive adult–child relationships	> Friendships
> Low distress	> Affectionate ties with alternative caregivers in the absence of parents	> School
> Active, alert		> Teachers and mentors
> Sociable	> Maternal competence	
> Easy temperament in early childhood	> Good socialization practices	
> Self-help skills	> Positive socialization	
> Problem-solving skills	> The child's required helpfulness and responsibilities	
> Sociable	> Faith	
> Low frustration level		
> Good language abilities		

Sources: Werner, E. (2000). Protective factors and individual resilience. In J. Shonkoff & S. Meisels (Eds.), *Handbook of early childhood intervention* (pp. 115–132). Cambridge, UK: Cambridge University Press; and Werner, E. (1995). Resilience in development. *Current Directions in Psychological Science, 4*(3), 81–85.

> A child's self-help skills may buffer against poverty and multiple risks at school and with family.
> Maternal competence may buffer against teenage motherhood, poverty, and multiple risks with the family and at school.

Protective Factors within the Child

During infancy, resilient children are characterized by their caregivers as having a positive temperament. These infants feed and sleep well, and are described as being active, affectionate, alert, cuddly, good-natured, and easy to deal with (Werner, 1995, 2000). Resilient infants seem to be robust, alert, easy to soothe, responsive, and able to express feelings and elicit support from their caregivers. These patterns have been observed even in some infants with neurodevelopmental problems (Werner, 2000).

During preschool years, resilient children have been described as being cheerful, responsive, self-confident, and independent (Werner, 2000). Young children who are found to be resilient have good problem-solving and self-help skills. They are able to express thoughts, emotions, and needs well. They have a low frustration level and seem to be socially mature.

Protective Factors within the Family

Protective factors that exist within the family help to promote resilience in the child in two ways. First, the child is provided with positive psychological and emotional reserves for use in times of need; and second, the child learns from the positive behavioral models that exist within the family.

Adult–Child Relationship

Resilient research agrees that all children who have been found to be resilient have had an opportunity to establish a close bond with at least one member (whether parents or nonparents) who provided them with appropriate attention and emotional support during the first year of life (Vanderbilt-Adriance & Shaw, 2008; Masten et al., 1991; Werner, 2000). Because of responsive caregiving during infancy, these children are able to form a secure attachment and a basic sense of trust early on (Werner, 1995, 2000; Masten et al., 1991; Anthony & Cohler, 1987).

In families where parents are absent, a strong and positive relationship with an alternative caregiver, such as an extended family member, grandparent, or sibling who can provide stable physical and emotional care for the child serves as the buffer against risks for the child (Vanderbilt-Adriance & Shaw, 2008; Werner, 2000). Grandparents can form a strong source of emotional support in cases of divorce or teenage parenthood for children. Siblings are also strong sources of loyalty and emotional support during divorce. Positive sibling relationships are especially protective when the sibling's caregiving does not substitute for parenting and is rather supplementary (Werner, 2000).

Maternal Competence

A mother's competence is a strong protective factor throughout childhood. Competent caregiving during the first year of life contributes to secure attachment in the child. In addition, competent mothers (such as those gainfully employed) are shown to be important protective factors for their preschool children by becoming their children's role models and motivational figures (Werner, 2000).

Positive Socialization Patterns

Families in which independence and appropriate social behavior are emphasized seem to promote resilience in their children (Werner, 2000). A well-structured environment with a clear routine, behavioral limitations, clear rules, and adult supervision provides a protective environment for all children. In addition, young boys who have a male role model, such as a father, brother, grandfather, or uncle, seem to be more likely to develop resilient characteristics (Werner, 1995, 2000).

A Child's Required Helpfulness and Responsibilities

A number of resilience studies show that when children are assigned specific chores, roles, and responsibilities, they tend to become more resourceful and strengthened (Masten et al., 1991; Anthony & Cohler, 1987). Helpfulness in children seems to become a source of competence and positive self-concept for resilient children (Masten et al., 1991; Anthony & Cohler, 1987).

Faith

Families of children who are considered to be resilient often hold some kind of spiritual or religious beliefs, and provide stability and meaning to their children during times of crisis or hardship (Werner, 2000; Anthony, 1987). The spiritual beliefs of these families vary and cover different faiths and religious or spiritual practices.

However, all of these families have in common a conviction that there is a meaning behind every occurrence and things will work out in the end (Werner, 1995, 2000).

Protective Factors in the School and Community

In addition to the child and family factors, resilience scholars have identified several other protective factors that exist in the school and community that can promote resilience in children who grow up facing adversity (Webster-Stratton, Reid, & Stoolmiller, 2008; Werner & Smith, 1992; Werner, 1993, 1995, 2000; Anthony, 1987).

Friendships

Even when sources of emotional support and strength are absent within the family, resilient children draw needed support from sources outside their families (Werner, 1993; Anthony, 1987). Friends form important protective factors for children, usually providing emotional support when needed. In some instances, friends who have stable families provide a surrogate family for children who live in families with serious risk conditions. Friends are also stable sources of emotional support for children whose parents are going through divorce (Werner & Smith, 1992).

School

Most resilient children seem to enjoy school (Werner, 2000). Schools are safe, organized, structured, and predictable. For most at-risk children, school provides the only safe environment in which they might freely explore, learn, be nourished, and develop.

Teachers and Mentors

The protective function of a positive adult–child relationship is repeated in later childhood years in school, when one or more teachers form positive relationships with their students (Webster-Stratton et al., 2008; Pianta, 1999). Teachers can be strong buffers for children against the negative effects of poverty, violence and maltreatment, parental substance abuse, parental mental illness, divorce, and other multiple risks. In addition, a positive teacher–child relationship protects children against school risk factors associated with learning (Birch & Ladd, 1997).

Teachers who establish strong and positive relationships with their students during early childhood years and beyond not only can create a love of learning in children, but become positive role models for them. Strong teacher–child relationships are also an important motivating factor for children who have learning problems or have low English language proficiency. The teacher–child relationship is known to be predictive of further academic success in children (Webster-Stratton et al., 2008; Pianta, 1999).

INTERVENTION FOR CHILDREN AT RISK

A number of prevention and compensatory programs have been designed to provide intervention for at-risk children and their families in the United States. These programs receive funding from federal and state agencies, or private sources, and can have a variety of program goals. In general, prevention and compensatory programs for young at-risk children can be divided into three major categories: (1) family health and education programs, (2) parent education programs, and (3) prevention and compensatory programs.

Family Health and Education Programs

These programs usually target mothers and their children. Their aim is to provide supplemental food and nutrition to low-income pregnant women or mothers of infants and young children, as well as basic education on nutrition, health, and child care to these families. An example of such a program is Women, Infant, and Children (WIC), which provides federal grants to states to establish such preventive services (Food and Nutrition Services, U.S. Department of Agriculture, 2008). Parents and children are eligible to receive services for the child from the prenatal period *up* until the child reaches the age of 5.

Parent-Focused Education Programs

Parent training programs focus on family literacy and education, or aim at improving parent–child relationships. Family literacy and education programs are usually offered through local community agencies or schools (Casp, 2003). Their goal is to provide a variety of adult literacy services, such as English language learning, basic and secondary education, and job preparation training for parents.

Many of these programs offer multiple services together in one setting. An example of such programs is the Even Start Family Literacy program, which provides grants to local schools and agencies under the Adult Education and Family Literacy Act of 1988 for low-income families with children ranging in age from birth to age 7 (U.S. Department of Education, 2008). The Adult Education and Family Literacy Act mandates enhancement of workforce investment by delivering a one-stop delivery system in which an array of training programs are offered to eligible families.

Another group of parent training programs are parent–child programs. These programs might be offered at home, in a center, or utilize a combination of both (Brooks-Gunn, Berlin, & Fuligni, 2000). They might target teenage or nonteenage mothers of children from birth to age 3, or preschool- and kindergarten-age children. The goal of programs for teenage parents or parents of children from birth to 3 years of age is to improve parent–child relationships. These programs help parents consistently watch and monitor their babies' cues and respond in ways that facilitate their children's emotional, cognitive, and physical development. Throughout these programs, parents learn how to appropriately interact and play with their children to promote positive development (Brooks-Gunn et al., 2000).

Parent–child programs for preschool- and kindergarten-age children have a goal of training parents to become partners in the education of their children (Reynolds, Temple, Robertson, Mann, & Ou, 2003). Parents participate in a variety of training programs, focusing on parent–child activities that will enhance a child's literacy learning. Some programs focus on training parents in child behavior management, disability training, or special education advocacy.

Early Childhood Education Compensatory Programs

As explained in Chapter 1, early childhood education compensatory programs provide early educational opportunities for at-risk children in order to reverse the possibility of negative educational and developmental outcomes. The most notable among early childhood compensatory programs are Early Head Start and Head Start, established in the early 1960s.

ENHANCING THE TEACHER–CHILD RELATIONSHIP

Because a positive teacher–child relationship is a protective factor, interventions that aim at establishing, maintaining, and improving teacher–child relationships should be considered a necessary part of any early school programming for young at-risk children. As we saw in this chapter, research has shown that children with whom teachers have formed positive relationships are less likely to fail in school (Birch & Ladd, 1997; Pianta, 1999). Because early school success depends to a great degree on the positive emotional experience of children during the early school years, teachers' efforts to communicate openly, interact with children in a positive way, and form healthy attachments with them, builds self-esteem and creates an interest in learning and schooling that protects children from school and family risk factors (Webster-Stratton et al., 2008; Pianta, 1999).

EXCEPTIONAL CHILDREN WHO ARE GIFTED

Children who are gifted and talented are another group of exceptional children. These children are considered exceptional because, by the virtue of their giftedness, they require individualized education that is appropriate and meets their intellectual and emotional needs. Unlike the education of children with disabilities, the education of gifted children in the United States has not been articulated or mandated in the language of U.S. federal laws. The U.S. federal laws do not promote, require, or fund gifted education in public schools. Rather, it is up to the states and local school systems to determine policy and provide funding for the education of gifted children (Brown, Avery, Van Tassel-Baska, Wolrey II, & Stambaugh, 2006).

Currently, although all 50 states cite some form of legislation regarding the education of gifted children, it is the decision of local school districts as to whether or not funding should be allocated in educating gifted children in each district (National Association for Gifted Children, 2006). However, not all states' legislations have articulated provisions governing appropriate education for gifted and talented children.

Because no federal guidelines are available in regard to the education of gifted children, states with specific gifted education laws usually have a different interpretation of what is necessary and what is not for the education of children who are gifted (Brown et al., 2006). By the same token, differences usually exist in the

Gifted and talented
children, by virtue
of their giftedness,
require individualized
education that
is appropriate
and meets their
intellectual and
emotional needs.

levels of services provided among the states. In addition, within each state that does provide programs for gifted children, the local schools themselves are not necessarily consistent.

A lack of legislation does not mean there are no federal resources for gifted children. Currently, a federal program called the Jacob Javits Gifted and Talented Student Education Act provides funds for research and grants relating to children who are gifted and talented. This program, which was established by Congress in 1994 and reauthorized in 2001, supports projects of scientific research and innovative strategies related to the education of gifted children.

In general in the United States, there is some ambiguity regarding the education of children who are considered gifted and talented. This uncertainty is to some degree due to a lack of agreement on the definition of giftedness and what might be considered an appropriate education for these types of children (Brown et al., 2006).

The History of Gifted Education

Throughout history, gifted individuals have been acknowledged and admired in a variety of ways. In his book, *The Republic,* Plato recommends that the ruling of countries be assigned to those who have natural gifts and whose minds can tolerate the higher academic exercises necessary for the education of kings (Karnes & Nugent, 2002). During the Dark Ages, the study of different sciences provided by the Roman Catholic Church was reserved for the most gifted students in theological seminaries (Summers, n.d.). In the Middle Ages, universities were similarly reserved for the most intelligent and gifted students who could afford it. During the Renaissance, gifted and talented writers, poets, and artists were recognized and promoted by their respective governments (Karnes & Nugent, 2002).

During the early 20th century, although many gifted scholars, artists, and statesmen arose around the world, specifically in Europe and America, not much emphasis was put on the acknowledgement of gifted individuals, or the promotion of their education (Folsom, 2006). In general, there were only a privileged few who could afford a university education. In this era, the ideas of Sir Francis Galton (1822–1911) regarding the heredity of intelligence received scholarly and popular attention in Europe and the United States. Shortly, the Eugenics movement and the idea of intelligence testing and the calculation of mental capacity were established by Alfred Binet and his colleagues and followers (see Chapter 11).

A prominent scholar of the time, Lewis Terman (1877–1956), developed the Stanford–Binet version of the intelligence test at Stanford University, and advanced the idea of the intelligence quotient (IQ). Terman proposed to use the IQ test to classify children. He contended that the top 2 percent of children measured by this test (scoring above 135) were gifted (Jolly, 2003). He believed that by identifying children at a very young age who were gifted, society could ensure their appropriate place in leadership positions. In 1921 and 1922, Terman began a genetic study of giftedness with more than 1,000 boys and girls who had an IQ of more than 135 (Jolly, 2003). This study continued after his death and is ongoing today at Stanford University as one of the longest-lived research studies available to date. See Text Box 14.1 about Terman's study.

Text Box 14.1   The Lewis Terman Study at Stanford University

In the 1920s, Lewis Terman began a longitudinal study of gifted children at Stanford University. His original intention was to find out if gifted children maintained their intelligence over a period of 10 years. He later expanded his question into the adult years and the total life cycle of gifted children.

Terman chose 857 boys and 671 girls, ages 3 to 19 years, from different areas of California, mainly from white middle class families. These children had IQs above 130. For each child enrolled in the study, Terman maintained a data file containing information regarding physical health, interests, ancestry, reading and play habits, and the parents' income and occupation. He used regular surveys and home interviews of his subjects to study how these children developed and carried on their daily lives. In 1925, he published his first report in *The Mental and Physical Traits of a Thousand Gifted Children.* His report indicated that, in general, gifted children were emotionally healthy, well-rounded, and happy, hence dispelling the myth that gifted children have emotional problems. Terman decided to continue his study of these children, and every 5 to 10 years collected data from the group.

Children in the study group, commonly known as "Termites," remained loyal to the study, and through various societal and historical events, such as World War II, stayed in touch and mailed completed surveys and questionnaires regarding different aspects of their lives. So far, 13 waves of data collection have been conducted using this group.

Some members have achieved remarkable feats and become well-known scholars, researchers, and public figures, whereas others have remained ordinary.

In general, Termites have had the same emotional and health profile as the general public. For example, they have the same rate as the national average in divorce, suicide, and alcoholism. However, they are distinguished in that they received a higher education overall compared with the general public. Two-thirds of the men and women in the study received bachelor's degrees—10 times the national average—with the majority getting their degrees during the Depression. Of the participants in the study, 97 received PhDs, 57 received MDs, and 92 became lawyers. As of the year 2000, about 200 members of the original study group were still alive.

Many methodological and ethical criticisms have been directed at Terman's study. For example, the study has been thought to have sample and test biases. In addition, some of Terman's interpretations are considered to be biased regarding both gender and race. Terman's work has been frequently criticized for his attitude toward nonwhites, given that Terman considered nonwhites inferior in intelligence compared to Caucasians. Nevertheless, Terman's study remains an unprecedented empirical exploration of giftedness.

Source: Stanford Magazine. (2000, July/August). Available at http://www.stanfordalumni.org/news/magazine/2000/julaug/articles/terman.html

A contemporary of Terman's, Leta Hollingworth (1886–1939) furthered the cause of gifted children (Folsom, 2006). Hollingworth believed that IQ tests were valid measures of intelligence and that children scoring 130 and above were gifted (Klein, 2000). Hollingworth is considered the founder of gifted education, having invented ways to identify, educate, and counsel children who were highly gifted (Klein, 2000). She designed an experiment and established a curriculum for the gifted to be carried out in the Speyer school in New York City. The Speyer school provided separate curricula for exceptional children, both highly gifted children and those with cognitive delays.

Hollingworth believed that gifted children should be identified as early as possible and be educated through an accelerated and enriched curriculum. From her perspective, gifted children wasted more than 50 percent of their time in a school with a general curriculum, and highly gifted children wasted almost all of their time in a typical school (Jolly, 2003).

In 1959, Jon Paul Guilford published his studies on the structure of the intellect. Guilford rejected that intelligence could be represented by a numerical value (Karnes & Nugent, 2002). He believed that the area of creativity, or divergent thinking, played a role in intelligence. His ideas eventually led to the development of creativity tests, as well as further explorations of the relationship between intelligence and creativity (Klein, 2000).

The ideas of Terman, Hollingworth, and Guilford remain the most influential ideas of giftedness. Over time, the concept of gifted children as an exceptional group with specific educational needs has been established and accepted.

In 1969, Congress mandated a study by the U.S. Commissioner of Education, Sydney Marland, to determine whether or not, and to what extent, the needs of the most able students were being met. The result of the study was published in what is known as the Marland report, which was presented to the U.S. Congress in 1972. The report provided a definition of giftedness, which has been widely adopted and adapted by scholars, as well as by various states with specific educational policies for gifted children. This report forms the foundation of laws governing the education of gifted children in the United States.

What Is Giftedness?

There is no single agreed-upon definition of the concept of giftedness or its measurement and what might be considered an appropriate education for gifted children. The challenges with defining and measuring giftedness in children are similar to those previously discussed in relationship to the definition and measurement of intellectual disability in children.

The parameters of giftedness have been construed differently by various individuals, institutions, and cultures. Terman and Hollingworth believed in the IQ score as the measure of giftedness (Jolly, 2003). Standardized tests of intelligence are heavily reliant on the linguistic and mathematical abilities of an individual. Guilford added creativity as an additional criterion (Klein, 2000). Other scholars, such as Gardner have suggested culturally competent and multidimensional performance-based criteria as important considerations in determining intelligence and giftedness (Gardner, 2006). Finally, some have argued that any criteria for a definition of giftedness should look at both performance as well as potential in various areas in children (Harrison, 2003; Cigman, 2006).

The Marland report defined gifted children as those "children identified by professionally qualified persons who by virtue of outstanding abilities are capable of high performance. These are children who require differentiated educational programs and/or services beyond those normally provided by the regular school program in order to realize their contribution to self and society" (Marland, 1972). The Marland report (1972) included six criteria for children with giftedness. Based on these criteria, children who are gifted should demonstrate any of the following abilities:

> General intellectual ability
> Specific academic aptitude
> Creative or productive thinking
> Leadership ability
> Visual or performing arts aptitude
> Psychomotor ability (integration of cognitive and motor process, such as pairing numbers to symbols)

The current federal definition of giftedness is a modification of Marland's definition. It describes gifted children and youth as those who have high achievement abilities in academic fields or in intellectual, artistic, leadership, or creative areas (National Association of Gifted Children, 2008). This definition acknowledges

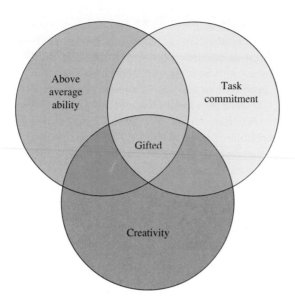

FIGURE 14.3
Renzulli's Three-Ring
Model of Giftedness

the need of gifted children for specialized services and activities that will fully develop their capabilities.

The Three-Ring Model of Giftedness

Renzulli (1978, 1994) presented the most influential model of giftedness, which is used extensively by scholars, educators, and school agencies in Western countries. The Renzulli model, also known as the **three-ring model of giftedness** (Figure 14.3), determines three basic traits as characteristics of giftedness:

> Above average, though not necessarily superior, general ability
> A high level of task commitment and intrinsic motivation
> Creativity

Renzulli believes that children who are capable of developing these traits and applying them to any area of performance are gifted children. These traits are equally important and interact with each other to create what is considered gifted qualities. For example, it is not sufficient to be motivated or be highly intelligent; rather, for a child to be considered gifted, the child should also be able to use creativity to utilize his or her other traits in order to perform well in any given area.

CHARACTERISTICS OF YOUNG GIFTED CHILDREN

Not all gifted children have the same traits or characteristics in development. However, some common behavioral, emotional, and developmental characteristics are evident among children who show gifted behavior during their early childhood years. For example, in terms of language development, most young gifted children often have extraordinary language abilities, with advanced expressive language development and a complex vocabulary by age 2 or 3 (Morrissey & Brown, 2009; Rotigel, 2003). Many young gifted children enjoy participating in adults' conversations of daily events and may seem more mature for their age. They often become interested and absorbed in a specific topic until they exhaust all avenues of information about that topic and learn all there is to know about it (Rotigel, 2003).

Gifted children often have one or more unusual interests and might be uninterested in the play repertoire that other children their age are typically interested in. Thus, they may become isolated from their peers (Rotigel, 2003). Some gifted children might be ridiculed and teased by their peers regarding their unusual interests, to which they may react with anger or aggression (Rotigel, 2003). Such behaviors have often resulted in professionals mistakenly labeling gifted children with emotional and behavioral disorders, even though research has shown that, by and large, gifted children have a typical social emotional development.

The perceived emotional or behavioral problems often result because of the social adjustment and competency problems that can begin during the early childhood years within typical early childhood education settings. For example, gifted children might wonder why they do not fit in with their peer groups. Often, when the teacher asks a question, gifted children might look at the problem on a deeper level; therefore, giving the wrong answer—or one the teacher is not looking for. This might cause a feeling of self-inadequacy in gifted children (Rotigel, 2003). Gifted children might also defy teachers' assumptions when concepts and problems are being introduced and discussed, and thus be considered oppositional and defiant. The behavioral and developmental characteristics of gifted children are listed in Table 14.4.

Asynchronous Development

Gifted children usually have an uneven development in different domains. For example, when one or more areas, such as cognitive or language abilities, develop at a rate that is ahead of the norm, another area, such as physical or emotional

TABLE 14.4   Developmental and Behavioral Characteristics of Young Gifted Children

Language Characteristics	Cognitive Characteristics	Behavioral Characteristics
Early verbal abilities	Extreme curiosity	Might possess high energy level
Good vocabulary	Intense interest in specific topics	Might have intense emotions
Might be able to read before age 4 without picture cues	Able to recognize patterns and see relationships early on	Might be a perfectionist
Early ability to understand abstract concepts	Accelerated rate of learning without a need for repetition	Displays various patterns in play

Source: Rotigel, J. (2003). Understanding the young gifted child: Guidelines for parents, families, and educators. *Early Childhood Education Journal, 30*(4), 209–214.

development, might develop on a par with typical children in the same age group (Silverman, 2002). The term **asynchronous development,** coined by Silverman, refers to this pattern of uneven development in gifted children. Silverman (2002) believes that asynchrony with chronological peers often presents serious social emotional stress for gifted children. For example, to have the intelligence of an adult and the body of a child—physically looking like a 3-year-old and speaking like a 20-year-old—poses great challenges for many highly gifted children to adjust socially and fit in with their peers. The younger the child, the greater the challenge for the child to adjust socially.

Terrassier (1985) coined the term **internal dyssynchrony** to refer to emotional and psychological problems that can result in gifted children because of an uneven development. For example, a child who can read but is not able to write might experience frustration—experience an internal dyssynchrony—as a result of this developmental discrepancy.

The Identification of Young Gifted Children

The identification of young gifted children is important, because without identification a general curriculum is less likely to meet the needs of these children. In addition, when gifted children are not challenged appropriately, they might become bored and resort to challenging behaviors, conform to low expectations, or develop negative attitudes toward school and school authorities (Robinson, 2003; Hodge & Kemp, 2006).

Teachers' observations and parental reports are usually the first steps in the identification process of gifted children. Manning (2006) recommends that early childhood teachers ask several questions regarding the child whom they believe might be gifted before making a referral for formal assessment procedures:

> ➤ Does the child use art materials in creative or unique ways?
> ➤ Is the child highly verbal in her spoken or written language?
> ➤ Is the child able to comprehend, synthesize, and evaluate materials from stories in unique ways?
> ➤ Does the child solve problems in unique ways?

Intelligence testing continues to remain a part of the identification and assessment procedure for gifted children. Most states set the criteria for the IQ score to be no lower than 130 or 135. Children's performance portfolios, academic achievement records, parental interviews, and teachers' observational reports form other pieces of information that are necessary for the assessment of gifted children (Robinson, 2003).

Gifted Children Who Are at Risk

Some children with disabilities, such as those with specific learning disabilities, ADHD, cerebral palsy, blindness, deafness, or sensory processing difficulties might also meet the criteria for giftedness. Because gifted children often have uneven development, it is possible that a child who is gifted in some areas will have weaknesses

The identification of young gifted children is important. Children's performance portfolios, academic achievement records, parental interviews, and teachers' observations form pieces of information necessary for the assessment of gifted children.

or a disability in another. Such children have been referred to as **twice exceptional children** (Seeley, 2004). Children with disabilities who are gifted are often overlooked due to stereotypical thinking that disabilities are usually accompanied by cognitive problems (Seeley, 2004). Having a disability puts gifted children at risk for underachievement.

Low income and cultural diversity are other risk factors for gifted children. Many gifted children who have limited English proficiency may not be identified due to their language difficulties (Seeley, 2004). A lack of available linguistically and culturally compatible standardized IQ testing measurements is another reason why this population might be overlooked. Most states do not have a specific identification process or differentiated programming for disadvantaged gifted children (Seeley, 2004). Finally, inappropriate curricula, negative relationships with teachers, and inadequate school policies regarding gifted children put gifted children at risk for underachievement or loss of interest at school.

STRATEGIES AND ADAPTATIONS FOR INCLUSIVE CLASSROOMS

Two terms that are commonly used in the education of gifted children are **acceleration** and **enrichment.** Acceleration refers to educational interventions, which move the student through an educational program at a faster rate than usual (Colangelo, Assouline, & Gross, 2004). In acceleration, the emphasis is on the strengths and abilities of the child. For example, a 4-year-old who can read and count might enter kindergarten. Similarly, another gifted student might skip a whole grade or be placed in advanced classes for certain subjects. Acceleration is recommended for gifted children who show evidence of high academic achievement or mastery of the content of the general curriculum used for their current grade level (Colangelo et al., 2004).

Curriculum enrichment refers to the process of modifying a curriculum by adding to its content or adding new learning opportunities. Curriculum enrichment

Encourage gifted children to work cooperatively with their peers. Young children enjoy learning from one another and gifted children often enjoy taking on leadership roles in different activities.

might include project-based learning, field trips, scientific experimentations, use of multimedia, and active learning. Although curriculum enrichment is often mentioned in relation to the education of gifted children, it is recommended for the education of all children.

Acceleration, enrichment, accommodation, and modification are qualities of a *differentiated instruction,* which should be used for the education of all exceptional children, including gifted children. Ongoing assessment is another aspect of working with exceptional children (Colangelo et al., 2004). Assessment guides Individualized Education Plan (IEP) goal setting, the integration of a variety of methods, curricular activities, and the utilization of appropriate materials. Though dependent on the state's policies, the education of gifted children might not require IEP development, since the breadth and depth of the education of gifted children does not differ from that of other exceptional learners. Therefore, the education of young gifted children should be designed based on the abilities, strengths, and developmental characteristics of the child. Programming and curricula for young gifted children should not only be grounded in developmental knowledge, but in the understanding of pedagogical approaches recommended for gifted children.

Specific curricular activities and strategies are highly recommended for use with preschool children who are gifted (Rotigel, 2003). For example, project-based learning guided by the children's input and interests, which is the hallmark of the Reggio Emilia approach (see Chapter 6), is one method that can benefit young gifted children since it allows creativity and multifaceted avenues of inquiry and learning.

Activities that include creative thinking should be encouraged for preschool children who are gifted. Gifted children should be encouraged to use creativity in problem solving, visual arts, writing, musical projects, and in their dramatic play themes. A wide variety of toys, manipulatives, and art materials should be available for a range of productive and play activities (Rotigel, 2003). Gifted children should be encouraged to work cooperatively with their peers, since young children tend to enjoy learning from one another, and gifted children often enjoy taking on leadership roles in different learning and play activities.

Research Corner

Resilience Research

The National Resilience Resource Center (NRRC) is a prevention and intervention research and resource center at the University of Minnesota. The center assists schools, the community, and organizational leaders in enhancing resilience in children and their families. Its philosophy is grounded in resilience research and the center advocates for the recognition of innate capacities in children which leads to a view that considers all children as "at promise" instead of "at risk." The NRRC disseminates information on resilience and provides training on systematic resilience enhancement for organizations and community leaders.

Through its services in the community, the NRRC seeks to answer the following questions:

> Are all children, youths, and adults at promise?
> If so, what are the conditions of empowerment that research and best practice support?
> What program models, approaches, and conditions will provide these conditions?
> What results can we realistically expect for children, youth, adults, and communities who learn to tap their natural resilience?

More information is available at the National Resilience and Resource Center at http://www.cce.umn.edu/nrrc/.

SUMMARY

Children at risk are a large group of children who due to environmental and family factors might be at risk for negative developmental and learning outcomes. Poverty is the greatest environmental risk factor threatening the healthy development of children. Family factors such as child maltreatment, substance abuse, education, mental health, divorce, and teenage- and single-parenthood are other risk factors that might have adverse effects on the development of children. Child risk factors, such as biological problems and difficulties with English language proficiency, also put the child at risk for learning problems. Other factors that might contribute to the child's learning and behavioral problems are the teacher's poor quality of instruction and the teacher's lack of behavioral management skills.

Not all children who are at risk will have a negative developmental outcome. Some children living with a variety of adverse conditions grow up to become caring and successful contributing members of their communities. These children are considered resilient children. In these children, a number of protective factors—such as positive adult–child relationships, the child's personality and temperament, and good friends—might buffer the child from risk factors.

Gifted children are another group of exceptional children who by virtue of their giftedness require specialized education and services that should meet their needs. No mandated federal laws exist for the education of gifted children. States, however, can choose to have legislation regarding the education of gifted children carried out by local education agencies. Gifted children are children who have an above average intelligence, have high task commitment, and are creative. Gifted children exhibit asynchronous development, in that, while they are above their peers in some areas of their development, they might be on a par with (or below) the developmental level of their peers in other areas of development. Accelerated and enriched curricula have been recommended for gifted children. Gifted children should be challenged appropriately based on their ability levels. If gifted children are not identified and appropriate programming is not provided, they might be put at risk for underachievement.

Review Questions

1. What is the relationship between risk and outcome?
2. Who are children at risk?
3. Describe how poverty might put children at risk for negative learning and developmental outcomes.
4. Describe two parental risk factors, and how they might put children at risk for developmental problems.
5. Name two forms of child maltreatment.
6. What are different forms of child neglect?
7. What is child abuse?
8. What are some effects of child abuse?
9. What are different forms of child abuse?
10. How might limited English language proficiency be a risk factor?
11. What is the socialization mismatch hypothesis?
12. What are some school-related risk factors?
13. Who are resilient children?
14. What are protective factors? How might protective factors result in resilience?
15. How does a positive adult–child relationship contribute to resilience in children?
16. Who are gifted children?
17. What is Renzulli's three-ring model of giftedness?
18. Who are twice exceptional children?

Out-of-Class Activities

1. With the permission of parents and the early childhood teacher, visit an early childhood inclusive classroom and:
   a. Identify children who are from diverse linguistic and cultural backgrounds.
   b. Design at least three activities that are culturally and linguistically responsive to these children.
   c. With the help of the teacher, carry out the activities in the classroom.
   d. Record your observations of the children during these activities in your journal, and answer the following questions:
      1. How did children who are not from these cultures respond to these activities?
      2. How did children from these cultures respond to these activities?
      3. How might you change and modify these activities to become more responsive to the linguistic and cultural needs of these children?

2. From our discussions in Chapters 6 and 9, conduct a Banking Time or a Floortime session with a 3- to 6-year-old child whom you know.
   a. Record your observations during the play sessions.
   b. How does the child react to your interactions?
   c. How does the behavior of the child change or not change during your interactions within the session?
   d. How do you think the child might benefit from regular sessions like the one you conducted with him or her?

3. With the permission of the parents and the teacher, visit a gifted program in a local elementary school, observe the children's activities in that program, and make detailed notes of your observations:
   a. How do the behaviors of gifted children differ from their typical peers?
   b. How are the behaviors of gifted children similar to that of their peers?

Recommended Resources

Carnegie Mellon Institute for Talented Elementary and Secondary Students (CMITES)
http://www.cmu.edu/cmites/

Center for Gifted Education Policy, American Psychological Association
http://www.apa.org/ed/cgep.html

Center for Talent Development at Northwestern University
http://www.ctd.northwestern.edu

Child Welfare Information Gateway
http://www.childwelfare.gov/can/

Children, Youth, and Families at Risk (CYFAR) Program USDA Cooperative State Research, Education, and Extension Service
http://www.csrees.usda.gov/nea/family/cyfar/cyfar.html

Duke University Talent Identification Program
http://www.tip.duke.edu/

Education Program for Gifted Youth at Stanford University
http://www-epgy.stanford.edu/epgy/

Jacob K. Javits Gifted and Talented Education Program
http://www.ed.gov/programs/javits/index.html

National Association for Gifted Children
http://www.nagc.org

National Center for Children in Poverty: Columbia University
http://www.nccp.org/

National Data Archive on Child Abuse and Neglect: A Project of the Family Life Development Center, College of Human Ecology, Cornell University
http://www.ndacan.cornell.edu

North Central Regional Educational Library (Resources for at-risk students)
http://www.ncrel.org/info/sitemap.htm

Northwest Regional Educational Laboratory
http://www.nwrel.org/nwedu/fall%5F97/

Prevent Child Abuse America
http://www.preventchildabuse.org

Raising Resilient Children Foundation
http://www.raisingresilientkids.com/

Resilience Net: Information for Helping Children and Families Overcome Adversities
http://resilnet.uiuc.edu/

Safe Child Program
http://www.safechild.org

The Center for Gifted Education at the College of William and Mary
http://cfge.wm.edu/

The Center for Talented Youth at The Johns Hopkins University
http://www.jhu.edu/~gifted/

The Child Abuse Prevention Network
http://child-abuse.com/

U.S. Department of Health and Human Services: Administration for Children and Families
http://www.acf.hhs.gov/programs/cb/

University of Connecticut National Research Center on Gifted and Talented
http://www.gifted.uconn.edu/nrcgt.html

University of Minnesota National Resilience Resource Center
http://www.cce.umn.edu/nrrc/

View the Online Resources available to accompany this text by visiting http://www.mhhe.com/bayat1e

References

Amato, P. R., & Keith, B. (1991). Parental divorce and the well-being of children: A meta-analysis. *Psychological Bulletin, 110,* 26–46.

Anthony, E. J. (1987). Children at high risk for psychosis growing up. In E. J. Anthony & B. J. Cohler (Eds.), *The invulnerable child* (pp. 147–184). New York: Guilford Press.

Anthony, E., & Cohler, B. (Eds.). (1987). *The invulnerable child.* New York: Guilford Press.

Anthony, E. K, Alter, C. F., & Jensen, J. M. (2009). Development of a risk and resilience-based out-of-school time program for children and youths. *Social Work, 5*(1), 45–55.

Asawa, L., Hansen, D., & Flood, M. (2008). Early childhood intervention programs: Opportunities and challenges for preventing child maltreatment. *Education & Treatment of Children, 31*(1), 73–110.

Barry, T. D., Dunlap, S. T., Cotten, S. J., Lochman, J. E., & Wells, K. C. (2005). The influence of maternal stress and distress on disruptive behavior problems in boys. *Journal of the American Academy of Child Psychiatry, 44,* 265–273.

Bayley, C., & King, K. (1990). Father–daughter incest: Degradation and recovery from degradation. In T. Putman & K. Davis (Eds.), *Advances in descriptive psychology* (vol. 5, pp. 285–305). Boulder, Co: Descriptive Psychology Press.

Birch, S. H., & Ladd, G. W. (1997). The teacher–child relationship and children's early school adjustment. *Journal of School Psychology, 35*(1), 61–80.

Brooks-Gunn, J., Berlin, L. J., & Fuligni, A. S. (2000). Early childhood intervention programs: What about the family? In J. P. Shonkoff & S. J. Meisels (Eds.), *Handbook of early childhood intervention* (pp. 549–588). Cambridge, UK: Cambridge University Press.

Brooks-Gunn, J., & Duncan, G. (1997). The effects of poverty on children. *The Future of Children, 7*(2), 55–71.

Brown, E., Avery, L., Van Tassel-Baska, J., Wolrey II, B., & Stambaugh, T. (2006). Legislation and policy: Effects on the gifted. *Roeper Review, 29*(1), 11–23.

Campbell, F. A., & Ramey, C. T. (1995). Cognitive and school outcomes for high-risk African-American students at middle adolescence: Positive effects of early intervention. *American Educational Research Journal, 32,* 734–772.

Carleton, R. A. (2006). Does the mandate make a difference? Reporting decisions in emotional abuse. *Child Abuse Review, 15,* 19–37.

Casp, M. (2003). *Family literacy: A review of programs and critical perspectives.* Cambridge, MA: Harvard Family Research Project.

Chan, J. S., Elliott, J. M., Chow, Y., & Thomas, J. I. (2002). Does professional and public opinion in child abuse differ? An issue of cross-cultural policy implementation. *Child Abuse Review, 11*(6), 359–379.

Child Welfare Information Gateway. (2008). *Mandatory reporters of child abuse and neglect: State statutes series.* Retrieved December 7, 2008, from http://www.childwelfare.gov/systemwide/laws_policies/statutes/manda.cfm

Christ, M. A., Lahey, B., Frick, P., Russo, M., McBurnett, K., Loeber, R., et al. (1990). Serious conduct problems in the children of adolescent mothers: Disentangling confounded correlations. *Journal of Consulting and Clinical Psychology, 58*(6), 840–844.

Cigman, R. (2006). The gifted child: A conceptual inquiry. *Oxford Review of Education, 32*(2), 197–212.

Colangelo, N., Assouline, S. G., & Gross, M. U. M. (2004). *A nation deceived: How schools hold back America's brightest students.* Iowa City, IO: The Connie Belin & Jacqueline N. Blank International Center for Gifted Education and Talent Development. Retrieved December 21, 2004, from http://www.nationdeceived.org/

Conger, R., McCarty, J., Yang, R., Lahey, B., & Burgess, R. (1984). Mother's age as a predictor of observed maternal behavior in three independent samples of families. *Journal of marriage and the family, 46,* 411–424.

Cummings, E. M., & Davis, P. T. (1994). Maternal depression and child development. *Journal of Child Psychology and Psychiatry, 35*(1), 73–112.

Daniel, B. (2004). Introduction to issues for health and social care in neglect. In J. Taylor & B. Daniel (Eds.), *Child neglect: Practice issues for health and social care* (pp. 11–25). London: Jessica Kingsley Publishers.

De Bellis, M. D. (2005). The psychobiology of neglect. *Child Maltreatment, 10*(2), 150–172.

Enwefa, R. L., Enwefa, S.C., & Jennings, R. (2006). Special education: Examining the impact of poverty on the quality of life of families of children with disabilities. *Forum on Public Policy, 2*(1), 1–27.

Espinosa, L. M. (2007). English-language learners as they enter school. In R. C. Pianta, M. J. Cox, & K. L. Snow (Eds.), *School readiness and the transition to kindergarten in the era of accountability.* Baltimore: Paul H. Brookes.

Faltis, C. (1998). *Joinfostering: Teaching and learning in multilingual classrooms* (3rd ed.). Upper Saddle River, NJ: Merrill/Prentice Hall.

Federal Child Abuse Prevention and Treatment Act, 42 U.S.C.A. §5106g (1996).

Fields, J. (2003). *Children's living arrangements and characteristics: March 2002* (Current Population

Report N. P20-547). Washington, DC: U.S. Bureau of the Census.

Fitzgerald, M. M., Schneider, R. A., Salstrom, S., Zinzaw, H. M., Jackson, J., & Fossel, R. V. (2008). Child sexual abuse, early family risk, and child parentification: Pathways to current psychosocial adjustment. *Journal of Family Psychology, 22*(2), 320–324.

Folsom, C. (2006). Making conceptual connections between gifted and general education: Teaching for intellectual and emotional learning. *Roeper Review, 28*(2), 79–87.

Food and Nutrition Service, U.S. Department of Agriculture. (2008). *About WIC.* Retrieved July 7, 2008, from http://www.fns.usda.gov/wic/aboutwic/wicataglance.htm

Garbarino, J., Gottmann, E., & Seeley, J. (1987). *The psychologically battered child.* San Francisco: Jossey-Bass.

Gardner, H. (2006). *Multiple intelligences: New horizons, completely revised and updated.* New York: Basic Books.

Gimpel, G. A., & Holland, M. L. (2003). *Emotional behavioral problems of young children: Effective interventions in the preschool and kindergarten years.* New York: Guilford Press.

Gough, D. (2004). Research for practice in child neglect. In J. Taylor & B. Daniel (Eds.), *Child neglect: Practice issues for health and social care,* (pp. 43–56). London: Jessica Kingsley Publishers.

Graham-Bermann, S. A., & Seng, J. (2005). Violence exposure and traumatic stress symptoms as additional predictors of health problems in high-risk children. *Journal of Pediatrics, 146,* 349–354.

Grant, B. F. (2000). Estimates of U.S. children exposed to alcohol abuse and dependence in the family. *American Journal of Public Health, 90,* 112–115.

Harrison, C. (2003). *Giftedness in early childhood* (3rd ed.). Sydney, Australia: GERRIC.

Hart, B., & Risley, T. (1995). *Meaningful differences in the everyday experience of young American children.* Baltimore: Paul H. Brookes.

Hart, B., & Risley T. (1999). *The social world of children learning to talk.* Baltimore: Paul H. Brookes.

Hart, S. N., & Brassard, R. (1987). A major threat to children's mental health: Psychological maltreatment. *American Psychologist, 42,* 160–165.

Hernandez, D., Denton, N., & Macartney, S. (2009). *Children in immigrant families—the U.S. and 50 states: Economic need beyond the official poverty measure.* Research brief series. Publication # 2009–19. Child Trends: William and Hewlett Foundation.

Hetherington, E. M., Bridges, M., & Isabella, G. M. (1998). What matters? What does not? Five perspectives on the association between marital transitions and children's adjustment. *American Psychologist, 53,* 167–184.

Hodge, K. A., & Kemp, C. R. (2006). Recognition of giftedness in the early years of school: Perspectives of teachers, parents, and children. *Journal of the Education of the Gifted, 30*(2), 168–204.

Horning, L., & Gordon-Rouse, K. (2009). Resilience in preschoolers and toddlers from low-income families. *Early Childhood Education Journal, 29*(3), 155–159.

Jacobson, S., & Jacobson, J. (2001). Alcohol and drug-related effects on development: A new emphasis on contextual factors. *Infant Mental Health Journal, 22*(3), 416–430.

Jolly, J. L. (2003). Pioneering definitions and theoretical positions in the field of gifted education. *Gifted Child Today, 28*(3), 38–44.

Kaplow, J. B., & Widom, C. (2007). Age of onset of child maltreatment predicts long-term mental health outcomes. *Journal of Abnormal Psychology, 116*(1), 176–187.

Karnes, F. A., & Nugent, S. A. (2002). Influential people in gifted education. *Gifted Child Today, 25*(2), 46–49.

Kilpatrick, D. G., Saunders, B. E., & Smith, D. (2003). *Youth victimization: Prevalence and implications, Research in brief.* Rockville, MD: National Institute of Justice/NCJRS, U.S. Department of Justice.

Klein, A. (2000). Fitting the school to the child: The mission of Leta Stetter Hollingworth, founder of gifted education. *Roeper Review, 23*(2), 97–103

Kroll, B. (2004). Living with an elephant: Growing up with parental substance misuse. *Child and Family Social Work, 9,* 129–140.

Kyunghee, L. (2009). The bidirectional effects of early poverty on children's reading and home environment scores: Associations and ethnic differences. *Social Work Research, 33*(2), 79–94.

Lewin, D., & Herron, H. (2007). Signs, symptoms and risk factors: Health visitors' perspectives of child neglect. *Child Abuse Review, 16,* 93–107.

Logsdon, M., Birkimer, J., Ratterman, A., Cahil, K., & Cahil, N. (2002). Social supports in pregnancy and parenting adolescents: Research, critique, and recommendation. *Journal of Child and Adolescent Psychiatric Nursing, 15,* 75–84.

Magee, T., & Roy, S. C. (2008). Predicting school-age behavior problems: The role of early childhood risk factors. *Pediatric Nursing, 34*(1), 37–44.

Manning, S. (2006). Recognizing gifted students: A practical guide for teachers. *Kappa Delta Pi Record,* 64–68.

Marland, S. (1972). *Education of the gifted and talented.* Report to the Congress of the United States by the U.S. Commissioner of Education. Washington, DC: Government Printing Office.

Masten, A., Best, K., & Garmezy, N. (1991). Resilience and development: Contributions from the study of children who overcame adversity. *Development and Psychopathology, 2,* 425–444.

McDaniel, B., & Dillenburger, K. (2007). Can childhood neglect be assessed and prevented through childcare skills training? *Child Abuse Review, 16,* 120–129.

Mittendorfer-Rutz, E., Rasmussen, F., & Wasserman, D. (2004). Restricted fetal growth and adverse maternal psychosocial and socioeconomic conditions as risk factors for suicidal behaviour of offspring: A cohort study. *Lancet, 364,* 1135–1140.

Molnar, B. E., Cerda, M., Roberts, A. L., & Buka, S. (2008). Effects of neighborhood resources on aggressive and delinquent youth behaviors among urban youth. *Research and Practice, 98*(6), 1086–1093.

Morrissey, A., & Brown, M. (2009). Mother and toddler activity in the zone of proximal development for pretend play as a predictor of higher child IQ. *Gifted Children Quarterly, 53*(2), 106–120.

National Association for Gifted Children. (2006). *State of the Nation 2006–2007.* Retrieved December 26, 2007, from http://www.nagc.org/uploadedFiles/Gifted_by_State/state%20of%20nation%20(for%20website).pdf

National Research Council, Institute of Medicine. (2000). *From neurons to neighborhoods: The science of early childhood development.* Washington, DC: National Academy Press.

Oats, M. (1997). Patients as parents: The risk to children. *British Journal of Psychiatry, 170*(Suppl. 32), 22–27.

Otto, B. (2006). *Language development in early childhood* (2nd ed.). Upper Saddle River, NJ: Merrill/Prentice Hall.

Patterson, S., & Albers, A. B. (2001). Effects of poverty and maternal depression on early child development. *Child Development, 72,* 1794–1813.

Pianta, R. (1999). *Enhancing relationships between children and teachers: School psychology book series.* Washington, DC: American Psychological Association.

Pianta, R. C., La Paro, K. M., & Hamre, B. K. (2004). *Classroom Assessment Scoring System [CLASS].* Unpublished measure, University of Virginia.

Raghaven, C., & Kingston, S. (2006). Child sexual abuse and posttraumatic stress disorder: The role of age at first use of substances and lifetime traumatic events. *Journal of Traumatic Stress, 19*(2), 269–278.

RAND. (2005). *Children at risk: Consequence for school readiness and beyond.* Retrieved December, 5, 2007, from http://www.rand.org/pubs/research_briefs/2005/RAND_RB9144.pdf

Renzulli, J. S. (1978). What makes giftedness: Reexamining a definition. *Phi Delta Kappan, 60*(3), 180–184.

Renzulli, J. S. (1994). *Schools for talent development: A practical plan for total school improvement.* Mansfield Center, CT: Creative Learning Press.

Reynolds, A. J., Temple, J. A., Robertson, D. L., Mann, E. A., & Ou, S. R. (2003, April 26). *Prevention and cost-effectiveness in the Chicago child–parent centers.* Paper presented at the Meeting of the Society for Research in Child Development, Tampa, Florida.

Robinson, N. M. (2003). Two wrongs do not make a right: Sacrificing the needs of gifted students does not solve society's unsolved problems. *Journal of the Education of the Gifted, 26,* 251–273.

Rodriguez, C. D., & Higgins, K. (2005). Preschool children with developmental delays and limited English proficiency. *Intervention in School and Clinic, 40*(4), 236–242.

Rotigel, J. V. (2003). Understanding the young gifted child: Guidelines for parents, families and educators. *Early Childhood Education Journal, 30*(4), 209–214.

Rouse, H., & Fantuzzo, J. (2009). Multiple risks and educational well being: A population-based investigation of threats to early school success. *Early Childhood Research Quarterly, 24*(1), 1–14.

Rutter, M., & Quinton, D. (1984). Long-term follow-up of women institutionalized in childhood: Factors promoting good functioning in adult life. *British Journal of Developmental Psychology, 18,* 225–234.

Rutter, M. (2000). Resilience reconsidered: Conceptual considerations, empirical findings, and policy implications. In J. P. Shonkoff & S. J. Meisels (Eds.), *Handbook of early childhood intervention* (pp. 651–682). Cambridge, UK: Cambridge University Press.

Seeley, K. (2004). Gifted and talented students at risk. *Focus on Exceptional Children, 37*(4), 1–8.

Seidman, E., & Pedersen, S. (2003). Holistic contextual perspectives on risk, protection, and competence among low-income urban adolescents. In S. S. Luthar (Ed.), *Resilience and vulnerability: Adaptation in the context of childhood adversities* (pp. 318–342). New York: Cambridge University Press.

Seligman, M., & Darling, R. B. (2007). *Ordinary families, special children: A systems approach to childhood disability* (3rd ed.). New York: Guilford Press.

Silverman, L. K. (2002). Asynchronous development. In M. Neihart, S. M. Reis, N. M. Robinson, & S. M. Moon (Eds.), *The social and emotional development of gifted children: What do we know?* (pp. 31–37). Washington, DC: Prufrock Press Inc.

Smith, M. (2004). Parental mental health: Disruption to parenting and outcomes for children. *Child and Family Social Work, 9,* 3–11.

Stevenson, O. (2004). Forward. In J. Taylor & B. Daniel (Eds.), *Child neglect: Practice issues for health and social care,* (pp. 9–10). London: Jessica Kingsley Publishers.

Stormont, M. (2007). *Fostering resilience in young children at risk for failure: Strategies for grades K–3.* Upper Saddle River, NJ: Pearson/Prentice Hall.

Summers, E. (n.d.). *A brief history of the education of the gifted child.* Retrieved December 21, 2007, from http://www.hunter.cuny.edu/gifted-ed/documents/summersgiftedhistory_000.doc

Terrassier, J. C. (1985). Dyssynchrony-uneven development. In J. Freeman (Ed.), *The psychology of gifted children: Perspectives on development and education* (pp. 153–159). New York: Wiley.

The National Commission on Excellence in Education (April, 1983). *A nation at risk: The imperative for educational reform.* Retrieved December 21, 2007, http://www.ed.gov/pubs/NatAtRisk/index.html

Thomlinson, B. (2003). Characteristics of evidence-based child maltreatment intervention. *Child Welfare League of America, 5,* 541–569.

Turner, H. A., Finkelhor, D., & Ormrod, R. (2007). Family structure variations in patterns and predictors of child victimization. *American Journal of Orthopsychiatry, 77*(2), 282–295.

U. S. Department of Commerce, Bureau of the Census. (1997). *Census brief: America's children at risk.* Retrieved December 5, 2007, from http://www.census.gov/prod/3/97pubs/cb-9702.pdf

National excellence: A case for developing America's talent. Retrieved December 21, 2007, from http://www.ed.gov/pubs/DevTalent/toc.html

U. S. Department of Education. (2008). *Even Start: Program description.* Retrieved July 7, 2008, from http://www.ed.gov/programs/evenstartformula/index.html

VanDeMark, N., Russell, L., O'Keefe, M., Finkelstein, N., Noether, C., & Gampel, J. (2005). Children of mothers with histories of substance abuse, mental illness, and trauma. *Journal of Community Psychology, 33*(4), 445–459.

Vanderbilt-Adriance, E., & Shaw, D. (2008). Protective factors and development of resilience in the context of neighborhood disadvantage. *Journal of Abnormal Child Psychology, 36*(6), 887–901.

Webster-Stratton, C., Reid, M., & Stoolmiller, M. (2008). Preventing conduct problems and improving school readiness: Evaluation of the incredible years teacher and child training programs in high-risk schools. *Journal of Child Psychology & Psychiatry, 49*(5), 471–488,

Weissbourd, R. (2009). The "quiet" troubles of low-income children. *Education Digest: Essential Readings Condensed for Quick Review, 74*(5), 4–8.

Werner, E. (1993). Risk, resilience, and recovery: Perspectives from the Kauai longitudinal study. *Development and Psychopathology, 5,* 503–515.

Werner, E. (1995). Resilience in development. *Current Directions in Psychological Science, 4*(3), 81–85.

Werner, E. (2000). Protective factors and individual resilience. In J. P. Shonkoff & S. J. Meisels (Eds.), *Handbook of Early Childhood Intervention* (pp.115–132). Cambridge, UK: Cambridge University Press.

Werner, E., & Smith, R. (1992). *Overcoming the odds: High-risk children from birth to adulthood.* Ithaca, NY: Cornell University Press.

Westby, C. E. (2007). Child maltreatment: A Global issue. *Language, Speech, and Hearing Services in Schools, 38,* 140–148.

Wyman, P. E. (2003). Emerging perspectives on context specificity of children adaptations and resilience: Evidence from a decade of research with urban children in adversity. In S. S. Luthar (Ed.), *Resilience and vulnerability: Adaptation in the context of childhood adversities* (pp. 293–317). New York: Cambridge University Press.

Issues of Consideration in Kindergarten through Third Grade Special Education

Education of Children with Disabilities in Primary School Years: Kindergarten through Third Grade

Objectives

Upon completion of this chapter, you should be able to:

> Understand developmental and environmental changes that might occur as children enter primary grades.

> Discuss learning disabilities and their history in the United States.

> Understand Response to Intervention (RTI).

> Distinguish between different types, causes, and characteristics of learning disabilities.

> Discuss strategies and adaptations for working with children with learning disabilities in the primary grades.

> Understand issues pertaining to curriculum in primary grades.

> Identify school-wide issues related to the education of children in primary grades.

Key Terms

community-based instruction (532)	functional academics (531)	Response to Intervention (RTI) (520)
critical thinking (516)	music therapy (532)	systematic instruction (529)
curriculum-based assessment (517)	number sense (530)	temporal-sequential ability (524)
curriculum-based measures (517)	peer-mediated instruction (536)	visual-spatial ability (525)
data-driven (522)	peer tutoring (536)	working memory (525)
explicit instruction (528)	prereferral intervention (PRI) (521)	

Reflection Questions

Before reading this chapter, answer the following questions to reflect upon your personal opinions and beliefs that are pertinent to early childhood special education.

1. How do you think issues concerning the education of primary level children with disabilities might differ from those in earlier grades?

2. What are some issues that parents of children with disabilities might be concerned about as their children prepare to enter elementary school?

3. As an early childhood educator who might be working with children with special needs in primary grades, what are some questions you have?

Looking into the Future

When my son, Seena, was 2½ years old, he received a diagnosis of Autism Spectrum Disorders. During those early days of diagnosis, as my husband and I were adjusting to the idea of our child having a disability and dealing with many immediate demands, we were also concerned about the future. Every day, we asked ourselves questions such as:

1. Is our son going to grow out of his disability as he matures?
2. What is going to happen to him?
3. Where and how will he be educated?
4. Would he ever graduate from an elementary or a high school?
5. Would he grow up to have a job?
6. Would he ever get married?
7. What would happen to him when we are no longer living?

You might believe that parents should not think about such far removed future concerns, but these are very legitimate questions, and parents of children with disabilities usually ask them as early as the first day of the diagnosis. Through the years, we have found answers to some of these questions, especially the ones related to our son's education, but others still remain unknown, and we find ourselves asking them often as he continues to develop and mature.

As it turned out, in our son's case, Seena's needs were best met through a preschool specialized autism program that was available in our area's local public school. Although our son has been, and continues to be, included in all regular family affairs and community activities since his early childhood years, the severity of his disability compelled his educators and us to move him to a specialized classroom for his elementary education.

Throughout his elementary school years, he received special education in a structured classroom along with other children with autism. When appropriate, he was included in school activities within and outside the school settings with his peers without disabilities. Last year, he transitioned into a specialized high school for students with developmental disabilities.

In our son's case, he has received—and is likely to continue receiving—his education in specialized classrooms for the remainder of his schooling. However, this is not necessarily the case for many young children who are diagnosed with moderate to severe disabilities today. In fact, it is hoped that those young children who are deemed best suited for special education preschool classrooms today, will in time, because of their positive developmental gains from high-quality early intervention and preschool programs, be placed in inclusive classrooms as they enter elementary school. The success of children with disabilities in elementary school is an important predictor of their academic success and their future transition into the community.

INTRODUCTION

Predicting the future developmental course of young children with special needs is not an easy task. As we have learned throughout this book, achieving a positive outcome for children depends on many complex biological, environmental, and educational factors. However, when young children with special education needs receive appropriate early intervention and early childhood special education, the possibility that they might no longer qualify for special education or be placed in inclusive elementary classrooms becomes extremely high (Bailey, Scarborough, Hebbeler, Spiker, & Mallik, 2004).

The point needs to be made that after completing their preschool years, no matter what kind of educational placements children with special needs transition into, whether inclusive or specialized, we should continue to be prepared to use appropriate methods and make suitable adaptations to meet their developmental and academic needs.

Since early childhood education encompasses intervention from infancy through third grade, in this chapter we will examine general issues concerning the education of children with disabilities during the primary school years: kindergarten, first, second, and third grades. Because learning disabilities are usually diagnosed during elementary and middle school years, we will first examine learning disabilities and related issues in this chapter. We will then focus on components of a curriculum that are more appropriate for children with special needs in both inclusive and special education classrooms from kindergarten through third grade.

PRIMARY SCHOOL YEARS

Primary school years include kindergarten through third grade. The transition from preschool to primary school signals a period of change for both parents and children. This period is a time in which children begin transitioning to middle childhood. Changes will occur not only in the children's physical, cognitive, language, and social emotional development, but in the academic environment they are now preparing to enter.

The transition of children from a preschool environment, as shown here, to primary school, signals a period of change for both parents and children.

Changes in Development

The last years of early childhood are the beginning of a period of slow but steady and consistent growth (Santrock, 2006; Feldman, 2007). During the elementary school years, children grow about 2 to 3 inches in height and gain 5 to 7 pounds in weight every year (Feldman, 2007). Between ages 6 and 12, children's fine and gross motor skills become more coordinated. During these years, children learn to skip, balance on one foot with their eyes closed, and perform actions like jumping jacks and rhythmical hopping. By age 7, girls can throw a small ball an average of 33 feet, and boys can throw a small ball an average of 59 feet (Feldman, 2007).

In terms of cognitive abilities, children's long-term memory increases (Santrock, 2006). Children begin to think reflectively and productively, and learn to evaluate the evidence that they can see, what we call **critical thinking** (Santrock, 2006). Upon entering the elementary school years, children discover the need to become independent. They not only master taking care of their own physical needs, they become motivated to learn the rules and customs of their classroom, school, community, and culture (McDevitt & Ormrod, 2007). For example, children learn to read, write, to use a computer, and to help in household tasks.

The primary school years also bring forth the importance of friendship to children. Peer relationships and having friends become extremely important to children, especially between children of the same age and gender (McDevitt & Ormrod, 2007). Behaviorally, children begin to internalize the limitations and expectations that had earlier been set for them by adults, and frequently try to follow rules and live up to those expectations.

For children with severe special needs, the primary school years are often a relatively calmer period compared to their earlier years (Marcus, Kunce, & Schopler, 1997). During this time, most children with disabilities show some improvement in sociability, emotional control, and attention span (McAdoo & DeMyer, 1977). For most families, this period is a time to build consistent routines and daily living skills. Typically, children with disabilities might show gains in the areas of daily living skills, and the family who had previously been

The primary school years bring forth the importance of friendships. Having friends becomes extremely important to children, especially between children of the same age and gender.

frustrated in teaching cognitive tasks to their child may find this period gratifying (Marcus & Schopler, 1987).

Changes in Teachers' Expectations and the Environment

Educators teaching primary grades usually have a different set of expectations for children—academically and behaviorally—than child care providers or preschool teachers do. Although many primary classrooms are similar in physical structure to preschool classrooms, there are usually more structured classroom rules for children to observe in kindergarten and beyond (Downing, 2008).

With kindergarten and first grade, children begin to engage in formal academic activities and are assessed more frequently by **curriculum-based measures** compared to developmental assessment instruments. A **curriculum-based assessment** is a procedure in which the student's academic performance is broken down into measurable pieces and evaluated in a systematic way through the use of standardized criterion-referenced measurement instruments (Mindes, 2010). In this approach, teachers assess a student's performance in specific subject areas based on the curriculum's learning goals.

Some children who are transitioning to kindergarten might have a difficult time meeting the demands and expectations of their new environments, whereas others adjust quickly and learn academic and social skills that are appropriate for elementary classrooms. It is usually during the elementary or middle school years that children who have difficulties meeting the academic expectations of their grade level might be identified as having a learning disability.

Under IDEA, children with learning disabilities are eligible to receive special education services. In the following sections, we will learn about children with learning disabilities and some useful adaptations regarding reading and math instruction in primary grades.

CHILDREN WITH LEARNING DISABILITIES

The number of children with learning disabilities (LD) has been on the rise during the last three decades. Some reports indicate that a staggering number of U.S. children, from 5 percent to about 9.7 percent (about 1 in every 10), have a learning disability (Altarac & Saroha, 2007; Donovan & Cross, 2002; Lyon et al., 2001). Among typically developing children 5.4 percent (about 2.7 million) have learning disabilities, whereas 27.8 percent (about 3.3 million) of children with special needs have learning disabilities (Altarac & Saroha, 2007). Children with learning disabilities form the largest group (about half) of children with disabilities who receive special education services in the United States (Donovan & Cross, 2002; Lyon et al., 2001).

Various types of learning disabilities exist; for example, those in reading, writing, mathematics, and specific subject areas (Levine & Barringer, 2008; Lyon et al., 2001). Learning disabilities are seldom diagnosed prior to kindergarten or first grade, since these are the formal grades in which children begin to engage in academic activities such as literacy, math, social studies, and sciences. A learning disability is a specific problem related to oral and written language. In the following section, we will examine learning disabilities and related issues.

The History of Learning Disabilities

The history of learning disabilities has been traced back to Franz Joseph Gall, an 18th-century anatomist and physiologist (Fletcher, Lyon, Fuchs, & Barnes, 2007; Hallahan & Mercer, 2001). Through observation of injured soldiers, Gall discovered the relationship between brain injury and a subsequent expressive language disorder (Hallahan & Mercer, 2001). He established that patterns of strength and weakness in oral and written language might be related to damage in specific areas of the brain (Fletcher et al., 2007).

In 1877, Adolph Kussmaul, a prominent German physician, identified a specific learning disability, referring to it as "word blindness" to describe patients who, despite being able to see, could not read written words (Hallahan & Mercer, 2001). In the years that followed, two other physicians, John Hinshelwood and Pringle Morgan, reported on further cases of adults and children with word blindness. These two studies identified what today are known as dyslexia and developmental dyslexia.

Inspired by these European discoveries, in the 1920s U.S. researchers began to study individuals who, despite their obvious cognitive abilities, were not able to read and/or write. The American scholars focused their efforts on speech and reading difficulties, perceptual problems, and attention difficulties. With the advent of IQ testing, most of these scientists were intrigued by the fact that many children who had learning and reading problems actually had average to above average IQ scores (Gallego, Duran, & Reyes, 2006; Hallahan & Mercer, 2001).

Notable among the U.S. scientists are Grace Fernald, an educational psychologist, and Samuel Orton, a physician. Grace Fernald established the first remedial clinic for individuals with learning problems at the University of California, Los Angeles. Samuel Orton studied reading problems. Both Orton and Fernald advocated multisensory training, or visual-auditory kinesthetic methods, by which children traced letters with their fingers while sounding them out loud (Fernald & Keller, 1921; Orton, 1937).

Although many individuals contributed to the identification and remediation of learning disabilities, it was Samuel Kirk who appeared as the most prominent figure in the field of learning disabilities. Kirk was a psychologist who, as a graduate student in 1929, encountered and worked with a child with a learning disability (Kirk, 1976).

Kirk conducted research on learning and reading problems in children, devised methods of working with children with learning problems, created a special education program for graduate and undergraduate students at the University of Illinois, established the first experimental preschool for children with intellectual disabilities, and designed an instrument to diagnose differences in individual cognitive and language abilities—the Illinois Test of Psycholinguistic Abilities (ITPA) (Kirk, McCarthy, & Kirk, 1961).

In 1961, Kirk for the first time used the term "learning disabilities" in his book *Educating Exceptional Children,* and in 1963, while addressing a group of parents, he formally used the term as a label for children who had problems with oral and written language (Hallahan & Mercer, 2001). For a small synopsis of Kirk's historic speech, see Text Box 15.1.

The label of learning disabilities that Kirk proposed did not have the negative connotations other previous labels had, such as mental retardation or brain injury. Despite previously known disabilities, learning disabilities did not imply having low intelligence or behavioral problems. Rather, children with learning

The Birth of Learning Disabilities	Text Box 15.1

In 1963, Samuel Kirk, a professor of Special Education at the University of Illinois, addressed a group of parents at the *Conference on Exploration into Problems of the Perceptually Handicapped Child.* This speech marks the introduction of the term *learning disabilities.* Kirk's remarks began the learning disability movement, resulting in the establishment of various parent and professional organizations and special education legislations. In his talk, Samuel Kirk explained his reason for employing the label to be his lack of satisfaction with the term *brain injury,* which had been used up to that time to describe the condition of children with learning difficulties. His term learning disabilities described children who had specific language-related problems, such as in the areas of speech, reading, and social interactions. He pointedly excluded children with intellectual disabilities from this group.

Source: Kirk, S. A. (1963). Behavioral diagnosis and remediation of learning disabilities. In *Proceedings of the conference on exploration into problems of the perceptually handicapped child* (pp. 2–3). Chicago: Perceptually Handicapped Children.

disabilities had normal intelligence and adaptive skills, yet had problems with learning (Fletcher et al., 2007). Inspired by Kirk's speech, a group of parents established the Association for Children with Learning Disabilities (ACLD). This association is today known as the Learning Disabilities Association of America (LDA).

Definition of Learning Disabilities

Professor Kirk's speech was important in establishing learning disabilities as a group of disorders affecting many children who struggle with learning in school. The movement that followed prompted Congress to create a legislative policy for the definition, assessment, and intervention for children with learning disabilities.

In 1969, Congress amended the Elementary and Secondary Education Act to include Children with Specific Learning Disabilities. This act, which is also known as the Learning Disabilities Act (LD Act) of 1969, has remained unchanged throughout the iteration of IDEA (Gallego et al., 2006). The Federal definition of learning disabilities appeared first in the All Handicapped Children Act of 1975, and later in IDEIA 2004. (For the current definition of learning disability, as used in IDEIA 2004, see Text Box 15.2.) The original definition of *specific learning disability,* iterated in 1968 by the Office of Education, is as follows:

> A disorder in one or more of the basic psychological processes involved in understanding or in using language, spoken or written, which may manifest itself in an imperfect ability to listen, speak, read, write, spell, or do mathematical calculations. . . . The term does not include children who have learning disabilities, which are primarily the result of visual, hearing, or motor handicaps, or mental retardation, or emotional disturbance, or of environmental, cultural, or economic disadvantage (U.S. Office of Education, 1968).

The federal definition and identification procedures for learning disabilities have generated much debate among scholars in the field since the 1970s. In 1977, the

| Text Box 15.2 | Specific Learning Disabilities in Individuals with Disabilities Education Improvement Act (2004); Section 300.7. |

Specific learning disability is a disorder in one or more psychological processes involved in understanding or using spoken or written language, that may be manifest as an imperfect ability to listen, think, speak, read, write, spell, or do math: it does not include learning problems primarily resulting from visual, hearing, or motor disabilities, mental retardation, emotional disturbance, or environmental, cultural, or economic factors.

U.S. Office of Education defined learning disabilities to be the discrepancy between achievement and intellectual ability in different academic areas to be measured by IQ testing and other standardized tests.

The use of IQ discrepancy as a measure of learning disabilities has become a major source of controversy in the field, however. The main objection against using IQ and achievement discrepancy is that—in the view of many educational researchers—IQ is still considered an arbitrary measure of intelligence and thus may lead to inappropriate decisions regarding a child's educational placement (Francis et al., 2005). In addition, the impressive body of research in neuroscience has now pointed to specific dysfunctions in the brain that are not revealed through traditional IQ and achievement tests (Levine & Barringer, 2008).

Since the 1980s, the rise in the number of English language learners (ELL) who are routinely identified as having both learning disabilities and limited English proficiency has added fuel to the existing debate about the identification of LD (Gallego et al., 2006). The ever-increasing number of children identified with learning disabilities has made educators and scientists concerned that many children are misdiagnosed and inadequately placed (Francis et al., 2005; Lyon et al., 2001; Gresham, 2001).

Critical Thinking Question 15.1   Refer to the story presented at the beginning of this chapter. Considering the questions that we as parents asked at the time of diagnosis, what do you think is the best way of responding to parents when they ask you questions regarding the developmental and educational future of their young child with special needs?

RESPONSE TO INTERVENTION

With the emphasis that the No Child Left Behind Act and IDEIA 2004 put on scientific based teaching methods, an approach known as **Response to Intervention (RTI)** (also known as Response to Instruction) has been progressively advocated by researchers and educators as a method of identifying learning disabilities instead of using IQ discrepancy measures. RTI was defined in the 1990s as a procedure to measure the change in the behavior or academic performance of a child as a result of an intervention (Gresham, 1991).

Response to Intervention is a part of a **prereferral intervention (PRI)** process, which has been established since the 1980s in many schools to reduce the number of students who were referred for special education (Carter & Sugai, 1989). PRI is a team-based approach in which a prereferral intervention team (PIT)—usually consists of special educators and a school administrator—is created to collaborate and consult with the classroom teacher to enhance the teacher's competence and skills in order to provide nonspecial education intervention for the child who is struggling academically, before he is referred for special education (Tam & Heng, 2005; Truscott, Cohen, Sams, Sansborn, & Frank, 2005).

Concerns have arisen that the prereferral intervention processes currently in place across various states have not been effective as preventive measures (Buck, Polloway, Smith-Thomas, & Cook, 2003). Response to Intervention has therefore been proposed as both an identification and prevention model to improve the prereferral process (Mastropieri & Scruggs, 2005). The RTI procedure usually begins with an academic screening for possible learning problems. Children who are found through screening to struggle with learning would receive intervention. Different RTI approaches exist, which vary in structure and setting.

Most RTI approaches use a three-tier framework (Ehren & Nelson, 2005). In a three-tier model, a typical procedure is as follows (Reschly, 2003; Vaughn, Wanzek, & Denton, 2007):

> **Tier 1:** A child who is struggling in one or more academic areas is identified through an academic screening. The teacher will begin using a research-validated curriculum targeting specific skills and monitors the child's progress closely.
> **Tier 2:** If the child continues to have difficulties, parental consent is obtained for the child to receive private tutoring and a more intense intervention, in addition to the Tier 1 intervention. If the child does not make appropriate progress, the child might continue to remain in Tier 2 with more intense individual tutoring and classroom monitoring. If the appropriate mastery level in the targeted skill is not reached after a more intense intervention, the child is referred for a diagnostic evaluation.
> **Tier 3:** The child receives diagnostic and evaluation services for eligibility determination to receive special education services. See Figure 15.1 for an illustration of a three-tier RTI model.

Although, historically, RTI was intended for use with school-age children who have possible learning disabilities, it is now being increasingly considered for preschoolers who have other issues, such as challenging behaviors (Fox & Hemmeter, 2009). In a preschool setting, the RTI team should consist of early childhood educators, special educators, developmental psychologists, and family members (Beganto, 2006). For a successful RTI process in preschool, an ongoing play-based or curriculum-based authentic assessment, along with parental observation reports, should be used for monitoring progress and data collection, as well as to understand every child's strengths and needs within his everyday learning experiences and environment (Beganto, 2006; Coleman, Roth, & West, 2009).

FIGURE 15.1
Three-Tier Model of
RTI

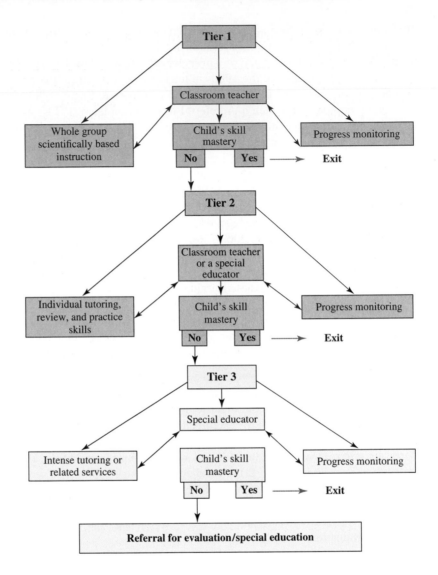

RTI is a **data-driven** process. This means that through all tiers of RTI, assessment data is collected and reviewed regularly and systematically. The progress monitoring data in each of the tiers provides the basis for decision making regarding further intervention and services. See Text Box 15.3 for an example of RTI for a kindergarten student.

Response to Intervention has gained increasing support from school districts and local agencies. In fact, the Individuals with Disabilities Education Improvement Act of 2004 specifies that (1) states cannot require districts to use IQ tests for identification of students with learning disabilities, and (2) states should permit school districts to implement assessment models that incorporate RTI (Fletcher et al., 2007).

Example of a Response to Intervention Model in Kindergarten

Text Box 15.3

Rhoda Elementary School has begun adopting a Response to Intervention model since the previous year. As part of the RTI program, in September, Ms. Ponce screened all children in her kindergarten classroom using Phonological Awareness Literacy Screening-Kindergarten (PALS-K), a literacy screening tool for kindergarten students.

Tier 1

Ms. Ponce's screening results indicated that three of her students, Jamal, Malcolm, and Natasha scored below the cut-off point used to identify possible reading problems. These students had a hard time blending phonemes, recognizing letters in words, and hearing specific sounds in words. Ms. Ponce began using *Ladders to Literacy,* a research-based validated reading curriculum for all children, ensuring to spend some individual time in small group activities with the three students, as well as individually for review and practice. Using a curriculum-based assessment procedure to monitor her students' progress, she systematically documented these three students' progress for several weeks. Based on Ms. Ponce's data, Jamal's response to her reading intervention was minimal, falling below the desired mastery level; whereas Malcolm and Natasha made considerable progress, indicating that they had almost reached mastery at the grade level after several weeks of intervention.

Tier 2

Ms. Ponce and other members of the prereferral intervention team met with Jamal's parents to discuss their concerns regarding Jamal's reading problems. Jamal's parents gave consent so that the school could begin the second tier of RTI in reading intervention with Jamal.

Jamal was to receive private one-on-one tutoring sessions with a reading specialist everyday for 30 minutes for the next 8 weeks, in addition to the classroom intervention he was receiving from his teacher. A progress report was to be sent home every other week. The data collected during the second tier of intervention would inform the school professionals whether or not Jamal should be referred for a formal evaluation.

The school personnel informed Jamal's parents that at any time during Tier 2 of the intervention period, if the parents were dissatisfied with Jamal's progress reports, and suspected a learning disability, they could request a formal evaluation process to begin.

Jamal responded positively during Tier 2 of the RTI. He made improvements in phonological awareness and beginning reading, and was able to achieve the mastery level by January. Ms. Ponce continued to monitor Jamal to make sure he succeeded in all academic areas. In case Jamal indicated difficulties in any subject, Ms. Ponce would recommend his entry into Tier 2 of the RTI program again.

AREAS OF LEARNING DISABILITIES AND CAUSES

In brief, learning disabilities are difficulties in understanding and using either written or oral, or both written and oral language, which impede children's learning. Children with learning disabilities might have problems with listening, speaking, reading, writing, spelling, reasoning, or doing mathematical calculations. Difficulties in reading and writing usually are caused by underlying neurodevelopmental dysfunctions (Levine & Barringer, 2008; Levine, 2003).

Levine and Barringer (2008) describe dysfunctions in eight neurodevelopmental mechanisms that underlie common learning disabilities in reading and writing. These areas consist of attention, temporal-sequential ordering, spatial ordering, memory, language, neuromotor functions, social cognition, and higher-order cognition, which are described in the following sections. Table 15.1 displays some common learning disabilities related to language, motor, and memory.

Attention

Attention includes the ability to concentrate, focus on one thing rather than another, complete tasks, and control what one says and does. Attention deficits are common in children with learning disabilities, and as mentioned in Chapter 8, a large number of children who are diagnosed with ADHD also have learning disabilities.

Temporal-Sequential Ordering

Performing most tasks, from counting from one to ten, to typing on a keyboard, depends on the child's ability to understand the time and sequence of pieces of information (Levine & Barringer, 2008). The **temporal-sequential ability** enables the child to organize and remember information in the order it has been presented. This ability is needed for understanding the concept of time and following multistep

TABLE 15.1   **Learning Disabilities**

Learning Disabilities in Oral and Written Language	
Dyslexia	Problems with reading, specifically in phonological processing (the manipulation of sounds). Children with dyslexia have problems with single word decoding, might reverse words or read from right to left, might write letters back to front, or might have difficulties remembering the sequence of letters in a word
Dysnomia	Problems with remembering names or recalling words for oral or written communication
Dysgraphia	Problems with producing handwriting that is legible and is written with a speed that is appropriate based on the child's age
Dyscalculia	Problems with understanding mathematical symbols and concepts
Dysarthria	Problems with fine motor muscles involved in speech, which impedes the child's ability to speak with normal muscular speed, strength, or precision. In some children, the problem is so severe that the speech is unintelligible

directions. Children who have problems in the area of temporal-sequential ordering will have difficulties arranging and organizing their ideas.

Visual-Spatial Ordering

The **visual-spatial ability** enables the child to identify the differences between shapes, sizes, and volumes, and recognize complex and multidimensional objects or images (Levine & Barringer, 2008). For example, recognizing the difference between a circle and a triangle depends on the child's visual-spatial ability. Children with weak visual-spatial ordering have difficulties figuring out how things are built, or how specific parts could be put together to form an object.

Memory

Memory is the child's ability to store information and recall it when needed. Having a good memory is necessary for all kinds of learning activities. Short-term memory mechanisms enable the child to receive information through visual, auditory, or sequential memory and store it for a short time for immediate retrieval. Some children with a learning disability might have difficulties registering the information that they receive through their short-term memory (Fletcher et al., 2007; Levine, 1987, 1990). Others might have problems organizing the correct information for storage in the long-term memory. Yet another group of children might have a hard time retrieving or recalling the information that they have stored.

Problems with **working memory** are very common among children with learning disabilities (Fletcher et al., 2007). Working memory is active when a person recalls different parts of information that they need to perform a task, such as writing the alphabet down as one recalls the letters, or putting words into sentences to make a paragraph as one is writing. It is part of the information processing system that enables the child to hold several facts or thoughts in memory temporarily while he or she is performing the task. Some children with learning disabilities, who have problems with working memory, forget the required information for a task as they are performing that very same task. See the case of Cory presented in Text Box 15.4 for an example.

Language

Most learning disabilities are related to written or oral language. Specific language functions that are elemental in academic learning are abilities such as pronouncing sounds, distinguishing between different phonemes that are heard, and understanding the written symbols (Levine & Barringer, 2008). Listening and reading comprehension, which are common problems among children with learning disabilities, relate to the child's ability to think about what they hear and read and understand their meanings.

Children who have language-based learning disabilities might have the following problems (Levine & Barringer, 2008):

> Difficulty in understanding spoken or written instructions or explanations
> A weak vocabulary

➢ Difficulty recognizing sounds and phonemes and blending them together (see the case of Martin in Text Box 15.4)
➢ Problems expressing ideas in words or sentences
➢ Various problems in writing and spelling (see the case of Amy in Text Box 15.4)
➢ Remembering words, sentences, or numbers
➢ Problems with the pragmatic or social aspect of language, which might lead to difficulties in making friends or being accepted by others

Neuromotor Function

The brain controls movements and coordination in large and small muscles. Motor movement and coordination control abilities such as writing, cutting with scissors, playing, typing on a computer, or running. All tasks require some kind of fine or gross motor ability, or hand-eye coordination. Many children with learning disabilities have problems with motor coordination, such as having difficulties with balance.

In addition, graphomotor function might be impaired in some children with learning disabilities (Levine, 2003). Graphomotor function relates to the abilities required for writing. Many children with a learning disability, although able to do fine motor tasks such as working with beads or constructing small objects, have problems with writing. Their pencil grip might be inappropriate and their writing might be labored, slow, or illegible, indicating graphomotor function problems.

Higher-Order Cognition

Higher-order thinking involves the ability to solve problems, think logically and systematically, think creatively, and explore new areas of learning. Higher-order

Children who have language-based learning disabilities might have various problems in writing and spelling.

| **Different Children, Different Learning Disabilities** | **Text Box 15.4** |

Martin: Martin is in first grade and is approaching the end of the school year. Throughout this school year, he has constantly struggled with reading. Martin's problems in reading have to do with phonological awareness. He has trouble distinguishing between the sounds (phonemes) he hears. Martin also has difficulties recognizing the sounds of the letters in the words that he sees on paper. Martin often has trouble understanding that words can be divided into segments of sounds. When he reads, he struggles to match letters to sounds, and to blend them together to form words. This is called decoding. Since Martin cannot accurately decode words, he has problems with recoding or spelling words.

Cory: Cory is a third grader. Unlike Martin, Cory can decode words. He is able to read words and sentences, and pronounce them well. However, he has a hard time understanding what he is reading. Often, he forgets what he is reading while he is reading it. Cory has problems with his working memory. This means Cory has trouble keeping the information which he reads together as he is reading. He also has problems with math. Although he knows the multiplication tables, it takes him a long time to remember them while he is doing math problems.

Amy: Amy is another third grader. She seldom volunteers to answer any questions that the teacher asks the class. Amy knows most of the answers, but does not like to volunteer to answer because she has a hard time finding the words as quickly as she needs them. Amy has good ideas, but she gets embarrassed in class when she is unable to say the words she wants to speak. Amy also has a spelling problem. She spells words that look like words but are not English words. For example, Amy might spell *alligator* as *aligiter.*

cognition requires the ability to infer and generate conclusions, to apply rules, to find solutions to problems, and to manipulate ideas at an abstract level (Baker, Gersten, & Scanlon, 2002; Levine, 1987). As children enter the primary grades, they are increasingly required to use higher-order thinking. Some children with learning disabilities might lack underlying abilities, such as classification or information processing, which are required for higher-order thinking (Levine, 1987). Many children with learning disabilities fail to utilize simple cognitive strategies in solving problems. They might have poor inferential reasoning and lack the ability to apply rules when necessary and appropriately (Levine, 1987)

Relationships and Social and Emotional Competencies

Although often overlooked, academic learning and achievement is influenced by the child's ability to succeed in social relationships with peers and adults in the home and the community, such as working in a group, making friends, and coping with peer pressure (Levine & Barringer, 2008). Three key areas in social and emotional competencies have been identified as the main source of difficulties in children with learning disabilities: recognizing emotions in themselves and others, regulating

Academic learning and achievement is influenced by the child's ability to succeed in social relationships with his peers.

and managing strong emotions (positive and negative), and recognizing their own strengths and areas of need.

In addition, problems with the social aspect of language often creates a lack of ability in these children to use appropriate words, communicate their feelings, choose a suitable topic, or allow for an exchange of ideas. Children with learning disabilities might also deal with self-esteem issues, the lack of an appropriate self-image, and peer rejection. Many children with learning disabilities experience a learned helplessness and a lack of motivation not only to learn, but to socialize as a result of previous academic and social failures.

STRATEGIES AND ADAPTATIONS FOR WORKING WITH CHILDREN WITH LEARNING DISABILITIES IN THE PRIMARY GRADES

Children with learning disabilities are usually educated in general education classrooms. Because learning disabilities vary in nature and cause, a variety of instructional methods and strategies have been articulated (Fletcher et al., 2007; McNary, Glasgow, & Hicks, 2005; Chard et al., 2005; Mastropieri & Scruggs, 1998; Levine, 1998) to address different areas of learning disabilities, such as improving phonological awareness, reading and listening comprehension, spelling, writing, mathematics, memory, and attention. In addition, a curriculum that addresses building social emotional competencies and peer relationships is also considered beneficial to children with learning disabilities who might struggle with such issues.

Explicit and Systematic Instruction

To address the difficulties within academic areas, it is recommended that the primary teachers use explicit and systematic methods of instruction, utilizing research-based curricula (Spear-Swerling, 2005). **Explicit instruction** is an intentional teaching method where all steps needed to complete a task are taught clearly and overtly (Vaughn et al., 2007).

The same way in which task analysis is used to teach various adaptive and pre-academic tasks to children, **systematic instruction** similarly refers to breaking down complex academic learning tasks into smaller units and teaching each learning unit in a sequence, one at a time. To teach explicitly and systematically, the teacher overtly imparts important skills by explaining, modeling, and demonstrating in sequential steps, and by providing appropriate scaffolding and support for students to demonstrate their learning. Here, we will briefly mention some strategies that are appropriate for enhancing reading and math in primary grades through explicit and systematic instruction.

Improving Reading in Primary Grades

In primary grades, several areas of reading abilities need to be addressed (Spear-Swerling, Brucker, & Alfano, 2005; Spear-Swerling, 2005):

1. **Phonological awareness:** Distinguishing various sounds which children hear in spoken words
2. **Phonics knowledge:** Recognizing that letters have sounds, distinguishing letters and common patterns of letters, and applying the knowledge of letters to read words
3. **Reading fluency:** Being able to read with ease and appropriate speed
4. **Vocabulary:** The knowledge of words and what they mean
5. **Comprehension:** Understanding what children read or hear

Explicit and systematic teaching of each area will prevent reading problems and help children who have reading disabilities. The following is one example of the explicit and systematic instruction steps required for phonics knowledge (Fitzsimmons, 1999):

1. Demonstrate the connection between sounds and letters and the connection between sounds and words.
   a. Use index cards with written words, highlighted letters in words, individual letter shapes to form the words, and representational pictures of words for visual aid.
2. Ask the student to produce words that have similar beginning or ending sounds to the model words that you produced.
3. Pay attention to the way in which the student:
   a. Makes individual sounds
   b. Identifies letters in isolation and within the words
   c. Blends sounds
   d. Reads words on the cards or the text
   e. Produces words that rhyme or have the beginning sound as compared with the model word
4. Give immediate feedback.
   a. Correct errors promptly.
5. Model new sounds and words.
   a. Correct errors promptly.

6. Sequence presenting and reading words from easy to more difficult.
    a. Repeat the feedback and correction process.
7. Practice and review each task, based on the student's needs.

Improving Math in Primary Grades

A child's mathematical learning depends on his or her **number sense.** Number sense is the child's fluidity and flexibility with numbers, a sense of what numbers mean, and an ability to perform mental mathematics, such as quantity comparisons (Gersten & Chard, 1999). In other words, it is the child's awareness and intuitive sense of what numbers mean. This ability enables the child to make mental quantitative calculations automatically and with ease (Morin & Frank, 2010; Chard et al., 2008). The importance of having a number sense in developing mathematical skills has been likened to the necessity of having a phonological awareness in developing reading abilities (Gersten & Chard, 1999). In fact, learning disabilities in mathematics have been linked to a lack of number sense during primary grades (Geary, Bow-Thomas, & Yao, 1992).

Acquiring a number sense usually occurs informally as children interact with people and objects in their natural environment. Children who are at risk, or have cognitive impairments or learning disabilities, often fail to acquire a number sense informally (Geary et al., 1992). Children's mathematics difficulties are not usually identified in primary grades. Rather, it is during later elementary grades that a child's mathematical problems are usually noticed. One way to improve mathematics learning in children with learning disabilities is to provide effective, explicit, and systematic math instruction that focuses on enhancing the children's number sense during primary grades (Morin & Frank, 2010; Chard et al., 2008).

Chard and colleagues (2008) have recommended that number sense activities in the primary grades be simultaneously integrated with measurement concepts, simple plane geometry, and related mathematical vocabulary. In a proposed math curriculum model called the Early Learning in Mathematics (ELM) program, they advocate explicit and systematic instruction of a research-based mathematical curriculum at the primary grade level. In this model, children are introduced to mathematical models starting with three-dimensional models (e.g., shapes, blocks), leading to two-dimensional representations (e.g., number lines), and finally moving to mathematical symbols. Children work in small peer groups, as well as independently.

Once children have been introduced to math models through working with manipulatives, Chard and colleagues (2008) recommend the following instructional and content components be added:

1. Numbers should be represented to children in three different ways:
    a. Conventional mathematical symbols (digits, addition, equal sign, etc.)
    b. Horizontal number lines
    c. Hundreds chart displays
2. Mathematics vocabulary, geometry, and measurement should be explicitly taught and reviewed.
3. Math concepts and skills should be systematically practiced and reviewed both in small peer groups and individually.

CURRICULAR ISSUES OF CONSIDERATION IN KINDERGARTEN THROUGH THIRD GRADE INCLUSIVE EDUCATION

In the past in special education, the focus of a curriculum has been on matching the curriculum content and outcomes of the curriculum to the developmental and functional needs of children with special needs (Rose, 2007). A typical curriculum for children with moderate to severe disabilities, for example, might have focused mainly on functional academics and daily living skills. Currently, however, the emphasis on inclusion has compelled us to think of ways in which a curriculum can equally address the educational and functional needs of all students, with and without disabilities. The promotion of an equitable educational experience within inclusive settings for all students has become the forefront of developments in special education today (Rouse & McLaughlin, 2007).

In Chapter 4, we presented a universal design model of a curriculum that would meet the challenge of addressing the needs of all students, yet acknowledge the necessity for individualization and adaptation of instruction and curriculum content (Figure 15.2). As a reminder, an appropriate curriculum contains multiple dimensions that form the cornerstones of professional practice in school and the classroom. These dimensions are influenced by the overall philosophical framework and theories underlying professional behaviors and teaching practices (see Chapter 4 for details).

During the primary and later grades, several issues pertaining to the education of children with disabilities gain special importance, items which might not have been of immediate concern to parents and educators in the earlier years, such as sexual education. These issues influence both the content and delivery of the curriculum. Keeping our curriculum model in mind, in the following sections we will discuss some of the most important issues.

Functional Academics and Daily Living Skills

The education of children with moderate to severe disabilities in both inclusive and specialized classrooms requires an emphasis on **functional academics** and daily living skills. Functional academics refers to literacy and math skills needed for

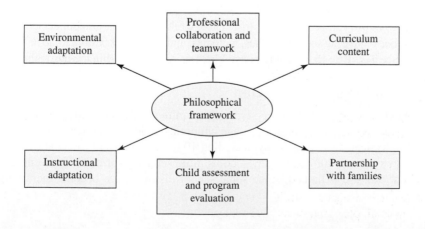

FIGURE 15.2
Seven Components of an Effective Primary Curriculum in Inclusive and Specialized Settings

everyday functioning, such as following a recipe, being able to use money for a purchase, or reading a restaurant menu (Taylor, Smiley, & Richards, 2009).

Teaching functional academics is not exclusive to middle and high school levels (Bouck, 2004). Academic skills that are meaningful to children and are functional should be taught during early childhood years. For example, whereas functional math in early and later primary grades might focus on money denomination values and simple addition and subtraction skills, in high school it might target writing a check or managing daily money exchanges.

In primary grades, functional academics should be taught within the daily classroom activities and practiced during neighborhood and community field trips. For example, a second grade field trip to the neighborhood supermarket might focus on practicing a series of math, literacy, and functional communication skills that had been previously learned in the classroom, such as students following individualized grocery lists, approaching and interacting with the cashier, and paying for the items independently at the checkout counter.

The instruction that takes place in the community is called **community-based instruction.** Community-based instruction for primary grade children usually takes place in nearby neighborhood restaurants, stores, or recreational places via classroom field trips and recreational and leisure activities. These extracurricular activities provide opportunities for children with special needs, specifically those with moderate to severe intellectual disabilities, to be included with their peers without disabilities, extend their academic skills, and form friendships. Community-based instruction increases the likelihood that children with disabilities will be integrated into the community after high school (Kleinert, Miracle, & Sheppard-Jones, 2007).

Integrating Music Activities in the Curriculum

Music has been widely used in early childhood education and in special education. It allows all children to join in group activities at their appropriate level and therefore promote a sense of community among them (Press, 2006). In special education, teaching musical skills has not necessarily been the focus, and **music therapy** has traditionally been used to teach children appropriate behaviors or academic skills (Standley, Walworth, & Nguyen, 2009; Gallegos, 2006).

In primary grades, music can be used to promote specific academic areas as well as socialization behaviors in all children (Press, 2006). For example, as a part of academic activities, music can be connected to science. Children can learn about acoustics and the science of hearing sounds, pitches, melodies, and harmonies (Conderman & Woods, 2008). See Text Box 15.5 for some ideas about using music within the curriculum.

Adapted Physical Education

During elementary years, children typically acquire physical activities through daily play in recess or in the gym. School-age children should have at least 30 to 60 minutes of physical activity each day, including 10 to 15 minutes of moderate to vigorous activity (Frey, 2007). In many schools, time set aside for children to engage in physical exercise is limited, since some school districts have become increasingly

Ways to Use Music in Primary Grades

Use Songs to Teach Vocabulary

Put the major word(s) that is(are) repeated in a song on large index cards (accompanied by pictures if needed). Explicitly teach the meaning of the words first. Give each student the vocabulary cards. Play the song and have students sing along. Have the students raise the vocabulary card and shout the word when it comes up in the song.

Use Music for Transitions between Activities

Use specific music, or make up your own transition song, and have students sing or play the music while transitioning from one activity to the next.

Play Music during Independent Work Time

When appropriate, play reading or relaxation music during individual time.

Have Children Sing Directions That They Need to Follow

Have children follow directions while singing them. Use a well-known tune, or make up your own, "It's time, it's time, it's time to line up."

Make up Specific Movement Activities to Match the Music

Enhance gross and fine motor activities by integrating specific large motor and fine motor movements into musical activities.

Have Children Create Their Own Books Based on Music

Decide on a song that you will play in class. Have students make up their own books—integrating art and literacy activities—about the song that they have been listening to.

Have Children Create Their Own Tunes or Lyrics

Have children interact with simple musical instruments, creating their own tunes. Have them add lyrics.

Have Children Create and Play Their Own Instruments

Using simple art and daily living items, such as paper towel rolls or egg cartons, have children create and play their own instruments.

Use Music to Teach Appropriate Behavior

Make up simple tunes to help children improve behavior. Have children sing the tune and model the behavior, "This is the way we sit in our chair, sit in our chair, sit in our chair . . ."

Have Children Draw to Music

Play mood music and have children draw how they feel.

Source: Press, M. (2006). Use music in the classroom. *Intervention in School and Clinic, 41*(5), 307–309.

concerned with academic achievement, and as a result have eliminated recess. Therefore, the opportunity for children to engage in physical activities during the school day has become minimal.

Children with disabilities often are less active than their typically developing peers (Pitetti, Beets, & Combs, 2009; Kozub & Oh, 2004; Longmuir & Bar-Or, 2000). Children with disabilities, especially those with physical and special health needs, are at a higher risk for developing obesity compared to other children. Unfortunately, despite a need for integrating physical activities for children with disabilities, physical education has been a neglected aspect of the curriculum for children with special needs (Gehring, 2007).

Appropriate adaptations to physical education instruction, equipment, and the environment to allow full involvement of children with special needs in physical activities are usually lacking in the inclusive and specialized curricula (Menear & Smith, 2008). Therefore, participation in physical education activities for children with special needs has often been a negative experience (Frey, 2007). As a result, children with special needs are less likely to participate in sports and team activities compared to their typically developing peers.

The Individuals with Disabilities Education Improvement Act of 2004 identifies adapted physical education as a direct service option. IDEIA defines physical education as the development of physical and motor fitness, fundamental motor skills and patterns, and skills in aquatics, dance, and individual and group games and sports, including intramural and lifetime sports (IDEIA, Sec. 300.308, 2004). A successful integration of physical education in the curriculum during primary grades will promote not only emotional and physical well-being in children with disabilities, but a sense of belonging to the group and community (Pitetti et al., 2009; Frey, 2007).

Promoting Peer Relationship and Friendship

As children begin to enter middle childhood, their need for friendship and socialization with their peers increases. Forming friendships is a natural process and seldom requires facilitation from adults. However, in children with special needs, socialization and friendship do not necessarily occur automatically and without intervention. This is especially the case with children with moderate to severe disabilities and those with social relatedness and communication problems. In fact, parents of children with disabilities have often expressed concern about the absence of friends in their children's lives (Turnbull & Ruef, 1997).

To just place children with disabilities along with peers without disabilities does not necessarily lead to children having meaningful interactions with one another (Buysee, Goldman, West, & Hollingworth, 2008). Children without disabilities need to understand how to communicate and interact with their peers with disabilities who do not have the necessary skills for communication and meaningful conversation (Van Norman, 2007).

Special education has seldom concerned itself with facilitation of reciprocal friendships (Turnbull, Pereira, & Blue-Banning, 2000). In fact, the emphasis of a typical special education curriculum has generally been on academics or functional academics. Lacking support from schools, teachers and parents have not been enthusiastic about facilitation of friendship among children with special needs with their typically and atypically developing peers. In reality, developing friendships between children with disabilities and their peers is not only possible, but beneficial to both children and adults.

Schaffner and Buswell (1992) have proposed a model for facilitating friendship among children with and without disabilities. In their model, they suggest teachers use three strategies to facilitate friendship between children:

1. Find opportunities to bring children together. These opportunities can include field trips, school events, after-school programs, recreational activities, and community programs.
2. Provide interpretation for children's behavior. Teachers can articulate values such as respect, affirm and acknowledge individual children's strengths, and point out common interests and behaviors among them.
3. Make accommodations for children based on their needs. To make accommodations, teachers should provide the necessary modifications and changes that will facilitate interaction between children.

Facilitating friendships between children depends on the active participation of teachers and parents. Teachers and parents in partnership can do much to facilitate friendship among children in the community and school (Turnbull et al., 2000).

Another curriculum model, Circle of Friends, has also been successful in promoting communication and friendship between children with disabilities and their typically developing peers (Frederickson, Warren, & Turner, 2005; Kalyva & Avramidis, 2005). See Text Box 15.6 for a description of Circle of Friends. Figure 15.3 is a diagram of the members in a Circle of Friends.

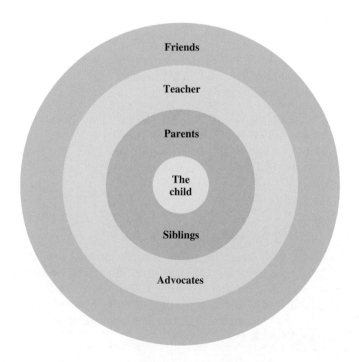

FIGURE 15.3
Diagram of Members in a Circle of Friends

Friends

Teacher

Parents

The child

Siblings

Advocates

Text Box 15.6	Circle of Friends

Circle of Friends is an intervention for promotion of friendship between a child with special needs and typically developing children. The intervention has four components.

Establish the Circle of Friends: To establish the Circle, the teacher and the school first make the commitment to the intervention. A team of two or more professionals (the Individualized Education Plan team, therapists, or other support staff) are designated to carry out the intervention along with the teacher. The team selects a focus child for the intervention. The school personnel obtain permission from the parents to begin the intervention.

Discussion with the Class to Form the Circle of Friends: The team facilitates the first discussion with the class. The focus child or his or her parents consent for the focus child to be absent from the first discussion. The facilitator talks to all students in a circle or group session. After setting up some ground rules, the facilitator asks children to talk about friendship and how it might feel for one not to have a friend. Allowing for all children to take part in the discussion, the facilitator links the focus child to the discussion. Possible behavior difficulties of the child are discussed at this point. The facilitator asks for volunteers to form a Circle of Friends as a support group for the focus child.

First Meeting of the Circle of Friends: After the first discussion, a facilitator meets with the Circle members along with the classroom teacher and the focus child. Target goals are set for the Circle to work on. Ground rules, such as respect, listening to each other, and seeking adult help when needed are established. Resources and support are provided by the school for the Circle to carry out its activities.

Circle of Friends Meets Regularly: The Circle members meet every week or every other week. Meetings are facilitated by an adult.

a. The Circle activities include games, celebrations, field trips, and extracurricular activities with the focus child.
b. Periodic meetings might serve as a way to discuss what worked and didn't work, and can be used for problem solving, role-playing, and planning for future activities.

The Peer Tutoring System

When children teach each other, the rate of success for both academic and social skills learning is likely to increase. One way to facilitate learning in academic and nonacademic areas in children with and without disabilities is **peer tutoring.** Peer tutoring or **peer-mediated instruction** is a model in which an older or a more proficient child teaches communication skills or academic content to another child (Gardner, Nobel, Hessler, Yawn, & Heron, 2007).

Peer tutoring is not a new concept and has been used in the education of children with and without disabilities throughout the history of education around the world. Over the past 30 years, peer tutoring has gained considerable interest among U.S. educators and scholars. Research in peer tutoring has led to the development of several peer tutoring systems which educators have successfully used for all children as early as the kindergarten level (Van Norman & Wood, 2007).

In special education, peer tutoring has been used as both a method of instruction and a vehicle to promote inclusion. Peer tutoring has been successfully utilized to teach typically developing children, children at risk, children with visual and hearing impairments, children with learning disabilities, and children with autism and other disabilities (McDuffie, Mastropieri, & Scruggs, 2009; Bouck, 2004; Harper & Maheady, 2007; Van Norman, 2007; Herring-Harrison, Gardner, & Lovelace, 2007; Gardner et al., 2007). In a system of peer tutoring, children without disabilities as young as kindergarten age are taught how to interact with and tutor their peers who have disabilities (Wood, Mackiewicz, Van Norman, & Cooke, 2007).

An effective peer tutoring system requires training for the tutor in specific skills, such as how to teach, prompt, and model. Teachers who have used peer tutoring in their classrooms have utilized a variety of training vehicles, such as role-playing, cartoon scripts, and audio and video webcasting technologies to teach children how to take on tutoring roles (Heron, Guy, Heron, Villareal, & Yao, 2002; Gardner et al., 2007; Wood et al., 2007).

Training children without special needs to become tutors can become part of the learning activities within the school community. Gardner and colleagues (2007) propose a training model where school districts provide video and audio materials for teachers to be used with tutors. Integration of a peer tutoring system into the curriculum requires that both the teacher and students understand tutoring to be a part of the natural daily activities of the classroom. Peer tutoring not only facilitates a productive inclusion, but promotes a positive sense of community in the classroom.

Sexual Education

Children with disabilities, specifically those with intellectual disabilities, usually have a delayed development of sense of self. Their toilet training and understanding of body parts and their functions take place at a much slower rate (Craft & Craft, 1982). Children with moderate to severe cognitive impairments often lack an ability to differentiate between the sexual and nonsexual parts of their bodies (Ballen, 2001). Like children without disabilities, as children with disabilities grow up, they too begin to explore their sexuality (Black, 2005). During the early childhood years, children with special needs usually depend on parents and other caregivers for personal and hygiene care.

Typically developing children learn about sexuality and personal hygiene through informal means—for example, via their environments, through peer conversations, or by exposure to the media—usually during early and middle childhood. Since children with disabilities are included in regular classrooms and community activities more frequently, they are therefore exposed to the peer, public, and media sexual conversations without necessarily completely understanding or interpreting the information correctly. Teachers and parents of children with special needs are usually concerned about their children's lack of appropriate knowledge, which might put them at risk for becoming victims of sexual abuse. In addition, educators believe that children with disabilities have a right to sexual education and being provided with accurate information about sexuality and reproduction (Kreinin, 2001). However, not all educators integrate sexual education into their curriculum for children with special needs.

Parents often ask about the right time to begin teaching children with disabilities about sexuality and self-hygiene. The appropriate time to begin teaching children with disabilities about basic sexual education is in the early childhood years. During the primary grades, age-appropriate sexual education should be incorporated within the curriculum on a regular basis, and should continue through middle and high school. An appropriate integrated program teaches cognitive, literacy, social, adaptive, drama and art activities regarding body parts, as well as personal hygiene and care, privacy, and appropriate versus inappropriate touches.

Age-appropriate information for early primary grades includes information about appropriate ways of physically expressing feelings toward others, such as allowing to be hugged or hugging others. Figure 15.4 displays a modified diagram of Circle of Friends that was previously presented. This adapted diagram might be called "people in my circles" and could be used to teach children with disabilities appropriate behaviors with people around them. The people in my circles could be presented as a group activity that consists of making multiple circles of various sizes and colors to form a concentric circular shape. It is recommended that the activity be done with the child and family members, and can be integrated within the art activities in the classroom, or be used as a child–family activity during orientations and special events with families.

The child's name or picture is placed in the most inner circle—the center. The pictures or names of different people with whom the child interacts are placed in each outer circle. In the first outer circle from the center, pictures of the immediate family members—people that the child could allow or have embraces and kisses with—are placed. The more distant a circle is to the center, the less intimate the people located in that circle are to the child. The child is taught to have or allow different behaviors with the members in each circle based on the distance and color of the circle. Decisions about whose pictures should be included and in which circle must be made in partnership or consultation with the parents.

Self-Advocacy

Self-advocacy refers to the ability of the child to articulate one's own dreams, strengths, needs, desires, interests, and vision for the future (Amerman & Carr-Jones, 2007). Self-advocacy is related to self-determination (discussed in Chapter 11). Both require that the child has a self-knowledge.

Self-knowledge includes the child's ability to understand their own strengths, as well as own needs, and to have a realistic picture of what he or she can and cannot do (Amerman & Carr-Jones, 2007). To protect their children, families of children with

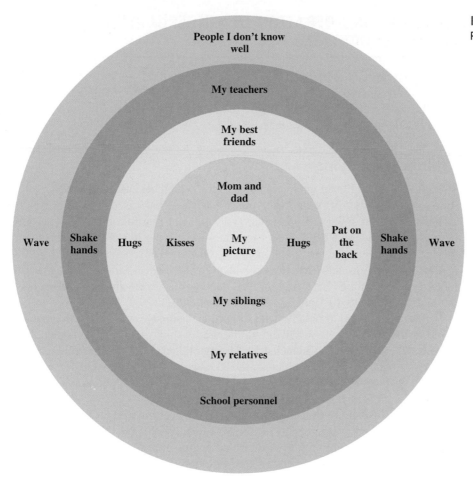

FIGURE 15.4
People in My Circle

disabilities may not want their child to know about their own disabilities. However, self-awareness is the first step toward developing self-advocacy.

Since part of self-advocacy is having the child participate in his or her Individualized Education Plan, it is important that the child knows his or her own strengths and needs, and is able to articulate his or her own interest (Danneker & Bottge, 2009). Participating in one's IEP should take place as early as it is realistic for the child to do so. Primary school years might be a good time for the parents and teachers to begin discussing this possibility. In addition, teachers should ask family members how to approach the issues related to self-knowledge and self-advocacy with the child. Steps for self-advocacy and self-determination can be articulated in the child's IEP so it takes place gradually and over several years. Although many students might not be able to advocate for themselves until they are much older, establishing the building blocks of independence, self-determination, and self-advocacy should occur during early childhood years. Research shows that children with disabilities are capable of contributing important information about their disabilities and their ideas for accommodating them during their IEPs (Danneker & Bottge, 2009).

SCHOOL-WIDE ISSUES OF CONSIDERATION IN KINDERGARTEN THROUGH THIRD GRADE EDUCATION

Aside from curriculum issues in primary grades, several school-wide problems merit consideration in order to maximize success in all children. Childhood bullying, parental involvement in school activities, and homework success are three pertinent school-wide issues in primary grades.

Childhood Bullying

Childhood bullying is an international problem, which has gained increasing attention during the past 30 years. Bullying has been defined as repetitive aggressive behaviors to overcome a targeted victim, who for some reason cannot defend himself easily (Smith & Brain, 2000). Most research on bullying in schools has been conducted in European countries and in Japan (Olweus, 1991; Smith & Brain, 2000). Childhood bullying, however, is as prevalent in the United States as it has been in other countries around the world. In fact, one in every seven children reports being bullied in schools in the United States (Crockett, 2003).

Because of their problems with cognition, language, and social relatedness, children with moderate to severe disabilities are less likely to be able to defend themselves and are therefore at higher risk of being bullied. On the other hand, children who have social-emotional problems, ADHD, depression, oppositional defiant disorder, and conduct disorder are at higher risk of becoming the perpetrators of bullying (Kumpulainen, Rasanen, & Puura, 2001).

Bullying usually begins in elementary school, peaks in middle school, and falls off in high school (Viadero, 1997; Morris, Taylor, & Wilson, 2000). Therefore, a whole-school anti-bullying intervention that begins in primary grades is critical in preventing and reducing the incidence of bullying (Crothers & Kolbert, 2008). To prevent the incidence of bullying in children with and without special needs, early childhood educators can use a variety of activities that might sensitize children to the problem (Crothers & Kolbert, 2008; Morris et al., 2000). Preschool and primary grade teachers might act out bullying scenarios, use puppets to role-play the victim

Due to problems with cognition, language, and social relatedness, children with moderate to severe disabilities are less likely to be able to defend themselves against bullying, and are therefore at higher risk.

Suggestions to Stop Bullying Problems in School	**Text Box 15.7**

Help Parents to Take Anti-bullying Actions at Home

1. Ask parents to talk to their children about bullying.

    a. Ask parents to advise their children to:

    - Be involved and stay with groups.
    - If in a bullying situation, scream to get others' attention.
    - Tell parents and teachers immediately if bullied.

2. Encourage parents to raise awareness in school and among other parents.

Write Out IEP Goals That Address Bullying

1. Focus IEP goals on:

    a. Building self-esteem
    b. Appropriate socialization skills, sharing, taking turns, expressing feelings, and expressing preferences
    c. Thinking before acting out
    d. Ways to avoid bullying situations

Promote Peace in the Classroom through Curriculum

1. Create a peaceful, caring, nonviolent classroom environment through your own behavior.

    a. Use books and stories to demonstrate:

    - Positive problem solving and conflict resolution
    - Friendship skills
    - Kindness skills: caretaking, gentleness, helping, and generosity
    - Compassion toward and understanding of those who are different

and bully situations, read books on bullying, or have children perform plays that portray bullying situations.

Parent involvement in anti-bullying education is another important component in preventing bullying. Crothers and Kolbert (2008) suggest that parents be encouraged to think about ways to promote self-confidence and healthy social development in their child by involving him or her in social organizations that relate to their child's strengths, as well as enhancing their child's physical development by supporting participation in individual sports such as karate, bicycling, swimming, and running as a way of building self-esteem and personal strength.

Because children with special needs are less likely to defend themselves, as a part of inclusive best practices, typically developing peers could be encouraged to form groups that take on advocacy roles for their peers who have disabilities in order to prevent bullying. Peers could teach each other anti-bullying strategies, such as staying with groups and screaming for help when someone bullies another, as part of a peer tutoring program. Text Box 15.7 provides suggestions for anti-bullying actions.

Parental Involvement in School

We have learned that working with families is one of the most important aspects of educating children with exceptional learning needs. Parent involvement at school is related to a range of positive outcomes for all children. For example, when parents get involved at schools, children tend to have improved academic performance, better attendance, and a more positive attitude toward school and school authorities (Eccles & Harold, 1996; Henderson & Mapp, 2002).

For families of children with disabilities, aside from the IEP meetings, there are a range of other activities that will enable them to get involved in school activities. Examples of different ways parents of children with special needs might get involved in their child's school include the following: parent–volunteer activities during field trips or in the classroom, periodic class or school events (such as science and culture fairs), occasional school meetings, local school council activities, and parent–teacher conferences.

Some possible barriers can prevent parental involvement in school. These barriers include lack of transportation, finding appropriate child care, conflict with work, lack of compatibility with the school culture, and miscommunication that might occur during the IEP meetings (Smrekar & Cohen-Vogel, 2001). Despite these barriers, the U.S. Department of Education reports that families of children with disabilities are more likely than other parents in the general population to participate in school-based activities, such as general school meetings and parent–teacher conferences (Office of Special Education Program, U.S. Department of Education, 2005). Just as it is the case in the general population, when parents of children with disabilities get involved in school activities, their children have more positive outcomes both in academic performance and in social behaviors (OSEP, U.S. Department of Education, 2005). It is important for the programs to understand and respect a family's cultural values as they relate to parental involvement in children's schooling (Giovacco-Johnson, 2009).

Homework Assignments and Completion

Children who have moderate to severe disabilities seldom receive academic homework assignments. Instead, teachers might ask parents and family members to supervise their children in self-help and adaptive skills. Early research shows that during elementary school years, most families of children with disabilities help their children build consistent routines and daily living skills (Marcus & Schopler, 1987).

For children with learning disabilities, homework completion can be an ongoing problem, however. Parents usually have two sorts of complaints: teachers either give too little or too much homework to children (Bryan & Burstein, 2004). Most parents have problems establishing a homework routine and monitoring their children's homework activities. Parents usually describe their busy work schedule as a barrier to monitoring their children's homework. In addition, some parents might have difficulties understanding the learning concepts embedded within their child's homework (Balli, Demo, & Wedman, 1998).

In addition, most teachers (about 80 percent) do assign academic homework for children with learning disabilities (Salend & Schliff, 1989). However, there are very few teachers who modify homework tasks for these children to match their skill level and abilities (Salend & Schliff, 1989). As a result, about 56 percent of children with learning disabilities have problems completing homework assignments (Polloway, Epstein, & Foley, 1992).

Several strategies have been recommended that are useful in helping children complete their homework assignments (Bryan & Burstein, 2004). Among the strategies suggested, those that apply to children with disabilities consist of:

1. Using positive reinforcement with the child to motivate and encourage them to complete their homework
2. Modifying assignments based on the developmental and skill level of the child
3. Assigning real-life and functional assignments
4. Encouraging families to set specific routine times for homework completion, when they can monitor their child

Bryan and Burstein (2004) recommend a school-wide homework team be created, which can be responsible for designing developmentally appropriate homework assignments and methods for systematically evaluating the effect of homework assignments on students. Although implementing this recommendation might be far reaching, individual teachers can do much to provide homework support for their students. Teachers can work with parents to understand the amount of time it takes to complete homework at home as a starting point to modify homework assignments. Success in homework completion depends on the teachers' willingness to work with families and to make necessary homework changes to help their students complete their homework tasks.

Teachers should encourage parents to set specific routine times for homework completion that allow parents to monitor their children's work.

Research Corner

The Special Education Elementary Longitudinal Study

The Special Education Elementary Longitudinal Study (SEELS) is a study of school-age children with disabilities. This study was conducted by SRI international and funded by the U.S. Office of Special Education programs in the U.S. Department of Education. The study collected data from 1,300 children with disabilities (ages 6–13) and their families from 2000 to 2006.

SEELS surveyed students, family members, and educators, and collected three waves of data, documenting changes in the children's educational, social, adaptive, and personal development as they transitioned from elementary to middle school, and then to high school. Although the study has ended, the final reports and findings have not yet been published. Preliminary data and reports are available on SEELS web site at http://www.seels.net/seelsfaq.htm.

SUMMARY

Primary grades signal a transition to middle childhood. Many changes both in the development of children and in their academic environment occur as they begin to leave the early childhood period. Issues surrounding the education of children in primary grades differ in nature from those in preschool and earlier classrooms. For one thing, during primary or later grades children who might have learning disabilities are identified, since they will be required to perform more challenging academic tasks.

Children with learning disabilities are those who have learning difficulties in different academic areas such as reading, writing, and math. Specific strategies to help them build foundation skills, improve memory, and to decode and encode reading and oral materials have been used to enhance their learning. Response to Intervention is a model of preventing over-identification of children with learning difficulties, as well as intervening to help children maximize their potential.

Other issues of consideration in primary grades are the integration of appropriate areas of learning in the curriculum, such as music, physical education, functional academics, sexual education, and self-advocacy. Additional areas of concern are those related to school-wide problems such as childhood bullying, parental involvement in school, and homework completion.

Review Questions

1. What are some changes in the school and classroom environment in primary grades as compared with preschool?
2. What is a learning disability, and what are some problems with its identification?
3. What is *Response to Intervention (RTI)?*
4. Describe a three-tier model of RTI. What are some benefits to this model?
5. What are some major areas of learning disabilities?
6. How can teachers promote successful learning in children with learning disabilities?
7. What is a number sense, and what are some recommendations for improving math skills in primary grades?
8. What are functional academics, and why is it important that they be part of the curriculum in primary grades?
9. Can friendship be promoted among children with and without disabilities?

10. What is peer tutoring, and how might it benefit children with disabilities?

11. Why is sexual education an important part of the curriculum in primary grades?

12. What are some recommendations to stop bullying in schools?

13. What are some recommendations to promote success in homework completion for children with disabilities?

Out-of-Class Activities

1. With the permission of parents and teachers, interview at least three elementary grade children who have been identified with learning disabilities. Address questions that deal with their school experience, their learning difficulties, their relationships with their peers, and what has helped them be successful.

   a. Write a report about your findings and share it with the class.

2. Visit some resource or classrooms (kindergarten through third grade) in which teachers have been making successful adaptations to academic content and the environment to promote learning in children who have learning difficulties.

   a. Write a report describing some of the specific adaptations these teachers have made in their classrooms.

3. Design an lesson plan focusing on sexual education that is appropriate for one of the primary grade levels.

   a. Conduct the lesson in a role-play format in class in order to share it with your classmates.

4. Conduct Internet and library research to find at least five books that deal with bullying in childhood.

   a. Make a list of these books and distribute it to your class as an anti-bullying resource.

5. Design an anti-bullying lesson plan appropriate for one of the primary grade levels.

   a. Choose team members to role-play the lesson in order to share it with your class.

Recommended Resources

American Music Therapy Association (AMTA)
http://www.musictherapy.org/

CAST (on differentiated instruction)
http://www.cast.org/publications/ncac/index.html

Learning Disabilities Association of America
http://www.ldanatl.org/

Learning Disabilities Association of America (history)
http://www.ldaamerica.org/about/history.asp

Learning Disabilities Summit
http://ldsummit.air.org/paper.htm

National Center for Learning Disabilities
http://www.ncld.org/

Pacer Center's Kids Against Bullying
http://www.pacerkidsagainstbullying.org/

View the Online Resources available to accompany this text by visiting http://www.mhhe.com/bayat1e

References

Altarac, M., & Saroha, E. (2007). Lifetime prevalence of learning disability among U.S. children. *Pediatrics, 119,* 577–583.

Amerman, T., & Carr-Jones, J. (2007). Self advocacy. In A. M. Bursztyn (Ed.), *The Praeger handbook of special education* (pp. 24–26). Westport, CT: Praeger.

Bailey, D., Scarborough, A., Hebbeler, K., Spiker, D., & Mallik, S. (2004). *Family outcomes at the end of early intervention.* Menlo Park, CA: SRI International. Retrieved March 13, 2008, from http://www.sri.com/neils/pdfs/FamilyOutcomesReport_011405.pdf

Baker, S., Gersten, R., & Scanlon, D. (2002). Procedural facilitators and cognitive strategies: Tools for unraveling the mysteries of comprehension and the writing process and for providing meaningful access to the general curriculum. *Learning Disabilities Practice, 17*(1), 65–77.

Ballen, M. (2001). Parents as sexuality educators for their children with developmental disabilities. *SIECUS Report, 29*(3), 14–19.

Balli, S. J., Demo, D. H., & Wedman, J. F. (1998). Family involvement with children's homework: An intervention in the middle grades. *Family Relations, 47,* 149–157.

Beganto, S. J. (2006). Of helping and measuring for early childhood intervention: Reflections on issues and school psychology role. *School Psychology Review, 35*(4), 615–620.

Black, K. (2005). Disability and sexuality. *Pediatric Nursing, 17*(5), 34–37.

Bouck, E. C. (2004). State of curriculum of secondary students with mild mental retardation. *Education and Training in Developmental Disabilities, 39*(2), 169–176.

Bryan, T., & Burstein, K. (2004). Improving homework completion and academic performance: Lessons from special education. *Theory into Practice, 43*(3), 213–219.

Buck, G. H., Polloway, E. A., Smith-Thomas, A., & Cook, K. W. (2003). Pre-referral intervention processes: A survey of state practices. *Exceptional Children, 69*(3), 349–361.

Buysee, V., Goldman, B., West, T., & Hollingworth, H. (2008). Friendships in early childhood: Implications for early education and intervention. In W. Brown, S. Odom, & S. McConnell (Eds.), *Social competence of young children: Risk, disability, and intervention* (pp. 77–97). Baltimore: Paul H. Brookes.

Carter, J., & Sugai, G. (1989). Survey on prereferral practices: Responses from state departments of education. *Exceptional Children, 55*(4), 298–302.

Chard, D. J., Baker, S. K., Clarke, B., Jungjohann, K., Davis, K., & Smolkowski, K. (2008). Preventing early mathematics difficulties: The feasibility of a rigorous kindergarten mathematics curriculum. *Learning Disability Quarterly, 31*(Winter), 11–20.

Chard, D. J., Clarke, B., Baker, S., Otterstedt, J., Braun, D., & Kata, R. (2005). Using measures of number sense to screen for difficulties in mathematics: Preliminary findings. *Assessment of Effective Intervention, 30*(2), 3–14.

Coleman, M. R., Roth, F. P., & West, T. (2009). *Roadmap to Pre-K RTI: Applying Response to Intervention in preschool settings.* National Center for Learning Disabilities, Inc. Retrieved July 7, 2009, from http://www.florida-rti.org/Resources/_docs/roadmaptoprekrti.pdf

Conderman, G., & Woods, S. C. (2008). Science in the inclusive classrooms. In M. Larocque & S. M. Darling (Eds.), *Blended curriculum in the inclusive K–3 classroom: Teaching all young children* (pp. 309–347). Boston: Allyn & Bacon.

Craft, M., & Craft, A. (1982). *Sex and the mentally handicapped: A guide for parents and carers.* London: Routledge and Kegan Paul.

Crockett, D. (2003). Critical issues children face in the 2000s. *School Psychology Quarterly, 18*(4), 446–453.

Crothers, L. M., & Kolbert, J. (2008). Tackling a problematic behavior management issue: Teachers' intervention in childhood bullying problems. *Intervention in School and Clinic, 43*(3), 132–139.

Danneker, J., & Bottge, B. (2009). Benefits and barriers to elementary student-led individualized education programs. *Remedial & Special Education, 30*(4), 225–233.

Donovan, M. S., & Cross, C. T. (2002). *Minority students in special and gifted education.* Washington, DC: National Academy Press.

Downing, J. E. (2008). The elementary school student. In J. E. Downing (Ed.), *Including students with severe and multiple disabilities in typical classrooms: Practical strategies for teachers* (3rd ed., pp. 117–152). Baltimore: Paul H. Brookes.

Eccles, J. S., & Harold, R. D. (1996). Family involvement in children's and adolescent's schooling. In A. Booth & J. F. Dunn (Eds.), *Family school links: How do they affect educational outcomes?* (pp. 3–34). Mahwah, NJ: Erlbaum.

Ehren, B. J., & Nelson, N. W. (2005). The responsiveness to intervention approach and language impairment. *Topics in Language Disorders, 25*(2), 120–131.

Feldman, R. S. (2007). *Child development* (4th ed.). Upper Saddle River, NJ: Pearson/Prentice Hall.

Fernald, G. M., & Keller, H. (1921). The effect of kinesthetic factors in the development of word recognition in the case of non-readers. *Journal of Educational Research, 4,* 355–377.

Fitzsimmons, M. (1999). Beginning reading. *ERIC Clearinghouse on Disabilities and Gifted Education Reston VA.* ERIC/OSEP Digest # E565. Retrieved April 3, 2008, from http://www.eric .ed.gov/ERICDocs/data/ericdocs2sql/content_ storage_01/0000019b/80/15/63/fc.pdf

Fletcher, J. M., Lyon, G. R., Fuchs, L. S., & Barnes, M. A. (2007). *Learning disabilities: From identification to intervention.* New York: Guilford Press.

Fox, L., & Hemmeter, M. L. (2009). A program-wide model for supporting social emotional development and addressing challenging behavior in early childhood settings. In W. Sailor, G. Dunlap, G. Sugai, & R. Horner (Eds.), *Handbook of positive behavior support* (pp. 177–202). New York: Springer.

Francis, D. J., Fletcher, J. M., Stuebing, K. K., Lyon, G. R., Shaywitz, B. A., & Shaywitz, S. E. (2005). Psychometric approaches to identification of LD: IQ and achievement scores are not sufficient. *Journal of Learning Disabilities, 38*(2), 98–108.

Frederickson, N., Warren, L., & Turner, J. (2005). Circle of friends: An exploration of impact over time. *Educational Psychology in Practice, 21*(3), 197–217.

Frey, G. C. (2007). Physical activity and youth with developmental disabilities. In S. L. Odom, R. H. Horner, M. E. Snell, & J. Blacher (Eds.), *Handbook of developmental disabilities* (pp. 349–365). New York: Guilford Press.

Gallego, M. A., Duran, G. Z., & Reyes, E. I. (2006). It depends: A sociohistorical account of the definition and methods of identification of learning disabilities. *Teachers College Record, 108*(11), 2195–2219.

Gallegos, J. (2006). Judith A. Jellison: Music and children with special needs. *Intervention in School and Clinic, 42*(1), 46–50.

Gardner III, R., Nobel, M., Hessler, T., Yawn, C. D., & Heron, T. (2007). Tutoring system innovations: Past practice to future prototypes. *Intervention in School and Clinic, 43*(2), 71–81.

Geary, D. C., Bow-Thomas, C. C., & Yao, Y. (1992). Counting knowledge and skill in cognitive addition: A comparison of numeral and mathematically disabled children. *Journal of Experimental Child Psychology, 54,* 372–391.

Gehring, J. (2007). Moving in a special direction. *Education Week, 24*(9), 36–39.

Gersten, R., & Chard, D. (1999). Number sense: Rethinking arithmetic instruction for students with mathematical disabilities. *The Journal of Special Education, 33*(1), 18–28.

Giovacco-Johnson, T. (2009). Portraits of partnership: The hopes and dreams project. *Early Childhood Education Journal, 37*(2), 127–135.

Gresham, F. (2001). Responsiveness to intervention: An alternative approach to the identification of learning disabilities. Retrieved March, 20, 2008, from http:// ldsummit.air.org/download/Hallahan%20Final%20 08-10-01.pdf

Gresham, F. M. (1991). Conceptualizing behavior disorders in terms of resistance to intervention. *School Psychology Review, 20*(1), 23–36.

Hallahan, D. P., & Mercer, C. D. (2001). *Learning disabilities: Historical perspectives.* Retrieved March 20, 2008, from http://ldsummit.air.org/ download/Hallahan%20Final%2008-10-01.pdf

Harper, G. F., & Maheady, L. (2007). Peer-mediated teaching and students with learning disabilities. *Intervention in School and Clinic, 43*(2), 101–107.

Henderson, A. T., & Mapp, K. L. (2002). *A new wave of evidence: The impact of school, family, and community connections to student achievement.* Austin, TX: Southwest Educational Development Laboratory.

Heron, T. E., Guy, A., Heron, K. M., Villareal, D., & Yao, M. (2002, September). *Cross-age tutoring in an inclusive classroom: Preliminary findings with typically developing students and students with autism.* Paper presented to the Ohio State University's Third Focus on Behavior Analysis in Education Conference, Columbus, OH.

Herring-Harrison, T. J., Gardner III, R., & Lovelace, T. S. (2007). Adapting peer tutoring for learners who are deaf or hard of hearing. *Intervention in School and Clinic, 43*(2), 82–87.

Kalyva, E., & Avramidis, E. (2005). Improving communication between children with autism and their peers through the "Circle of Friends": A small-scale intervention study. *Journal of Applied Research in Intellectual Disabilities, 18,* 253–261.

Kirk, S. A. (1976). Samuel A. Kirk. In J. M. Kauffman & D. P. Hallahan (Eds.), *Teaching children with* learning disabilities: Personal perspectives (pp. 239–269). Columbus, OH: Charles E. Merrill.

Kirk, S. A., McCarthy, J. J., & Kirk, W. D. (1961). *Illinois Test of Psycholinguistic Abilities* (Experimental ed.). Urbana, IL: University of Illinois Press.

Kleinert, H. L., Miracle, S. A., & Sheppard-Jones, K. (2007). Including students with moderate and severe disabilities in extracurricular and community recreation activities. *Teaching Exceptional Children, 39*(6), 33–38.

Kozub, F. M., & Oh, H. K. (2004). An exploratory study of physical activity levels in children and adolescents with visual impairments. *Clinical Kinesiology, 58,* 1–7.

Kreinin, T. (2001). Sexuality education for the disabled is priority at home and in school. *SIECUS Report, 29*(3), 4.

Kumpulainen, K., Rasanen, E., & Puura, K. (2001). Psychiatric disorders and the use of mental health services among children involved in bullying. *Aggressive Behavior, 27,* 102–110.

Levine, M. D. (1987). *Developmental variation and learning disorders.* Cambridge, MA: Educators Publishing Service, Inc.

Levine, M. D. (1990). *Keeping ahead in school: A student's book about learning abilities and learning disorders.* Cambridge, MA: Education Publishing Service Inc.

Levine, M. D. (2003). *Myth of laziness.* New York: Simon and Schuster.

Levine, M., & Barringer, M. D. (2008). Getting the lowdown on the slowdown: Brain-based research is providing new strategies for identifying and treating the many causes of slow learning. *Principal,* (January–February), 14–18.

Longmuir, P. E., & Bar-Or, O. (2000). Factors influencing the physical activity levels of youths with physical and sensory disabilities. *Adapted Physical Activity Quarterly, 17,* 40–53.

Lyon, G. R., Fletcher, J. M., Shaywitz, S. E., Shaywitz, B. A., Torgensen, J. K., Wood, F., et al. (2001). Rethinking learning disabilities. In C. E. Finn, A. J. Rotherham, & C. R. Hokanson (Eds.), *Rethinking special education for a new century* (pp. 259–287). Washington, DC: Thomas B. Fordham Foundations and the Progressive Policy Institute.

Marcus, L. M., & Schopler, E. (1987). Working with families: A developmental perspective. In D. Cohen A. Donnellan, & R. Paul (Eds.), *Handbook of autism and pervasive developmental disorders* (pp. 499–512). New York: John Wiley & Sons.

Marcus, L. M., Kunce, L. J., & Schopler, E. (1997). Working with families. In D. Cohen & F. Volkmar (Eds.), *Handbook of autism and pervasive developmental disorders* (2nd ed., pp. 631–649). New York: John Wiley & Sons.

Mastropieri, M. A., & Scruggs, T. E. (1998). Constructing more meaningful relationships in the classroom: Mnemonic research into practice. *Learning Disabilities Research and Practice, 13,* 138–145.

Mastropieri, M. A., & Scruggs, T. E. (2005). Feasibility and consequences of response to intervention: Examination of the issues and scientific evidence as a model for identification of individuals with learning disabilities. *Journal of Learning Disabilities, 38*(6), 525–531.

McAdoo, W. G., & DeMyer, M. K. (1977). Research related to family factors in autism. *Journal of Marriage and the Family, 41,* 236–244.

McDevitt, T. M., & Ormrod, J. E. (2007). *Child development and education* (3rd ed.). Upper Saddle River, NJ: Pearson/Merrill.

McDuffie, K., Mastropieri, M., & Scruggs, T. (2009). Differential effects of peer tutoring in co-taught and non-co-taught classes: Results for content learning and student–teacher interactions. *Exceptional Children, 75*(4), 493–510.

McNary, S. J., Glasgow, N. A., & Hicks, C. D. (2005). *What successful teachers do in inclusive classrooms: Research-based teaching strategies that help special learners succeed.* Thousand Oaks, CA: Corwin Press.

Menear, K. S., & Smith, S. (2008). Physical education for students with autism: Teaching tips and strategies. *Teaching Exceptional Children, 40*(5), 32–37.

Mindes, G. (2010). *Assessing young children* (4th ed.). Upper Saddle River, NJ.: Prentice Hall.

Morin, J., & Frank, D. (2010). Why do some children have difficulty learning mathematics? Looking at language for answers. *Preventing School Failure, 54*(2), 111–118.

Morris, V. G., Taylor, S. I., & Wilson, J. T. (2000). Using children's stories to promote peace in classrooms. *Early Childhood Education Journal, 28*(1), 41–50.

Office of Special Education Program, U.S. Department of Education. (2005). *Family involvement in the education of youth with disabilities: A special topic report of findings from National Transition Study-2 (NTS-2).* Menlo Park, CA: SRI International.

Olweus, D. (1991). Bully/victim problems among school children: Some basic facts and effects of a school-based intervention program. In D. Pepler & K. Rubin (Eds.), *The development and treatment of childhood aggression* (pp. 411–438). Hillsdale, NJ: Lawrence Erlbaum.

Orton, S. T. (1937). *Reading, writing, and speech problems in children.* New York: W. W. Norton & Company, Inc.

Pitetti, K., Beets, M., & Combs, C. (2009). Physical activity levels of children with intellectual disabilities during school. *Medicine & Science in Sports & Exercise, 41*(8), 1580–1586.

Polloway, E. A., Epstein, M. H., & Foley, R. (1992). A comparison of the homework problems of students with learning disabilities and non-handicapped students. *Learning Disabilities: Research and Practice, 7,* 203–209.

Press, M. R. (2006). Use music in the classroom. *Intervention in School and Clinic, 41*(5), 307–309.

Reschly, M. (2003, December). *What if ID identification changed to reflect research findings?* Paper presented at the National Research Center on Learning Disabilities Responsiveness-to-Intervention Symposium, Kansas City, MO.

Rose, R. (2007). Curriculum considerations in meeting special educational needs. In L. Florian (Ed.), *The SAGE handbook of special education* (pp. 295–306). London: SAGE publication.

Rouse, M., & McLaughlin, M. J. (2007). Changing perspectives of special education in the evolving contest of educational reform. In L. Florian (Ed.), *The SAGE handbook of special education* (pp. 85–103). London: SAGE publication.

Salend, S. J., & Schliff, J. (1989). An examination of the homework practices of teachers of students with learning disabilities. *Remedial and Special Education, 12,* 18–27.

Santrock, J. W. (2006). *Life-span development* (10th ed.). Boston: McGraw-Hill.

Schaffner, C. B., & Buswell, B. E. (1992). *Connecting students: A guide to thoughtful friendship facilitation for educators and families.* Colorado Springs, CO: PEAK Parents Center, Inc.

Smith, P. K., & Brain, P. (2000). Bullying in schools: Lessons from two decades of research. *Aggressive Behavior, 26,* 1–9.

Smrekar, C., & Cohen-Vogel, L. (2001). The voices of parents: Rethinking the intersection of family and school. *Peabody Journal of Education, 76,* 75–100.

Spear-Swerling, L. (2005). *Components of effective reading instruction.* Retrieved April 2, 2008, from http://www.ldonline.org/article/5589

Spear-Swerling, L., Brucker, P. O., & Alfano, M. P. (2005). Teachers' literacy-related knowledge and self-perceptions in relation to preparation and experience. *Annals of Dyslexia, 55*(2), 266–296.

Standley, J., Walworth, D., & Nguyen, J. (2009). Effects of parent/child group music activities on toddler development: A pilot study. *Music Therapy Perspectives, 27*(1), 11–15.

Tam, K. Y., & Heng, M. A. (2005). A case involving culturally and linguistically diverse parents in prereferral intervention. *Intervention in School and Clinic, 40*(4), 222–230.

Taylor, R. L., Smiley, L. R., & Richards, S. B. (2009). *Exceptional students: Preparing teachers for the 21st century.* Boston: McGraw-Hill Higher Education.

Truscott, S. D., Cohen, C. E., Sams, D. P., Sansborn, K. J., & Frank, A. J. (2005). The current state(s) of prereferral intervention teams: A report from two national surveys. *Remedial and Special Education, 26*(3), 130–140.

Turnbull, A., Pereira, L., & Blue-Banning, M. (2000). Teachers as friendship facilitators: Respeto and personalismo. *Teaching Exceptional Children, 32*(5), 66–70.

Turnbull, A. P., & Ruef, M. B. (1997). Family perspectives on inclusive lifestyle issues for individuals with problem behavior. *Exceptional Children, 63,* 211–227.

U.S. Office of Education. (1968). *First annual report of the National Advisory Committee on Handicapped Children.* Washington, DC: U.S. Department of Health, Education, and Welfare.

Van Norman, R. K. (2007). "Who's on first?" Using sports trivia peer tutoring to increase conversation language. *Intervention in School and Clinic, 43*(2), 88–100.

Van Norman, R. K., & Wood, C. L. (2007). Innovations in peer tutoring: Introduction to the special issue. *Intervention in School and Clinic, 43*(2), 69–70.

Vaughn, S., Wanzek, J., & Denton, C. (2007). Teaching elementary students who experience difficulties in learning. In L. Florian (Ed.), *The SAGE handbook of special education* (pp. 175–186). London: SAGE publication.

Viadero, D. (1997, May 28). Bullies beware. *Education Week,* 19–21.

Wood, C. L., Mackiewicz, S. M., Van Norman, R. K., & Cooke, N. L. (2007). Tutoring with technology. *Intervention in School and Clinic, 43*(2), 108–115.

acceleration Educational interventions which move students through programs at a faster rate as compared with other students.

acquired deafness Deafness which occurs after birth as the result of an event or an illness.

acquired immunodeficiency syndrome (AIDS) A life-threatening disease that makes it difficult for the body to fight infections.

adaptive skills Development of skills necessary to control one's environment, such as hygiene and self-care, feeding, dressing, play, and simple daily problem-solving abilities.

affect attunement A pattern of reciprocal behavior and emotional harmony shared between the caregiver and infant that helps the infant develop and sustain self-regulation.

alternative assessment The use of informal techniques to measure a child's abilities, including performance, oral presentation, demonstration, exhibition, portfolio, and others.

American Eugenics movement A widespread belief in the 1920s and 1930s that certain problems such as feeblemindedness, epilepsy, alcoholism, and criminality are biological traits of the inferior type and are inherited from generation to generation.

American Sign Language (ASL) A manual/gestural language system that is used by the majority of children and adults who are deaf.

Americans with Disabilities Act (ADA) The first comprehensive civil rights law for people with disabilities. This act was signed by President George H. W. Bush in 1990. The act prohibits discrimination against individuals with disabilities in employment, public services, public accommodations, and telecommunications.

annual goals Broad statements relating to domains of development or to various academic areas that indicate what the child is to achieve in one year.

antecedent Anything that happens before a behavior occurs.

Apgar score A score describing the overall well-being of the newborn right after birth, by measuring the heart rate, breathing, appearance, and reflexes of the infant.

applied behavior analysis (ABA) A systematic approach to understanding, predicting, and changing human behavior.

apprenticeship The concept based on the idea that children develop as active constructivists of their knowledge with the guidance and ongoing support of adults in their culture and within their cultural routines, and via use of different cultural tools available to them.

assessment An ongoing process of gathering information about the child, based on which intervention and activity plans might be designed, revised, refined, or modified.

assistive listening device Any type of device that helps individuals hear sounds better and therefore better communicate.

asynchronous development Uneven development, where there is a disparity in levels of growth and ability within various developmental areas.

at risk Children who because of various environmental and biological risk factors (such as poverty, lack of educational resources, or biological conditions) are at jeopardy to develop special needs, or are less likely to succeed in school and in the community.

attachment A developmental process consisting of an emotional tie and binding affection that a child has with his or her caregiver and other people.

atypical development Patterns of slow, unhealthy, or atypical development in children.

auditory system A part of the overall sensory processing system that is responsible for sound perception and the processing of the auditory sensory input.

augmentative and alternative communication (AAC) An intervention strategy that utilizes manual as well as low- and high-technologies such as sign language, pictures, symbols, and computerized devices, in conjunction with the child's language abilities, in order to enable the child to communicate with others.

behavior A behavior refers to an observable action of an individual. What an individual *does* or *says* is a behavior. Therefore, behaviors can be verbal or nonverbal.

body mass index (BMI)   A measure of the relationship between length and weight across age.

causal theory   Theory that provides explanations for originating roots of a disease or a condition. A causal theory also provides information about designing appropriate treatment plans.

cell   The basic building blocks of all living things. The human body has more than 100 trillion cells.

cephalocaudal   A type of motor development in which control over motor skills progresses from the head downward toward lower portions of the body.

child abuse   Unreasonable acts that may endanger a child or cause a child unnecessary physical and emotional pain, or threaten the child's health and development.

child advocate   A person who would argue on behalf of the parents and the child.

Child Find   A system consisting of organized efforts in each state to locate and identify children who might have developmental delays or might be at risk for developmental problems.

child neglect   Failure of parents or caregivers to provide the minimal age-appropriate care necessary for the child's physical, emotional, and mental growth and development.

children at risk   Children who, due to poverty and other adverse conditions, are in danger of having negative developmental outcomes.

children with special needs   Also referred to as exceptional children. Those children who due to a variety of conditions, such as a diagnosed disability, require special care and education.

chromosomes   Threadlike structures located in the nucleus of each cell.

circles of communication   Back and forth communicative signals between the infant and the caregiver. Circles of communication can be verbal or nonverbal.

cognitive development   Refers to the development of general awareness and thought processes such as problem solving and memory. Cognitive development includes the development of communication and language.

cohesion   The degree to which family members are close together or are far apart from one another.

collective empowerment   Also known as family professional partnership. Occurs when parents and professionals come to a mutual appreciation of each other, thereby creating a synergy that brings together each others' expertise and knowledge to work successfully together.

combined type   A subtype diagnosis under categories of ADHD, characterizing children who display symptoms of inattention, hyperactivity, and impulsivity.

comments   Simple sentences that provide additional information about events or actions that are or are about to take place.

communication   The exchange of ideas, thoughts, or information via sending and receiving messages between two or more parties.

community-based instruction   Teaching children specific skills within their environments, and through related required skills.

comorbidity   The coexistence of two or more disorders together.

Compensatory or preventive programs   Also called prevention programs. Programs designed for at-risk children to give them opportunities to change their life course.

conductive hearing loss   Hearing loss caused by damage to the outer or middle ear, marked by a lack of sensitivity to faint or certain sounds.

congenital   Infant's diseases, disorders, or conditions that are present at birth.

congenital blindness   Blindness that has been present from birth.

congenital deafness   Deafness that is present at birth and caused by genetics factors, hereditary conditions, or as a result of a prenatal event or condition.

consequence   Event or events following the behavior that would affect its future occurrence.

context of child development   The environment in which the child develops, and the people with whom the child interacts. A developmental context includes the family members, ethnicity, and community in which the child lives.

contextually based assessment   Assessing children in their various contexts, such as home, community, and early childhood settings, and as they perform different activities.

contingent praise   A specific praise delivered that is contingent upon the occurrence of a target or desired behavior.

control sentences   Sentences that provide analogies related to one or more appropriate responses in the child to help the child remember the appropriate course of action to take.

convergent assessment   An assessment process in which information about the child is collected from multiple sources and over a certain period of time to get an accurate picture of the child's condition.

critical period hypothesis   States that unless one is exposed to language and social stimuli within the first few years of life, one will lose much of his or her abilities to learn a language, in particular its grammatical system.

critical thinking　Mental processes consisting of reflection, analysis, and evaluation of tangible and nontangible evidence.

cultural codes　Ways in which people conduct their various daily living practices.

cultural competence　Understanding and respecting basic cultural and family values of individuals from a different perspective than one's own, and to reserve judgment about what is right or wrong, or what is better or worse as compared to one's own cultural or family background. In its broad sense, it refers to an ability to work effectively with a diverse group of people.

cultural reciprocity　A model established and promoted by professionals, in which both parents and professionals come to a mutual and true understanding of each others' cultural beliefs, values, and attitudes as it relates to the child with special needs.

culture　Values and beliefs that dictate how people should behave within their family and in the larger society.

curriculum-based assessment　Assessment procedure that is based on students' achievement of the curriculum learning goals in specific subjects.

curriculum-based measures　Assessment instruments that measure knowledge in specific subject areas.

data-driven　All decisions regarding any course of action are based on results obtained from systematic collection of data throughout intervention and progress monitoring.

deaf　With a lowercase "d," deaf refers to any individual or child who cannot utilize hearing to use language.

Deaf　With a capital "D," Deaf refers to a child or individual who is a member of a distinct cultural and linguistic group.

Deaf community　Deaf individuals who perceive themselves as a linguistic minority group who have their own culture and language (American Sign Language [ASL]).

decibel (dB)　A logarithmic unit used to measure sound level by describing a ratio of power, sound pressure, voltage, or intensity.

deinstitutionalization　A trend leading to the rapid downsizing of institutions and hospitals that previously cared for children and adults with intellectual disabilities and mental illnesses.

deoxyribonucleic acid (DNA)　DNA is the nucleic acid that is the genetic material determining the makeup of all living cells. It consists of two long chains of nucleotides twisted into a double helix and joined by hydrogen. DNA determines individual hereditary characteristics.

descriptive sentences　Sentences that describe a story's details, such as the time and location.

development　Refers to the process in which human behavior changes in a predictable way, provided certain conditions are met, throughout the life cycle.

developmental care　An early intervention strategy used for premature infants that focuses on caregiver and infant interaction, through which the caregiver learns to understand the infant's cues and devises ways to increase the infant's self-regulation.

developmental delay　Delay in development in two or more areas as measured by testing. Usually a specific percentage of delays, set by states, should be present for the child to be eligible for services.

developmental domains　Major dimensions of development that encompass specific abilities. There are three major domains: physical, cognitive, and social emotional.

developmental milestones　Specific behavioral markers that indicate development of a certain skill around a particular time (child's age).

developmental screening　A short standardized test usually conducted to allow professionals to identify children who might need further assessment or careful monitoring.

developmental theories　Systems of explanations and principles for the evolving and gradual process of human development.

diagnostic test　An assessment instrument that helps confirm or exclude the presence of a specific condition for which the test has been designed.

differential attention (DA)　An approach marked by attending to the child's behavior when the behavior is acceptable or appropriate, and ignoring the child's behavior when the behavior is inappropriate or unacceptable.

differentiated instruction　A flexible approach to teaching that allows for change of instruction, as well as different materials, procedures, and assessment protocols for students based on their individual learning needs.

differentiation　A principle of motor development in which infants' motor skills become more defined and develop into a set of distinguished skills, each with a different function.

DIR model　Developmental, individual difference, relationship-based model of intervention, also called the Floortime model, is a play-based framework for the assessment and intervention of children with developmental disabilities, specifically children within the Autism Spectrum Disorders. The focus of DIR is to build healthy social, emotional, and intellectual capacities in the child.

directive sentences   Sentences that give the child suggestions as to one or more appropriate responses in a given situation.

discrete trial teaching (DTT)   Consists of systematic and intensive one-on-one instruction and reinforcement procedures between the child and the behavior interventionist.

due process hearing   A legal process that entitles the parents of children with disabilities to have legal counsel and to contest decisions made in regard to the education and placement of, and services for, their children.

dynamic systems model   A theory of development that explains that motor development occurs as a result of the interaction of many factors, such as sensory and cognitive processing, biomechanical and physical development, environment, and the demands of a specific task that the child is to perform. In this model, development is a dynamic system that is marked by variability, instabilities, regressions, discontinuity, and jumps.

early childhood education (ECE)   A system of care and education of children from birth through age 8 or third primary grade.

early childhood intervention (ECI)   Includes the system of care and education addressing the needs of children at risk and children who are diagnosed with disabilities or developmental delays from birth through age 5.

early childhood special education (ECSE)   The system of intervention that provides specialized instruction and supporting services for children (from birth through 8 years of age) who have diagnosed disabilities.

early intervention (EI)   A system of intervention consisting of a range of developmental services and programs designed for infants and toddlers (birth to age 3) who are diagnosed with developmental delays or disabilities.

early onset   The appearance of a disease at the earliest age (usually from birth).

echolalia   A condition marked by echoing, or repeating, the words that one hears.

elementary special education   Special education services (specialized instruction and support services) for children with disabilities from age 6 through 14 (kindergarten through eighth grade).

emotional competence   The child's ability to regulate self-emotions, understand feelings and emotions of self and others, and apply this knowledge to form and maintain relationships with others.

enrichment   Modifying the curriculum by adding learning activities or providing new learning opportunities in addition to what the regular curriculum might require.

evaluation   A formal process that occurs at the time of diagnosis and periodically after that to determine if a child is eligible and continues to be eligible to receive early intervention and special education services.

evidence-based   Practices and strategies that have been grounded in research and have empirical validity.

evidence-based practices   Those educational practices that are supported by research findings.

exceptional children   Children who by virtue of their special needs require special educational services and instruction in order to be successful in school.

executive function   A mechanism in the brain circuits, located in the frontal cortex of the brain, that prioritizes, integrates, and regulates other cognitive functions, such as the planning and execution of an action.

expansion   A language stimulation technique that recasts the child's utterance into a correct syntactic form.

experimental   Scientific inquiry in which all factors under study are controlled, and the researcher tests a hypothesis under controlled conditions.

explicit instruction   An instruction in which the teacher overtly teaches all steps needed to complete a task.

extension   An advanced form of expansion in which the teacher expands the child's utterance into a correct sentence, then adds an additional and related comment.

externalizing behaviors   Behaviors that are easily observable, such as acting out, defiance, noncompliance, or aggression.

extremely low birth weight (ELBW)   A newborn weighing less than 1,000 grams (2.25 pounds).

false negative   The results of the test indicate the absence of certain risk factors, when in fact those risk factors are present.

false positive   The results of the test indicate the presence of certain risk factors in the individual, when in fact no risk factors are present.

family   Any unit whose members consider themselves to be a family and provide support and care for each other on an ongoing basis.

family directed assessment   Involving family in evaluating the resources, priorities, and concerns of the family and the child, and in developing a plan of action accordingly.

family functioning   The ongoing relationships between adult members and between the adults and children in fulfilling the family's functions.

family resilience   The concept describing the phenomenon that some families cope with stress and adversity in a positive way, and become strengthened as a result.

family structure   Refers to the configuration of the family based on the members within the family unit.

field of vision   The area around the person, which one can see when looking ahead. A normal field of vision is 160 degrees.

fine motor   The development of small muscles in the arms and hands; required in the manipulation and handling of objects.

flexibility   The degree to which family members are willing to change their roles and responsibilities as situational changes in the family might demand.

Floortime model   A relationship-based philosophy and procedure, pioneered by Stanley Greenspan, that refers to a set of child-centered techniques based on the child's interest and developmental level, by which the therapist aims to help the child overcome any developmental problems.

formative evaluation   An ongoing assessment throughout the daily operation of a program, gathering statistical information as well as qualitative information about the program.

free appropriate public education (FAPE)   Special education and related services that are provided at public expense, meet state standards, are appropriate, and are provided in conformity with an IEP.

functional academics   Academic skills necessary so students can function independently within the home and community settings.

functional behavior analysis   Analysis of the components of events taking place prior, during, and after the problem behavior. Functional analysis determines the behavior's functions and consequences that might increase or reduce the behavior in the future.

functional behavioral assessment (FBA)   A system of behavioral assessment that focuses on identifying cognitive, social emotional, or environmental factors, which contribute to the occurrence of a child's behavior.

functional vision assessment (FVA)   Assessment of how the child uses his or her visual abilities within his or her natural environment.

genes   The basic physical and functional unit of heredity.

gestational diabetes   Diabetes that is contracted during pregnancy without a prior history of that disorder.

giftedness   Children identified by professionals, who by virtue of their various abilities and higher-performance capabilities require special education services or programs to realize their potentials.

graphomotor   The abilities necessary for drawing and handwriting.

grasping   A child's ability to use fine muscles in the finger to hold, pick, or grasp objects.

gross motor   Development of the large muscles of the trunk and limbs, involving locomotion, posture, and balance.

growth   Refers to an increase in weight or height, or the maturation of an organism.

guided participation   A process of interpersonal transaction between children and adults, through which children participate in learning, as the adults guide and support their learning and development.

gustatory system   A part of the sensory processing system that is responsible for detecting and processing taste input.

handedness   A person's preference for using one hand over the other, and that hand's precision and proficiency in performing skilled tasks, such as writing, drawing, and object manipulation.

hard of hearing   A child or individual who has sufficient hearing for communication and language use.

Head Start   A compensatory program funded in 1965 by the office of Economic Opportunity to give children who, due to socioeconomic conditions, are at risk for school failure a head start in education, so that the disparities in education of these children and their peers are eliminated.

hearing impairment   A term used by IDEA to describe hearing loss or deafness in children.

hearing loss   Any degree or type of hearing damage.

hertz (HZ)   Named after a German physicist, Heinrich Hertz, who demonstrated the existence of radio waves in 1886, hertz is the unit of measurement expressing the frequency in one cycle per second.

human immunodeficiency virus (HIV)   The virus that causes AIDS by damaging part of the body's defenses against infection.

hyperactivity   A state in which the child is easily excitable or overactive.

hyperlexia   An advanced ability to read, while the ability to understand speech is below the typical developmental level.

hypertonia   An increased tightness of the muscles. Also called spasticity.

hypotonia   A decreased or lack of adequate level of muscle tone.

IFSP outcomes   Statements of major outcomes expected to be achieved for the child and the family based on the child's current developmental level and the family's priorities. IFSP outcomes include criteria for achieving the outcome, the type of services or activities needed to achieve the outcome, and a timeline for revision of the outcome if necessary.

implants   Small electronic devices that are inserted surgically underneath the skin. Based on their type, implants help provide hearing sensations, transmit sounds, process auditory information, and amplify sounds.

impulsivity   Resorting to an action without thinking first, or considering the consequences of one's action.

inattention   Having a short attention span, or not being able to sustain attention for more than a short period of time.

incidental teaching   An approach that uses naturally occurring opportunities in the child's environment for teaching and instruction, while utilizing the child's interests and motivations.

inclusion   The concept in which children with disabilities are educated in the same educational settings along with their peers without disabilities, while special education and support services are provided for them in that environment.

inclusive classrooms   Classrooms in which both children with and without special needs are educated, and support services, such as adaptation to a curriculum, are available to meet all the children's needs.

indirect language stimulation   Language stimulation techniques to be used through daily activities where the goal is to carry out a discussion while increasing the language comprehension of the child.

Individualized Education Plan (IEP)   A written plan developed by professionals and parents outlining the education plan for the child on an annual basis.

Individualized Family Service Plan (IFSP)   An annual plan written by professionals and parents outlining outcomes for the infants and toddlers and their families.

Individuals with Disabilities Education Act (IDEA)   The Individuals with Disabilities Education Act (PL 101-476) is the amendment to the previous law, the All Handicapped Education Act. IDEA adopted a language of "child first" and provided a set of guidelines regarding the legal rights of children with disabilities, and their families, to support and services.

intellectual disability   Problems in the area of cognitive development and adaptive skills to the degree where day-to-day functioning is adversely influenced.

intelligence   Refers to a range of abilities, including reasoning, problem solving, thinking abstractly, planning, and learning from experiences in one's environment.

intelligence quotient (IQ)   A score indicating the ratio between an individual's chronological age versus their mental age.

interdisciplinary team model   A team approach, in which the members consists of parents and professionals from several disciplines. In interdisciplinary teams, formal channels of communication exist that promote sharing information and the exchange of ideas on an ongoing basis.

internal dyssynchrony   Emotional and psychological problems that might occur because of asynchrony in development.

internalizing behaviors   Behavior characteristics that may not be easily observable, such as depression, anxiety, or withdrawal.

itinerant teacher   A special educator, therapist, or specialist who is designated by the Board of Education to provide consultation or direct services to a child in a private or public school.

labeling   The written and oral labeling of objects, toys, and materials that are within the young child's environments.

language   A socially shared system of rules for sounds, signs, and written symbols to be used for the purpose of communication among members of a human group.

language disorder   Problems with receptive expressive language.

language modeling   Providing linguistic models for children beginning with isolated sounds and moving to modeling words, phrases, sentences, and uttering sentences.

large for gestational age   An infant's weight that is more than 4,000 grams (8.5 pounds).

late onset   Appearance of a disease two or more years after birth.

lead   An environmental toxin found in some old buildings, which can cause cognitive impairment in children.

learned helplessness   A psychological condition in which a person has learned that he or she has no control over a situation no matter what he or she does, even if in reality the situation is easily changeable.

least restrictive environment (LRE)   An educational setting where to the maximum extent possible, a child with disabilities can receive an individualized, free, and appropriate education along with his or her peers without disabilities.

legally blind   Children and individuals whose vision is 20/200 or less, or whose field of vision is 20 degrees or less.

locomotion   Refers to movements that change the child from one location to another in a natural, spontaneous, and rhythmic pattern.

logo reading   A picture fading approach in which familiar signs in the environment are used to teach children letter and sound correspondence and word reading.

low birth weight (LBW)   A newborn's weight that is less than 2,500 grams (5.5 pounds).

low-incidence disabilities   Conditions that are not very common in children, and which include a variety of disorders, such as deafness, blindness, and a number of neurological and physical disabilities.

low vision   Refers to children who need optical aid in order to see and read print. These children might learn to read Braille.

mainstreaming   A concept in which children with disabilities are educated in a general education classroom with or without any special education resources.

manipulatives   Hands-on materials that are designed to teach shapes, numbers, letters, concepts, and mathematical operations, by means of active engagement with and manipulation of the materials.

manual or hand babbling   Sequence of hand gestures in infants, which resemble signs in a sign language.

matching   In a face-to-face interaction between infant and the caregiver, matching is referred to as the infant's ability to either imitate the facial expression of the caregiver, or respond to the caregiver's overtures with similar facial expressions or vocal behaviors.

mean length utterance (MLU)   A measure of language productivity in children, usually calculated by collecting the number of utterances of children and then dividing the number of morphemes by the total number of utterances. The higher the MLU of a child, the higher the proficiency in the child's language.

measurable   Clear criteria that specify how goals and all objectives and benchmarks are achieved.

mental retardation   A static condition marked by limited intellectual functioning and adaptive development that can not be changed or improved over time.

mercury   A toxic substance that can be ingested through contaminated food and cause neurological impairments.

micropreemie   A newborn who weighs less than 800 grams (1.75 pounds).

mixed hearing loss   Hearing loss caused by damage to a combination of the outer, inner, and middle ear, or to the auditory nerve.

mixed methodologies   Studies that employ both qualitative and quantitative methodologies to capture the details of experiences of subjects in the study and conditions in the field.

mobility   A child's ability to move about safely in their environment.

morpheme   The smallest meaningful unit in a grammar of a language.

motor or movement planning   The process of finding out how to accomplish a goal that involves sequential action, such as climbing stairs.

multidisciplinary team   A team composed of professionals from various disciplines that work independently of one another. Although team members might work side by side or share space together, they work and function separately.

multifactorial genetic disorders   Disorders caused by defects in one or more genes in combination with environmental factors.

musculoskeletal system (MSK)   Consists of bones, muscles, and joints that enable motor movements.

music therapy   A form of therapy established using music to address different developmental needs of the individual.

natural environment   The typical environment in which the young child develops, such as a child's home and community.

negative attention   Paying attention to the inappropriate behavior of a child by using negative statements or punishment.

negative reinforcement   Removal of an aversive stimulus that increases the likelihood of the behavior that lead to it.

neonate   The infant during the first 28 days of life.

neurobiological risk factors   Genetic or neurological factors that can lead to establishment of a developmental problem in a child before, during, or after birth.

neuromuscular system (NM)   Consists of spinal motor neurons, the peripheral nerves, and the junction between muscles and nerves. It enables the body to move through transferring messages to and from the brain and body.

neurotransmitters   Chemical messengers that are responsible for carrying information from one nerve cell to the next.

No Child Left Behind Act (NCLB)   A U.S. federal law signed by President Bush in 2002 that reauthorized the Elementary and Secondary Education Act, in addition to reauthorizing programs to improve the educational performance of students in primary and secondary schools by raising the standards of accountability for states, school districts, and schools. The act also gave parents flexibility in choosing schools that their children attended.

norm-referenced tests   Standardized measures that evaluate and compare each examinee's performance with the performance of other similar examinees.

number sense   An intuitive ability to understand what numbers mean and how to make mental calculation and comparisons about quantity.

objectives   Also referred to as benchmarks, objectives are smaller components of the annual goals that describe what the child should achieve by specific segments of the year.

observable   Any behavior that can be seen.

observation   A systematic watching and listening of children to gather information about them.

olfactory system   A part of the sensory processing system that is responsible for detecting and processing smell.

oral motor   Involves the development of orofacial musculature that is elemental in feeding and in speech development.

orientation   A child's ability to figure out where they are.

orientation and mobility specialists   A trained individual who helps children and adults with visual impairment find their way and move about safely in their environment.

parallel play   Children playing alongside one another.

parallel talk   Also called narrating. Parallel talk is describing the child's actions by matching words to the action as the child performs a task.

paraprofessional   Persons not certified to practice as licensed professionals or teachers, but who are trained to assist the teacher in a specialized or nonspecialized educational setting.

partially sighted   Children and individuals who have some vision, but need special education in order to succeed in school.

partnership with families   A framework outlining a working relationship between families and professionals that is based on an ongoing collaboration to benefit the child.

peer-mediated instruction   A system of teaching and learning that relies on training more proficient children to teach academic and social skills to their peers with learning difficulties.

peer tutoring   See peer-mediated instruction.

perception   The interpretation of what has been sensed.

perceptual motor skills   The ability to mentally organize and interpret, and then respond motorically to what one sees. It requires appropriate sensory processing and the development of balance, coordination, and fine and gross motor muscles.

performance-based assessment   The direct and systematic observation of a student performance and the rating of that performance based on previously set criteria.

perinatal period   The period surrounding child birth, beginning from about 5 months before to 1 month after birth.

perspective sentences   Sentences that provide perspective and insights into the thinking of the child as well as others involved in a social story scenario.

phonological awareness   The ability to hear and recognize the structure of sounds in a language.

phonology   The study of how sounds are organized and produced in a language.

physical development   Refers to the development of muscles, bones, motoric movements, and to the general health of a child.

pica   Eating nonfood items.

Picture Exchange Communication System (PECS)   A system of communication used for children with autism based on an exchange of pictures between the child and others.

picture fading   A phonics approach to teaching literacy in which single pictures and their associated words are used during play and instructed games and lessons. Over time, as children learn to identify words, pictures are removed while the word remains.

planned ignoring   A procedure in which the adult withdraws attention from the child for a predetermined period of time upon occurrence of inappropriate behavior.

play-based assessment   An assessment approach in which the child's performance is measured during play.

polygenic disorders   Disorders caused by defects in more than one gene without the influence of environmental factors.

positive behavior support (PBS)   A collaborative approach that uses educational methods to help the child develop new behaviors, and also employs systems change to redesign a child's environment so as to minimize the child's problem behavior and enhance the child's quality of life.

positive reinforcers Reinforcing stimuli that increases the likelihood of the behavior that produces it.

postnatal period The period beginning immediately after birth to about 4 to 6 weeks of the infant's chronological age.

postural and balance control A child's ability to move efficiently and perform actions such as standing, twisting, sitting, reclining, bending, swinging, and stretching—and to be able to balance, adapt, and adjust his posture as needed.

praxis One's ability to use sensory input to formulate goals, and to plan, sequence, and execute motoric and nonmotoric actions.

predominantly hyperactive impulsive type A subtype diagnosis under categories of ADHD, characterizing children who do not have attention difficulties, but who display symptoms of hyperactivity and impulsivity.

predominantly inattentive type A subtype diagnosis under categories of ADHD, characterizing children and individuals who have symptoms of inattention without having any symptoms of hyperactivity and impulsiveness.

prelinguistic foundations of language development Skills necessary for the child to begin language acquisition and use. These skills include eye contact, pointing, holding joint attention, gesturing, and vocalizing.

prelinguistic milieu teaching (PMT) A teaching strategy used for young children, consisting of a number of steps that are embedded within the child's natural environment to promote prelinguistic abilities, such as eye contact and gesturing, in the child.

prenatal period The period of development and growth of the baby before birth.

prereferral intervention (PRI) A team collaborative approach in which children who are identified as having learning problems receive intense intervention before they are referred for special education services.

pretend play Make-believe play or taking on a pretend role, while following a play theme.

prevalence A measure of the number of individuals with a specific disease or condition.

problem or challenging behaviors Behaviors that present a challenge to the child's development and learning, and those that present a threat to the safety of the child and others.

prompt An action provided by the adult that supports the learning of a task or behavior in a child. Prompts can be physical, verbal, or gestural.

prompt dependency When teachers routinely and repeatedly provide physical and verbal assistance without setting a goal for a child's independent functioning so that he begins to expect others to assist him even when he is able to perform a task independently.

prompt fading The gradual elimination of a teacher's scaffolding as the child learns to perform a task.

prompt hierarchy A system of prompts organized in an order from most to least or from least to most intrusive form.

proprioceptive system A part of the sensory processing system that uses information from various muscles and joints, and helps one be aware of the body's position in space.

protective factors Factors that buffer the effect of risk factors and protect the child against adverse conditions.

protodeclarative pointing Pointing to an object with the purpose of showing one's interest in that object to another.

proximity control The method of standing or sitting in close proximity to the child in order to encourage the child's focus and attention, and to monitor his or her behavior.

proximodistal A principle of motor development whereby an infant's control over his or her motor skills progresses from the center of the body to the extremities.

qualitative research Studies that use observational field studies and interview methods to understand the details and nature of the experience of subjects in the study.

quantitative research Research that uses structured and predetermined questions where a relatively large number of participants are involved. In quantitative research, measurement should be objective and results should be statistically sound and valid.

quasi-experimental A method of study that is usually used for field settings, such as educational programs. In this method, the experimenter might choose to control certain factors, or not manipulate any factors at all.

readiness skills Behaviors necessary for classroom participation that are essential to learning, such as sharing, sitting still for an appropriate length of time, expressing emotions, taking turns, and finishing tasks.

register Refers to variations in style of language that occurs in different contexts, such as the way one talks to a friend as opposed to the way one talks to a teacher.

reinforcement An experience, object, or event that increases the likelihood that a behavior will occur again in the future.

reliability   The accuracy by which a test measures what it targets to measure.

repetition   A language stimulation technique that helps the child learn correct articulation by repeating what the child says in its correct form.

resilient children   Children who, despite a biological or environmental high-risk status, have positive developmental outcomes, and grow up to become productive members of their communities.

Response to Intervention (RTI)   A research-based process that aims at improving academic performance. It consists of different tiers of intervention and progress monitoring used as the basis of assessment and intervention for children who have learning problems.

responsive teaching   A teaching method in which parents and educators participate in a child's activities and provide support for children by doing the things that are similar to what children are doing.

risk factors   Factors that might impede healthy physical, intellectual, and emotional development in the child.

scaffolding   Active assistance of a more able person in helping the child learn a specific task. It ranges from verbal, gestural, or physical cueing and modeling, to a complete physical motoring of an act.

scientific research–based   Practices and strategies that have been grounded in research and have empirical validity.

screening test   A test that screens an individual for specific risk factors for which the test has been designed.

self-determination   The child's ability to act autonomously and independently in regulating his or her behaviors to respond to events, as well as initiate his or her own responses to events.

self-regulation   A developmental task related to brain development, marked by the ability of the child to manage arousal, emotion, attention, and self-reaction in response to different conditions, situations, and sensory stimuli in their environments.

self-stimulatory behaviors   Repetitive movements of limbs or the entire body, which might have neurobiological and sensory causes.

self-talk   Describing one's actions carefully and in simple language as one is going through the action.

sensation   Reception of information from the sensory receptors in ears, eyes, skin, tongue, and nose.

sensorineural hearing loss (SN hearing loss)   Hearing loss caused by damage to the inner ear structure, marked by a lack of sensitivity to environmental or speech sounds.

sensory diet   A comprehensive plan that would provide the child with sensory input needed for self-regulation and sensory processing.

sensory integration   A theory developed by Jane Ayers to explain the process of organizing sensations from the body and environment to be used. Sensory integration is the brain's ability to integrate information received from the various senses by balancing and adjusting the flow of sensory input to the nervous system.

sensory-kinesthetic approach to phonics   A strategy to enhance phonemic awareness in children by having them touch letters with rough textures while saying the sound.

sensory modulation   The ability to respond appropriately to ordinary levels of sensory input.

sensory motor   Involves the physiological and sensory processing mechanisms that reside within the nervous system.

sensory processing   The ability to receive sensory information and to organize and make sense of the information received from senses.

sensory processing dysfunction   The inability of the brain to correctly process information received from the senses.

service delivery model   The model indicating what types of services and where services are to be provided for a child with disabilities. Services can be home-based, center-based, or home- and center-based.

setting events   Factors that might not be immediately noticeable and could contribute to a child's behavior.

shared attention   Takes place when two persons are interested in, and are looking at, the same object at the same time.

single-gene disorders   Abnormalities that affect only one gene, such as PKU.

social competence   A child's ability to self-regulate so that she can engage in and have effective interactions with others.

social emotional development   The development of emotions, personality, temperament, and relationships with others.

social games   Interactive games that require children to cooperate with one another, while following specific sets of rules pertaining to that game.

socialization mismatched hypothesis   The hypothesis that states that children are more likely to succeed in school when socialization patterns and linguistic interactions at home match those that society uses and values.

social story   A cognitive method that has been used for children with autism to teach them theory of mind skills related to specific behaviors as well as teaching academic content.

socioeconomic status (SES)   The status of a family in society based on education, income level, and class association.

spasticity   Lack of flexibility; rigidity in muscles.

special education   Specially designed instruction for children who have unique learning needs.

special education classrooms   Specialized and highly structured classrooms in which children with disabilities are educated.

special education regulations   Explanations published by the U.S. Department of Education that clarify the U.S. code that governs the education of children with disabilities.

specific praise   Describes the behavior that is being praised.

speech   The spoken form of language, requiring the production of specific sounds of language.

speech and language delay   Lateness in the emergence of speech and aspects of language use.

speech disorder   An inability in the production of speech sounds, fluency, or voice projection.

stuttering   Disruptions in the production of speech sounds, usually beginning in early childhood.

subsystems   Smaller systems within the family consisting of specific members.

summative evaluation   Information gathered at the end of a specific time period about the effectiveness of an intervention program. It analyzes qualitative and quantitative results obtained through formative evaluation against the outcome of the program.

systematic instruction   A method of instruction based on task analysis—breaking down complex skills into smaller steps, and teaching each step in its logical sequence.

systems theory   A theory of development that explains a child's growth and development within multiple systems. Interactions within the system and between the systems and the child influence and shape a child's development.

tactile defensiveness   Having an over-sensitive tactile processing system. This makes certain touches aversive to the child.

tactile system   A part of the sensory processing system that is responsible for feeling different sensations of temperature, texture, pain, and pressure.

temporal-sequential ability   The ability to organize and remember information in the specific order that the information is presented. This ability underlies understanding the concept of time.

terotogen   Any toxin that can pose a threat to the developing fetus.

theory of mind   A human's ability to understand that others can think and have beliefs. It enables the individual to understand that others can have different mental states than one's own state of mind.

three-ring model of giftedness   A model proposed by Renzulli in which giftedness is composed of three interlocking clustered abilities in an individual: above average intelligence, high level of task commitment, and creativity.

tics   Repetitive motor movements or sounds that individuals may make without realizing or having control over them.

TORCH   Named for **t**oxoplasmosis, **o**ther (HIV, syphilis, and others), **r**ubella, **c**ytomegalovirus, and **h**erpes; an acronym used to describe a group of infections that can cause specific disabilities in the child.

totally blind   Children and individuals who cannot receive any meaningful information through their visual sense.

transdisciplinary team   A team composed of parents and professionals from several disciplines. In a transdisciplinary team, members communicate, cooperate, and collaborate with one another on an ongoing basis. Mutual and cross training across disciplines are common in this team model.

transition   A plan of action that outlines specific services for children with disabilities as they reach the age to exit early intervention and enter preschool special education or another appropriate early childhood program.

twice exceptional children   Gifted children who have learning or other kinds of disabilities.

umbilical cord prolapse   The condition that occurs when the umbilical cord descends through the birth canal in advance of the infant.

universal health precautions   A set of guidelines that are recommended to prevent the spread of infections and transmittable diseases.

universal model of curriculum   An early childhood curriculum model that is comprehensive enough that it takes into account various developmental and educational needs of all students.

validity   The extent to which a test actually measures what it claims to measure.

values Standards to judge specific actions or thoughts as proper or improper.

very low birth weight (VLBW) Newborns weighing less than 1,500 grams (3.33 pounds).

vestibular system A part of the sensory processing system that coordinates the movement of eyes, body, and head through space, and helps with the body's movement and balance.

visual acuity The accuracy of vision to see things at far and close ranges.

visual impairment Vision loss that is significant enough that the child's visual acuity is 20/60 even with corrective lenses and glasses.

visual-spatial ability The ability to mentally understand and manipulate two- and three-dimensional objects and figures.

visual system A part of the sensory processing system responsible for visual perception and processing of the visual sensory input.

working memory An active memory system in the information processing area of the brain that enables the individual to hold several facts in the memory temporarily while solving a problem or performing a task.

zone of proximal development A concept brought by Vygotsky who believed that with adults' help children can learn to do different tasks without any assistance. ZPD refers to the difference between what a child is able to do and what the child is not able to do without an adult's assistance.

Photo Credits

Chapter 1

Opener: © Liquidlibrary/Jupiterimages RF; p. 8: © IT Stock Free/Alamy RF; p. 12: © BananaStock/PunchStock RF; p. 16: © Library of Congress Prints and Photographs Division; p. 17: © The McGraw-Hill Companies, Inc./Jill Braaten, photographer

Chapter 2

Opener: © IT Stock Free/Alamy RF; p. 42c: © Brand X Pictures/PunchStock RF; p. 49: © Blend Images/Alamy RF

Chapter 3

Opener: © Getty RF; p. 76: © MedioImages RF; p. 77 and p. 81: © BananaStock/PunchStock RF; p. 96: © Gaetano Images Ind./Alamy RF

Chapter 4

Opener: © Digital Vision/Getty RF; p. 122: © The Center for AAC & Autism; 4.5a: From *First Words Sterling Edition*, © Language Links ® Syntax Assessment & Intervention Level 1, Laureate Learning Systems, Inc. Used with permission; 4.5b: From *Exploring Nouns Sterling Edition*, Laureate Learning Systems, Inc.,© Language Links ® Syntax Assessment & Intervention Level 1, Laureate Learning Systems, Inc. Used with permission; 4.5c: Language Links®: Syntax Assessment & Intervention Level 1, Laureate Learning Systems, Inc., Used with Permission; p. 128 bottom: © Corbis RF

Chapter 5

Opener: © Image 100 Ltd RF; p. 150: © IT Stock Free/Alamy RF; p. 160: © Somos Images/Corbis RF; p. 161: © Blend Images/Getty RF

Chapter 6

Opener: © image 100/PunchStock RF; p. 178: © Thinkstock Images/PictureQuest/Jupiter RF; p. 186: © Historicus Inc.; p. 202: © Katrina Wittkamp/Getty RF

Chapter 7

Opener: © Laurence Mouton/Photoalto/PictureQuest RF; p. 226: © IT Stock Free/Alamy RF; p. 228: © PictureQuest/Corbis RF; p. 234 (a–e), p. 235 (a and b), p. 236 (a and b), p. 242 (a and b), and p. 243: © Mojdeh Bayat

Chapter 8

Opener: © RubberBall/Alamy RF; p. 261: © Image100/PunchStock RF

Chapter 9

Opener: © Corbis RF; p. 291: © Floresco Productions/Corbis RF; p. 292: © IT Stock Free/Alamy RF; p. 293: © Image Source/PunchStock RF; p. 301: © Ariel Skelley/Blend Images/Corbis RF; p. 317: © Pixland/PunchStock RF; p. 318: © Photodisc/Getty RF

Chapter 10

Opener: © PhotoAlto/PictureQuest RF; p. 351: © Bob Daemmrich/Photo Edit; 10.2 (a–d): Reprinted with permission of Erika Ash

Chapter 11

Opener: © BananaStock/AGE Fotostock RF; p. 379: © Digital Vision/PunchStock RF; p. 385: © George Doyle/Stockbyte/Getty RF; 11.2 (a–d): Reprinted with permission of Erika Ash; p. 390: The Denny's name and logo are registered trademarks of DFO, LLC

Chapter 12

Opener: © Image Source/PunchStock RF; p. 407: © Photodisc/Getty RF; p. 411: © Corbis RF; p. 412: © Steve Hamblin/Alamy RF; p. 417: © PunchStock RF; p. 419: © Comstock/PunchStock RF; p. 427: © Historicus, Inc.

Chapter 13

Opener: © Ed-Imaging; p. 445: © Pixland/PunchStock RF; p. 458: © World Health Organization; p. 459 (left and right): © Dennis MacDonald/Photo Edit; p. 463: © BananaStock/PunchStock RF

Chapter 14

Opener: © BananaStock/AGE Fotostock RF; p. 476: © Corbis RF; p. 493: © Comstock/PunchStock RF; p. 500: © Corbis RF; p. 501: © PhotoLink/Getty RF

Chapter 15

Opener: © BananaStock/AGE Fotostock RF; p. 515: © IT Stock Free/Alamy RF; p. 516: © BananaStock/PunchStock RF; p. 526: © BananaStock/AGE Fotostock RF; p. 528: © SuperStock RF; p. 540: © Photodisc/Getty RF; p. 543: © Paloalto/Laurence Mouton/Getty RF

Note: Page numbers followed by *f* and *t* indicate figures and tables, respectively. Text boxes are indicated by *b*.